Bernardino Luini
and Renaissance Painting in Milan

Bernardino Luini and Renaissance Painting in Milan

The Frescoes of San Maurizio al Monastero Maggiore

edited by Sandrina Bandera and Maria Teresa Fiorio

SKIRA

Editor
Francesco Porzio

Graphic design
Marcello Francone

Editing
Doriana Comerlati

Layout
Eliana Gelati

Translations
Rhoda Billingsley
Adrian Hartley Cook
Andrew Ellis
David Stanton

Photographs
Paolo Manusardi

Plans
Margil srl, Milan

First published in Italy in 2000 by
Skira Editore S.p.A.
Palazzo Casati Stampa
via Torino 61
20123 Milano
Italy

Printed and bound in Italy. First edition

ISBN 88-8118-736-1

Distributed in North America and Latin America by Abbeville Publishing Group, 22 Cortlandt Street, New York, NY 10007, USA.
Distributed elsewhere in the world by Thames and Hudson Ltd., 181a High Holborn, London WC1V 7QX, United Kingdom

Grandi Libri Skira

This collection has been created with the ambitious aim of illustrating the greatest works of art of all time with reproductions of the highest quality that can be offered in book form.
Quality of image, in the first place, true to the best Skira tradition. Quality of interpretation — which signifies an examination of the work at close quarters and paying special attention to its material and aesthetic qualities. Last but not least, scientific quality, meaning constant care over the choice of authors and of historical and documentary materials, as demanded by the ever increasing sophistication of international studies.
Each volume is devoted to a single work, cycle or series of works linked together by their author, theme, date or location. In each case, the masterpieces in question will be ones that have left a profound mark on the history of art and culture. However celebrated or obscure, they are revealed in a new light, offering a different perspective to experts and bringing them to the attention of a broader public.

To the Reader

This volume is devoted to the decorative cycles of San Maurizio al Monastero Maggiore, one of the most important churches of Milan. The frescoes were carried out in the course of the sixteenth century by some of the finest painters then active in Lombardy, and are among the most striking examples of Milanese art of the period in question.
Given the complexity of the subject treated, the book has been divided into four large sections that follow the chronological sequence of the separate phases of work on the frescoes. The first section focuses on the earliest phase of decoration in the aula claustrale*, or convent hall. The second illustrates the esteemed cycle by Bernardino Luini. The third is largely devoted to the frescoes executed in the later sixteenth century by the Piazza and Luini families. The fourth section discusses the last phase of decorative work, which was carried out under Cardinal Borromeo.*
Each section contains a relative plan of the church as a guide for identifying the precise position of the pictorial episodes under discussion within each specific decorative itinerary. The bold numbers found in the captions refer to those in the plan.
The final part of the book comprises the complete records of all documents relating to the paintings, decorative works, and church furnishings.

The first edition of this book
was published
under the auspices of

Banca Popolare
di Milano

Contents

Introduction

Maria Teresa Fiorio

Few churches in Milan can boast a tradition comparable to that of San Maurizio, which is linked to the most celebrated Benedictine convent in the city. The legend of the house's foundation by St Sigismund, King of Burgundy, and the fact that its benefactors included Desiderius, the last of the Lombard kings, and Emperor Otto I indicate that, from the outset, the complex of the Monastero Maggiore was aristocratic in nature.
Its history, which begins between the eighth and ninth century is recounted by Giovanni Battista Sannazzaro in this volume: making use of thorough archive research and the results of archaeological investigations carried out with modern criteria, this account outlines the vicissitudes of the convent, giving the lie to legends and groundless traditions and placing the events in a more convincing perspective. But the reconstruction of the foundation of this Benedictine convent and the dedication of the church to the Virgin Mary and St Maurice — as well as that of life in the convent up to the end of the fifteenth century — constitutes the prehistory of the theme with which this book is concerned. The leading protagonist is, in fact, the present church of San Maurizio, which, standing on the site of the earlier one, was refounded in 1503 and, from the beginning of the second decade of the sixteenth century, was adorned with the frescoes that are unique in Milan both for their richness and their coherence with the architectural frame bearing them.
Not only has the long process of conservation — started some years ago and now almost completed — restored much of the original brightness to the frescoes in San Maurizio but, by allowing them to be examined at close quarters, it also has led to further discoveries that, together with in-depth studies of relevant documents carried out in recent years, offer a new interpretation of the whole complex. The starting-point for this volume was, naturally, the monograph by Angela Ottino Della Chiesa (*San Maurizio al Monastero Maggiore*, Milan 1962), who must be credited with having for the first time written a major study dealing with all the aspects of the church. But the forty years that have passed since it was published weigh heavily on this pioneering work, inevitably making it appear out of date.
There is no wish on the part of the authors to claim that this new volume will provide answers to all the questions that have been raised hitherto, first and foremost the one regarding the authorship of the design of the building. It is indeed curious that the identity of the architect of a church of this magnificence, constructed according to a design that is notable for its confidence and harmony, as well as for the range of stylistic elements it comprises, should still be unknown. Capable of absorbing the most vital and innovative ideas proposed by Bramante, this anonymous architect then adapted these to a style that was still distinctly Lombard. Yet, despite painstaking research in the archives, the paternity of the church of San Maurizio has, to date, remained a mystery, although it is clear that the outstanding quality of this building is a major element in this inquiry, suggesting that attention should focus on the great names of Milanese architecture in the early Cinquecento.
In his essay, Sannazzaro expounds the various hypotheses

regarding the church's authorship, retrieving the name of Giovanni Giacomo Dolcebuono, who, having been excluded previously due to his conflicts with the nuns and because the supposed date of his death (1506) is too close to the beginning of the work, has once again been taken into consideration on the basis of recent archive discoveries. After it had been ascertained that the quarrel with the Benedictine nuns was, at a certain point, patched up and the date of his death was actually 1510 — as documentary evidence revealed — Dolcebuono now seems to be one of the most likely candidates for the design of this church, in which the great Lombard architectural tradition is renewed as a result of Bramante's spatial innovations.

However, what is not clear is the extent to which the intimate relationship between architecture and painting — one of the most significant features of San Maurizio — could have developed without close collaboration between the architect and the artists working on the decorative scheme. Since the work on the first series of frescoes in the convent section of the church may be assigned to the beginning of the second decade of the Cinquecento, Dolcebuono's death in 1510 seems to argue against his being the architect and supervisor of the project — unless, that is, when designing the church, he was also able to establish the general principles for its decorative scheme.

The works of art adorning the walls and ceilings of San Maurizio offer an overview of almost a century of Milanese painting, bearing witness to the salient stages of a period that, starting from the Sforza rule, lasted until the age of Borromeo. The old guides to Milan, however, only recorded the most outstanding of the artists whose work may be admired in the church: while the name of Bernardino Luini appeared frequently, sometimes accompanied by that of Antonio Campi, they ignored other, less important artists, who, nonetheless, played a major role in the decoration of the building, helping to create its unique appearance.

Long before Luini's arrival, work had already started on the decoration of the uncluttered Bramantesque architecture in the convent section of the church, adorning its severe structures with the bright colours of the frescoes. The first series of frescoes is analysed by Sandrina Bandera, who, although she does not propose a precise attribution for the paintings on the bridge (the arched structure adjacent to the partition wall, linking the galleries) and the lunettes in the side chapels — but it must be stressed that works painted before Luini arrived are the most problematic in the church — provides sufficient information for them to be identified stylistically and given a chronological order. It may be cause for surprise that these cycles, attributed in the past to specific artists, are now once again anonymous, despite numerous studies that have led to a better knowledge of Renaissance art in Milan. But this very understanding, together with the evidence of documents informing us of the presence in Milan of hitherto totally unknown painters,[1] cannot but advise the greatest possible caution when making attributions.

This is the case with the monochromes on the pilasters, which were assigned to Luini by Ottino Della Chiesa, while more recent studies of the artist have excluded them from his œuvre. And the same may be said of the supposed participation of Giovan Antonio Boltraffio in the series of female saints painted in the gallery and the *Annunciation* on the front of the bridge, a hypothesis that was regarded with favour by Ottino Della Chiesa. However, even if in some of these it is possible to note similarities with the artist's style, such as, for example, the veiled Leonardism of the faces of the Virgin and the archangel Gabriel, it is quite improbable that the painter actually worked here. The total lack of documentary evidence that Boltraffio worked as a fresco painter, the fact that the artist, at the supposed date of this cycle, was working less frequently as a painter and, finally, the fact that the fresco cycle painted in the gallery — where the same cartoons appear to have been used a number of times and there are clearly a number of different hands (at times very cursory) — was evidently the result of teamwork, are all elements that prevent us from attributing any of these works to this refined Milanese painter. It is, however, possible that the artists who painted this cycle used cartoons supplied by Boltraffio or, more simply, that their style was influenced by his works already existing in Milan, such as *St Barbara* then in Santa Maria presso San Satiro.[2]

It is probable, as Sandrina Bandera suggests, that the need to complete the work in a short space of time meant that more than one artist was employed at a time, and, in fact, within the various frescoes painted in the convent section of the church during the execution of the first stage of the decorative scheme, some differences in tone may be noted. This tone appears to be particularly refined in the case of the artist who painted the arch of the bridge, so much so that Ottino Della Chiesa even suggested it might be the work of Vincenzo Foppa. Although this hypothesis is untenable — apart from any other considerations — for chronological reasons, it is, in any case, indicative of the quality of these paintings.

What these first frescoes have in common — and what lends homogeneity to the different works — is the fact that the various artists involved belong to a traditional current that followed in the footsteps of Bergognone and Bernardo Zenale. The taste that, in the star-studded vault of the bridge, has prompted the artist to avail himself of iconography of Late-Gothic origin is traditional — but then so is the technique used. As Paola Zanolini explains, the use of precious colours such as malachite and lapis lazuli, and the free handling of the paint, independently of whether sinopie or engraved outlines have been employed, is fully in keeping with Quattrocento practice.

And it is indeed the examination of the technique that allows us to confirm what has been revealed by stylistic analysis: in particular, the fact that the artists who worked on the vault under the bridge are not the same as the ones who painted the *Annunciation* on the spandrels of the arch, and yet another group of artists were responsible for the decoration of the lunettes in the side chapels with the series of saints flanking the oculi. In fact, the simplified handling of the paint and the repetitive use of the same cartoons suggest that the presence in this area of such great masters as Bergognone or Zenale may be excluded, although these may well be works by their followers. These observations are, however, simply intended to illustrate the cultural climate in which the oldest frescoes in San Maurizio were executed and should not, therefore, be interpreted as judgements on the quality of these paintings.

Nonetheless, it seems surprising that the Benedictine nuns of San Maurizio, belonging to the leading, most cultured families of the Milanese aristocracy, should have turned to painters whose style was decidedly *retardataire* for an initiative of such great importance as that of the decoration of their church, which had certainly been designed, as we have seen, by an architect of considerable standing. In the period when the work is believed to have started — the beginning of the second decade of the sixteenth century — Leonardo da Vinci was still in Milan, while the tradition represented by Bramantino, who had just completed the first series of tapestries of the *Months* for Marshal Gian Giacomo Trivulzio, had emerged as an original alternative to Leonardism. And, in the city, there was no lack of the early examples of a style that combined Leonardesque elements with the central-Italian style of Baldassarre Peruzzi and Jacopo Ripanda, such as the fresco cycle of the *Creation* — now in the Castello Sforzesco — painted in or before 1508 in the monastery of Sant'Antonio. In San Maurizio, on the other hand, it is as if the patrons, rather than run the risk of accepting innovatory ideas, had wished to seek refuge in tradition, creating a sort of continuity with other Milanese monastic establishments such as San Pietro in Gessate or Santa Maria delle Grazie — that is, the places where a "conventual style" respectful of tradition had developed.

It was thanks to Bernardino Luini that the "modern manner" burst into the tranquillity of the convent. His entrance was facilitated by the presence of patrons with a high social position, Alessandro Bentivoglio and his wife, Ippolita Sforza, who, as Dario Trenta explains, can now be identified without a shadow of doubt as the two donors portrayed by Luini in the lunettes on the side of the partition wall facing the lay worshippers' section of the church. It is they, not their daughter Violante and her husband, Gian Paolo Sforza, who must take the credit for the choice of an artist who was already established and capable of producing much better works than the all-too-predictable decorative scheme realized hitherto. And it was due to them that the church virtually became a family mausoleum, because other members of the noble family and their relatives were subsequently buried in San Maurizio and assumed the patronage of the side chapels.

As far as Luini's presence in the church is concerned, its chronology has been the subject of scholarly debate. Having abandoned the hypothesis that he started on the frescoes in 1513–15,[3] that is at the same time as the artists working on the bridge and lunettes, art historians have agreed on a date at the beginning of the 1520s, both on stylistic grounds and for reasons linked to the career of the patron, who achieved political success with the rise to power of Francesco II Sforza, consequently becoming a senator in 1522. Another problem that still has to be addressed is, however, the order in which Luini's frescoes were executed — that is to say, did the artist begin with the convent section of the church, painting the scenes of the Passion on that side of the partition wall, or did he, as a tribute to his patrons, start his part of the decorative scheme with their portraits?

Pietro Marani contributes to this debate by linking Luini's activity in San Maurizio to the wider context of his experience in other decorative schemes in Lombardy, without, however, forgetting the important role played by his patrons' cultural milieu. This very timely contextualization has allowed this scholar to offer a new interpretation of Luini's fresco cycle, the execution of which appears to be interwoven with other contemporary commissions undertaken by the artist. Contrary to the widely held opinion that the upper panels were painted before the lower ones — as was usual practice — Marani believes that Luini started with the frescoes on the lower part of the side of the partition wall facing the lay worshippers' section of the church, and then executed the ones on the lower part of the opposite side, facing the convent section. There is a gap between this first stage, which was completed before 1524 or even before 1523, and the next one, which began in 1525. Marani advances the hypothesis that, in this interval, Luini went on a journey to Rome, the consequences of which may be seen in the last two panels he painted on the partition wall facing the lay worshippers' section — those at the top depicting St Maurice. Marani's essay also refers to other attributions that are no longer accepted: for instance, the *Assumption* in the centre of the upper level has now been excluded from Luini's œuvre and tentatively ascribed to Bernardino Ferrari.[4] Sandrina Bandera, on the other hand, suggests that the monochromes on the pilasters in the convent section may be the work of the follower of Luini and Zenale who painted the *Annunciation* formerly in the Cappella di San Giuseppe in Santa Maria della Pace, now in the Pinacoteca di Brera.[5] And justice has finally been done to "pure landscapes" — that is, the ones with neither figures nor architecture — painted in the side chapels of the convent section of the church. Ascribed to Luini by Ottino Della Chiesa, they have turned out to be modern, probably late nineteenth-century (or even post-1917, as Sannazzaro suggests elsewhere),[6] having been painted over the original decoration with geometrical motifs that emerged during the conservation work.

The frescoes in the Cappella Besozzi, painted by Bernardino Luini in 1530, and commented on here by Marani, mark the end of the first stage of the decoration of San Maurizio, which was suspended for a long period after the artist died in 1532. Luini left four sons, three of whom became painters: but Aurelio and Giovan Pietro, born around 1530, were very young when their father died, while the eldest, Evangelista (documented from 1532 onwards), must have been in his early adolescence. This was too early, therefore, to ensure immediate continuity.

Naturally, the painter's death was not the only reason for this standstill in the work: the excommunication of Alessandro Bentivoglio — which was only revoked in 1541 — and, above all, the creation of new family alliances and the addition of new patrons (albeit still linked to the Bentivoglio) are also factors that may have contributed to a hiatus lasting over ten years.

When work did finally start again it was in a very different cultural atmosphere, which Valerio Guazzoni examines in his perceptive essay, where he also proposes new attributions. Apart from the frescoes by the Piazza in the Cappella Simonetta and their *Marriage at Cana* on the partition wall facing the convent section of the church — where Sandrina Bandera has identified the predominant (and weaker) hand of Callisto Piazza's son — the leading protagonist of the decoration of the side chapels and much of the convent section is the workshop of Luini's sons.

The lukewarm judgements pronounced with regard to their work in the past have weighed heavily on the reputation of these artists, while more recently art historians have credited Aurelio, who was much more talented than Giovan Pietro, with the qualities for which he was praised in the sixteenth century by the artist and writer Giovan Paolo Lomazzo.

The problem of the distinction, within this workshop, between the contributions of the three brothers is addressed by Guazzoni in a rigorous manner that has produced important results. I am referring to the attribution of the two Carreto chapels — the first to be frescoed after work started again in 1545 — to Evangelista Luini, whose participation, previously suggested by Ottino Della Chiesa, has hitherto been purely a hypothesis, without any documentary evidence. Now, however, Guazzoni's observations, deriving from his reading of Lomazzo, who describes Evangelista as a specialist in grotesques — and the walls of the Cappella di Santo Stefano abound with sphinxes, masks and candelabra — together with the fact that Evangelista's presence is recorded in Genoa in 1544 (thus justifying the paraphrase of Giulio Romano's Genoese altarpiece seen here in the *Stoning of St Stephen*), lend credibility to the identification of his hand in the two chapels commissioned

by the Carreto brothers, who were related to the Bentivoglio through Ginevra, one of Alessandro Bentivoglio's daughters.
Moreover, the choice of Evangelista — who, as the eldest son must have been the first to follow in his father's footsteps — seems to be perfectly logical: it reflects, in fact, the desire of the new patrons to confirm Alessandro Bentivoglio's preferences by availing themselves of what was probably the only workshop able to ensure continuity in the decoration of the church.
The younger brothers started work in San Maurizio in 1555; their training had provided them — especially Aurelio — with a wide-ranging, variegated artistic background that combined an urge for renewal with loyalty to tradition. Guazzoni's essay recounts the stages in their work, throwing light on the iconographic programme and recognizing the contributions of each of them, with careful distinction between the two hands and linking their activity to the influence that Mannerism began to have on Milanese art in this period. This was stimulated, in San Maurizio, by a sort of rivalry with the workshop of the Piazza family, who came from Lodi, close to the orbit of the Venetian Republic.
A turning-point came at the beginning of the 1570s, when the last spaces still without frescoes were entrusted to artists from outside Lombardy. The climate was that of the Borromean reform, which required adherence to dogma, attention to the values of the faith and stimuli for prayer and repentance. This is already perceptible in Aurelio Luini's rendering of the frescoes in the Cappella Bentivoglio, the accents of which, by reflecting the tenets of the Counter-Reformation, tend to suffocate the work of this inventive member of Lomazzo's Accademia della Val di Blenio, whom the Milanese writer greatly admired for his originality. While, on the entrance wall, Simone Peterzano, here at the beginning of his long Milanese career, displays the Venetian style — still immune from devotional overtones — he had previously assimilated, the frescoes of the Genoese Ottavio Semino in the Cappella Fiorenza, like Antonio Campi's altarpiece in the high altar, meet Cardinal Charles Borromeo's requirements regarding the decorum and simplicity to which, as Sandrina Bandera underlines, sacred images had to rigorously adhere.

[1] I am referring to what may be learnt from the documents published by Janice Shell, especially the one dated 2 February 1481, in which the members of the Scuola di San Luca appoint their procurators, and the one of 13–22 May 1511 in which a large group of painters sign a protest to the Scuola di San Luca defending Bernardo Zenale (J. Shell, *Pittori in bottega. Milano nel Rinascimento*, Milan 1995, pp. 203–205, 213–217.)

[2] Strong affinities with the compositional schema and modelling of the faces of the female saints in the gallery of San Maurizio are to be found in the figure of St Catherine painted in a *Pietà* formerly in Santa Maria della Pace (now in the Museo di Sant'Agostino, Genoa). Executed in the first decade of the Cinquecento by an anonymous Lombard painter, the fresco — where Blessed Amadeo da Silva is portrayed while writing his prophetic text — is evidence of how certain inflections of Leonardesque origin are a characteristic of many Lombard paintings at the beginning of the Cinquecento, without implying they are the work of artists of Boltraffio's calibre. For the fresco mentioned here, see E. Parma, "Rapporti artistici tra Genova e le Fiandre nella prima metà del Cinquecento", in *Fiamminghi a Roma 1508–1608. Atti del convegno internazionale, Bruxelles 24–25* Febbraio 1995, ed. N. Dacos (published in *Bollettino d'arte*, supplement to no. 100, 1997, pp. 44–45).

[3] M.T. Binaghi Olivari, in *The Dictionary of Art*, London and New York 1996, s.v. "Bernardino Luini".

[4] See G. Bora, "Bernardino Luini", in *I leonardeschi. L'eredità di Leonardo in Lombardia*, J. Shell, Milan 1998, p. 350.

[5] The artist responsible for this mysterious painting — which appears to be the work of either Luini or Zenale, without being by either of them — has been identified by Grazioso Sironi in a document (to be published shortly) kept in the Archivio di Stato in Milan: this document confirms the provenance of the work from the Cappella di San Giuseppe in Santa Maria della Pace.

[6] G.B. Sannazzaro, "Per la decorazione pittorica nella chiesa di San Maurizio al Monastero Maggiore di Milano: suggerimenti di studio", in *Arte lombarda del secondo millennio. Saggi in onore di Gian Alberto Dell'Acqua* Milan 2000, p. 148–149.

The Architecture of San Maurizio

Giovanni Battista Sannazzaro

The great quantity of studies devoted to the church of San Maurizio and the neighbouring Benedictine convent, the Monastero Maggiore,[1] has recently brought to light a document recording the sale of a parcel of land, transacted on 20 May 1503, appointed "pro fabricatione fiendæ ecclesiæ"[1] (for the construction of church property).[2] By comparing maps of Milan,[3] one can see that part of the new church was built on the newly acquired land, lying contiguous with today's Corso Magenta — then the busy *via ad Vercellas* (road to Vercelli), subsequently named Corso di Porta Vercellina — and just outside the vestigial circuit of the ancient city walls.[4] For centuries this curtain of defence had enclosed all the church buildings together with a large tract of land attached to the monastery; these buildings have since either been completely transformed or dismantled, but originally arose on the remains of pre-existing structures of signal importance, namely, the Roman circus and the city walls built in Roman imperial times.[5] The areas lying outside the later republican enceinte were undoubtedly developed in the first century A.D., as testified by traces of a former *domus* unearthed during excavation work in 1961, and still visible in the seventeenth-century cloister to the right of the church, now the adjacent entrance to the Museo Archeologico (1965). While a lingering reminder of the former circus, built for horse-races probably in A.D. 293–94, has reached us in the name of the street, Via Circo, the layout itself of the public arena remained pure guesswork until an accurate reconstruction was made in the 1930s on the basis of traces of walling found in the basements of houses fronting the present streets of Cappuccio, Vigna, and Sant'Orsola; similar circular walls had meanwhile come to light in Via Circo and Via del Torchio. In conformance with tradition, Milan's circus (measuring around 470 × 85 m) was laid along a north–south axis and encircled by an escarpment and a reinforced containing wall (south end) equipped with loopholes coinciding with the city walls, beyond which ran the Nirone stream, now covered up. Upon the order of the linesmen, the drivers of the quadriga chariots bolted from the *carceres* (cells, north end), and it is here at the race's former starting line that the buildings of the Monastero Maggiore were raised. In accordance with the tradition of Roman circus building, the structural limit of the *carceres* was marked by two towers, of which one, built on a rectangular trapezoidal plan, has survived behind the apse of the church of San Maurizio; of the other, towards the south, there is no trace.

Formerly considered the work of the city's archbishop, Ansperto (r. 869–881), owing to insufficient historical knowledge, the tower, long since absorbed into the structures of the Monastero Maggiore, has proved to have foundations in rubble similar to that used for the Roman circus, therefore suggesting its being contemporary. Detailed studies and stratigraphic tests performed on the tower, one of the most sturdy in Milan, have revealed at least two key phases of building, fairly close to each other, and both effected in Roman times.[6]

When, in the year A.D. 286, Milan became the northern capital of the Western Empire, this corner of the city was transformed by the construction of defensive walls raised by Emperor Maximian, along with reinforcements to the

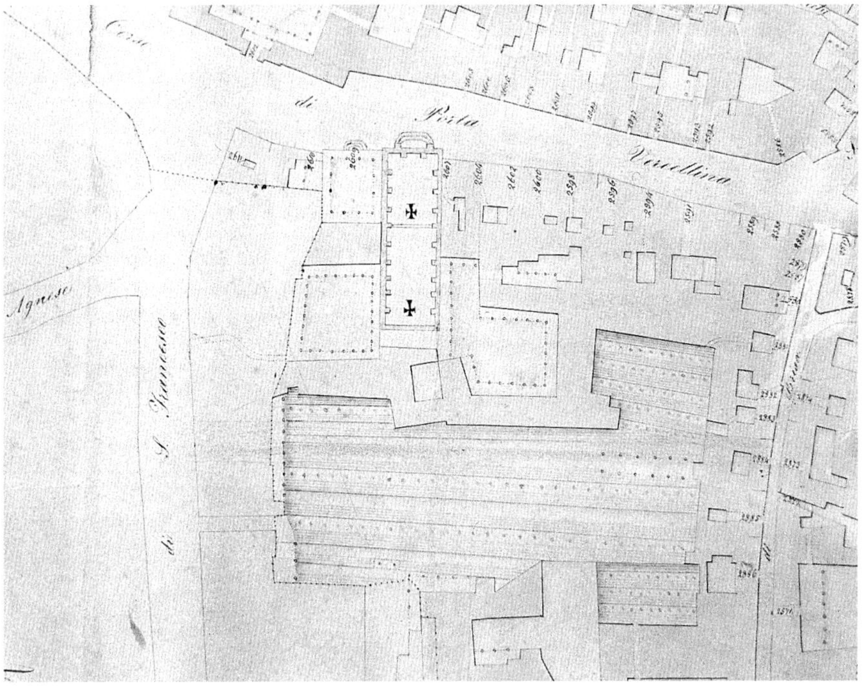

Ground plan of the Monastero Maggiore, nineteenth century
Archivio di Santa Maria alla Porta, Milan

existing ramparts built during the republic, subsequently enveloping the circus. The limit of the new curtain of fortifications lies to the northwest, with sections on Via Nirone, and more particularly, on Corso Magenta, the path that would thenceforth until 1503 demarcate the property boundary of the Monastero Maggiore. Portions of similar city walls, surviving solely by dint of the longevity of the monastic buildings themselves, can be seen in the little seventeenth-century cloister to the south, now the entrance to the Museo Archeologico, and also in the museum's basement exhibition rooms and the crypt of the neighbouring church of San Maurizio. Tests have revealed traces of rubble foundations mixed into the building mortar, a feature that recurs in the foundations of the two surviving towers erected to guard the city's defence system. While only the foundations remain of the said tower at the corner of the northeast wall, between Via Nirone and Corso Magenta, the other tower, which would later delimit the area west of the monastery, is today enclosed in what remains of the sixteenth-century cloister — behind, on the south, the smaller, seventeenth-century cloister — which now serves as the back garden of the museum.

Believed once to be associated with Archbishop Ansperto, and, according to an ancient legend,[7] to be the prison of the city's early Christian martyrs Gervase, Protase, Nabor, and Felix, this tower rises on a course of cement (discovered during excavation work in 1954), and comprises masonry walling considered for the most part to be of Roman origin, bar the crown and roofing. The only such structure in Milan still standing at its full height, the tower has twenty-four brick faces set on a polygonal base outside, with a circular internal section, and tapers upward (from 7.4 to 6.5 m) with a remarkable sense of thrust (height 16.6 m); the trunk is pierced at different levels by six embrasures and loophole windows, its defensive front looking out to what was once the countryside. On the same base course, as in the trench running along the tower's foundations, one can see remains of stone bridgework linking the two towers. Similar masonry was erected at a later stage, to keep the city's defence systems up to date, perhaps coinciding with the empire's fall, or more likely to repair the heavy damage received in the siege of the Goths of Uraia (A.D. 538), based nevertheless along a path that would subsequently be followed by the inner cloister of the monastery.

In light of archaeological research on the ancient circus,

it is now believed that the beginnings of the Monastero Maggiore date back to between the eighth and ninth centuries — that is, to the end of Longobard rule — or at most to the start of the Carolingian period, when, moreover, the circus may have been exploited as a convenient quarry for building or lime-furnace material — several false seventeenth-century diplomas referred to this period. Come what may, at a date not much earlier than A.D. 823, when the monastery must have already been in existence, on 3 June that year a deed of exchange cites a patch of monastery land ("terra de Monastero Maiore") to be exchanged for land in the town of Carpiano. In 853, some thirty years later, though without any further indication of place, archives cite certain "monachas monasterii Magiore"(nuns from the Monastero Maggiore), a name that suggests a special status for the monastery, at civic level also, perhaps owing to the considerable renown of its founder.

Even today there is general agreement that the Maggiore was the most famous of all the Benedictine monasteries built in Milan under Charlemagne. Fourteenth-century maps of the city show for the first time the position of the four churches that were once dependent upon each other: Santa Maria al Circo, San Pietro alla Vigna, San Quirico, and, not far off, Santa Valeria.[8] Meanwhile, within this enclave the monastery buildings must have lain between the two towers and the city walls, while to the south stretched the expanse of pasturage serving as a kitchen garden and orchard, that is later (1862) recorded as containing over two hundred grape vines (a fact echoed in the name of the nearby Via Vigna) and as many fruit trees (apricot, peach, plum, and various raspberry espaliers), at the time covering an estimated 13 hectares.[9]

Confirmation of the date of the foundation and of the importance of the monastery can be inferred from the reinforcement work done on Maximian's walls, carried out in the ninth century by Archbishop Ansperto[10] in order to render less vulnerable (both within and without the curtain) the city and the monastery itself, with its associated churches in this stretch of land extending over the former ancient Roman circus — walls of which Morigia would write in 1641 made "all of Milan like a cloister".[11] To the same century we owe the loggetta that encloses the quadrangular tower, whereas of Romanesque origin is the installing of Roman columns in the entrance archway;[12] conversely, no record is known of the activity of the monastery *scriptorum*, or copy-room, apart from an old fragment of a *Sacramentary* (end ninth century), while doubts remain as to its provenance.[13] It is possible that among the items donated by Otto I in the tenth century to the monastery was a relic of St Maurice[14] — to whom he was as devoted as he was to St Sigismund — presumably confirms the importance of the monastery. It may be that while Otto was in Milan in 965, Empress Adelaide — lodged in the guest quarters of the Monastero Maggiore with her son — made him a gift of the famous *Placchetta Trivulzio* (now in the Musei Civici, Castello Sforzesco, Milan), an ivory plaque carved with a complete illustration of the imperial triad being presented to the Almighty by St Mary and St Maurice, the protectors of the imperial family.[15]

The first historically reliable document relating to the monastery, a deed (1027), opens with a dedication to the Virgin Mary, in memory of "Gerechilda, abbess of the so-called Maggiore monastery of Mary, Holy Mother of God, founded in this city of Milan". Similar dedications appear in the will (1034) of Archbishop Heribert of Intimiano,[16] in which not only is the monastery indicated for the first time as being among the seven convents scattered across the city, but, also present in the commission of clergymen appointed as dutiful executors of the will, are the abbot of Sant'Ambrogio and the abbess of the Maggiore, the only woman cited: the woman's station corroborates her distinction and prominence, elected thus as a guarantor of the future Monastero Maggiore, with a position of considerable rank in Milan's clergy and in the city itself. The entitlement to the Virgin Mary is reiterated around mid-eleventh century (1042, 1060),[17] and again in 1078 we find the joint dedication to St Mary and St Maurice,[18] after which the monastery would be known simply as San Maurizio, starting with the bestowal of papal privilege — the first known distinction accorded to the monastery — addressed by Pope Eugenius III on 29 July 1148 to the abbess of the monastery, Margherita da Lampugnano.[19] Besides the bestowal of apostolic protection, an endorsement was made for the rights to the property and its assets in Milan and *contado*, or countryside,[20] and for legitimate purchase in the future. Effectively, the convent owned the four church properties within the city limits,[21] with relative appurtenances, assorted buildings and plots of land. It is not documented whether at this point the monastery's church was the original one, or whether it was radically altered or completely rebuilt in the proto-Romanesque

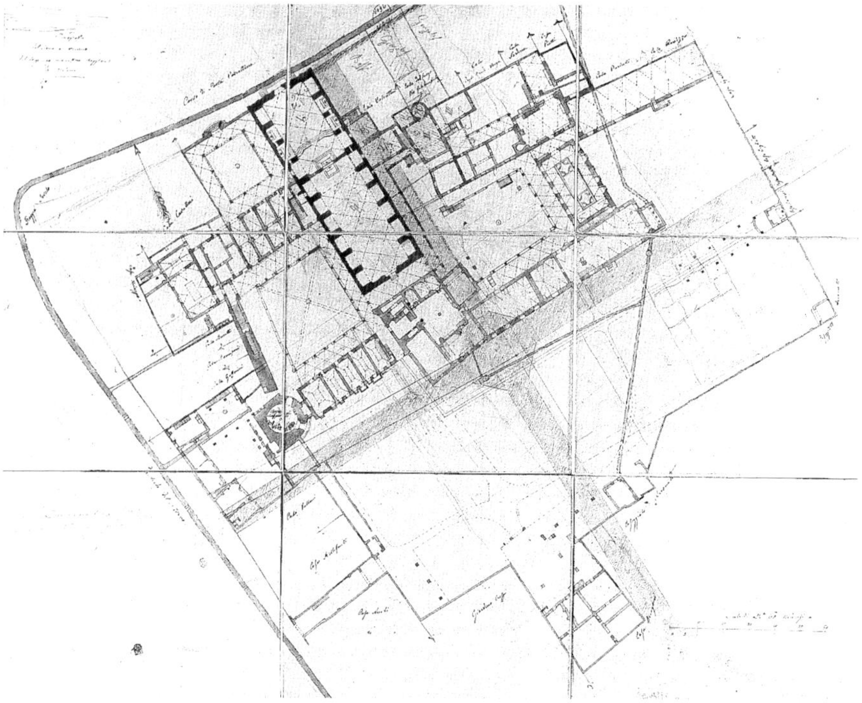

Ground plan of the Monastero Maggiore, with pencil shading for the planned Via Ansperto and Via Luini
P 42, Raccolta Bertarelli, Milan

or Lombard style; the grounds, considering the pre-existing structures and the continuity of its existence, must have generally coincided (but on a reduced scale[22]) with the temple's current site plan: the fact that the church today consists of two contiguous vessels, divided by a partition raised along the ancient walls and acquiring a slight deviation in the course of alterations to existing convent building stock, suggests the reutilization of structures belonging to Santa Maria just outside the ramparts themselves. In the meantime, the need for a twin vessel offering separate churches dividing the lay congregation from the convent nuns may have influenced the construction of the early church according to a divided scheme which, it is generally accepted, must date back to the early days of Christianity, when some churches had an iconostasis (dividing icon screen) separating the main hall from the bema, or inner sanctum, thereby parcelling up the church according to function.[23] Given that in the late Middle Ages such dividing walls screening off the women's choir from the main hall were common also in Cistercian convents, it is likely that the first church to adopt this setup — perhaps one of the very earliest — is Santa Maria d'Aurona, which, like the Maggiore, is also of Benedictine foundation. From the thirteenth century several Benedictine convents had employed simplified forms of division, such as the addition of a small lay worshippers hall to an earlier oratory in churches today no longer standing such as Santa Radegonda and Santa Maria del Lentasio. Owing to the growing practice of retrieving unused land within the now obsolete city defence walls, progressing from the ramparts inwards toward the city, near the original church there may have been at least two cloisters, around which the monastery itself was gathered. Gothic vestiges of these structures can still be seen in Via Luini (no. 5),[24] comprising a section of arcading on the left. Described in 1851 as an "irregular courtyard [...] on the north side: arcade [...]. Pointed archways with 7 Gothic columns", the ruins also appeared in a nineteenth-century *veduta* (Museo di Milano), which showed them already assimilated into the sixteenth-century convent buildings (no longer extant).[25] Moreover, the layouts themselves, another nineteenth-century *veduta* (Raccolta Bertarelli, Milan) and photographs taken both before World War II and during the subsequent clearance after bomb damage[26] reveal how other convent buildings surrounded Maximian's polygonal tower, hugging the city walls, in a logical reutilization of existing structures on land still vacant for development.[27]

In the fifteenth century, while still recoiling from the grim years of the previous century, the monastic orders all across Lombardy were plagued not so much by decadence as by exhaustion. The effects were felt in the Monastero Maggiore in economic terms due to the documented slackening of the rural seignories' hold, but first and foremost repercussions were felt at a religious level. Towards 1444 the inhabitants of the monastery complex comprised the abbess and ten Benedictine nuns "viventes cum parva aut potius nulla clausura aut regulari observantia, ymmo satis cum infamia" (who evinced little or almost no respect for their vows and for regular observance, indeed they lived dishonourably).[28]
During the subsequent rapid recovery of the Benedictine community the number of members began to rise, starting in 1479, as testified in chapter deeds of the congregation of Santa Giustina, which reports insufficient room to accommodate the stream of newcomers.[29] To judge from the wood model built to illustrate the proposed design (a standard practice at the time), probably dating to before 1503, and given the purchase of land "pro fabricatione fiendæ ecclesiæ" (20 May), and from the foundation stone in the church itself, it is credible that plans were already afoot for the construction of a new church. For three centuries the church's design was attributed, also by Carlo Torre (1674) and Serviliano Latuada (1738), to Bramantino (Bartolomeo Suardi);[30] whereas in 1776 Abbot Albuzio attributed it to the architect Giovanni Giacomo Dolcebuono, regarding as an eminently tenable source "a book of memoirs conserved in the monastery" (as yet unfound).[31] Engaged in building activity in Milan and the duchy, together with Giovanni Antonio Amadeo, Dolcebuono actually lived in the vicinity of the monastery itself. At the time working jointly with the cousins Guiniforte and Giovanni Solari, the attribution to Dolcebuono was dismissed by some scholars as unlikely, given that in 1474 he was involved in a legal dispute with the monastery order over the use of the nearby Nirone watercourse (as disclosed in documents long since available). The alleged untenability of the attribution is however controverted by the subsequent settlement of the dispute, in 1492, involving the intervention of another architect very active at the time, Bartolomeo della Valle, a suggestion further endorsed by new finds among the archives that established the death of Dolcebuono in 1510 rather than 1506 as previously believed (at any event too close to the date of 1503).[32]

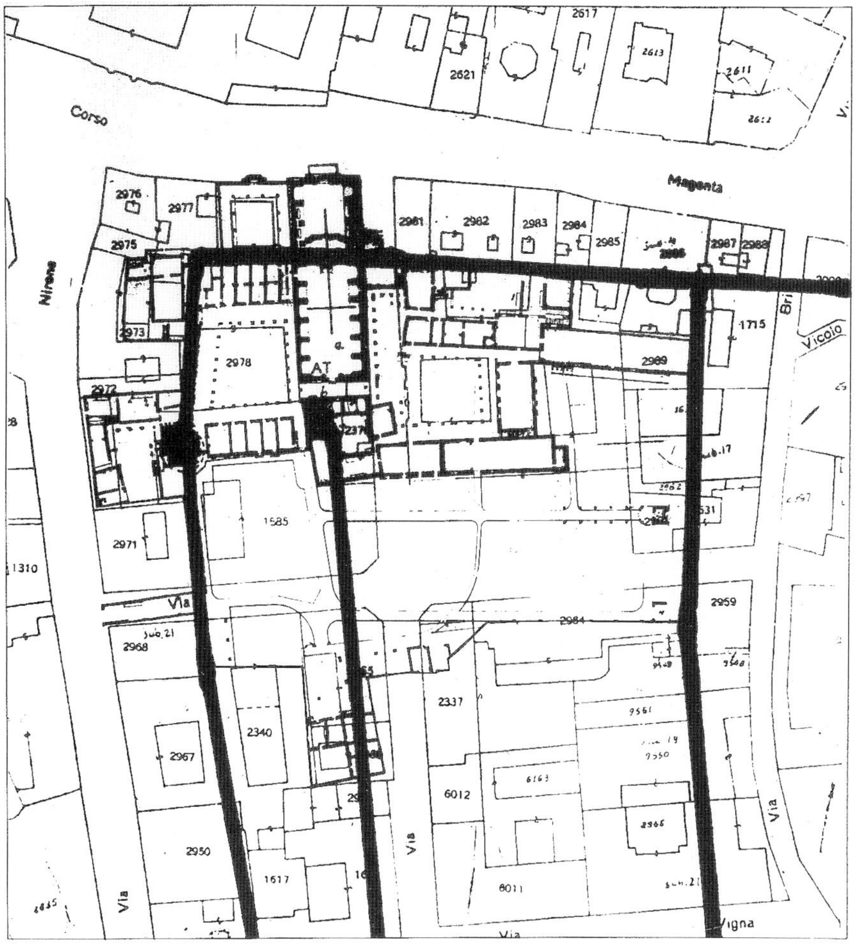

Present-day ground plan of the Monastero Maggiore, showing the original path of the ancient Roman structures (circus, city walls) From G. Pertot, "Contributi per la storia edilizia del Monastero Maggiore di Milano: nuove indicazioni da documenti del periodo 1798-1858", in *Rassegna di Studi del Civico Museo Archeologico e del Civico Gabinetto Numismatico di Milano*, suppl. XVIII, 1997, pl. V

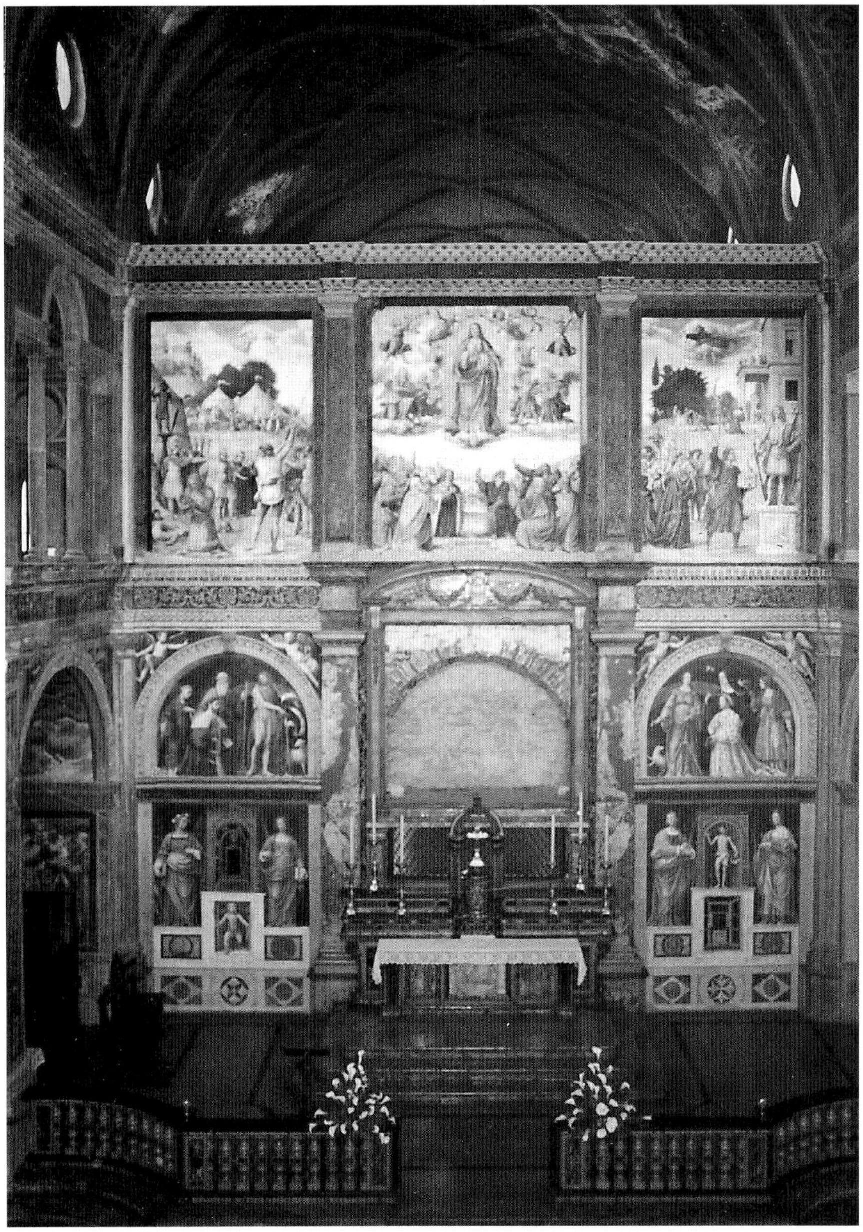

Lay worshippers' hall view
including the central arch of the
dividing wall without the altarpiece

Consequently, the recent discovery of the deed of sale effected that year has brought to light the first name of any architect linked to the sixteenth-century construction of San Maurizio, appearing among the *testes*, as "magister Antonius de Bodiis de Lonatis filius quondam domini Ambrosii porte verceline parochie sancte marie ad portam mediolani" (Master Antonio da Lonate, son of the late Ambrogio of the parish of Porta Vercellina at Santa Maria alla Porta, Milan), that is, in the shadow of the church itself.[33]

In the meantime, the attribution to Dolcebuono has been flanked by others, largely to architects whose common denominator was their documented involvement in the cathedral,[34] not least Amadeo,[35] Cristoforo Solari and Cesare Cesariano.[36] On the basis of close links detected between the architecture and pictorial programme of San Maurizio,[37] work has also been attributed to Bernardo Zenale.[38] Given that, in the absence of a more certain attribution, even one of the enigmatic "anonimi sforzeschi" (anonymous Sforza architects) has been proposed as the building's architect,[39] it is now held that the church's design is at any event the work of a major architect active in Milan during the period in question, a hypothesis amply borne out by the ingenious idea of making good the area outside the perimeter of the ancient walls, whence the buildings' slight angle of deviation, and of land external to the convent buildings, at the time not all demolishable, together with the dimensions permitted by the available acreage, wedged into a rectangle of 49.2 × 16.4 m. Added to this is the requirement for two separate areas for worship, monastic and public. The early solution of a "double church" constitutes the first complete realization of the system of a single nave divided transversely into two separate contiguous chambers, one reserved for members of the order, the other for lay worshippers; in architectural terms, the resulting scheme not only resembles that adopted for other monastery churches like San Vittore in the town of Meda, and the Milanese churches of San Vincenzino alle Monache (no longer extant), and later San Paolo Converso, but also complies with the provisions laid down by Bishop Charles Borromeo in his *Instructiones fabricæ et suppellectilis ecclesiasticæ*, issued when the Counter-Reformation was well under way (1577).[40]

Raised to the height of the vault's imposts, this transverse dividing wall separates the front four-bay chamber accessed by the lay community from the six-bay rear section reserved for the nuns. The full ten bays proceed uninterruptedly with lateral buttresses supported on two orders of Tuscan pilasters, rising to a discreet continuous entablature that serves as a springing course. Set into the lower order of each bay, the chapels have a barrel vault and round arch, whereas the field between the pilasters of the second order accommodates an Ionic Serlian window (ratio 1:1) set into the parapet of the triforium (women's gallery) the same depth as the chapels below. The arrangement is surmounted by a depressed arch resting on a stepped cornice from which rise tall lunettes (these too pierced with circular windows slanting downwards, diam. 1 m), which distribute the load of the main vault above. A similar orchestration of elements is reiterated for the entire perimeter of the church — lending grandeur to what would otherwise have seemed like a long corridor given the vessel's restricted dimensions — including the entrance wall and apse, in a tripartite arrangement, though shallower, and a fully arcaded third order. The roof itself is an orthodox barrel vault perfectly inscribed in a semicircle (height 5 m; diam. 10 m) ranged with fictive ribbing of double intersecting arches.[41] These ribs have no static purpose and are merely a decorative device to give a sense of lift to the vessel below and to draw attention to the ceiling's continuing perspective sequence beyond the dividing wall. By contrast, the enormous thrusts entailed by the main vault are distributed through the buttress but in correspondence with the anchoring of the dividing wall (which is without any foundation course, as discerned from the crypt below); further counter-thrust is provided by the "bridge" (or arched platform literally bridging the two sides of the church), which rests on a single, vast, slightly depressed elliptical three-centred arch (span 10 m), and is directly braced for the breadth of one bay to the corresponding buttresses comprised of similarly designed arches. The thrusts of the huge vault counter those of the twenty-two buttresses, which are structurally connected through the chapel vaults (true load-bearing arches), and distributed along the entablature and arch systems of the loggia and the said bridge — all in all a delicate system of structural stability whose calculation took account of the counter-thrusts afforded at the time by the convent's existing buildings alongside the nuns' chamber (which were in turn already within the consolidated path of the old city walls). Included in this solution of complex construction loads — achieved undoubtedly at the hands of accomplished builders — is a double presbytery built in the bays at either side of the dividing wall, one in the fourth bay for

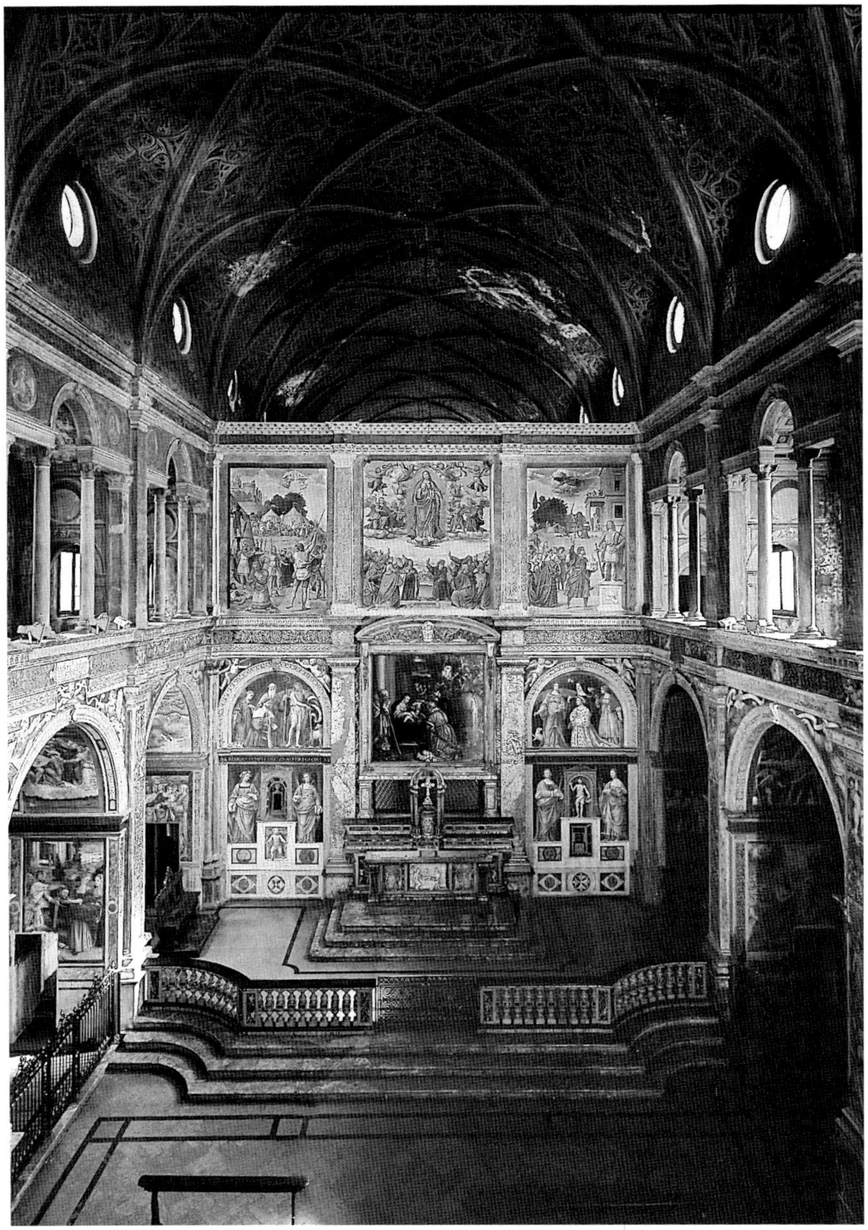

Lay worshippers' hall

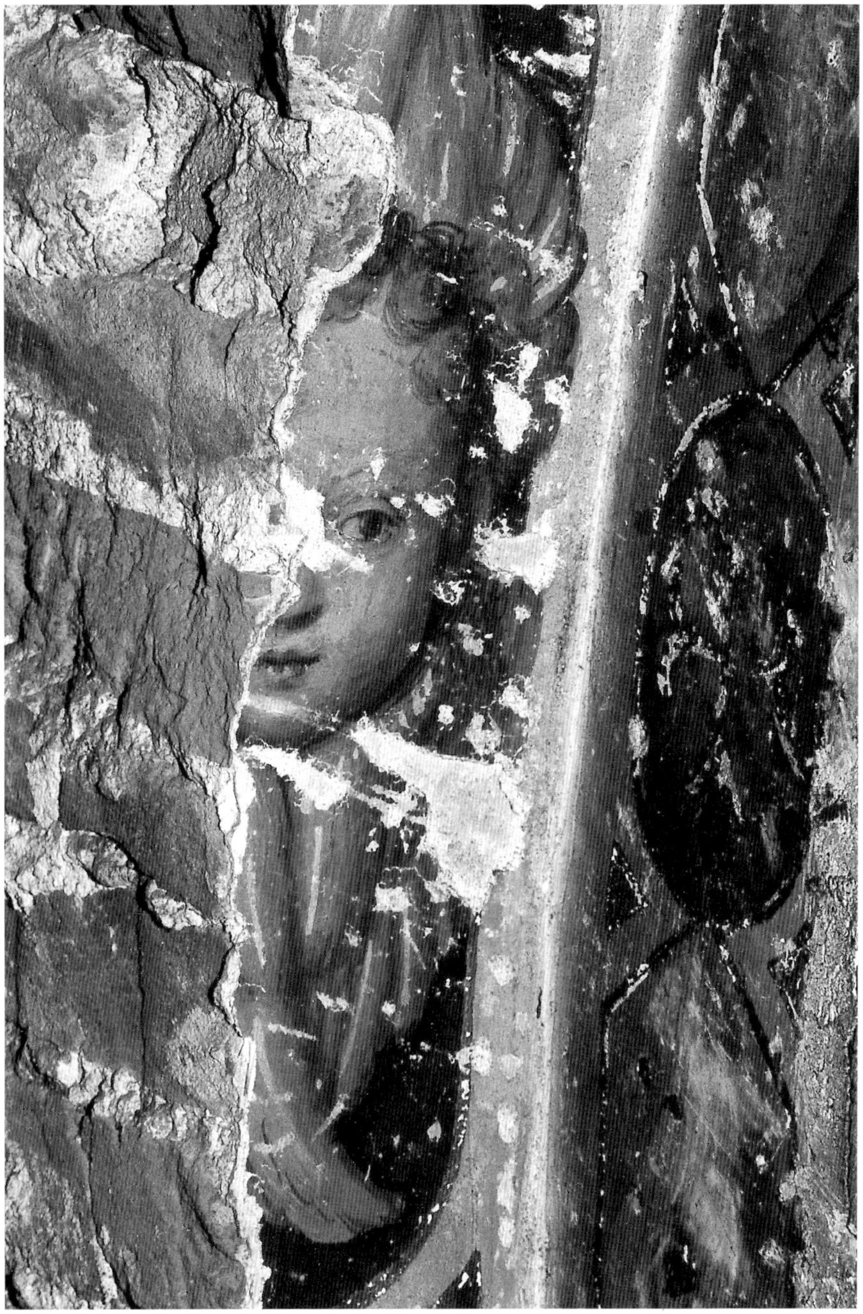

Painted angel in the main arch above the high altar, now hidden by the painted altarpiece

the lay congregation, the other for the nuns below the bridge-arch (formerly with an altar); the floor of this area is raised uniformly half a metre above the basic floor level on the nuns' side and above the crypt (implicating a total of seven bays).[42]

In compliance with the specifications for joint worship between the two congregations during liturgical practices later prescribed by St Charles in his *Instructiones* the raised floor enabled the Benedictine nuns (unobserved) to follow Masses performed in the lay half of the church by means of a window, still present over the high altar, and therefore the focal point of religious attention and the architectural focus of the entire church. In 1545 a special iron grating (now lost) was fitted to the aperture, fashioned to designs by Cristoforo Lombardo ("ferrata una ante altare maius");[43] and some thirty years later (1577) the window was reduced in size, at St Charles' behest, and a painted altarpiece set before it (1579); some two centuries thereafter the marble section of the altar was added (1790–93), comprising stone pilasters and a cornice. These alterations concealed the initial opening cut into the centre of the wall, painted (as moreover recently revealed[44]) so as to accentuate the unitary and circular nature around which the entire church was designed. As would subsequently be stressed in the cardinal's *Instructiones*, on the dividing wall, delimiting beyond the dais the nuns' presbytery too, on the opposite side of the wall lie the two doorways through which the nuns were able to pass in order to receive the Host ("communicate", on the Gospel side) and adore the Holy Father (on the Eucharist side). According to the original project, these doorways, plus a third opening on the left (east) wall of the presbytery were the only forms of access from one half of the church to the other, hitherto linked indirectly by the double sacristy that was demolished with the creation of Via Luini (after 1865, with the opening of an interior door). According to the earlier liturgical scheme, whenever sacred music was being played — whose performance by the nuns was greatly appreciated — access may have been available via the transitional space of the said platform on the extrados of the bridge in the cloister choir, hidden from the lay congregation by the second order of the dividing wall (as suggested by the greater wear on the central part of the floor), allowing meanwhile internal circulation among the various passageways in the second-story loggia, whose only point of access was via the staircase in the square tower alongside.

The interior of the church closely reflects the architectural exterior, despite alterations carried out over time, notably, the demolition of the outlying convent building on the left; in the upper portion, at the height of the third order, the vessel's sides were set back and lightened by ten large arches in line with the bays inside, and also pierced with roundels; the second order was ranged with narrow arched openings, each one in line with the Serlian windows of the women's choir parapet inside. Almost one third taller than the breadth of the vessel, the church façade (over 22 m at the fourth cornice, and around 24 m at the crown) is aligned with the road, and slightly angled with respect to the nuns' hall; the resulting effect is of a façade arranged on a framework that rests on a high base course (raised level with the interior floor, containing a basement of tombs) and subdivided into five vertical fields profiled with tapering pilaster strips (two marking the lateral chapels, and three the central section of the entrance wall); and vertically into three orders framed by stepped horizontal courses respectively demarcating the chapel level, the loggias, and the vault, in ascending order. The entire façade is clad in Ornavasso stone with mouldings in marble; only the two lower orders are coeval with the original structure, and are mentioned in a resolution passed in 1507 by the deputies of the Fabbrica del Duomo di Milano (Cathedral Board of Works) who, "lecta supplicationem dominarum ab[batiss]e et monialium monasterii maioris Mediolani" (having read the appeal of the abbess and the nuns of the Monastero Maggiore, Milan), adhered to their request for "petia sedecim marmoris fini pro ornatu faciate ecclesiæ earum monasterii" (sixteen pieces of fine marble for the decoration of the façade of their monastery church), provided Amadeo (then *capomastro* of the cathedral building site) could spare his men for the year in question.[45] After the first two façade orders were completed, respectively Doric and Ionic — reflecting those inside the church, which by now must have been near completion — the front prospect remained unfinished, most likely due to a lack of further funds or to the mood of uncertainty that gripped the region, a period during which possession of the duchy was contended by France and Spain, leading to the capture (1500) and death (1508) of Ludovico il Moro, thence to the reinstatement of Ludovico's firstborn, Massimiliano (1512), followed by the second-born, Francesco II, whose eventual death (1535) spelt the demise of the Sforza dynasty's legitimate claim to the duchy.

Completed, therefore, before the date (1509) carved on the tombstone of Martino Curzio (formerly set into the floor of the laypersons' hall inside the church but since dispersed), and at any event, long before the church's consecration (traditionally ascribed to 1519),[46] the subtle, graceful architecture of San Maurizio belongs to the creative universe of Bramante and Leonardo da Vinci and the emergence of a universal classical idiom which heralded the gradual enfranchisement from the contemporary "Lombard" tradition. Also influential was the dialectic pluralism that had characterized a great deal of expression in Italy in the preceding period, each region with its own canons. In substance, ideas were evolving away from the Sforza architectural tradition in favour of a new classicizing grammar, a change testified by such works as Bramantino's Cappella Trivulzio at San Nazaro, the arcaded atrium of Santa Maria presso San Celso, and Santa Maria alla Fontana, all three in Milan; other further-flung models include San Pietro Po in Cremona; the apse tribune of the cathedral at Como; the scale model for the new cathedral of Vigevano; and not least the façade of the Certosa of Pavia.

In this respect, the façade of San Maurizio would seem to subscribe to an intellectual approach in which, after firmly establishing the layout and elevations, the whole is announced in an orchestration of surface planes. While observing the standards of hierarchy and closely respecting the building's framework, the architectural orders do not convey the static forces at play, but instead assume a more electively decorative pattern, layered onto those structures as it were: the mouldings are more drawn than actually modelled, obeying a sequence that turns the elevation into a rhythmic surface expressing a dynamism more intent on eliciting a feeling, than on positing classical canons by means of clever references to established formulas, which were to some extent remote in both time and space. Such canons were still only conceptual, and not yet fully formulated into precise rules of proportion, allowing a compositional dynamics that was based on a two-dimensional, surface organization of planes.[47]

The available sources of references that served as models for San Maurizio are legion: the Arch of Constantine, for the architectural sequence of the church's dividing wall;[48] the Roman thermal baths for the chapels turned into giant niches; the triforium motif for the loggia, whose Serlian windows were a complete novelty; the tripartite formula of the traditional Lombard octagon for the

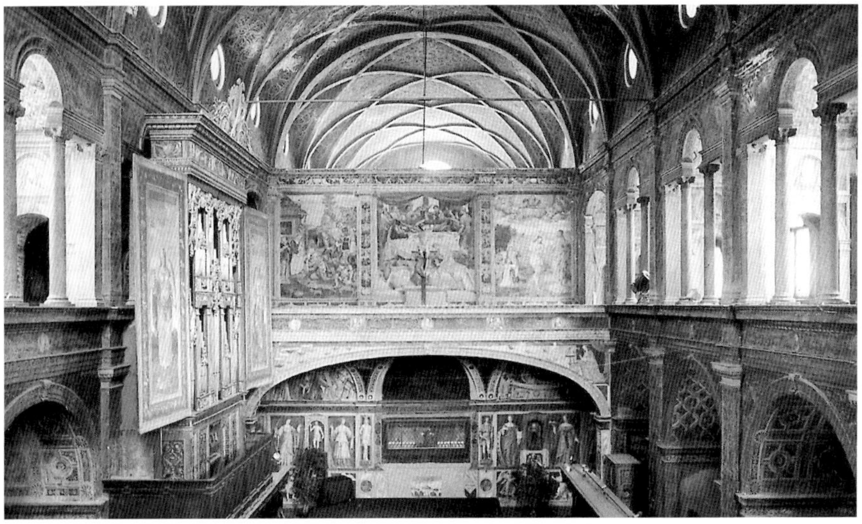

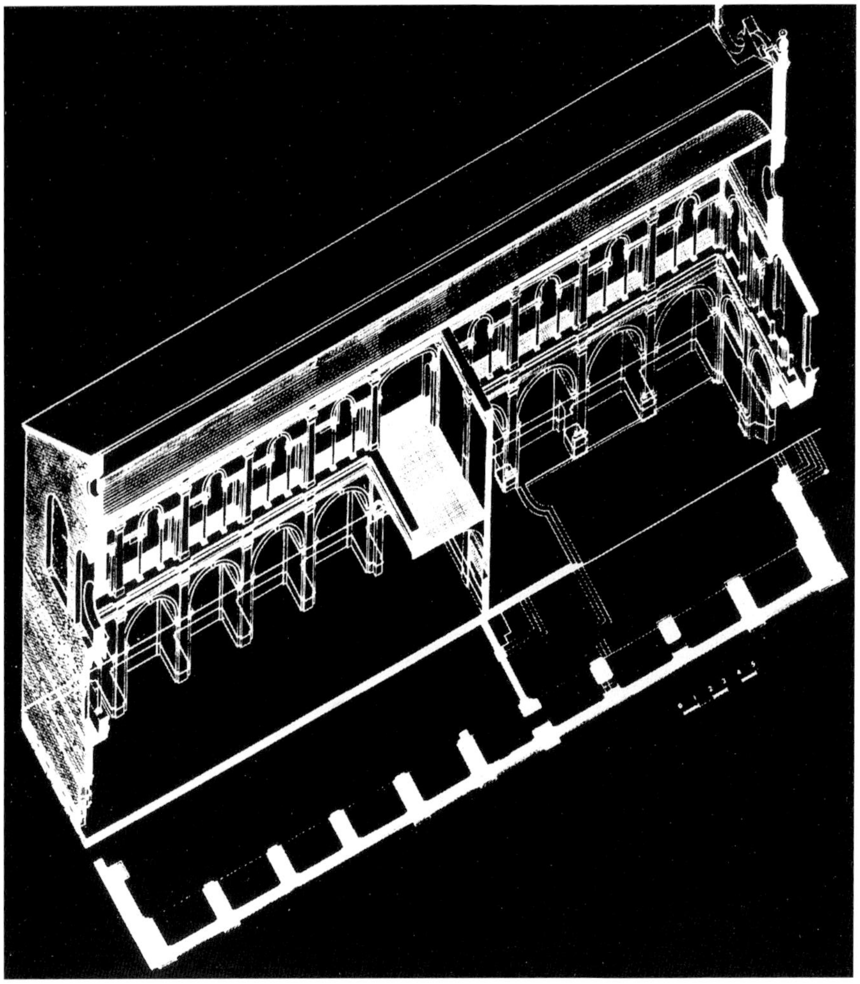

Convent hall

Axonometric of the church
From L. Grassi, *Medioevo, Rinascimento, Manierismo, Barocco*, Milan 1965, pl. 179

triple-order bays; Romanesque-type arches for the third external order; Albertian spatial formulas for the scheme of lateral chapels flanking an aisleless vessel, with shallow pilasters marking the rhythm of each module, and an unbroken pattern running through into the nuns' hall with a continuous barrel vault over the nave; Florence, for the spatial circularity of the interior as represented in Lorenzo di Credi's *Annunciation* in the Uffizi,[49] and for the lower-order profiles of the church façade, as in Alberti's Palazzo Rucellai;[50] Rome (the spatial division of the Sistine Chapel before Julius II;[51] the scheme of the façade as shown in the hand of the frescoed figure of St Sigismund in the last left chapel of the nuns' section, perhaps with the initial idea involving a large triangular pediment with statues at each point; the background of Botticelli's *Temptations of Christ* in the Sistine Chapel, and Cesariano's drawing illustrating the temples of Antiquity according to Vitruvius;[52] the Rome of Raphael for the Serlian window feature);[53] Venice: the façade of Santa Maria dei Miracoli; and not least Milanese (the floor plan of Santa Maria presso San Celso; the apse tribune of Santa Maria della Passione for the Serlian windows; Santa Maria alla Fontana for the external capitals; Milan Cathedral itself for the overall upward movement and vault painted with flamboyant-Gothic openwork; and elsewhere in the Duchy of Milan (San Sigismondo in Cremona for the general layout of the interiors; the façade of the Certosa of Pavia for the polyptych arrangement of the dividing wall; the sanctuary of Saronno for the Serlian motif; the churches in Soncino and San Vittore in Meda for the barrel vault).

Other expressly Bramantesque sources present both in Milan and in the duchy that may have served as models for San Maurizio include: Bramante's studies for church façades provided references for the pattern of the church's architectural elements;[54] the interior first-order Doric capitals with staggered acanthus flowers on the apse wall of Santa Maria presso San Satiro along Via Falcone; and the Canonica cloister at Sant'Ambrogio for the external Ionic corner capitals;[55] the sacristy and interior of Santa Maria presso San Satiro for the initial pictorial schemes in the church's cornices; Pavia Cathedral for the façade.

Bramante's works in Rome also provided essential models for San Maurizio, namely for the discriminating layout and the *stiacciato* (bas-relief) of the windows at either side of the high altar; in Emilia for the ranging of arches between Tuscan pillars surmounted by a Serlian window;[56] the device also has associations with Serlio's design for a Venetian gentleman's mansion.

The sheer wealth of references to be seen in San Maurizio and the still uncertain attribution have prompted scholars to draw comparisons with other churches of the same period across the duchy, such as Santa Maria di Canepanuova (Pavia), Santa Maria di Piazza (Busto Arsizio), San Rocco (San Colombano al Lambro), San Magno (Legnano), and the Incoronata (Lodi).[57]

All in all, the church's architecture manifests a discerning effort to accent the decorative, outward aspects rather than the more rational, lucid features of the structure; contributing to this surface approach are the earlier fresco cycles (after 1511),[58] densely distributed like a page of manuscript illuminations,[59] while maintaining an exacting subdivision and decomposition of space, achieved by freighting the composition with illusionistic features. In fact, the church's decorative painting cycles afford a compendium of the region's artistic history, along the lines of Amadeo's chromatic and decorative philosophy and the constants underlying the fundamental humanist idea first introduced by Bramante (in the so-called *Prevedari engraving*), in a bid to master the laws of space through calculated illusion of perspective, in a substantially classicizing key. Given the striking overall unity of purpose and continuity that links the architecture of San Maurizio with its decorative cycles, such that it was lauded as a "cofano prezioso" (jewel-casket),[60] there is evidence that — given the context of fecund cultural exchange at the time — whoever the project's originator may be, he was most likely influenced by a certain, as yet unnamed, theologist friar — "reverendum sacræ theologiæ professorem dominum fratrem Johannem Pagnanum ordinis [esp.] predicatorum in monasterio domine sancte marie de gratis ibidem [mediolani]" (reverend professor of sacred theology, father Johannem Pagnanum, member of the priesthood of the monastery of Santa Maria delle Grazie, Milan) — who appears to have worked alongside Antonio da Lonate (1503), a conjecture borne out by the precise iconographic programme applied uniformly to the entire church.[61] The consistent recurrence of certain pictorial ideas, in some cases quite far apart, confirms the overall coherence of the project, which was doubtlessly rapidly executed under the direction of a single master mason who, incidentally, may be the same person portrayed in the caricature of a painter that appears inside the loggia, or in the small grisaille profile in one of the panels on the inside of the parapet (nuns' hall).

Having finished all the relative building work on the church, convenient use was made of the scaffolding (usually working from the top down), the main vault and its piers must have been immediately decorated with Gothic openwork, providing a seamless visual and symbolic union of the two halls (with one difference, in that the central lozenges in the lay worshippers' ceiling bore the Sforza *sole raggiante* and stars emblem).[62] Test patches of cleaning carried out on both old and more recent areas of painting have confirmed an original layer of lime-whiting, the same used as a preparatory undercoat of the loggia mural paintings, which was probably meant to symbolize the light filtering from the first order of windows: inside the loggia corridor, painted mouldings lend emphasis to the rhythm of the architecture, outlining the passage archways, including one — the first from the nuns' hall, on the right (west) side — in which the studied integration of the architecture with the pictorial scheme can be noticed in the stretch of wall with a slight deviation of direction, where the mural attempts to optically correct the effect of the ensuing archways of the loggia, which would otherwise reveal the divergence caused by the two halls' being set slight askew from each other. This ingenious perspective device is furthermore emphasized by the cornice mouldings that frame the archways, each embedded with a winged cherub-head painted in grisaille (the name near one such head may be the signature of one of the decorators, Paolo da Pavia), and surmounted by fictive "open" roundels (whereas in the nuns' hall the roundels contain a series of martyrs and Benedictine nuns), all the mouldings being thus closely meshed with both the real and the fictive architecture.[63]

Due to a global revision of practices in monastic communities, the Monastero Maggiore was annexed to the order of Montecassino (1506),[64] a fact that enabled the completion of work on the building. During this period it is likely that religious services were held in the old oratory contained in the polygonal tower situated within the confines of the complex and accessed via the cloister (1569, "oratorio di devozione, nel qual però non s'habbia da celebrar più messa, com si soleva": devotional oratory, in which Mass can no longer be held as in the past).[65] In 1521, when the nuns were still held in great esteem[66] — and among these one Perpetua da Birago, who compiled the texts for the order's liturgical practices (1522)[67] — an economic upturn heralding the relative enlargement of the monastery's estate made possible the piecemeal continuation of the church's decorative programme. This programme is likely to have been the reason for a donation of 1,173 Lire (to the "ven. dom. Alexandre Sfortie de Bentivolis filie me professe in monast. Majori Mediolani" (to my daughter Alessandra Sforza Bentivoglio, reverend sister at the Monastero Maggiore, Milan) from Ippolita Sforza Bentivoglio in 1521, whose consort was granted the title of senator by the newly reinstated Francesco Sforza (1522–24), and whose entire family was behind the patronage of the lay half of the church. Numerous tombstones and plaques — one entitled to Gabriele Velasco, struck down in 1551, a mere twenty-three years old, "in a harquebus battle in the war of Parma"[68] — and, similarly, documents like the contract stipulated in 1554 by the Chapter of the Maggiore, by then comprising ninety-three members, "ad ferratam foresterie dicti Monasteri, ubi solent pro similibus negociis congregari"(at the iron gate of the said monastery, where they are wont to gather for such activities),[69] each testify to the progression of works in both church and convent.

Lying adjacent to the east cloister (and coinciding with the rooms of today's archaeological museum), a stone's throw from the "porta dei carri" (carriage gateway) and close by the *parlatorio*, or parlour — in turn mentioned in the pastoral visit of St Charles (1569), whose somewhat stringent directives included an exhortation that, as a penitence, "D. Paula Antonia be cloistered among the nuns, and that Monastero Maggiore pay 250 Lire per year while she lives" — the said *foresteria*, or guest-quarters, were presumably additions requested by the abbesses, intent on improving the decorations and devotional conditions of the entire convent.[70]

Shortly thereafter other works were carried out in the "Monastery [...] corresponding to the sumptuous views of the church,"[71] recorded as starting in 1571 on the large east cloister, and effected "as per our agreement with signor Francesco Pirulla, engineer from Milan", meaning Francesco Pirovano who, according to Girolamo Pobia, belonged to a family of stonemasons engaged on the monastery building site at least since the end of the century.[72] Working to designs by Pirovano on convent buildings whose actual state at the time was detailed in Lafréry's illustrated *Grande città di Milano* of 1573, the monastery underwent extensive building works that engulfed the polygonal tower (and were later demolished), and the renovation of all the buildings around the large east cloister, which were reworked in the classicizing style and orchestrated with vaulted corridors supported by Doric columns (of which scant remains are still visible alongside the Museo Archeologico). Besides the new buildings of the *foresteria*, documents relate the construction of dormitories, at least until 1590, of a refectory in the west cloister, formerly frescoed by Giovan Paolo Lomazzo (before 1571), "with its double cells and cellar [...] ornamented chimneypiece [...] with *scartozono* in terracotta emblazoned with three relief saints with pyramids [...] 16 lunettes and plaques with array of ornamentation", and a dormitory with a trussed ceiling, all recorded in an accounts ledger (5,647.24 Lire) by Cesare Pobia, with an estimate from the engineer Gio. Battista Strazza. To judge from the floor plans of the monastery, the constructions were almost entirely vaulted; whereas the upper elevations devised by Pirovano were ranged with openings and with moulded subdivisions and courses whose scheme suggested the distribution and proportions of the arcading; other characteristics include a classicizing repertoire of features such as stone doorways sculpted on-site (visible only in the courtyard at the back of the museum). This same architectural and decorative pattern was reiterated, fictively, on the cladding of the remaining stretch of Roman wall bordering the east cloister, with blind arcading, aedicules and portals. As illustrated by Ronchus (1610), this invention was intended to make the new constructions blend with the existing fabric.

Other works executed to designs by Pirovano to the same purpose include the main prospect of the church abutting the street, until then only partially faced; the continuation of the façade is documented in a contract — whose *testes* comprised the designer-engineer himself — drawn up by the master mason on 6 August 1574, one year after the completion of the frescoes commissioned by the nuns from Simone Peterzano for the entrance wall inside. That same day, moreover, Pirovano was also contracted to design a silvered statue of *St Sigismund*.[73] Recent restoration efforts (1985) on the front prospect — with its third Corinthian order reduced to three elements, and the much-maligned gable ornament[74] — have disclosed stylistic discrepancies and differences in the materials and techniques employed in two lower orders, of demonstrably finer workmanship. Coherently corre-

lated with the vessel's framework, the lower part is arranged and articulated to reflect the plan of the interior; the jutting stonework of the roof is partially hidden by the crowning volutes. The lower terminations of these volutes were once adorned with two slender pyramids, a decorative feature popular at the time (witness contemporary designs tendered for the cathedral façade); these were removed for safety reasons in 1825, but appear in eighteenth-century illustrations by G.B. Riccardi (city plan, 1739) and Marc'Antonio Dal Re (c. 1740). Remaining on the upper tier, however, are the lateral pinnacles and the moulded pediment, which was once capped with further volutes, respectively flanked and counterbalanced, together with the crowning emblem in embossed metal bearing the Sforza *sole raggiante* motif upheld by the crowns of the two titular martyrs. Once the façade and the two large courtyards beyond the course of the old city walls were completed, towards 1590, with the involvement of the static engineer Giovan Ambrosio Pissina,[75] in the city maps draughted by Galiti in 1578 and 1582 (comprising at least twenty-eight "double" churches) the church is shown to be connected with the convent buildings by an unadorned wall inset with a portal, shown at an angle (Ronchus: 1610), and delimited by the courtyard, while on the left the temple was still flanked by the early Gothic building fabric (Dal Re).
In the seventeenth century, in front of the two ample cloisters — illustrated in the town plan by Barateri (1629), and coming shortly before the *veduta* of Milan Cathedral by Lampugnani (1640) — a third cloister was added, built to plans by Benedetto Quarantini on the site of the courtyard already illustrated by Ronchus and at the time described by the architect himself ("The courtyard extends at street level, on an irregular plan, with its wall along the street, in which stood the unadorned entrance, a single arcade facing the monastery, paved in terracotta, and one ascended upon stone steps");[76] the said third arcaded cloister (1680–83) on Corso Magenta, recalled by Torre ("evidence of the magnificence of the monastery [...] the Atrium [...] affords a fine frontage of arcading on marble columns, beyond which lie the *parlatorij* [parlours] and outer rooms for guests"). Payments for the adjacent doorway to Giacomo Muttone in 1682–83 are on record, upon the installation of "that vague ancona wrought from fine silver plates" (Latuada) by the goldsmith Federico Perego (also at work on the cathedral *scurolo*) are a sign of the monastery's growing

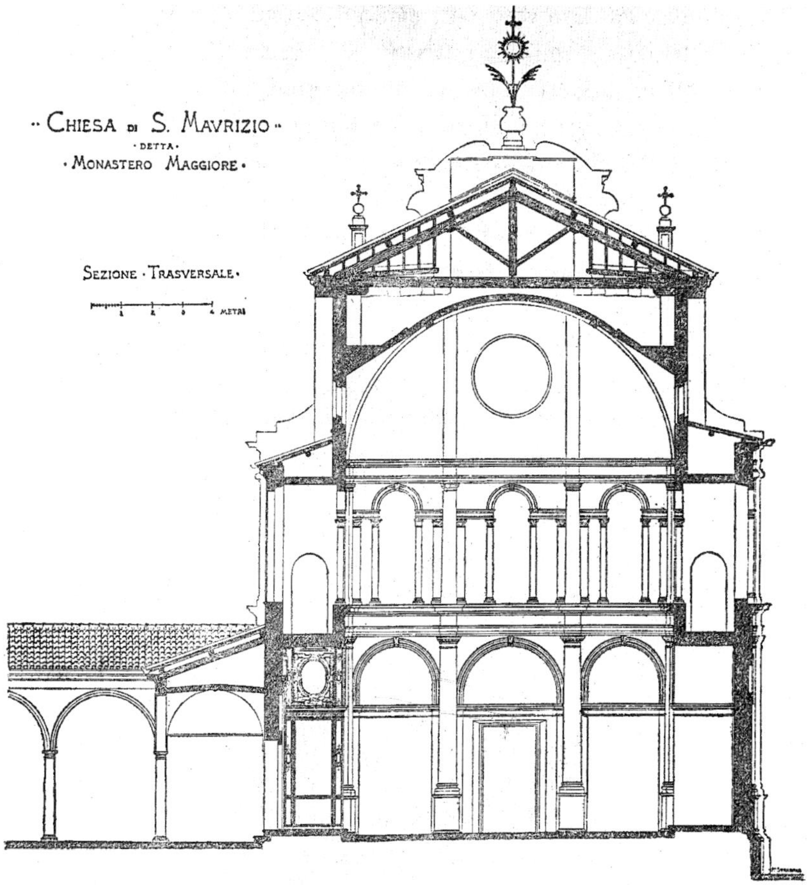

Transverse section of the church

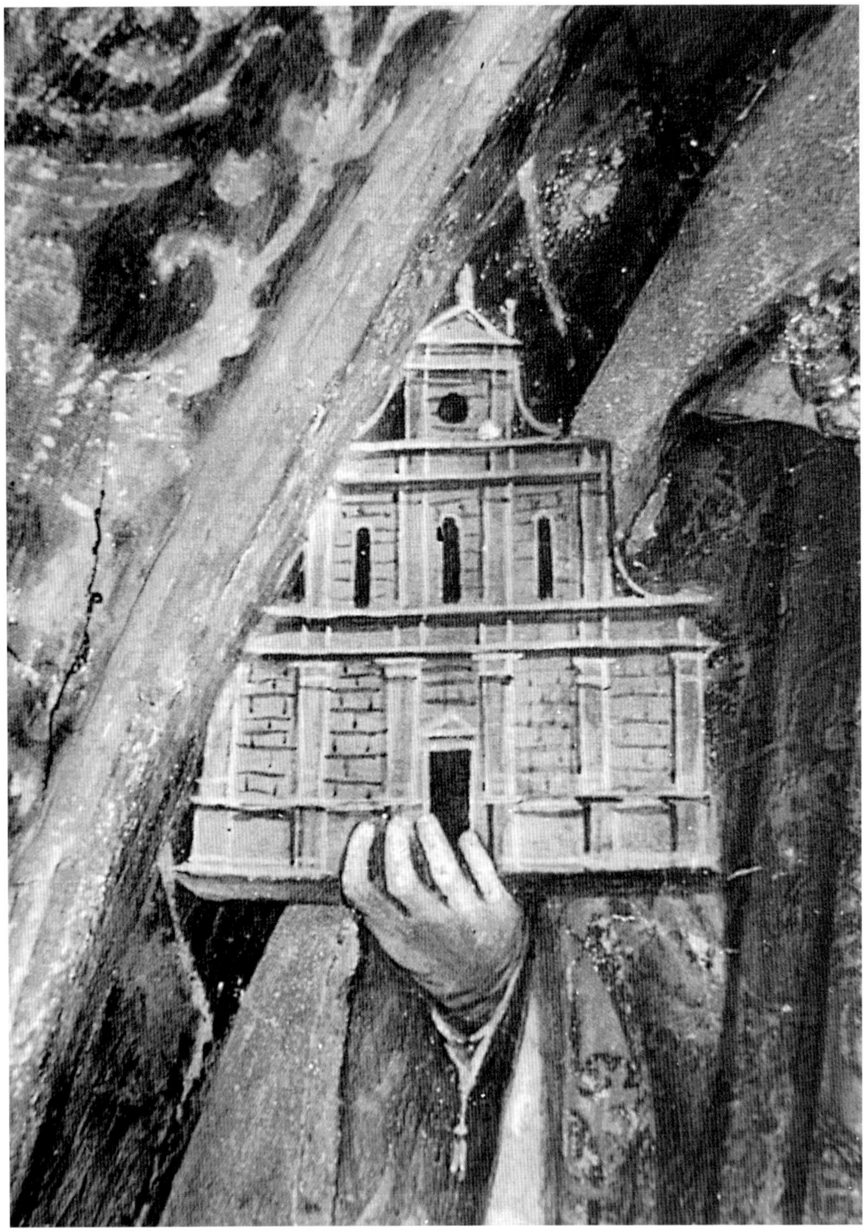

Convent hall, apse chapel (left), model of the church held by St Sigismund, detail of fresco

fortune. The "cloister doorway, made from fine marble" (Latuada), illustrated by Marc'Antonio Dal Re, announces itself harmonically with a reversed broken pediment, an idea perhaps prompted by the counterbalanced volutes crowning the church façade alongside, and subsequently taken up by Bolli in the frontage of the Palazzo Litta (1752–63) opposite: the scroll inserted between the brackets alludes to the imperial foundation, while the elegant grating with its spirals is the contemporary work of Gio. Pietro Alegrino.[77] The cloister and the doorway onto Corso Magenta are part of the last commission undertaken on the church of San Maurizio, where in the eighteenth century after the pastoral visit of Cardinal Filippo Archinto (1705–06), the entrance steps of the front prospect of the church were rebuilt (1762), together with the high altar (1790–92), with a reduction in size of the window overhead and the insertion of the marble pilasters made to designs by Giuseppe Antonio Pissina (engineer and architect), son of Giovanni Ambrogio, and the engravers Giuseppe Maria Buzzi and Antonio Giudice, all documented as present on the cathedral site);[78] other work included the steps around the altars in the laypersons' hall (1793) — where the nuns were permitted to enter "once only" after the Ave Maria, with special permission from Cardinal Filippo Visconti, to see the work so far carried out — up until the suppression of the monastery, decreed on 20 November 1798 by the Cisalpine Republic "to address the present needs of State".[79] Although the enclave was officially ceded to the Exchequer's Office, the nuns (now numbering 59, plus five boarders, in 1796) were allowed to remain as residents. From a petition presented at the time, one can detect premonitory misgivings about the ensuing events in the nuns' definition of "the space in question, being of such irregular shape and so awkwardly built, was the least suited for the public office", such that "it would reduce the risk of damage to the church alongside, which deserves careful conservation owing to the sublime paintings it contains".[80]

In both monastery and church — the latter made a subsidiary of Santa Maria alla Porta from 17 April 1799 — from the 1800s onwards a great many alterations were made. These are currently the subject of in-depth studies, including some of recent date, which have shed light on the alterations' correspondence with the ideas and practices of the evolving currents of art and architecture for each successive stage of development on the build-

ing. Once the complex's original destination as a monastery came to an end and the need arose for a change of use, the convent buildings in particular tended to lose their historical prestige and subsequently suffered drastic alterations and demolitions, right up until after World War II. As many archives concerning the site of the monastery show,[81] after attempts to disband the buildings for private use through auction, various sections were converted,[82] substantially as a result of the creation of Via Luini and Via Ansperto (laid right through the complex; (as of 1864, including a plan for a piazza with a new vegetable market and the conversion of the refectory for warehouse space); at all events, the alterations were definitive, and formed part of the implementation of a new master plan for the whole of Milan. In the monastery the nuns were confined to rooms overlooking the garden (rented out as market gardens); hanging on as if by a miracle, by 1847 the convent had dwindled to a mere twenty-two souls, paling to no more than nine by 1853.[83] In the second half of that century the evolving discussions in the field of town planning led to a wider vision of conservation issues, eliciting the participation of such bodies as the Consulta del Museo Patrio Archeologico, and the Ufficio Regionale per la Conservazione dei Monumenti (two major heritage and conservation departments), and the involvement of scholars and researchers such as Camillo Boito, Gaetano Moretti, Luca Beltrami, Ambrogio Annoni, plus the boards of the newly founded regional superintendencies, notably Augusto Brusconi (Soprintendenza ai Monumenti della Lombardia), who supervised work carried out by Giuseppe Vandoni.[84]
In the meantime, among the numerous documented nineteenth-century alterations made to the church, the most ostensible came after the creation of Via Luini in 1869 by Colla. While substantially a mere reiteration of the extant mouldings along the front prospect, Colla's operation was criticized at the time, for having destroyed remains of early pictorial works described in 1872 by Mongeri as embellishing the blind arcading of the third order ("these arches, standing ten in a row, still betray traces of paintwork where the surfaces were shielded under the arch, one bearing a large half-figure with a phylactery bound to his head, the rest adorned with chiaroscuro coffering in the intrados").[85] In the twentieth century (1941) Baroni also criticized the work as having jeopardized any further study of the church, lamenting

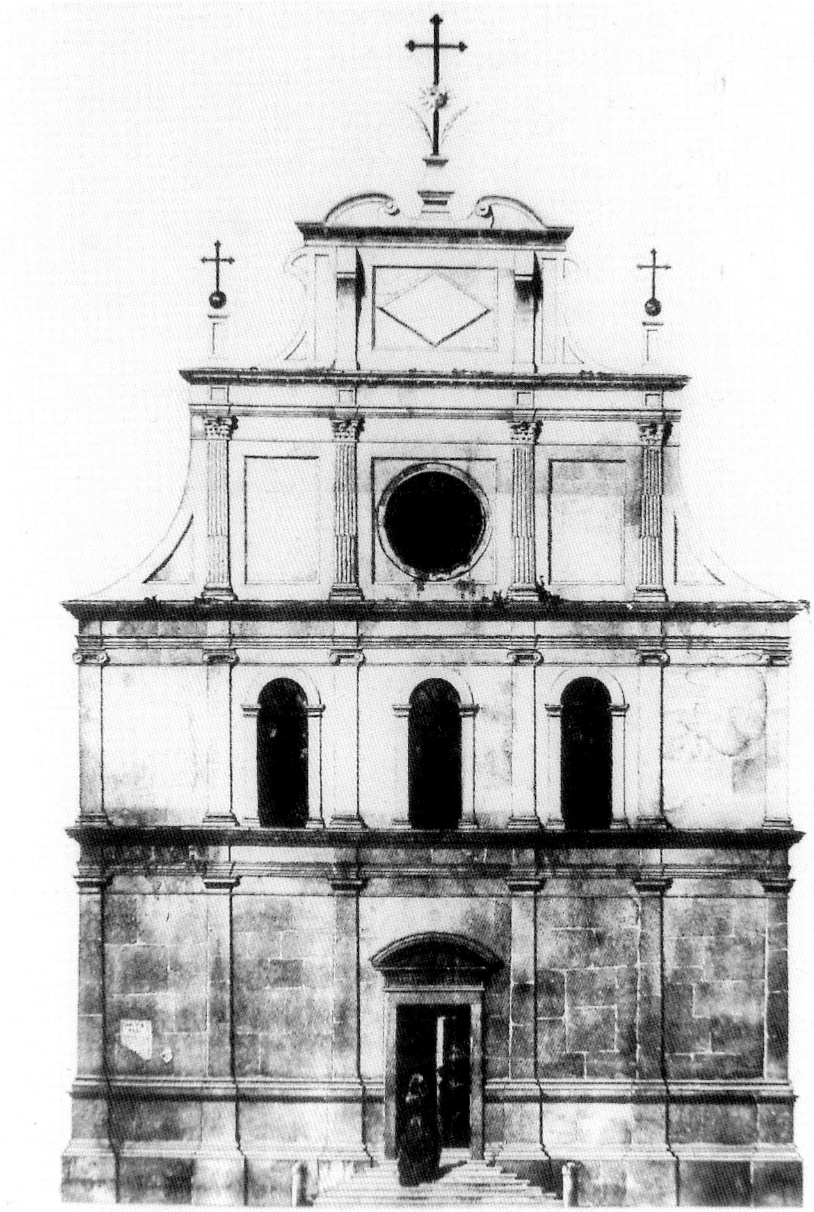

A. Colla, survey of front prospect
Mappe e disegni, Archivio di Stato, Piacenza

that it was symptomatic of the building's fate "that in all the standard manuals of art history the only views offered are of the front prospect and side along Via Luini — the former belonging to works realized quite independently in the sixteenth century, the latter a product of the mind of the architect Colla".[86]

[1] At present the indispensable reference works are I. Rossi, *La chiesa di San Maurizio in Milano. Il Monastero Maggiore e le sue due torri*, Milan 1914, and A. Ottino Della Chiesa, *San Maurizio al Monastero Maggiore*, with extra historical background information by P. Reina, Milan 1962. For a more complete up-to-date study, note also the present author's *San Maurizio al Monastero Maggiore*, 2nd ed., Milan 1992.

[2] Archivio di Stato of Milan (henceforth ASM), *Notarile* 4586, 20 May 1503.

[3] The nineteenth-century town plans of the Monastero Maggiore — of which the best are in the Raccolta Bertarelli, P 42, containing elevations of all the interior vaults of the convent buildings, and the planned courses of Via Ansperto and Via Luini — are reproduced in G. Pertot, *La torre "quadrata" del Monastero Maggiore di Milano. Contributi alla lettura del manufatto dalle fasi romane ai restauri moderni attraverso l'analisi stratigrafica delle murature*, Milan 1995; Idem, "Contributi per la storia edilizia del Monastero Maggiore di Milano: nuove indicazioni da documenti del periodo 1797–1858", in *Rassegna di Studi del Civico Museo Archeologico e del Civico Gabinetto Numismatico di Milano*, suppl. XVIII, 1997, pl. V; Idem, "Le fabbriche del monastero attraverso i secoli", in *San Maurizio al Monastero Maggiore in Milano. Guida storica-artistica*, Milan 1998, pp. 18–27.

[4] Also Milan, Archivio Storico Diocesano (henceforth ASD), sez. X, *Visite. Santa Maria alla Porta*, III ("Pianta per il censimento del C.so di P. Vercellina fino al Monastero Maggiore e a San Rocco sull'angolo di via Nirone, e rispettivamente al palazzo Arese poi Litta"): M. Bendiscioli, "Vita sociale e culturale", in *Storia di Milano*, X, Milan 1957, p. 357 ill.

[5] For a wider discussion of the Roman circus and the towers, see also Pertot, *La torre "quadrata"*.

[6] The first phase saw the construction of the atrium, with a vaulted ceiling resting on sturdy corner piers, together with walls raised to a height of 14 m above ground level; the second came in the ensuing century, and comprised the loggia and the decorative work along what is now Via Luini, which involved razing some of the ancient fabric of the monastery complex in 1866–70; similarly Via Ansperto saw the erection of columns in cipollino marble, plus two brick pediments, and a leafed ledge in white marble, perhaps supplemented by a second course with a column linking the two on the front prospect.

[7] *Liber Notitiae sanctorum Mediolani*, no. 300, col. 283 B.

[8] Map published by Monneret de Villard and Magistretti, overlaid on the present street map covering a quadrilateral bordered by part of Corso Magenta (N), Via Brisa (E), Via Vigna and a stretch of Via Santa Valeria (S), and Via Nirone (W).

[9] ASM, *Catasto* 2045, 9 September 1862.

[10] While in 1123 mention was made of a so-called "antique" wall plus a different "new" wall built over the existing fabric but soon implicated in "restoration" work, Ansperto may well have been responsible for the rehabilitation of the monastery's square tower: Pertot, "Le fabbriche del monastero attraverso i secoli", p. 22.

[11] P. Morigia, *Il santuario della città di Milano*, Milan 1641, p. 129.

[12] Once work on the structure was terminated by progressively raising the walls in successive stages, the loggetta, built along similar lines to those of the bell towers of San Satiro in Milan and Sant'Apollinare in Baggio, dates from the ninth century and comprises apertures in the *arcus productus* fashion, three per side, on slender white marble columns, each bearing a different capital (recycled elements for the two on the south side, respectively from the third and eigth centuries); while on the upper register small anthropomorphic and zoomorphic features formed a corbel table in brick (no longer extant). Work executed in the Romanesque period in the entrance arch of the said tower includes the setting in place of ancient Roman columns in cipollino marble; and likewise in the archways above, the construction of the relieving arches.

[13] A. Ambrosioni, "Le abitanti del monastero: il medioevo", in *San Maurizio al Monastero Maggiore in Milano. Guida*, pp. 9–12.

[14] See also Reina, *San Maurizio al Monastero Maggiore*, p. 119.

[15] See also G.P. Bognetti, "Pensiero e vita a Milano e nel Milanese durante l'età carolingia", in *Storia di Milano*, II, Milan 1954, p. 855; G. Rosa, "Le arti minori dalla conquista longobarda al Mille", in *Storia di Milano*, p. 673.

[16] C. Manaresi and C. Santoro, *Gli Atti privati milanesi e comaschi del secolo XI*, II, Milan 1960–65, pp. 296, 323–325.

[17] "Monasterium sancte Dei genitricis Marie, quod dicitur magiore", "monasterium Beate Virginis Marie quod dicitur maius" (E. Occhipinti, "Appunti per la storia del Monastero Maggiore di Milano in età medioevale. Il problema delle origini e la configurazione giuridico-patrimoniale", in *Studi di storia medioevale e di diplomatica*, II, Milan 1977, p. 74).

[18] In a deliberation issued by the magistrate for Milan, Stefanardo da Vimercate, regarding a dispute between Gisla, the abbess "Sancte Marie et Sancti Moricii sive eius monasterium dictum Magiore", and the brother Marcolo and Curio, tenants of a wood at the time owned by the monastery.

[19] P. Jaffé and G. Wattenbach, *Regesta pontificum romanorum ab condita Ecclesia ad annum post Christum natum 1198*, II, Leipzig 1885, p. 59, no. 9286; J.P. Migne, *Patrologia latina*, Paris 1844–55, 20, col. 1360.

[20] That is, in the city ("ecclesiam sancte Marie ad Circulum, ecclesia sancti Petri in Vinea, ecclesia sancti Quirici, ecclesia sancte Valerie cum pertinentiis suis") and in the *contado* ("curtem de Aroxio cum ecclesia sancti Nazarii et ecclesia sancti Petri; curtem de Circlate; curtem de Purletia; Castrum de Robiate cum pertinentiis suis. Possessiones quas idem monasterium habet in Varedeo, in Magnicago, in Septimo, in Baradeglo, in Legniano, in Arconate, in Pistirago et in Tazono; Braidam de Monte Vulpe; Braidam que dicitur Ticinello et alia que idem monasterium possidet in Gardesana, in Valle de Bubledeira et in Ulmeto et in valle Sarriana cum suis honoribus et aliis omnibus supradictorum pertinentiis"): see also Reina, *San Maurizio al Monastero Maggiore*, p. 109.

[21] Regarding which the abbess was entitled to appoint the rector of

Santa Maria al Circo, despite the objections of locals, but according to rights endorsed after the dispute documented 29 May 1148 (see also G. Giulini, *Memorie spettanti alla storia, al governo e alla descrizione della città e campagna di Milano nei secoli bassi*, Milan 1760, 1854–57 ed., III, p. 364; E. Cattaneo, "Istituzioni ecclesiastiche milanesi", in *Storia di Milano*, IX, 1961, p. 603).

[22] Among the scant early drawings related to San Maurizio is a seventeenth-century ground plan, probably draughted in the studio of Francesco Maria Ricchino, the architect of Cardinal Federico Borromeo, and thereafter in the collection of an erudite eighteenth-century scholar who studied the church, Venanzio De Pagave (G. Struffolino Kruger, "Disegni inediti d'architettura relativi alla collezione di Venanzio De Pagave", in *Umanesimo*, Milan 1971, pp. 287–288); the plan illustrates the two juxtaposed churches, each having four bays instead of the existing plan of four in the lay section and six in the nuns'. Given that the slight deviation between the two sections of the church suggests the existence of previous structures from the earlier church sited just outside the old line of the defensive walls and coinciding with the nuns' hall, it may be that this plan of the seventeenth century is an indication of an initial scheme to maintain the same basic dimensions of the older church, which may have corresponded to the space covered by the present four bays.

[23] See especially L. Grassi, "Iconologia delle chiese monastiche femminili dall'alto medioevo ai secoli XVI-XVII", in *Arte lombarda*, 42/3, 1975, pp. 131, 136–137.

[24] *Catasto* 1950: mapp. 2375, and 2989 (east cloister).

[25] Thus described in ASM, *Genio Civile* 2704, f. 8, such a painting (Museo di Milano, ill. in C. Spellanzon, "I primi anni della restaurazione austriaca in Lombardia e il movimento politico e culturale a Milano", in *Storia di Milano*, II, 1960, p. 31) illustrates, in considerable adherence to contemporary ground plans for the monastery, a *veduta* of the current state that comprises — together with the arcade of six octagonal pillars, with bases and leafed capitals in *serizzo* granite supporting a series of ogival arches, probably restored in part — also the construction grafted onto the main entrance of the quadrangular tower, as portrayed in elevation in the illustrations published by Grazioli (1735) and Giulini (1760). As may be observed from the plans, the extension of the building along the remains of the Gothic arcade could coincide with the end of the fourth bay of the present nuns' hall, perhaps confirming the original layout of the early church.

[26] See also Spellanzon, "I primi anni della restaurazione austriaca", p. 49; P. Mezzanotte and G.C. Bascapé, *Milano nell'arte e nella storia*, Milan 1948, p. 619; Reina, *San Maurizio al Monastero Maggiore*, p. 106; P.M. De Marchi, "Nota preliminare sul Monastero Maggiore e l'inserimento delle strutture romane preesistenti negli edifici conventuali", in *Scritti in ricordo di Graziella Massari Gaballo e di Umberto Tocchetti Pollini*, Milan 1986; Pertot, *La torre "quadrata"*.

[27] The fact that the nineteenth-century surveys and plans only provide a generic outline (each according to its specific purpose) of the different phases of construction of the monastery complex prevents us from obtaining a clear picture of the pre-existing fabric prior to extensive alterations carried out repeatedly from the sixteenth century and affecting all aspects of the site. It is likely that the earliest buildings, already in place before the purchase in 1503, were clustered against the old city walls; hence the two refectories recorded in the nineteenth century, the one to the east (beyond the Gothic cloister, parallel with the city walls) being the older of the two, identified in nineteenth-century survey work (1851), and declared at the time as being extant.

[28] As declared in 1442 by Monsignor Francesco della Croce, primicerius of the cathedral.

[29] E. Occhipinti, "San Maurizio al Monastero Maggiore di Milan", in *Monasteri benedettini in Lombardia*, Milan 1980, p. 74.

[30] Morigia, *Il santuario della città di Milano*, p. 129; C. Torre, *Il Ritratto di Milano*, Milan 1674, p. 212; S. Latuada, *Descrizione di Milano*, IV, Milan 1738, pp. 410–425; N. Sormani, *Passeggi storico-topografico-critici nella città, indi nella diocesi di Milano*, III, Milan 1751, p. 30; C. Bianconi, *Nuova guida di Milano*, Milan 1787, p. 271; G. Caselli, *Nuovo ritratto di Milano in riguardo alle belle arti*, Milan 1827, pp. 160–161; Ottino Della Chiesa, *San Maurizio al Monastero Maggiore*, p. 33.

[31] A.F. Albuzio, *Memorie per servire alla storia de' pittori scultori e architetti milanesi*, 1776, MS in the Archivio della Fabbrica del Duomo di Milano (chapter on Dolcebuono), transcribed by G. Nicodemi in "Le 'Memorie per servire alla storia de' pittori, scultori e architetti milanesi' raccolte dall'abate Antonio Francesco Albuzzi", in *L'Arte*, 1951, pp. I-VIII, 1–44; F. Pirovano, *Nuova guida di Milano*, Milan 1831, pp. 153–157; G.L. Calvi, *Notizie sulla vita e sulle opere dei principali architetti, scultori e pittori che fiorirono in Milano durante il governo dei Visconti e degli Sforza*, II, Milan 1865, pp. 185–187; L. Beltrami, "Arte antica. La chiesa di San Maurizio in Milano e le pitture di Bernardino Luini", in *Emporium*, 49, 1899, pp. 51–61; F. Malaguzzi Valeri, *La corte di Ludovico il Moro*, II, Milan 1915, p. 262; Rossi, *La chiesa di San Maurizio in Milano*; A. Pica, "Il Monastero Maggiore", in *Per l'arte sacra*, III, 1926, pp. 29–45.

[32] ASM, *Religione p.a.* 2147, 4 June 1474 (F. Malaguzzi Valeri, "Contributi alla storia di San Maurizio", in *Archivio Storico Lombardo*, XXXV, s. IX, 1908, pp. 325–339); *Notarile* 1561, 10 May 1493; C. Baroni, *L'architettura lombarda dal Bramante al Richino*, Milan 1941, p. 37; G. Borlini, "Gian Giacomo Dolcebuono", in *Rendiconti dell'Istituto Lombardo di Scienze e Lettere*, LXXXVII, 1954, pp. 67–69; M.L. Rizzardi, "La chiesa di San Maurizio in Milano non è opera del Dolcebuono", in *Istituto Lombardo di Scienze e Lettere. Rendiconti*, LXXXVII, 1–2, 1956, pp. 53–71; E. Arslan, "Le opere mature dell'Amadeo. Gli ultimi bramanteschi. L'architettura civile", in *Storia di Milano*, VII, 1956, p. 680; R.V. Schofield, J. Shell and G. Sironi, *Giovanni Antonio Amadeo*, Como 1989, p. 58.

[33] For more on Antonio da Lonate, see also *Dizionario del duomo di Milano*, Milan 1986, pp. 45, 84, 381; G.B. Sannazzaro and G. Sironi, "Antonio da Lonate", in *Dizionario della Chiesa ambrosiana*, I, Milan 1987, pp. 179–180; A. Cattaneo Cattorini, "Antonio da Lonate e il modello ligneo del duomo di Vigevano", in *Bramante a Milano*, conference proceedings (Milan 1985), in *Arte lombarda*, 86/87, 1988, p. 160. Although the lack of any further records makes confirmation impossible, in another notarial deed recently discovered, dated 1574 but relative to the completion of the main prospect of San Maurizio, among the *testes* cited is the selfsame technician Francesco Pirovano, this time quoted as an engineer in charge. Although still needing research, Antonio da Lonate's name crops up in records as a "ducal engineer", i.e., as having the right technical background for resolving

the statics of the church. Working as such Lonate is mentioned as engaged on the cathedral, and he receives at least one mention in relation to San Maurizio, together with references to other works undertaken, such as Santa Maria di Piazza in Busto Arsizio, and the wooden model for Vigevano Cathedral. In the likely event that, as for the cathedral of Vigevano, a scale model was built to illustrate the architectural scheme for the new church of San Maurizio — a common practice in this period — this model may have inspired the first of the three models frescoed in the nuns' hall (last chapel on the left, toward the entrance wall), held by St Sigismund, the legendary founder of the Monastero Maggiore.

[34] It is possible that for sixteenth-century alterations to San Maurizio the twin church scheme was actuated by using at least the longitudinal walls of the existing vessel, no longer large enough or adequate for the new devotional practices. If the purchase of new land in 1503 made available a new space along today's Corso Magenta — just beyond the earlier boundary of the monastery formed by the city walls and including the church itself — the fact that the new dividing wall coincides with a similar line, and that the two halls connected on this line are slightly at an angle to each other, would seem to substantiate the idea of the re-employment of existing fabric. A similar deviation in alignment is discernible along the Via Luini flank (though only completed in 1867), in the attic, and in several recent ground plans (including street maps); this deviation stems from the need to align the new façade of the church properly with Corso Magenta, which lay in a different direction from the city walls: this option (also involving progressive adjustments to accommodate the new buildings in the convent's existing fabric) would have involved meeting the needs of the town's planning programme and the recycling of available fabric without forgoing the spatial coherence of the new ground plan.

[35] C. Baroni, *Documenti per la storia dell'architettura a Milano nel rinascimento e nel barocco*, Florence, I, part I, 1940, p. IX; Idem, *L'architettura lombarda dal Bramante al Richino*, Milan 1941, p. 37; Mezzanotte and Bascapé, *Milano nell'arte e nella storia*, p. 62; P. Mezzanotte, "L'architettura milanese dalla fine della signoria sforzesca alla metà del Seicento", in *Storia di Milano*, X, 1957, p. 567.

[36] Ottino Della Chiesa, *San Maurizio al Monastero Maggiore*, pp. 32, 46; C. Verzone, "Cesare Cesariano", in *Arte lombarda*, XVI, 1971, pp. 203–210.

[37] The aforementioned fresco featuring St Sigismund in the nuns' hall — part of the church's earlier and vaster decorative cycle undertaken shortly after it was built — confirms the close links between the architecture and the pictorial works inside, both complying to a single project, in which the decorative lines respect, and occasionally complement, the architectural concepts of the building itself by means of ingenious fictive panels and mouldings. Although, as one may legitimately surmise from operations on other building sites in and around Milan at the time, work on the church underwent the changing tenure of successive *capomastri* and phases of execution, the resultant project is nevertheless uniform.

[38] M.L. Ferrari, "Zenale, Cesariano e Luini: un arco di classicismo lombardo", in *Paragone*, 211, 1967, pp. 26–28.

[39] L. Grassi and P. Portaluppi, "Scuola e 'maniera' nell'architettura lombarda del Cinquecento", in *Quaderni dell'Istituto di Storia dell'Architettura*, 1965, p. 225.

[40] Grassi, *Iconologia delle chiese monastiche femminili*, pp. 136–137.

[41] For speculations as to the architecture of Borromini see P. Portoghesi, *Borromini*, 1967, p. 20; B. Adorni, "L'architettura a Milano dalla caduta di Ludovico il Moro a Carlo V", in *Guide di architettura. Milano*, Turin 1990, p. 89.

[42] The floor of the presbytery (fourth bay in the laypersons' hall) and the nuns' hall is raised roughly half a metre above the church floor level to set the nuns kneeling in prayer at the same height as the officiating priest and hence not visible to the lay congregation. This difference of level also applies to the lower crypt, now hosting rooms of the Museo Archeologico, whose extension coincides with the length of the seven bays of the church above; beneath the lay hall on the side of Corso Magenta lies a small hall, now filled in, that may have been for burials. A similar raised section affects one of the bays of the convent's hall, creating a presbytery for the nuns with an altar for private services (as testified by old photographs), whose technical peculiarities and building features have prompted attributions for the church's design to Dolcebuono and Amadeo, given their involvement in several of the city's more signal building projects, notably the *tiburio*, or crossing tower, of the cathedral, considered at the time to be the very symbol of the cathedral's ties with the city.

[43] ASM, *Notarile* 10021, 11 March 1545.

[44] G.B. Sannazzaro, "Per la chiesa di San Maurizio al Monastero Maggiore di Milano", in *Raccolta vinciana*, XXVII, 1997, pp. 573–576. The only stonework insert present in the entire church, a similar instance of eighteenth-century masonry can be detected in the central bay of the tripartite sequence of the dividing wall, up to the second order: at the sides the sections terminate in round arches rising level with the cornice of the impost line of the side chapels; whereas above the tall intermediate fascia delimiting the fastigium of the altar the second order contains three large panels, aligned with the geometry of the space below. The recent temporary removal of the painted altar revealed unexpected traces of an early arch, initially created at the same level as those on either side, and bordering the upper part of the window, and most likely the one to which Lombardi's grate was fixed. In this way, the former tripartite subdivision of the dividing wall conveyed a greater sense of unity and circularity than the present arrangement affords, features moreover that were intrinsic to the original design of the church and are repeated in modular fashion throughout the rest of building with appreciably greater cogency than is manifest today.

[45] Archivio della Veneranda Fabbrica del Duomo di Milano (henceforth AVFDM), *Ordinazioni capitolari* 5, f. 131r (Schofield, Shell and Sironi, *Giovanni Antonio Amadeo*, p. 404).

[46] Respectively, V. Forcella, *Iscrizioni nelle chiese e negli altri edifici di Milano dal secolo XVIII ai giorni nostri*, III, Milan 1890, p. 450; and Albuzio, *Memorie per servire alla storia*.

[47] Likewise Ferrari, "Zenale, Cesariano e Luini", pp. 27–28; E. Tea, *Quattrocento e Cinquecento*, Turin 1968, pp. 27–28; L. Grassi, "Gli Sforza e l'architettura del ducato", in *Gli Sforza a Milano*, Milan 1978, p. 254; Idem, "Trasmutazione linguistica dell'architettura sforzesca: splendore e presagio al tempo di Ludovico il Moro", in *Milano nell'età di Ludovico il Moro*, conference proceedings, Milan 1983, pp. 466, 471. My thanks for discussion and fertile exchange of ideas on this topic to the superintendent, architect Sylvia Ponticelli Righini.

[48] The same sequence — particularly as revealed upon the removal of the altarpiece, and when compared with the entrance wall — reveals a layout whose prototype derives from the Arch of Constantine in Rome, as confirmed by the central bay's being greater in width to the lateral bays. Similar echoes of classical architecture recur in the frescoes painted by Bernardino Luini in 1522–24, not only in their general layout (having bases ranged with four statue-like saints, and the lunettes above, in which gift-bearers and saints stand out against the backdrop like statues), and in the insertion of angels within the pendentives (similar to the winged Victories of the triumphal arch system), or the general spaciousness of the central panels, visually linked with the airy brightness of the adjacent loggiato, but even in certain compositional details: as in the galloping horses and the soldier in profile in the left panel; or the altar and votive statue in the opposite panel, both faithfully rendered within the same arch; and the St Ursula (or Justina?) and, directly opposite, the St Lucy, whose poses and cloak folds in both cases derive from the Victory figures sculpted on the base of the triumphal arch, as if to substantiate that "faultless classicism" noted in these very frescoes by Luini (F. Frangi, "Una traccia per la storia della pittura a Milano dal 1499 al 1535", in *Pittura a Milano. Rinascimento e manierismo*, Milan 1998, p. 35). The sequence of windows and painted fields of the second order of the Sistine Chapel appear in fact to have visual parallels in the Serlian arrangement of San Maurizio, and similarly other Sistine frescoes carry various references to the Arch of Constantine. Furthermore, studies have revealed details such as landscapes (for the landscape in the nuns' presbytery — see S. Bandera, "I cicli pittorici", in *San Maurizio al Monastero Maggiore in Milano. Guida*, pp. 60–61 — compare also with the background of the *Assumption* in the Portinari Chapel); other parallels include the compositional details which seem to stem from the scheme of the lost *Assumption* by Perugino in the Sistine Chapel, in the aforementioned frescoes on the dividing wall of San Maurizio by Luini, who had just made a trip to Rome for the purpose of study (G.B. Sannazzaro, "Per la decorazione pittorica nella chiesa di San Maurizio al Monastero Maggiore di Milano: suggerimenti di studio", in *Arte lombarda nel secondo millennio. Saggi in onore di Gian Alberto Dell'Acqua*, Milan 2000, p. 140).

[49] G.B. Sannazzaro, "L'Amadeo e Santa Maria alla Fontana", in *Giovanni Antonio Amadeo. Scultura e architettura del suo tempo*, conference proceedings, Milan 1993, pp. 305, 308, 323 (also for comparative studies of Santa Maria alla Fontana).

[50] Ottino Della Chiesa, *San Maurizio al Monastero Maggiore*, p. 28.

[51] Sannazzaro, "Per la decorazione pittorica", p. 139.

[52] A certain resemblance has been observed (ibid., p. 143) between the front prospect of San Maurizio and the façade design of the temple in Botticelli's Sistine *Temptations of Christ*, which in turn stems from Baccio Pontelli's Santo Spirito hospital in Rome. While the Sistine façade can be assimilated with the second and third orders of San Maurizio's, the way the façade's crown is represented is quite different from that actually built; completed in 1574 with a profiled fastigium, the fresco shows a broad triangular pediment. The fact that this triangular pediment crops up again in the frescoed church in St Sigismund's hand in one of the earlier cycles in the nuns' section would seem to suggest an initial but subsequently altered scheme for the façade, confirming the close ties between the church's architecture and the earlier decorative cycles. The painted statues at the top of the triangular pediment in the aforementioned fresco cannot however be assimilated with the Sistine painting, but come closer to Cesariano's drawing — to which the church has hypothetical connections — devoted to the temples of Antiquity according to Vitruvius, and to another church design also seen in the hand of St Sigismund in one of the outer panels of the Antegnati organ in the convent part of San Maurizio, dated to the mid-1500s, providing almost a painted record of the existence of a wooden model (no longer extant) — a standard practice at the time, as exemplified by Antonio da Lonate's model for Vigevano Cathedral. Contextually, in this same façade the adherence to Roman classicism and to Bramante's type of classicism in particular is manifest in the capitals of the first order (described as the "ornatu faciate" whose marbles were delivered in 1507 with the consent of Amadeo), similar not only to those of Santa Maria alla Fontana — also by Amadeo — but also to those of the lower walls of San Pietro in Montorio in Rome, begun by Bramante in 1052.

[53] Grassi, "Trasmutazione linguistica", pp. 466, 471; L. Patetta, "La tipologia della chiesa 'doppia' (dal medioevo alla Controriforma)", in Idem, *Cinque studi sull'architettura del passato*, Milan 1990, p. 32.

[54] C.L. Frommel, "Il progetto del Louvre per la chiesa dei Fogliari e l'architettura di Cristoforo Solari", in *Quaderno di studi sull'arte lombarda dai Visconti agli Sforza*, Milan 1990, p. 61.

[55] A.E. Werdehausen, "Bramante e il convento di Sant'Ambrogio", in *Bramante a Milano*, conference proceedings (Milan 1985), in *Arte lombarda*, 1986, pp. 35, 42; C. Denker Nesselrath, "I chiostri di Sant'Ambrogio. Il dettaglio degli ordini", in *Bramante a Milano*, pp. 54–56.

[56] Still on the question of the links between the building's architecture and the painting cycles, the triumphal arch provides further endorsement of the aforementioned unitary and cyclic nature of the church's design, recurring not only in the arrangement of the dividing wall and the repetition in each wall of the building (particularly in section), but also in the series of Serlian windows. In each of these the tripartite sequence of lintel-arch-lintel harks back to the triumphal arch pattern, a motif much appreciated among Lombard sculptors and stonemasons at work in Venice in the late fifteenth and early sixteenth centuries. See also R. Wittkower, *Principles of Architecture in the Age of Humanism*, London 1962, pl. 59; K. De Jonge, "La serliana di Sebastiano Serlio. Appunti sulla finestra veneziana", in *Sebastiano Serlio. Sesto seminario internazionale di storia dell'architettura* (Vicenza 1987), Milan 1989, p. 54; S. Frommel, *Sebastiano Serlio architetto*, Milan 1998, p. 69.

[57] Grassi and Portaluppi, "*Scuola e 'maniera'*", p. 225.

[58] At any event, the attribution belongs among the Lombard workshops, in which whole families of artists handed down a legacy of drawings and models — of a range that now eludes assessment — including the *Small Passion* by Albrecht Dürer, dated around 1511, the period in which at least part of the said frescoes were executed. Scholars have associated these works to artists of rank then at work in Milan, whose work tends to pivot on architectural schemes, whether rendered through painting or in actual constructions: in addition to Zenale and Bramantino, others such as Vincenzo Foppa, Bergognone, and Giovan Antonio Boltraffio have been named, and more recently the young Bernardino Luini himself, who later in 1523–24 went on to

paint the dividing wall, maintaining the close union between the architectural and pictorial features; in 1530 he continued with the Cappella di Santa Caterina. For comparisons of the illusionistic decoration in San Maurizio with that of San Sigismondo in Cremona, and San Paolo Converso in Milan, see M.L. Ferrari, *San Sigismondo di Cremona*, Milan 1974, p. 146, no. 112.

[59] A. Venturi, *Storia dell'arte italiana*, VIII, Milan 1924, part 2, p. 671.

[60] Painted decorative features of the older and more extensive fresco cycles of the two halls were thereafter realized structurally for the sections above the first intermediate cornice for the whole church, and for the section above the imposts of the lower arches over the side chapels in the nuns' hall — an undertaking that was repeatedly requested by the nuns themselves — together with the intermediate pilasters (first order).

[61] Also related to this, together with the relative religious structure, are the evident links with the numerous lines of saints depicted, all enclosed in mouldings — a visual cue, as it were, of the initial unfied scheme intended — still visible in the nuns' hall, that is, in the section of the church appointed specifically for meditation and prayer. Similarly, the couples painted on the arched backgrounds of the side chapels are portrayed like statues against an open sky that is visually delimited by the roundel in the upper order and the perspective of the fictive coffered vault above. An ample stretch of similar open sky at the same height is embellished with a large *Annunciation*, a theme that recurs in the triumphal arch arrangement over the presbytery. Framed in gilded fictive borders is the corresponding lunette vault over which the so-called bridge arches (this time against a star-spangled ground), whose structure determines the arrangement of the traditional themes that appear on the iconostasis (icon screen) above the altar: *God the Father*, the four *Evangelists*, the choir of angels, together with fictive medallions containing scenes from the lives of the Ancestors. Though exclusive to the nuns' hall, set once more against an open sky and framed within fictive windows is the set of saints in the painted roundels of the loggia — alongside which, denoting accessories to their vocation as it were, appear garlands of flowers and fruit frescoed as if strung from flowing ribbons (these too against a backdrop of open sky) on the adjacent fictive Serlian windows. Other busts appear in the central medallions of the early volutes of the intermediate cornice; whereas grisailles accentuating the architecture are featured both within the double order of candelabras — together with scenes from the life of Christ and angels in the intermediate dados (first order only, nuns' hall), and Christian symbols — and also inside the clipei in the panels of the entire second order of the church. On the outside walls of the church, coinciding with this second order, the richly articulated fictive framework once included frescoes integrated with the original blind arches, comprising a series of architectural details and prophets (G. Mongeri, *L'arte in Milano*, Milan 1872, p. 240): witness similar well-known works such as Bramante's *Philosopher* (Palazzo della Ragione, Bergamo), the *Prophets* (Santa Maria Incoronata, Milan), and in the Cappella della Madonnina in the church of San Paolo, Cantù. Still level with the second order, perhaps denoting a theme of critical importance that was previously inserted and iconographically linked to motifs assimilated into the original architectural framework, were what the superintendent Angelo Brusconi observed in 1915–16 as still visible in a dominant position on the entrance wall, under three large seventeenth-century canvases (still present): "Scant traces of decoration outlining the rose window and the upper section of a saint, life-size" (perhaps the titular saint of the church, painted while the scaffolding was still in place), but by that time "retouched and repainted several times over", such that it is now no longer legible (Archivio Soprintendenza ai Beni Artistici e Storici, Milan, 1915–16). The artists at work during the sixteenth century continued to respect the structural features of the building, filling the remaining free space on the walls of both halls with painted decorations. But the first frescoes that Bernardino Luini executed in 1522–24 on the dividing wall (nuns' side) — most likely at the behest of Ippolita Bentivoglio (6 May 1521: ASM *San Maurizio – benedettine* 461; Rossi, *La chiesa di San Maurizio in Milano*, p. 34), whose daughter Bianca was a convent member — were complemented on the lay worshippers' side with new commissions from the nobility, linked almost exclusively to the Bentivoglio dynasty. The new works were largely of a votive nature, with images of patron saints, portraits of the church's benefactors, coats of arms, and dedicatory inscriptions, which, together with correlated archive material, have provided new insights into the sequence of commissions. In the meantime, in the nuns' hall the paintings — all commissioned by the Benedictine order — always tended towards a meditation mood (in particular those relating the Passion) and prayer, in keeping with what would appear to be the original intentions of the entire programme of decoration.

[62] The ribbing of the vault groins are decorated with continuous volutes, with openwork discs at each intersection. The latter — albeit simply moulded and superimposed — recur in the triumphal arch above the high altar, emphasizing the semi-circular concept on which the main vault rests.

[63] The coffering of the side chapel vaults (nuns' hall and the upper vaults throughout the loggia); the front volutes in the panels (first order of nuns' hall); the double order of candelabras on the intermediate and upper pilasters; what remains of the earlier decorative work of the intermediate voluted cornice with intermediate medallions; the fictive marble panels, outlined with central clipeus, on the prospects of the Serliana windows; panels orchestrating each wall of the loggia, including the fictive Serlianas, frescoed on the perimeter walls on either side of the arched one-light apertures, or fictive windows — documented as once having actually existed — largely obscured from view below, but only in the corridor of the loggia, confirming the general integrity of the building's painted architecture.

[64] See also M.A. Winkelmes, *Benedectine Nuns in Milan: Claustration and Innovation at St. Maurizio*, in *Picturing Women in Renaissance and Baroque Italy*, Cambridge 1997, p. 102; D. Zardin, "Le abitanti del Monastero: l'età moderna", in *San Maurizio al Monastero Maggiore in Milano. Guida*, pp. 13–17.

[65] Milan, Biblioteca Ambrosiana, D 348 Inf. (R. Beretta, "Il Monastero Maggiore di Milano e la riforma operatavi da san Carlo Borromeo il 23 febbraio 1568", in *Rivista storica benedettina*, XI, 1916, pp. 132–141).

[66] F. Chabod, *Lo Stato e la vita religiosa a Milano nell'epoca di Carlo V*, Turin 1971, p. 378.

[67] *Officium hebdomadae sanctae cura sororis Perpetua da Birago*, Milan 1522, ed. Gottardo Pontano (Cattaneo, "Istituzioni ecclesiastiche milanesi", p. 604).

[68] Forcella, *Iscrizioni nelle chiese*, p. 457.

[69] Contract for the Antegnati organ: ASM, *Religione p.a.* 2147; *Notarile* 10026 (Malaguzzi Valeri, "Contributi alla storia di San Maurizio", pp. 332–333).

[70] For the same reasons other works for the laypersons' hall were carried out in rapid succession over the ensuing decade, such as the decoration of the Cappella di San Paolo (1571), the creation of the silver candle-holders for the high altar "in the prescribed fashion" (1572, 1577), and the frescoes of the entrance wall (1573), the reduction in size of the dividing wall's window, and the commission for the altarpiece from Antonio Campi, Cardinal Borromeo's favourite painter, for both the altar steps and the "wooden tabernacle" (1578); similarly, it is likely that the hanging of curtains to screen the adjacent window of the *comunichino* (since lost, but testified by the fixing rings in the cornice above), and not least for paintings commissioned by the order to complete the decoration of the nuns' hall (upper part of the dividing wall and the apse area).

[71] Torre, *Il Ritratto di Milano*, p. 198.

[72] ASM, *Religione p.a.* 2147, 9 July 1571 (Malaguzzi Valeri, "Contributi alla storia di San Maurizio", p. 329), 2 July 1590; for more on Pirovano, see also L. Grassi, *Province del barocco e del rococò. Lessico di architetti in Lombardia*, Milan 1966, p. 259, and the *Dizionario del duomo di Milano*, p. 45.

[73] ASM, *Notarile* 10030, 6 August 1574.

[74] See especially Mezzanotte and Bascapé, *Milano nell'arte e nella storia*, p. 622; Ottino Della Chiesa, *San Maurizio al Monastero Maggiore*, p. 29.

[75] For further data on Giovan Ambrogio Pissina (or Pessina), see also Grassi, *Province del barocco e del rococò*, p. 253.

[76] ASM, *Religione p.a.* 2147, 19 January 1680, 2 February, and 15 March 1683; for Quarantini see Grassi, *Province del barocco e del rococò*, p. 277.

[77] Torre, *Il Ritratto di Milano*, p. 198; Latuada, *Descrizione di Milano*, pp. 420–421; Ottino Della Chiesa, *San Maurizio al Monastero Maggiore*, p. 18.

[78] ASM, *Religione p.a.* 2147, 6 February 1790 (first design for the ancona signed by the prior: "Resta fissato il dis[s]egno più alto con la testa di Angelo sotto al timpano [...] Giuseppe Maria Buzzi ac[c]etto"); 29–31 May 1792 (design for high altar, elevation with notes on materials, signed by "Giuseppe Antonio Pissina ing.re e Architetto", and plan, signed by Pissina, Giuseppe Maria Buzzi, and Antonio Giudice); see also Rossi, *La chiesa di San Maurizio in Milano*, p. 52 (ill.); for all three artists see also AVFDM, *Occorrenze particolari*, regesto MS; for more on Pissina (or Pessina), see also Grassi, *Province del barocco e del rococò*, p. 253, and *Dizionario del duomo di Milano*, p. 46.

[79] ASM, *Religione p.m.* 2460.

[80] Respectively, ASD, sez. XII, *Ordini religiosi e congregazioni* 101, 1705 (October, November, December), 1706 (January); Milan, Archivio Storico Civico (henceforth ASC), *Località milanesi* 230 (1762); ASD, sez. XII, *Ordini religiosi e congregazioni* 101, 26–28 September 1794; ASC, *Località milanesi* 230, 8 December 1796; ASM, *Religione p.m.* 2460, 20 November 1798; ASM, *Culto p.a.* 1926, 24 November 1798.

[81] See also Sannazzaro, *San Maurizio al Monastero Maggiore*; Pertot, *La torre "quadrata"*, pp. 115–135.

[82] One option considered was the possibility of endowing the conservatory of Santa Maria della Passione to the Monastero Maggiore (1843), which had successively served as a girls' school, a barracks, a gaol for political dissidents (1852), a police station, a military hospital (before 1865), and a grain market (1866).

[83] Besides the initial idea of laying new roads through the monastery complex (1813), other works recorded include alterations to the church itself: the almost contemporary erection of a small belfry and the nearly immediate consolidation of surrounding fabric threatened with instability (1814), followed by rebuilding (1837) and repairs (1854) to the campanile, subsequently replaced (1864) to designs by the Civil Engineers Department with the more stable one presently standing (above the nuns' presbytery, pierced with slits for the bell-cords on the west side). Providing certain background information for the church's architecture are the records covering the removal of the pyramids crowning the façade, subsequently replaced by pinnacles (1825–26); also, works undertaken by the Fabbrica di Santa Maria alla Porta for the replacement of flooring in the first three bays in the lay worshippers' hall (1827), namely, for the so-called *vespaio*, "dig up the ground and deposit gravel, and given the presence of various graves the vaults must be demolished and filled in with earth, to make it all damp-proof" — this in light of the proximity of the Nirone stream — which confirms that the area north of San Maurizio was even then recognized as burial ground, though now greatly modified (owing also to extensive works carried out in 1911). Some twenty years later (1848) the first of three separate instances in which the quadrangular tower was threatened with demolition (at the hands of the Civil Engineers) fell through due to insufficient funds; the second threat came when the parish priest voiced the need for more light in the apse behind (1864); and the third with a scheme to forestall further structural instability (1892). The year 1856 saw certain pictorial additions to the church — whose importance is evident both from a note made earlier in 1791 by Domenico Aspari, then professor of drawing at the Brera Academy (ASM, *Autografi* 92, 12; 13 December 1791; see also G. Ferri Piccaluga, "Eugenio di Beauharnais, conoscitore e collezionista di dipinti leonardeschi", in *I leonardeschi a Milano. Fortuna e collezionismo*, exhibition catalogue, Milan 1990, p. 219), and the series of engravings made from drawings of Fumagalli in 1811 — by the "doratore e verniciatore" (gilder and painter) Felice Valenzani, both to the frescoes in the Cappella di Santa Caterina, and the altarpiece which, however, the Brera Academy noted had suffered abrasions and repainting, for which consequently in 1857 the academy contracted a then famous restorer, Giuseppe Knoller, to carry out due repairs. A general scheme of repairs to the frescoes, never carried through, was drawn up by a new commission which included Francesco Hayez and Federico von Schmidt, or Gaetano Mongeri, the author of a city guide (1872) which contains detailed descriptions that have proved immensely useful for the study of the church. On several occasions around mid-century, the church — and the nuns' hall in particular — was a regular subject for students of painting at the Brera Academy, and for the Scuola di Prospettiva (School of Perspective), and for exhibitions (L. Goffi, in *Pinacoteca di Brera. Dipinti dell'Ottocento e del Novecento. Collezioni dell'Accademia e della Pinacoteca*, II, Milan 1994, p. 310; see also G.B. Sannazzaro, "Per la chiesa di San Maurizio al Monastero Maggiore di Milano: ritrova-

menti e nota di studio", in *Studi in onore di Renato Cevese*, Vicenza, forthcoming, regarding references to a painting by Luigi Bisi, from which the famous engraving was taken).

[84] When in 1856 the church was ceded by the Fabbriceria to the Pubblico Erario Demaniale, in 1864 the latter made the convent building over to the municipal authorities, thereby triggering a process of dismemberment that would lead to the creation of Via Luini, approved by the Accademia in 1865. In view of the new street, the double sacristy was demolished, and with it the only form of linkage between the two halves of the church; to remedy the division, a small grilled window was converted into a doorway at the left of the presbytery. Also dating to 1864 is the decision of the Commissione d'Arte Archeologica to build a small courtyard, still present at the foot of the square tower, on Via Luini. In light of this, the left flank along the new street was given a new stone facing devised (1869, 1888) by Angelo Colla, an innovation that entailed the destruction of the surviving early decorative work on the church's exterior (duly described by Mongeri); the operation was much criticized at the time, particularly as the murals had been documented in studies on the church on several occasions. Colla was also responsible for new work on the church façade (1879, following the rejection in 1876 of another project by Dossena), a few years after the design for the stairway up to the *coretti* (1869). Ensuing renovation works include repairs to the crypt (1893), with its fine depressed arches spanning seven bays of the church above, formally used as storage for firewood, and now housing part of the Museo Archeologico; through the sale of four important tapestries (used as ceremonial drapes on the front of the church during feast days), with the approval of the Ministero per il Culto (1896), further work was effected including repairs to the roof and the application of tie-bars in the nuns' hall (an operation which had originally been opposed by Beltrami in 1894), together with the cleaning of all the frescoes (1897, by the renowned restorer from Bergamo, Giuseppe Stefanoni). To this same period belong several detailed inventories of the furnishings present in San Maurizio, particularly those in the nuns' hall, many of which had also featured in nineteenth-century paintings of the church. Upon the formation of a new governing body that included numerous notables, a new motion for improvements was passed — actuated, as was the going custom, with public subscription — which saw the adherence of Vandoni, Annoni, and Beltrami, together with the directors of the two superintendences involved, Brusconi (who conceived the stairway to the nuns' hall) and Ettore Modigliani (Soprintendenza alle Gallerie). As had happened in the past, in order to stem the humidity spreading from the ground, the crypt below the first bays along Corso Magenta was cleared, resulting in the discovery of a burial vault divided into two chambers, 3 cm from the church entrance; here arches and gratings to ensure proper aeration were inserted (in line with the first bay). Meanwhile, above ground the ancient paving in terracotta was replaced with the present marble flags, level with the doorframe — with the elimination of what yet remained of the old windows, reported several times in early records, including visual documents (witness the little *veduta* by Marc'Antonio Dal Re); likewise, restorative measures were taken on the canvas of the entrance wall (1915, by Luigi Boccalari from Mantua), and on the frescoes (1917, on the ceiling of the nuns' presbytery, restorer Luigi Cavenaghi, on-site inspections by Annoni and Beltrami, operations to which most probably belongs the retouching of the paintings comprising various landscapes in the central chapels of the nuns' hall, 1936–40, funded by the engineer Antonio Chizzolini: see Mezzanotte and Bascapé, *Milano nell'arte e nella storia*, p. 622). The buildings of the west cloister, hit by bombs in World War II, were subsequently (1952) razed, allowing a clear view of the polygonal tower they had almost completely obscured. In the meantime, along with the reconstruction of some of the cloister's bays (four are original) and of part of the ground storey of the former dormitory annexed to the square tower (now the lodge for the museum's security corps), the site of the former *parlatori* was assigned for the new Museo Archeologico (1959–64). Since what remained of the monastery was spared further alterations that had been tabled in the new Master Plan, in the 1970s intensive restoration programmes were applied in stages to the church, the roof, the exteriors, the Antegnati organ, the paintings (including those in the polygonal tower); no solution has been found, however, for the grievous damage caused by the removal of the early convent fabric, whose very existence determined the original static calculations guaranteeing the delicate structural stability of the church itself.

[85] Mongeri, *L'arte in Milano*, p. 240; C. Ponzoni, *Le chiese di Milano*, Milan 1930, p. 209; Mezzanotte and Bascapé, *Milano nell'arte e nella storia*, p. 624.

[86] Baroni, *L'architettura lombarda dal Bramante al Richino*, p. 55.

Alessandro and Ippolita Bentivoglio's Commission for San Maurizio

Dario Trento

The Coats of Arms and the Chronology of the Commissions

The names of Alessandro Bentivoglio and Ippolita Sforza Bentivoglio appear on the dividing wall of the church of San Maurizio, on the convent side. They can be identified with certainty owing to their association with the two escutcheons alongside bearing the Bentivoglio family emblem, the *sega* (saw). In this case, the emblem is coupled with the Visconti's own device, the *vipera* (serpent), though it is worth noting that in addition to being the Lombard dynasty's symbol, the serpent motif also stood for the Duchy of Milan. The same device was assumed by the Visconti's successors to the duchy, the Sforza, and specifically by Cardinal Ascanio Sforza, for his coat of arms; it also appears on coinage minted under Francesco II Sforza, Duke of Milan from 1521 to 1535.[1] In order to ally the ducal insignia with his own badge, Alessandro Bentivoglio needed to hold an appropriate office in state affairs — a position he enjoyed in 1529, when he was awarded the title of vice-duke. Though retouched in 1578, the two coats of arms that adorn the wall today must be faithful replicas of the originals painted some time after 1529.[2]

In the front portion of the church, reserved for lay worshippers, the pilasters delimiting the presbytery also still bear the Bentivoglio family arms, this time with the saw emblem quartered with that of the eagle, recording the imperial bestowal of the city of Bologna on the family.[3] The devices therefore indicate the Bentivoglio family's patronage of the main vessel of the church, comprising both the lay and the convent halls. With these variants, the armorial bearings have two different meanings: the one on the nuns' side celebrates the accession of the head of the family to the powers of the Duchy of Milan; whereas the emblem in the lay portion of the church bears witness to his provenance from the family that had held power in Bologna, with which they were entrusted by imperial decree. Although painted in the mid-1550s, the emblems in the presbytery must perforce refer exclusively to Alessandro Bentivoglio, as the nobleman outlived his direct male issue. This date becomes an essential clue for identifying the patrons' portraits here in the church's presbytery.[4]

Portraits of a Nun and a Court Lady

The *Entombment of Christ* frescoed by Bernardino Luini in the convent church includes the portrait of a nun. A close likeness to this face can be identified in a fresco in the lay part of the church, showing the figure of St Scholastica engaged in the presentation of the lady benefactor. These heads link the two halves of the church, providing another pair of references associating the names of Alessandro and Ippolita with the portraits. If the contemporary figure inserted into the sacred scene on the nuns' side is a member of the family of Alessandro and Ippolita, it may well be their daughter Alessandra, one of the convent nuns; if this is the same person featured on the other side of the dividing wall, then this is further endorsement for the identification of the two donors with the Bentivoglio couple. Further confirmation lies in the third portrait, featuring a nun, that resembles the same person (formerly Museo Civico Gaetano

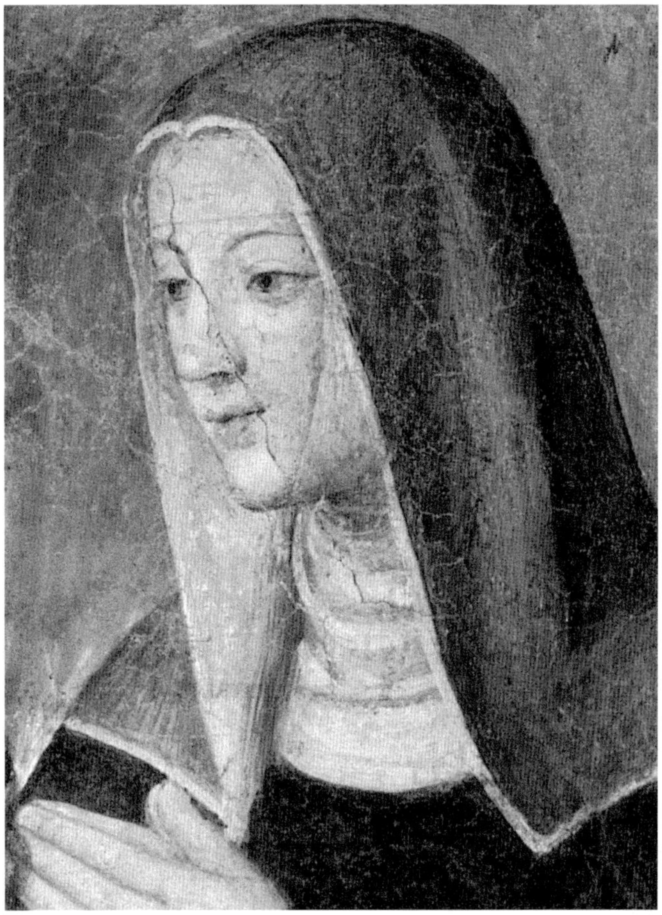

Bernardino Luini
Entombment of Christ, c. 1530, detail
Convent hall, San Maurizio, Milan

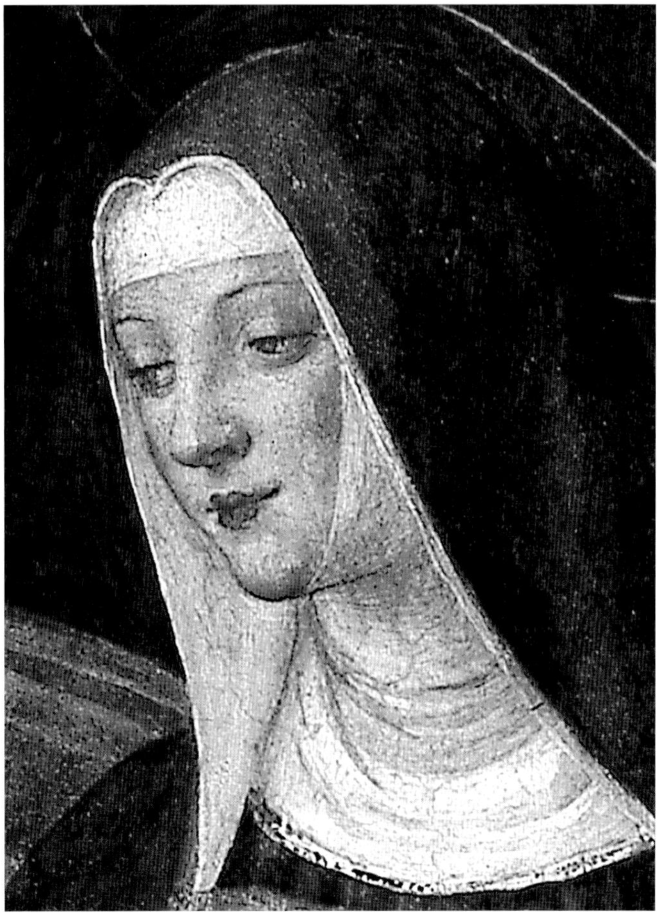

Bernardino Luini
St Scholastica, detail of the lunette showing the patron accompanied by three saints
Lay hall, San Maurizio, Milan

Filangieri, Naples). Executed by Luini on a devotional panel, this last rightfully belongs among the devices contained in the double portrait on the church's dividing wall.[5]

A comparison of the three nun's portraits helps solve several other questions regarding the wall's frescoes. Although the paintings belong to different periods, in each one the nun's features are similar: the Neapolitan portrait dates around 1520; the St Scholastica figure to 1522–24; and the figure in the *Entombment of Christ* around 1530. It appears that only the panel painting was done from life, and the others were merely copied from it. If this is the case, the features of the nun must have changed by the time the third portrait was made.

This fact offers a useful aid to similar questions affecting the portraits of the two patrons on the dividing wall. Over the period 1515–19 the manuscript illuminator G. Ambrogio Noceto embellished a codex with portraits of twenty-seven ladies of the Milanese nobility,[6] a gift from the city's aristocracy to Francis I, king of France; among the ladies featured is Ippolita Bentivoglio, shown in profile in the same pose as the church's benefactress and in similar white apparel.[7] The manuscript portrait predates the fresco by three or five years, and yet the same personage appears older. From this one can reasonably surmise the use of an original model painted some years earlier.

A Key Witness: Matteo Bandello

The aforementioned codex from the Biblioteca Trivulziana provides other clues. In his *Novelle*, Matteo Bandello closes one of his accounts on the scandalous affairs of Filippo Maria Visconti's daughter and heir, Bianca Maria Sforza, countess of Challant, with an unexpected invitation to the reader: "Whomsoever might wish to see her portrait taken from life may visit the Monastero Maggiore, wherein hangs her likeness".[8]

Since the Romantic period, this quote has been associated with the scene of the *Beheading of St Catherine* in the Cappella Besozzi, painted by Luini in 1530. It is certain that the writer never saw the painting in person, having left Milan in 1526, returning perhaps only once, albeit very briefly in 1528.[9] Even if he had only had indirect knowledge of the painting, it is altogether unlikely that a woman who had died in such disreputable circumstances would have her likeness hanging in a place of worship. The portrait of the countess allegedly "painted from life" must have hung in San Maurizio in an early period of the church's history, when she was still "esteemed among the honourable and righteous women of Milan". That period corresponds to her marriage with Ermes Visconti, from 1514 to 1519,[10] when Bandello was able to glimpse the couple from the privileged viewpoint of Alessandro and Ippolita Bentivoglio's home. The plot of the entire novella must be taken into account, in which in a dedicatory letter Bandello declares himself a direct witness to the period of the lady's virtuousness, whereas in the narrative that follows he tells of her degeneracy: the last mention of the portrait in San Maurizio harks back to the opening passage, in which the narrator is an eyewitness. It is this very context that leads one to suspect that the portrait of Bianca Maria Visconti in San Maurizio was inserted into an iconographic project associable with the Bentivoglio family. The decoration of the part for the lay congregation between 1514 and 1525 (the part Matteo Bandello may have seen) resembled the cycle still visible in the nuns' section. But a fair amount of the decoration of the presbytery may have been already completed by Luini by the mid-1510s, given that his stylistic approach is close in manner to the Passion cycle at San Giorgio al Palazzo, Milan. The portrait that Bandello invites his reader to witness may have hung in one of the niches that were later transformed into chapels and repainted, but also in Luini's first decorative system in the presbytery. The contemporary portrait of Bianca Maria in the Biblioteca Trivulziana nonetheless affords a more tenable basis on which to reconstruct the one cited by Bandello as hanging in San Maurizio.

The Benefactor: Alessandro Bentivoglio

The first known portrait of Alessandro Bentivoglio appears in a large votive canvas painted by Lorenzo Costa in 1488 for the family chapel in San Giacomo, Bologna, the family's native city. Third from the left, after the firstborn Giovanni II Annibale, and the second-born Antongaleazzo (in clerical vestments), the fourteen-year-old Alessandro is set amid the grandeur of his father's court.[11] This portrait accompanies all successive documented appearances, from his nuptials with Ippolita Sforza in 1492, to his assignments as ambassador, ceremonies and other gatherings.[12] An unusual painting by Lorenzo Costa of five years later shows us Alessandro once more, engaged in song with two brothers, some townsmen and the painter himself.[13] The resemblance of

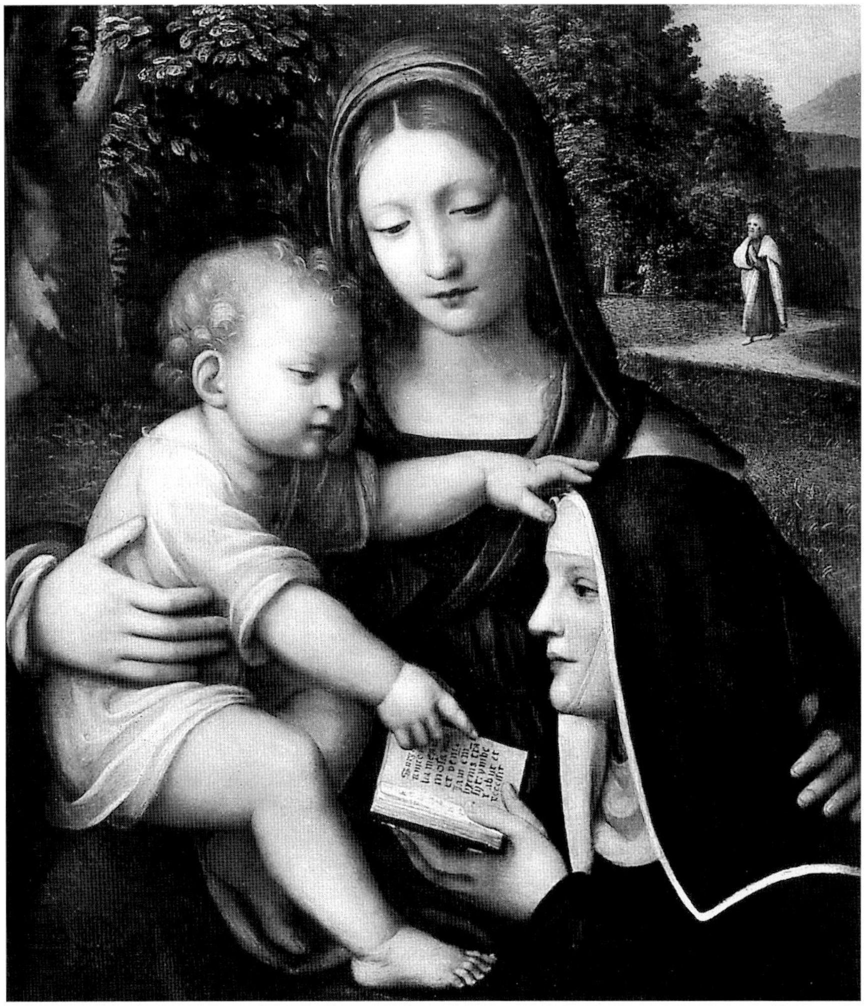

Bernardino Luini
Virgin and Child with Nun in Adoration
Formerly Museo Civico Gaetano Filangieri, Naples

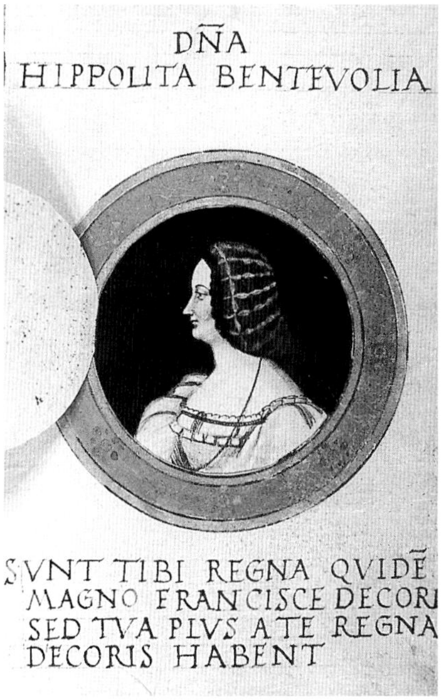

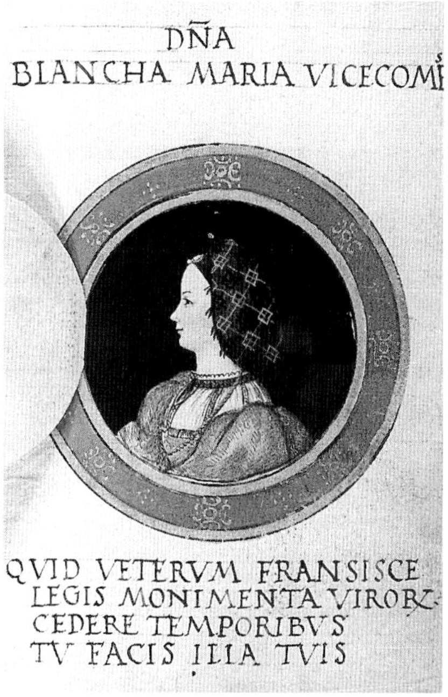

G. Ambrogio Noceto
Portrait of Ippolita Bentivoglio
MS 2159, Biblioteca Trivulziana, Milan

G. Ambrosio Noceto
Portrait of Bianca Maria Visconti (then Duchess of Challant)
MS 2159, Biblioteca Trivulziana, Milan

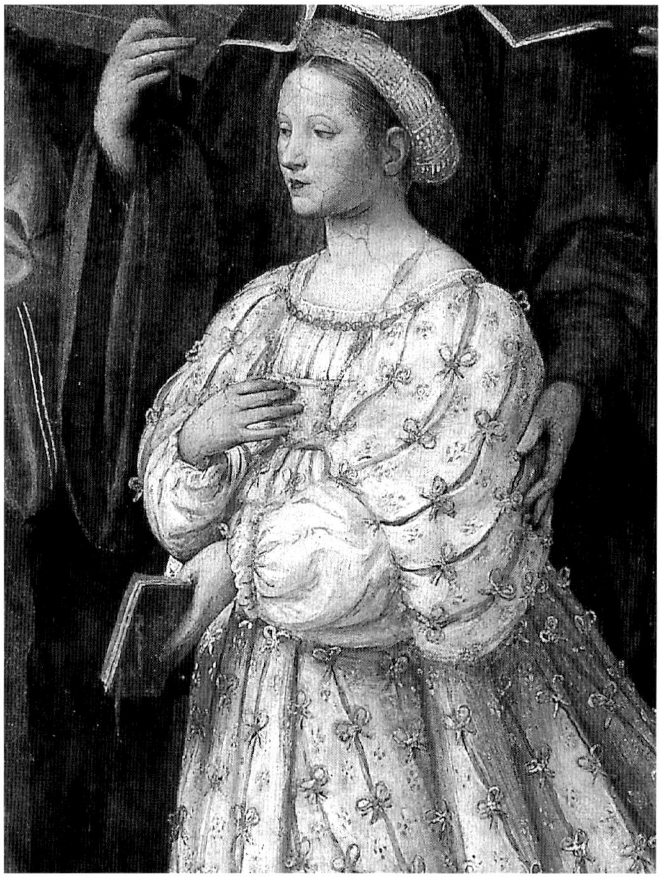

Bernardino Luini
Portrait of the Benefactress
Lay hall, San Maurizio, Milan

the male profile here with that of the minister dressed *all'antica* and crowned with an oak-garland, visible in the altarpiece commissioned by his brother from Francesco Francia in 1499 as a votive offering for his safe return from Palestine, has led to its identification as Alessandro.[14] At this time the young Bentivoglio was twenty-five years old, and hence twenty years from the benefactor portrayed in San Maurizio.

In 1499 Alessandro could hardly have envisaged the abrupt reversals of fortune that overtook his family and led to the confiscation of Bologna and their subsequent exile. With the loss of the city in 1506, and having by 1512 abandoned any hope of regaining it, the young nobleman decided to make good the connections acquired through his marriage, and entered the government of the Duchy of Milan. By 1513, during the reign of Massimiliano Sforza, son of Ludovico il Moro, Alessandro had established himself securely in the duchy's aristocracy. His family ties with the Sforza enabled him to remain in the city when, in 1521, under Spanish tutelage, Francesco II Sforza rose to power. From this moment on political fortunes of the Bolognese lord went from strength to strength: in 1522 he was appointed to the senate, and in 1529, as already noted, he was bestowed the title of vice-duke. Meanwhile, further intermarriage increased bonds with the Sforza family: his daughter Violante married Gian Paolo Sforza (1497–1535), half-brother of Francesco II and heir apparent to the dukedom.[15]

Ippolita Sforza Bentivoglio

A lively and detailed account of Alessandro and Ippolita Bentivoglio is contained in Bandello's *Novelle*. The couple are said to possess a "house or palace" in the "borgo de la Porta Comense" (III, 9), complete with garden where, in due conformity with the customs of Milanese courtly life, they received guests and held social gatherings. Some time between 1513 and 1515, Bandello had readied a "Ragionamento" divided up into nine days that aired discussions held during the dinners,[16] but Ippolita seems to have prompted the collection of the writer's novellas in vernacular Italian. This explains the work's dedication, indeed, the first dedicatory letter is addressed to her: "Many years ago I began writing a number of novellas, prompted by the entreaties of [...] the virtuous lady Ippolita Sforza, consort of the most enlightened Alessandro Bentivoglio".[17] The gentlewoman in question appears in numerous different instances of the collection. In her house in Milan, "there come many squires who, true to the praiseworthy custom, come to amuse themselves, competing in all kinds of daily events, discourses on love, and other such happenings", and the lady of the house is equal to any form of discussion: "Each day it is customary to see the depth of knowledge of *belles lettres*, due to your constant immersion in books, now towards texts in Latin, now in the vulgate, of which you with a single reading manage to grasp, such that you seem to do little else but attend to your studies".[18]

The lifestyle upheld by the couple soon led to the purchase of the "Palagio", a country residence near the Adda river, and in the places that the Milanese gentry and intelligentsia was wont to gather. In her time Ippolita was a formidable social figure, and even receives a mention in Ludovico Ariosto's *Orlando Furioso* among the noble women readers who admit the author into their company at the end of his epic poem;[19] she is also documented in a literary exchange with Gian Giorgio Trissino over the period 1510–12.[20] While there is no trace of any literary output of her own, this same female figure features with equal prestige in other works by Bandello, stressing the vital importance of the exchange that took place between the courtly man of letters and the noble Ippolita.

Bambaia and Luini, a Model and a Dating

The date 1522 was carved by Agostino Busti, called Bambaia, on the Birago funerary monument in the church of San Francesco Grande.[21] The tall statue of St John the Baptist, one of several large figures once adorning it, recurs in the closely similar pose of the figure before the donor in Luini's fresco in San Maurizio. The monument was a crucial point of reference for Luini's intellectual mastery of his style, developing it beyond his classicism of Raphaelesque stamp; rather than displace earlier artistic attainments, it entailed the addition of greater articulation. Compared with the rest of the wall, the poses in the two lunettes in San Maurizio are more dynamic: line prevails over colour, the folds of the drapery are thick and nervous, and some of the profiles evince a vein of classicism. The impact Bambaia's work had on Luini remained steady after this episode; the *Evangelists* in Saronno have resumed the postures of the *Apostles* from the tomb of Gaston de Foix, the *Sibyls* echo the headdresses, anatomy, and clothing of the *Virtues* of the same monument; while in the scenes depicting *Jesus among the*

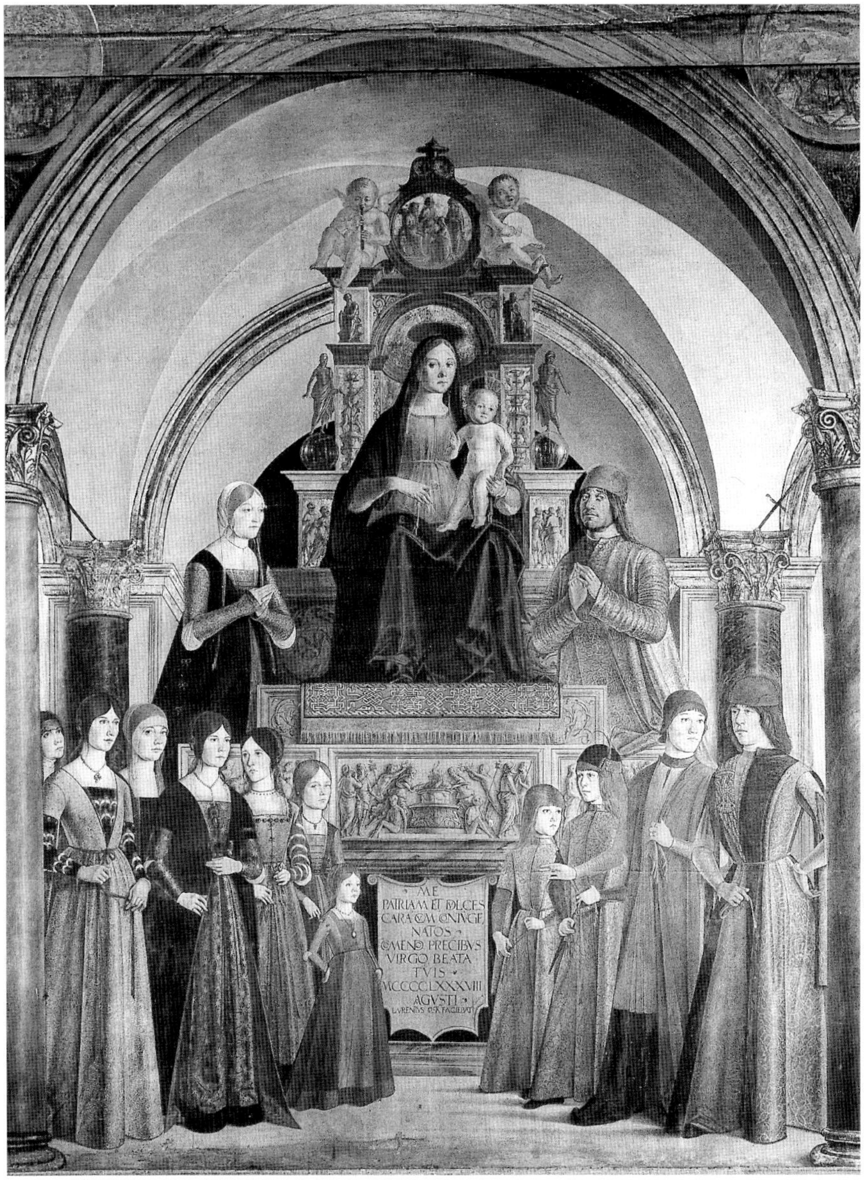

Lorenzo Costa
The Family of Giovanni II Bentivoglio at the Feet of the Virgin, 1488
Cappella Bentivoglio, San Giacomo, Bologna

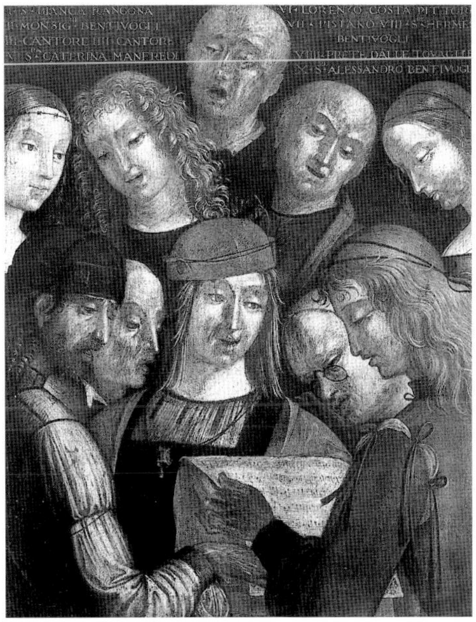

Lorenzo Costa
Concerto Bentivoglio, 1493
Fondación Colleción Thyssen-Bornemisza, Madrid

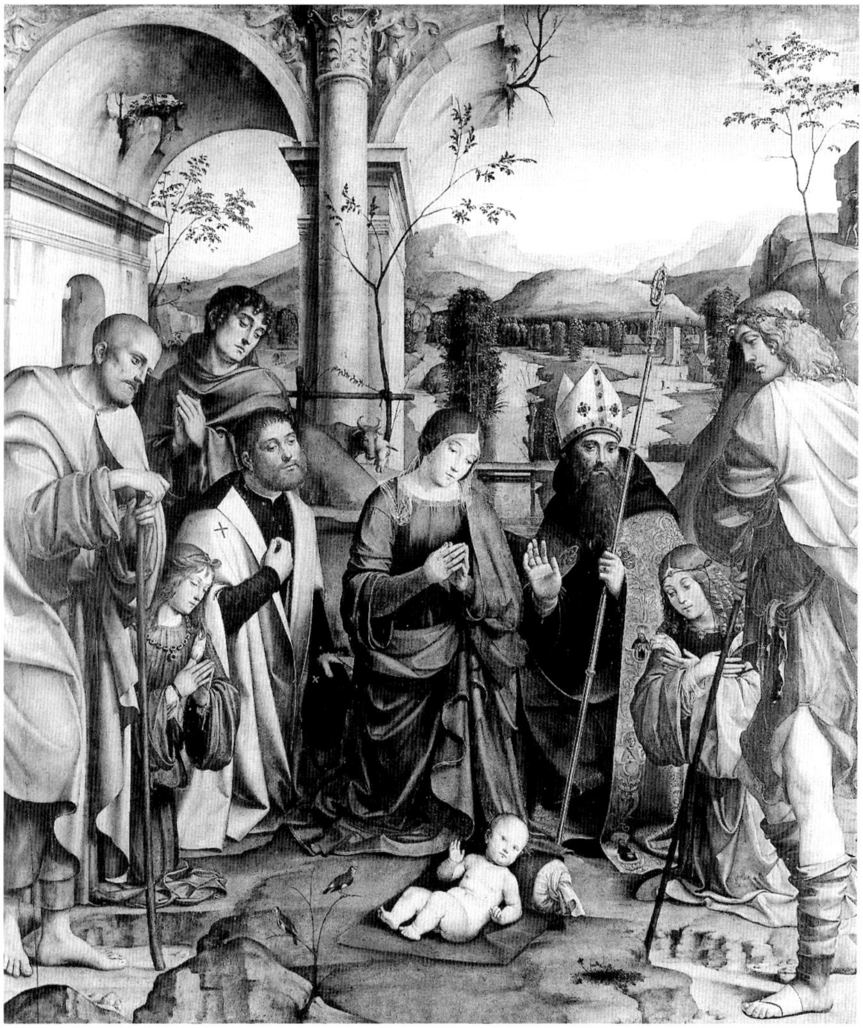

Doctors, and the *Marriage of the Virgin* we find inserts and emphasis typical of classical statuary manifested in the profiles, clothing, and spatial arrangement.[22]

To return to the two lunettes in San Maurizio, it is worth noting that the direction of the gazes and gestures of the figures depicted seem to focus on a point towards the high altar, the place where the rite of Christ's sacrifice is enacted, or to where there was most likely a Crucifix resting on the grating, thereby providing the indispensable iconographic completion of the representation of the Passion, in both public and monastery halls. Is there some explanation for Luini's introduction of one of the Passion's themes on the wall of San Maurizio? Given that shortly after 1521 Ippolita Sforza met her death, one could surmise that the lunette with the donors was a form of funerary monument.

If this were true, it would dispel many lingering doubts surrounding the paintings.[23] First of all it would explain the noticeable difference in age between Alessandro and Ippolita, the woman's features presumably having been copied from an earlier picture. Similarly, the white cloth of her dress, in stark contrast with that of her consort Alessandro, seems to hint at a "phantom" presence, that the lady was being portrayed in retrospect, so to speak, in an idealized image (corresponding, therefore, to Bandello's own account in his *Canti XI*).

Francesco Francia
Thanksgiving Altarpiece, 1499
Pinacoteca Nazionale, Bologna

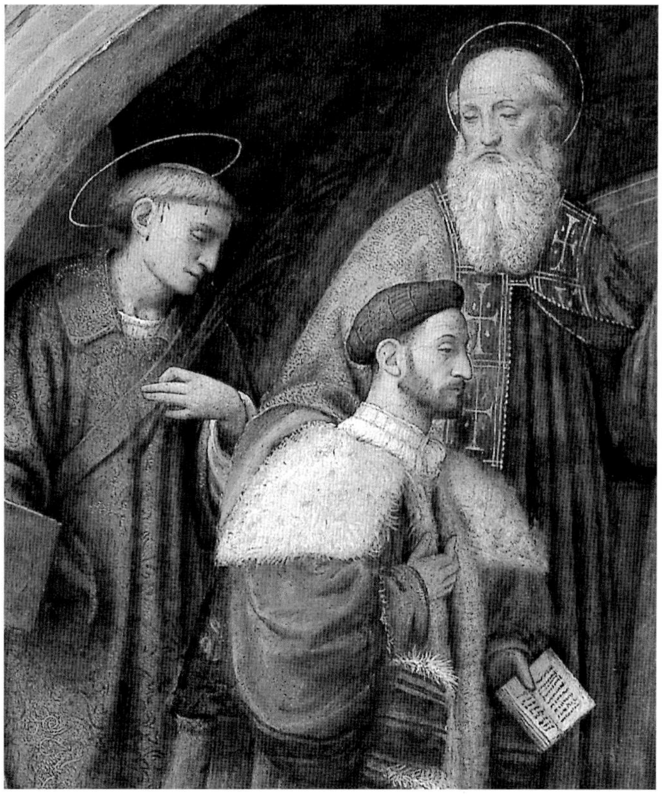

Bernardino Luini
Portrait of the Benefactor, c. 1522
Lay hall, San Maurizio, Milan

San Maurizio, a Family Mausoleum

In a letter dated 26 January 1541 Cardinal Gaspare Contarini announced to Alessandra Bentivoglio, then living under vows at the convent, the definitive annulment of the papal excommunication of the remains of her father, dating from the time of Bologna's seizure.[24] This event doubtlessly marked a watershed in the handling of the family's remains in San Maurizio. The eminent personage who had had his name and emblem carved into the frame of the grate in the dividing wall, had also commissioned his portrait for the lay side of the wall and had been honoured by his daughter with a stone plaque that exalted above all his moral probity. Dying with no direct male heir, he had strengthened his dynastic ties with the family reigning over the Duchy of Milan by marrying his daughter Violante to Gian Paolo Sforza to the step-brother of Duke Francesco II; another daughter, Ginevra, was joined in wedlock to Giovanni Carreto, scion of the Finario marquises. These marital ties had afforded the Bentivoglio family a position of rank among the Milanese hierarchy; from the 1540s, San Maurizio became the chosen site for the family burials. In 1541 the Carreto family became the benefactors of one of the church's chapels as a sepulchral shrine to Ginevra Bentivoglio, daughter of Alessandro and wife of Giovanni Carreto,[25] and in 1551 the chapel alongside became the sepulchre of another member of the latter's family, Francesco Giacomo.[26] Documents relate that the chapel whose decoration was commissioned from Aurelio and Giovan Pietro Luini in 1555, was dedicated to the "loving memory" of Bona, wife of Giovan Pietro Bergamini and sister of Gian Paolo Sforza.[27] That same year Bernardo Simonetta, bishop of Perugia and cousin of Ippolita Bentivoglio, assumed the patronage of a chapel and began preparing his own tomb; his death brought a halt to the work, which was later completed by his brother.[28]

A tomb slab of 1572 attests the Bentivoglio family's patronage of the lay worshippers' hall of San Maurizio; the vessel is dedicated variously to Alessandro Bentivoglio, *signor* of Milan and Cremona, to his nephew Giovanni, to his daughter Ginevra, marchioness of Finario, to the two nuns Francesca and Violante, and lastly, to Alessandra, six times abbess of the monastery.[29] The inscription designated the shared entombment of these members of the family. The original placement of the slab is not known, but the heavy wear of its surface suggests a position in a well-trod passage — not the presbytery area, which contained a crypt beneath, but more likely the lay church itself, just before the presbytery. The emblem engraved on the slab corresponds with that on the side pilasters of the presbytery, its saw motifs clearly visible, whereas the eagles have a chiselled look. The engraved tombstone marking the place where Alessandro Bentivoglio was buried with four children and a nephew is a keystone for unravelling the line of patronage accrued in the course of San Maurizio's history as a mausoleum to the Bentivoglio-Sforza family, and has remained an immutable testament to the present day.

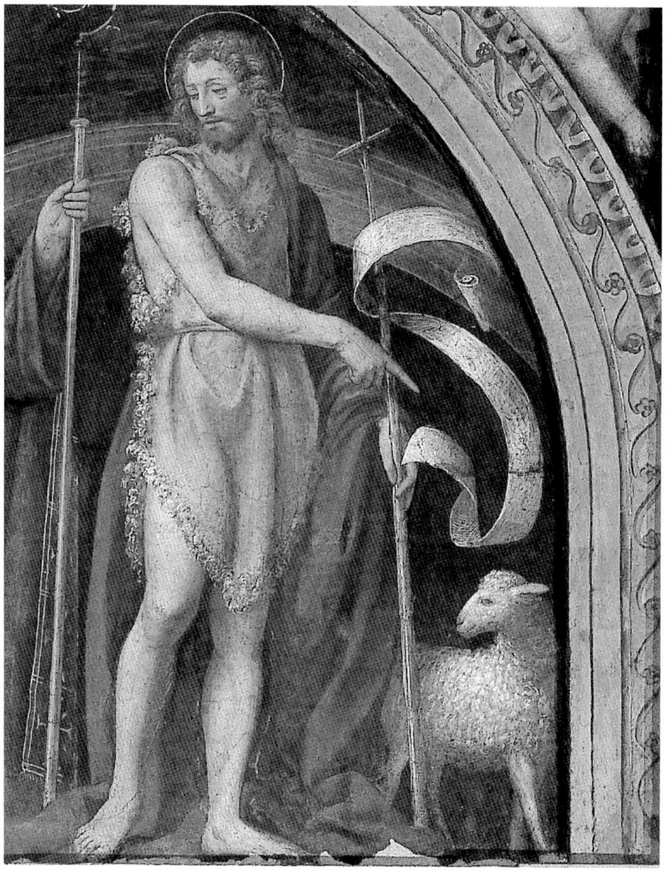

Bernardino Luini
St John the Baptist, c. 1522
Lay hall,
San Maurizio,
Milan

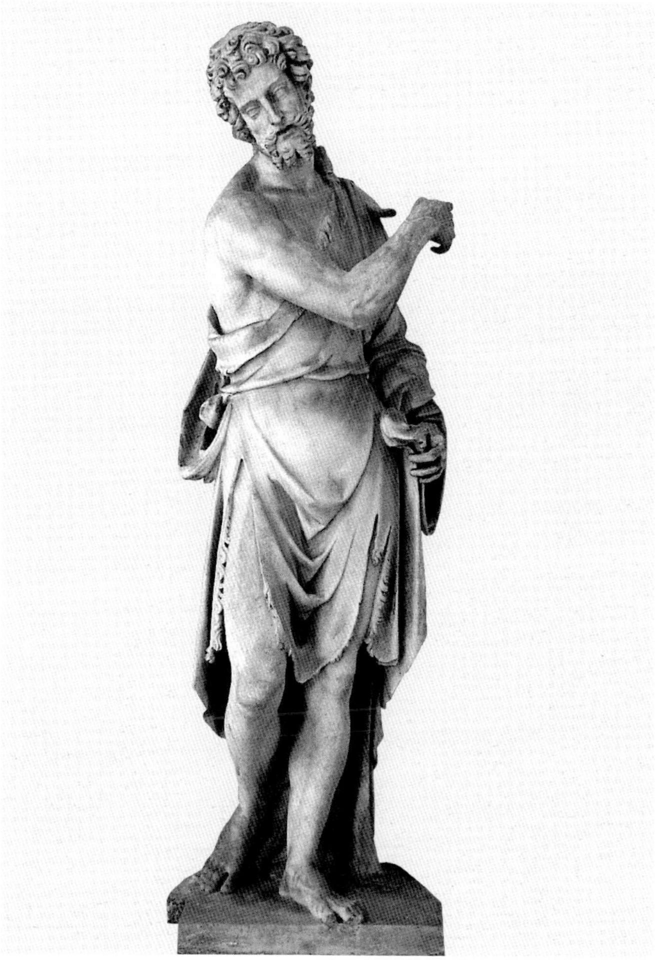

Agostino Busti,
called Bambaia
St John the Baptist,1522
Chapel, Palazzo Borromeo, Isola Bella

[1] P. Litta, *Famiglie celebri di Italia*, Milan 1819, entry "Attendolo di Cotignola in Romagna, poi Sforza", pls. V and I, no. 10. Regarding the coat of arms located on the funerary monument of Cardinal Ascanio Sforza in Santa Maria del Popolo, Rome, 1500, Litta notes that "Cardinal Sforza was from the branch of the Dukes who had adopted the Visconti device, namely, the viper".

[2] I. Rossi, *La chiesa di San Maurizio in Milano. Il Monastero Maggiore e le sue due torri*, Milan 1914, p. 23.

[3] P. Litta, *Famiglie celebri di Italia*, Milan 1834, entry "Bentivoglio di Bologna", pl. I: "The coat of arms used by *Bentivoglio* was always

what the Bolognese called the seven-toothed red saw in a gold field [...]. On 15 July 1460 the Emperor Frederick III conferred on Gio. *Bentivoglio* and his descendants the title of Count Palatino and of the S.R.I. with the black eagle on gold ground quartered with the saw". This ensign was often on the reverse of coins minted by Giovanni II Bentivoglio, father of Alessandro: cf. pl. IV, nos. 2, 4, 5, 7–12, 14, 17–20.

[4] Arguing against the identification of the portrayed benefactors with Alessandro and Ippolita Bentivoglio is M.T. Binaghi Olivari, "I francesi a Milano (1499–1525): arti figurative e moda", in *Annali dell'Istituto storico italo-germanico in Trento*, V, 1979, pp. 85–116, especially pp. 104–106. The author maintains that the ages of the figures portrayed cannot correspond with those of Alessandro and Ippolita, and may therefore refer to other members of the family, namely, Gian Paolo Sforza and Violante Bentivoglio, or Giovanni Carreto and Ginevra Bentivoglio. The basis of the argument (coats of arms and plaques) linked to the portraits does not admit the identification, while the lack of correspondence of their ages (itself somewhat hard to resolve), can be explained in another way, as shown further on in this essay.

[5] Cf. L. Beltrami, *Luini 1512–1532. Materiali di studio*, Milan 1911, p. 362; and A. Ottino Della Chiesa, *Bernardino Luini*, Novara 1956, p. 122.

[6] Biblioteca Trivulziana, Milan, MS 2159; cf. Binaghi Olivari, "I francesi a Milano", pp. 95–113.

[7] Binaghi Olivari in "I francesi a Milano", p. 104, claims the painting to be a portrait of Ippolita, "one of the four daughters of Alessandro Bentivoglio and Ippolita Sforza", but on 3 August 1529 (date of Alessandro's will) the girl was around 10 years old (Rossi, *La chiesa di San Maurizio*, p. 26; see also C. Godi, *Bandello. Narratori e dedicatari della prima parte delle "Novelle"*, Rome 1996, p. 85) and therefore was not yet born at the time of the codex's composition.

[8] Bandello, *Tutte le opere*, ed. F. Flora, I, Milan 1934, p. 65 (Novella I, 4).

[9] A.C. Fiorato, *Bandello entre l'histoire et l'écriture. La vie, l'expérience sociale, l'évolution culturelle d'un conteur de la Renaissance*, Florence 1979, pp. 340–341.

[10] F. Neri, "La contessa di Challant", in Idem, *Storia e poesia*, Turin 1926, pp. 63–95. Bandello dedicates Novella I, 27 to Ermes Visconti.

[11] C.M. Ady, *I Bentivoglio*, Milan 1965, pp. 190–192 and 198–240.

[12] Ibid., p. 195.

[13] D. Von Halden, "Das Bentivoglio-Conzert von Lorenzo Costa", in *Pantheon*, 1934, pp. 338–340.

[14] The identification of the shepherd with Alessandro Bentivoglio, argued at length by M. Reggiani Rajna in "Un po' d'ordine tra tanti Casii", in *Rinascimento*, II, 3–4, 1952, pp. 350–351 (and 343–344), ill. 6, is endorsed with different motives by G. Romano, "Verso la maniera moderna: da Mantegna a Raffaello", in *Storia dell'arte italiana*, vol. VI, t. I, Turin 1981, p. 51, ill. 46.

[15] Violante Bentivoglio Sforza is the dedicatee and protagonist of the dialogue by Ludovico Domenichi, *La nobiltà delle donne*, Venice, Giolito de' Ferrari, 1549, set in the Milanese residence of the Caravaggio marquises on the occasion of the marriage of their son Muzio to Faustina Sforza.

[16] Bandello, *Tutte le opere*, II, pp. 167 and 302 (Novelle II, 48, and III, 9); see also Fiorato, *Bandello entre l'histoire et l'écriture*, pp. 141 and 227–228.

[17] Bandello, *Tutte le opere*, I, p. 3.

[18] Ibid., pp. 5–6.

[19] L. Ariosto, *Orlando furioso*, XLVI, st. 4 (Canto XL, st. 4 of the 1516 edition).

[20] Fiorato, *Bandello entre l'histoire et l'écriture*, pp. 226–227.

[21] M.T. Fiorio, *Bambaia*, Florence 1990, pp. 73–106, especially p. 73, and Idem, "La 'buona maniera moderna' del Bambaia e lo 'sperperato avello' dei Birago", in M. Natale (ed.), *Scultura lombarda del Rinascimento. I monumenti Borromeo*, Turin 1997, pp. 277–292, especially p. 277.

[22] See the detailed illustration of the cycle published by P.C. Marani, "Pittura e decorazione dalle origini fino al 1584. Giorgio da Saronno, Alberto da Lodi, Bernardino Luini e Cesare Magni", in M.L. Gatti Perer, *Il Santuario della Beata Vergine dei Miracoli di Saronno*, Cinisello Balsamo 1996, pp. 142–175, to be compared with Fiorio, *Bambaia*.

[23] A definite date for Ippolita's death is not known; mention of the lady's "premature death" recurs several times in Bandello's *Novelle*, giving rise in part to the traditional date of around 1520: N. Ratti, *Della famiglia Sforza. Parte II. Donne illustri di casa Sforza*, II, Rome, Salomoni, 1795, p. 94: "This rare creature died a premature death, as testified by Bandello in his Foreword. We do not know exactly what year this took place, perhaps around 1520, or shortly thereafter, such a date possibly being inferred from the dedication of Novella XXXVI of Tome III, which talks of the wedding of her daughter Violante to Gio. Paolo Sforza, Marquis of Caravaggio, held around that date allegedly in the house of Signor Alessandro Bentivoglio, father of the bride". The date is carried through in commentaries of Bandello: Godi, *Bandello. Narratori e dedicatari*, in which the previous literature is supplemented by new archival and bibliographical material; cf. pp. 85, no. 20; 147, no. 3; 185, no. 23; 248, no. 2; 292, no. 3. The will of Ippolita Bentivoglio bears the date 6 May 1521.

[24] A. Giulini, "Per la sepoltura di Alessandro Bentivoglio," in *Archivio Storico Lombardo*, IV, 39, 1912, pp. 255–256; cf. Rossi, *La chiesa di San Maurizio*, p. 25.

[25] G.B. Sannazzaro, *San Maurizio al Monastero Maggiore*, 2nd ed., Milan 1992, p. 121, nos. 68 and 69.

[26] Ibid., pp. 121–122, no. 75.

[27] Ibid., p. 122, no. 80.

[28] Ibid., pp. 122–123, no. 85.

[29] Rossi, *La chiesa di San Maurizio*, p. 119; Sannazzaro, *San Maurizio al Monastero Maggiore*, pp. 65–66, no. 36. The plaque is now in the women's gallery, on the Gospel side, above the first arch of the presbytery. (My thanks to Roberto Cassanelli for his assistance.)

The Decoration Project

Sandrina Bandera

In San Maurizio it seems as though the history of Milan has stopped at the sixteenth century. In the two divisions of the church, the one for lay worshippers and the other for the Benedictine nuns of the Monastero Maggiore, the pictorial decoration entirely covering the articulated architecture of the church provides an opportunity to study the history of the painting, society, liturgy, politics, faith, fashions and the collectivism of sixteenth-century Milan.

The frescoes as a whole were executed in a number of different phases, each separated by a certain period of time, not to mention changes in taste and culture. However, one is bound to admit that the stamp given to architecture by Bramante established the structural framework into which the frescoes and decorations were woven with an extraordinary sense of unity.

The very careful painting of festoons and pilasters, some of them dating from the first phase of the convent church's decoration, i.e. during the second decade of the sixteenth century, allows us to conjecture that the overall decoration project had been thought out, on general lines at least, ever since work began on reconstructing the old Benedictine church in 1503, as we read on the *lapis primarius* now placed on the wall of the convent church.

Considering that the first phase of decoration was launched in the convent church beneath the bridge, on the triumphal arch and on the upper registers of the chapels, more precisely in the lunettes around the *oculi*, one can only presume the existence of an integrated, unified project. Organized on the same Bramantesque principles that underlie the architecture of the church, the decoration is characterized by various scenes, all designed on a scale of Renaissance proportions. Although created by different painters and techniques according to the practices and procedures of the various *botteghe* involved, after nearly a century of decoration the result is one totally integrated scheme, linked by a series of pilasters bearing grotesques. But in spite of repainting and the inroads of continuous maintenance, the decorations in the convent church remain, fundamentally, those of the original concept, which in part can be dated to around 1513–14.

The conspicuous presence of decorative elements such as fascias and classical motives can be ascribed to the culture and informed taste of the nuns who commissioned the work. As we know, they belonged to the most important Milanese families, and obviously possessed a fresh classical culture and sensibility. Equally important however must have been the status of the city of Milan itself, which ranked high among the great capitals of Europe. After Ludovico il Moro was driven out in 1499, it took Milan until the Peace of Cateau-Cambrésis in 1559 to begin settling down to peace and quiet. But even with the many and unexpected changes that occurred throughout this period, there was one activity which continued to flourish in the Lombard capital, and this was the buoyant manufacture of "sumptuous" arts. In Milan the goldsmiths, the silversmiths and the weavers of cloth of gold exported their production all over Europe, constituting a bridge with the Empire, and with transalpine Europe and the great merchants of the Nordic countries.[1]

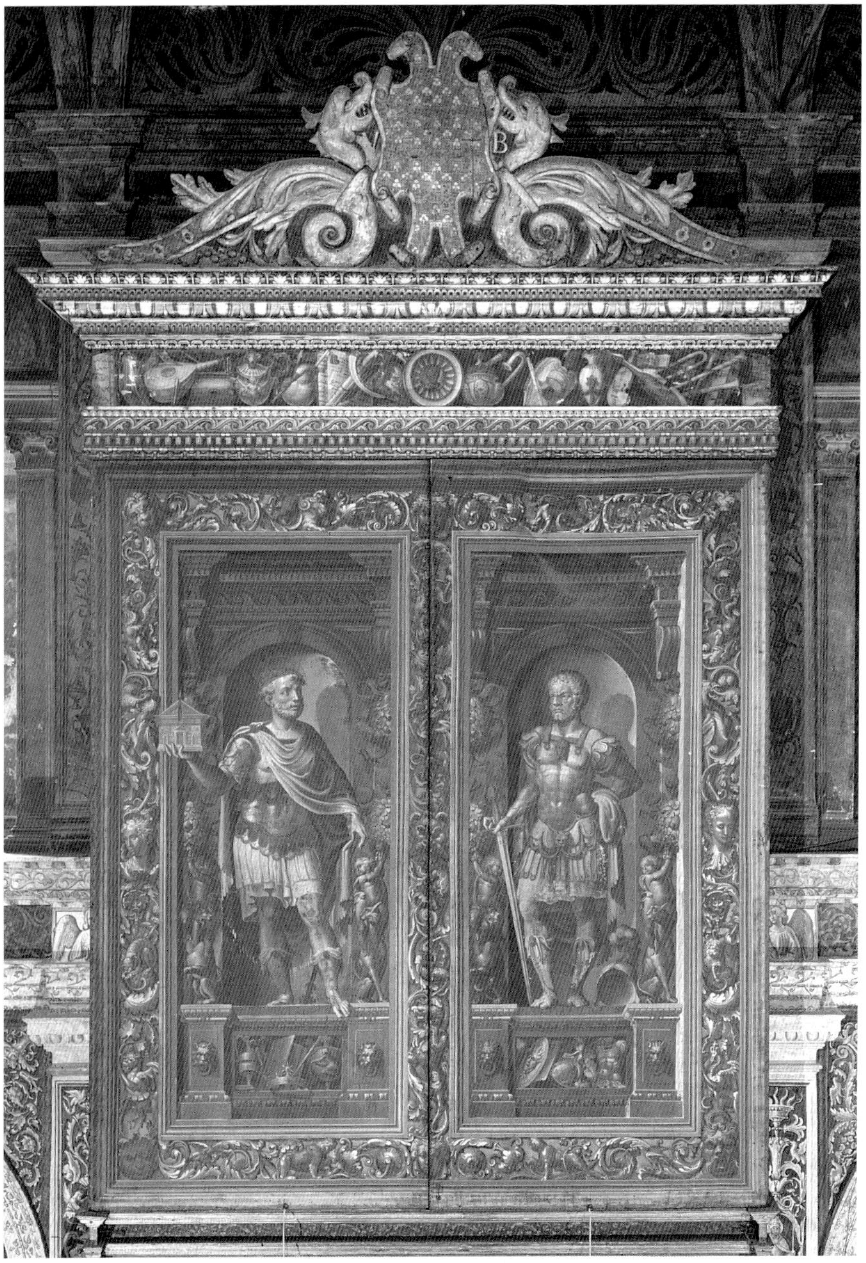
Organ by Gian Giacomo Antegnati, 1554
Convent hall, San Maurizio, Milan

Although disappearing into the past chronologically, from a strictly artistic point of view the Sforza epoch made its importance and ineluctable heritage felt in the pictorial decoration of San Maurizio. The interior had the air of a grandiose solemn space. At the same time it demonstrated orderly composition through the series of partitioning elements which form the skeletal framework of an artistic language where painting joins with architecture in horizontal and vertical scansions that structure the interior in the manner of music; and this is the most profound, if indirect, legacy which Bramante left to Milan. At the same time, in spite of the subjects from the scriptures, the extensive freedom in decoration conceived with profane sensibility is the expression of an aristocratic and neo-feudal society. And this is what Leonardo left behind for assimilation in the local humus. His must be the merit for having carried Milanese culture through to the modern manner.
Independent of their date of execution, the distribution of scenes painted in the two divisions of the church respects the architectural structure to such an extent that we cannot help being reminded that the decoration project was conceived by a mind imbued with Bramatesque culture, and formed with the idea, already current in Milan since the innovative "Prevedari engraving" of 1481, of the necessity of subdividing and decomposing space in order to have it conform to knowledge, thus expressing a wholehearted adhesion to humanism. The cultural wave that carried the San Maurizio decoration is the one fixed by Bramantino in his concept for the Trivulzio tapestries (begun 1501), where architectural arrangement becomes the basic common denominator.
At all events, it should be noted that each of the decoration projects, beginning with the painting of *God the Father* among the *Evangelists* below the bridge that adjoins the partitioning wall, shows a certain tendency to soften the rendering through a harmonious sense of colour. And gradually, as the decoration progressed, it achieved a Raphaelesque sensibility, recalling the Urbino master's early work painted in Florence in the years 1507–08. But once again we cannot help noticing insistent references to Leonardo, which is so typical of Milanese culture.

Iconography of the Decoration of the Monastic Churches

Documentary sources and an examination of surviving fragments in the museums of Milan make it clear that the subdivision of San Maurizio into a double church, as an expression of monastic reform to promote a perfect community life, was particularly successful in Milan. In this very same period, parallel to the recuperation of the religious orders which began in the mid-fifteenth century, and contemporaneously with the spirituality which became widespread in Milanese social life at the turn of the century, many other convent churches were decorated on very similar iconographic lines.[2] Good examples are the lost Dominican convent of Santa Maria della Purificazione, commonly referred to as "delle Vetere", and the convent of Augustinian nuns at Santa Marta, whose detached frescoes, are still preserved in the Pinacoteca di Brera.[3] One has the impression that the development of the decoration followed themes and subjects associated with meditation and prayer, almost as though batches of images were being invented to encourage contemplation and deepen a personal *lectio*.

Apart from references to life in a cloistered community, one should also bear in mind the two monasteries which were the first to adopt the pictorial language of Bramante: the Benedictine San Pietro in Gessate, and the Dominican Santa Maria delle Grazie, because of their importance in establishing the basic iconographic schemes employed by the painters of San Maurizio. Both these churches, built in an archaic style (the Solarian nave in Santa Maria delle Grazie), were painted at the end of the fifteenth century in the course of a project where the forms were inspired by a Bramantesque sense of space; both possessed successful illusionistic and architectural effects by way of *oculi* framed in painted marble in order to break up and transform the imprint of the former, simple church, a leftover from the Gothic tradition.[4]

Early Chronology of the Decoration

Begun in 1503, as we read on the inscription still existing in the apse of the convent church, the construction of the church of San Maurizio must have been completed before 1509, according to the date reported by V. Forcella[5] on the tombstone of Marti Curzio, placed in front of the first chapel to the left on the lay worshippers' section. It is most likely that the pictorial decoration was begun around 1510–11, according to what can be gathered from details of the frescoes from the first decoration projects that are clearly influenced by Albrecht Dürer's *Small Passion*, a woodcut of 1511.[6] The initials and crests

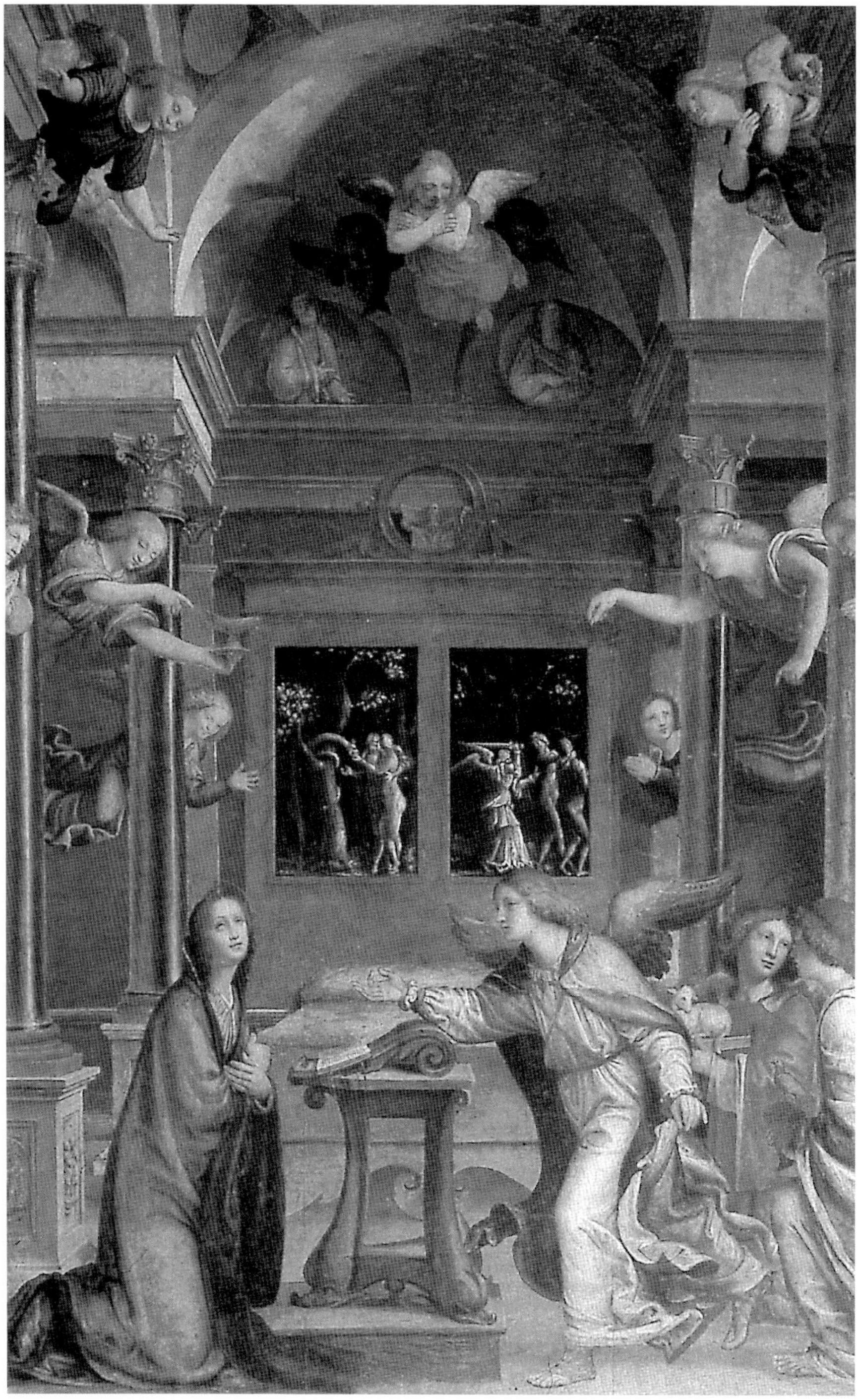

School of Bernardino Luini
Annunciation
Pinacoteca di Brera, Milan

on the partitioning wall refer to Alessandro Bentivoglio and his wife Ippolita Sforza, while the couple themselves are solemnly represented in the centre of the wall opposite the public entrance. (Their identity seems certain in spite of M. Teresa Binaghi Olivari's suggestion,[7] that they are actually portraits of Bentivoglio's daughter, Violante, and her husband, Gian Paolo Sforza.) This would certainly confirm the close connection between the Bentivoglio family and the building and decoration of the church. It is also true that a daughter of this couple became a nun at the convent, where she held the position of abbess six times during these years. The fact that the building was commissioned by nobles reflects the elitist character the convent of San Maurizio enjoyed in the sixteenth century, when its doors were open to the female descendants of the most illustrious local families.[8] This was also evident in the overall decoration of the cells and other rooms of the convent, now destroyed, and in the refectory where there existed a large-scale decoration by Giovan Paolo Lomazzo.

[1] Even at the end of the sixteenth century, Milan was still extremely important for the production of luxury goods, such as textiles in gold and silver, ornamentation and elaborate art works, precious metalwork, artistic objects and bronze statues, cameos, marbles and precious stones, filigrees, etc. (E. Sestan, introduction to F. Chabod, *Lo stato e la vita religiosa a Milano nell'epoca di Carlo V*, Turin 1971, p. XVII; M. Gregori, "Notizie storiche sulla Lombardia tra Cinque e Seicento", in *Il Seicento Lombardo*, 1973, p. 22).

[2] L. Grassi, "Iconologia delle chiese monastiche femminili dall'alto medioevo ai secoli XVI-XVII", in *Arte lombarda*, 42/3, 1975, pp. 131, 134–136; L. Patetta, *L'architettura del Quattrocento a Milano*, Milan 1987, pp. 62–66; F. Autelli, *Pitture murali a Brera*, Bergamo 1989; M.T. Fiorio, "La pittura nel Cinquecento nei territori di Milano e Cremona", in *La pittura in Italia. Il Cinquecento*, I, Milan 1997, pp. 72–73; F. Frangi, "Una traccia per la storia della pittura a Milano dal 1499 al 1535", in *Pittura a Milano. Rinascimento e manierismo*, ed. M. Gregori, Milan 1998, pp. 32-33.

[3] See *Pinacoteca di Brera. Scuole lombarda e piemontese 1300–1535*, Milan 1988 (entries by M.T. Binaghi Olivari, P.C. Marani and F. Frangi).

[4] P.C. Marani, "Resistenze locali e affermazione della 'maniera moderna': pittura a Milano dal 1480 al 1500 circa", in *Pittura a Milano*, p. 16.

[5] V. Forcella, *Iscrizioni nelle chiese e negli edifici di Milano dal secolo XVIII ai giorni nostri*, III, Milan 1890, pp. 449–451.

[6] P. Viotto Pedroli, "Reminiscenze düreriane nella chiesa claustrale di San Maurizio al Monastero Maggiore", in *Arte cristiana*, 732, 1989, pp. 99–103; C. Terribile, *Dürer e i battuti. Sala dei Battuti del duomo di Conegliano*, 1999, p. 12.

[7] M.T. Binaghi Olivari, "I francesi a Milano (1499–1525). Arti figurative e moda", in *Jahrbuch des italienisch-deutschen historischen Instituts in Trent*, V, 1979, pp. 85–116.

[8] On this subject see the document of 4 September 1554 (Milano, Archivio di Stato, *Religione p.a.* 2147, "Locale chiesa culto"), where the names of the nuns at this date are listed on almost five sheets of paper. See also L. Beltrami, *Luini 1512–1532*, Milan 1911, p. 355; A. Ottino Della Chiesa, *San Maurizio al Monastero Maggiore*, with historical notes by P. Reina, Milan 1962, p.124.

The First Phase of the Decoration in the Convent Section of the Church

Sandrina Bandera

The convent section of the church was very probably the first to be built and used for worship; consequently it was the first to be decorated. Constructed on the same level as the presbytery of the public church, its architectural layout is typical of the convent churches which, shortly after, came to be institutionalized under the *Instructiones* of St Charles Borromeo.[1] This single-nave church possesses six *campate* (areas between each pair of columns down the aisle), instead of the four *campate* in the lay worshippers' section, and a series of side bays similar in form and spacing to the chapels in the lay church. There are no altars here, however, in compliance with the liturgical usages of a nunnery where the obligation to celebrate the Eucharist, as in monasteries for monks, did not exist. The central altar, as documented in old photographs, was not the original. As the most recent restoration has revealed, it was added later, covering up a landscape, today in ruinous condition, at the bottom centre of the dividing wall, on the side facing the nuns' hall. It may easily belong to the same phase of decoration as the frescoes painted on this wall by Bernardino Luini,[2] or a little later on, as Marani claims.

In order to guarantee speedy completion for the decoration in the convent section where, for various exigencies, the work needed to be finished ahead of time, it is feasible to suppose that at least two or three masters were called in to work at the same time. The aim was to create premises worthy of one of the largest convents in Milan, moreover frequented by the élite of the city's society, including the most representative families of the neo-feudal hierarchy which characterized Milanese history in the sixteenth century.[3]

The Decoration beneath the Bridge

The central group painted with impressive solemnity on the vaults of the ceiling, below the arched platform supported by the partition wall on the convent side, forms part of the first cycle of paintings to be executed in San Maurizio. It represents *God the Father* and the *Evangelists* set in medallions and surrounded by angels, against a midnight-blue background (painted on a preparatory composition which recent restoration has identified as resinous) and studded with stars in gilt *pastiglia*. The decorative borders contain monochrome *Episodes from the Story of Adam and Eve,* beginning with the *Creation* and ending with the *Punishment of Cain*. From an iconographical point of view, this theologically central representation should be considered the nucleus from which the succeeding frescoes develop: the depiction in the same area of *God the Father* and the *Evangelists* was no doubt intended to provide a reference point for the meditations of the Benedictine nuns, constituting a sort of *summa theologica* of the Holy Scriptures, from Genesis to the New Testament.

The upper sections of the entire convent side must have been painted at the same time, if not slightly before: pairs of saints at the sides of the lunettes in the highest register; classically inspired grisaille clypei, now barely visible in their Serlian frames, bear images of a number of saints (among them: Sts Sebastian, Vittore, Eustace, Gervase, Matthew the Evangelist and Agatha); the faces of women painted inside the illusionistic marble tondi on the dividing walls of the gallery, except for the six which date from the following decade; the *Annunciation* painted on the parapet of the bridge; the trophies surrounding the Serlian windows with their countless decorative and figurative details; and the small monochrome medallions with *Episodes from the Life of Christ*, including the *Passion* cycle,[4] whose style recalls the episodes from the Old Testament: these too are monochromes within painted borders on the ribs of the smaller vaults above the bridge which adjoins the partition wall, where, as already mentioned, the fresco cycle began.

The central group, distinguished by a particular tenderness in the rendering of the Evangelists, shows an iconography linked to fifteenth-century Lombard tradition, and which met with considerable approval at the end of that century. The reference to the frescoes in the Cappella della Vergine of Santa Maria delle Grazie, attributed to the circle of Giovanni Donato, Montorfano,[5] though purely on iconographic grounds confirms the success — at the end of the fifteenth century — of an iconography already adopted by Michelino da Besozzo, as in the Cappella Visconti in Sant'Eustorgio[6] (where the Evangelists are represented only by their zoomorphic symbols), and by Bonifacio Bembo, as in the ducal chapel of the Castello Sforzesco [7] which bears a large central representation of *God the Father Surrounded by Angels.* The persistence into a later epoch and into the context of the Paduan Renaissance, of Late-Gothic iconographies characterized by celestial representations isolated against a sky-blue background, and tending towards a two-dimensional figurative scheme, whose colours include lavish use of sky-blue and gold, also appears to have met with remarkable success at the end of the fifteenth century and beginning of the sixteenth, especially with Bergognone's circle. One can mention the decoration, now lost, painted above the main arch of the sanctuary of Santa Maria Incoronata in Lodi between 1497 and 1500, the year when the church was inaugurated,[8] and the grand and solemn scene created in the same church in 1507.[9]

The painter, who was certainly trained in a Sforza culture, may be traced to the circle of Bergognone's followers, already active in the last decade of the fifteenth century. A certain tenacity in the use of archaic elements suggests the earliest phase of the young Vincenzo Foppa, in particular the *Young Cicero Reading*, now in the Wallace Collection in London, which comes from the fresco cycle the Brescia master painted for Pigello Portinari's Milan office of the Banco Mediceo.[10] Although he proved himself a keen observer of the work of Foppa and the masters in his circle who were working on the stained glass windows of the cathedral — such as, for example, Nicolò da Varallo — the painter of this cycle appears to have directed most of his attention to the art of Bergognone and Bernardo Zenale. The softness with which he painted the serene round faces, the composure, the simplicity of the narration and the luminous colour, where the earthy shades, so typical of Foppa, are totally absent, lead us to presume that the anonymous painter of this cycle belonged to the circle of Bergognone or Zenale, at a time when we know there was a particular symbiosis between the two artists.[11]

The anonymous painter of this cycle can also be distinguished by certain contradictions in style: on the one hand, his incisive drawing in outlining the figures, which tends to flatten the forms, rendering them almost two-dimensional, pertains to a culture that is still Late-Gothic; on the other hand, his capacity for softening anatomical details with skillful and delicate shading, e.g. the necklines, the hair and the luminous rotundities of the brow. But this is not all. In spite of his incisiveness in outlining, this master shows considerable skill in placement of the volumes of the figures, and above all in filtering these volumes in accordance with squared forms. These aspects allocate the artist to the point where Late-Gothic culture begins to turn into the Renaissance. A host of details reveal how he was able to add, to an early training in a vaguely Bembo style of fifteenth-century painting, a knowledge of Foppa, Leonardo, Bramante and Zenale. Very probably the painter of this cycle can be traced to masters who were active in the side chapels of the Certosa of Pavia, painted between 1489 and 1491 by Bernardo Zenale, Bernardino Bergognone, Pietro da Velate, and Jacopino de' Mottis. The most convincing references could in fact be seen in the work of Jacopino de' Mottis, whose painting personality has only recently been reconstructed on the basis of the identification of a triptych representing the *Madonna and Child between Sts Hugh of Grenoble and Hugh of Lincoln,* dating from 1491 and now in the church of San Giusto in Susa. However the recently disclosed fact that the artist was reported dead in 1505 prevents us from accepting this proposal, since it is absolutely impossible that the pictorial decoration of San Maurizio could have begun as early as two years after its foundation.[12]

The Early Decoration on the Lateral Walls

The decoration painted in the convent section was probably proceeding at the same time on the upper mouldings of the lateral walls. On the gallery, a series of women's faces look down from illusionistic clypei, with such intensity that one suspects they were intended as portraits, rather than mere iconographic reference to some saintly martyrs, and addressed directly to the nuns of the community. The character of a privileged élite which distinguished the Monastero Maggiore, when it was chosen as the cloistered retreat for some of the most illustrious nobility of Milan, allows one to conjecture that beneath the severe habits of the sisters dwelt an aristocratic sensibility imbued with courtly ceremony, in perfect accord with Milanese history in the first years of the sixteenth century. The vigour of some of these *clypei*, their three-quarter length together with a vague allusion to a culture stemming from Leonardo, have led Angela Ottino Della Chiesa to propose, for some of them at least, an attribution to Boltraffio.[13] Generic though it may be, this reference is the only proposal on a critical level that has been advanced until the present. It should be emphasized that there is still no trace of any documentation capable of unravelling the philology of San Maurizio's earliest decoration. However it is enough to bear in mind that some of these faces, particularly those of the six female saints in the apse, show a much greater advancement in style in what appears to represent creative experience that is not only Lombard, but central Italian as well, and which we find particularly in the works Raphael produced in Florence; for such is the memorable intensity of the harmonious composition of his *Madonna with the Goldfinch*, or the *Madonna Belvedere*. Consequently these female saints should be assigned to the following decade and to the hand of the artist who painted the most important fresco cycles: Bernardino Luini.

The Lunettes

The frescoes painted inside the lunettes of the various chapels, to the left and right of a central oculus, belong to the very first project for the decoration, i.e. before 1520. From the first to the fourth chapel, starting from the left-hand side and then from the right, we see: the *Visitation*, *St Peter and St Paul*, the *Noli me tangere*, *St Ambrose and St Gregory the Great*, *St Sigismond and St Maurizio*, *Sts Placidus, Maurus and Benedict*, *St Cecilia and St Juliana*, *St Martin and St Bernard*, the *Archangels Michael and Raphael*. Their full-length figures stand out with steadfast assurance. Previously attributed by Angela Ottino Della Chiesa to Boltraffio and Zenale,[14] this cycle, with its late fifteenth-century style, is certainly reminiscent of Zenale, and in particular seems to relate, generically at least, to the panels with *Sts John the Baptist and Victor* in the museum of Grenoble (side panels of the *Madonna and Child* in the Pinacoteca Malaspina in Pavia),[15] attributed to the Treviglio master towards the last decade of the fifteenth-century (around 1494); and the great clipeus, also by Zenale, which recently reappeared from under the whitewash of the chapterhouse in the Certosa of Garegnano.[16] Ever since they were singled out by Ottino Della Chiesa, these figures have always been examined *en passant*, except for M.L. Ferrari's attribution to the circles of Boltraffio, and that of G. Carlevaro to the sphere of Zenale.[17]

Although much repainted, the figures in these lunettes deserve special attention, because they probably belong to the original and earliest phase of the project, linked as they are to the severity of the San Maurizio Bramantesque architecture. They are distinguished by a particular tension in the representation of volumes, by a limpid definition of their spatial relations and by the particular precision of placement in their proper setting.[18]

Moreover these figures constitute the expression of an iconography in San Maurizio that is strictly connected with the return to religious observance typical of the monastic orders from the fifteenth century on. Each of them, like the file of Dominican saints painted in Santa Maria delle Grazie, was intended to provide an occasion for the personal meditation of the nuns.

The Annunciation

Though previously attributed to Boltraffio by Ottino Dalla Chiesa,[19] the *Annunciation* painted on the bridge parapet towards the convent section, should probably be assigned to the same master. Once the dark layer covering it had been removed by a fairly recent restoration, it was now characterized by strong, intense colour. The technique is very simple, using a lime binder mixed with the paint and executed almost directly onto the brickwork. It seems clear that the artist was raised in the school of Zenale and open to the modern style of figuration. In this *Annunciation* we recognize the influence of a meditation on a Bramantesque sense of space, while the three-quarter length of the figure appears to allude, albeit guardedly, to Leonardo as well.

The Monochromes on the Pilasters

The monochromes on the pilasters of the convent side of the church also belong to a rather early phase of the decoration.

Each pilaster bears two monochromes: the upper ones representing episodes of the life of Christ before the Passion, while the ones below mostly illustrate the Way of the Cross. So above we have the *Flight into Egypt,* the *Circumcision,* the *Dispute in the Temple,* the *Baptism*, and the *Rising of Lazarus,* all painted in grey against a sky-blue background; while, below, the *Washing of the Feet*, *Christ in the Garden*, the *Betrayal of Christ,* the *Way to Calvary* and the *Crucifixion* are presented on a dark brown background. As already mentioned, in the subjects from the Passion there is an extremely close reference to the *Small Passion* cycle of Albrecht Dürer, dating from 1509 to 1511, and which won him great success in northern Italy from 1513 on.[20] All these monochromes could well be assigned to the hand of a single artist. This very modern painter — as is borne out by his, almost certainly, direct knowledge of German woodcuts in contrast to other derivations from sixteenth century work — reveals a particular freedom in expression and a rapid and synthetic use of the sketch and monochrome, together with the capacity to imitate effects attained by woodcut and drawing techniques.
The artist, who belonged to Bernardino Luini's workshop, could be identified with the Zenalian painter who produced an *Annunciation*, now in the Pinacoteca di Brera, in the second decade of the sisteenth-century. Its former attribution to Luini only emphasizes the strong affinities between Bernardo Zenale and Bernardino Luini around 1516–17.[21] It is considered extremely doubtful that this painting originally came from the Cappella di San Giuseppe in Santa Maria della Pace. But there is not much doubt about the fact that, as an expression of the insertion of the Zenale circle in the context of the famous Luini frescoes in the Pinacoteca di Brera (ill. p. 47), this altarpiece[22] can be seen as having the closest affinities with the monochromes in San Maurizio.

[1] St Charles Borromeo, *Arte sacra*, (1577), ed. C. Castiglioni and C. Marcora, Milan 1952, pp. 95–100; M. Bendiscioli, "Politica, amministrazione e religione nell'età dei Borromei. Vita sociale e cultura", in *Storia di Milano*, X, Milan 1957, p. 1566 ff.; E. Gombrich, "Recent Concepts of Mannerism. Introduction: the Historiographic Background", in *Renaissance and Mannerism. Studies in Western Art*, II, Princeton 1963, pp. 160–165.
[2] In this same volume Marani actually dismisses the attribution of this small fragment to Bernardino Luini.
[3] For the text on this subject see: F. Chabod, *Lo stato e la vita religiosa a Milano nell'epoca di Carlo V*, Turin 1971, with introduction by E. Sestan; and for the influence on the arts: M. Gregori, "Notizie storiche sulla Lombardia tra Cinque e Seicento", in *Il Seicento lombardo*, 1973, I, pp. 19–46.
[4] See below, the paragraph "*The* Annunciation".
[5] F. Mazzini, *Affreschi lombardi del Quattrocento*, Milan 1965, p. 480; P.A. Caccin, *Santa Maria delle Grazie e il Cenacolo vinciano*, Milan 1983, pp. 63–64.
[6] S. Bandera, "Il tardogotico a Milano. La corte, le famiglie nobili e il duomo", in *Pittura a Milano. Dal tardo medioevo al tardogotico*, ed. M. Gregori, Milan 1997, pp. 233–234. The decoration of the Cappella Visconti can be dated to c.1440.
[7] M. Natale, "Magnificenza e ragione: la pittura a Milano al tempo di Francesco e di Galeazzo Maria Sforza", in *Pittura a Milano. Rinascimento e manierismo*, ed. M. Gregori, Milan 1998, p. 8. The decoration of the chapel was commissioned from a group of painters, including Zanetto Bugatti and Stefano de' Fedeli, under the direction of Bonifacio Bembo after 1473. The painting of *God the Father Surrounded by Angels* appears to be attributable to Bonifacio Bembo.
[8] S. Bandera, in *Ambrogio da Fossano, detto il Bergognone. Un pittore per la Certosa*, exhibition catalogue, Pavia, Castello Visconteo, 1998, pp. 342–344.
[9] F. Frangi, "Una traccia per la storia della pittura a Milano dal 1499 al 1535", in *Pittura a Milano. Rinascimento e manierismo*, p. 29.
[10] A.G., in *Pittura a Milano. Rinascimento e manierismo*, p. 189.
[11] On the other hand, this cycle was attributed by Angela Ottino Della Chiesa (*San Maurizio al Monastero Maggiore*, Milan 1962, pp. 19–20) to Foppa himself.
[12] For Jacopino de' Mottis see R. Battaglia, "La Certosa", in *Pittura a Pavia dal romanico al Settecento*, ed. M. Gregori, Milan 1988, pp. 228–229, 262–263, and M. Albertario, ibid., pp. 292–294 (entry relating to the frescoes of the left transept in the Certosa).
[13] Ottino Della Chiesa, *San Maurizio al Monastero Maggiore*, p. 92.
[14] Ibid., pp. 38–42, 92.
[15] See the entry by M. Natale, in *Zenale e Leonardo*, exhibition catalogue, Milan, Museo Poldi Pezzoli, 1982, pp. 96–99.
[16] S. Bandera, "Inattese e gratificanti sorprese di una campagna di restauro: la scoperta di un affresco sconosciuto. Bernardo Zenale alla Certosa di Garegnano", in *Arte lombarda nel secondo millennio. Saggi in onore di Gian Alberto Dell'Acqua,* Milan 2000, pp. 106–110.
[17] M.L. Ferrari, "Zenale, Cesariano e Luini: un arco di classicismo lombardo", in *Paragone*, 211, 1967, p. 37, note 19; G. Carlevaro, "Materiale per lo studio di Bernardo Zenale", in *Arte lombarda*, 633, 1982, pp. 105–106.
[18] For the influence of Bramantesque spatial concept on Milanese painting at the end of the fifteenth century, see: P.C. Marani, "Resistenze locali e affermazione della 'maniera moderna': pittura a Milano dal 1480 al 1500 circa", in *Pittura a Milano. Rinascimento e manierismo*, pp. 15–17.
[19] Ottino Della Chiesa, *San Maurizio al Monastero Maggiore*, pp. 38–39.
[20] P. Viotto Pedroli, "Reminiscenze düreriane nella chiesa claustrale di San Maurizio al Monastero Maggiore", in *Arte cristiana*, 732, 1989, pp. 99–103; C. Terribile, *Dürer e i battuti. Sala dei Battuti del duomo di Conegliano*, 1999, p. 12.
[21] G. Romano, in *Zenale e Leonardo*, p. 104.
[22] For a critical history of this painting see the entry, updated and complete with bibliography, initialed S.B., in *Pittura a Milano. Rinascimento e manierismo*, pp. 234–235.

Bernardino Luini's Frescoes in San Maurizio: Literary Circles, the Lombard Tradition and Central-Italian Classicism

Pietro C. Marani

"Because of the superb paintings by the Luini and Vinci adorning it, [the church of San Maurizio al Monastero Maggiore] deserves to be preserved." With this surprising declaration, the central administrative headquarters of the department of the Olona responded favourably, on 24 November 1798, to the petition presented by the Benedictine nuns of Monastero Maggiore in Milan, in which they requested that they should be allowed to continue living there.[1] The convent of the Benedictine nuns of San Maurizio had, in fact, been suppressed on 20 November, just four days before they were authorized to remain, with explicit instructions that the decree should be notified "to each and every one of the aforesaid nuns" who had to be informed individually that the convent "remains perpetually suppressed and abolished".[2] The lukewarm acknowledgement on the part of the French government of Lombardy of the importance of the paintings by the Luini preserved here — highlighted by the fact that, as if the name of the Lombard artist and his sons alone were not sufficient to ensure their survival, it was necessary to add phantom paintings by Leonardo da Vinci, of which no other documentary evidence exists — sounds like dutiful recognition at a local level. This was, however, tardy if one thinks that the first, prestigious appreciation of these paintings by writers from outside Lombardy was that of Vasari, although he too pointed out that they were heavily influenced by Leonardo. It is following the reference to Leonardo's *Last Supper* in Milan, in his *Lives* relating to the Ferrarese painters Benvenuto Garofalo and Girolamo da Carpi and other Lombard painters, that Vasari mentions the frescoes by "Lupino" in the Monastero Maggiore in Milan, which he had evidently visited in 1566 when preparing the second edition of the *Lives*: "But returning to the Milanese painters, after Leonardo da Vinci had painted the abovementioned *Last Supper*, many sought to imitate it, including Marco d'Oggiono and others.[...] Bernardino del Lupino, reference to whom was made above, then painted the house of Signor Gianfrancesco Rabbia near San Sepolcro, in Milan. Here he painted the façade, the loggias, the *saloni* and other rooms, depicting many scenes from Ovid's *Metamorphoses* and other fables with beautiful, delicately executed figures. In the Monastero Maggiore he painted the whole of the large altar-wall with different scenes; and likewise, in a chapel, Christ at the Column, and many other works, all of which are agreeable".[3] Whereas Vasari described them as "delicate" and "agreeable", in the same period Luini's paintings in Casa Rabia and San Maurizio must have seemed "excellent" to the artist and writer Giovan Paolo Lomazzo, both as regards their colours and the rendering of the drapery, and despite the fact that he does not mention them specifically.[4] The other important tribute Lomazzo paid to Luini was to call him a "perspective painter", a skill that was evident in many of the other works of the artist's maturity (such as the paintings in San Giorgio al Palazzo in Milan, the polyptych in San Magno in Legnano and the frescoes in the sanctuary of the Beata Vergine dei Miracoli in Saronno). And it was also noticeable in Luini's frescoes in San Maurizio, with the daring foreshortening of some of the figures, the use of *sottinsù* in some scenes and the inclusion of perspective views of a number of buildings, as in the upper scenes on the partition wall, on the side facing the section for lay worshippers, representing episodes from the life of St Maurice. According to Lomazzo, "Bernardino Lovini, too, used to say that a painter without perspective was like a doctor without grammar".[5] Subsequently the frescoes were frequently mentioned and praised by guidebooks to Milan: in 1671 the painter Agostino Santagostino even went so far as to affirm that in San Maurizio "almost the whole church has been painted by Bernardino Luini in both oils and fresco", but perceptively adding immediately afterwards that "among the most exceptional things in it are two portraits flanking the high altar" — in other words, the portraits of the Bentivoglio painted by Luini in the section for lay worshippers, the only one that visitors could see.[6] Mentioned by such writers as Carlo Torre, Serviliano Lattuada, F. Bartoli, Carlo Bianconi, L. Bossi and F. Pirovano,[7] Luini's frescoes were, in the nineteenth century, subjected to the careful scrutiny of the art critics of Romanticism and the connoisseurs of the day, who began to distinguish between the parts of the frescoes in San Maurizio executed by Luini himself and those by his assistants and followers. Thus, in 1869–70, G. Lafenestre was already able to strike the *Assumption*, in the centre of the upper register of the partition wall facing the lay worshippers' section of the church, off the list of Luini's works (it had, in fact, been previously assigned by Stefano Ticozzi to Bergognone),[8] and, fifty years later, L. Beltrami was to consider the possibility that Luini had been assisted by another artist.[9] Unfortunately, these developments were not taken into account by Angela Ottino Della Chiesa, who, in her meritorious volume on the church of San Maurizio, in one of the excesses of affectionate generosity that characterize this work, confirmed the attribution to Luini.[10] The result is that Luini's paternity of the *Assumption* has continued to weigh heavily on the hypotheses attempting to give a chronological order to Luini's frescoes in San Maurizio. This is because, since the *Assumption* is on the upper part of the partition wall of the church, it was thought that it could have been precedent to the lunettes below with the Bentivoglio portraits and the figures of *Female Saints*, usually associated with the period, about 1522–23, when Alessandro Bentivoglio was at the zenith of his political power and his daughter Bianca was present in the convent, as we shall see later. And, since the *Assumption* is located between the two panels, almost certainly autograph, depicting, on the left, the *Martyrdom of St Maurice*, and, on the right, *St Sigismund Offering the Model of the Church of Agaunum to St Maurice*, it has usually been inferred that these two side scenes were painted before the lunettes and panels below.[11] The later style of the *Assumption* and its facture, absolutely unworthy of Luini, oblige us today to definitively omit this work from his oeuvre.[12] This omission will, it is hoped, allow the sequence of Luini's works in the church of San Maurizio to be interpreted more clearly.

But, given that other proposals for attributions involving Luini have yet to be clarified, I believe that, before starting to examine the frescoes that are definitely ascribable to the artist, it is worth further reducing the attributions, made some time ago, by Ottino Della Chiesa and other contemporary art historians. I am referring to two series of frescoes: the landscapes painted in the six side chapels in the convent section of the church and the monochromes depicting episodes from the life and Passion of Christ (above the pilasters, in grey on a blue ground; below the pilasters, on a dark sepia ground), partly derived from Albrecht Dürer.[13] Paradoxically, the fact that in 1798 the whole complex was taken over by the state seems, because the convent part of the church then became accessible, to have facilitated the study of the paintings in this part of the building, allowing them to be compared — at least as regards the ones by Luini — with those in the section for lay worshippers. But, for example, the silence of contemporary sources and the guides to Milan from the sixteenth to the eighteenth centuries with regard to the landscape scenes in the convent part of the church is explained simply by the fact that lay visitors were not admitted to the convent section, and thus cannot in any way be interpreted as a judgement on their merits or the expression of a desire to exclude them from the artist's œuvre. The rediscovery by art historians of these scenes — secular landscapes with neither architecture nor figures — dates back to only about forty years ago, when they were ascribed to Luini. Today this attribution must be regarded as perplexing — astonishing, even — although it was, in fact, challenged at the time.[14] Despite this, it is still given credence on the basis of a comparison with a number of landscapes appearing in some of the frescoes in Santa Maria dei Ghirli at Campione d'Italia that are also attributed to Luini and, in part, derive from engravings by Dürer.[15] If these historians had paid greater attention to events in the nineteenth century and the history of the "restoration" work and the completion of the left side of the building in the second half of that century,[16] they would have been more cautious and might, perhaps, have taken into account the possibility that the restoration of the landscapes in the chapels in the convent section of the church — in which Giuseppe Knoller well may have been involved[17] — dated from after that period.

A disenchanted glance at the style and type of paint adopted for these landscapes, greater scientific knowledge with regard to the pigments used, as well as core-sampling recently carried out on one of these panels to find out whether there were older layers of painting in fresco under the surface (they have, in fact, been found, as is recounted elsewhere in this book), allow us to finally address, without any distractions, the issue of the real extent of Luini's work in the church of San Maurizio. This is a problem regarding which art historians have, in recent times, maintained a discreet silence, except for when they seek to justify Ottino Della Chiesa's singular and now long-standing theory and attempt to track down at least one authentic example of a landscape, independent of the other paintings, by Luini's hand.[18] However, the attribution to Luini of the series of small monochrome panels, mentioned above, painted on the pilasters dividing the chapels in the convent section of the church depends on the ascription of the landscapes to the same artist. Indeed, it has also been hypothesized that, at an early stage, Luini executed the small panels, despite their exiguity, hoping he would then receive the commission to paint the landscapes in the larger panels of the chapels. It must, therefore, be stressed that it seems improbable that Luini, now a mature artist, can be credited with the execution of these small scenes (*Kiss of Judas*, *Christ and Lazarus's Sisters*, *Christ Washing his Disciples' Feet*, *Raising of Lazarus*, *Baptism of Christ*, *Flight into Egypt*, etc.), which have been rightly assigned to another artist elsewhere in this book. Now that we know more about the various stages of Luini's artistic career, it is not possible to ascribe these paintings to any of the stages during which the artist was working in San Maurizio and, in particular, to the one that coincided with the execution of the paintings on the partition wall, or the later one when he was painting the frescoes in the Cappella Besozzi. Moreover, on the basis of what we know at present, it is not even possible to date these monochromes to an earlier stage of his career because, during his formative years, Luini's art was very different in character. Further problems regarding the nature of his painting will be addressed later in the descriptions of the other frescoes traditionally attributed to Luini, in which an attempt will be made to reconstruct the chronology of the decoration of San Maurizio and these attributions to the artist will be confirmed.

Contrary to the received wisdom opinion prevalent among art historians — according to which Luini began to work in San Maurizio, starting from the convent section of the church, according to a programme, possibly prepared by the Benedictine nuns — I intend to commence with the frescoes on the side of the partition wall facing the lay worshippers' section. And, for the moment, I shall leave aside the question of the female saints in the tondi frescoed in the gallery, for some of which Bernardino Luini's name has recently been put forward, although the attribution to Giovan Antonio Boltraffio continues to prevail; I consider neither of these to be reasonable candidates.[19] The idea that the decoration of the whole building began with the painting of the convent section, as might be supposed on the basis of the style of the frescoes in the gallery (tondi with figures of female saints) and in the intrados of the vault behind the partition wall (*God the Father*, *Evangelists*, examined elsewhere in this book), does not, however, mean that Luini did not work in the church. Indeed, it would have seemed illogical to employ the artist if he had to begin in the part not visible to the public. Once the situation regarding the paintings not attributable to Luini has been clarified, as I believe I have done in the preceding remarks, the information regarding the commissioning of the work and, above all, stylistic elements clearly indicate that the artist's role in the church of San Maurizio was a leading one and that, when he started work there, he was at the height of his career and had the backing of an important patron. The latter charged Luini with giving visual form to the prestige and eminence that he wished to assume and with bringing this to his contemporaries' attention through the artist's refined, classicizing style. It has recently been acutely observed that, by commissioning the frescoes on the partition wall and admitting the patronage and artistic commissions of relatives and aristocratic families linked to them, the Bentivoglio sought to manifest their desire to appropriate the church, which, in practice, they regarded as "a noble fief dedicated by the Bentivoglio or families close to them".[20] The depiction of their coats of arms, with the initials of Alessandro and Ippolita ("AL" and "HIP") in the convent section of the church and their portraits in the lay worshippers' section appear to be, in effect, an expression of their approval of this appropriation and confirmation of their patronage of the decoration of the church that had yet to be carried out. The coats of arms appear twice at the sides of the grating that permitted the nuns to participate in the services celebrated in the lay worshippers' section and, although they were repainted in 1794, they are legible as those of Alessandro (a golden saw on a red field) and Ippolita (the Visconti-Sforza serpent). The artist chosen to interpret their needs was Luini. He had already worked for religious orders, such as the Cistercians for whom he frescoed an *Enthroned Madonna* in the abbey of Chiaravalle, near Milan, in 1512; the Augustine nuns of Santa Marta, Milan, for whom he painted an altarpiece, now lost, in 1516, and, perhaps a little later, also the frescoes now in the Pinacoteca di Brera; for the convent of Santa Maria della Purificazione or "delle Vetere", Milan; and for the oratory of Santa Corona, in Milan, for which, in 1521–22, he painted a large fresco representing the *Brothers Adoring Christ Crowned with Thorns*. He had also worked for eminent members of the aristocracy or of the emergent Milanese society, such as Gerolamo Rabia, for whom, on various occasions — according to the recent studies by Giulio Bora, in the first and second decade of the Cinquecento — he decorated his house in Milan and the suburban Villa della Pelucca; Luca Terzago, for whom he decorated the chapel of the Santissimo Sacramento in the church of San Giorgio al Palazzo, Milan, in 1516; and Agostino Busti, for whom he painted, in 1521, an altarpiece to be placed in his chapel in Santa Maria di Brera, Milan. These paintings tended to reflect what was often open disagreement with orthodox religious practices and official culture on the part of the aristocrats and members of Milanese society, who became involved with the new French rulers or emerged briefly as a result of the political and military upheavals to which Lombardy was subjected in the first two or three decades of the Cinquecento.

L. Beltrami rightly observed that "all this superb work was commissioned from Luini by Alessandro Bentivoglio when his daughter Alessandra took the veil in the Monastero Maggiore around 1522".[21] Alessandra, who became the abbess in 1522 with the name of Bianca, was not, however, the only daughter of Alessandro to enter the convent; another daughter of his, Ippolita, took vows with the name of Sister Francesca and another two, Ginevra and Violante, were admitted after they had become widows, thus constituting a sort of family appendage in San Maurizio. Born in 1474, of Giovanni II Bentivoglio, Signore of Bologna, and Ginevra Sforza, daughter of Alessandro Sforza, Signore of Pesaro, Alessandro Bentivoglio was obliged to follow his father to Milan, then to Genoa and finally back to Milan, when his father was expelled from Bologna by Julius II. Alessandro devoted himself to the cause of Massimiliano Sforza, one of Ludovico il Moro's sons, and particularly distinguished himself fighting as a condottiere for the Swiss, who had been hired by Massimiliano, in the battle of Novara of 6 June 1513, which allowed the duke to reconquer Milan. Shortly after it had been retaken by the king of France, Francis I, in 1515, Milan was claimed by Charles V, Holy Roman Emperor, who intended to restore the duchy to the Sforza. Francesco, Ludovico's second son, was in Trent when, with the support of Pope Leo X and the emperor, he decided to reconquer Milan, which he did successfully on 19 November 1521. It is not known whether Alessandro Bentivoglio was already in Milan with the victorious army at that date or whether he entered the city with Duke Francesco Sforza on 4 April 1522. At the height of his personal success, Alessandro thus reaped the rewards of his long-standing support for the Sforza, immediately becoming senator and later, in 1529, vice-duke. Also in 1522, his daughter Alessandra took vows in San Maurizio, "perhaps in order to release herself from a vow, since fortune now seemed to smile on her father".[22] Sister Alessandra had, however, already been in the Monastero Maggiore for at least a year — possibly somewhat longer — because, in her will of 6 May 1521, her mother, Ippolita Sforza, in addition to specifying that she should be buried in the church of Santa Maria degli Angeli, outside the walls of Milan, assigned the sum of 1,173 ducats to her and the Monastero Maggiore of San Maurizio where Sister Alessandra lived.[23] Thus it may be deduced that both Ippolita and her daughter, and probably the rest of the family, already lived in Milan before Francesco Sforza reconquered the duchy in November 1521 and his entry into Milan in the following year. Although instructions contained in wills may be disregarded after the testator's death and "declarations of intention in a will [...] cannot be relied on as a direct chronological reference for the execution of the frescoes" in San Maurizio,[24] it has been observed that the donation of 1,173 ducats to her daughter Sister Alessandra was "presumably intended for the decoration of the church".[25] The usual association of the frescoes in the lay worshippers' section of the church of San Maurizio with the personal success of Alessandro Bentivoglio in 1521–22 has so far overshadowed the role played by Ippolita, who may have been Luini's real patron prior to 1521, which is thought to have been the year of her death, or just before this.

However, in order not to give a forced interpretation of the chronology that has been available up to now, and keeping to the known historical facts, a more important role in the decision to commission Luini to paint the partition wall must be now be assigned to Ippolita Sforza Bentivoglio than has hitherto been thought appropriate. Contemporary sources describe Ippolita as a very cultured person, a patron of literature who associated with individuals that are known to have been leading figures in the Milanese society of the first two decades of the Cinquecento, either as patrons or connoisseurs. She was the inspirer of the *Novelle* (totalling 214, they were published 1554–75) of Matteo Bandello, who asserted that he decided to write them after the sudden death of Ippolita, to whom he dedicated all his stories until she died. We know from other sources, however, that Bandello wrote some of his stories — at least those set in Milan and Mantua — between 1506 and 1524. Ippolita Sforza, thought to have been born around 1481, was often referred to by Bandello as a patron of literature and an erudite Latinist, "a woman unequalled in any age", in whose *palace* the cultured ladies and Milanese gentlemen gathered,[26] including Cecilia Gallerani (the *Lady with an Ermine* Leonardo portrayed in a painting now in Cracow), Camilla Scarampa, a famous poetess, the Florentine Ludovico Alemanni (brother of Luigi, a poet and man of letters), Girolamo Cittadino, Niccolò Amanio[27] and other noblemen such as the Atellano. The latter were also patrons of Luini; with the aid of assistants, the artist decorated a room in their palace (with portraits of the ducal family in tondi, now in the Castello Sforzesco, in Milan),[28] located opposite the church of Santa Maria della Grazie, where Ippolita was a frequent visitor together with Cecilia Gallerani. Another great friend of Matteo Bandello, who dedicated several of his novelle to him, was Lucio Scipione Atellano, one of the most outstanding members of the Milanese aristocracy, whose

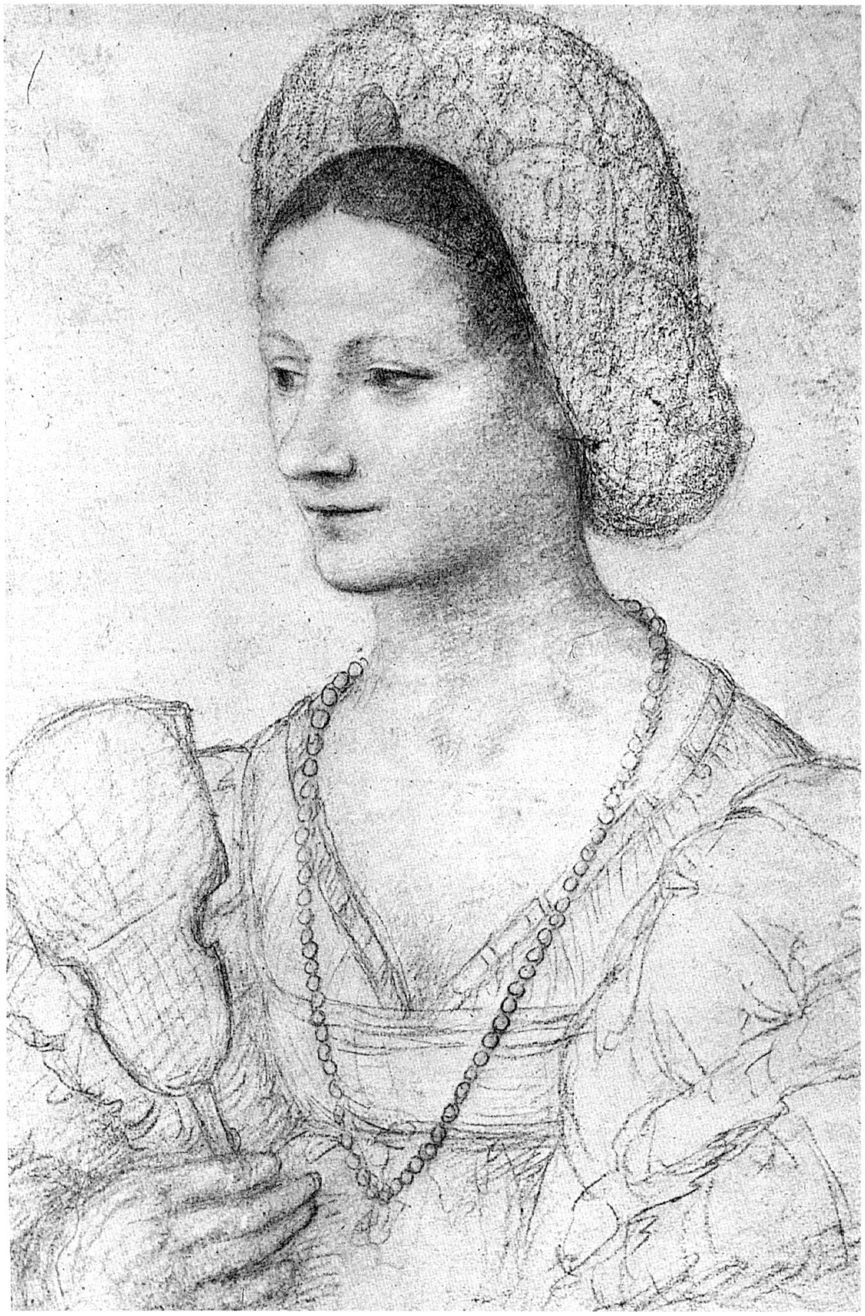

Bernardino Luini
Study for the portrait of Ippolita Bentivoglio
Graphische Sammlung Albertina, Vienna

father had been secretary to Ludovico il Moro. In his house it is easy to imagine "the peerless heroine Ippolita Sforza Bentivoglio, who spends the whole day learnedly discussing obscure passages of the Latin language [...] a latter-day Sappho, Signora Cecilia Gallerana, Countess Bergamina, who, apart from the Latin language, writes magnificent verses in the Italian idiom [...] Signora Camilla Scarampa Guidobona, whose rhymes are so highly valued". And, above all with regard to Ippolita Bentivoglio — to whom the novelle that must have been read in these houses were dedicated — "the world [was not] worthy of such a noble and illustrious spirit".[29]

Bandello dedicated to Lucio Scipione Atellano, a patron of art and literature who himself "composed fine verses", a long novella that he then presented "to our two Muses, Countess Cecilia Gallerana and Signora Camilla Scarampa, who are, in fact, two great luminaries of the Italian language in this age".[30] In this novella his description of a sumptuously furnished *salone* in a Lombard palace — "the room was splendidly adorned with paintings by the hand of Master Leonardo da Vinci" — gives us an insight into the luxury of the Milanese society of the day and probably refers to a house belonging to a member of this literary circle, in view of the wit and culture of the two protagonists of the novella, who are, however, given pseudonyms. Another famous novella is dedicated to one of the sons of Alessandro Bentivoglio and Ippolita Sforza. In this, recounting the sojourn of Cecilia Gallerani at Acquario, reference is made to the visit paid to her by Antonio Fregoso Fileremo, the author of a book entitled *Dialogo di fortuna* that was published in 1519 and had been "discussed in Milan for nine days" in the presence of Ippolita Sforza Bentivoglio herself. Bandello referred to this visit in other novelle,[31] and also to that of Lancino Curzio, perhaps the most outstanding exponent of the new poetry now in vogue that was "free from the constraints of the Petrarchan and humanistic tradition".[32] As proof of the fact that this was Ippolita Sforza Bentivoglio's cultural and social milieu, it should also be mentioned that Bandello, when he was about to narrate the sad tale of Bianca Maria, countess of Challant, in another famous novella, mentions that the latter always had to ask her first husband, Ermes Visconti, for permission to visit other houses, while the only one she was, in fact, allowed to frequent was that of Ippolita Sforza Bentivoglio. At the end of this account of the life of the countess of Challant, who was beheaded on the ravelin of Milan Castle on 20 October 1526, Bandello reminds his readers — and Isabella d'Este, the marchioness of Mantua, to whom the novella was dedicated — that "whomsoever might wish to see her portrait taken from life may visit the Monastero Maggiore, wherein hangs her likeness".[33]

It has often been suggested that Bandello was referring to Luini's fresco in the Cappella Besozzi in the church of San Maurizio depicting the *Beheading of St Catherine*, but this is, in fact, almost certainly not the case.[34] Luini worked in the Cappella Besozzi around 1530, as we shall later see: Bandello, who had left Milan in late 1526 (taking refuge firstly at Castel Goffredo, near Mantua, then, perhaps after a fleeting visit to Milan in 1528, in Verona from 1529 to 1536), could not, in all likelihood, have seen the frescoes in the chapel after they had been completed. It is evident, therefore, that the portrait of the countess of Challant to which he was referring was one of the heads or figures that Luini had previously painted on the partition wall facing the lay worshippers' section of the church. Due to her close friendship with Ippolita Sforza Bentivoglio, it is quite possible that her portrait is, in fact, the face of one of the female saints flanking Ippolita in the right lunette of the partition wall: *St Agnes* on the left and, on the right, *St Catherine*, seen in profile facing the centre of the scene. Because it is not sufficiently idealized, this profile has all the characteristics of a portrait, like the other female faces in the lunette, including that of *St Scholastica* (in the centre), which it seems reasonable to suppose is a portrait of Sister Bianca, Alessandra Bentivoglio. Apart from that of Ippolita, the face of *St Agnes* also seems to be a portrait painted from life. As further proof of Luini's use of real models, it has been observed that even Ippolita's dress — made of white brocade decorated with gold ribbons, it resembles the one worn by Isabella d'Este in Leonardo's drawing of her now in the Louvre — is of a type Bona Sforza described as being "in a new style" in a letter to Isabella d'Este, dated 16 June 1523.[35]

The two lunettes with the kneeling figures of the Bentivoglio must, therefore, have been the first paintings that Luini executed in San Maurizio, together with the lower register of this side of the partition wall. Thus these were intended to be visible from the whole of the lay worshippers' section, signalling the family's patronage of the church to the general public and, above all, the social élite of Milan who came there. This is borne out by stylistic and technical factors: in fact, they are the most outstanding of all Luini's frescoes in San Maurizio from the point of view of their style and facture. The order in which he executed these works seems to be all the more logical if it derives from a desire to honour Ippolita Bentivoglio's bequest to her daughter of 1521 and Alessandro's appointment as senator in 1522. Moreover, there is no need to assume that the two upper scenes — as I have already stated, the central one depicting the *Assumption* cannot be attributed to Luini, and may perhaps be the work of Bernardino Ferrari (after 1532) — were painted before the two lunettes, following a sequence of execution, because of the use of scaffolding, from the top towards the bottom. The upper area, in fact, may have been left free from figurative scenes — although it might have been decorated with plant or other motifs — while awaiting other funds. Otherwise it may have been surrounded by geometrical patterns executed soon after the wall was built; this was the case with the decoration of the dome on the sanctuary of the Beata Vergine dei Miracoli in Saronno, painted by the architect and sculptor Giovanni Antonio Amadeo with geometrical motifs and only twenty-five years later, in 1534–35, frescoed by Gaudenzio Ferrari, when Luini had already painted, about ten years earlier, the parts below.[36] Yet another possibility is that it was painted by the same artists who had begun to decorate the convent section of the church, and only later was it repainted or adapted to meet the requirements of subsequent patrons, as, in fact, occurred in the case of the Bentivoglio.

Be that as it may, the two superb lunettes, with the portraits of the kneeling Bentivoglio — which the painter Agostino Santagostino considered to be "among the most outstanding things" in the church — and the saints presenting them (on the left, *St Stephen*, *St Benedict*, the founder of the monastic order named after him, and *St John the Baptist with a Lamb*; on the right *St Agnes with a Lamb*, *St Scholastica*, St Benedict's twin sister, and *St Catherine*), simulate illusionistic apertures in the walls by representing two arches *sottinsù* in the backgrounds at the same height as those of the side chapels. Thus it is almost as if they were intended to give a sense of depth to the huge wall and create the effect of two gigantic semicircular arches holding up the "bridge" that both links and supports the two side walls of the church. In other words, they reveal unity of conception and complete understanding of the spaces available, offering a specta-

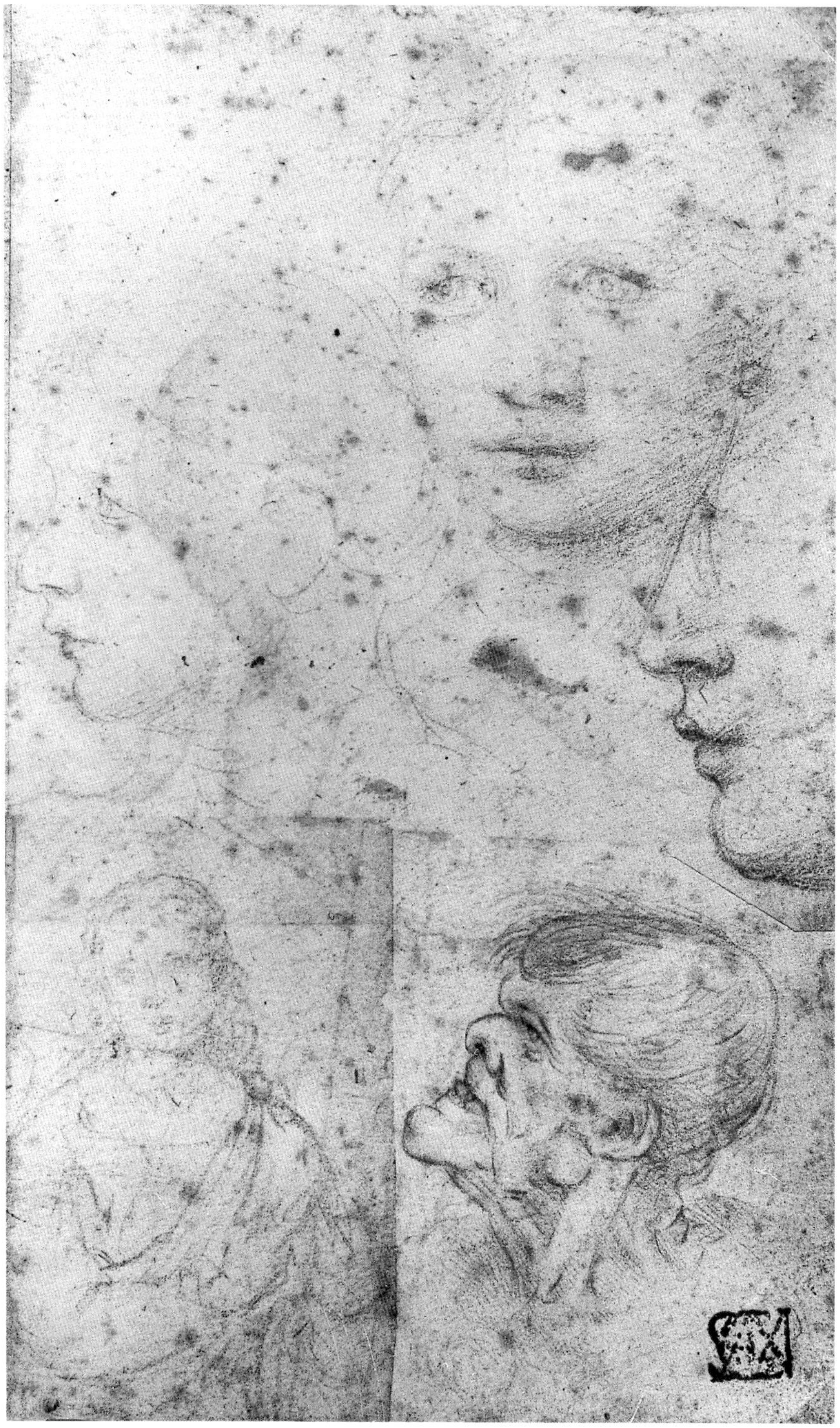

Bernardino Luini
Study for a female figure (probably for *St Apollonia* on the partition wall facing the lay worshippers' section of the church), *for other female faces and for a caricature*
Biblioteca Ambrosiana, Milan

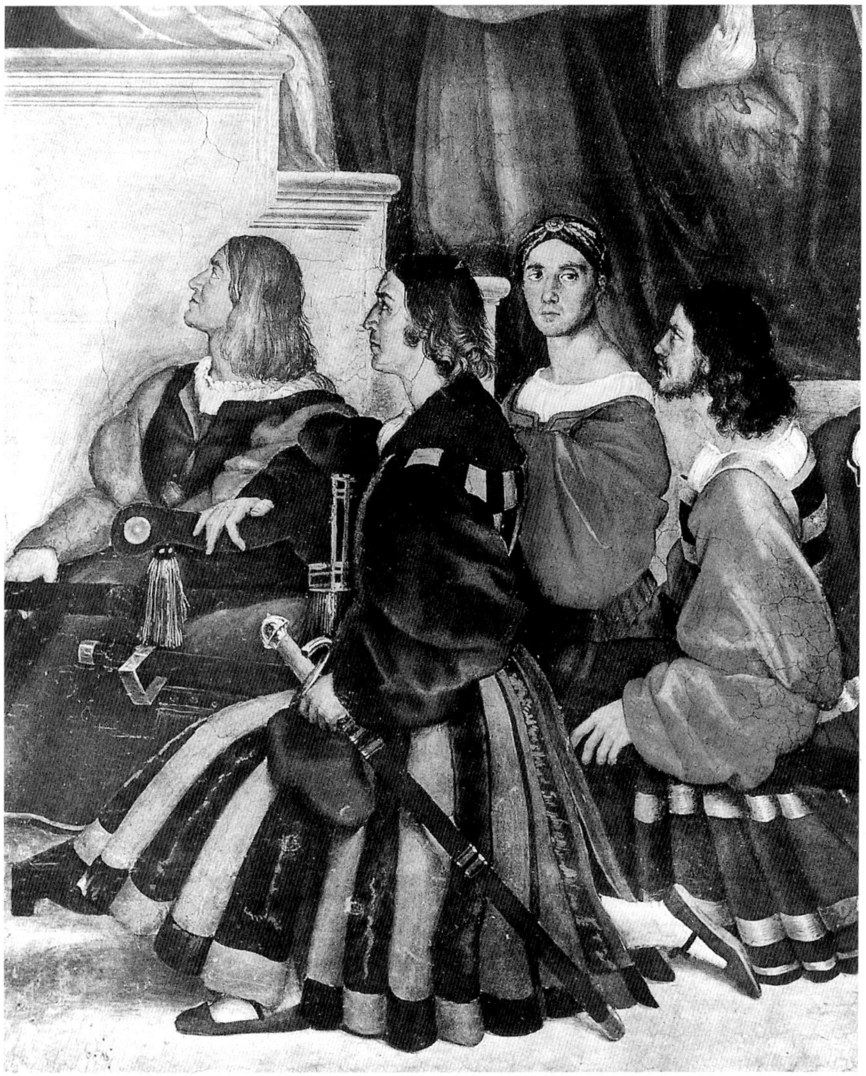

Raphael
Mass of Bolsena, detail
Stanza d'Eliodoro, Vatican

cle that is both architectural and theatrical. If one tries to imagine the original appearance of the church — before, in 1578, Antonio Campi's altarpiece closed the large central arch that must have formed a passage between the two sections (further alterations were made in 1790–93)[37] — the two side lunettes appear to flank a larger, real semicircular arch, so that all three form what is virtually an imposing triumphal arch, with the wider central semicircular arch rising behind the high altar. Hence the patrons — and their patron saints — are incorporated into the real space of the church, almost as if they could observe, through the metal grating installed in the central arch (an expedient used in a similar manner by Verrocchio in the Old Sacristy of San Lorenzo in Florence, in the tomb of Piero de' Medici), their daughters participating in the services, while remaining in the convent section. On the other hand, the lay worshippers perceive Alessandro and Ippolita Bentivoglio as always being present, located in a sort of loggia of which the depth is visible (especially that of the arches, seen with the intradoses in perspective) and from which the other figures, animals and objects project, seemingly about to fall off the edge as they protrude into real space. The illusionistic space painted in the lunette is supported by the solid, flat walls of the lower register where, nevertheless, Luini has simulated two sculpted and gilded tabernacles, echoing, on the left, the real door slightly recessed in the wall and representing, on the right, the *Man of Sorrows* — the figure of Christ spurting blood into a chalice — inserted in a much deeper niche that appears to be almost as profound as the small door set in the wall below. The latter corresponds to the almost cubical niche on the left — where perspective is used with equal skill — containing a young angel with candles: note how the latter appear to project from the wall, even casting their shadows on the painted frame of fictive white marble surrounding the recess. In the four standing figures of female saints (on the left, *St Cecilia* and *St Justina*, or perhaps *St Ursula*; on the right, *St Apollonia* and *St Lucy*) — which foreshadow the figures of saints frescoed by Luini in the apse of the Cappella Maggiore in the sanctuary of Saronno, of three or four years later — the rotundity of the faces dear to Bernardo Zenale and Bramantino is apparent, although it is mitigated by the artist's familiarity with the counterpoint characteristic of Leonardo's portraits, for instance in the *Lady with an Ermine*. In the portraits of the Bentivoglio in the lunettes above, however, the same features are combined with the influence of Lorenzo Lotto and the compositions of certain famous paintings by Raphael, such as the *Mass of Bolsena* (Stanza d'Eliodoro, Vatican), although the artist had already experimented with the theme of the portraits of twelve kneeling donors in the *Brothers Adoring Christ Crowned with Thorns*, a fresco in the oratory of Santa Corona in Milan (now incorporated in the Biblioteca Ambrosiana) that he executed between October 1521 and March 1522. And if the realism of the portrait of Ippolita Bentivoglio, despite its Leonardesque and Raphaelesque accents, would cut a fine figure beside that of Lotto's *Lucina Brembati* (Accademia Carrara, Bergamo), the date of which was recently confirmed as being around 1518, that of Alessandro Bentivoglio is truly memorable for its Veneto-Lombard mode and acute psychological insight. Indeed, there seems to be an attempt on Luini's part to vie with Lotto in the naturalism of his portraits and, in this case, he foreshadows the latter's *Young Man in his Study* in the Gallerie dell'Accademia in Venice, datable to around 1530, and — almost twenty years earlier! — the portraits of *Febo da Brescia* and *Laura da Pola* (in the Pinacoteca di Brera). And he foreruns Lotto also in his mimesis of reality, with his splendid rendering of the fabrics (white, grey, black and gold) and the fur.[38]

The next frescoes we shall examine here, following the probable chronological order, are those on the side of the partition wall facing the convent section: on the left, *St Apollonia* and *St Lucy*; on the right, *St Catherine* and *St Agatha*; between the first two is another figure of Christ as the *Man of Sorrows*; *St Sebastian* and *St Roch* are painted on the pilasters flanking the central arch. Compared with the female saints in the lay worshippers' section of the church, these appear to be more loosely handled and structurally less substantial. However, the less elegant style and the more modest facture indicate, in my opinion, not the hand of assistants (as Ottino Della Chiesa believed in 1956), but that they were executed at a slightly later date than the decoration of the other side of the partition wall. The rest of the decoration is, however, still excellent, with the wainscot in fictive marble, recesses and projections, projecting brackets and fictive niches, and illusionistic effects disposed with masterly skill in a composition arranged as if the female saints were situated, on the left and on the right, in two recesses flanking two niches (on the left, a fictive one with the *Man of Sorrows*; on the right, the real one with the little door). These rest on a plinth in front of which is placed a paint-

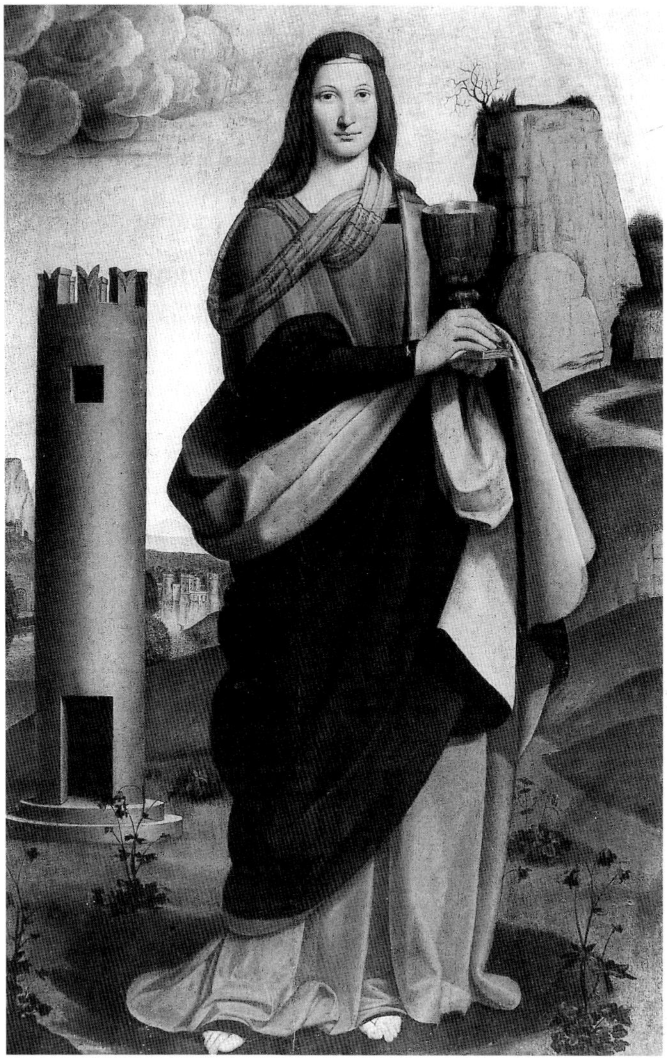

Giovan Antonio Boltraffio
St Barbara
Staatliche Museen, Berlin

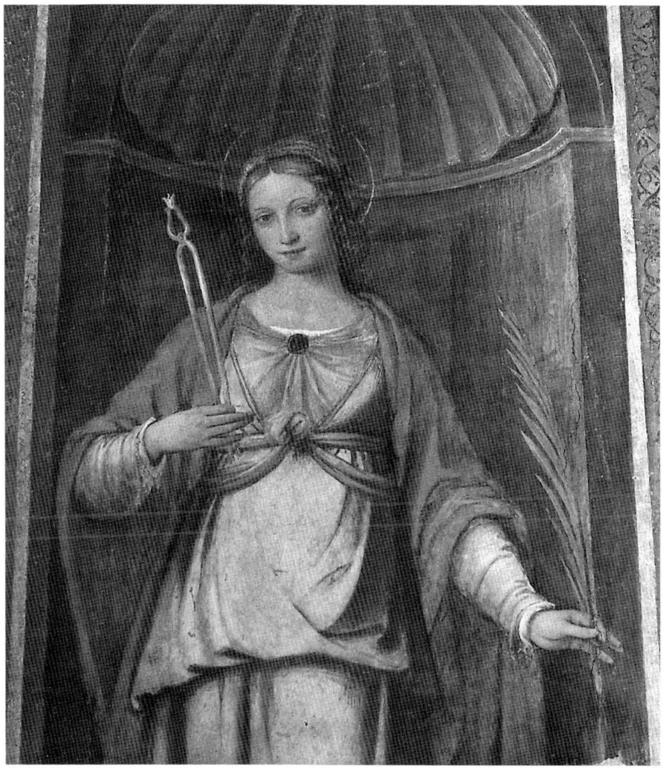

Bernardino Luini
St Apollonia
Sanctuary of the Beata Vergine dei Miracoli, Saronno

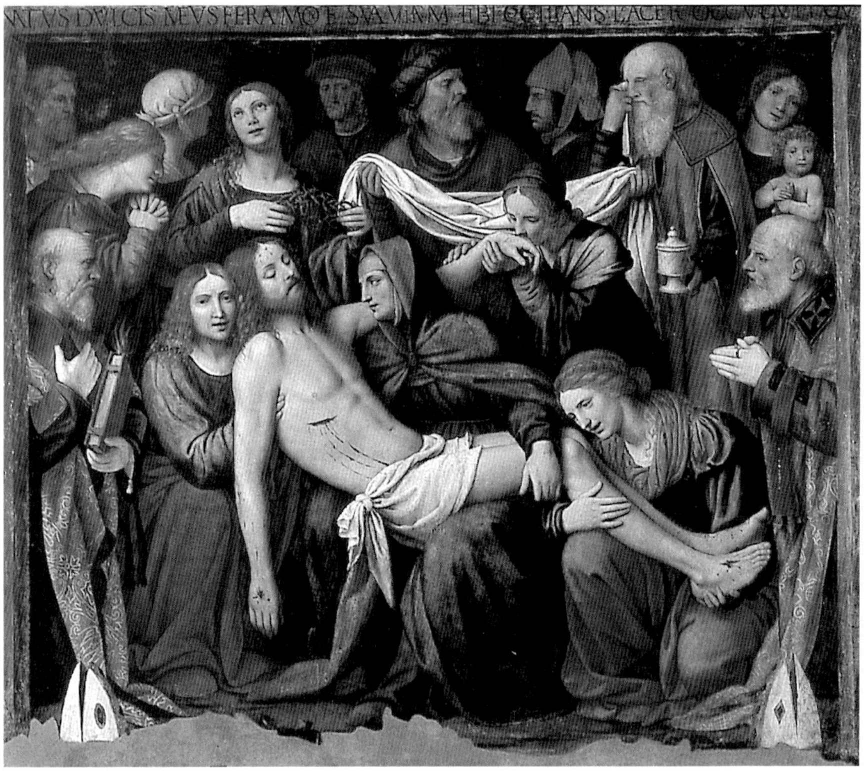

Bernardino Luini
Lamentation over the Dead Christ
San Giorgio al Palazzo, Milan

ed dais, shaped to form a concavity (in the centre of this are two notable medallions depicting, on the left, the monochrome bust of *St Barbara* and, on the right, that of *Salome with the Head of St John the Baptist*), on which young angels are posed.

Despite its illusionism, the scenographic structure of the partition wall facing the convent section of the church, still resembling the configuration of a Lombard polyptych, appears to be less complex than that in the lay worshippers' section. Here, in fact, the more modest projections are not intended to suggest the depth of the prominent openings, such as the three semicircular arches on the other side of the wall, but to allow the nuns to approach the wall, almost as if they were to kneel close to it, as is suggested by the painted daises and concavities close to the small window from which they could peep into the other section of the church. Luini continued to adopt the refined style he had used in the decoration of the lay worshippers' side of the wall, seeming to favour not only Bergognonesque models (the female saints painted in the niches of San Satiro, in Milan, now in the Pinacoteca di Brera, or the figures in the refectory of Santa Maria della Passione, also in Milan)[39] and Boltraffesque ones (such as *St Barbara*, also painted for San Satiro, now in the Staatliche Museen, Berlin)[40] but also those of an up-to-date follower of Leonardo such as Andrea Solario. The latter's *Christ Blessing* in the Metropolitan Museum in New York[41] may have suggested a more solemn and majestic representation of the figure in the illusionistic space than Bergognone, while Luini combined his own well-tried models with Solario's depictions of Salome.[42] Here the style is, nevertheless, influenced by the modes of Bernardo Zenale and Leonardo rather than those of Raphael, as if Luini had yet to carry out a further survey of central Italian classicism. Elsewhere I have hypothesized that Luini must have gone to Rome just before he executed the decoration of the sanctuary in Saronno, one of the panels of which (*Presentation of Jesus in the Temple*) is dated 1525, which means that he made the journey in 1523 or 1524,[43] perhaps because, at this time, plague was rife in Milan. I believe, therefore, that the decoration of the lower part of the partition wall in the convent section of the church, concluding Luini's first period in San Maurizio, was completed before 1524 or even before 1523, the year in which the polyptych in the church of San Magno in Legnano[44] is thought to have been finished. In the latter work, as in San Maurizio, the

influence of Baldassarre Peruzzi, Sodoma and Raphael on Luini is not evident, as it was, however, in the frescoes in Saronno.
The decoration of the convent section of the church must have continued, mainly after 1525, with the scenes of the Passion, although it cannot be excluded that some panels, in the first chapel on the right, were begun or executed at the same time, or immediately after, the decoration of the walls of the convent section — that is, between 1523 and the artist's return from Rome and Saronno. The works in the chapel include *Noli me tangere*, which was still composed — like some of the frescoes in the Villa della Pelucca — with a high horizon and the construction of the space with superimposed planes; the *Resurrection of Christ*, consisting of a lower panel with the soldiers and an upper lunette with Christ forming a continuous space despite the intervening fascia (as Zenale had already done in the Cappella Grifi in San Pietro in Gessate), where exercises in perspective and foreshortening of the figures, clearly deriving from Zenale and Bergognone, predominate; and, finally, the *Entombment of Christ*. The Christ in the lunette, for example, recalls a *Resurrection of Christ*, now in a private collection, which similarly shows soldiers thrown down before the tomb, or the older one, also by Bergognone, in the National Gallery in Washington.[45] The other frescoes, especially those in the chapel opposite, comprising the *Betrayal of Christ*, the *Agony in the Garden* and *Christ before Pilate*, and the two lunettes on the partition wall showing, on the left, the *Way to Calvary* and, on the right, the *Lamentation over the Dead Christ*, must certainly be assigned to the second half of the 1520s. Thus they were painted just before the frescoes in the Cappella Besozzi, as is evident from the composition of the scenes, especially the one of the *Agony in the Garden* with the sleeping disciples and that of the *Way to Calvary*, which are reminiscent of the late works of Raphael and his assistants, as will be explained in more detail later.
The more fluent pictorial style, the lower horizons, the dominance of the figures in space, composed in the so-called modern manner — note Christ praying before the Eucharistic chalice, combining, in an extraordinary manner, Leonardo's "science of the emotions" with the Raphaelesque depiction of a devotional image — but with some differences of atmosphere (in *Christ before Pilate*, together with evident derivations from Leonardo's caricatures and grotesque heads, there are also

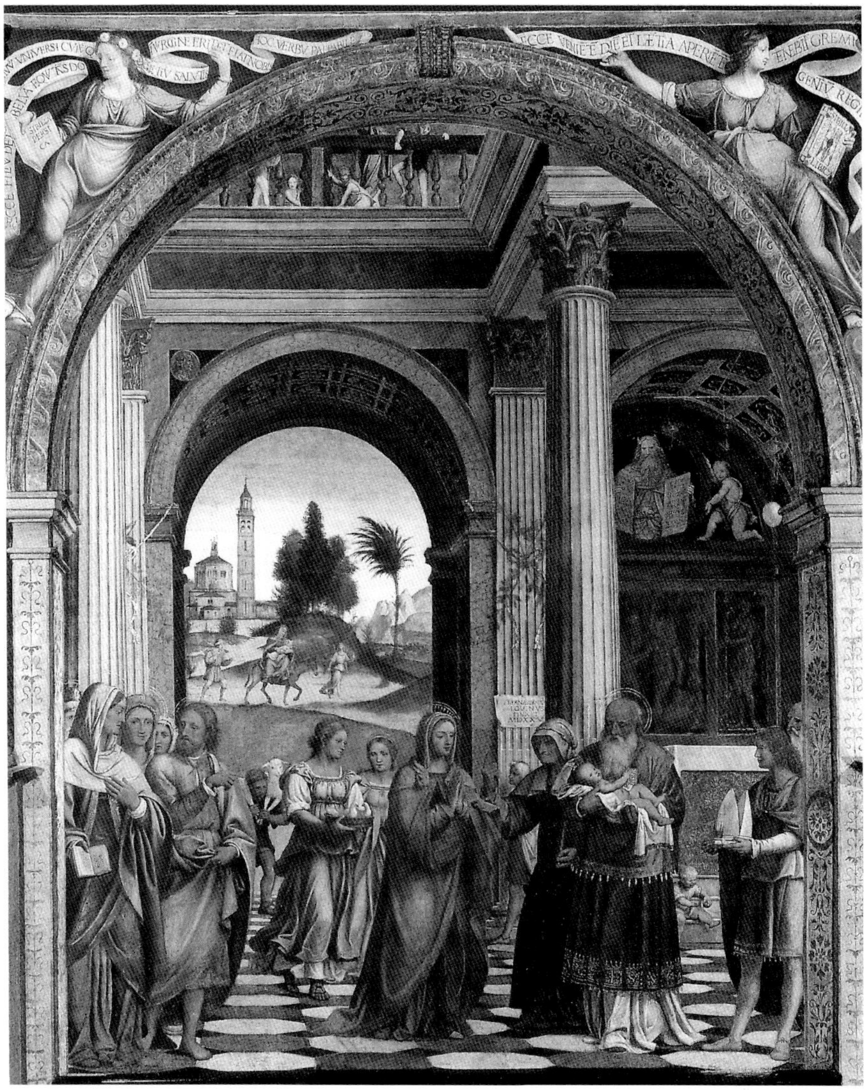

Bernardino Luini
Presentation of Jesus in the Temple
Sanctuary of the Beata Vergine
dei Miracoli, Saronno

Raphael
Disputa
(Disputation over the Sacrament),
detail
Stanza della Segnatura,
Vatican

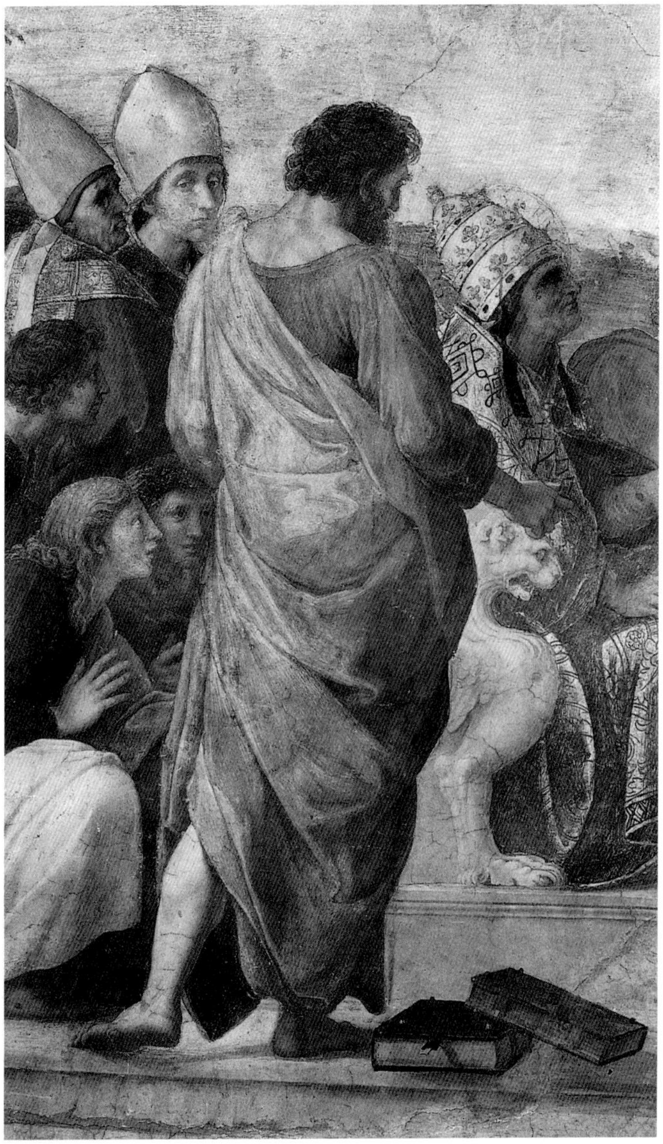

echoes of German prints and paintings), indicate that the artist worked on these paintings over a long period. In fact, he probably alternated them with the two upper panels on the wall facing the lay worshippers' section — that is, the ones representing, on the left, the *Martyrdom of St Maurice* and, on the right, *St Sigismund Offering the Model of the Church of Agaunum to St Maurice*. These two panels — so different as regards the conception of space and their composition from the illusionistic scenes below — are very similar, because of the choice of stylistic and architectural models, to the two large frescoes painted in the sanctuary of Saronno in 1525, the *Presentation of Jesus in the Temple* and the *Adoration of the Magi*, or the *Adoration of the Magi* in Como Cathedral, executed in the early 1520s.

From the point of view of perspective, all these scenes seem to be unbalanced: the main actors are placed on the edge, in the foreground, and the secondary figures are brought to the centre, while the architecture, seen in perspective, is mainly situated on one side, forming theatrical wings. The depth of the scene is no longer suggested by the superimposition of two or three registers in which the figures are depicted as decreasing in size towards the background, but thanks to a rapid rising up of the ground plane, which, as if it were a real slope, leads to the representation of the scenes in the distance. In the *Martyrdom of St Maurice* the executioner, portrayed from behind, seems almost to be dancing (the position of the legs is exactly the same as that of the figure shown from behind on the left in Raphael's *Disputa* [*Disputation over the Sacrament*] in the Stanza della Segnatura in the Vatican). The commander clad in a cuirass with his left arm outstretched and right arm bent with the finger pointing upwards, the gilded statue standing on a bronze column depicted immediately behind and, lastly, the scene with horsemen and martyrs before the tents in the background are all elements of antiquarian and central-Italian origin, in some cases deriving directly from Raphael — for instance, the young man walking on the right who is being stopped by a soldier comes straight from the *School of Athens*. And in *St Sigismund*, in addition to the *all'antica* relief on St Maurice's dais, the building seen in perspective on the right seems to be based on a scenographic drawing by Baldassarre Peruzzi, now in Turin, datable to c. 1515.[46]

As in Luini's works after 1525, in these two important scenes there is the development of new spatiality seeking "a profounder fusion of figures and landscape, which is now of much greater importance",[47] resulting in a greater degree of narrative clarity and composure. It is almost as if the concept of the Albertian *historia*, or the now long-standing scenographic experience compromised by "pre-Mannerist" tendencies proposed by, for example, Zenale, were being applied to these scenes. Often, moreover, they are overcrowded with figures, as in the autograph panels frescoed in the Cappella di San Giuseppe in Santa Maria della Pace, or in the works executed together with Zenale, such as the *Annunciation* in Brera,[48] paintings which can all be assigned, probably, to 1515–20.[49] And, while the Raphaelism noticeable in his works between c. 1515 and 1525 could be explained as being the consequence of a new propagation of this mode, imported into Lombardy by Cesare da Sesto, the Roman and antiquarian tone of the upper panels on the partition wall facing the lay worshipper's section of San Maurizio, their oratorical and declamatory style, the breadth of the gestures and the precision of the quotations (as a final example, see the cloaked figure in the centre of the middle ground in the *Martyrdom of St Maurice*, which seems to be derived from the first figure on the left in Leonardo's unfinished *Adoration of the Magi* in Florence, further illustration — and this is no coincidence — of the Albertian precepts regarding the painting of *historiæ*) are confirmation of the artist's new, fully-conscious interpretation of the Tuscan and Roman models and the fact that these two panels were executed later than the lunettes and *Female Saints* below. Thus, even the most evident Leonardism that may be noted in Luini's painting after 1524–25, his making use "at a deep level of the values of chiaroscuro naturalism that had marked the turning-point of the 'modern manner', rendering them with masterly refinement",[50] must also be seen as the consequence of renewed acquaintance with the works of Leonardo, and not only those brought to Milan by Francesco Melzi and Salai after his death, but also those remaining in Florence, which Luini must certainly have seen.

Having painted two altarpieces in 1526 and the following years (the painting now in the Courtauld Institute Galleries in London, and the Della Torre polyptych formerly in San Sisinio at Mendrisio, now in a private collection in Turin), Luini returned to Saronno in 1528 and then, in 1529, frescoed the partition wall of Santa Maria degli Angeli in Lugano with the *Crucifixion* and *Scenes from the Passion*. The influence of Venetian painting that pro-

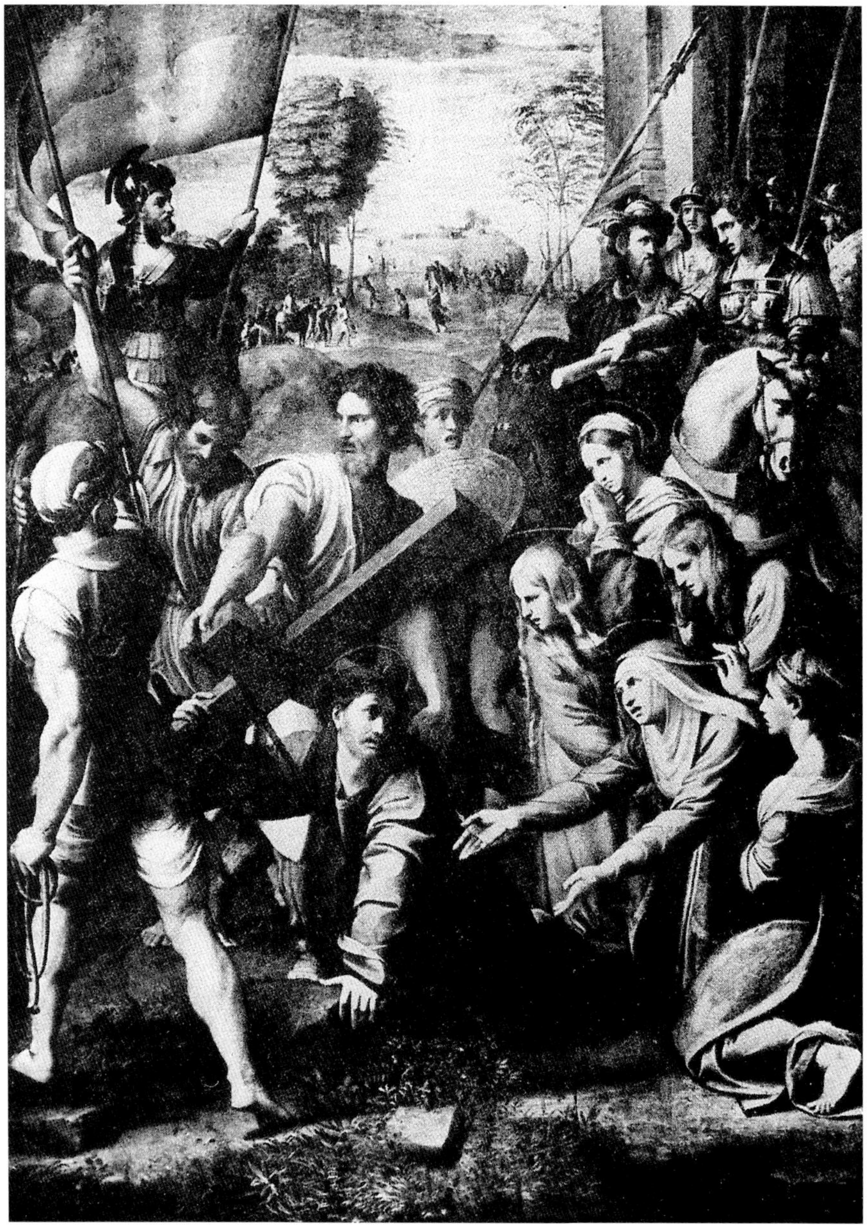

Raphael and assistants
Spasimo di Sicilia
(Christ Fallen beneath the Cross)
Prado, Madrid

duced quasi-Titianesque accents in the *Adoration of the Magi* in Saronno (a fresco that was also studied by Moretto) is replaced in Lugano by an expressive force that is almost Romaninesque in character. Here the realism of the facial features and the inflections of an artistic language are no longer constrained by classical moderation (note the remarkable group of soldiers casting lots for Christ's clothes, towards the lower-right corner of the wall), but are given the archaic form of an immense polyptych in which the figures thrash about — as if they were confined by a grid and two clearly marked registers, one above the other — then emerge with a new combination of Gaudenzio Ferrari's style and Leonardesque models.

Observing the frescoes in the first chapel on the right in the convent section of San Maurizio — especially those depicting the *Betrayal of Christ* and *Christ before Pilate*, as well as the lunettes mentioned previously, the *Way to Calvary* and the *Lamentation over the Dead Christ* — one realizes that the great fresco sequence on the partition wall in Lugano was created by assembling separate scenes that here, in San Maurizio, were tried out for the first time as adaptations of Raphaelesque compositions to an emotionally charged mode of that was typically Lombard and popular in its nature. It was, in other words, of the type indicated by Gaudenzio, and was the first formulation in the expressive and stylistic terms described above. Reminiscences of Raphael's late manner remain in these frescoes in San Maurizio: in the *Way to Calvary*, for instance, familiarity with the *Spasimo di Sicilia* (*Christ Fallen beneath the Cross*, Prado, Madrid), emerges. This *terminus ante quem* for this work is 1517 (the year in which Agostino Veneziano's engraving reproducing it was executed), and it is from it that the gesture of the Virgin holding out her arms towards Christ is derived. But an artistic language characterized by a degree of coarseness had already started to appear (see *Christ before Pilate*, with the strongly expressive grotesque heads of the captors). In Lugano, where it was absorbed by the "great mountain theatre" of the huge, incredibly populated scene, this was transformed into a superb, universal description of the drama and infinitely varied traits of human beings.

The same technique adopted by Luini in these penultimate frescoes in San Maurizio suggests that they were executed shortly before he went to Lugano — that is, a date around 1528–29. And this toing and froing by Luini when he was working at San Maurizio should not be cause for surprise (even if it is not documented) if it is remembered that the decoration at the Villa della Pelucca and that in the sanctuary in Saronno were carried out in exactly the same way — in various stages, that is — and, in the case of Saronno (except that it was begun at a later date) almost at the same time. Started in 1525 with the large panels in the Cappella Maggiore, the decoration of the sanctuary in Saronno continued, as I have said, in 1528 with the execution of a coat of arms on the façade of the Cappella della Croce (now lost, this was paid for on 9 August 1528) and, after 1529 — as the result of an interruption probably due to the artist's presence firstly in Lugano, then at San Maurizio (in 1530, when he decorated the Cappella Besozzi) — when Luini painted the ceiling of the Cappella del Sepolcro, for which he was paid on 15 October 1531, and the large figures of *Saints* under the dome, which were paid for on 9 July and 22 October of the same year.[51]

In Luini's career between 1526 and 1529 there would, therefore, have been sufficient time for him to complete the paintings in the convent section of the church of San Maurizio. The style and facture of the works mentioned above seem to foreshadow, not only the frescoes on the partition wall in the church in Lugano, but also the works in Saronno after 1529: the *Putti with the Symbols of the Passion*, the *Figures Peering over a Balustrade* on the dome of the Cappella del Cenacolo (a now distant and limited reminiscence of Mantegna's Camera degli Sposi in the Palazzo Ducale, Mantua) and, above all the monumental figures of *Saints* are all indicative of Luini's more popular and realistic style at the end of the 1520s. This is particularly evident in the emphasis on the facial features and the use of chiaroscuro and stronger flesh-colours, in which there are clearly echoes of Sodoma and the late Giampietrino. These are the same stylistic features that can be observed in the *Lamentation over the Dead Christ* in the right lunette on the partition wall facing the convent section of San Maurizio. I do not, however, believe that Luini deliberately intended the style of the scenes of the Passion in the convent section to differ from the more refined and aristocratic one used in the lay worshippers' section. This stylistic transformation, which corresponded to one that was taking place in his own personality, was perhaps more in keeping with the tastes of the times — and, presumably, was related to the patrons' control of the purse strings: one wonders whether

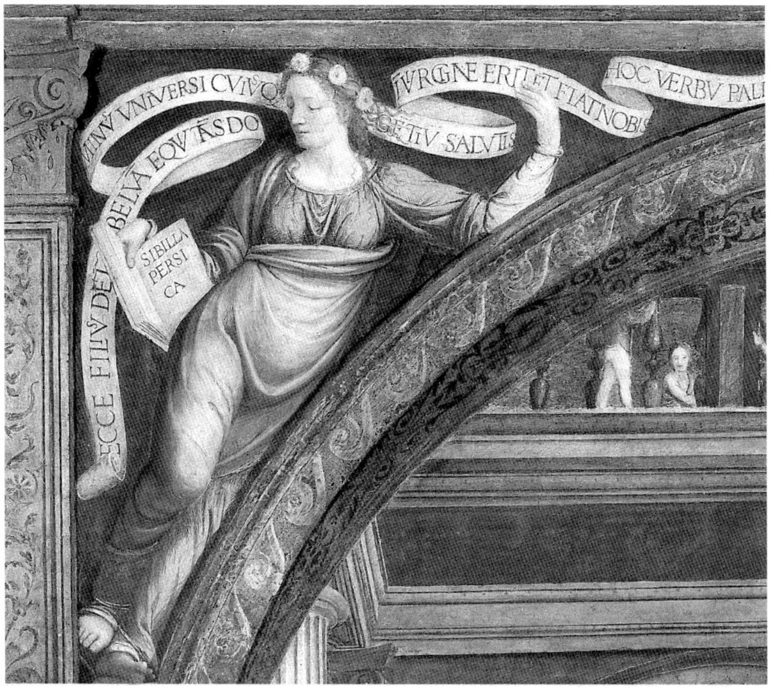

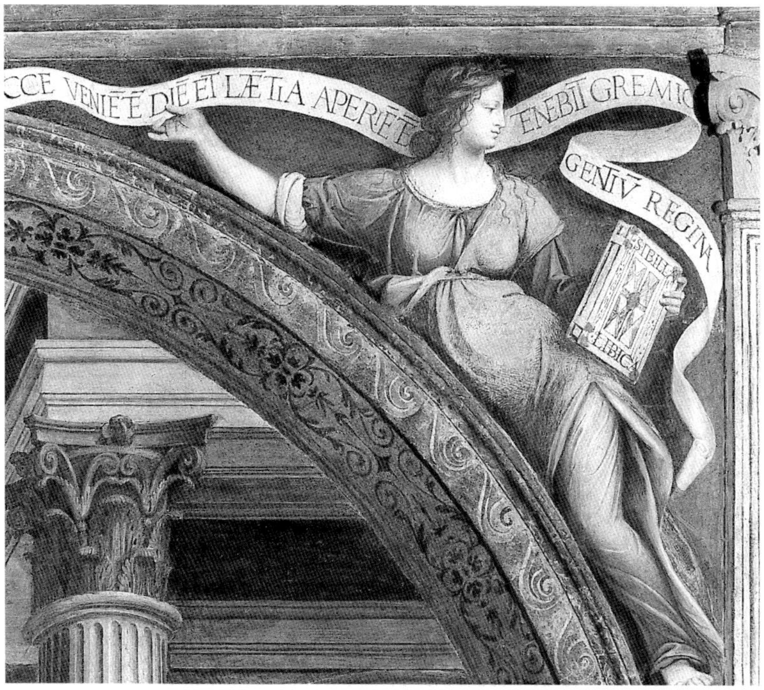

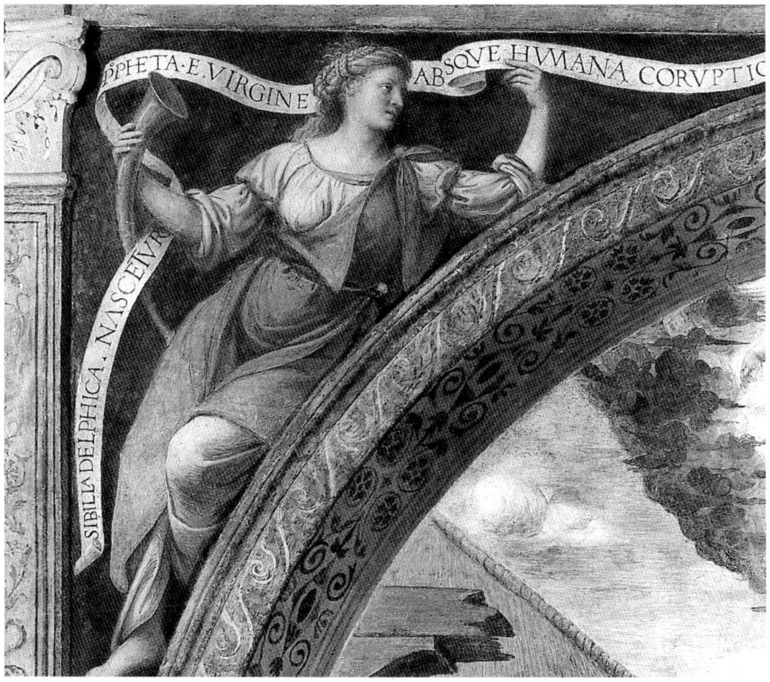

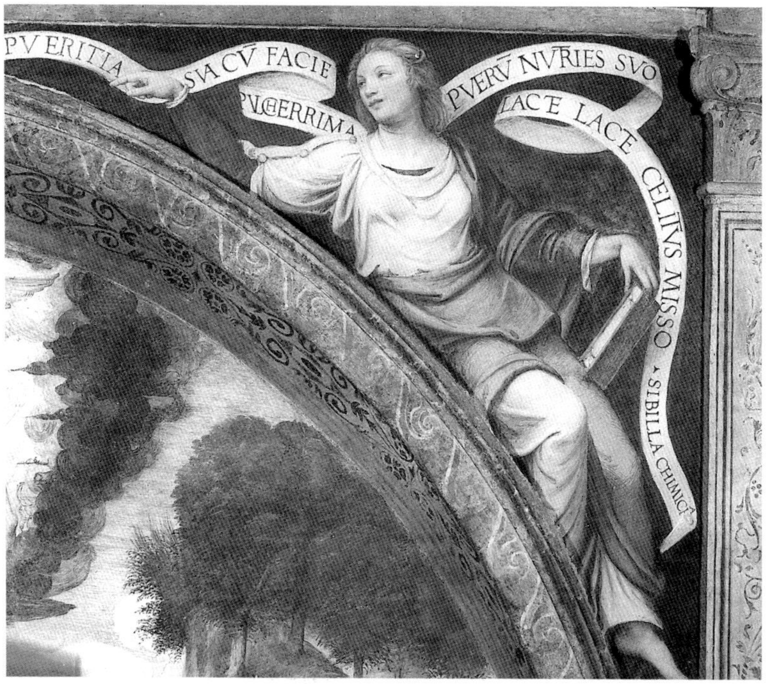

Bernardino Luini
Persian Sibyl
Libyan Sibyl
Delphic Sibyl
Cimmerian Sibyl
Sanctuary of the Beata Vergine
dei Miracoli, Saronno

the bequest of 1,173 ducats made by Ippolita Sforza in 1521 to Sister Bianca was sufficient to continue the decoration — which were changing rapidly.
The chronology of the various stages of Luini's decoration of San Maurizio, which I have sought to reconstruct here, will undoubtedly require further clarification and verification. Nevertheless, I felt it essential to attempt to assign the artist's very different frescoes located in the two distinct sections of the church to the various periods in which they were executed: differing in technique, style and circumstance, even without taking into consideration the final episode constituted by the Cappella Besozzi, they required him to be present in San Maurizio on and off for almost a decade. Despite the lack of certain chronological data for a number of frescoes — those, for example, on the partition wall facing the convent section of the church and those in the first chapel on the right in this section — I believe that, to put it briefly, there are two main stages. Firstly, there is the one before 1525, which, starting in 1521–22, comprises the decoration of the lower part of the partition wall on the side facing the lay worshippers' section and, immediately after this, the decoration of the lower part of the side facing the convent section. The second one, after 1525, includes, first of all, the two notable frescoes flanking the *Assumption* (this is now no longer attributed to Luini) on the lay worshippers' side of the partition wall — that is, the *Martyrdom of St Maurice* and *St Sigismund, Offering the Model the Church of Agaunum* — which reflect the artist's experience in Saronno and bear witness to his new understanding of antiquity and the spatial relationships of the figures, architecture and landscape. This stage extends to the first chapel on the left in the convent section and the lunettes on this side of the partition wall with the memorable frescoes of the *Way to Calvary* and *Lamentation over the Dead Christ*, containing numerous borrowings from Raphael; with minimal variations, these scenes were then reproduced on the partition wall in Santa Maria degli Angeli in Lugano.
Although it is perhaps unrealistic to expect to assign precise dates to the works executed in this second stage, which served to complete the decoration of San Maurizio, the commission for these frescoes might be linked to the nomination of Alessandro Bentivoglio as vice-duke in 1529, or else, if we prefer a slightly longer period, to his consolidated position as senator. This would certainly have allowed him to ensure a continuous financial contribution to the convent to which his three daughters had retired, while, after the death of Ippolita, he may well have wished to commemorate this event with the commission of the frescoes of the Passion cycle and the death of Christ in the convent section of the church. Thus, if we knew the exact date of Ippolita's death, this would probably be of assistance in dating part of Luini's frescoes. The absence of Alessandro Bentivoglio from Milan from 1524 (when the second French invasion of the duchy caused him to take refuge in Ferrara) to 1529 may, in fact, explain why the completion of the frescoes on the partition wall in the convent section overlapped with the decoration of the Cappella Besozzi.
The Cappella Besozzi, the first on the left in the lay worshippers' section coming from the altar, was dedicated on 15 August 1530 by the Milanese procurator Francesco Besozzi, Ippolita Sforza's uncle, as the inscription in lapidary lettering on the fascia — now ruined on the left side and only partly legible — states: FRANCISCVS BESVTIVS MDXXX DIE XI AVGVSTI DIVAE CATERINAE NOBILIS FRANCISCVS BESVTIVS VIVENS POSVIT (Francesco Besozzi 1530, 10 August. The living nobleman Francesco Besozzi dedicates to St Catherine...).[52] It is known that from 1524 onwards Besozzi offered oblations here, but this does not mean that at this date the chapel was already decorated.[53] The date of the dedication is the first decisive element in favour of a very late date for these frescoes. It would not make sense for Besozzi to wait five or six years before having the dedicatory inscription painted in his name: it is more logical to suppose that the chapel was begun in 1529 or 1530 and that the inscription was added as soon as it was completed, in August 1530. Moreover, stylistic and technical elements indicate that this was one of Luini's last works, and that it was certainly subsequent to the decoration of the partition wall in the church in Lugano. The chapel is conceived as a perforated architectural structure: for the first time in San Maurizio, on the front, in the spandrels over the extrados of its arch there are two figures of *Sibyls* (with "Eritrea" and "Agrippa" inscribed on the fluttering cartouches they bear aloft), evidently derived from the sanctuary in Saronno. It should be noted that, instead of figures of Sibyls, the extradoses of the two arches with the frescoes representing the Bentivoglio on the partition wall of the church are decorated with those of *Young Angels*, perhaps because the space was too small to contain larger reclining figures or, more probably, because the models

for these *Sibyls* (and those in Saronno) are to be found in Raphael's paintings, or drawings deriving from these, such as those of Innocenzo da Imola,[54] and it is likely that Luini only became familiar with them after his journey to Rome around 1523–24. The ceiling of the chapel is decorated, in the centre, with the head of *God the Father* and, on each side, with *Angels Bearing the Symbols of the Passion*, seen through rounded openings and resting on the cornice or on clouds. Closely related to those frescoed on the ceiling of the Cappella del Sepolcro in the sanctuary of Saronno, they have faces and expressions characterized by noticeable pathos and strong flesh-colours. The end wall of the chapel is a daring exercise in illusionism: the fresco depicting *Christ at the Column between St Laurence and St Catherine with Francesco Besozzi* is situated on a projecting podium. On this stands a gigantic column; attached to a wall with two side openings, it reaches up to the chapel ceiling, stressing its three-dimensionality and load-bearing function, and overcoming the division between the upper and lower registers found in the other frescoes. At the sides of the column, apparently beyond the chapel in a low-horizoned landscape, are two frescoes representing, on the left, *St John and the Virgin* and, on the right, the *Denial of Peter*, illustrating Luini's absorption of Raphael's "tragic style", with echoes of the figures in the cartoons for tapestries in the Sistine Chapel and, especially in the female figure in the panel on the right, models by Andrea del Sarto.

In the central fresco, almost as if it were required to counterbalance the erudite scenes in the background and attract a sense of piety of the faithful and render their participation in the Passion of Christ more direct, Christ's limp body, anti-classical and almost disarticulated (although the chiastic form of the legs is certainly an allusion to Christ himself), the caricatured expressions of the three tormentors (a third one appears behind St Laurence) and the naturalistic, almost realistic, modelling (note the rivulets of blood on the column and its plinth, the thick ropes, the wounds on Christ's body) indicate that Luini was inspired by the same artistic tenets that had animated his decoration of the partition wall in Santa Maria degli Angeli in Lugano, and that he diversified his style from one scene to another according to the subject-matter, in tune with the patron's tastes and requirements and the characteristics of the site. Certainly, there could hardly be a greater contrast with regard to

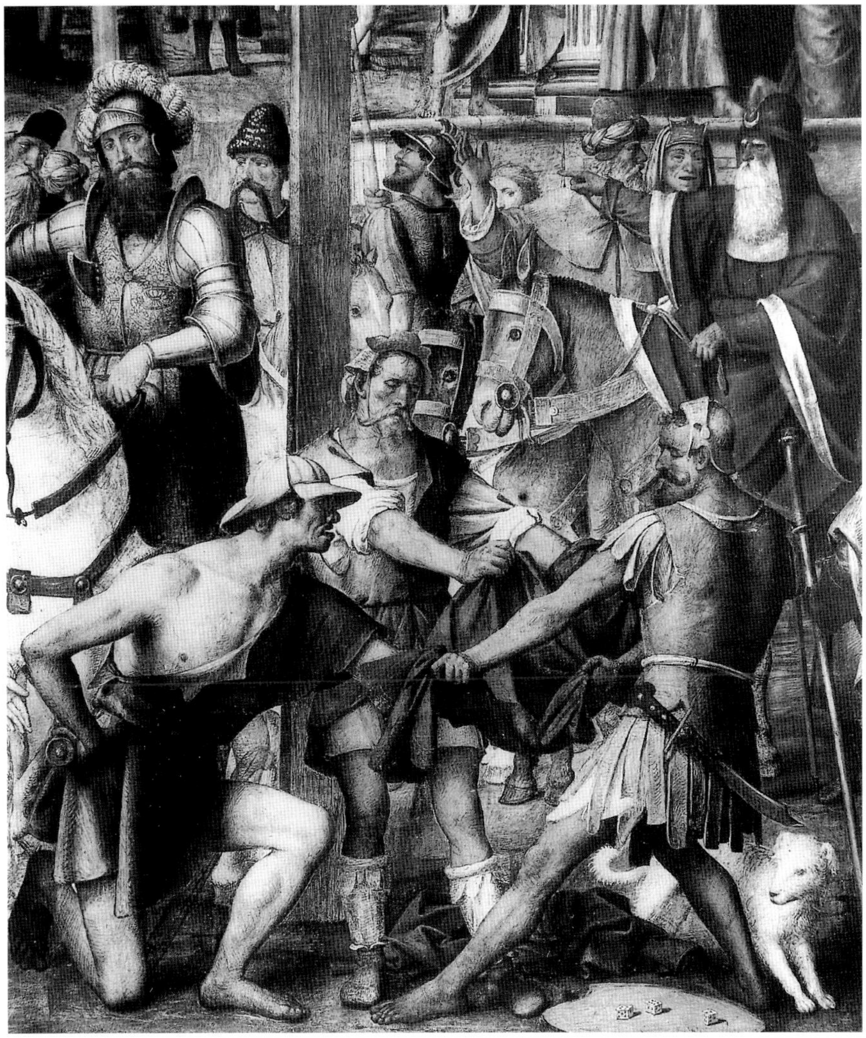

Bernardino Luini
Crucifixion and *Scenes from the Passion*, detail
Santa Maria degli Angeli, Lugano

their ideals, ideologies and artistic language between this *Christ at the Column* and the aristocratic figures represented nearby on the partition wall facing the lay worshippers' section of San Maurizio less than ten years previously. But there it was necessary to depict the cultured patrons as they appeared when they were alive, while here there was a need to provide the faithful with the means to participate directly, with suitable devotional orientation, in the Passion of Christ. Here Besozzi himself, portrayed on the left, seems to be astonished by so much violence and coarseness, while St Laurence, on the opposite side, invites the faithful to contemplate the scene and feel compassion for such suffering.

Finally, observation of Luini's technique, especially his brushwork in the figures in the two upper scenes,[55] will reveal his remarkable ability to modify his style and surpass himself in accordance with the subject matter of his paintings: thus the ladies' dresses are no longer embellished with elegant designs and less attention is paid to superficial detail, while forms are rendered more succinctly (in *St Peter*, whose face seems to have been derived from the disciple kneeling in the centre of Raphael's *Transfiguration*, one might almost describe his style as Michelangelesque), and the nerveless Leonardesque chiaroscuro has been abandoned in favour of a definition of the image that is more cursory, but with greater contrast.

On the side walls of the chapel, Luini has painted two fictive windows: beyond these we can see, on the left, the *Martyrdom of St Catherine* and, on the right, the *Beheading of St Catherine*. In the *Martyrdom* the device of concealing behind the wall part of the figure of an executioner, who is fleeing in fear after a thunderbolt has destroyed the martyr's wheel — shown in the left background as if it were an exploded diagram of the gearwheels in a machine (exactly as in a famous drawing by Leonardo) — has the task of stressing the three-dimensionality of this scene, the centre of which is dominated by the kneeling figure of the saint wearing a red cloak. Andrea Solario and Giampietrino seem to have provided the model, but the artist's rendering of it produces a type of naturalism resembling that of the Lombard works of Gaudenzio Ferrari, who, however, only came to Saronno for the first time in 1534, two years after the death of Luini. Nonetheless, this scene is not wholly convincing: the dramatic effects of the explosion of the wheel, with the victims strewn on the ground, draw the spectator's attention away from the saint, but gratify, one presumes, the taste of a public that had already thronged to watch the beheading of the countess of Challant on the ravelin of Milan Castle in 1526. The traditional story according to which this episode is represented in the *Beheading of St Catherine*, on the right wall and that the saint's face is, in reality, a portrait of the countess — as a passage by Matteo Bandello, to which reference has already been made, seems to suggest — does not seem to be credible. This fresco, in which both style and composition are much superior to those of the one just described, seems to offer Luini's own interpretation of Raphael's "tragic style", with its total concentration on the event that is about to take place in the foreground and the two leading actors, with, in the middle ground, the onlookers, one of whom is indicating the martyrdom of the saint, and, in the distance, the transport of her body by two angels to the top of a mountain. In these scenes, the artist has paid greater attention to the use of colour, which is now more refined, with slight iridescence in the fabrics — note, in the clothes of the executioner (who is the one fleeing in the panel of the *Martyrdom* directly opposite), the juxtaposition, of which Luini became fond after he had worked in Saronno, of yellow and purple-blue, almost periwinkle. Here, too, there is a new change in tone with regard to the main scene in the chapel, as if Luini always wanted to go one better and as if he intended, in the final stage of his career, to measure himself with the great masters of the day.

And, taking into account these last two scenes and, above all, the figures in the two succinct upper compositions flanking the huge column, it can certainly be affirmed that the artist had finally felt the need to update his style to that of the High Renaissance and that he had — almost with amazement — seen, emerging from his brush, solemn figures that were, however, alive and sorrowful. Perhaps for the first time appearing to be made of flesh, blood and tears, they were now worthy of Raphael and Michelangelo.

[1] See Archivio di Stato di Milano (henceforth ASM), *Culto p.a.* 1926. The nuns were still living in the convent in 1847 and 1853.

[2] ASM, *Religione p.m.* 2460. See I. Rossi, *La chiesa di San Maurizio in Milano. Il Monastero Maggiore e le sue due torri,* Milan 1914, p. 149; G.B. Sannazzaro, *San Maurizio al Monastero Maggiore*, Milan 1992, p. 161, note 36; G. Pertot, "Interventi di restauro al Monastero Maggiore. Note in margine a una campagna di lettura stratigrafica", in

Milano restaurata. Il monumento e il suo doppio, conference proceedings, Florence 1995, p. 115.

[3] See G. Vasari, *Le vite de' più eccellenti pittori scultori e architettori nelle redazioni del 1550 e 1568*, ed. R. Bettarini, explanatory notes by P. Barocchi, V (text), Florence 1984, p. 435.

[4] See G.P. Lomazzo, *Trattato dell'arte della pittura*, Milan 1584 (see also *Giovan Paolo Lomazzo. Scritti sulle arti*, ed. R.P. Ciardi, II, Pisa 1973–74, pp. 201 e 305). The adjective "excellent", in fact, refers in general to Luini as regards his use of colour and representation of the drapery, especially in the figures of the saints. It is, therefore, probable that he was thinking of the figures of saints, particularly female ones, depicted on the partition wall of San Maurizio, where the fabric and the colours, especially in the figures in the lay worshippers' section of the church, are rendered with a truly remarkable and realistic technique.

[5] Lomazzo, *Trattato dell'arte della pittura*, p. 20.

[6] See A. Santagostino, *L'immortalità e gloria del pennello*, Milan 1671, p. 91. See also *Agostino Santagostino. L'immortalità e gloria del pennello. Catalogo delle pitture insigni che stanno esposte al pubblico nella città di Milano*, ed. M. Bona Castellotti, Milan 1981, p. 48. The Benedictine nuns could not enter the section of the church for lay worshippers without special permission. For example, in a document of 26 September 1794 Archbishop Filippo Visconti consented that "for just once" the Benedictines could "go into the external church of the convent [...] in order to observe the splendid, recently constructed high altar and the other lesser altars, and paintings" on condition that the outer doors were closed and that two delegates of the archbishop were present. See also ASM, *Archivio diplomatico*, sez. XII, *Ordini religiosi e congregazioni* 101.

[7] For the church of San Maurizio and Luini's frescoes see, for example, C. Torre, *Il Ritratto di Milano,* Milan 1674, 1714 ed., pp. 211–212; S. Latuada, *Descrizione di Milano*, IV, Milan 1738, pp. 17, 31 and 410–425; F. Bartoli, *Notizie delle sculture, pitture e architetture che ornano le principali città d'Italia*, I, Venice 1776, p. 204; C. Bianconi, *Nuova guida di Milano*, Milan 1787, p. 271 (1795 ed., p. 313; 1796 ed., p. 312); L. Bossi, *Guida di Milano*, Milan 1818, pp. 155–157; F. Pirovano, *Nuova guida di Milano*, Milan 1831, pp. 153–157. For other bibliographical references see A. Ottino Della Chiesa, *Bernardino Luini*, Novara 1956, p. 112, and F. Frangi, in *Pittura a Milano. Rinascimento e manierismo*, ed. M. Gregori, Milan 1998, p. 229.

[8] See G. Lafenestre, in *Gazette des Beaux-Arts*, II, 1869, pp. 441–451, and I, 1870, pp. 47–57, with preceding biography.

[9] See L. Beltrami, *Luini 1512–1532, Materiale di studio*, Milan 1911, pp. 463–468.

[10] A. Ottino Della Chiesa, *San Maurizio al Monastero Maggiore*, Milan 1962, pp. 52–54. See also Eadem, *Bernardino Luini*, cat. 151/2, p. 111: "Lafenestre has struck the *Assumption* of the list of Luini's works, but this exclusion is quite unjustified".

[11] The *Assumption* was again attributed to Luini by G.B. Sannazzaro in the second edition of his guide (1992, p. 107: "As is usually the case in Luini's paintings, in the *Assumption* the carefully pondered classical rhythm in the disposition of the Apostles — recalling Raphael or Luini's frescoes formerly in the Villa della Pelucca... — helps to exclude all dramatic violence or expressive characterization and favours the respectful, rational representation of religious dogma") and, while admitting that there is "a certain weakness in the composition and a diminished resemblance to Luini's works", by S. Bandera in "I cicli pittorici", in *San Maurizio al Monastero Maggiore. Guida storico-artistica*, Milan 1998, pp. 46 and 62.

[12] See G. Bora, "Bernardino Luini", in *I leonardeschi. L'eredità di Leonardo in Lombardia*, essays by G. Bora, M.T. Fiorio, P.C. Marani, J. Shell, Milan 1998, p. 350, which very opportunely links it to a generically Luinesque circle in Milan, Pavia, Lodi and Vigevano; the artist responsible could perhaps be Bernardino Ferrari, who, because of his stylistic affinities with the artist, may have been commissioned to complete the wall Luini left unfinished.

[13] See Ottino Della Chiesa, *San Maurizio al Monastero Maggiore*, pp. 42–46, pls. 17–22 and 25–30.

[14] See R. Bossaglia, review of A. Ottino Della Chiesa's book in *Arte lombarda*, VII, 1, 1963, pp. 165–166, which in any case dates them to the sixteenth century. Also M.T. Fiorio, *Leonardeschi in Lombardia*, Milan 1982, p. 78, refers ambiguously to these works, asserting that "his [Luini's] hand has also been noted in the older series of silent landscapes in the choir, a mysterious and early insertion of pure landscape in a period in which this type of painting was not yet in vogue. Another possibility is that they are the work of a specialist in the genre, who was certainly neither Flemish nor Leonardesque, judging by the serene poetry of these corners of Lombardy"; here it is not clear if the writer is referring to the oldest landscapes or those painted after Luini's works. See also the following note. Ottino Della Chiesa, in *Bernardino Luini*, 1956, pp. 111–112, makes no reference to them.

[15] See Sannazzaro, *San Maurizio al Monastero Maggiore*, p. 56. For the frescoes of Santa Maria dei Ghirli, see F. Mazzini, *Santa Maria dei Ghirli*, Milan 1988, pp. 128–135. The figures in the *Temptation* derive from Dürer's *Adam and Eve* of 1504; the background of the *Expulsion from the Garden of Eden* is derived from his *Small Passion* of 1511. The frescoes at Campione d'Italia may be dated to c. 1514.

[16] In 1869 and 1871, after the preparation of the projects, work was carried out on the left side of the church, involving the demolition of walls and the opening of new windows on both the ground and upper floors ("to be carried out with the greatest care and attention in order not to damage the paintings in the interior"): see ASM, *Pergamene per fondi* 44/ II (unpublished). It is reasonable to suppose that, after this, the frescoes (especially the landscapes) were "restored" and, possibly, totally repainted. It should also be remembered, moreover, that in 1827 the floor of the church was replaced due to problems caused by rising damp (Archivio Storico Civico, Milan, *Ornato fabbriche*, I, 15, application of 14 June 1827), which may well have badly affected the frescoes and, as a consequence of this, "artistic" restoration work may have been undertaken. See also the following note.

[17] In 1857 Giuseppe Knoller was involved in the conseravtion of Luini's frescoes in the Cappella di Santa Caterina in San Maurizio, which had already been badly restored in 1856. See ASM, *Pergamene per fondi* 44/1, and with reference to this, Rossi, *La chiesa di San Maurizio*, pp. 57 and 62. It should be noted that Knoller himself was not averse to carrying out work involving restoration of the decorations, as he was to do in the refectory of Santa Maria delle Grazie in Milan, the walls of which were "artistically restored" by him in 1872: see P.C.

Marani, "Il Cenacolo di Leonardo", in P. Brambilla Barcilon and P.C. Marani, *Leonardo. L'Ultima Cena*, Milan 1999, p. 49 and notes 76 and 78 on p. 88. The landscape paintings may, however, have been executed at an even later date, in the the late nineteenth and early twentieth centuries, as Sandrina Bandera and Paola Zanolini seem inclined to believe, in another part of this book as a result of the analyses carried out during the recent conservation work.

[18] The fragment in question is a landscape which came to light on the side of the partition wall facing the convent section of the church after the recent removal of the altar installed there during the Counter-Reformation. Bandera ("I cicli pittorici", p. 58, plate on pp. 60–61) describes it as being "in the purest Peruginesque and Raphaelesque tradition.[...] This remarkable landscape, painted in *buon fresco*, is in a distinctly classical style that is very different from the Lombard landscapes painted by Bergognone, and confirms that Luini's art is the most subject to the influence of the central-Italian art of the Renaissance". Nonetheless, I doubt whether this work is by Luini: the hand is descriptive rather than analytical, and the style is that of a mediocre painter of the mid-Cinquecento. Naturalistic and landscape details painted by Luini may be seen close at hand, in the rocks of the *Christ Carried to the Tomb*, in the flower on a tall stem on the lower right of the *Resurrection*, or in the backgrounds of the same panels. Thus there are hills clearly outlined with a sure hand and their rotundity and volume carefully rendered (with an effect resembling risen bread, true enough, rather than the humid, verdant earth – but this is Luini's poetry!), and trees and foliage analytically depicted. And this is quite the opposite of what we see in the landscape fragment on the partition wall, executed in a cursory, superficial manner.

[19] See Sannazzaro, *San Maurizio al Monastero Maggiore*, p. 53. In fact, none of these figures (including those in the apsidal gallery, all reproduced by Sannazzaro, pp. 78–82) is in Luini's style. Some bear a resemblance to *St Sigismund* and *St Maurice* in the chapels in the convent section (Ottino Della Chiesa ascribed them with reservations to Bernardo Zenale), or to the figures of Christ and Mary Magdalen in *Noli me tangere*, or to the archangel Gabriel and the Virgin in the *Annunciation* frescoed on the spandrels of the arch in front of the partition wall in the convent section, all usually attributed to Boltraffio (but, alas, they are not his). Leaving aside the state of conservation and the repainting, probably dating from the nineteenth century and clearly visible in the faces of a number of female saints, it must be observed that, like other figures in the lunettes of the convent section (for example, *St Michael and the Devil*, *Tobias and the Angel*, *Charity of St Martin*, *Temptation of St Anthony*, *St Exuperius* and *St Candidus*), or like the monochrome tondi depicting saints on the spandrels of the serliane, the artist may have been a member of one of the "companies" working with Bergognone and perhaps Zenale on the decoration of the transept and chapels of the Certosa of Pavia in which painters such as Jacopino de' Mottis or Pietro da Velate emerged. The issue is, however, complex and requires further investigation and specific comparisons that lie outside the province of this essay. For the various artists and "companies" working at the Certosa of Pavia, see the essays by P.C. Marani and R. Battaglia, and the entries by M. Albertario, published in the catalogue *Ambrogio Bergognone. Un pittore per la Certosa*, ed. G.C. Sciolla, Milan 1998.

[20] See Sannazzaro, *San Maurizio al Monastero Maggiore*, p. 43.

[21] Beltrami, *Luini 1512–1532*, p. 359.

[22] Rossi, *La chiesa di San Maurizio*, pp. 19–23, also for the reconstruction of the historic events mentioned. For the Bentivoglio family see C.M. Ady, *I Bentivoglio*, Milan 1965, and P. Litta, *Famiglie celebri italiane*, Milan 1819–38, "Bentivoglio", pl. V.

[23] The document in ASM, *Pergamene, Fondi* 461, is partially published in Rossi, *La chiesa di San Maurizio*, p. 34.

[24] See Bandera, "I cicli pittorici", p. 54.

[25] See Bora, in *I leonardeschi*, p. 347.

[26] See *Matteo Bandello. Novelle*, with an essay by L. Russo, notes by E. Mazzali, Milan 1990, p. 529. Ippolita, Alessandro Bentivoglio's second wife, was the daughter of Carlo di Galeazzo Sforza.

[27] These are only some of the personages mentioned in the first novella: see *Matteo Bandello. Novelle*, p. 89 ff. For the complete edition of Bandello's novelle, see M. Bandello, *Tutte le opere*, ed. F. Flora, Milan 1934. For Cecilia Gallerani, her fame as a poetess, her culture and artistic tastes, see the essays by J. Shell and P.C. Marani in *Leonardo. La Dama con l'ermellino*, exhibition catalogue, Milan 1998. For the possible classical sources that may have inspired Leonardo da Vinci for the portrait of Cecilia Gallerani now in Cracow and, in particular, for the reference to Lucian (perhaps suggested by the cultured sitter herself, or one of her learned friends?), apart from his symbolic and political links with Ludovico il Moro, see P.C. Marani, *Leonardo. Una carriera da pittore*, Milan 1999, pp. 171–173.

[28] For this controversial series, which, in the past, was attributed to famous artists, but which has now been relegated — perhaps unjustly, given the poor state of conservation — to a work by an anonymous painter, see G. Cavalieri, in *Museo d'arte antica del Castello Sforzesco – Pinacoteca*, II, Milan 1999, pp. 235–245.

[29] *Matteo Bandello, Novelle*, p. 87.

[30] Ibid., I, novella III, pp. 97–109.

[31] The one dedicated to the son of Alessandro Bentivoglio and Ippolita Sforza is novella XXI in part I, *Matteo Bandello, Novelle,* pp. 138–158; those in which Fregoso's work are mentioned are novelle XLVIII in part II and IX in part III. Fregoso is also the author of two poems: *I doi Philosphi* (1505) and *La cerva bianca* (1510). Mentioned by Ludovico Ariosto, he died in 1530. See also *Matteo Bandello, Novelle,* p. 558, note 6.

[32] Ibib, p. 559, note 7. Lancino Curzio, who died in 1512 and is famous for his *Epigrammi,* had dealings with Giovan Antonio Boltraffio, Cristoforo Solari, Andrea Solario (Curzio wrote the elegiac distich on his *Portrait of Cristoforo Longoni*, now in the National Gallery, London), the physician Giovanni Marliani mentioned by Leonardo, the Grifi and Benedetto Briosco (who sculpted Ambrogio Grifi's tomb in San Pietro in Gessate) and, lastly, Agostino Busti, known as Bambaia, Cristoforo Lombardi (he commissioned his tomb from the latter two) and Leonardo himself, whose equestrian monument to Francesco Sforza he mentioned. For Lancino Curzio's role in the Milanese milieu see C. Pedretti, "Leonardo's Studies for the Sforza Sepulchre. II", in *Gazette des Beaux-Arts*, January 1978, pp. 1–20; Idem, *Leonardo architetto*, Milan 1978 (2nd ed. 1988), p. 100–103, figs. 143–147; Idem, "A Proem to Sculpture", in *Achademia Leonardo Vinci. Journal of Leonardo Studies and Bibliography of Vinciana*", II, 1989, p. 20 ff.; G. Agosti, *Bambaja e il classicismo lombardo*, Turin 1990, pp. 120 ff.; Idem, "Scrittori che parlano di artisti, tra Quattro e

Cinquecento in Lombardia", in *Quattro pezzi lombardi (per Maria Teresa Binaghi)*, ed. S. Lombardi, Brescia 1998, pp. 57–62.

[33] *Matteo Bandello, Novelle,* part I, novella IV, pp. 109–118; Agosti, *Scrittori*, p. 66.

[34] See F. Neri, "La contessa di Challant" (1931), in *Storia e poesia*, Turin 1936, p. 78, for the preceding literature and the questioning of this belief ("it is not certain, nor even likely, that it is the portrait of Bianca Maria").

[35] See R. Levi Pisetzky, "L'apogeo dell'eleganza milanese durante il ducato", in *Storia di Milano*, VIII, Milan 1957, pp. 750–751; Sannazzaro, *San Maurizio al Monastero Maggiore*, p. 106. See also M.T. Binaghi Olivari, "I francesi a Milano (1499–1525): arti figurative e moda", in *Annali dell'Istituto storico italo-germanico di Trento*, V, 1979, p. 106. However, the latter writer suggests that the kneeling woman depicted in the lunette on the right of the partition wall facing the lay worshippers' section of the church is not Ippolita Sforza, but rather her daughter Violante, and that the kneeling man in the lunette on the left is not Alessandro Bentivoglio but rather Gian Paolo Sforza di Caravaggio, Violante's husband, judging by the apparent age of the couple portrayed, which does not seem to correspond with that of Alessandro and Ippolita around 1521–22. The writer also suggests that the portrait of the countess of Challant may be the face of one of the female saints depicted in tondi in the gallery in the convent section of the church, which have traditionally been attributed to Boltraffio (but, because of its location in the convent section, it would have been difficult for Bandello to see it). Although it is possible that the female portrait on the right painted by Luini makes Ippolita seem younger, in 1521 she must in any case have been just over forty, and she seems to be roughly this age in the corresponding drawing by Luini in the Albertina in Vienna (Binaghi Olivari, "I francesi a Milano", fig. 13). Moreover, it can hardly be said that the male portrait on the left appears to be that of a gentleman much younger than Alessandro Bentivoglio was in 1521 (he was forty-seven), because the man portrayed appears to be of mature years and somewhat drawn. Indeed, the sumptuous lined black cloak with a large sable collar seems to allude to the office of senator to which he was appointed in 1522. Besides, the prominent position assigned to the two portraits in the church would seem to be unjustified if they represented Violante and her husband Gian Paolo Sforza, who do not appear — at least from available documentary evidence — to have donated anything to the convent of San Maurizio, nor do they seem to have had any kind of role in the rich and cultured circle of artists and humanists within which Ippolita seemed to be perfectly at her ease. For other reasons, linked to the chronology of the frescoes on the partition wall facing the convent section, Bora, in his essay in *I leonardeschi*, pp. 346–347, rejects the identifications proposed by Binaghi Olivari. Furthermore, it is, in my opinion, quite possible that the portrait of "Ippolita Sforza" by G. Ambrogio Noceto in codex 2159 of the Biblioteca Trivulziana in Milan (datable to after 1515, since it is dedicated to Francis I, the king of France) represents — together with the portraits of twenty-six other Milanese ladies — Ippolita Sforza Bentivoglio and not, as Biraghi affirms (pp. 104–105, fig. 11 on p. 103), her daughter Ippolita, who, although she was betrothed to Roberto Sanseverino, entered the convent of San Maurizio under the name of Sister Francesca. It would, indeed, be somewhat strange if Noceto's "portable gallery", with its dedication to the king of France, contained, rather than the portrait of Ippolita Sforza Bentivoglio, who had relations with all the most important ladies of her day, that of her daughter. The lady is, in fact, portrayed, in the codex in the Biblioteca Trivulziana, in a similar pose to Isabella d'Este in Leonardo's portrait now in the Louvre, and is wearing the same style of dress. This not only indicated the social status of the sitter, but also the fact that she kept up with the fashion set by Isabella, whose political instinct and diplomatic prowess were a byword. In fact, she came post-haste to Milan to meet the king of France, Louis XII, and dance with him, as soon as he had deposed Ludovico il Moro in 1499.

[36] For this sequence of decorative schemes, then replaced by Gaudenzio Ferrari's frescoes, see P.C. Marani, "Amadeo inedito. La cupola del santuario di Saronno prima di Gaudenzio", in *Il santuario della Beata Vergine dei Miracoli di Saronno. Arte, religiosità popolare, tradizioni*, conference procedings, ed. C. Saccardo, Milan, forthcoming.

[37] When Campi's altarpiece was recently removed for restoration, fragments of paintings portraying heads of putti were revealed on the intrados and front of the arch that temporarily became visible. See G.B. Sannazzaro, "Per la chiesa di San Maurizio al Monastero Maggiore", in *Raccolta Vinciana*, XXVII, 1997, pp. 573–576. Campi's altarpiece, with its figures larger than life-size and its incongruous inventions (for example, the off-centre perspective of a colonnaded building and the large irreverent horse seen from behind), disturbs the equilibrium and proportions of Luini's frescoes at the sides, making it difficult today to appreciate their notably illusionistic effects.

[38] For these portraits by Lotto see M. Lucco and P. Humfrey, in *Lorenzo Lotto. Il genio inquieto del Rinascimento*, exhibition catalogue, Milan 1988, pp. 115–116, 173–174 and 206–207 (English ed. Washington 1977).

[39] For Bergognone's *Saints* in San Satiro (c. 1495), see J. Shell, in P.C. Marani and J. Shell, *Ambrogio Bergognone. Acquisizioni, scoperte, restauri*, exhibition catalogue, Florence 1989, pp. 66–74; for the *Saints* in the chapter house of the church of Santa Maria della Passione, see S. Bandera (in the same catalogue), pp. 123–125; G. Bora, "Due secoli d'arte a Milano: la pittura in Santa Maria della Passione", in *Santa Maria della Passione e il Conservatorio Giusppe Verdi a Milano*, Milan 1981, pp. 76–161.

[40] For Boltraffio's *St Barbara* from San Satiro, see *Gemäldegalerie Berlin. Gesamtverzeichnis*, ed. H. Bock et al., Berlin 1996, cat. 1808, p. 20 and ill. on p. 418. This panel is datable to c. 1502. See also M.T. Fiorio, *Boltraffio*, forthcoming.

[41] For Solario's *Christ Blessing* in New York see F. Zeri and E.E. Gardner, *Italian Paintings. A Catalogue of the Collection of the Metropolitan Museum of Art*, New York 1986, pp. 59–60, pl. 31; D.A. Brown, *Andrea Solario*, Milan 1987, pp. 285–286, cat. 71. This is a late work by the artist (early 1520s).

[42] For Luini's paintings of *Salome* and their relationship with those of Salario, see Bora in *I leonardeschi*, pp. 354–356.

[43] P.C. Marani, "Pittura e decorazione dalle origini al 1534: Giorgio da Saronno, Bernardino Luini, Alberto da Lodi e Cesare Magni", in *Il santuario della Beata Vergine dei Miracoli a Saronno*, ed. M.L. Gatti Perer, Milan 1996, p. 140 ff.

[44] For the polyptych in San Magno in Legnano, see my entry in *Pittura tra Ticino e Olona. Varese e la Lombardia nord-occidentale*, ed. M. Gregori, Milan 1992, pp. 248–249.

[45] See *Ambrogio Bergognone. Un pittore per la Certosa*, ed. G.C. Sciolla, Milan 1998, cat. 39, pp. 228–229, and cat. 63, pp. 338–339. The latter work is clearly derived from Zenale, while the former is still influenced by Bramantino's *sottinsù* views.

[46] Biblioteca Reale, Turin, no. 15728; see also C.L. Frommel, in C.L. Frommel, S. Ray and M. Tafuri, *Raffaello architetto*, Milan 1984, p. 226. For the Peruzzesque echoes in Luini's late work see Marani, "Pittura e decorazione", p. 154 and note 38 on p. 183. The Saronno fresco cycle does not imply a journey at an indeterminate date by Luini to Rome, a hypothesis attributed to me by Bora (in *I leonardeschi*, p. 360), but one that took place immediately before 1525, about 1523–24, perhaps before the execution of the two organ shutters for Sant'Eustorgio in Milan (now, modified, in the parish church of Paderno Dugnano, near Milan) in 1524. For the use of antiquarian motifs in the two panels flanking the *Assumption*, see also G.B. Sannazzaro, "Per la decorazione pittorica nella chiesa di San Maurizio al Monastero Maggiore di Milano: suggerimenti di studio", in *Arte lombarda nel secondo millennio. Saggi in onore di Gian Alberto Dell'Acqua*, ed. F. Flores d'Arcais, M. Olivari and L. Tognoli Bardin, Milan 2000, p. 146 ff., who refers to the reliefs on the arch of Constantine and, in particular, the Great Trajanic Frieze and the roundel showing *Trajan Offering a Sacrifice to Apollo*.

[47] Bora, in *I leonardeschi*, p. 364.

[48] For this problematic painting, which I believe to be mainly by Zenale himself, see G. Bora, "Firenze 1510–Milano 1515", in *Settanta studiosi italiani. Scritti per l'Istituto germanico di storia dell'arte di Firenze*, ed. C. Acidini Luchinat, L. Bellosi, M. Boskovits, P.P. Donati and B. Santi, Florence 1997, pp. 239–246, who identifies — assisted by a previous analysis by myself — the simultaneous presence of two or three different hands, one of them being Luini's.

[49] For this cycle, see M.T. Binaghi Olivari, in *Pinacoteca di Brera. Scuole lombarda e piemontese 1300–1535*, ed. F. Zeri, Milan 1988, pp. 266–316; Bora, in *I leonardeschi*, pp. 334–340.

[50] See Bora, in *I leonardeschi*, p. 354.

[51] For the documents recording Luini's presence in Saronno, see E. Sala, "Siste viator. Dagli archivi la storia del Santuario 1400–1600", in *I Quaderni del Santuario*, 6, 1995; for the last works see pp. 79–80 and 86. See also Marani, "Pittura e decorazione", p. 169. For the execution in various stages of the frescoes in the Villa della Pelucca, see Bora, in *I leonardeschi*, pp. 328–332, with a reconstruction of the stages (the first may even have been in the first decade of the Cinquecento) that must certainly be confirmed.

[52] See Sannazzaro, *San Maurizio al Monastero Maggiore*, p. 118, note 44, which quotes Rossi's transcription in *La chiesa di San Maurizio in Milano*, p. 59; I have, however, replaced the Us with the Vs that are still legible in the right part of the inscription.

[53] Sannazzaro, *San Maurizio al Monastero Maggiore*, p. 109 and note 46 on p. 119. A document of 18 May 1524 (ASM, *San Maurizio* 465) refers to the "donationem facio, pro dote capellæ Beatæ Catharinæ construendae in Ecclesia monalium [...] et sub altare ejus capellæ volo fiat locus sepulchri [...] in quo volo reponi cadaver meum", and Sannazzaro has interpreted this as being the beginning not of the building work, but rather of the pictorial decoration. In fact, the work could not have been that of the construction of the chapel, which must have existed already, but it must have involved the preparation of the walls and surfaces for the frescoes that were to be executed on them and, above all, for the tomb of Besozzi (who died in 1539).

[54] See Marani, "Pittura e decorazione", fig. 32 on p. 150. For Raphael's *Sibyls* in Santa Maria della Pace in Rome, see, for example, P.L. De Vecchi, *Raffaello. La pittura*, Florence 1981, pl. CXXI, p. 220.

[55] Excellent details of *St Peter* and the *Virgin* are reproduced in Ottino Della Chiesa, *San Maurizio al Monastero Maggiore*, pls. 76 and 77.

The Cappella Simonetta by Callisto and Fulvio Piazza

Sandrina Bandera

At the same time that the decoration for San Maurizio was resumed, which had been interrupted after the death of Bernardino Luini, that of the Cappella Simonetta also began. The artist entrusted with the commission, who was neither from Milan nor of Milanese formation, was Callisto Piazza of Lodi, who was assisted by his son Fulvio. It is of significance that Callisto was called to work in one of the most important chapels of the lay worshippers' section in the same months that Giovan Pietro and Aurelio Luini were reopening their family workshop in the church where their father Bernardino had left such ample evidence of his artistry. Callisto Piazza had studied in Brescia under Romanino and Moretto, and by the time he returned to Lodi, in 1530, his interests had turned to the current models from Rome and the work of Pordenone, as can be seen at the sanctuary of the Incoronata in Lodi (1534–38), where festoons and sturdy putti stand out in the vigorous decoration.

In 1542, he began his Milanese career with the altarpiece of *St Jerome* in Santa Maria presso San Celso. Here, he abandoned the stylistic accentuation of his Lodi period in favour of a style that would characterize his later Milanese years, one based on the models of Gaudenzio Ferrari, but filtered through Leonardo so as to neutralize the grandiloquence of Gaudenzio through his own learned and contained interest in naturalism.

The calm, temperate manner of the Lodi painter together with a certain gentleness, similar also to the work of Bernardino Lanino, proved to be particularly fortuitous, earning him important religious commissions in Milan. He painted a fresco, the *Marriage at Cana,* for the Cistercians in the refectory of Sant'Ambrogio, and a *Madonna between Two Saints and Monks* in the cloister of the abbey at Chiaravalle.[1] Still unpublished, and belonging to Piazza's Milanese period, are the fresco decoration of the second altar on the right of the abbatial church of the Umiliati at Viboldone, and a small oil painting in the church of San Lorenzo in Milan representing the *Pietà of Christ*, the colourism of which is reminiscent of Moretto and Brescia.

On his arrival from Lodi, Piazza became part of that circle of non-Milanese artists, together with Gaudenzio Ferrari and the Cremona painters, who were receiving important commissions from the noble families of Milan. "On the other hand, its centralized power and role as the administrative capital had brought an increasing number of artists to Milan from the rest of Lombardy, but this was also a consequence of the diminishing prestige and autonomy of the other cities in that state."[2] What is more, such an exodus marked the decline of local schools in favour of a common style that was to unite the courts of Europe.

Once work had begun in the different sites, in the third quarter of the century almost all of the decoration was completed. Although the final result of the entire church decoration (the lay and the convent halls) is unified in its general effect at first sight, it should be pointed out that the initial project called for the iconography to be related to the architectural plan and based on themes that conformed both to the liturgical and public functions of the church. This was not true for the second project which was not as rich in subject matter. In the middle of the century, the decoration was probably meant to prevail over an emphasis on the liturgical role or an exaltation of the architecture, unlike the first project in which these were considered differently. The expansion of the Milanese nobility, both in number and increased power, during the era of Charles V, resulted in an increase in the number of commissions for the pictorial works in the church of San Maurizio. These were divided into a series of fresco cycles corresponding to each chapel commission. The various decorative undertakings were no longer the appanage of the Bentivoglio family, but were distributed among a group of families who were related, on the other hand, more or less directly to the Bentivoglio family; a situation that reflected the changing political and cultural climate.

The decoration of the Cappella Simonetta (the second on the right) was commissioned by Monsignor Bernardino Simonetta — a former bishop of Perugia, cousin of Ippolita Sforza Bentivoglio and nephew of the Sforza ducal secretary Cicco Simonetta — who was buried in San Maurizio in 1550. The entire chapel decoration, including the frescoes (*St James and St Lawrence* on the left, *St George and the Dragon* on the right, and in the upper lunette, *St Francis*, with festoons and trophies), stuccoes and a painting on canvas in the centre representing the *Deposition of Christ*, was executed by Callisto Piazza and his son Fulvio. The two marble tablets inserted in the pilaster strips on the sides of the chapel bear information relative to the donor and the execution date of the fresco: MDLV.[3] By 1555, Callisto Piazza of Lodi occupied a position of particular prestige. Set against the background of contemporary Milanese culture, he represented a new departure; one that envisaged a broader reality, more varied and vibrant than the Luini brothers' workshop had ever been.

Thoroughly versed in Venetian painting, he had distinguished himself in Milan with a series of large paintings, mentioned above, in which he qualified himself by his rich colourism, a talent for fluent narration (probably owing to his training at Romanino's workshop in Brescia), a mastery of Renaissance drawing and a dexterity in the realization of festoons and putti, as well as an awareness of the innovations that Giulio Romano had brought to northern Italy.

The Lodi painter received the commission for the paintings in San Maurizio the same year that he was working in the nearby monastery of Sant'Ambrogio (today the Aula Magna of the Università Cattolica). His work for the Benedictine nuns was distinguished in general by the presence of motifs that had already been tried and tested for a decade after the Incoronata of Lodi, and which were widely used due to the circulation of preliminary drawings.

He decorated the bases of the two pilaster strips with the busts of virile figures and putti with festoons, heads, armour and animals; the frieze and cornice with a lively procession of putti, and on the arch — aided by his son and workshop assistants — two prophets. The *St Francis* in the lunette inside the chapel, rich in chromatic subtleties and characterized by a careful rendering of the details, was probably executed with the help of a preparatory drawing that is now visible under the layer of flaking colour. The saints painted on the side walls — in particular, *St George* on the right — are reminiscent, albeit they are slightly clumsy and repetitious, of models that Piazza had abandoned some ten years before,[4] which leads one to think that they may be the work of his son Fulvio. The latter was probably also responsible for part of the centre painting of the *Deposition*, although the composition seems to be the work of Callisto. Even though it is in a ruined state and some missing sections have been repainted, one notes a particular modernity in this painting, and the presence of themes that would emerge a few years later, with the Reformation of the Catholic Church. While the naturalistic details, rendered with great attention, are reminiscent, on the one hand, of the painter's early training in Brescia,[5] they are an anticipation, on the other hand, of the imminent renewal of painting during the Counter-Reformation.

It should be noted that perhaps for the first time there is evidence in this cycle of a certain autonomy on the part of Fulvio, whose presence at his father's side seems to have been documented for the first time in a letter[6] written by Callisto in 1554 to the vestrymen of Santa Maria presso San Celso (although it is very likely that his activity in the workshop began much earlier).[7] In his work at San Maurizio, Fulvio displayed all the qualities of a good workshop assistant in following his father's drawings and cartoons. His workmanship is explicitly revealed in some formal characteristics, namely, the round, expressionless faces that are usually found in his œuvre. A variation of the *Deposition* of San Maurizio exists in the parish church of Pandino, as M. Marubbi has pointed out,[8] which was signed by Callisto, but probably executed for the most part by Fulvio according to his father's cartoons.[9]

From Piazza's workshop also came the varicoloured, animated fresco of the *Marriage at Cana,* which was executed in 1565 for the Abbess Donna Maura Taverna in the centre of the upper part of the partition wall between the *Adoration of the Magi* (on the left) and the *Baptism of Christ* (on the right), painted by Aurelio and Giovan Pietro Luini. This representation of the *Marriage at Cana*, which has been attributed to Callisto Piazza,[10] appears to be a "clumsy remake" — to quote G. Bora[11] — of an analogous composition by the same painter in the refectory of Sant'Ambrogio (1545). Its lack of intensity, in fact, would suggest that his son Fulvio,[12] or some anonymous painter in the Piazza workshop, had intervened here as well.

[1] G. Bora, "La cultura figurativa a Milano 1535–1565", in *Omaggio a Tiziano. La cultura artistica milanese nell'età di Carlo V*, exhibition catalogue, Milan 1977, p. 48.
[2] Ibid.
[3] Confirmation of the date of the chapel decoration is to be found in the document *Legato per messe fatto da mons. Simonetta vescovo perusino*, of 1555 (Archivio di Stato di Milano, *Religione p.a.* 2147, *Compre, spese...*).
[4] G. Bora, "I Piazza e la fortuna della 'maniera'", in *I Piazza da Lodi. Una tradizione di pittori nel Cinquecento*, exhibition catalogue, Lodi 1989, p. 255; M. Marubbi, "L'officina dei Piazza fra comprimari e presenze esterne", in *I Piazza da Lodi*, p. 325.
[5] Bora, "I Piazza e la fortuna della 'maniera'", p. 257.
[6] The letter, part of the San Celso papers, is to be found in the Archivio della Curia Arcivescovile of Milan. It was published by Marubbi in "L'officina dei Piazza", p. 376.
[7] Ibid., p. 335.
[8] Ibid.
[9] The attribution to Fulvio was expressed for the first time by Marubbi, while previous criticism tended towards Callisto (M.L. Ferrari, "Calisto de la Piaza", in *Paragone*, 185, 1965, p. 40; G.C. Sciolla, "L'arte dei Piazza", in A. Novasconi, *I Piazza*, Lodi 1971, p. 28.)
[10] A. Ottino Della Chiesa, *San Maurizio al Monastero Maggiore*, with historical notes by P. Reina, Milan 1962, p. 62.
[11] Bora, in *I Piazza*, p. 261, note 24.
[12] G.B. Sannazzaro, *San Maurizio al Monastero Maggiore*, 2nd ed., Milan 1992, p. 59.

The Sons of Bernardino Luini

Valerio Guazzoni

After an interval of some considerable length, work on the decorative programme of San Maurizio was resumed in the mid-1550s, once again under commission from the ramified Bentivoglio family, one of the Milanese aristocracy's foremost noble houses, which, like those of the Bergamini and Simonetta, was closely tied to the power of the Sforza, by then on the wane.

The new phase of decoration largely involved the lateral chapels in the lay worshippers' hall, continuing a comprehensive programme initiated in the 1520s by Bernardino Luini with the Cappella Besozzi (last but one, right), that proceeded in the mid-1540s with the frescoes for the two Carreto chapels dedicated respectively to St Stephen and St John the Baptist (second and third, left). Also dating to the new phase of commissions — this time contracted by Mother Maura Taverna — was the resumption of fresco work on the wall separating the two sections of the church, which had until then only reached as far as the large arched platform on the convent section. Dating to the year 1556 is the fresco attributed to Fulvio Piazza depicting the *Marriage at Cana*, executed concurrently with the painting of the doors of the Giacomo Antegnati organ by the artist Francesco de' Medici da Seregno.

The fresco cycle for the chapels of the Bergamini and Simonetta families ushered in a new phase of decoration to San Maurizio that witnessed new stylistic characteristics which, while faithfully adhering to the existing pictorial cycles carried out over several decades as part of a programme initiated by Luini himself, testified to sweeping changes under way and denoted a marked departure from Luini's idiom. That change of direction is not discernible in the Carreto chapels, whose decoration was effected by less accomplished exponents of a style that was both dated and, for the most part, derivative. While it is hardly surprising to find evidence of this new direction in the Cappella Simonetta frescoes by Callisto Piazza and followers — that is, by painters of a different background and quite foreign to Milanese tradition — one cannot say the same for the Cappella Bergamini, painted by Luini's sons Giovan Pietro and Aurelio, who continued to contribute to the church's cycles at various stages thereafter. Although their work may be associated with a heritage that was amply acknowledged by their patrons, the two artists soon began to show signs of independence, and quickly assimilated outside stimuli into their work, each one striving to innovate his art which, though expressed in separate ways, resulted in a personal and often original idiom in line with the advances then under way in contemporary painting in Lombardy.

It is curious to note how the two artists' work in San Maurizio, now considered a crucial document of their joint labours, has been completely overlooked by past scholars of art, and that their appreciation is a relatively recent development, initiated by Gaetano Mongeri[1] and only really established with studies of more recent date, particularly those of Giulio Bora.[2] To attribute the entirety of the pictorial works to Bernardino alone (as Carlo Torre[3] had specified: "da Bernardino Lovini venne tutta dipinta a tempera", i.e., all was painted in tempera by Bernardino Luini), the early commentaries had entirely overlooked the role of his sons, whose activity in other churches in Milan is nonetheless amply documented. It was not until Francesco Pirovano's guide of 1822 that Aurelio received his first mention, though mistakenly assigned the authorship of the frescoes in the Cappella di Santo Stefano, undoubtedly by another artist; also mentioned is Aurelio's pupil Pietro Gnocchi, allegedly at work in the convent hall.[4] Even the first printed *Cenni* devoted to the monastery church mention Aurelio as the likely author of the frescoes in the "tribuna superiore" (the convent section of the dividing wall), and posit Pietro Gnocchi once more for other unspecified works.[5] Finally, on the basis of a contract for lodgings in 1555 which referred only to his being present (published by Achille Ratti[6] in 1895), in 1872 Mongeri acknowledged Aurelio and Giovan Pietro as authors of the frescoes in the Cappella Bergamini. In what can rightly be called the first critical commentary on the frescoes in the Monastero Maggiore, Mongeri went a step further and identified the brothers' handiwork elsewhere in the church, namely, in the decoration of the entrance wall of the convent section, and the hand of Aurelio alone in the *Adoration of the Magi* and the *Baptism of Christ* on the dividing wall.

Mongeri's opinion of the two brothers' level of competence was severe, even disparaging, accusing them of being engaged in a "gara miseranda" (pitiful contest) and even guilty of an "opera indegna" (ignoble workmanship), as evinced by the *Marriage at Cana*, which successive studies would later assign to another artist altogether.[7] Mongeri's censure inevitably stemmed from direct comparisons with the frescoes of Bernardino, and a trend for imputing painting from the later Cinquecento as involuted compared to the classical simplicity to which Luini was brilliant testimony in the first half of the century.

Over the years, the criticism first voiced by the Lombard scholar Mongeri and his limited assessment remained virtually unchallenged. Although to some extent this was attenuated by Adolfo Venturi in his profile of the two brothers (1934),[8] opinion remained unchanged at least up until the appearance of Angela Ottino Della Chiesa's monograph on San Maurizio (1962). While remaining generally critical and even berating Aurelio for "blatantly paying lip-service to a vision not his own [i.e., that of his father Bernardino], and turning to the Mannerists of Rome and Florence for his muscles, torsions and violent gesture",[9] the scholar did however prompt a wholesale revision of opinion on the two painters' roles, advancing new ideas, especially as regards the decoration of the two Bentivoglio chapels (last chapels on both left and right in the lay church), which Mongeri had attributed to Giovan Paolo Lomazzo and she now reassigned (though not without misgivings) to the Luini brothers' circle.[10] This was a new and significant step in the reappraisal of the brothers' contribution to San Maurizio, a contribution that was made clear in subsequent studies, starting with Giovanni Battista Sannazzaro's guide and Bora's commentaries up until the recent recapitulation published by Francesca Debolini.[11] In particular, Bora delved into the complexities of differentiating the input of the two brothers, ascertaining plausible distinctions in technique, and publishing drawings by Aurelio that confirm him as the more inventive and creative mind of the two, as part of a general reassessment of the artist's personality in the context of early Milanese Mannerism.

While the frescoes in the Cappella Bergamini (1555) are the first reliable evidence of their activity in San Maurizio, it must be said that, in the past, the handiwork of the two painters had been detected in the two Carreto chapels, frescoed some years earlier. The decoration of the second of these, entitled to St John the Baptist, dates from 1545, a fact validated by a gilded inscription on the wall overhead that also mentions the patrons, Marquis Alfonso Carreto of Finale and his brothers. The side walls carry frescoes depicting the *Naming of St John*, and the *Beheading of St John*; while the back wall is decorated with a *Baptism of Christ* and the vault with *Musician Angels*. Angela Ottino Della Chiesa correctly identified the author of the first two scenes, which evinced greater consistency in quality and narrative coherence, distinguishing them from the author of the *Baptism* and *Angels*, wich she imputed to a somewhat lame imitator of Luini identified as Giovan Pietro or the other brother, Evangelista.[12] While the attribution is not confirmed by the known characteristics of Giovan Pietro, the author may still be Evangelista, who in 1544 — one year earlier — is recorded as active in Genoa where he received payment for painting the armorial bearings on the Faro, the city lighthouse.[13]

In the preceding chapel dedicated to St Stephen, the left wall is dominated by a large *Portrait of Francesco Carreto*, knight of the Order of St John of Jerusalem, who is shown kneeling in offering and portrayed as an elderly man. The stone plaque commemorating his death in 1551, at the age of eighty-five,[14] suggests the portrait was made when he was already advanced in years, or even after his death, which would date the frescoes to around mid-century. For the same reasons the earlier attribution to Aurelio's pupil Pietro Gnocchi, advocated by Mongeri is also invalid, owing to the strange date MDCVIIII traced into the frame over the portrait; and equally negated is Pirovano's attribution to Aurelio, with whose work there are no perceivable parallels.[15] The somewhat makeshift execution of the painting on the back wall with the *Stoning of St Stephen*, evidently derived from Giulio Romano's altarpiece in Santo Stefano, Genoa, are the same traits detected in the *Baptism of Christ* and the *Angels* in the other chapel, and seem to my mind the work of a single painter, confirming the comparable figurative and decorative conception the chapels share. While the alleged links with the Genoa altarpiece favour the attribution to Evangelista Luini, documented as active in that city during the previous years (as noted above), the activity of this painter, who tended to work separately from his brothers, and largely as a decorator, requires further research in order to validate the supposition, albeit not in itself entirely unfounded. It is worth noting the qualities Lomazzo attributes to Evangelista in his *Trattato dell'arte de la pittura* in the chapter on "composizione dei fregi" (composition of ornament), where he relates the painter as a specialist in grotesques: "Skilled and capricious in their representations of entangled scrolls, shields, epitaphs, festoons and the like were Gio. Battista Bergamo and Evangelista Lovini, a rare talent in these and other parts".[16] Evident in both the vault and the walls of the Cappella di Santo Stefano is a certain emphasis on the elaborate and imaginative embellishment of the gilded pilaster strips framing the walls and the bands delimiting the vault, forming an intricate network of candelabra with inserts of grotesque faces, sphinxes and leering masks, and putti heads.

All the frescoes in this chapel, including the *Angels* in the vault's tondi, the *St Stephen Preaching* on the left, the *Portrait of Francesco Carreto* on the right, and perhaps the two *Angels* on the extrados of the entrance arch, are without doubt the work of a single artist whose dense chiaroscuro — together with a rather heavy definition of figures, inert and stiff drapery, but also a certain feeling for landscape of Luinesque derivation — can be detected likewise in the background of the *Baptism* of the adjacent Cappella di San Giovanni Battista. The artist's lack of invention — largely owing to his use of prints and drawings as models, and also the backdrop of the *Baptism* borrows from figures in the *Battle of Cascina* cartoon — epitomizes the stagnation of Milanese paintings observed in the 1550s by the painter-writer from Faenza, Giovanni Battista Armenini, who declared local artists to be "more interested in adorning themselves with fine garments and glistening armour than to take pen and brush in hand", and likewise averse to study, slow in operation, and too reliant on prints.[17]

As for the two *Stories from the Life of St John the Baptist* frescoed on the side walls of the third chapel, works that betray a more accomplished grasp of both form and expression ("these two small frescoes, so rapt and dry, busy at a pictorial level but weak in illustration"),[18] it is worth returning to an observation made by N. Forti Grazzini, based on observed similarities with the tapestries in Monza Cathedral, belonging to the circle of Biagio Arcimboldi and his son Giuseppe, whose possible connection is borne out by documents linking Biagio with the Luini, and particularly with Evangelista.[19]

While these observations would appear to endorse the attribution of the two Carreto chapels to Luini's eldest son (along with the two *Sibyls* frescoed outside the Cappella di San Giovanni Battista, which betrays an analogous stiffness in the drapery), further confirmation can be found in the likely propensity of the chapel's benefactors to choose Luini's heirs to complete an undertaking so closely associated with the name and prestige of the master, their father. If this were the case, then work on the church's decoration — suspended upon the death of Luini immediately after the Cappella Besozzi — may have been resumed in the mid-1540s by his son Evangelista, who nevertheless had to forego the family's exclusive rights to the church's frescoes, and found himself working in parallel with the "outsider" Callisto Piazza, commissioned to paint another chapel nearby.

Another factor linking the two Carreto chapels, is the insertion of the large portraits of the patrons (the figure of Zacharias intent on writing the Baptist's name in the first is in all probability Alfonso II Carreto, Marquis of Finale) as part of a grandiose homage to the family and its social status, in imitation of the nearby example of Alessandro and Ippolita Bentivoglio, who had had themselves portrayed by Bernardino Luini in the lunettes of the dividing wall in such a prominent position (visible from anywhere in the lay worshippers' hall) that even the rows of patron saints around them seem deferential in comparison. Similarly, Francesco Besozzi, Ippolita's uncle, was depicted at the foot of the column in *Christ at the Column* in his own chapel (1530).

Various inscriptions and documents enable us to untangle the complex braid of family ties that bound the Bentivoglio to the Carreto, the Simonetta and the Bergamini, that is, the families that spurred the reprise of the church's decorative programme. Together with his brothers, Marquis Alfonso II Carreto dedicated the family chapel entitled to St John the Baptist to the memory of their parents, and had himself depicted in the role of Zacharias; being the son of Giovanni and Ginevra Bentivoglio and hence the grandson of Alessandro Bentivoglio and his consort Ippolita Sforza; a more remote bloodline linked him to the other Carreto, Francesco, knight of the Order of St John of Jerusalem (depicted in the Cappella di Santo Stefano), cousin of his father Giovanni, Ippolita Sforza Bentivoglio, daughter of Bianca Simonetta was kinswoman moreover of Bishop Francesco Simonetta, buried in the family chapel, and of Countess Bona Bergamini, she too a Sforza (natural daughter of Ludovico il Moro), wife of Giovan Pietro Bergamini, Lord of San Giovanni in Croce (the names of both appear in the gilded inscription above the frescoes), and sister of Gian Paolo Sforza, who had married Violante Bentivoglio, another daughter of Alessandro and Ippolita.[20] Several decades after the decoration work was resumed, the Bentivoglio patronage of the lay worshippers' hall of San Maurizio, underscored by inscriptions and portraits, sanctioned the unitary strategy of their appropriation of the convent hall, though this was pursued with less conviction, owing to the growing control of the convent nuns over the subject matter and imagery allowed in their hall.

It is perhaps no accident that among the chapels frescoed in 1555 there are no further portraits. This seems to reflect the careful reassessment of the role of the commissioning patrons in light of the dawning historical and religious climate. By implication, the concerted effort to deliver a more specifically devotional message through subject matter must have also meant a diminution of the profane and gentile contents, as can be noticed in the first chapel on the left, entirely devoted to the Resurrection. This was commissioned on 6 May 1555 from the Luini brothers, not directly by the heirs of the chapel's patron Countess Bona Bergamini, but through the then abbess of the Monastero Maggiore, Gerolama Brivio, the same nun who was behind the commission for the new church organ, and to whom we owe the renewed activity on the church's pictorial works around 1555. The said contract outlines a precise programme of iconography which comprised six pendentives in the access archway ("from the architrave down"), two Sibyls; whereas "under the vault a dove with his golden rays outspread" and other ornaments in gold leaf both in the architrave and the imposts of the vault, together with "foliage and festoons and other appropriate features". On the wall above the altar they requested "a risen Christ and the three thieves at the tomb", while on the side walls, respectively "when Mary Magdalene finds our Lord dressed as a gardener" and "our Lord dressed as a pilgrim with the disciples on their way to Emmaus". To be painted alongside the central representation of the Mystery, with the Resurrection and guards at the tomb, the nuns commissioned two scenes of the resurrected Christ, respectively, one (left) appearing to Mary Magdalene, who mistakes him for a gardener; and one (right) disguised as a pilgrim appearing to the two disciples on their way to Emmaus. The contract entailed a fee of 60 golden *scudi*, and was signed by the two painters thus: "By my troth, this is written and signed in mine own hand. I, Pietro Lovino, confirm what is written herein. I, Aurelio, confirm what is written herein".

Applying his signature after that of his elder brother, when this contract was stipulated the twenty-five-year-old Aurelio was still perhaps a subordinate member of the Luini workshop. He was born around 1530, the fourth in line of Bernardino's children Tobia, Evangelista, and Giovan Pietro. His date of birth appears on the tomb slab formerly lodged in the church of San Gerolamo (1593), which states him dead at the age of sixty-three; and on his death certificate of 6 August 1593 ("Aurelius Lovinus annorum 63 vel circa ex febre longa obiit post menses quattuor").[21] A deed of 1534 declares him still an "infant" and resident with his family in the parish of San Marcellino.[22] While the birth-dates of his brothers are not documented, according to Beltrami Aurelio's brother Evangelista, who collected a debt left by his father in Lugano, was born around 1512, but in 1534 he had not yet come of age.[23]

Equally uncertain are the dates for Giovan Pietro, born perhaps in 1520 and active until the early 1580s (in 1581 he took part in the decoration of the new oratory of Luogo Pio di Santa Corona, Milan).[24] Documents testify to his working alongside Aurelio in partnership from

1555, the year of the contract for the Cappella Bergamini. A conflict of interests may have caused the two younger brothers to separate from Evangelista. As seen from a notarial deed of slightly earlier, in 1554 the latter, backed by Biagio Arcimboldi, was involved in a court case with his kinsmen, who had since moved from San Marcellino to the parish of San Pietro alla Vigna.[25]

In one of his *Rime* dedicated to Bernardino Luini ("Di Bernardino Lovino"), the painter-poet Giovan Paolo Lomazzo pays homage to the three brothers, from which one can infer the particular esteem Luini's sons enjoyed among Milanese painters, and the undisputed superiority of Aurelio: "Et à questa meta corre / Ciascun de i tre vostri figliuoli, trà quali / Evangelista e Pietro sono uguali / Nel pinger; ma più vali / Tu Aurelio, la cui mente più alto aspira, / Come per l'opere tue si vede e mira. / Oltre ch'in dolce lira / Dolce canti i pensier e i tuoi disegni, / Dispiegandogli in versi ornati e degni. / E perch'ognun vi insegni / Tutti tré siete di pel biondo e vago, / Qual fu del vostro genitor l'imago".[26] Lomazzo's references to Aurelio, who he claimed was the bastard son of Bernardino,[27] are numerous, and all endorse the artist's stature in each of his fields of activity — painting, anatomy, music, poetry — in line with the author's own ideal of what the cultivated artist should be. Lomazzo's admiration was based on a personal acquaintance with the painter at the Accademia della Val di Blenio (of which Lomazzo was director), which Luini had joined with the byname of "Compà Slureligl Lovign", then at the peak of his activity in San Maurizio.[28]

Too young to be direct pupils of their father, it is not easy to determine what sort of training Giovan Pietro and Aurelio received, but when they began working at San Maurizio they must have already been experienced painters, and sufficiently skilled to meet the church patrons' requirement to continue the cycles initiated by their father Bernardino. As for the work commissioned for the Cappella Bergamini, the patron's brief was to be followed to the letter: the emphasis was to be on the Resurrection, pictured through three moments or stations devised to educe meditation in the worshipper. The fresco on the wall over the altar is dominated by a large, severely iconic and statuesque representation of the risen Christ ascending victoriously from the sepulchre, one hand raised in blessing and in the other a standard, emerging amid the guards who start at the apparition, unsheathing their swords or staggering backwards, while in the broad landscape the presence of two pious ladies offers a counterweight to the commotion in the foreground. The guards — five instead of the three cited in the contract[29] — are particularly in evidence, whereas only two of the three intended ladies can be seen on their way to the sepulchre. The missing third lady, Mary Magdalene, is instead featured in the episode relating the *Noli me tangere* frescoed on the left wall, indicative of the patrons' concern (of which Bernardino was also apprised) to avoid creating discord between the two gospels of Luke and John. Central to female spirituality and the devotional rites of the convent, the theme of Christ's apparition to Mary Magdalene had already been undertaken by Bernardino in the convent section. In that case too, the saint was featured in the foreground to denote her privilege in receiving the Saviour's greeting, with the two other pious ladies distanced in the background. On the opposite wall the scene of the pilgrims journeying to Emmaus, in which the grouping in the foreground complies with a scheme amply reproduced in prints and drawings,[30] is paired with a miniature background representation of the journey's sequel, namely, the supper itself.

As pointed out earlier, it is symptomatic that one of the most significant testaments of Milanese painting during the critical period of alignment with the Mannerist currents in mid-century came under severe, restrictive criticism, levelled particularly at the large *Resurrection*. The work encapsulates a phase of transition and the pass to which the two painters involved had now come, vacillating as it were between their yearning for new forms of expression and a recalcitrant attraction to tradition. While the basics of the arrangement may stem, as F. Debolini has rightly observed, from Albrecht Dürer's engraving of the *Great Passion*,[31] it is primarily the figure of Christ that harks back to the past, foremost in its stark Bramantesque frontal vision and a sinuous anatomical construction greatly indebted to Bramante's *Argus* fresco, while the minute but withheld chiaroscuro sculpting of the forms has parallels with the contemporary solutions by Gerolamo Figino. The rapt stillness of the figure is offset, albeit not entirely successfully, by the animation of the guards, presented with marked foreshortening and a forceful Mannerist antithesis that was out of keeping with Milanese tradition, but which artists like Bernardino Gatti had already been experimenting with for some time, thereby acquainting Lombard art circles with its novel characteristics. In this respect Gatti's *Resurrection* (1529) on the entrance wall of Cremona Cathedral, probably known to the Luini, represents an important precedent. But the most stimulating source of comparison came from much closer quarters, from another painter at work in San Maurizio itself, the Lodi-born artist Callisto Piazza. Working in Milan, especially on the frescoes for the refectory of Sant'Ambrogio, since the late 1540s Piazza had been introducing new compositional vigour of Roman extraction that entailed the use of monumental layouts, a multiplicity of planes and foreshortening, a brilliant palette, and, above all, a more solid plasticity of forms that were still in part allusive of the school of Brescia, and of Moretto in particular.[32] The evident renewal of Luini's language that transpires in the Cappella Bergamini — notably in the group of guards and in the episodes recounted on the side walls, with their weighted plasticity and chromatic intensity (particularly in the *Noli me tangere*) — was in my view spurred by the artist's impulse to try and outdo his contender from Lodi. The body types themselves, echoing those characteristic of Piazza (for instance the figures of the guards on the right or the pilgrim on the left in the *Journey to Emmaus*), evince this decisive contact and a distinct phase in the two artists' development that signals their resolute departure from under the shadow of their father.

As for the sharing of tasks in the chapel's decoration, it seems without doubt that Aurelio was largely responsible for determining the new stylistic direction, while observing an almost equal division of duties. To judge from the payments for a following job, namely, the frescoes executed in 1578 for the church of Sant'Ippolito in Vigano Certosino, we learn that Aurelio had worked a total of 159 *giornate*, and Giovan Pietro 171, receiving equal daily pay.[33] This document, the only of its kind, implies that both tasks and earnings were shared between the two brothers, and that Aurelio's greater recompense did not dent a working relationship of many years' standing. Such was the basis upon which they assumed work on San Maurizio, and particularly in the Cappella Bergamini, where Aurelio's hand can be distinguished from that of his brother in the effects of a bolder plasticity and formal rendering, together with his trademark nervous painterly values. Bora has made a convincing argument for attributing the fresco of the *Resurrection* chiefly to Giovan Pietro (though Aurelio was doubtless responsible for the group of guards on the right), while the brother painted the *Noli me tangere* and the two graceful *Sibyls* (*Delphic* and *Cumana*) on the arch of the entrance, with their more concerted formal elaboration; to both artists are attributed the *Journey to Emmaus*,[34] in which Aurelio's workmanship can be detected at least in the figure on the left. At any event, Giovan Pietro may have completed the decoration of the vault in fictive stuccowork bordered by garlands of leaves and fruit (borrowed from Callisto Piazza's decorative repertoire), and the octagon at the centre, complete with the dove of the Holy Ghost cited in the contract.

Common to the three episodes is a landscape that recedes and dilates into the distance, particularly in the case of the *Resurrection*, creating a sense of visual continuity within the chapel; this feature is even more noticeable in the following chapels by the brothers, dedicated to St Stephen and St John the Baptist, both of which are painted with a similar landscape setting as part of the unified decorative scheme that corresponded closely to the style current among painters who trained in Milan when Luini was prominent,[35] and the kind of landscape that Bernardino left important examples of in San Maurizio itself.

Also set in a broad background landscape are the *Adoration of the Magi* and the *Baptism of Christ* frescoed on the convent side of the dividing wall in 1565. The date, which is inscribed in the medallion at the centre of the frieze of putti above the *Baptism*, provides the second reliable piece of evidence for the brothers' contribution to San Maurizio. The decoration of the upper part of the dividing wall was begun around ten years earlier in 1556, by a follower of Callisto Piazza, perhaps his own son Fulvio, who had frescoed the *Marriage at Cana* at the centre of the wall on commission from Mother Maura Taverna.[36] The pilasters flanking the central scene bear both the year and name of the patron, inscribed on fictive plaques hanging from ribbons. It must be excluded that the second date also refers to Aurelio's frescoes, as was once supposed, because both the pilasters and the frieze above the *Marriage at Cana*, painted with musician putti, ribbons and fruit garlands, are most likely the work of the same artist of the central scene, and are lacking the characteristic Luinesque traits evinced in the putti in the two lateral frieze sections. The commission from Mother Maura Taverna, a woman of high station whose name also crops up in the contract for the organ,[37] marked a new start to the decoration of the dividing wall, which had been left unfinished since the days of Bernardino's tenure, and followed a scheme that created — or, better, reiterated — the close parallels between this and the opposite side facing the lay congregation. The three large fields framed by pilasters correspond to the *Assumption* and episodes relative to St Maurice and St Sigismund which he had executed on the lay worshippers' side.

Ten years after their work on the Cappella Bergamini, the idiom of Aurelio and his brother shows evidence of change, a change that established itself as a truly original and clearly identifiable style acquired through a process of gradual evolution, whose successive stages can be followed in the pictorial works undertaken in that same decade, from the frescoes for San Vittore in Meda (1557) to those of the monastery of Cairate (1560), works which were actually signed by Aurelio alone. The painter's presence in San Vittore, the seat of a long-standing and authoritative Benedictine convent, is hardly a coincidence; in fact it confirms that he had been chosen by the order, which entrusted him with Milanese commissions not only for San Maurizio, but also for the monastic churches of Santa Maria Maddalena al Cerchio, Santa Caterina la Chiusa, and San Vincenzino.[38] In 1557 in Meda, the painter frescoed the second chapel on the right with a marbled ancona bearing the images of St George and St Roch, all emblazoned with sumptuous drapery held up by putti and elaborate decorative devices on the fiezes, the vault, and the pilasters at either side.[39] The sculptural, well-turned definition of the forms and the vibrant colours are once again reminiscent of the Cappella Bergamini, but the dense texturing of ornamental motifs — putti, ribbons, garlands of fruit, grotesques — accurately rendered in illusionistic relief, demonstrates a freshly acquired mastery of Mannerist repertoire; whereas in the figures of the saints, their noble, courteous mien suggests the influence of Gaudenzio Ferrari, but equally of the Veneto and Brescia schools. In that same church the artist would later paint (as surmised by F. Frangi) two large *Angels* — since removed and kept in the neighbouring Villa Antona Traversi — that once flanked an altarpiece by Antonio Campi, later substituted by the present one by Cerano.[40]

The apse frescoes of the Cairate monastery, which carry the signature of Aurelio alone (but could be another joint effort of the two brothers)[41], are an unequivocal statement of the swing toward Ferrari's realm of expression, not only in the "Piedmontese" type evinced in the Virgin of the *Assumption* (as noted by Frangi), but also in the freighted characterization, the almost earthy traits of the attendant Apostles, who are presented in a series of foreshortened poses and movements that derive from the later works of the said Ferrari and his circle. The cycle at Cairate denotes, furthermore, a renewal under way that is not entirely explained in the Mannerist monumentalism and fondness for coloured, minute narrative (as in the episodes alongside of the *Birth* and *Death of the Virgin*), nor in the expressive vivacity and more noble and sustained bearing of the figures.

In the two ensuing fresco commissions at the Monastero Maggiore, this awkward dialectic seems to be attenuated, and shows a prevalence for a narrative style of a more strict derivation from Ferrari that does not exclude — as testified by the luminous landscape of the *Baptism of Christ* — traits reminiscent of Luini himself. From the point of view of narrative technique, in the *Adoration of the Magi* one can sense echoes of the large fresco Bernardino did in the sanctuary of Saronno, particularly in the background populated with camels and other exotic animals, though more significant derivations from Ferrari can be inferred from the layout, which is particularly indebted to his *Adoration* in Santa Maria delle Grazie in Varallo, and in the great dignity of the figures, notably of the Virgin.[42] The more hallowed interpretation expressed in the general sumptuousness of the drapery tricked out with gold, of the jewels, and scimitars — visible in the picturesque entourage of the Magi, and the more overtly profane details such as the dwarf and tiger on a leash in the foreground — epitomizes the courtly aspirations and nostalgia for bygone feudal life, prevalent throughout Lombardy towards the end of the 1550s and early 1560s, hinting at, especially in the schools of Brescia and Bergamo, the imaginative variations on this theme explored by such painters as Giovan Battista Galeazzi, Luca Mombello, and Giovan Battista Moroni.

Notwithstanding Mongeri's correctly assigned the execution of the two frescoes to Aurelio, doubts over the attribution were still expressed by Ottino Della Chiesa, who advocated a painter of Lombard-Piedmont extraction for the *Adoration*, and Giovan Pietro working alone for the *Baptism*.[43] But while the stylistic variance from the previous Cappella Bergamini may seem considerable, the hand of Aurelio is unmistakable in the overall evenness of the choice of figure types and the narrative flair found in other works of the 1560s and 1570s.[44] This very consistency makes it difficult to ascertain whether he worked with his elder brother or not. While the possibility cannot be ruled out, his involvement may have been limited to marginal additions and is affected by a kind of stylistic osmosis that is not evident in his contributions elsewhere in San Maurizio.

Giovan Pietro's role in the *Scenes from the Passion* cycle frescoed on the apse wall in the convent hall, is a certainty — a cycle linked to that of Bernardino in the presbytery. The two works were in all likelihood completed in sequence, and offered the nuns a dual route through the mysteries of the Passion, Death, and Resurrection of Christ that involved the entire church. Instead of repeating themselves, the episodes are closely interwoven, despite manifest swings in narrative rhythm and tone of expression. The style evolves from the type of serene unfolding of the sacred story represented by Bernardino's frescoes, with their cogent pauses testifying to the different climate of devotion of the early decades of the century and the devotional exhortations of such convent luminaries as Perpetua da Birago in her *Officium* (1522),[45] proceeding towards a new form of narrative that evolves along a rapid sequence of episodes coloured by a more superficially dramatic tone. This cycle comprises the *Deposition* on the left, and the corresponding lunette showing the *Flagellation*; in the central lunette, the *Last Supper*; on the right, the *Betrayal of Christ*, and in the lunette above, *Christ before Pilate*, together with the *Angels with Instruments of the Passion* featured outside the three arches. Also worth noting is a deliberate iconographic correspondence that runs throughout the church, from the *Last Supper* at the centre of the apse wall to the *Marriage at Cana* at the centre of the dividing wall — that is, the meal that foreshadows the institution of the Eucharist.[46]

Endowed with less inventive flair than his brother, Giovan Pietro tends to lean on more well-tried schemes and draws from the many prints then in circulation, as can be observed in the *Deposition*, easily the most archaizing of the cycle's episodes, and therefore the closest to his father Bernardino's models, whence the "neo-classic profiles" of the women and the lighter-toned palette employed. The layout derives from a popular engraving by Marcantonio Raimondi after a drawing by Raphael,[47] a work that had been widely used already in Lombardy and interpreted by Giovan Pietro in the halting, controlled forms that were his custom, quite different from the immediacy and animation that distinguish the work of Aurelio, for example in the *Flagellation* above. In this lunette (below which runs the legend A PLANTA PEDIS USQUE AD VERTICEM NON EST IN EO SANITAS, from Job 2:7), the graceful ease of the figures and the expressiveness of gesture (note the scourger wrenching Christ by his hair) are evidence without doubt of the younger brother, who was reinterpreting ideas from Michelangelo's Cappella Borgherini. In the *Last Supper* — which, while taking a distance from Leonardo's work of the same scene, is rich in minute observations that include details of the table and the polychrome patterns of the Turkish carpet — one can see the customary traits of Giovan Pietro at their best, namely, as Bora notes: "Greater attention in descriptive minutiae, particularly in the drawing of types, showing a foreknowledge of developments in Cremona and Lodi from the second to the fourth decade".[48] Bora, who moreover considered Giovan Pietro the author of the entire cycle (excluding the *Betrayal*), correctly linked the *Christ before Pilate* in the last lunette to a drawing in the Gabinetto Nazionale dei Disegni e delle Stampe in the Palazzo Farnesina, Rome, in which the draughtsmanship, albeit less cursive and animated, is not substantially different from that of Aurelio's.[49] There is a slightly Venetian slant to the way the light catches the drapery and armour in this episode, a feature observable in the frescoes in Meda, whence incidentally the inclusion of the little dog on the right. The *Betrayal* scene is patently more lively in tone, this undoubtedly the handiwork of Aurelio, and very close in handling to the frescoes in the dividing wall in terms of the types adopted and the open, vivid narrative tone. Despite its autonomy, the invention freely re-employs elements plucked from Callisto Piazza's version of the same scene at the Incoronata in Lodi, inserting the latter's motif of the thug slipping the noose over Christ's head, proof of an awareness of his fellow artist from Lodi, no less now than at the time of his work on the Cappella Bergamini.[50]

Like the one above, this cycle is also datable to the same years as the *Adoration* and the *Baptism*, close to 1565, and therefore coinciding with the resumption of work on the decorative programme in the convent hall of San Maurizio. It is at this juncture that Aurelio seems to break new ground, and an authentic, personal side to his creative persona comes to the surface, bringing with it renewed narrative strengths and even a vein of diversion

— doubtless a side-effect of the jocund atmosphere at the Accademia della Val della Blenio — enabling him to express himself more fully. The change of mood that is most evident in the decoration of the two chapels to the right and left of the apse wall, one dedicated to the Flood, the other, I believe, to the sacred rite of the Eucharist. These episodes, of lesser gravity as it were, form part of a fairly complex iconographic programme which, by means of select cross-references and interrelated ideas, encompasses the entire space of the convent hall. The various scenes dealing with the *Flood* are effectively linked with the fresco of the *Baptism of Christ*, on opposite walls at some distance from each other, the latter an Old Testament scene foreshadowing a theme central to the idea of salvation, namely, the institution of the rite of baptism, that is, cleansing of one's sins, as disclosed in St Peter's First Epistle General (3:20–21: "The long-suffering God waited in the days of Noah, while the ark was a preparing, wherein few, that is, eight souls were saved by water. The like figure whereunto even baptism doth also now save us"); The celebration of the Eucharist in the other chapel is evidently linked to the theme of the Magi's adoration of the Infant Jesus illustrated in the corresponding fresco on the dividing wall. As if wishing to bypass the complex requisites of his patrons, Aurelio here makes a parenthetical excursus that sets aside the cultivated idiom of the scriptures and adopts a simpler vocabulary that addresses the commoner's heart directly as it were, taking advantage of the inherent immediacy of visual art to reach his audience. Though a great admirer of Aurelio's artistic persona, of that very immediacy and commitment to his craft as a painter ("E gli atti con decoro dintornando, / Con rara anatomia, con stil profondo, / Di lumi, d'ombre e di riflessi, il fondo / De l'arte e col pennel dotto toccando"),[51] Lomazzo did not fail to see the gently eccentric and playful side to the painter's character, a spirit consonant with the alternative trends expressed in the Accademia della Val di Blenio, where free rein was given to linguistic experimentation, a freedom he had used uninhibitedly in his *Grotesques* and *Rabisch*;[52] it was also a side he praised in his *Idea del tempio della pittura*, by describing a lost work most emblematic of Aurelio's temperament, the fresco crammed with "a great quantity of figures" formely on the façade of the Luogo Pio della Misericordia near San Tommaso in Terra Amara, with God the Father descending amid angels "above the charity of those painted below, who variously proffer bread and wine, and all kinds of vegetables scattered about them, with cripples, dwarves, the blind and the infirm or otherwise enfeebled",[53] a work that on the one hand complied with the Counter-Reformation's appeal for charity to the sick and poor, and on the other gave vent to a more blatantly earthy, caricatural idiom that the painter may have assimilated from Milanese circles and from Leonardo's own works, borrowing from drawings of "deformed old peasant men and women laughing", around fifty of which — according to Lomazzo — Aurelio apparently kept in a *libricciolo*, a sort of scrapbook.[54]

The tale of the *Flood* unfolds on the three walls of the chapel in discrete episodes, respectively relating the *Arrival of the Animals in the Ark*, the *Flood* itself, and the *End of the Flood* — this last with the addition of the *Drunkenness of Noah*. The ranking of small figures and the broad landscape setting may be indebted to earlier works by Bernardino, such as the frescoes of the Villa della Pelucca in which the background is peopled with tiny figures and episodes dotted about the landscape (for example, in the episodes from Exodus with the killing of the firstborn), but affording a more immediate source were contemporary prints and engravings — particularly those originating in northern Europe — from which derive the same fantastic and fabulous reworking of Bible stories common to international Mannerism, owing to a rise in cultural interchange with northern artists, particular in Lombard spheres. For the fresco showing the animals entering the Ark, the most obvious source is an engraving by Jost Amman for a Bible published in 1565, from which the overall layout of the scene (reversed) was appropriated together with a faithful replica of Amman's Ark.[55] Cues of secondary importance — for instance for some of the pairs of animals — may derive from a print by Giulio Bonasone showing the animals leaving the Ark (1544), but the more likely source is the former etching, with which the artist was probably acquainted soon after its publication. With an air of nonchalance, the artist fondly explores the picturesque variety of animals and birds, but carries his curiosity over into the dramatic detailing of the figures drowning or fleeing to save themselves from the rising waters, or the corpses scattered over the ground after the flood recedes; at any event, the Ark itself looms large, resting either on a green plain or among the waves, or balanced improbably atop Mount Ararat. Quite alien to the context of the convent hall, these frescoes are reminiscent of the type of decoration painted in various palazzi across Lombardy, where the theme of the Flood was particularly popular in this period. The idea returns, for example, in a frieze in The Palazzo Grattaroli in Bergamo, curiously close in arrangement to the episode presented here of the animals entering the Ark; another can be seen in the Palazzo Zurla in Crema by an unknown painter, tentatively attributed to Aurelio Busso.[56]

The other small chapel adjacent to the apse wall presents a decoration that admits no easy interpretation. The end wall carries a fresco of an altar with lighted candles flanked by cherubs drawing back heavy brocade drapes (a motif also found in San Vittore in Meda), while the side walls boast a *Fall of Man* on the left, and a *Sacrifice of Isaac* on the right. The disobedience of Adam and Eve and the obedience of Abraham are obviously correlated, but the second episode with Abraham about to sacrifice his son was also used as a Eucharistic message, often inserted in cycles representing the Holy Sacrament, and hence to be seen in relation to the altar motif. In the fresco in question, this feature appears oddly empty, dominated by a sort of tabernacle of false marble, but to my mind originally containing a true receptacle of the Holy Spirit, namely, a pictorial representation of the ostensorium or chalice. The cult of the Eucharist, a subject much dealt with in Luini's decorations of the dividing wall (the four tabernacles painted on either side), corresponded closely to rites specific to the religious activity in the convent ("Incende me tui amoris igne ut te sciam amare digne veniens mane in corde meo" wrote Perpetua da Birago),[57] and had therefore found a place in this corner of the church, claiming vital links with the neighbouring *Scenes from the Passion*. In the side frescoes — of which the *Fall* is particularly well conserved — Aurelio makes no departures from the semi-profane narrative key noted in the other chapel, and in his representations of Adam and Eve tempted by the serpent (pictured at either side of the Tree of Knowledge in deference to Dürer's example) he lingers on the enchanted reaches of Eden, in the cypresses, the rose espaliers, and the marble pavilions in the background.

The dating of the two, facing Bentivoglio chapels in the lay worshippers' hall (last on right and left) poses various problems. However, it is likely that, at least in part, the execution came at a later date, perhaps around 1570 or immediately afterwards, and therefore represents the closing chapter of the Luini brothers' work in San Maurizio. Dating to 1572 is the stone slab laid in the convent hall in memory of Alessandro Bentivoglio, by his nephew Giovanni and his daughters Ginevra (marchioness of Finale), Francesca and Violante (nuns), and Alessandra — six times abbess of the convent.[58] It cannot be by chance that this gesture of reverence coincided with the completion of the two family chapels, each one emblazoned with armorial bearings (on the pilasters), and wtih two commemorative plaques inserted above the arch, respectively in honour of Alessandro (1532) and of his nephew Giovanni (1531). The tone of the frescoes reflects the predominant Counter-Reformational idiom oriented to the theme of the Passion, and may have been occasioned by a visit to the monastery by St Charles Borromeo in 1569, and by the general tightening of monastic practices through proscriptions and prohibitions of astonishing severity, including the confiscation of books and the imposition of reading of an extreme penitential nature, such as of which the treatises on the conversions of Luis de Granada and Serafino da Fermo are a cogent example.[59] But at least part of the fresco betrays echoes of an earlier period, and therefore suggests two distinct phases of work.

Decorating the central wall of the left chapel is a large fresco of the *Deposition*, a preparatory drawing of which Bora has noted in the Art Institute of Chicago,[60] whereas on the side walls appear various groups of *Apostles* faithfully borrowed from Leonardo's *Last Supper*, and on the vault a *Gloria with Putti* similar to the one frescoed in the Carthusian church of Vigano (1578). In the extrados two *Prophets* portrayed in complex contrasting poses and gestures hold a scroll with the inscription: MORTEM MORIENDO DESTRUXIT, VITAM RESURGENDO REPARAVIT (from the Easter *praefatio*). Some sketches on the reverse of the Chicago drawing closely resemble one of the figures in the fresco. The dilation of forms, the emphasis of expression, the dramatic accentuation evinced particularly in the *Deposition*, painstakingly organized around a scheme referable to the Roman school, suggest a different period, probably anterior to the frescoes executed in the convent hall. A hint of hardness and some patent archaisms — due to the substantial contribution of his brother Giovan Pietro — together with certain idiosyncratic characterizations (the swollen or emphatic faces of some, or the stark head-on poses of others), seem to make patent reference to the frescoes at Cairate, and therefore belong close to 1560. That said, to a later date must belong work undertaken in the opposite chapel, which also carries a pair of *Prophets* on the outside wall (the inscription on the scroll reads: [VOS QUI] TRANSITIS P[ER] VIAM [ASPICITE ET VIDETE SI] EST DOLOR [SIC]UT DOLOR MEUS, taken from Lamentations 1:12), and inside three scenes from the Passion: an *Ecce Homo* on the right wall; a *Crowning with Thorns* on the left, and the *Christ Nailed to the Cross* in the lunette beneath the vault; added to these is a *Putto Drawing Back a Curtain* frescoed on the central wall, beside the door. In the decoration the fictive coffering of the vault contains landscape scenes with trees, ruins, and sfumato horizons, treated in the same luminous, transparent hues identified in autograph works by Aurelio, such as the *Noli me tangere* in the Cappella Bergamini, or the *Fall of Man*, evidence of the artist's keen interest in landscape noted by Lomazzo.[61] Aurelio's illusionistic skills are particularly remarkable in the *Putto*, one of his stock figures modelled on those of Campi (witness the *putti* of Giulio Campi at Santa Maria delle Grazie, Soncino), composed of soft pictorial strokes, the figure reveals the tighter control over form, a hallmark of his more mature work, and betrays certain precise affinities with *Rest on the Flight into Egypt* in the Gallarati Scotti collection in Arcore, a work that carries the date 1570, also drawn from Cremonese and Campesque models.[62] Whereas the *Christ Nailed to the Cross* alludes to the lunettes by Giovan Pietro in the section side of the church, a considerable contribution from Aurelio can be discerned in the side frescoes, whose distinctive features lie in his quest for new and animated compositional schemes, partially inspired by renowned models such as Titian's *Coronation*, formerly in Santa Maria delle Grazie, and in his realism accentuated by the foreshortening and a dynamic instability, the same found in the securely attributed frescoes by him in the church of Vigano, and particularly in the *Martyrdom of Sts Hippolytus and Concordia*.[63] For this reason the decoration of the second chapel for the Bentivoglio should be dated to the early 1570s — coinciding therefore with the last burst of work on San Maurizio's decorations and the commissions accorded to Semino and Peterzano — quite separately from the first chapel and especially from the *Deposition*. Like those in the Carthusian monastery in Vigano, this fresco marks a swing towards Mannerism in Aurelio's pictorial idiom, though not yet evincing the monumental manner typical of his later period that comprises the cycle in San Vincenzino, Milan, and the decorations of the apse of Santa Maria di Campagna in Pallanza, and the parish church of Trezzo.

[1] G. Mongeri, *L'arte in Milano. Note per servire di guida nella città*, Milan 1872, pp. 245, 248.

[2] For the two studies devoted specifically to the contributions of Aurelio and Giovan Pietro in the church of San Maurizio, see: G. Bora, "Da Leonardo all'Accademia della Val di Blenio: Giovan Paolo Lomazzo, Aurelio Luini e i disegni degli Accademici", in *Raccolta Vinciana*, XXIII, 1989, pp. 73–101; "Tradizione luinesca da San Vittore a Meda a San Maurizio al Monastero Maggiore", in *Raccolta Vinciana*, XXIV, 1992, pp. 155–179.

[3] C. Torre, *Il Ritratto di Milano*, Milan 1674, p. 212.

[4] F. Pirovano, *Milano nuovamente descritta*, Milan 1822, pp. 184–185.

[5] *Cenni intorno alla chiesa del Monastero Maggiore di Milano dedicata ai Santi Maurizio e Sigismondo ora sussidiaria a Santa Maria alla Porta*, Milan 1802 (2nd ed. Milan 1862), n.p.

[6] A. Ratti, "Del monaco cistercense don Ermete Bonomi milanese e delle sue opere", in *Archivio Storico Lombardo*, XXII, 1895, pp. 377–378. See also F. Malaguzzi Valeri, "Contributo alla storia artistica della chiesa di San Maurizio in Milano", in *Archivio Storico Lombardo*, XXXV, 1908, pp. 330–331. The document is in the Archivio di Stato di Milano (henceforth ASM), *Religione p.a.* 2147.

[7] Mongeri, *L'arte in Milano*; G.B. Sannazzaro, *San Maurizio al Monastero Maggiore*, Milan 1992, p. 59; S. Bandera, "I cicli pittorici", in *San Maurizio al Monastero Maggiore in Milano. Guida storico-artistica*, ed. C. Capponi, Milan 1998, p. 59.

[8] A. Venturi, *Storia dell'arte italiana*, IX, Milan 1934, part VII, pp. 503–531.

[9] A. Ottino Della Chiesa, *San Maurizio al Monastero Maggiore*, Milan 1962, p. 65.

[10] Ibid., pp. 77–79.

[11] F. Debolini, *La pittura manierista di Aurelio Luini*, specialist dissertation, Università degli Studi di Siena, 1995–96, pp. 21–49.

[12] Ottino Della Chiesa, *San Maurizio al Monastero Maggiore*, p. 69.

[13] L. Beltrami, *Luini 1512–1532. Materiale di studio*, Milan 1911, p. 604.

[14] V. Forcella, *Iscrizioni nelle chiese e negli altri edifici di Milano dal sec. XIII ai nostri giorni*, III, Milan 1890, p. 456, n. 601: FESSUS HIC TANDEM QUIESCIT / FR. IO. IACOBUS CARRETUS / CUI NEC GENTIS HONOR / NEC DECUS ORIS NEC HASTE / GLORIA DEFUIT SUB FABRITIO / PATRUO MAGNO MAGISTRO / MILITIE HIEROSOLIMITANE / MERUIT IN TURCAS / INDEFESSUS BELLATOR / PROMERITUS DUO RELLIGIONIS / BENEFICIA AGENS ANNUM / LXXXV MORITUR / MLAN. ANNO / M.D.L.I. / NONIS MAII / B. PINUS ALUMNUS. / B.M.P. ("World-weary here finally lies Francesco Giovanni Giacomo Carreto who lacked neither honourable lineage nor beauty of person nor the glory of command. Under [the command of] his uncle Fabrizio, grand master of the Order of St John of Jerusalem, indefatigable contender of the militant Turk, he valiantly attained two honours from the Order. He died aged 85 in Milan on 7 May 1551. His disciple B. Pino al benemerito pose.")

[15] Pirovano, *Milano nuovamente descritta*, p. 184; Ottino Della Chiesa,

San Maurizio al Monastero Maggiore, pp. 87–88; Sannazzaro, *San Maurizio*, p. 122, note 77; Bandera, "I cicli pittorici", pp. 68–69. As for the problem of the date MDCVIIII, we have to take into account that the neighbouring Cappella Bergamini likewise carries the incongruous date MDCVI, interpreted by Ottino Dalla Chiesa (*San Maurizio al Monastero Maggiore*, pp. 64–65) as a case of repainting, where the original date read MDLVI. It may even be that these dates were either inscribed or rewritten at the beginning of the seventeenth century.

[16] G.P. Lomazzo, *Trattato dell'arte de la pittura, scoltura ed architettura*, Milan 1584, ch. LXII, ed. G.P. Ciardi, *Gian Paolo Lomazzo. Scritti sulle arti*, II, Florence 1974, p. 366.

[17] G.B. Armenini, *De' veri precetti della pittura*, Ravenna 1586, ed. M. Gorreri, foreword by E. Castelnuovo, Turin 1988, p. 248. On the state of painting in Milan, see especially G. Bora, "Milano nell'età di Lomazzo e san Carlo. Riaffermazione e difficoltà di sopravvivenza di una cultura", in *Rabisch. Il grottesco nell'arte del Cinquecento. L'Accademia della Val di Blenio. Lomazzo e l'ambiente milanese*, exhibition catalogue (Lugano), Milan 1998, pp. 37–56.

[18] Ottino Della Chiesa, *San Maurizio al Monastero Maggiore*, p. 70.

[19] N. Forti Grazzini, "Gli arazzi", in *Monza. Il duomo e i suoi tesori*, Milan 1988, pp. 125, 133 (and also Sannazzaro, *San Maurizio*, pp. 111, 121, notes 71, 72). For a discussion of these documents, see R. Miller, "Note su Giuseppe Arcimboldo, Giuseppe Meda, Giovanni Battista Della Rovere detto il Fiammenghino ed altri pittori milanesi", in *Studi Monzesi*, 5, 1989, pp. 3–24, especially pp. 13–15. For more on the links between the Luini and the Arcimboldi, see also G. Berra, "Arcimboldi, le teste 'caricate' leonardesche e le 'grillerie' della Val di Blenio", in *Rabisch*, p. 61.

[20] I. Rossi, *La chiesa di San Maurizio in Milano. Il Monastero Maggiore e le sue due torri*, Milan 1914, pp. 70, 79–80, 83–86. The cited inscription in the Cappella Bergamini runs: BONA COMITISSA BERGAMINA CO. JO PETRI BERGAMINI UXOR MDCVI (Countess Bona Bergamini, wife of Count Giovan Pietro Bergamini) [for the date see note 15 above].

[21] Beltrami, *Luini 1512-1532*, p. 607; E. Motta, "Morti in Milano dal 1452 al 1552", in *Archivio Storico Lombardo*, XVIII, 1891, p. 243, note 1.

[22] ASM, *Notarile*, Bernardo Belloni, f. 7555, 9 November 1534. See Miller, "Note su Giuseppe Arcimboldo", p. 13.

[23] Ibid. (in 1534 only Tobia was of age). Beltrami, *Luini 1512–1532*, p. 603.

[24] P. Canetta, *Storia del Pio Istituto di S. Corona di Milano*, Milan 1883, pp. 16–17.

[25] ASM, *Notarile*, Gaspare Zavattari, f. 12915, 14 September 1554. See Miller, "Note su Giuseppe Arcimboldo", p. 13.

[26] G.P. Lomazzo, *Rime*, Milan 1587, p. 105.

[27] Lomazzo, *Trattato*, II, p. 200.

[28] See the dedication of Sonnet II, 35 of *Rabisch* (Milan 1589): *In ròd dor compà Slureligl Lovign dicc or Lovign* (G.P. Lomazzo and the Facchini of Val di Blenio, *Rabisch*, critical text and commentary by D. Isella, Turin 1993, p. 152).

[29] Five guards were also featured by Bernardino in his *Resurrection* frescoed on the convent side of the dividing wall.

[30] Debolini, *La pittura manierista di Aurelio Luini*, p. 25, links the composition to an engraving by Cornelis Cort.

[31] Ibid., p. 21.

[32] G. Bora, "Fra tradizione, maniera e classicismo riformato (1535–1595)", in *Pittura a Milano. Rinascimento e manierismo*, ed. M. Gregori, Milan 1998, p. 55; F. Rossi, "Il monastero di Sant'Ambrogio, i cistercensi e Callisto Piazza", in *I Piazza da Lodi. Una tradizione di pittori nel Cinquecento*, exhibition catalogue (Lodi), Milan 1989, pp. 293–301.

[33] Beltrami, *Luini 1512–1532,* p. 606.

[34] Bora, "Tradizione luinesca da San Vittore a Meda", pp. 170–173.

[35] On the diffusion of landscape painting in Milanese art of the time, see Bora, "Milano nell'età di Lomazzo", pp. 38–39; Idem, "La cultura figurativa a Milano, 1535–1565", in *Omaggio a Tiziano. La cultura artistica milanese nell'età di Carlo V*, exhibition catalogue, Milan 1977, pp. 49–50.

[36] Sannazzaro, *San Maurizio*, p. 59. Gandini (*Viaggi in Italia*, Cremona 1833, p. 199) attributed all the frescoes to Callisto Piazza.

[37] Malaguzzi Valeri, "Contributo alla storia artistica", pp. 332–333.

[38] Torre, *Il Ritratto di Milano*, pp. 132, 137, 225; A. Santagostino, *L'immortalità e gloria del pennello. Catalogo delle pitture insigni che stanno esposte al pubblico nella città di Milano*, Milan 1671, ed. M. Bona Castellotti, Milan 1980, pp. 37, 49–50; S. Latuada, *Descrizione di Milano*, Milan 1737, III, pp. 167–168; IV, pp. 48, 458–459.

[39] The first writer to mention Aurelio was Bora ("Un ciclo di affreschi, due artisti e una bottega a Santa Maria di Campagna a Pallanza", in *Arte lombarda*, 52, 1979, p. 92). F. Frangi, in *Pittura in Brianza e in Valsassina dall'alto medioevo al neoclassicismo*, ed. M. Gregori, Cinisello Balsamo 1993, pp. 43–44, 267–268, dated them to 1557, after a correct reading of the date inscribed by the painter (MDXXXXX7), formerly interpreted as 1587.

[40] G. Cirillo and G. Godi, *Contributi ad Antonio Campi*, Cremona 1982, pp. 28–29, and Frangi, *Pittura in Brianza*, p. 268.

[41] A possibility not ruled out by F. Frangi in *Pittura tra Ticino e Olona. Varese e la Lombardia nord-occidentale*, ed. M. Gregori, Cinisello Balsamo 1992, pp. 40, 264–265.

[42] See Debolini, *La pittura manierista di Aurelio Luini*, p. 54.

[43] Ottino Della Chiesa, *San Maurizio al Monastero Maggiore*, pp. 71, 76.

[44] As confirmed by Bora ("Un ciclo di affreschi", p. 92).

[45] *Officium hebdomadæ sanctæ Reverenda soror Perpetua de Birago Ordinis Sancti Benedicti Monasterij Majoris*, Milan 1522.

[46] Sannazzaro, *San Maurizio*, p. 72, nota 85.

[47] K. Oberhuber, *The Illustrated Bartsch. The Works of Marcantonio Raimondi and of His School*, vol. 26, New York 1978, p. 47. The print had been used, for example, by Bernardino Ricca for an altarpiece in San Pietro al Po in Cremona (1521).

[48] Bora, *Tradizione luinesca da San Vittore a Meda*, p. 167.

[49] Bora, "Da Leonardo all'Accademia della Val di Blenio", p. 91 (inv. F.C. 129580). Below the *Last Supper* runs an inscription thus: ELEGI VOSUT EDATIS ET BIBATIS SUPER MENSAM MEAM IN REGNO COELORUM (variant of Luke 22:30).

[50] As Debolini observed in *La pittura manierista di Aurelio Luini*, p. 48 (see also Bora in *Pittura a Milano. Rinascimento e manierismo*, p. 265, who stresses "the freighted dynamism and emphasis" of the composition). Over the fresco runs the incription: MORTE TURPISSIMA CONDEMNEMUS EUM (Book of Wisdom 2:20).

[51] Lomazzo and the Facchini of Val di Blenio, *Rabisch*, p. 152, vv. 5–8.

[52] For more on Aurelio's grotesques and caricatures see Bora's proposals in *Rabisch*, p. 182; Idem, "Da Leonardo all'Accademia della Val di Bregno", pp. 88–90.
[53] G.P. Lomazzo, *Idea del tempio della pittura*, Milan 1590, ed. G.P. Ciardi, *Gian Paolo Lomazzo, I*, p. 369.
[54] Lomazzo, *Trattato*, p. 315.
[55] *The Illustrated Bartsch. Jost Amman*, 20 (II), New York 1985, p. 249.
[56] B. Passamani, "Cristoforo Baschenis il Vecchio", in *I pittori bergamaschi dal XIII al XIX secolo. Il Cinquecento*, IV, Bergamo 1978, p. 66, fig. 4; G. Zucchelli, *Le ville storiche del Cremasco*, II, Crema 1998, p. 82. For a discussion of the Flood scenes, see especially S. Bandera, "Il recupero della Cappella del Diluvio", in *Terra Ambrosiana*, November-December 1995, p. 65; Bora, in *Pittura a Milano. Rinascimento e manierismo*, pp. 265–266.
[57] *Officium hebdomadae sanctae Reverenda soror Perpetua de Birago*, p. cxlv verso.
[58] Rossi, *La chiesa di San Maurizio in Milano*, pp. 119–120; Sannazzaro, *San Maurizio*, pp. 65–66, note 30.
[59] On the cardinal's visit to the monastery, see R. Beretta, "Il Monastero Maggiore di Milano e la riforma operatavi da san Carlo Borromeo il 23 febbraio 1568", in *Rivista storica benedettina*, XI, 1916, pp. 127–142; G. Palmieri, *Storia e storie del Monastero Maggiore di San Maurizio in Milano*, Milan 1996, pp. 33–40. Aurelio Luini ran into similar difficulties during the cardinal's bishopric, when he was termporarily forbidden from working as a painter (B. Besta, "Alcune notizie per una storia degli artisti milanesi del Seicento", in *Archivio Storico Lombardo*, LX, 1933, p. 451).
[60] Bora, "Tradizione luinesca da San Vittore a Meda", pp. 173–175.
[61] Lomazzo, *Trattato*, p. 409.
[62] G. Melzi d'Eril, "Opere del Rinascimento milanese nella Galleria Melzi", in *Arte lombarda*, XV, 1970, II, pp. 43–44, fig. 2; Idem, *La Galleria Melzi e il collezionismo milanese del tardo Settecento*, Milan 1973, pp. 108–109, pl. 26. The painting was in a Carthusian oratory in Porta Ticinese, Milan. Various documents cover Aurelio's relations with the Campi and the Cremona area in general. Early guidebooks on Milan relate that the painter had frescoed an *Adoration of the Magi* in Santa Caterina la Chiusa between two niches frescoed by Giulio Campi with *Sts Andrew and Bartholomew* (see Torre, *Il Ritratto di Milano*, p. 137). Besides having apparently collaborated with Antonio Campi in San Vittore, Meda, the painter was summoned in 1581 to San Colombano al Lambro to give his opinion of an altarpiece by Gervasio Gatti (F. Sacchi, *Notizie pittoriche cremonesi*, 1872, p. 201).
[63] For more on the Vigano frescoes, once believed lost but then rediscovered and discussed by Frangi (in *Pittura tra Ticino e Olona*, p. 263), see the detailed analysis by Debolini, *La pittura manierista*, pp. 72–84.
[64] For more on the frescoes in San Vincenzino, partly detached and divided up between the Pinacoteca di Brera and the Museo del Castello, see D. Pescarmona, in *Disegni lombardi del Cinque e Seicento della Pinacoteca di Brera e dell'Arcivescovado di Milano*, exhibition catalogue, Bologna 1986, pp. 53–55; M.T. Fiorio, in *Un museo da scoprire. Dipinti antichi della Pinacoteca del Castello Sforzesco*, exhibition catalogue, Milan 1993, p. 48; and the detailed catalogue entry by F. Cavalieri, in *Museo d'Arte Antica del Castello Sforzesco. Pinacoteca*, II, Milan 1999, pp. 100–104 (on the putti frieze reutilized by Cavenaghi for the decoration of the Palazzo Bagatti Valsecchi, see R. Pavoni, "I fregi parietali dipinti del palazzo Bagatti Valsecchi di Milano nella sistemazione dell'ultimo ventennio del XIX secolo", in *Studi di storia dell'arte*, Università di Genova, 1986–90, pp. 51, fig. 4, 59–60). On the fresco cycle in Pallanza, see Bora, "Un ciclo di affreschi". For the frescoes at Trezzo, executed in conjunction with Gnocchi, see G. Bora, "Aurelio Luini", in *Grafica del '500. 2. Milano e Cremona*, exhibition catalogue, Bergamo 1982, pp. 71–73, and G. Mulazzani, "Aurelio Luini a Trezzo d'Adda", in *Itinerari d'arte in Lombardia dal XIII al XX secolo. Scritti offerti a Maria Teresa Binaghi Olivari*, Milan 1998, pp. 207–216.

The Entrance Wall of Simone Peterzano

Maria Teresa Fiorio

Not much was written in the past about the frescoes on the entrance wall of San Maurizio — one of the last decorations executed in that church. Carlo Torre did not mention them, reserving his praise instead for the *Adoration of the Magi* by Antonio Campi,[1] nor did any of the other authors of the seventeenth- and eighteenth-century guides such as Santagostino, Biffi, Serviliano Latuada — another admirer of the painting on the high altar — Bartoli, and Bianconi, whose attention was constantly attracted to the most famous decoration of the church: that executed by Bernardino Luini on the partition and lateral walls of the Cappella Besozzi. At the most, some mention was made of Callisto Piazza, while the praise for Campi's canvas was untiringly repeated on the authority — one would say — of its more ancient admirers.

Nor did the pictorial cycle solicit comment during the nineteenth century. It was not until Gaetano Mongeri that the name of Peterzano finally appeared, but pronounced so cautiously as to lead one to believe that the reference to the Bergamo painter was insubstantial and had only been advanced as verification: "Unsigned works but clearly those of an imitator of Vecellio (Titian), as Simone Peterazano was and to whom, in fact, they are attributed".[2]

Such disinterest, which also transpired from the cursory definition of the painter as one of Titian's many followers, is not surprising: the document attesting to the very young Caravaggio's apprenticeship in the workshop of this neglected artist had not yet emerged. Starting in 1928, the year of Nikolaus Pevsner's[3] discovery, the critics suddenly began to take an active interest in Peterzano: studies proliferated and the artist was recognized in the panorama of late sixteenth-century Lombard painting, for that prestigious initiation if for nothing else. The investigations tended to be directed, according to Roberto Longhi's indications,[4] towards those characteristics that Caravaggio would later re-elaborate so brilliantly, individuating in the naturalistic inclinations of the artist those ideas on which the student would base his formation.

However, Longhi questioned Peterzano's apprenticeship at Titian's workshop; an experience that the painter was so proud of that he described himself as "Ticiani alumnus" ("student of Titian") not only when signing different works, but also when registering contracts.[5]

Although the illustrious scholar suspected that the artist was only boasting in order to create a more noble past for himself through an apprenticeship of that calibre, further studies proved his declaration to be correct. The presence of Peterzano's paintings in private Venetian collections,[6] mentioned in historical sources,[7] and above all the distinctly Venetian quality of his early Milanese works have by now dispelled Longhi's unjust suspicion.

For a long time it was impossible to accurately reconstruct Peterzano's early activity in Milan due to another equivocation regarding the *Deposition* now in San Fedele, Milan, but originally destined for the Cappella della Veronica in the church of Santa Maria della Scala which was demolished in 1776. The description that accompanied the painting at the exhibition *Caravaggio e i Caravaggeschi* in 1951 bore the artist's signature and the date 1591:[8] a date that had already aroused the suspicions

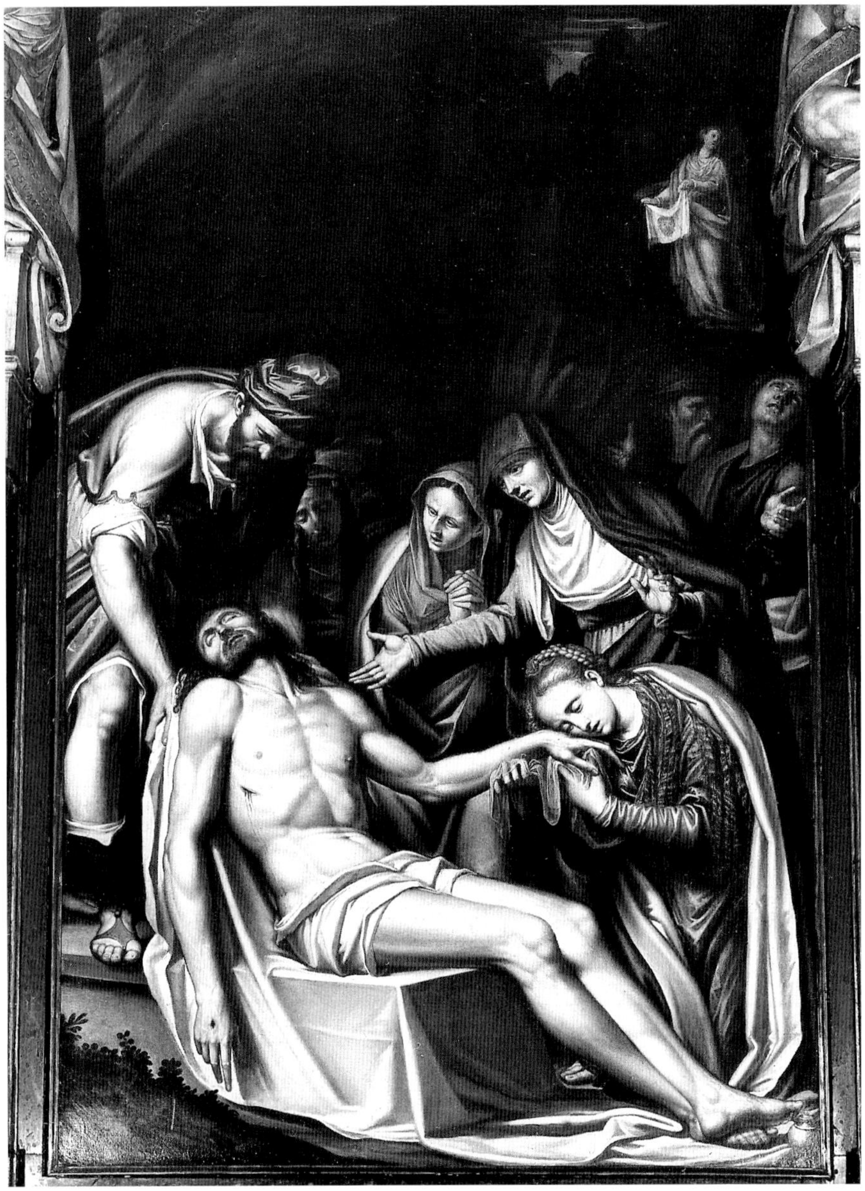

Simone Peterzano
Deposition
San Fedele, Milan

of Longhi and Costantino Baroni,[9] but which previous scholars had constantly cited. The guarantee of the exhibition confirmed the dating of the painting to Peterzano's later years, distancing it from the 1573 narrative cycle of San Barnaba, Milan, and placing it well after the frescoes of the Certosa of Garegnano. Thus the vibrant colourism, so typical of Veronese, of the *Deposition* seemed to be a return to youthful preferences, to a "Venetian-ess" after the turning point of his mature years during the period of the Counter-Reformation and Charles Borromeo.

The acceptance of such a late date for the San Fedele canvas capsized the entire chronology of Peterzano's activity: the San Maurizio frescoes were given the most disparate dates, fluctuating as much as fifteen years, since the documents regarding their payments had not yet been discovered.[10]

The restoration of the San Fedele painting in the early 1980s, has definitively excluded a date that has proven to be non-existent: Peterzano signed the painting, styling himself as a disciple of Titian, but he did not specify the year of execution.[11] The work could only be considered in light of the stylistic data which, however, were sufficiently eloquent in their Venetian character to place it in the early years of the artist's Milanese career. A comparison with the canvases painted by Peterzano in the presbytery of the church of San Barnaba — which can be dated 1573 according to a document of 1580 conserved in the parish archives[12] — indicates such a similarity in style as to consider it acceptable to date the San Fedele altarpiece to those same years. The impasto of colours, warm in tonalities and brilliant in harmony, is reminiscent of the rich colours of the two large compositions, while the important commission was indicative of the "foreign" painter's acceptance in the city. And that highly vaunted apprenticeship to Titian was perhaps relevant to such acknowledgement.

According to Longhi, the iconography of the San Fedele *Deposition* derived from Giovan Gerolamo Savoldo. At that time, such an interpretation was based on a reading of the artist in a pre-Caravaggesque key, one that later led critics to lay greater stress on the Lombard naturalistic elements which were present but certainly not exclusive. Textually, the composition is based on the great *Pietà* that Francesco Salviati painted for the church of the Corpus Domini in Venice about 1540.[13] The structure of Peterzano's painting is also organized on a diagonal which connects the three principal figures: Nicodemus, who stands on the tombstone, intent on supporting the weight of the lifeless body, the Christ, and Madeleine. Confirmation of this derivation is to be seen in a drawing by Salviati, today at the Uffizi,[14] where the theme of the abandoned body, with one foot over the other and the arms limp, according to the frequently imitated motif of Michelangelo, coincides to the letter with the Christ of Peterzano. This explicit reference to a Venetian painting is further confirmation of Peterzano's direct knowledge of it, and substantiates the painter's declarations about his apprenticeship to Titian. The Venetian environment must certainly have been very familiar to him, not only in regard to his probable maestro, but also in regard to his familiarity with Paris Bordon, Veronese, Tintoretto, and other foreigners — like Salviati — who were working in the lagoon.

The artist moved to Milan with this cultural background, ready to show off his experience in a city that years before had been attuned to what was new in Venice, welcoming a veritable cultural invasion from that city, and where a masterpiece by Titian — the *Crown of Thorns* — still dominated the altar of the Holy Crown in the church of Santa Maria delle Grazie. The suspicion arises that such a peremptory declaration of "Venetian-ess", pushed to the point of paraphrasing a composition that must have been well-known even outside of the Veneto region, may have been a way for Peterzano to introduce himself to the Milanese public. It was also a way to contrast with a local tradition that was dominated by the rivalry between the workshop of Bernardino Luini's children and that of Campi which was threatening the latter's position. In this light, it is possible to speculate that the San Fedele *Deposition* actually did represent the debut of the painter who had arrived in Milan ready to pick up the threads of the culture that had marked the reign of Charles V.

But even if the work was not Peterzano's first Milanese undertaking, there is no doubt that its execution was close to the date of 1573 given to the San Barnaba compositions. The previously mentioned document indicated that the two large canvases had been commissioned by Gian Giacomo Trivulzio, Count of Melzo, a sign that the artist's insertion in his new environment had been accepted at the highest level, that of the most exclusive aristocracy.

In those paintings, Peterzano took on the large dimen-

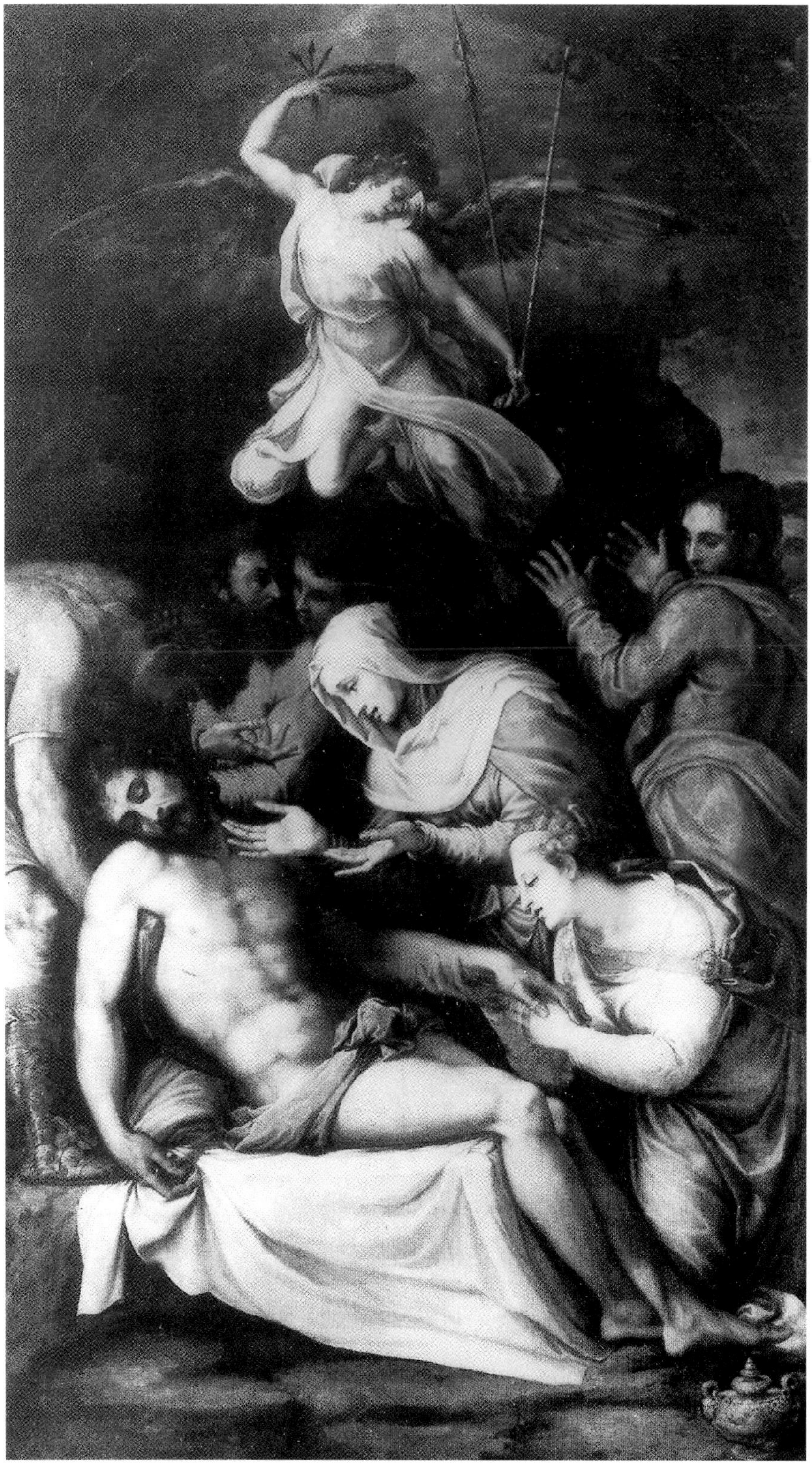

Francesco Salviati
Deposition
Pinacoteca di Brera, Milan

sion, setting the two scenes with a sure hand in vast landscapes where the figures, constructed according to the Mannerist forms of torsion and vivid contrasts, were characterized by an agitated expressivity. In the *Vocation of Sts Paul and Barnabas*, the painter staged a dramatic dialogue between the two saints, who are surrounded by a crowd, as the vortex of angels is broken by a sudden flash revealing the vision of the Holy Ghost. In the episode of *Sts Paul and Barnabas at Lystra*, the two protagonists balance each other in the centre of the scene, and dominate the multitude gathered to honour them as they harangue against the pagan sacrifices being made in their honour. Veronese's influence is evident in the brilliant palette where the colours are in sharp accord, while the composition is reminiscent of the great choral scenes of Tintoretto.

However, seeping through this complex scenic machine of Mannerist imprint are hints of the naturalistic, which Longhi interpreted as a return to Savoldo and the tradition of the Brescia hinterland to which Peterzano, who was originally from Bergamo, must have felt a particular affinity. And it is those very inserts depicting reality — the group of people on the left in the *Vocation* and, in the *Saints at Lystra* episode, the boy blowing on the fire, the other taking the flowers from the vase, and the old woman contemplating the young people's offer of flowers — that have been recognized as being the first revelations of a painting based on reality for Caravaggio.[15]

The San Maurizio frescoes were executed about the same time as the compositions of the church of San Barnaba, either just before them or parallel to them. Their chronology had disoriented the critics who were uncertain as to whether they were before or after the cycle of the Certosa of Garegnano which, according to the documents found by Costantino Baroni, made it possible to place them between 1578, the year in which the contract was stipulated, and 1582, the year in which the entire apse decoration was inspected.

Maurizio Calvesi[16] gave a later date, around 1591, to the entrance wall of San Maurizio, finding analogies there with the monochromes of the *Miracles of St Anthony* frescoed in the chapel of the same name at the Milanese church of Sant'Angelo. Calvesi justly excluded the traditional attribution of the entire cycle to Ottavio Semino in favour of Peterzano, and the exactness of the reference has been confirmed by some preliminary studies now conserved in the Castello Sforzesco Gabinetto dei Disegni, Milan. According to an extant memorial tablet still in loco, the chapel was built and dedicated in 1591, and the scholar has given that date to the San Maurizio paintings which are stylistically similar to those in Sant'Angelo.

Baroni, on the contrary, while taking into account both external data and linguistic factors, proposed a later dating. According to the documents, the construction of the church façade began in 1574, but it was not until 1579 that Antonio Campi painted the *Adoration of the Magi* for the high altar. The scholar argues that it was between those two dates that the entrance wall frescoes were executed, where "the Tintoretto-Veronese derivation is much more precise [with respect to the canvases in San Barnaba], even through the disastrous restorations, and leads back to the same Venetian environment".[17]

On the other hand, Baroni is responsible for the most lucid reconstruction of Peterzano's career. It had not escaped his eye, while he was studying the Garegnano frescoes, that the *Angels Bearing the Symbols of the Passion* in the segments of the dome showed no Venetian influence; and the precedent for the *Crucifixion* in the semi-dome of the apse was that which Giulio Campi had painted with "unusual leaden tones" in the vault of the Cappella Taverna alla Passione in 1560.[18] Baroni realized that the artist was present in a more severe form at Garegnano, limiting the seduction of colour and giving preference to a vigorous plasticism that was more in line with the northern interpretation of Michelangelo's Roman œuvre. Peterzano was, therefore, slowly moving away from his proudly vaunted Venetian training, so evident in the stylistic language of his earliest works, in order to assume those impeccable, accurate features that emerged in his production of the 1580s and 1590s.

Art historians have subsequently explained that this turning point reflected the climate of formal rigour that Archbishop Charles Borromeo had imposed in Milan in deference to the Tridentine principals, and which Peterzano conformed to from the time of the Certosa frescoes.[19] Baroni must also be given due credit for having distinguished with great clarity the initial "Venetian stage" from the successive one of the "Borromeo turning point". When he happened to come across that 1591 which had erroneously been ascribed to the *Deposition* at San Fedele, he revealed the incongruity more convincingly than Longhi. The fact that in 1596, in the last document regarding him, the painter was still being indicated as "de Titiani" (of Titian) was not sufficient enough evidence for him to accept "that date [...] which no one knows whence it comes".[20] Thus Peterzano's works in San Fedele, San Barnaba, and of course San Maurizio were grouped together and recognized by their Venetian stamp. While Angela Ottino Della Chiesa tended towards a later dating for the cycle at the Monastero Maggiore,[21] Mina Gregori argued that the decoration at Garegnano was not Peterzano's first attempt at wall painting, conjecturing other experiences. Although mentioned only cursorily, the frescoes at San Maurizio were identified as the precedents for those of the Certosa, and their date was ascribed to the mid-1570s, agreeing basically with that maintained by Baroni.[22]

All these uncertainties were finally dispelled when Giovanni Battista Sannazzaro discovered the documents relative to the payments made to Peterzano, the last of which — dated 22 August 1573 — constituted the full payment for the entrance wall decoration.[23] In addition to this fortuitous discovery, a more recent one has come to light: that of the contract for those same frescoes stipulated by Peterzano, in which the Milanese collector Gerolamo Legnani figures as the artist's guarantor.[24] The fact that Legnani was the painter's backer is very significant inasmuch as it demonstrates how well established Peterzano had become in a city that was new to him, indeed so much so that he was also well known to Lomazzo.

The frescoes are currently in a rather compromised state of conservation. Sixty years ago, Baroni spoke about "disastrous restorations", but the most serious problems have more recently been caused by the rising humidity that has seriously damaged the entire lower series of paintings. These are no longer legible today but may be partially recoverable by eliminating the salt. The others show traces of salt, previous restorations, a widespread loss of colour, and above all a general darkening of the pictorial surface that makes any appreciation of the original brilliant colourism of Venetian stamp quite difficult.

The narrative cycle is composed of four episodes painted on either side of the main portal. On the left, looking at the fresco, a lunette with *Isaac Blessing Jacob* is over the scene of the *Return of the Prodigal Son*; in the corresponding lunette on the right is *Moses Breaking the Tables of the Law*, and in the scene below the *Jesus Driving the Money-changers from the Temple*. There is no iconographic connection to the other decorative elements of that part of the church open to the faithful;

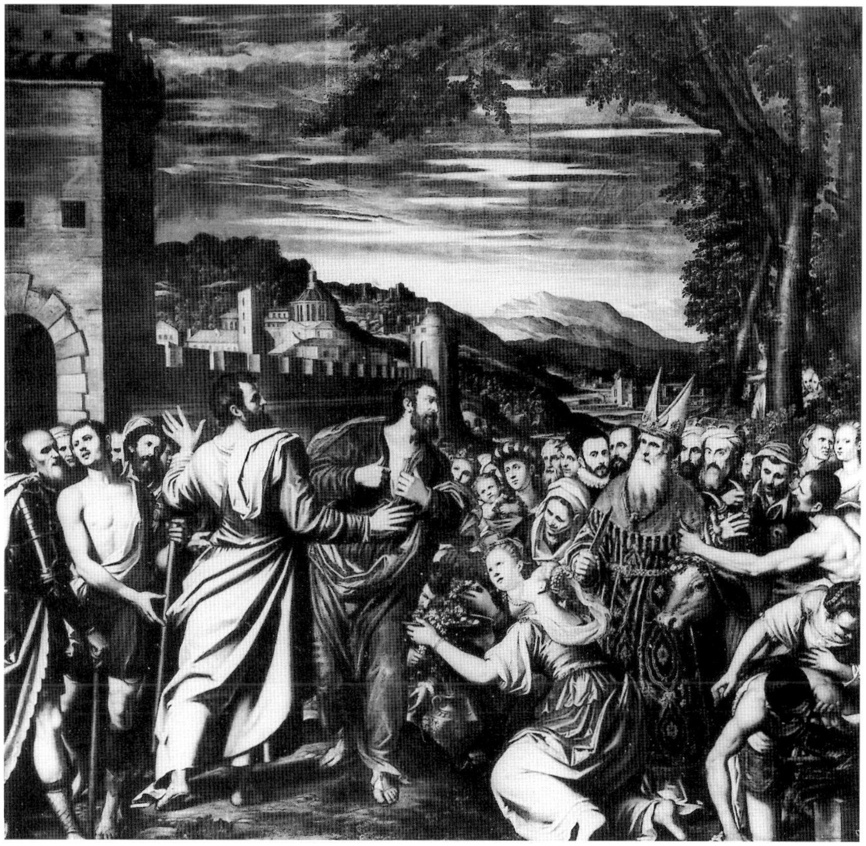

Simone Peterzano
Sts Paul and Barnabas at Lystra
San Barnaba, Milan

Simone Peterzano
Return of the Prodigal Son, detail
Entrance wall, San Maurizio, Milan

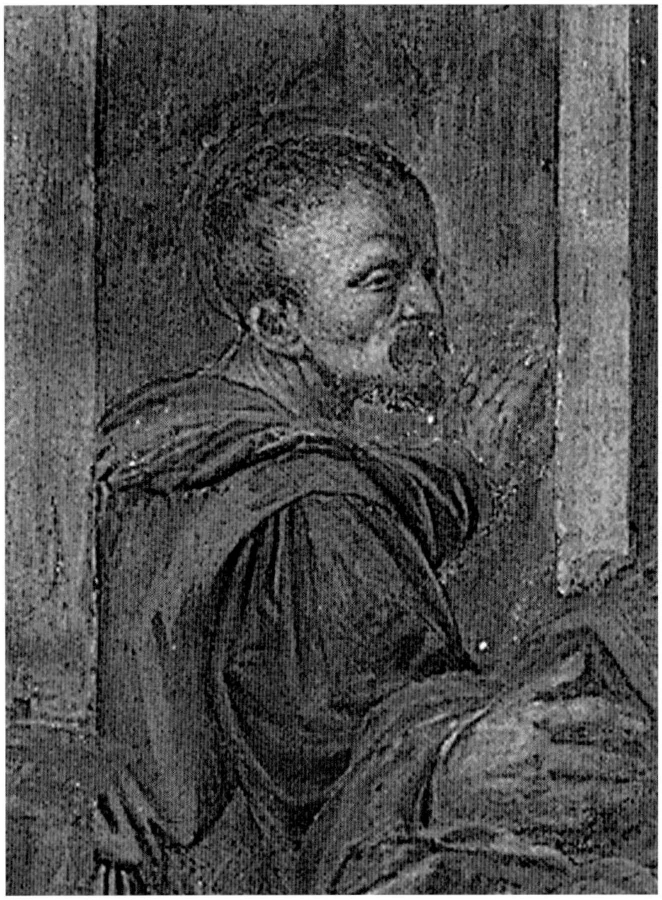

moreover, those who commissioned the different chapels had already suggested subjects that have nothing to do with one another. Here on the entrance wall, in a confrontation of the Old and New Testaments, filial devotion and paternal love are represented on one side, and anger against sacrilege and profanation on the other.
The scene of Jacob's blessing takes place in a bare domestic interior. Rebecca watches with affection as her favourite son obtains primogeniture, sanctioned by the gesture of the aged Isaac, ill and half-blind, who raises his hand to the head of his son kneeling at his bedside. In the background, beyond an arch, a male figure is running away: it is probably Jacob's brother Esau who is fleeing from his own humiliation. A few details suffice to create the atmosphere of this biblical episode: a simple still life on the table next to the bed, the protective, solemn gesture of the old man who places his hand on the young man's head while he blesses him with his other hand, the anxious participation of the mother. The unifying value of the light, something that the young Caravaggio most likely stopped to consider, emphasizes the intimacy of the scene.
Contrasting with the sobriety of the biblical episode is the dramatic excitement of the evangelical scene painted below it. Here, everything revolves around the central fulcrum of the father running to embrace his half-nude son. The bystanders comment his unexpected return and his father's pardon with eloquent gestures: one bolts in surprise, another points out the touching embrace to his neighbour, yet another interrupts what he is doing. As in the San Barnaba compositions, Peterzano creates an animated collective scene, knowledgeably structured against an architectural background of spacious loggias filled with people and minor events. It is a glimpse of life "in a villa", with servants laying the table, women carrying water, dogs, and everything else that makes up the comfortable life of a country gentleman. While the figures in the foreground are depicted with an incisive line and thick brushwork emphasizing their plasticity, in the background the touch is lighter and more rapid, yet always of impeccable technique.
Among the faces of the "extras", one in particular has attracted the attention of scholars. It is that of the man standing at the door of his house on the left who observes the encounter. This is a much more characterized face than the others, and must certainly portray a real person. At first it was thought to be a self-portrait of the artist,[25]

but the recent discovery of a painting that unequivocally represents Peterzano[26] makes this identification dubious. It is true that the self-portrait is dated 1589 when the artist was some sixteen years older, but the slightly bent profile of the man in the San Maurizio fresco with his hollow cheeks does not seem to correspond to the physiognomy that Peterzano has handed down of himself, although they do have the same cut of beard and moustache — slightly greying in the painting — and the same style of hair, albeit it is thicker in the fresco.

The recently discovered painting confirms, however, that Peterzano did portray himself in one of the San Barnaba canvases. He is standing behind the priest in the scene with the *Sts Paul and Barnabas at Lystra*, and can be distinguished from the crowd by his modern Spanish dress with a white ruff that stands out from the black of his outfit and hat.

In the corresponding lunette on the right, an enraged Moses grasps the tables of the Law, ready to hurl them to the ground at the sight of the Israelites in the act of worshipping the golden calf. Here, the constriction of space does not allow for a vast choral scene. The artist therefore brings the powerful figures of the patriarch and the person pointing to the encamped Israelites into the foreground, and opens the background onto the scene of the sacrificial banquet. And it is here that Peterzano displayed his extraordinary talent as a narrator, sketching rapidly and summarily with the tip of his brush the figures seated at the banquet table, those moving between the tents, and others gathering in groups. He seems to have fully assimilated the lesson of Tintoretto, that master in depicting distant scenes with flashes of colour.

Underneath in a studied chiasmic correspondence between the interiors and exteriors of the frescoes on the adjacent walls, the scene unfolds inside the temple. This is further confirmation of the ease with which Peterzano was able to create compositions filled with people and minor events, controlling the spaces and dimensional relationships perfectly. As in the corresponding fresco, the painter singles out the compositional fulcrum — here constituted by the figure of Christ brandishing a whip — and develops the story around it. One innovation is the bold definition of the temple architecture, depicted laterally in a rapid linear perspective. Tintoretto again comes to mind, especially for the expedient of the light flowing through the double openings of the oculus and the entrance, creating a "passage that illuminates with

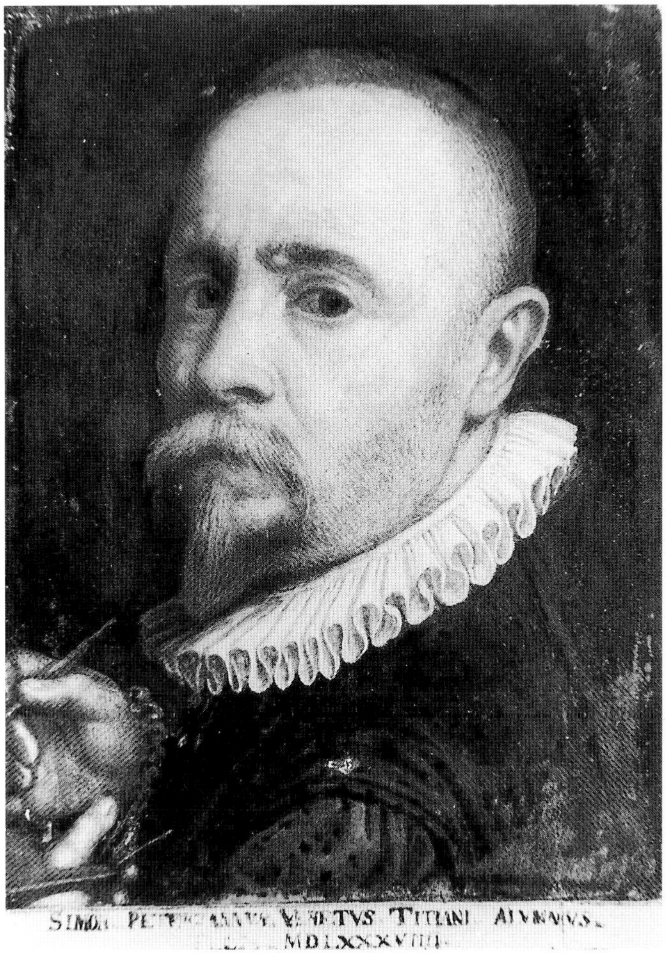

Simone Peterzano
Self-portrait
Private collection,
Rome

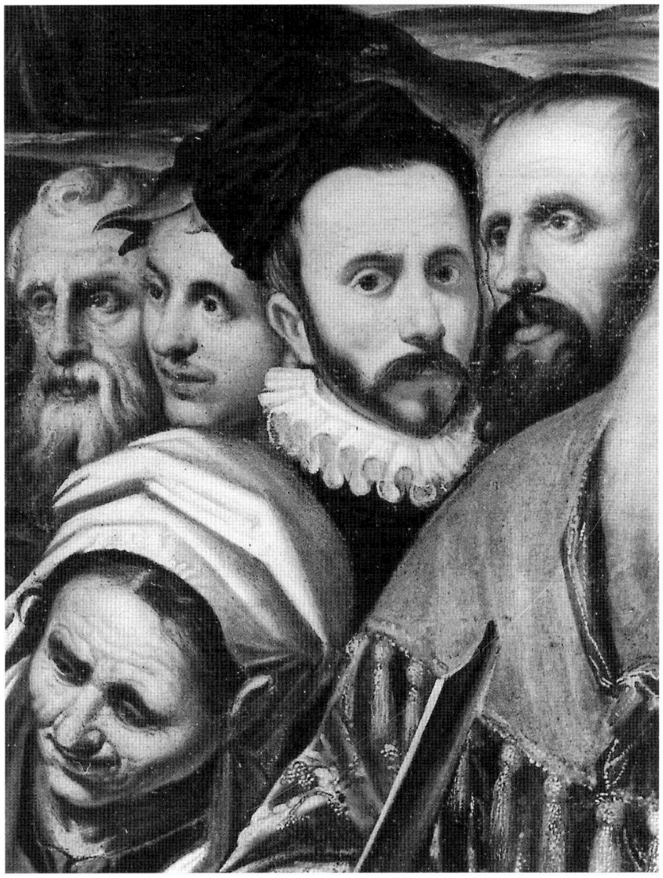

Simone Peterzano
Sts Paul and Barnabas at Lystra,
detail with
self-portrait
San Barnaba,
Milan

many reflections", as Vasari wrote with regard to the *Discovery of the Body of St Mark*, now at the Pinacoteca di Brera, Milan. The giant columns, the steep perspective of the coffered vault in the background, the contrast between the plasticity of the figures in the foreground and the immateriality of those in the distance, constructed with subtle threads of luminous colour, increase the spatial depth. The scene that unfolds is imbued with an extraordinary dramatic quality: the figure of Christ seems to rise out of a vortex as his threatening gesture, repelling the money-changers who are the closest to him, isolates him in a suddenly formed void. Caught by surprise, the profaners of the temple gather their belongings with febrile movements, clutching their money-bags, hoisting their filled panniers, driving out their sheep, and thronging towards the exit. On the right, under the ciborium, a priest observes the unexpected confusion.

As has been noted, this composition may also have given Caravaggio some ideas. The central figure of Christ, at whose feet lies a figure who tries to parry the blows, has been related to that of the executioner in the *Martyrdom of St Matthew*, as well as the figures of the woman seen from behind and the fleeing youth on the right who looks round in dismay at the commotion.[27] But in addition to these textual similarities, the student may have been inspired to re-elaborate themes based on his teacher's observations of reality and faithful representation of events.

In the frescoes of San Maurizio, Peterzano gives proof of his absolute mastery of the fresco technique: the architectural framework and the outlines of the figures are incised in the plaster with a sure touch, while the actual painting shows very few signs of *pentimento*. This raises the question of what previous experience Peterzano may have had before he took on the work at the Monastero Maggiore. We know nothing of his formation, apart from his apprenticeship to Titian which, however, remains undocumented. When did it take place? How long did it last? Did it follow a previous apprenticeship at some workshop in Bergamo or was it the painter's first formative experience? For the time being, these questions must remain unanswered, and the frescoes at San Maurizio represent the oldest documented and most reliably dated work that we know of to date. In any case, the publication of new documents — relative to the work carried out by Peterzano in the church of San Francesco Grande — may throw some light on the early years of the artist's Milanese career.[28]

As mentioned before, new information was provided by the discovery of the contract for the San Maurizio frescoes, a document in which Gerolamo Legnani was named as guarantor for the painter. The fact that Lomazzo mentioned him as Peterzano's patron is of interest: a sonnet composed probably some time before the publication of the *Rime* — which appeared in 1587 — was dedicated to "ona pinciura" (a painting) depicting *Angelica and Medoro*, a painting that Lomazzo described accurately.[29]

This was one of the artist's rare works dealing with a profane subject, and, as such, revealed an unusual aspect of a personality that was anchored primarily to a rich production of religious paintings that reflected the Tridentine precepts for sacred art, at least starting with the Garegnano frescoes. The canvas mentioned by Lomazzo, together with the *Venus with Satyrs* that Mina Gregori[30] noted, today at the Pinacoteca di Brera, revealed a worldly and cultivated Peterzano. The fact that he was remembered, together with his patron, by the Milanese writer and artist in a poem demonstrates that the artist was part of an intellectual circle which, under the vernacular label of "Facchini" (porters) of the Val di Blenio, gathered together the best brains in the city and its most fashionable writers.[31]

Gregori dated the *Venus with Satyrs* "around 1570–72 if not before", based on the evident influence of Titian in the reclining figure of the goddess, which repeated the scheme of the *Prado Venus* and the *Danae,* and in the treatment of the landscape and the two nude male satyrs depicted against the light. Indeed, this predominant Titianesque quality, seemingly of recent memory, had led the scholar to date the painting before *Angelica and Medoro*, in which memories of Veronese could be detected in a "naturalistic Lombard background", and in a less brilliant palette.

However, one is struck on rereading Lomazzo's sonnet by the description the poet gives of the painting; it is so accurate in the details ("the white hand poised over his neck") and so attentive to the lighting effects ("the trees tinged by the sun") that he could not have written such a description had he not seen the work. We do know that Lomazzo became blind in 1571, and therefore if he saw *Angelica and Medoro* in Gerolamo Legnani's house, the painting must have been finished before that date. It is true that in another verse of the *Rime*, Lomazzo mentions the San Barnaba paintings which he certainly could not have seen, but in this case the verses mention neither composition nor colour, and refer only to the subject matter of the two paintings.[32]

If this hypothesis is exact, it is anticipated both in the *Venus with Satyrs,* as Mina Gregori has already indicated, and in the *Deposition* at San Fedele, which, in my opinion, shares the luminous compactness and "Venetianess" of the Brera painting. In reconstructing the painter's first years in Milan — where he arrived when he was about thirty if indeed his date of birth can be placed around 1540[33] — these two works would therefore constitute his debut, followed by the Legnani painting, and, as his first public affirmation, the frescoes of San Maurizio.

Subsequently, Peterzano's career was increasingly successful: the paintings for San Barnaba, a thriving workshop,[34] the important commission for the Certosa of Garegnano, and other requests that came from the churches of Santa Maria della Passione, Sant'Angelo, and Santa Maria near San Celso all confirmed the leading role that the artist had managed to conquer for himself in the Milan of Borromeo together with such painters as Giovanni Ambrogio Figino, Aurelio Luini and Campi. There was, however, a shift in his later production towards a sort of "reformed classicism" with a predilection for compositional solutions of an archaistic stamp, as if the artist had forgotten the Mannerist lessons of his education and the narrative immediacy of his most successful attempts.

The frescoes of Garegnano, in which the vault is filled with a multitude of angels, prophets and sibyls and entirely resolved in a brilliantly Michelangelesque key, and whose narrative scenes make use of rich, luminous colours,[35] seem to conclude his first season of research with results of high quality. Later, in the frescoes of Sant'Angelo (1591), the narrative rhythm subsides, the composition settles on formally correct solutions but ones lacking impetus and inventiveness. The acute critical intelligence of the "little revolutionary" (Longhi) was quick to grasp the most fertile ideas present in the early Peterzano, the efficacious naturalist narrator, rather than in the measured creator of altarpieces.[36]

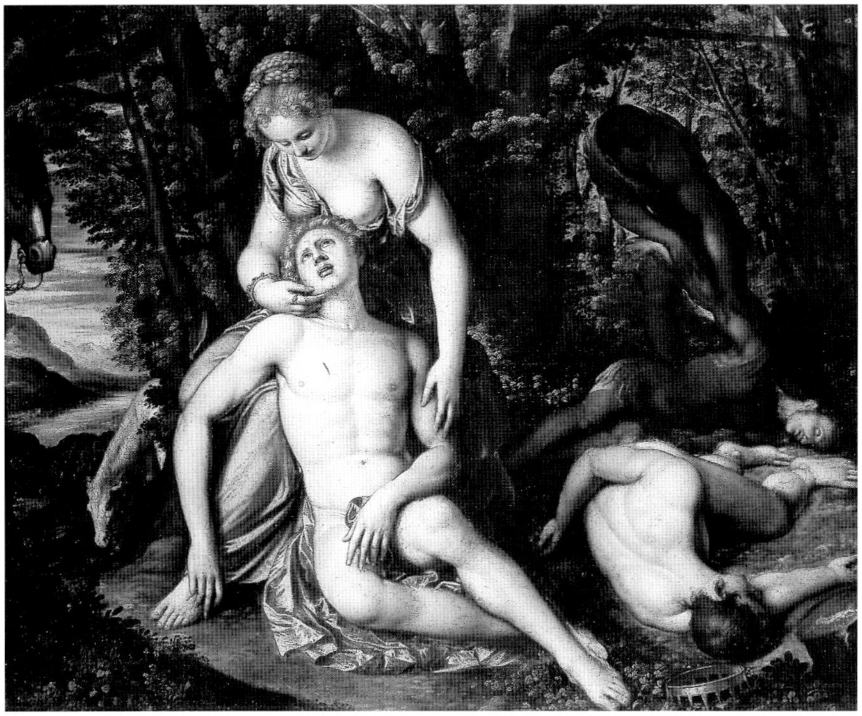

Simone Peterzano
Angelica and Medoro
Private collection

[1] "But the oil painting above the altar surpasses any other painting of his, representing the *Adoration of the Magi*, a painting worthy of eternal applause" (C. Torre, *Il Ritratto di Milano*, Milan 1674, 1714 ed., p. 198).

[2] G. Mongeri, *L'arte in Milano*, Milan 1872, p. 241.

[3] N. Pevsner, "Eine Revision der Caravaggio-daten", in *Zeitschrift für*

bildende Kunst, 1927–28, pp. 386–392. In this essay the scholar mentions the document which states that Caravaggio, then fourteen years of age, started his apprenticeship in Peterzano's workshop. The contract is to be found in the Archivio di Stato of Milan (henceforth ASM), sez. *Notarile*, notary Placido Borisio, 6 April 1584. Subsequently, Pevsner published another document, found in the parish archives of San Barnaba, from which it results that "Simone Petroianne the not unschooled Bergamo painter" had painted in 1573 the two large paintings of the *Life of St Barnabas* that are still today to be found in the presbytery of the church (N. Pevsner, "Der Lerhjahre des Caravaggio", in *Zeitschrift für bildende Kunst*, 1928–29, p. 285).

[4] R. Longhi, "Quesiti caravaggeschi", in *Pinacotheca*, 1928–29, pp. 311–312 (ed. of the complete works, IV, Florence 1968, pp. 130–132).

[5] In the contract dated October 1578 for the decoration of the chorus of the Certosa of Garegnano, Peterzano was called "dominus Simon Petrozanus de Ticiano pictor"; the commission for the altarpiece of Sant'Ambrogio in the cathedral of Milan was given, in 1592, to "Simone Peterzani de Ticianis"; a payment on behalf of the building supervisors of the Milan Cathedral was registered on 30 June 1596 to "Simone Peterzano de' Tiziani pittore". Furthermore, on the *Deposition* of San Fedele, the artist signed his name as SIMON PETRZANUS / TITIANI AL[UMNUS] (cf. E. Baccheschi, "Simone Peterzano. Regesti", in *I pittori bergamaschi dal XIII al XIX secolo. Il Cinquecento*, Bergamo 1978, pp. 474–475). Longhi's reservations, which this writer had already questioned (M.T. Fiorio, "Note su alcuni disegni inediti di Simone Peterzano", in *Arte lombarda*, XIX, 40, 1974, pp. 87–88), have by now been surpassed by all recent criticism (cf. M. Gregori, "Sul venetismo di Simone Peterzano", in *Arte/Documento*, 6, 1992, pp. 263–269; M. Calvesi, "Il Maestro del Caravaggio", in *Ars*, 19, 1999, pp. 84–87).

[6] The news that a painting by Peterzano was in the collection of Ambrogio Bembo in 1663, but originally came from the "studio of Moro della Zuecca", is to be found in A. Luzio, *La Galleria Gonzaga venduta all'Inghilterra nel 1627–28*, Milan 1913, pp. 311–312 (cf. M. Calvesi, "Simone Peterzano. Studio critico", in *I pittori bergamaschi*, p. 484).

[7] The source cited is the poem *La pittura trionfante*, published in Venice in 1615 by G.C. Gigli of Brescia, in praise of Andrea Schiavone. Peterzano is mentioned among the Venetian painters as a follower of Titian ("Simone Peterzano is still I discover / far behind his Maestro [Titian]", part I, p. 7).

[8] *Caravaggio e i caravaggeschi*, exhibition catalogue, introduction by R. Longhi, Milan 1951, p. 4.

[9] Longhi, "Quesiti caravaggeschi", p. 312 (1968 ed., p. 132); C. Baroni, "Aggiunte a Simone Peterzano", in *L'Arte*, 1940, p. 179.

[10] The payments for the San Maurizio entrance wall frescoes were found at the ASM by Giovanni Battista Sannazzaro ("Nuovi documenti per San Maurizio al Monastero Maggiore", in *Civiltà ambrosiana*, VI, 1, 1989, p. 61). The payments during the work were dated 10 November 1572 and 15 May 1573; the final payment was made on 22 August 1573. See also G. Bora, "Simone Peterzano", in *Pittura a Milano. Rinascimento e Manierismo*, Milan 1998, p. 276.

[11] The restoration of the San Fedele painting was carried out on the occasion of the 1985 exhibition (cf. M.T. Fiorio, in *Caravaggio e il suo tempo*, exhibition catalogue, Naples 1985, pp. 73–75). For the late 1570s dating of the San Fedele *Deposition,* see G. Bora, "Fra tradizione, maniera e classicismo riformato", in *Pittura a Milano*, pp. 60, 277.

[12] The document was published by N. Pevsner (cf. note 3).

[13] Regarding the *Deposition* by Salviati formerly at the Corpus Domini, today the property of the Pinacoteca di Brera, but on deposit at Viggiù, see A. Nova, in *Pinacoteca di Brera. Scuole dell'Italia centrale e meridionale*, Milan 1992, pp. 35–37.

[14] Regarding Salviati's drawing, now at the Uffizi, considered a preliminary drawing for the Corpus Domini *Pietà*, see E.A. Carrol, "Some Drawings by Salviati Formerly Attributed to Rosso Fiorentino", in *Master Drawings*, IX, 1971, p. 28.

[15] Regarding the Caravaggesque "anticipations" of Peterzano, see, in addition to Longhi ("Quesiti caravaggeschi", pp. 311–312), M. Calvesi ("Simone Peterzano maestro del Caravaggio", in *Bollettino d'Arte*, I, 1954, and *I pittori bergamaschi*); Idem, "Caravaggio o la ricerca della salvazione", in *Storia dell'arte*, 9–10, 1971, pp. 126–127); M.T. Fiorio (in *Caravaggio e il suo tempo*, pp. 73–75); M. Gregori (*Gli affreschi della Certosa di Garegnano*, n.d. [1973], *passim*; Eadem, "Simone Peterzano", in *Pittura a Bergamo dal romanico al neoclassico*, ed. M. Gregori, Milan 1991, p. 252).

[16] Calvesi, "Simone Peterzano maestro del Caravaggio", pp. 127–128. However, this scholar has subsequently stated that he was inclined to consider the problem of the dating of the San Maurizio cycle still open (cf. E. Baccheschi, "Simone Peterzano. Le opere", in *I pittori bergamaschi*, p. 530, no. 11).

[17] Baroni, "Aggiunte a Simone Peterzano", p. 180.

[18] Ibid., p. 174.

[19] Fiorio, "Note su alcuni disegni", pp. 92–93; Calvesi, in *I pittori bergamaschi*, pp. 488–489. See, in particular, Calvesi's observations about the Figino–Peterzano parallelism and Borromeo's commissions at Como and Pavia, in addition to Milan. Regarding the devotional aspects of Peterzano's paintings, see also M.T. Fiorio, "Simone Peterzano nella Milano borromaica", in *Osservatorio delle Arti*, 3, 1989, pp. 59–63.

[20] The equivocation about the date of the *Deposition* has been clarified by Calvesi: his initial dating was based on an erroneous reading of the *Guida del Touring* (1914), in which Bertarelli cited the date of 1591 (taken from the Ticozzi *Dizionario* which said "working in Milan in 1591") in reference to Peterzano's activity but not to the San Fedele painting.

[21] A. Ottino Della Chiesa, *San Maurizio al Monastero Maggiore*, Milan 1962, p. 96.

[22] Gregori, *Gli affreschi della Certosa*, p. 14.

[23] Cf. note 10.

[24] R. Miller, *Simone Peterzano in Milan: Contracts for Frescoes in San Maurizio and San Francesco Grande and Other Documents* (in press).

[25] Ottino Della Chiesa, *San Maurizio*, pp. 86, 96.

[26] The discovery of this painting is due to Maurizio Calvesi who had already mentioned its existence (in *I pittori bergamaschi*, p. 484), and tracked it down in a private Roman collection (Idem, "Il Maestro del Caravaggio", pp. 84–88, and, again, in "Sobre algunas pinturas de Caravaggio: la *Buenaventura*, el *San Francisco* de Hartford, el *David y Goliat* de la Borghese y las dos *Natividades* sicilianas", in *Caravaggio*, exhibition catalogue, Madrid 1999, pp. 12, 15).

[27] Calvesi, in *Bollettino d'Arte*, p. 131. However, I am not of the same mind with regard to the scholar's suggestion that the sketch at Castello Sforzesco (Ibid., p. 130) is a preliminary study for *Jesus Driving the Money-changers from the Temple* at San Maurizio. The small monochrome, in my opinion, refers to the Florentine ambient, as I have already suggested (cf. M.T. Fiorio, *Museo d'Arte Antica del Castello Sforzesco. Pinacoteca*, III, Milan 1999, pp. 374–375).

[28] In press by Robert Miller (cf. note 24).

[29] G.P. Lomazzo, *Rabisch*, critical text and commentary by D. Isella, Turin 1993, II, 36, pp. 153–154. Regarding the painting, see M.T. Fiorio, in *Rabisch. Il grottesco nell'arte del Cinquecento. L'Accademia della Val di Blenio. Lomazzo e l'ambiente milanese*, exhibition catalogue (Lugano), Milan 1998, pp. 284–285.

[30] M. Gregori, "Sul venetismo di Simone Peterzano", in *Arte/Documento*, 6, 1992, pp. 263–269.

[31] Regarding the Academy of the Val di Blenio and the role of Lomazzo, see D. Isella, in Lomazzo, *Rabisch*, pp. IX–LXII.

[32] "[...] those two stories, where / it shows how the Lord exhorts Paul, / and Saint Barnabas [...] to travel the world / and preach his divine faith" (G.P. Lomazzo, *Rime*, IV, Milan 1587, p. 293). Another painting by Peterzano that Lomazzo cited was the *Assumption* in the parish church of Vertemate, but in this case as well, although the description is very accurate, there are no annotations like "the shade and the lights" which make the reading of *Angelica and Medoro* so immediate (*Idea del tempio della pittura*, ed. R.P. Ciardi, *Scritti sulle arti*, I, Florence 1974, p. 367).

[33] In the absence of documents, Peterzano's date of birth had been fixed at approximately 1540. On the basis of the age — about sixty — of the painter in a recently found self-portrait (that bears the date 1589), Maurizio Calvesi suggests anticipating his date of birth to 1530.

[34] In 1575, Peterzano stipulated a contract committing himself to teach painting — and especially decoration and portraiture — to Francesco Alciati; therefore, he had a thriving workshop at least by that date. For this document, see Pevsner, "Eine Revision", p. 288.

[35] The paintings by Peterzano in the chorus of the Certosa of Garegnano have recently been restored, thus making it possible to fully appreciate their remarkable quality.

[36] The decoration of the entrance wall of San Maurizio is completed by four large oil paintings above the Serlian windows between the curve of the vault and the central oculus. Since it is impossible to make a close examination, no judgement can be made regarding their attribution. They are late with respect to the rest of the decoration, and possibly datable to the second half of the seventeenth century. Ottino Della Chiesa (*San Maurizio*, p. 87), uncertain about a single attribution, maintains that their author is to be found among the minor Lombard painters of the seventeenth century, and she suggests cautiously the ambit of Vespino. Not until such time as they are restored, will it be possible to study them properly.

The Early Furnishings

Sandrina Bandera

The Organ

The huge organ that rears its magnificent, multicoloured mantle of decorations, festoons and images of royal personages, is yet another indication of the nuns' nobility and their elaborate artistic tastes. The document for the commission of the organ in 1554[1] not only preserves for us the name of the master who built the instrument, Gian Giacomo Antegnati, and the painter commissioned for its decoration, Francesco de' Medici da Seregno assisted by his son Girolomo, but also provides us with a remarkable slice of convent life, evoking the elitist ambiance of this Benedictine community: as many as ninety-six nuns were present at the sealing of the document, all from the noblest families of the city; among them we find Angela Serafina da Terzago, Alessandra Sforza Bentivoglio, Francesca Violante Bentivoglio, Ottavia Pusterla, Judita and Prospera da Fiorenza, Polissena Simonetta, Faustina de Barzizza, Angela Francesca and Vittoria da Birago, Serafina, Gabriella and Adriana Resta, Sigismonda and Caterina Panigarola, Ippolita and Tarasia Gallarati, Laura Pellegrina Landriano and many others.

In accordance with the noble sisters who commissioned the instrument, the subjects painted on the wings of the organ case are all of royal lineage. On the open wings we see: *St Catherine* and *St Elizabeth of Hungary*, the latter given no less than three crowns as befitted a daughter and wife of kings, as well as her glorification in heaven; on the closed wings we see: *St Maurice* and *St Sigismund of Hungary*. The painter chosen for the decoration is practically unknown, apart from an archive reference of 1548, according to which he was present at a meeting in the University of Painting in Milan. Since the San Maurizio document makes explicit reference to the presence of his son as assistant, he may be presumed to have reached quite a mature age at the time.[2] The elegant placement of the female figures recalls the refined circle created around the court of Ferrante Gonzaga and the nobles of his entourage, while the abundance of festoons and extremely rich ornamentation links him to the tradition that had developed in Milan a few years before, with the preparations of solemn pomp and splendour to welcome the entry of Philip II into the city.[3]

However the drawings used by Francesco de' Medici for the execution of the female figures have been traced. As was often the case at that time, the creation of furniture and elements of decoration derives from the model of a more distinguished artist, Carlo Urbino. Urbino was one of the most brilliant exponents of the masters then working at the court of Milan, and very close to Bernardino Campi, a key figure for having introduced Milan to the Mannerist elegance and intellectual artifice of Parmigianino, apart from his constant endeavour to ape the affected ceremonial gesturing of an international court. Urbino's preparatory sheets, tracked down by Giulio Bora[4] to the Staatliche Graphische Sammlung in Munich (inv. 33097 and 33098), show two female figures drawn with intense refinement and fraught with vertical effects intended to override all natural proportions.

On the other hand the wooden decorations on the case, which is also painted, show considerable insistence on monstrous, redundant decorative elements from the classical repertory, such as masks, trophies, and burgeoning garlands. These seem more easily attributable to Francesco's son because of his affinity with the "imperial" climate established in Milan by Ferrante Gonzaga. The flowers and fruit ornamentation on the open wings were a much used motive in

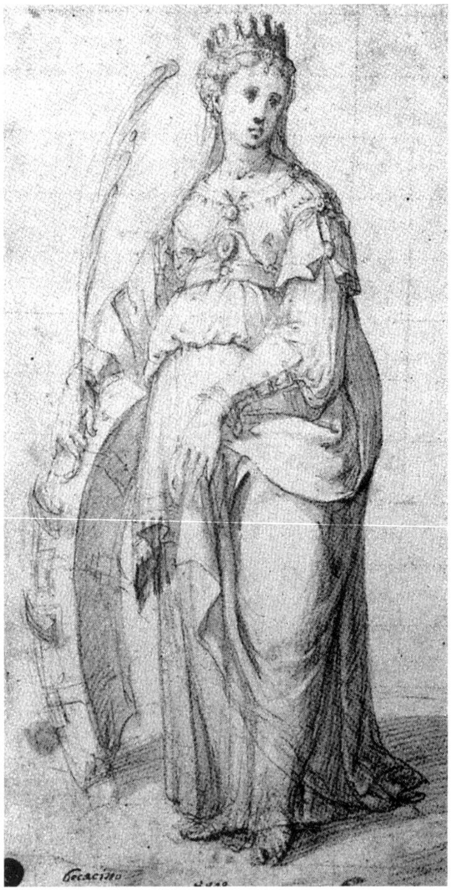

Francesco de' Medici
St Catherine
Staatliche Graphische Sammlung, Munich

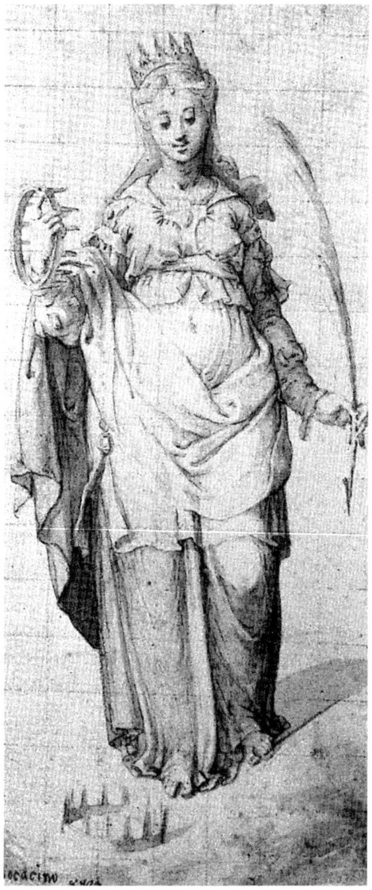

Francesco de' Medici
St Elizabeth of Hungary
Staatliche Graphische Sammlung, Munich

Milan around the mid century. Also the expanse of grassy mead upon which two female saints recline is rooted in the local post-Leonardo tradition.

The Wooden Choir Stalls

The monumental complex of wooden choir stalls was also executed in the sixteenth century. It has probably come down to us in a somewhat remodelled condition due to bouts of maintenance work, and may well be missing the abbot's seat. At present it is composed of a hundred stalls, and for this number of seats it must be one of the grandest in Lombardy, since the usual number of stalls is around seventy. Many elements assign the choir stalls to a date previous to 1530–40 and confirm the chronology proposed by Angela Ottino Della Chiesa, who puts it "before 1540".[5] Typical of the first quarter of the sixteenth century are the decorations on the armrests and the arrangement of the entire structure, including the form of a jutting canopy which presents characteristics existing in other early sixteenth-century furnishings, like those of Morimondo Abbey dating from 1522. The architectural structure may confirm an undocumented report that the stalls were designed by the same architect who created the church. Certainly the basic principle must have been the same that governed the furnishings in Santa Maria delle Grazie and Santa Maria presso San Celso, whose designs were certainly projected by the architects. The relation between architecture and furnishing — and in Lombardy we have numerous examples between the end of the fifteenth and the beginning of the sixteenth centuries — resulted from considerations concerning the value of a unified project introduced by Bramante ever since his work on Santa Maria presso San Satiro and Santa Maria delle Grazie.

[1] Archivio di Stato di Milano (henceforth ASM), *Religione p.a.* 2147, 4 September 1554. The document has already been mentioned by F. Malaguzzi Valeri, "Contributi alla storia di San Maurizio", in *Archivio Storico Lombardo*, XXXV, s. IX, 1908, pp. 323–333; I. Rossi, *La chiesa di San Maurizio in Milano. Il Monastero Maggiore e le sue due torri*, Milan 1914, p. 114; G.B. Sannazzaro, "Nuovi documenti per San Maurizio al Monastero Maggiore", in *Civiltà ambrosiana*, VI, 1, 1989, p. 62, note 29; Idem, *San Maurizio al Monastero Maggiore*, 2nd ed., Milan 1992, p. 661, note 92.
[2] G. Bora, in *I Campi e la cultura artistica cremonese del Cinquecento*, exhibition catalogue, Milan 1985, p. 300.
[3] For description, see G. Bora, "La cultura figurativa a Milano 1535-1565", in *Omaggio a Tiziano. La cultura artistica milanese nell'età di Carlo V*, exhibition catalogue, Milan 1977, pp. 49–50.
[4] Bora, in *I Campi*, p. 300.
[5] A. Ottino Della Chiesa, *San Maurizio al Monastero Maggiore*, Milan 1962, p. 97.

Church Reform under Cardinal Charles Borromeo

Sandrina Bandera

The historical situation during Cardinal Carlo Borromeo's (later St Charles) tenure of the bishopric of Milan wrought far-reaching changes on the monastic practices across the diocese, and was a determining factor behind the extensive building alterations and decorative cycles commissioned for the city's church of San Maurizio.

The cardinal's severe stance on religious matters was asserted in no uncertain terms through his *Instructiones fabricæ et suppellectilis ecclesiasticæ*, published in 1577, a position he restated in 1580 through the *Constitutiones et decreta condita in Provinciali Synodo Mediolanensis quarta.*[1]

By means of these texts, St Charles intervened directly in all questions concerning the production of religious art, paintings, furnishings, and architecture, which he deemed to be determining factors in the proper diffusion of the Faith. Moreover, the issuing of a set of tenets for devotional practices was a means of bringing the Milanese church in line with behavioural canons that delved beyond the outward manifestations of the Faith, and acted upon the very essence of the liturgy and practices observed in the various parishes. The cardinal was determined to establish a unitary, organic system across the diocese, thereby curbing the general disarray that had plagued it for some time, and forestalling possible outbreaks of unrest and self-determination among the parishes, which were fuelled by a leaning towards a pagan, mannered creative spirit sanctioned in intellectual circles and by the ruling families of the mid-sixteenth century, who were prone to flamboyance and outward display.[2]

Antonio Campi

On the question of religious painting, St Charles[3] did not advocate a merely generic orientation but laid down specific guidelines proscribing freedom of expression or leeway in the choice of subject matter, prohibiting the intrusion of imagery that lay outside a set of strict canons purged of all apocryphal content, superstition, and unorthodoxy: the purpose of art was to educe a sense of piety in the believer. This attitude explains the severity of the decrees issued by the bishop on his pastoral visit of 1569 to the convent of San Maurizio, a visit discussed elsewhere in detail by Giovanni Battista Sannazzaro.[4] Out of respect for the nuns' vows of seclusion, St Charles ordered the window in the wall dividing the two halls to be made much smaller, an operation that occasioned repair work to hide where the masonry had been added. The alterations were made in 1577, and the following year the convent commissioned an *Adoration of the Magi* from Antonio Campi, a Cremonese painter, who was already at work in Milan for the monastery of San Paolo, sponsored by the Sfondrati sisters (also from Cremona), and having particularly close ties with Cardinal Borromeo. While extant records provide fascinating data on the structural alterations carried out,[5] the iconography and the stylistic features of the work assigned to Campi reveal an equally compelling testament to the complete renewal of the nuns' choice of imagery and subject matter.[6] Despite its limited application, the change is of considerable significance.

Comparing the new commission with the fresco of the same subject, painted less than fifteen years earlier by

Antonio Campi
Flight into Egypt
San Marco,
Milan

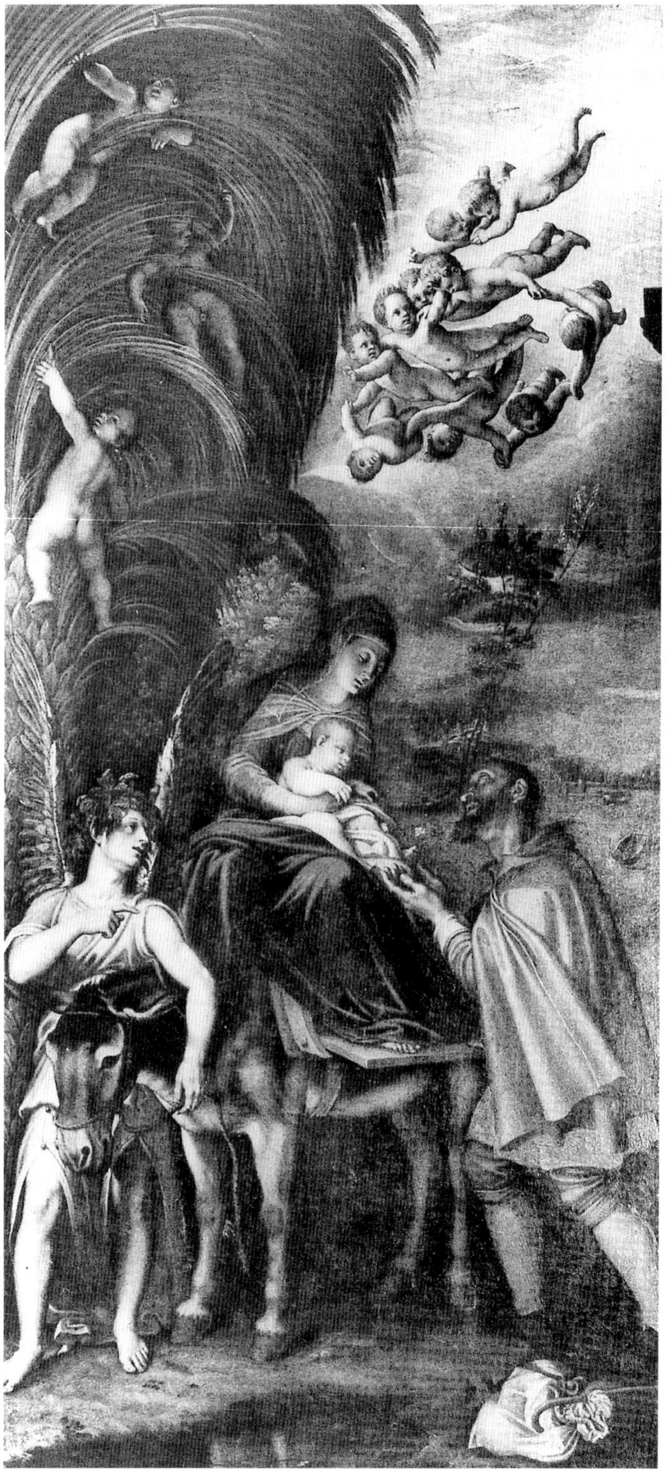

Aurelio Luini in the Cappella Bentivoglio (formerly attributed to Lomazzo), one can only marvel at the unexpected simplicity, humanity and sweetness of the gestures, the blended colours, and the quality of the details. Albeit in a revised form of his own, Antonio Campi had retrieved the compositional elements of Bassano's work,[7] emphasizing the impasto colouring and achieving a palette typical of the purest Venetian expression, as if to stress his tendency towards a simple, poignant narrative that did not implicate intellectual involvement. Something of this nature can be already detected in Campi's triptych in San Marco, Milan (1577), where, alongside the themes dear to the northern artists — particularly those of Albrecht Dürer and Giovan Gerolamo Savoldo — here he employs broad, steady compositional rhythms and warmer hues.[8]

Antonio Campi had already been in close contact with St Charles for some time. Both were intent on establishing a precise, vigilant control of subject matter, themes, and representation. In a letter to the cardinal dated 1575, Campi announces himself as deputy of the Cremonese oratory of Santa Maria della Stella, and interested in the church's restoration, laying bare his keen adherence to the scheme of renewal promulgated by Cardinal Borromeo.[9] From now on the timbres and hues employed, the everyday gestures of the figures, become the hallmark of Antonio Campi's work, typified by his *Flight into Egypt* in the Cappella Cusani in San Marco, dating from the 1580s.

Ottavio Semino

In the wake of the renewal that ensued the Council of Trent comes a series of late commissions around 1570 to complete the decoration of the public church: a set of frescoes relating the Passion for the Cappella Bentivoglio (fourth chapel from the entrance, left), formerly held to be the work of Giovan Paolo Lomazzo, but now attributed to the workshop of Aurelio Luini.[10] In addition, frescoes were ordered for the Cappella Fiorenza, and the large fresco of the entrance wall.

The abbess who initiated the renewal work on the church according to the new Counter-Reformation principles decreed by the cardinal was a member of the Fiorenza family. Previously she had commissioned a painter not of local origin to carry out decorations, including frescoes, of the altarpiece, and to design stuccowork (executed by Giovan Antonio Ferrari and Giuseppe Prevosti[11]) for the first chapel on the right side, dedicated to St Paul. Bora's earlier suggestion that the author of this classicizing tableau was a painter who had apprenticed in Genoa, Ottavio Semino, is confirmed by a document dated 24 i.e. July 1571 discovered by Sannazzaro.[12]

The artist was under obligation to finish the work by the end of November that year,[13] and to receive the sum of 40 *scudi*.

The frescoes relate events from the life of St Paul, with particular reference to the *Baptism* (left wall), and the *Conversion of St Paul* (right wall, now almost illegible), while the altarpiece at the centre shows the *Preaching of St Paul*. The discovered record states that the entrance arch carried two *Sibyls* (actually the figures painted were *Prophets*), with friezes and putti; and on the vault were figures of *Faith*, *Hope*, and *Charity* amid stuccoes (designed by Semino, and executed by Ferrari and Prevosti).[14] The painter was under obligation to employ "colori fini" (fine colours), and proof of his skills would be ascertained by "persone di Giuditio" (men of judgement), including Giovan Francesco Visconti.[15]

In conformance with the new dictates of the Counter-Reformation repertory, the compositional models were to be of a classicizing nature, with continuous references to the work of Raphael. From records we learn that the Genoese Semino's talents as a painter were highly regarded in Milan, a fact vouched for by the many important commissions, particularly the decoration for Palazzo Marino (Milan), and the Refectory of the Certosa of Pavia.

Be that as it may, Semino's frescoes in San Maurizio denote a complete departure from his previous work, until then freighted with an overt sumptuousness, and largely focused on profane subjects.

As Bora has already pointed out, Semino's undertaking in San Maurizio entailed considerable personal commitment, given the sheer quantity of Raphaelesque motifs employed for both the figures, and, more general, for the overall compostional organization (such as the foreground *Virgin and Child* in the central picture, after Raphael's in the Stanze Vaticane); others drawn from memory from the artist's travels in central Italy, referring to Jacopino del Conte's works in San Giovanni Decollato in Rome, and Giorgio Vasari's in the Palazzo Vecchio, Florence. This fondness for classical criteria in his compositions, based on his memories of central Italian painting, became a staple of Semino's work.

Despite the results — perhaps not altogether convincing — Semino's reputation lay in his adherence to the Reformation ideal, which he informed with a classical solemnity.[16] In one of his sonnets from the *Rabisch*, the poet and painter Giovan Paolo Lomazzo notes that Semino was considered superior in talent to the Milanese painters of his time, and much renowned for his adroit invention and compositional force, an ability that led to further significant commissions for the clergy, such as the *Life of St John the Baptist* cycle in Santa Maria delle Grazie (Milan), and frescoes for the vault of the Cappella Cusani in San Marco (Milan).[17]

[1] St Charles Borromeo, *Arte sacra* (1577), ed. C. Castiglioni and C. Marcora, Milan 1952, pp. 95–100; M. Bendiscioli, "Politica, amministrazione e religione nell'età dei Borromei. Vita sociale e cultura", in *Storia di Milano*, X, Milan 1957, p. 156 ff.

[2] L. Grassi, "Prassi, socialità e simbolo nell'architettura delle 'Instructiones' di San Carlo", in *Alto Milanese all'epoca di Carlo e Federico Borromeo. Società e territorio*, conference proceedings, Gallarate 1988, pp. 113–114.

[3] M.T. Fiorio, "Note su alcuni inediti di Simone Peterzano", in *Arte lombarda*, 40, 1974, p. 92.

[4] G.B. Sannazzaro, *San Maurizio al Monastero Maggiore*, 2nd ed., Milan 1992, pp. 17 and 26.

[5] Archivio di Stato di Milano (henceforth ASM), *Archivio spirituale*, X, fols. 56–57 (a. 1576); *Religione p.a.* 2147, 13 February, 25 June, 4 October 1578, and 25 May 1579.

[6] See the documented dated 25 June 1578 in the ASM, *Religione p.a.* 2147. The painting was supposed to be delivered within the year, for a fee of 125 gold *scudi*.

[7] G. Bora, in *I Campi e la cultura artistica cremonese del Cinquecento*, exhibition catalogue, Milan 1985, p. 183.

[8] Ibid.

[9] Ibid.

[10] G.B. Sannazzaro, *San Maurizio al Monastero Maggiore*, p. 110; D. Pescarmona, in *Disegni lombardi del Cinque e Seicento della Pinacoteca di Brera e dell'arcivescovado di Milano*, exhibition catalogue, Milan 1986, p. 55.

[11] See document dated 12 June 1573 at the ASM, *Religione p.a.* 2147.

[12] G. Bora, "La decorazione pittorica sino al Settecento", in *Santa Maria delle Grazie a Milano*, Milan 1983, p. 168; G.B. Sannazzaro, "Nuovi documenti per San Maurizio al Monastero Maggiore", in *Civiltà ambrosiana*, VI, 1, 1989, p. 60.

[13] G. Bora, "Fra tradizione manierista e classicismo riformato (1535–1595)", in *Pittura a Milano. Rinascimento e manierismo*, ed. M. Gregori, Milan 1998, p. 275.

[14] Bora, "La decorazione pittorica sino al Settecento", p. 168.

[15] See document in the ASM, *Notarile*, notary Galdo da Lodi, at dates 4 December 1573, and 24 July 1574.

[16] Bora, "Fra tradizione manierista e classicismo riformato", p. 61.

[17] Previously assigned to Antonio Campi; for references to Ottavio Semino, see Ibid., p. 61.

Wall Painting Techniques and Restoration

Sandrina Bandera and Paola Zanolini

The Changes Made by St Charles Borromeo

The first important reconstruction of the interior of the church could hardly be regarded as restoration. The work was commissioned by St Charles as part of the changeover in the planning of ecclesiastical architecture in accordance with the rulings of the Council of Trent. As far as the convent premises were concerned Cardinal Borromeo, following his pastoral visit in 1569, ordered a considerable reduction in the opening in the wall that partitioned the nuns' quarters from the lay section. This resulted not only in a series of new structural works but also a new scheme of decoration. The latter included the placement of a large painting, the *Adoration of the Magi*, on the lay section of the wall. It also meant filling up a space on the convent side and it was here, in the centre of the lunettes created by Bernardino Luini, that a canvas painting was set, the *Deposition of Christ*, a replica of the fresco already existing in the lay hall.

Previous Restoration

Over the years, restoration of the wall paintings which entirely cover the interior of the convent church and choir of San Maurizio has always been programmed as a single project, in keeping with the obvious homogeneity of the decoration scheme. Hence, we find documentation for operations such as fixing, reconstruction, repainting, dusting out and reintegration of the lacunae which are mostly due to infiltration of moisture either from the walls and roofage, but especially from capillary seepage from the ground.

The problem of rising damp is widespread in Milan, but it is particularly troublesome in San Maurizio because of the river Nirone which flows past the church. It has also been caused by modern structural restoration in the crypt below the convent which prevents natural evaporation through the masonry. Unfortunately waterproof plastering on the adjacent areas along the north wall and the church below, which corresponds to the crypt, easily transports dampness to the frescoed walls, causing serious damage through continuous eruption of greyish-white salts. This process is still causing problems in the church interior today. It became critical in 1964 when, during construction work on the new Museo Archeologico, the plaster was stripped off the lateral walls leaving the bare brickwork, thus exposing them for a considerable time to weather and air pollution (see *Corriere della Sera*, 8 February 1964).

Among the most important restoration work carried out before Ottemi della Rotta's in 1964, mention should be made of those conducted in the years 1792–93, 1856–57, 1897, 1911, 1917 and 1936. Many of these have been documented by I. Rossi[1] and Giovanni Battista Sannazzaro.[2] The first restoration work of 1792 was intended to repair the damage caused by the insertion of pilasters for the high altar. A document dated 2 October 1856, found in Santa Maria alla Porta parish archives, consisted of a series of articles and financial conditions relating to tender, signed by Giuseppe Knoller, and describing a list of items in need of restoration to be carried out in the following year.

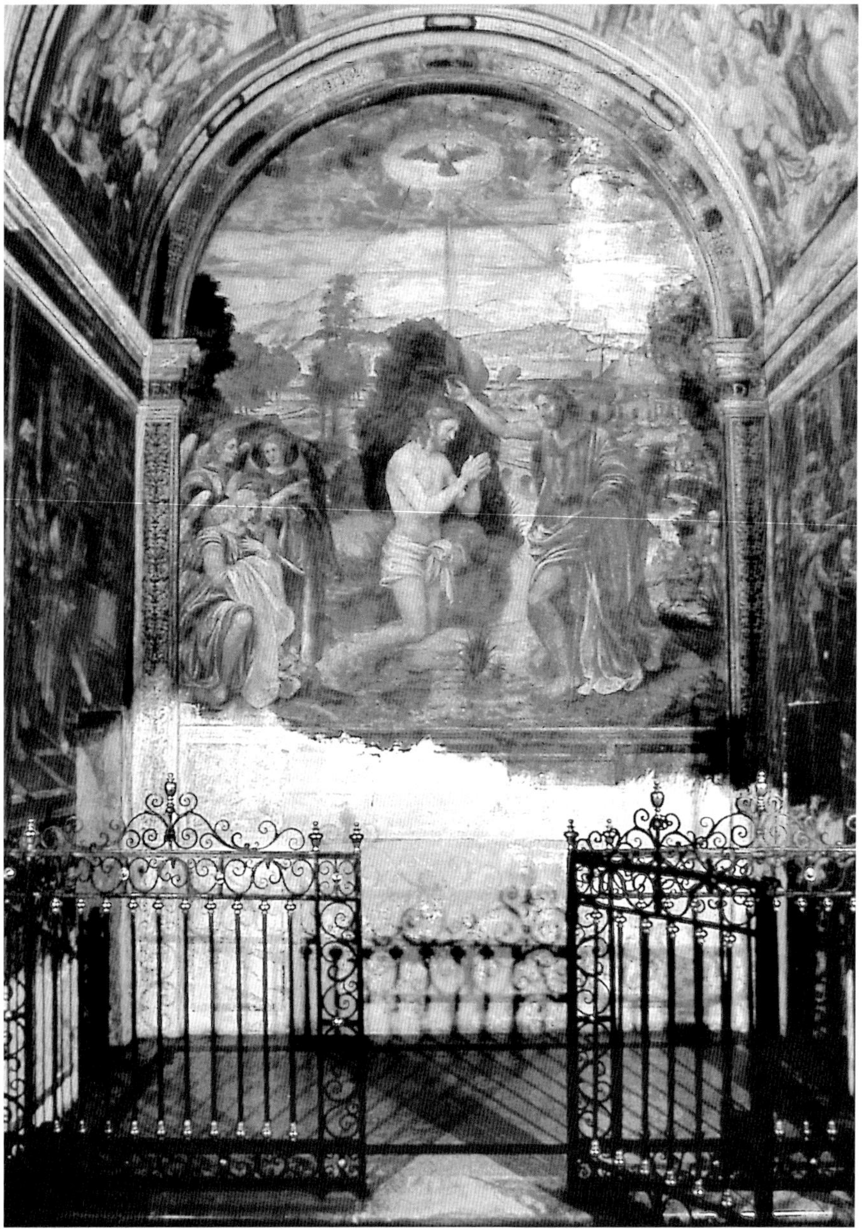

The effects of rising damp in the Cappella Carreto: the *Baptism of Christ*

This archives document leads us to suppose that, at the time, all the decoration showed serious problems of conservation. It also indicates that a certain amount of partial maintenance had been taken in hand. For example, it mentions the need to "reduce the amount of egg-white too thickly laid on", i.e. to cut down the over-abundant layer of albumin, a protein substance much favoured in the nineteenth century, used to consolidate colours and bring out brilliance in tone. It was probably this procedure that caused the worst damage of all. Even today it is extremely hard to counteract because oxidation and polymerization of organic substances produce halation and dark stains which are almost entirely incorporated throughout the channels of micro-cracks in the plaster, thus spoiling the harmonious luminosity of Luini's painting.
This process of alteration and oxidation of the egg-white could not have taken very long. Already by 1911 it can be clearly discerned in the illustrations of L. Beltrami's monograph on Luini.
New restoration work was carried out in 1892. This time some of the paintings in the church were frescoed over, and we can assume that many other restorations date from the same period. The paintings of landscapes on the two lateral walls of the nuns' church should actually date from 1917 (or not very long after).[3] The relevance of this important chapter in the decoration of San Maurizio will be revealed further on.
In 1896 the Ufficio Regionale for the conservation of monuments promoted a new restoration (document in the San Maurizio parish archives). The need for urgent action drove the Church authorities in Milan to authorize the sale of a series of four seventeenth-century tapestries depicting episodes from the life of Moses, by Jan Le Jamier (today in the Virginia Museum of Fine Arts, Richmond) The restoration, referred to as a "dusting out", but which must certainly have been far more substantial, was conducted by Giuseppe Stefanoni of Bergamo. It was followed by further restoration between 1915 and 1917 directed by Luigi Cavenaghi; this particularly concerned the painting on the vault of the convent presbytery and the four canvases on the entrance.[4]
Finally, mention must be made of the undocumented but highly important restoration financed by Engineer Chizzolini. The work (1936–40) is celebrated in a memorial tablet to the right of the nave in the lay section. It probably concerned the most famous frescoes in the lay hall, especially the ones by Bernardino Luini along the lateral

wall, with radical transformations of the borders and painted pilasters in order to link them to what remained of the original decoration.

Wall Painting Techniques

An examination of the techniques used in the San Maurizio frescoes, characterized either by individual painters or else the various workshops who participated in the church decoration, will allow us to formulate an initial research into the history of wall painting techniques in sixteenth-century Lombardy; although the results have been degraded and distorted by the succession of restorations. The most archaic technique, albeit as recent as the fifteenth century, is documented in the *cielino* in the vaulting above the top of the partitioning transverse wall of the convent church, and shows *God the Father* and the *Evangelists*. The most obvious technical archaism is the use of glazes and not impasto, the presence of resinous substances mixed with mineral powders to create stars in relief against the background, and a vast assortment of precious colours like lapis lazuli and malachite. In this section the technique is particularly loose and free, as we may deduce from the fact that there is no indication of sinopia or cut threads.

The *Annunciation* on the front of the triumphal arch of the same partitioning wall was also the result of archaic methods that can be traced as far back as the Middle Ages. It began by painting directly onto the recently finished brick coloured wall. Here too the presence of a high quality blue (azurite, not lapis lazuli), and compact material applied with the scrupulous care used for painting on wood, appear to belong to a method still in use in the late fifteenth-century. In regard to the vault with *God the Father* and the *Evangelists,* however, we should bear in mind that, from a technical rather than a stylistic point of view, the *Annunciation* cannot be considered a work from the same workshop. There are in fact noticeable differences in application, which here is more fluid and practically without glazes.

The series of saints at each side of the *oculi* on the upper register of the convent side chapels also belong to a late fifteenth-century decoration project, although it was not put into execution until the sixteenth century.

A certain carelessness in applying the layers of paint, and above all substantial restoration work prevent us from arriving at a precise description of the technique. To be sure, the simplicity noticeable in the preparatory drawing and in the application of colour shows the repeated use of

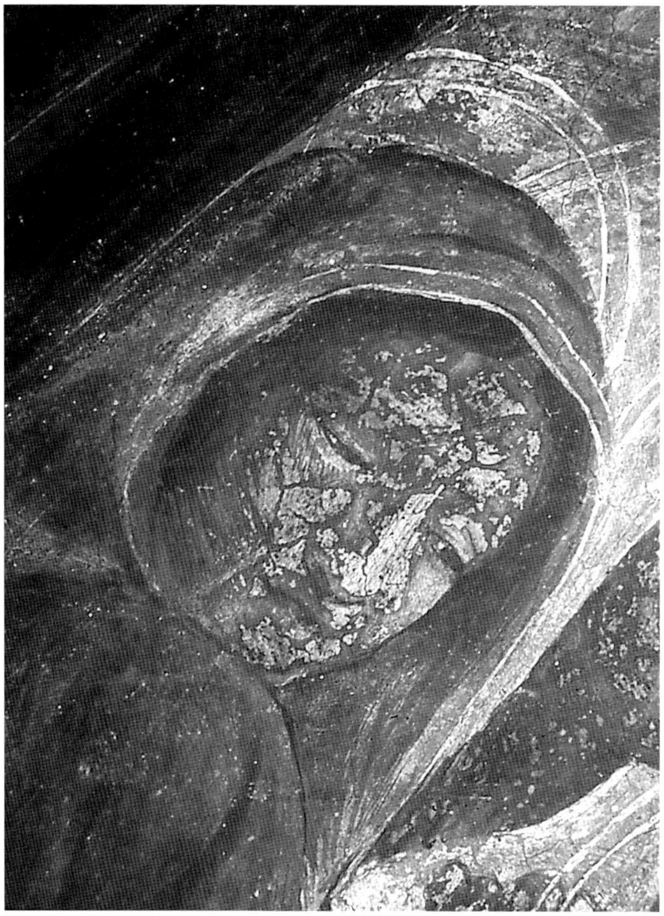

Dark stains on the flesh tones caused by chemical alteration of the protein fixatives

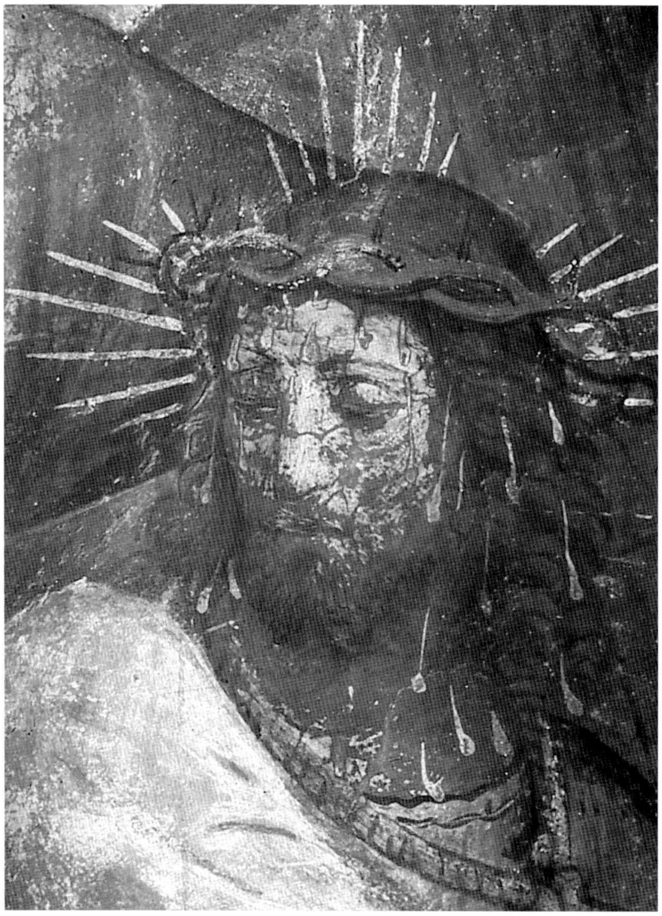

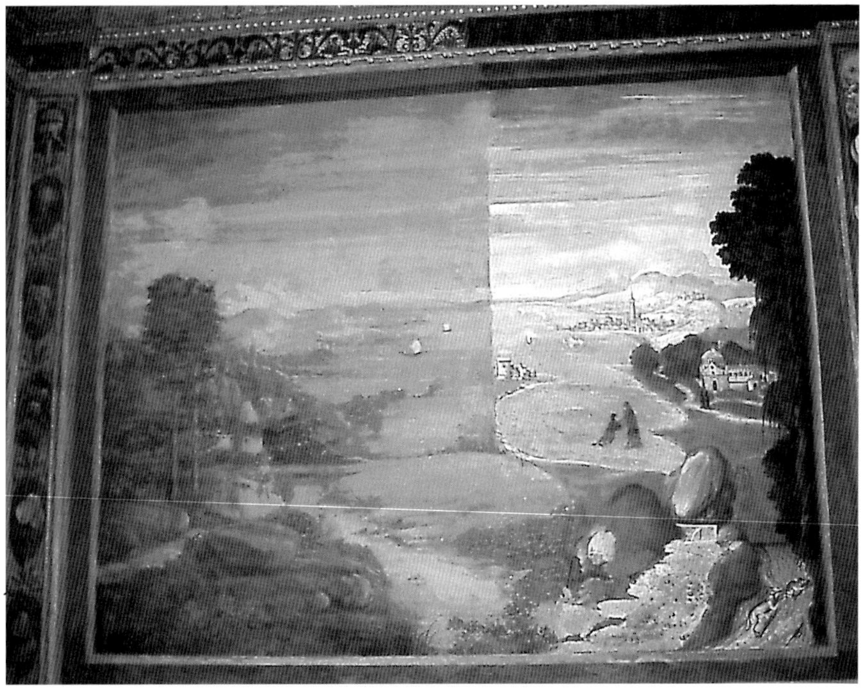

Convent section, fifth chapel on left: the left part of the fresco is an integration

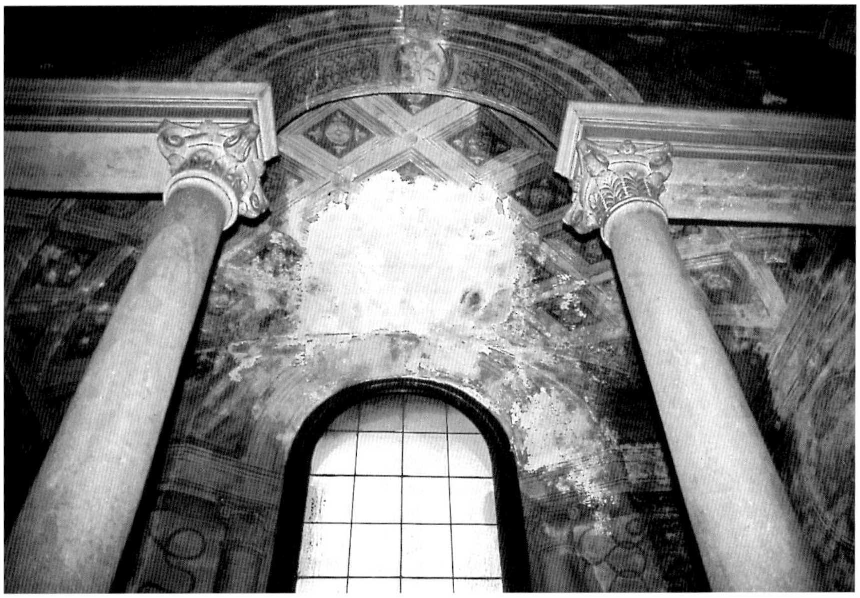

Water infiltrations in the gallery

cartoons, and most probably the presence of secondary masters. The only feature of any interest may be the architectural cast of the illusionistic corbels below, which are perfectly inserted into the architecture of the church. The technique of Bernardino Luini, who certainly painted the most interesting frescoes for the first decoration project, can be clearly distinguished from the technique employed in the frescoes of the very first years. It, on the whole, shows no particular character. It is half fresco painting, i.e. it follows procedures typical of the Lombard workshops of the fifteenth and sixteenth centuries: after a general laying out *a fresco* (normally done by pupils), the master sketches out the figure using the absorbent grip of the first surface (obviously still wet), while also adding a calculated quantity of animal glue. On the second surface the decorations (now almost completely lost) are painted, together with the clothes and the sumptuous features which are entirely painted *a secco* (when the plaster is dry), using no other binder but animal glue. The use of methods and techniques on these lines does not envisage *giornate*, which barely exist, but only a drawing produced with very subtle incision.
As far as technique is concerned, we notice a sharp difference on the wall facing the lay section. Here even in the topmost section the faces are handled with particular care and, unlike the others, appear to have been painted within an easily identifiable *giornata*. In regard to the whole of the frescoes on the dividing wall, the small landscape in the lower section of the wall facing the convent section is of special interest. It is entirely executed with a remarkable freshness, both in the dark glazes and the lighter transparencies. The extraordinary quality of this fragment allows us to comment on the technique and authenticity of the landscapes on the lateral walls which, as we shall see, were probably painted between the end of the nineteenth century and the first years of the twentieth.
Bernardino Luini devoted special attention to his final work in San Maurizio, which constitutes a unit in itself: the Cappella Besozzi on the right-hand side of the church. His extraordinary skill is already apparent in the architectonic partitioning wall upon which he had to begin his decoration for the chapel; his talent is particularly evinced in the drapery, where precious pigments, such as lapis lazuli and malachite, are applied in abundance.
As already mentioned, the Raphaelism which underlies Luini's work, and which generally informed European taste in the 1800s, meant that the major part of nineteenth-century restoration focused on his fres-

coes. In fact it is upon Luini's painting that the greatest concentration of egg-white is found; hence the stains due to alteration following restoration and over-energetic cleaning. Consequently, repairing Luini's original work has required very delicate application, and has been carried out only by means of sophisticated consultation and testing. Luini's sons did not automatically inherit their father's technique, mostly because of the wide generation gap that separated them.
On the whole the fresco painting of Aurelio and Giovan Pietro reveals a procedure based more on impasto than glazes, although there is a considerable difference between the two brothers in regard to execution (probably in accordance with the stylistic results). Giovan Pietro is quicker, more fluent and to a certain extent involved with "materials". For example, in the large-scale figures we notice execution *a giornate* where even the underlying plaster is applied according to the outlined form and muscular structure of the figure itself, as we gather from the lumps left by the trowel which seem to mold the figure in three dimensions. All this is done with a broad thick spatula, once again confirmation of fairly fast execution.
On the other hand Aurelio almost anticipated Simone Peterzano's technique in working on a perfectly smooth plaster, but he loves to heap an abundance of raised decorations in *pastiglia* with a consistently refined taste. We notice the copious use of gold, either in leaf or ribbon, and a particularly rich imagination in regard to colour. His careful execution is brought out not only in the infinite detail of the decorations, but perhaps above all in the way he handles shading with minute parallel brush strokes, almost giving the effect of sunbeams. It is a technique that also allows the artist to define the entire muscular structure, in so far as it is visible through the vibrant chiaroscuro, in perfect conformity to Mannerist taste.
The restoration, which is at present nearing completion after a decade of work on various surfaces, has also confirmed a theory concerning the landscapes painted on the lateral walls of the nuns' section, which had already been put forward on the basis of simple observation of style. These are the landscapes which Angela Ottino Della Chiesa, in her 1962 monograph on San Maurizio, saw as one of the first examples of large-scale sixteenth-century landscape painting, without insertion of figures or architecture. The fresco technique of some of these landscapes seems to confirm this theory.

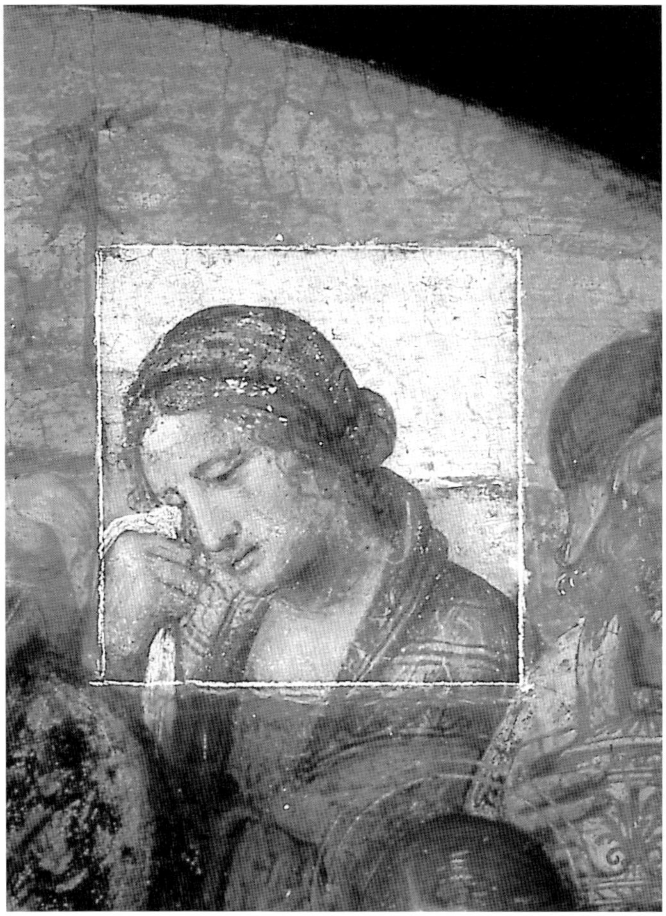

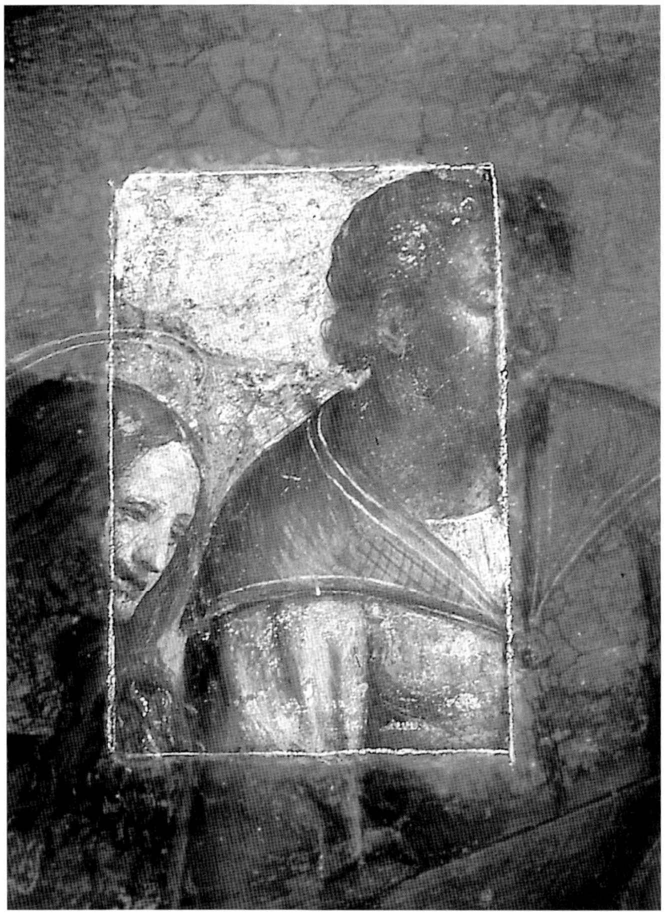

Test patches of cleaning

A careful examination of the layers of paint, and a series of samples submitted to stratigraphic tests, have clearly confirmed that they could not have been painted any later or earlier than the second half of the nineteenth century. The landscapes are fresco painted on two superimposed layers of plaster: the one underneath carrying the brush outlining of the *campiture* (large areas of uninterrupted colour), while the one on top bears the drawing in graphite and the final painting. This twofold stratum belonging to the same series of decoration is about 2 cm thick and could well have been executed during the restoration in 1917; but it was preceded by a report containing a programme for a future restoration written in 1892, referred to earlier in this text.

When fragments of paint were brought to light from beneath this plaster in the course of restoration, samples taken from all six chapels were submitted for stratigraphic examination to find out what the original decoration was like. It was then decided, in accordance with the civic and church authorities of Milan, to take out an entire square for investigation. Following the removal of the nineteenth-century plaster, it was discovered that originally the chapels had no decoration in terms of landscapes or figures, but only very simple painted compartments, probably the Bramante type, in brilliant colours that by now are severely damaged.

Restoration

The restoration of the frescoes launched in 1984, thanks to a generous private contribution, concerns both sides of the wall partitioning the lay section from the convent choir. This was followed up, again with financial backing from private sources, with restoration of the Besozzi and Carreto chapels. Funds raised by concerts made it possible to restore the wall at the entrance to the choir and the Cappella dell'Arca di Noè. In the past two years the financial institute which promoted the present publication has decided to complete restoration of the convent section with projects for the chapels and the gallery. A very similar principle of restoration has been adopted, since different types of damage were common to all the frescoes. The type of deterioration and resultant problems falls under two basic headings:

– damage caused by dampness infiltrating from walls, roofing and foundations, leading to the formation of highly dangerous sulfates, with consequent losses both to the painting and plaster;

– a very heavy overall darkening of all surfaces caused by stratification of deteriorating fixatives, candle smoke and particles of atmospheric pollution. In particular the fixatives, almost insoluble through chemical alteration and natural oxidation, appeared as dark, dirty stains, particularly noticeable on flesh tones.

Since here we have a mixed rather than pure fresco technique, the cleaning work has proved especially difficult and even hazardous in view of the fragility of the paint. With the help of tests conducted by technicians and institutes who kindly lent their services, highly complex cleaning methods have been developed, applying detergent cotton pads directly to the painted surface, the lengths of time and solvents varying according to type of pigment and cause of staining. Particular attention was given to decorations in gold, and these were very carefully fixed and isolated before proceeding to the general cleaning. Cleaning can be a very slow process. Sometimes it means waiting months before repeating the applications and completing the restoration to the original colours. The results however have been extremely satisfactory: these paintings have been successfully restored to their original vibrancy and colour.

Problems of dealing with long-established seepage of damp have been solved through consolidation of the plaster and the extraction of soluble salts. The serious problem of sulfate deposits has been dealt with using the tried and true method of barium hydroxide compresses.

On the whole, once the paintings had been freed from layers of deposits, the lacunae did not appear particularly extensive; but there was a general condition of abrasion owing to the nature of the paintings themselves, as well as to the careless cleaning they had been subjected to over the years. In consideration of the extremely decorative and homogeneous character of the decoration scheme it was decided to add minimal pictorial integration to the existing completeness of the overall composition.

[1] I. Rossi, *La chiesa di San Maurizio in Milano. Il Monastero Maggiore e le sue due torri*, Milan 1914, pp. 11–16.

[2] G.B. Sannazzaro, *San Maurizio al Monastero Maggiore*, 2nd ed., Milan 1992, pp. 162–179.

[3] G.B. Sannazzaro, "Per la decorazione pittorica nella chiesa di San Maurizio al Monastero Maggiore di Milano: suggerimenti di studio", in *Arte lombarda nel secondo millennio. Saggi in onore di Gian Alberto Dell'Acqua*, Milan 2000, pp. 148–149.

[4] Soprintendenza per i Beni Artistici e Storici per la Lombardia, *San Maurizio Maggiore*, correspondance of 1915–17.

Pictorial Decoration

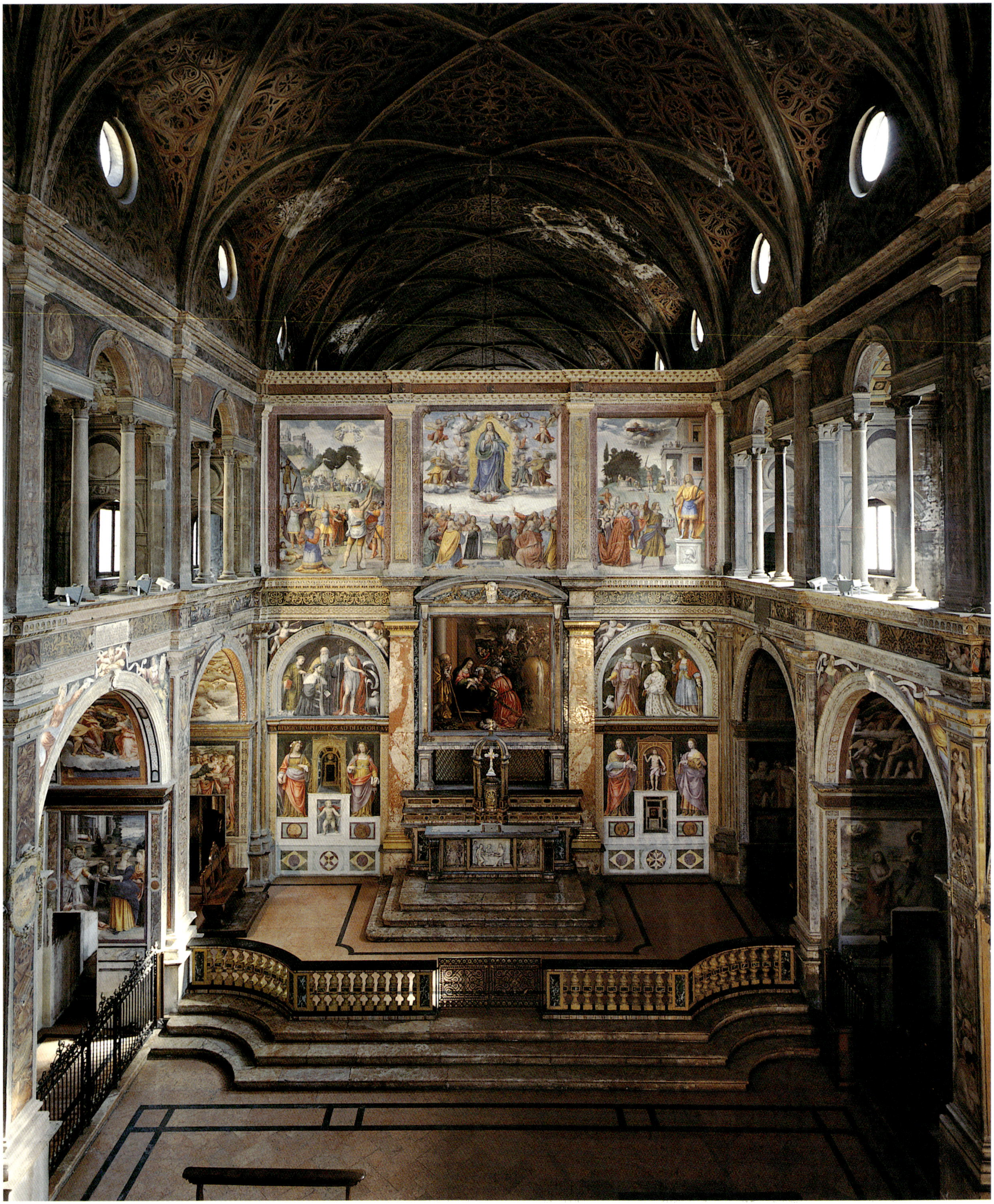

Opposite
Lay hall, general view

Convent hall, views towards the partition wall

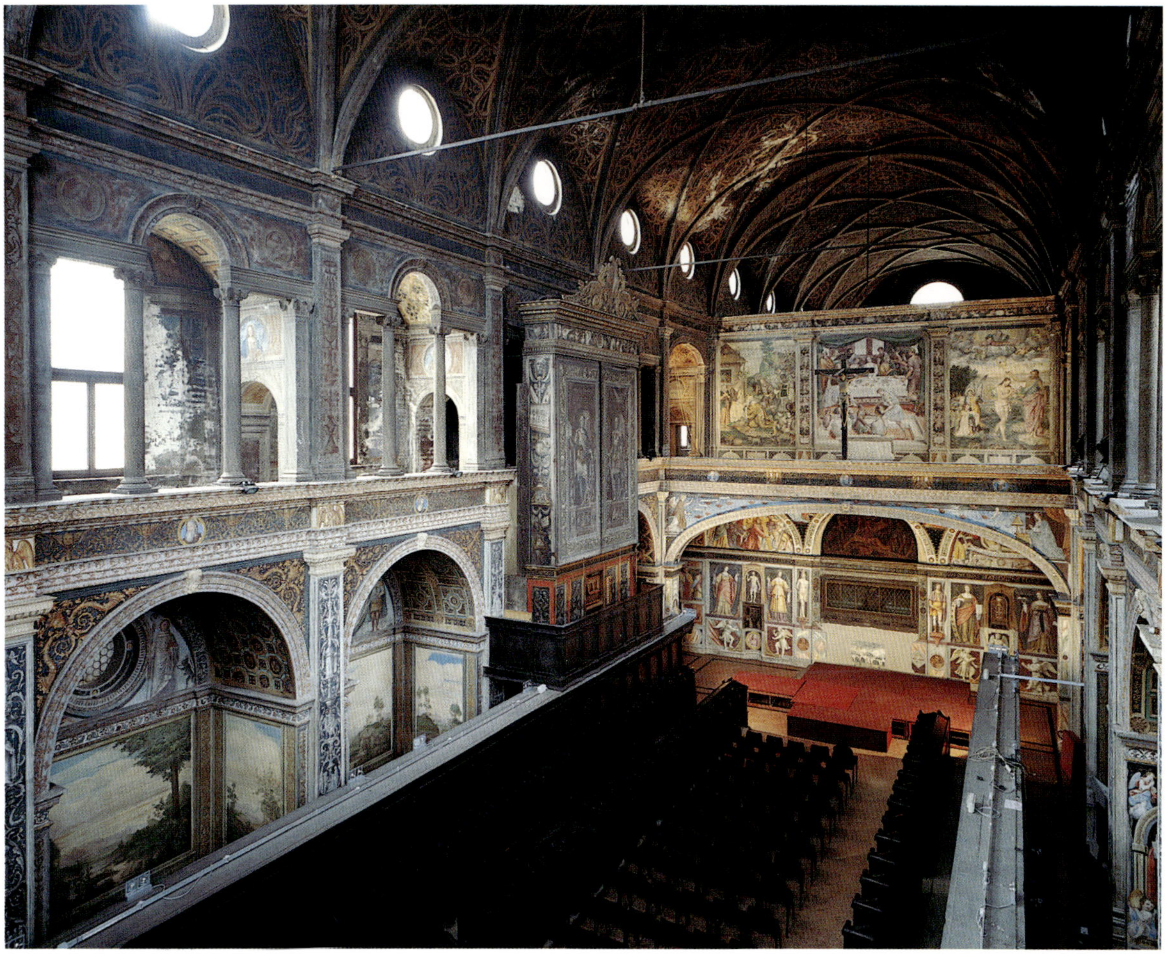

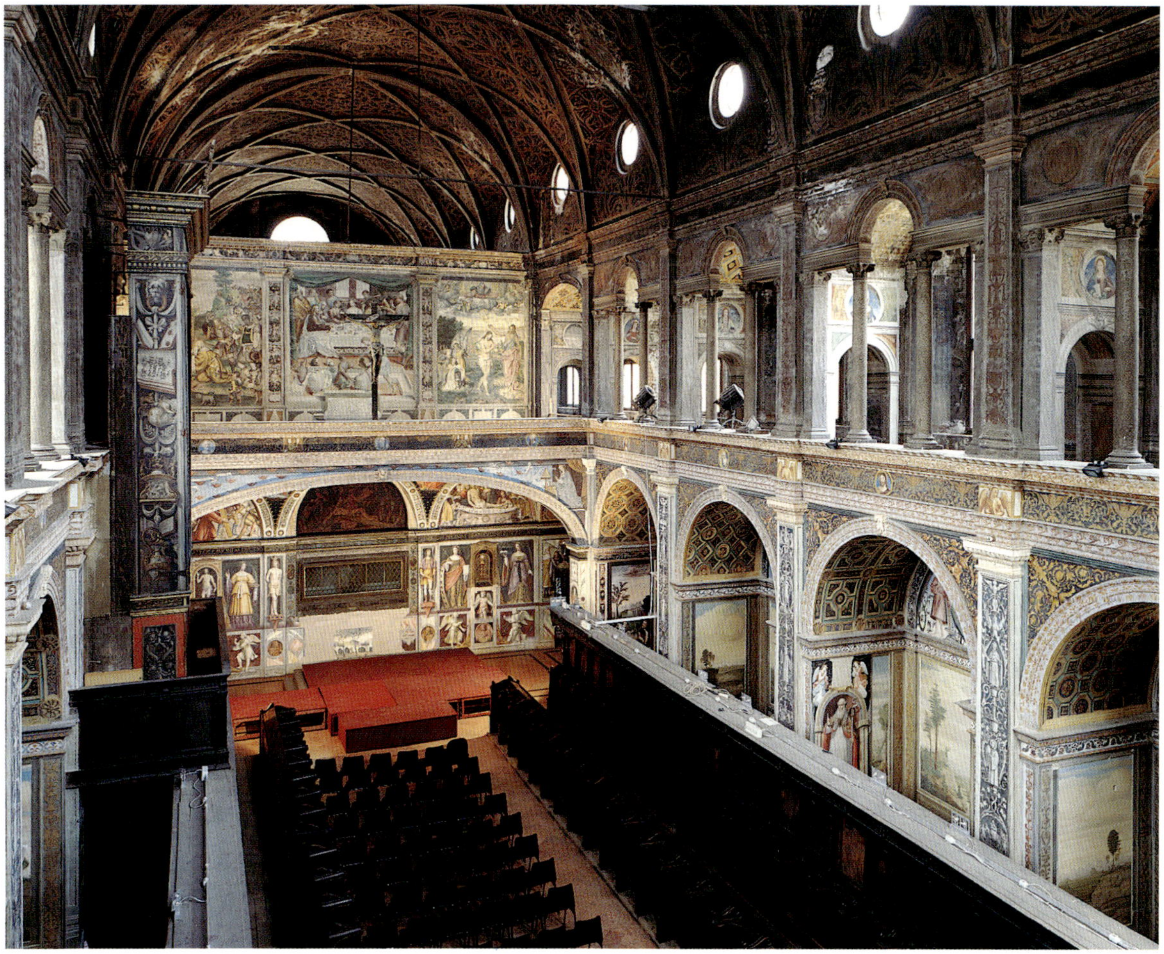

The First Phase of the Decoration in the Convent Hall

Ground plan of the church of San Maurizio al Monastero Maggiore

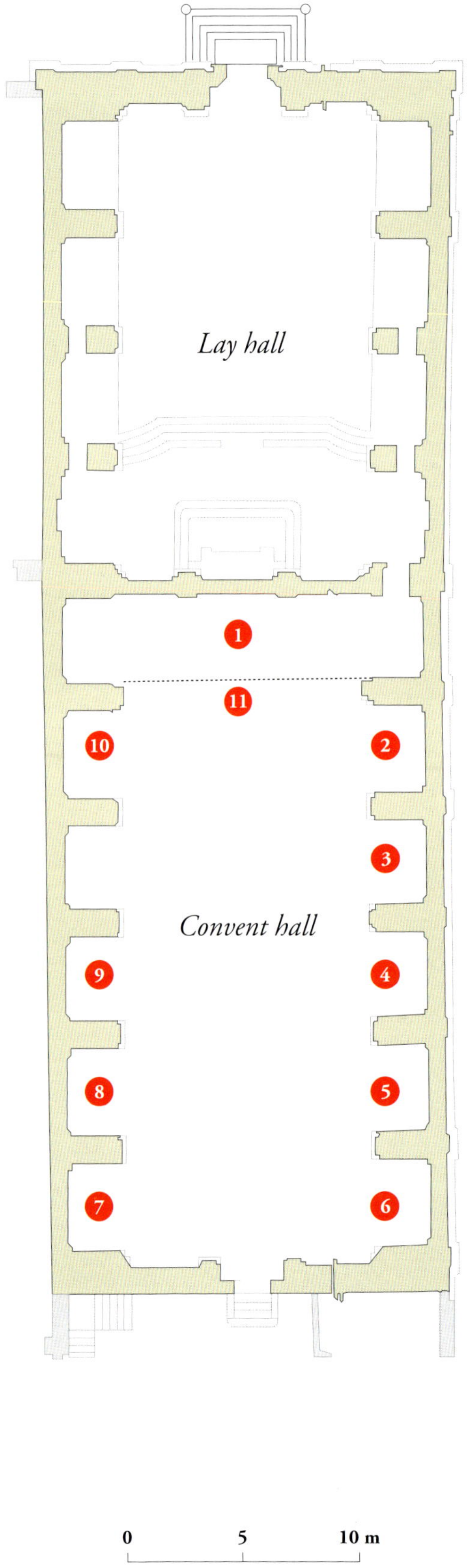

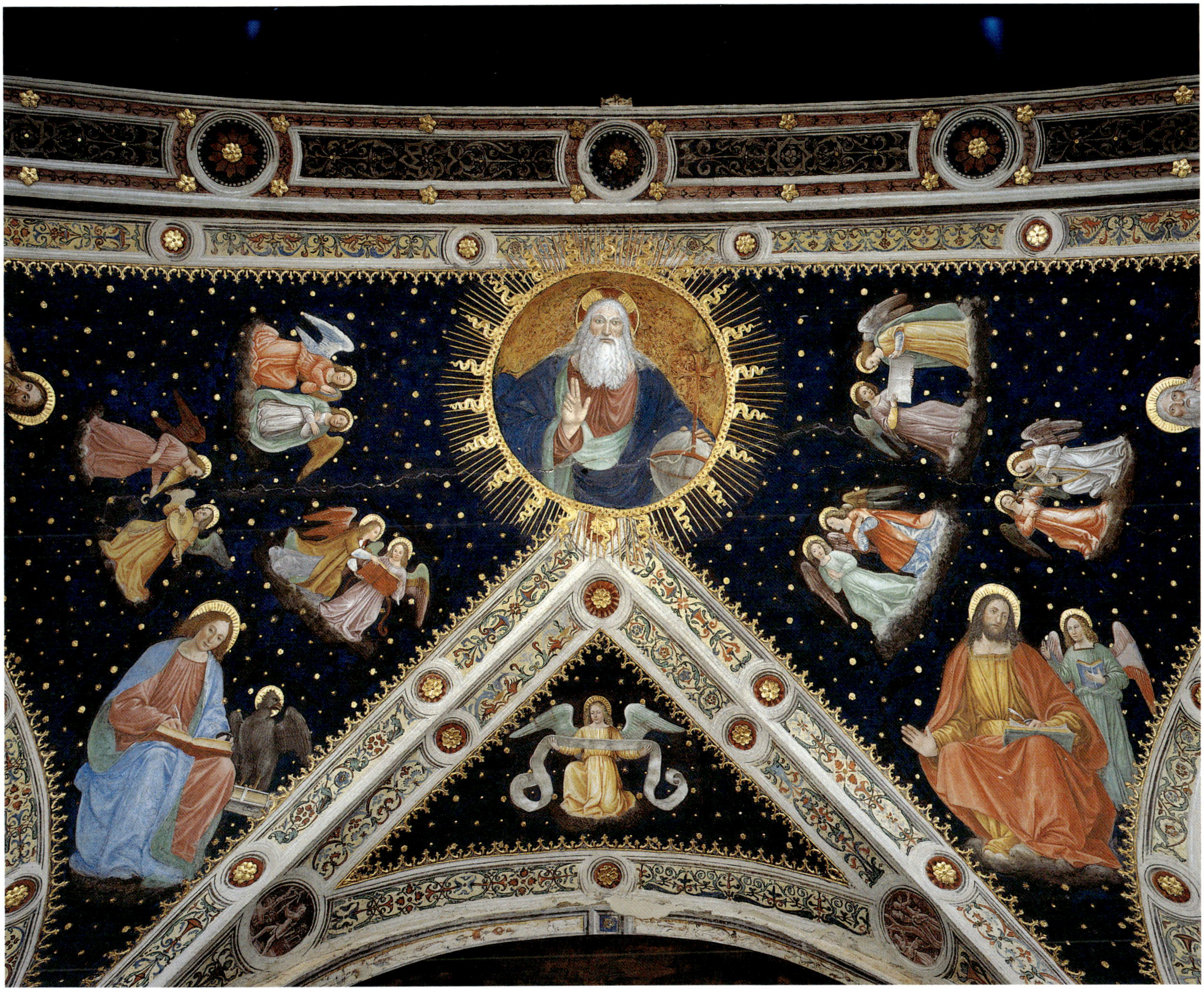

1. Lombard artist, early sixteenth century
God the Father among Evangelists and Angels
General view, bridge vault, convent hall

Pages 122–125
1. Lombard artist, early sixteenth century
God the Father among Evangelists and Angels, details

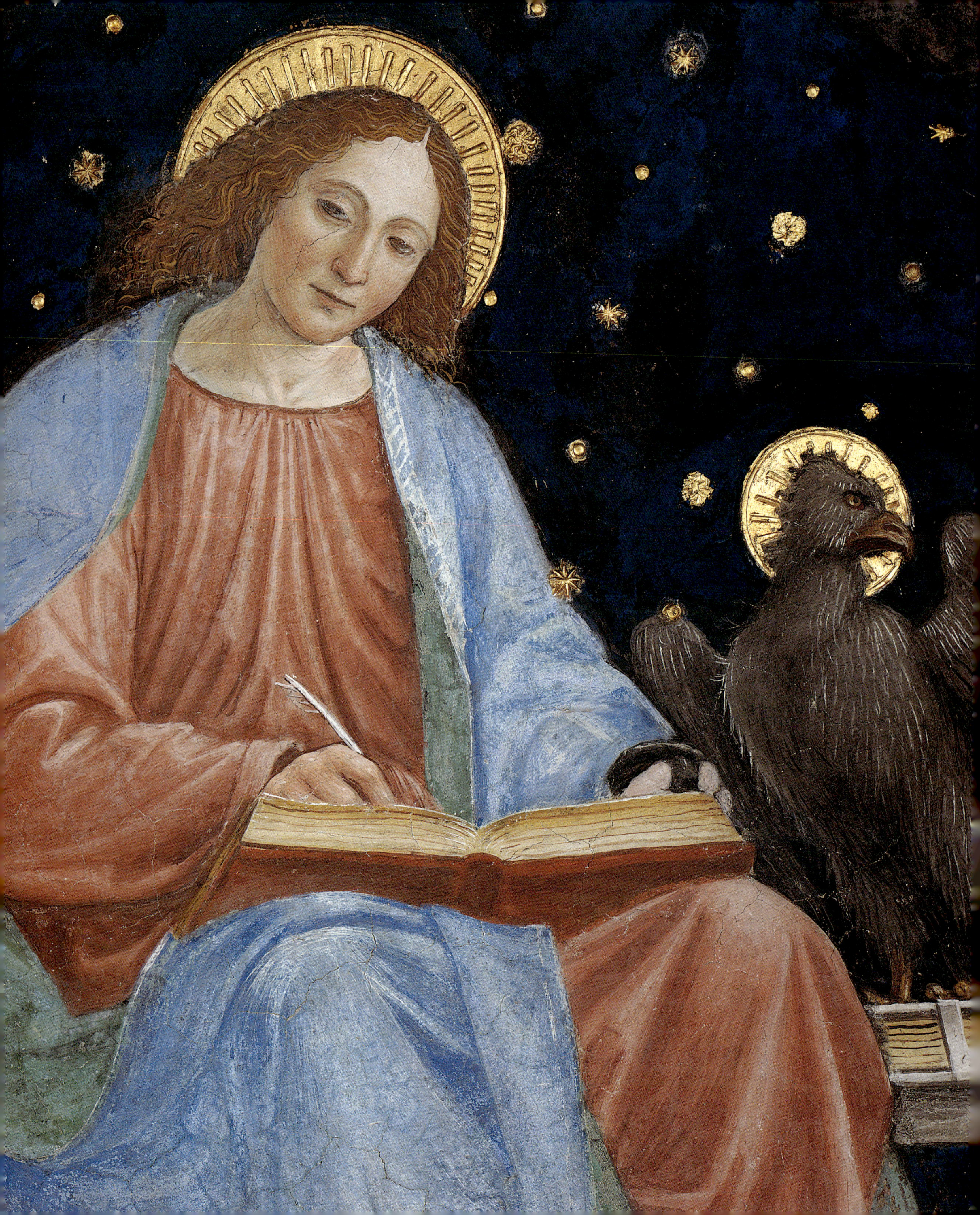

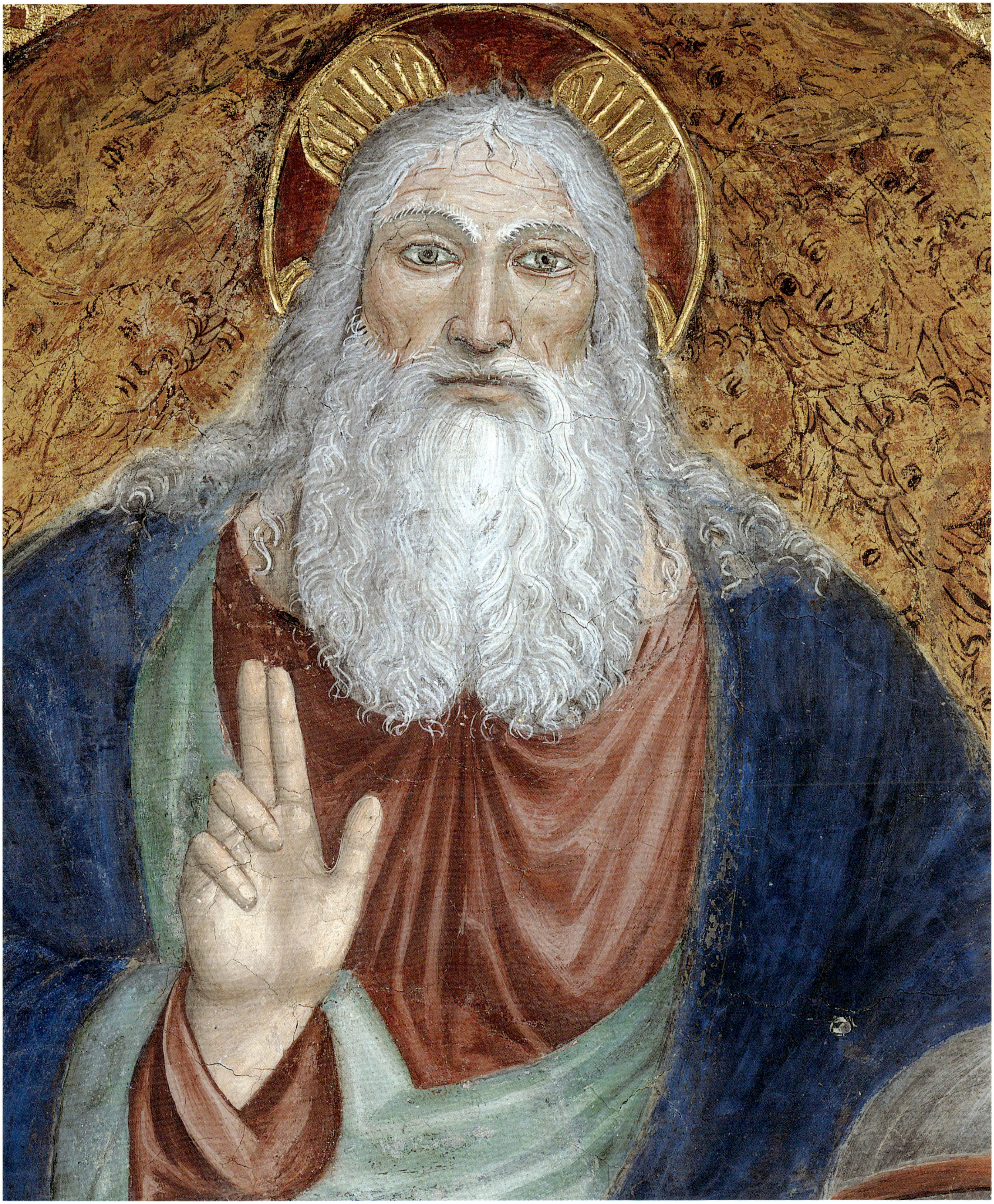

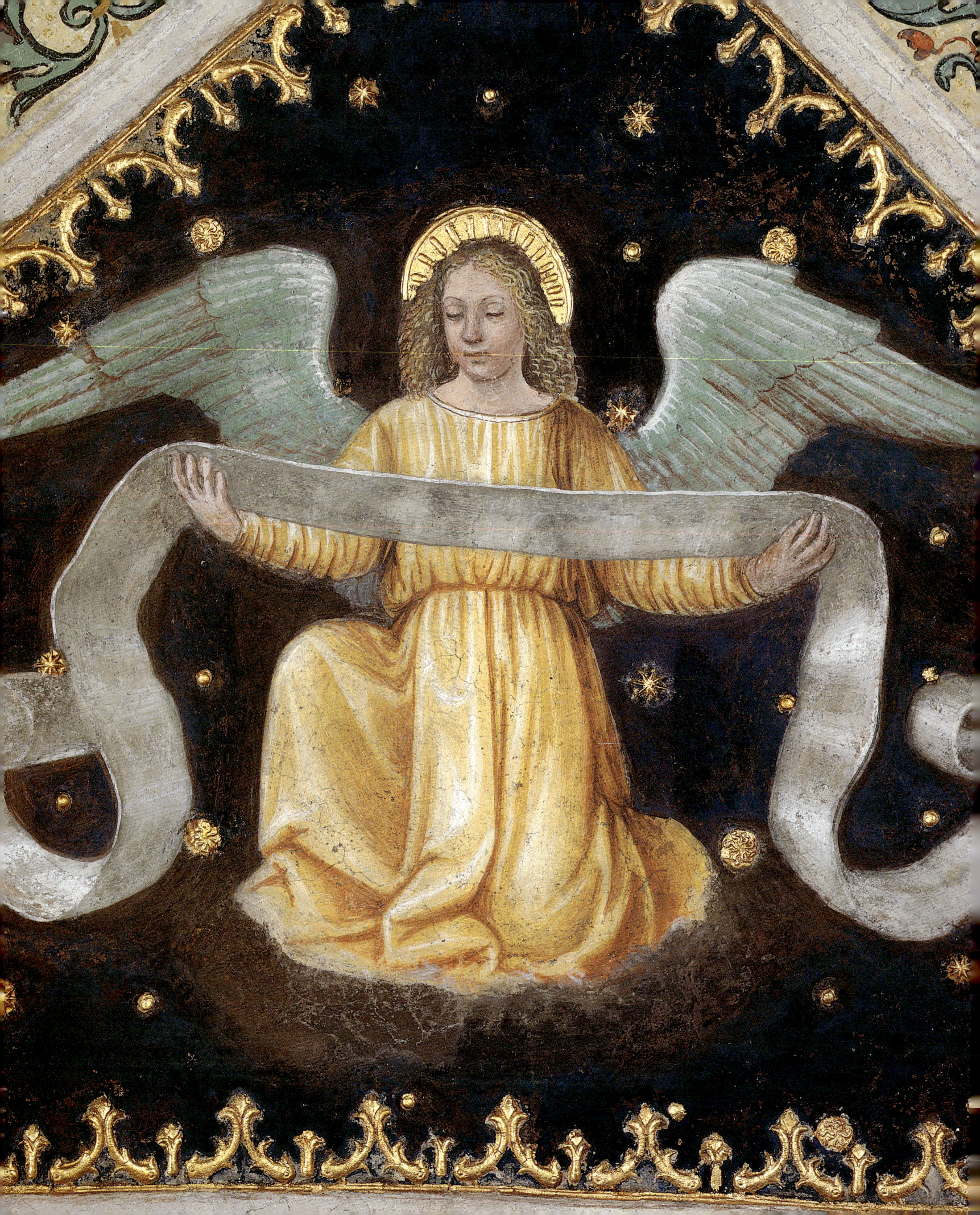

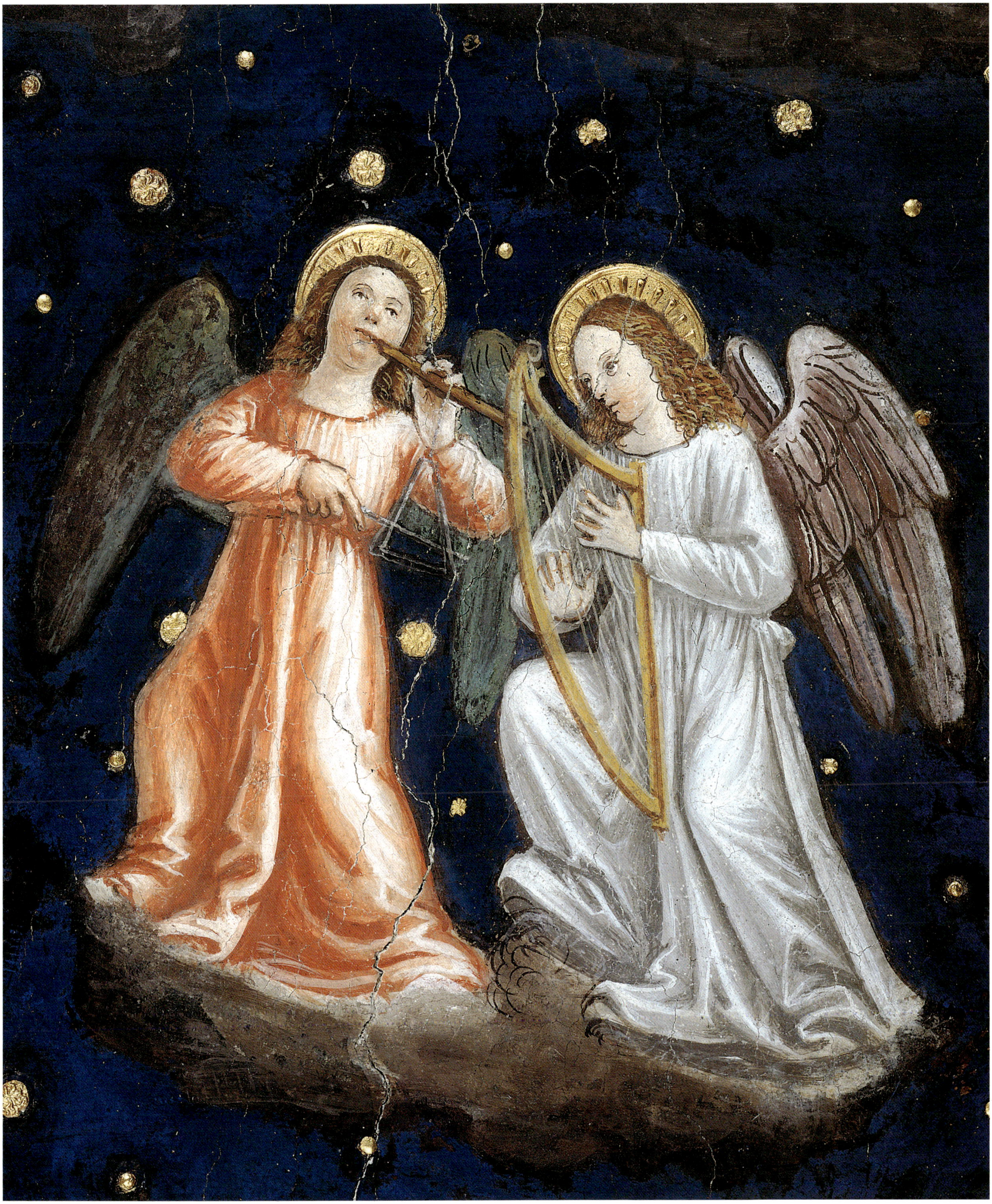

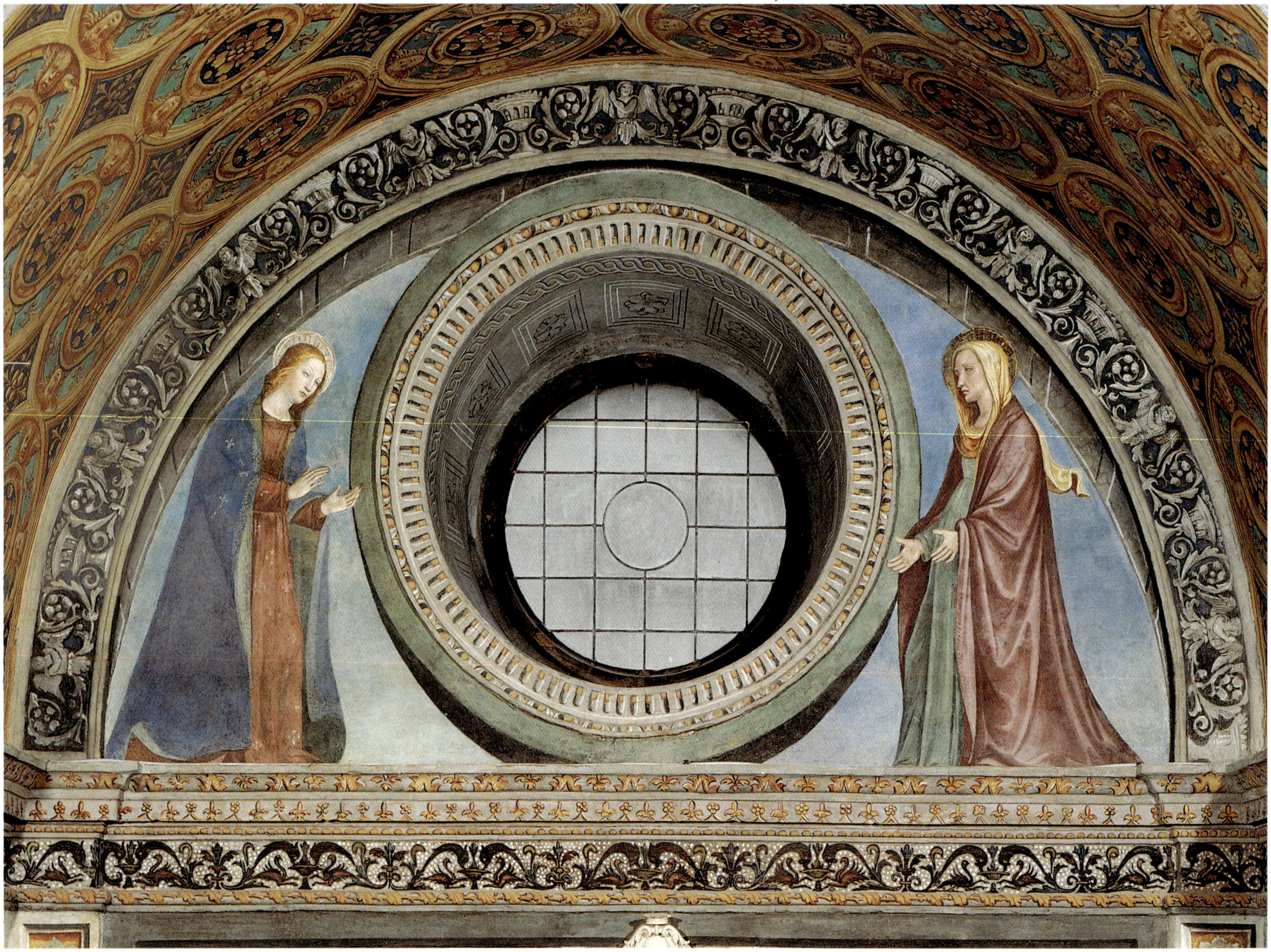

2. Lombard artist, early sixteenth century
Visitation
Convent hall

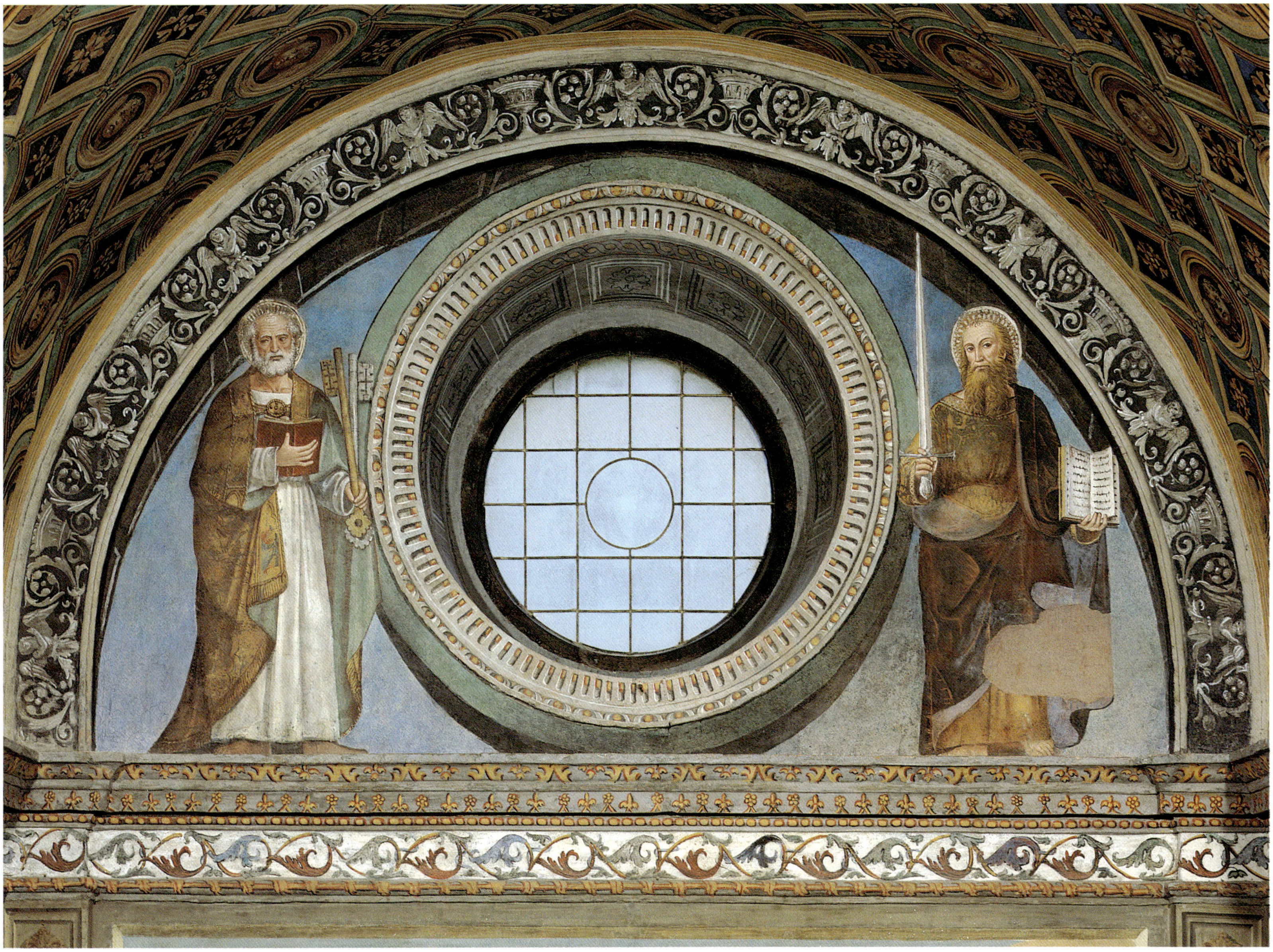

3. Lombard artist, early sixteenth century
St Peter and St Paul
Convent hall

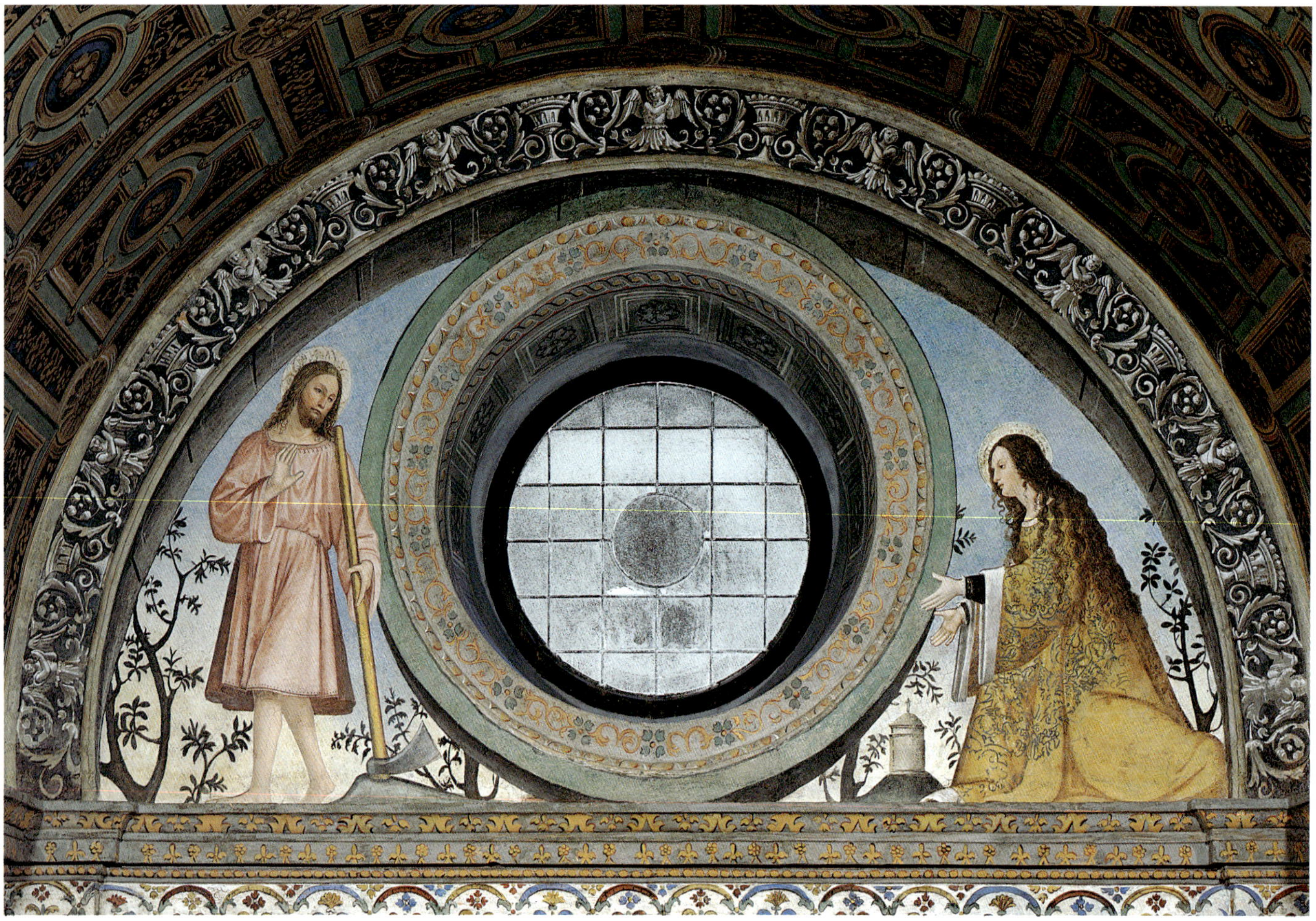

4. Lombard artist, early sixteenth century
Noli me tangere, with detail (*opposite*)
Convent hall

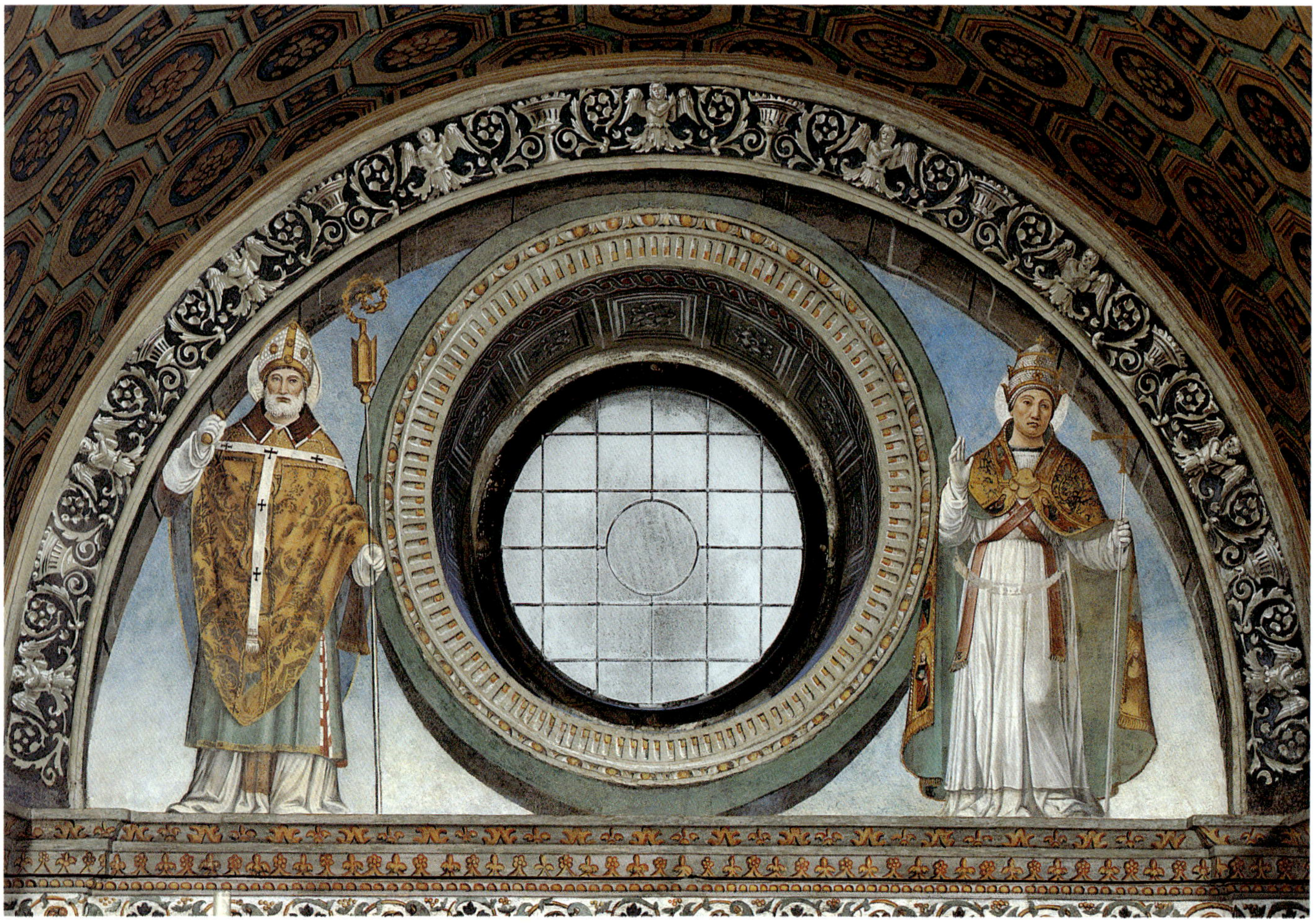

5. Lombard artist, early sixteenth century
St Ambrose and St Gregory the Great
Convent hall

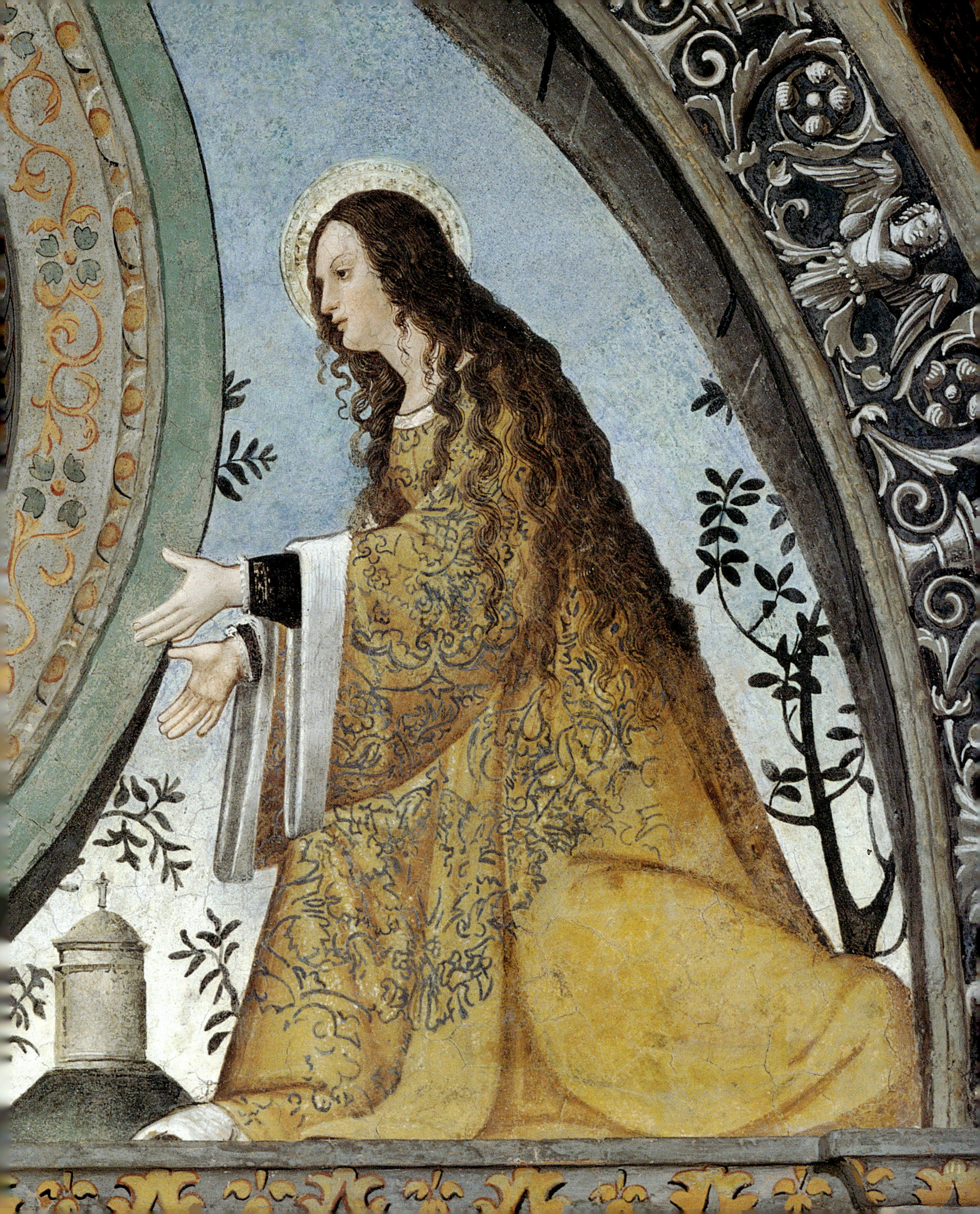

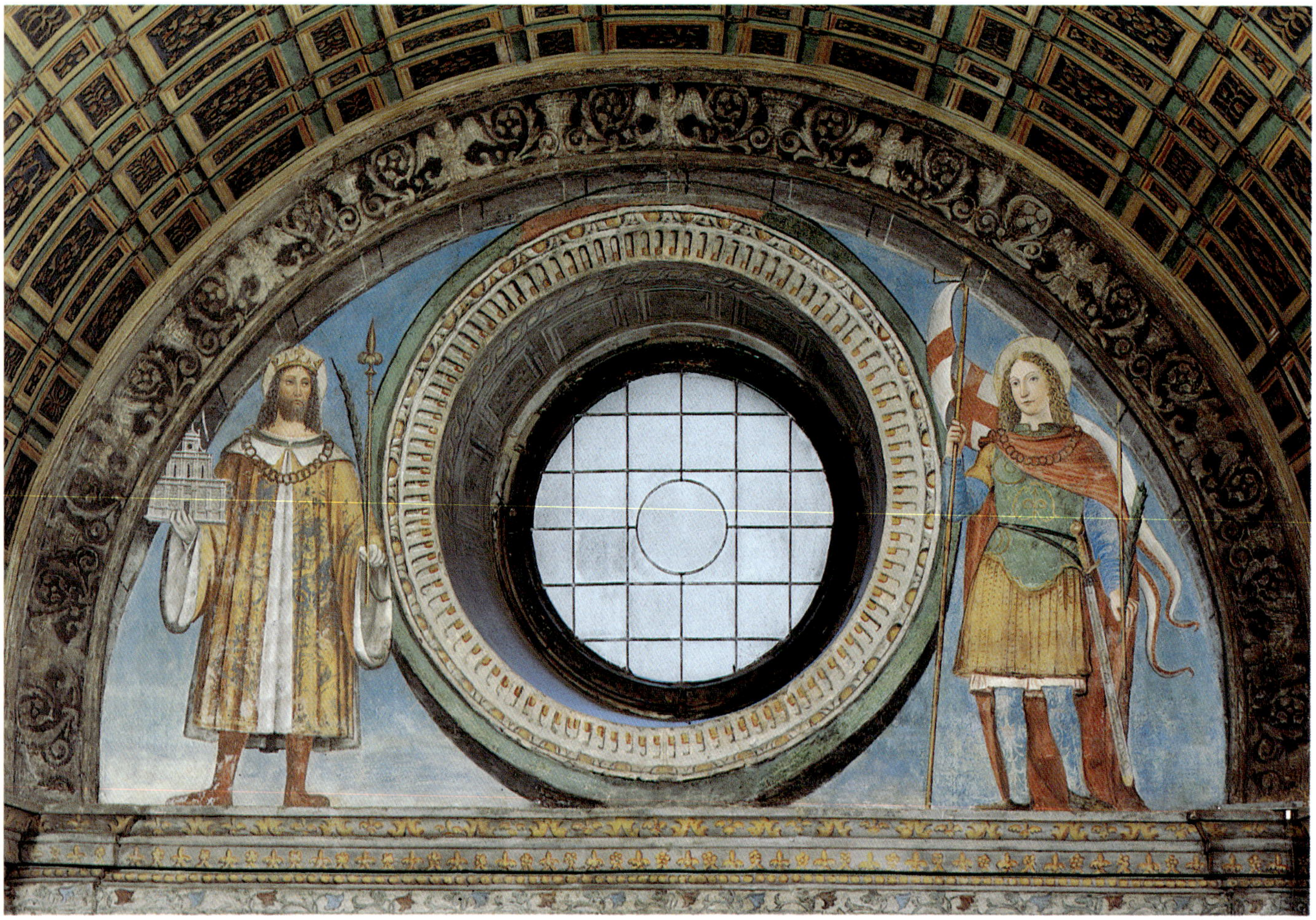

6. Lombard artist, early sixteenth century
St Sigismond and St Maurice
Convent hall

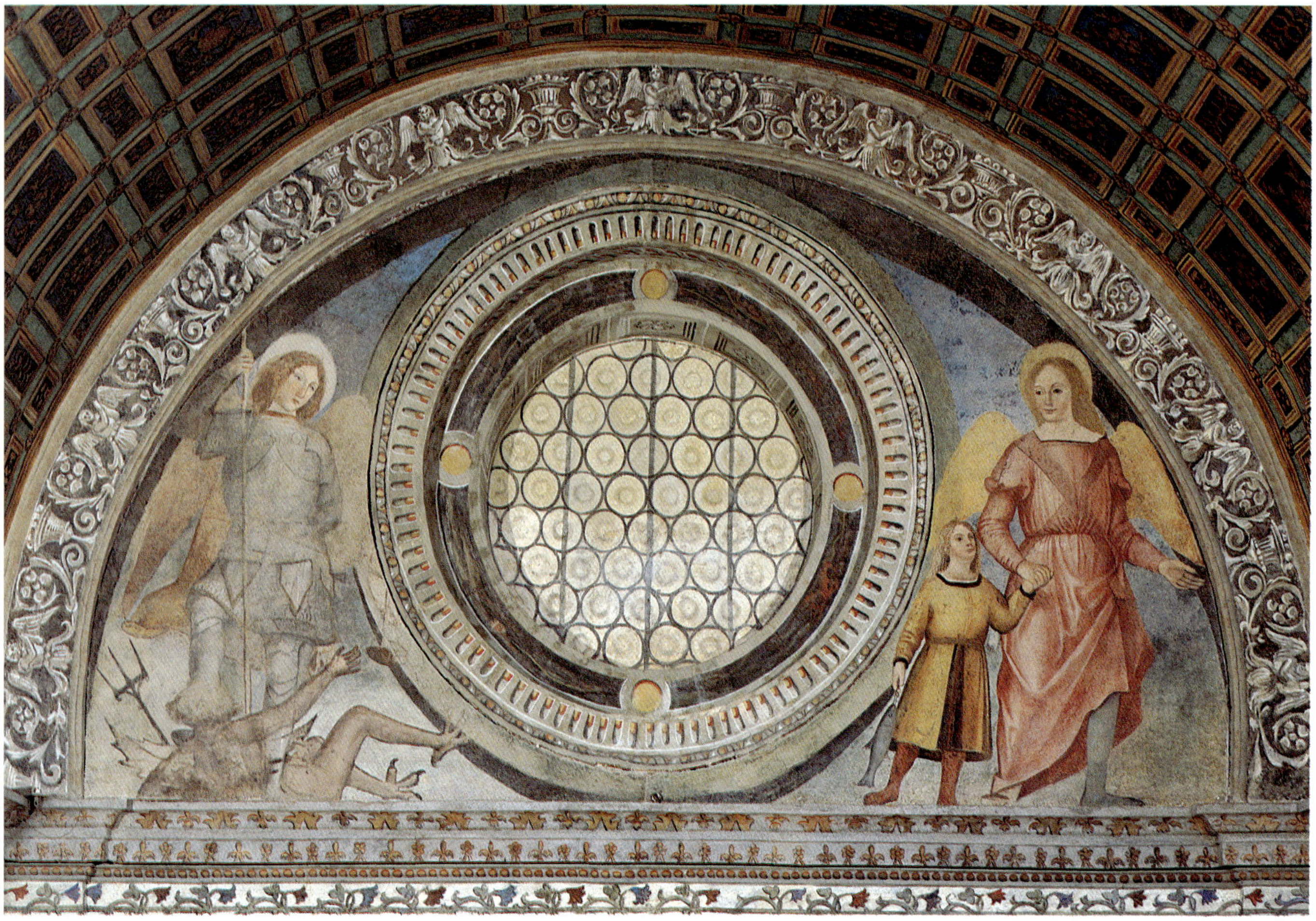

7. Lombard artist, early sixteenth century
Archangels Michael and Raphael,
with detail (*opposite*)
Convent hall

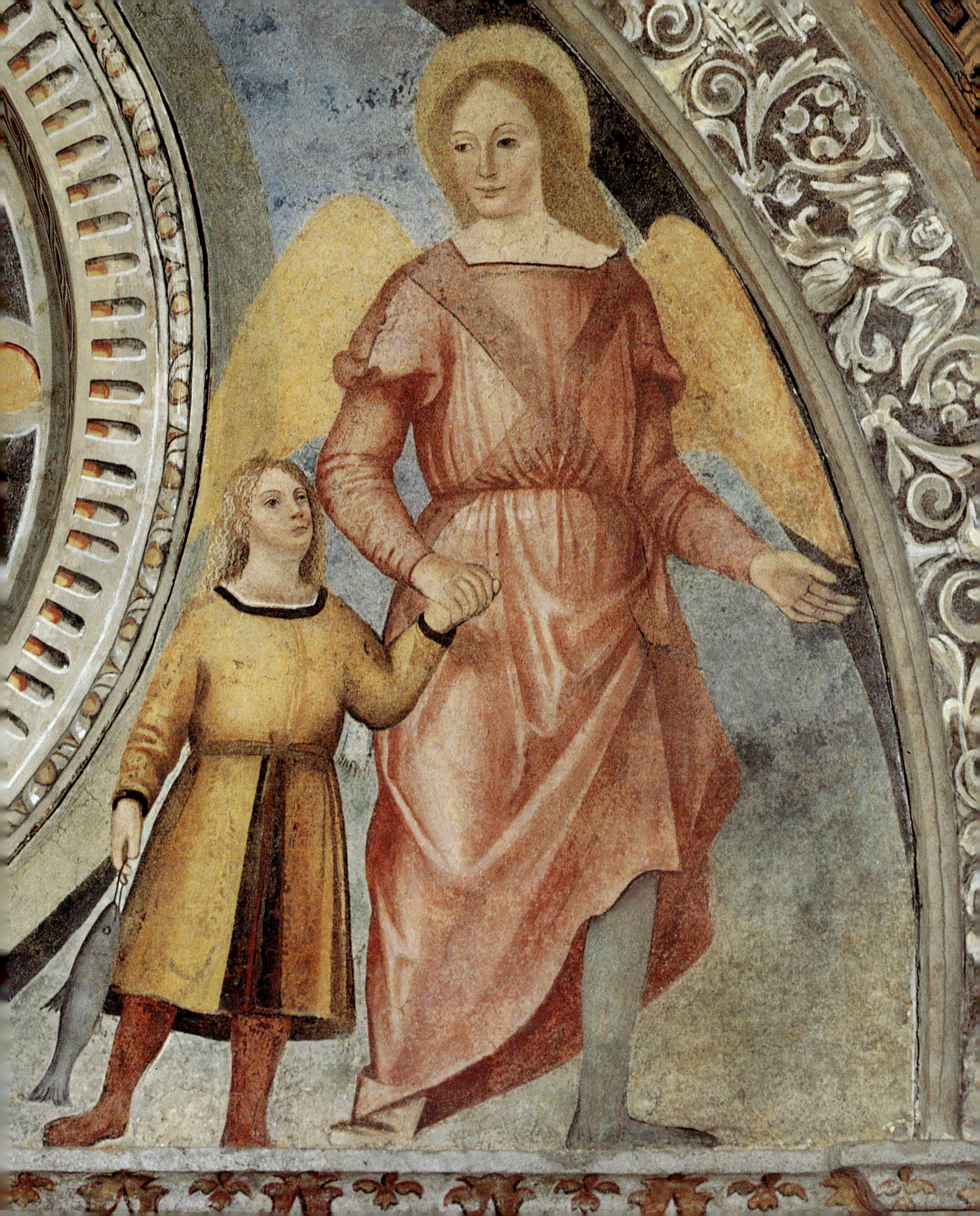

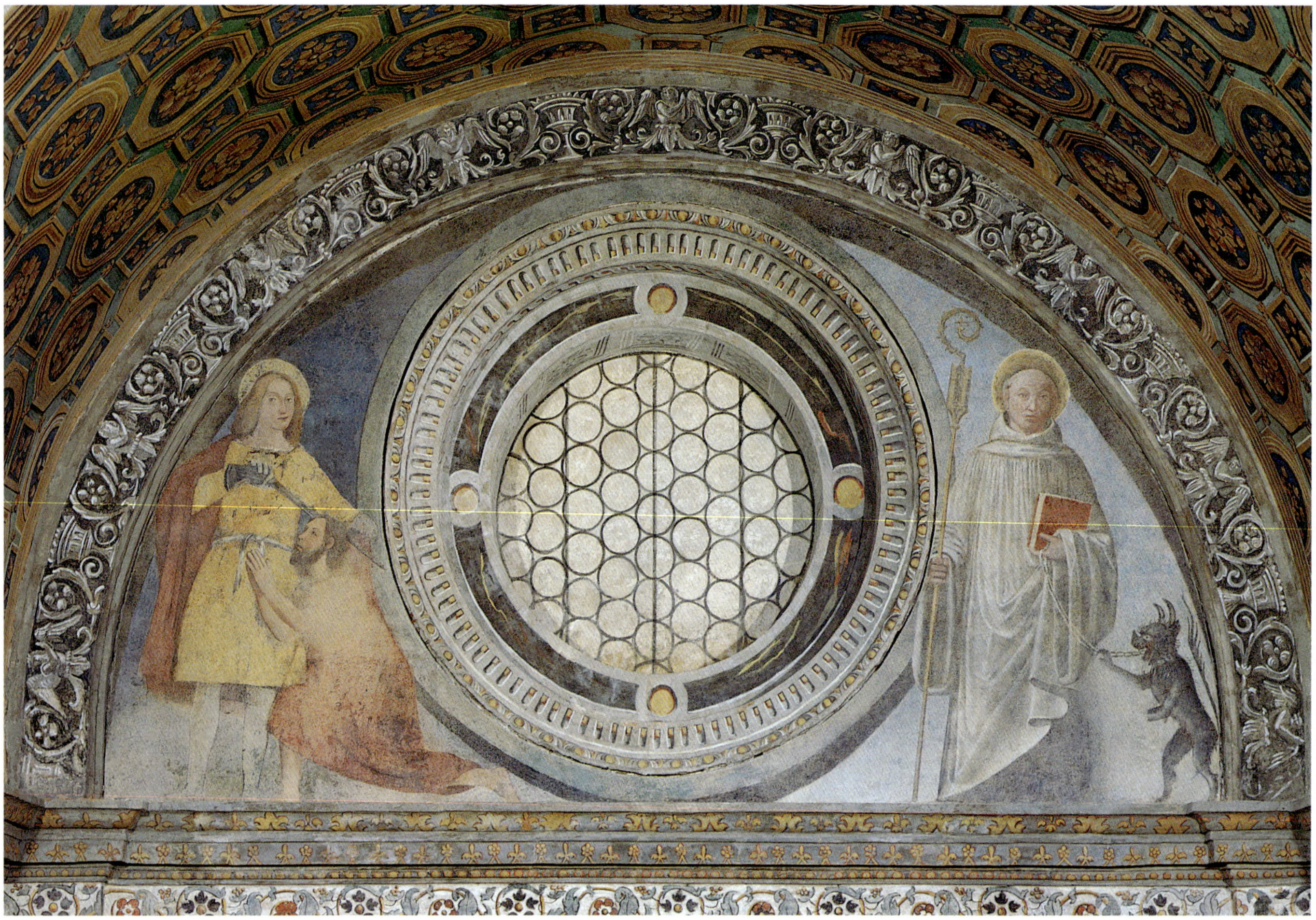

8. Lombard artist, early sixteenth century
St Martin and St Bernard
Convent hall

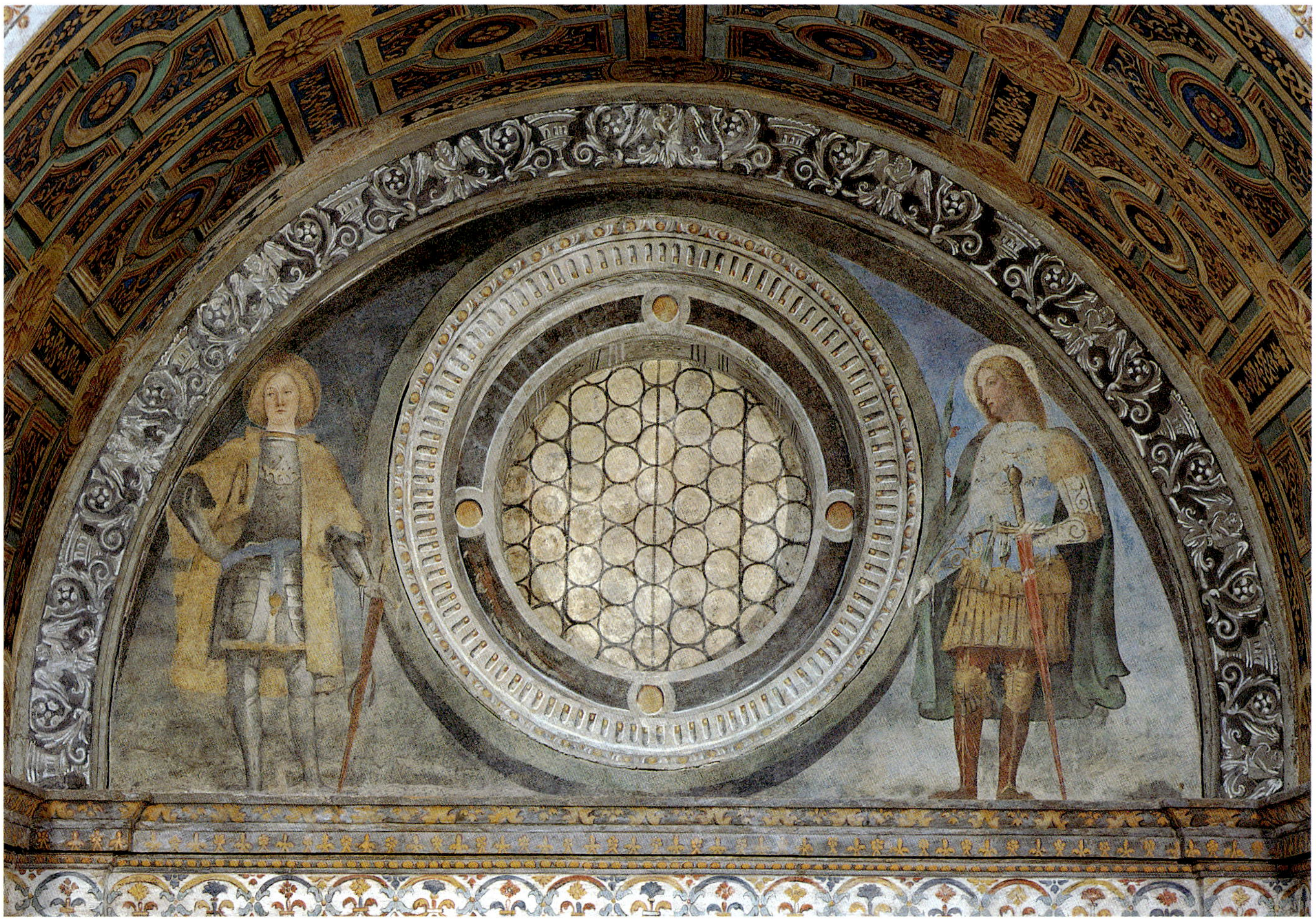

9. Lombard artist, early sixteenth century
St Exuperius and St Candidus
Convent hall

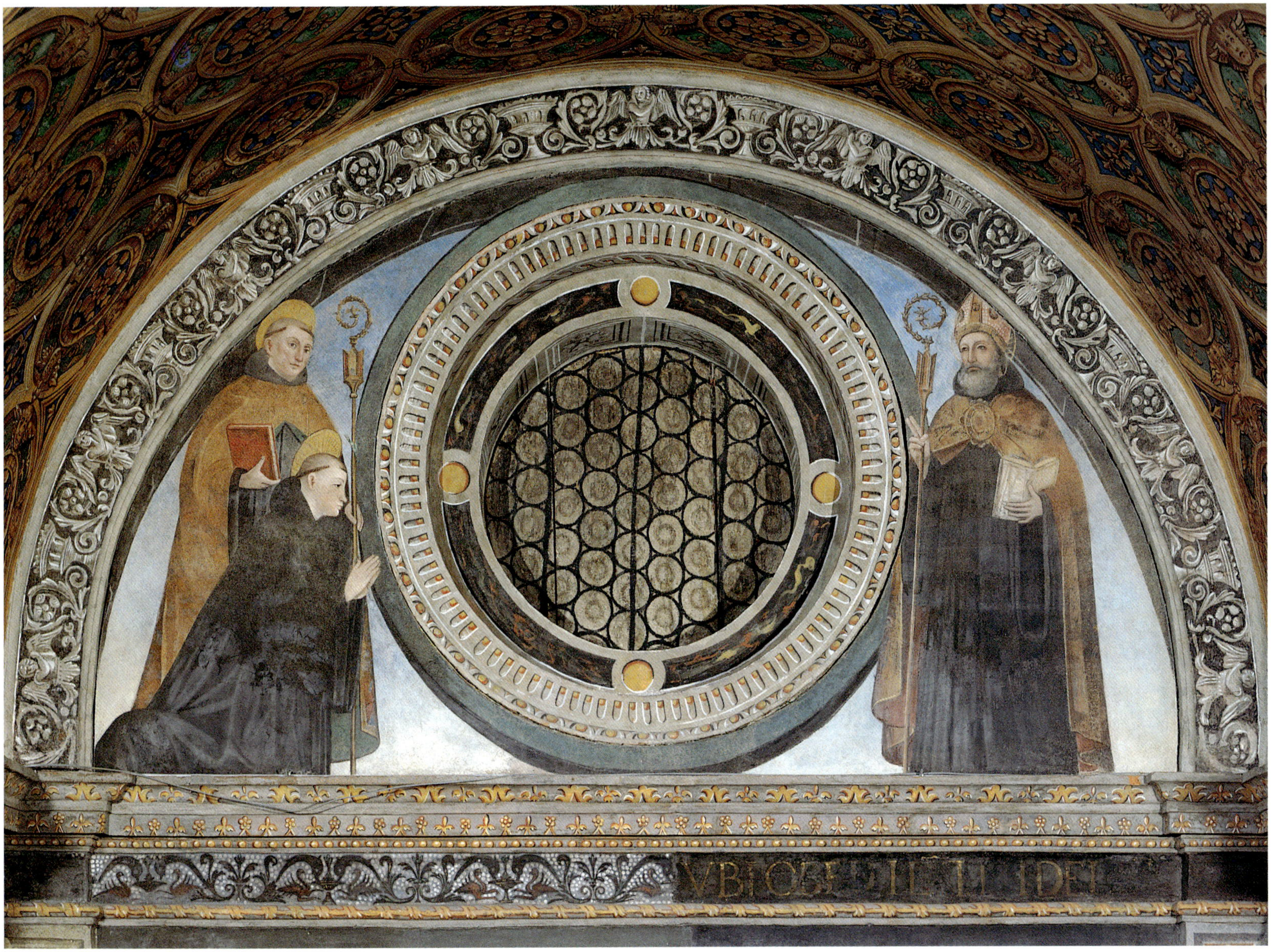

10. Lombard artist, early sixteenth century
Sts Placidus, Maurus and Benedict
Convent hall

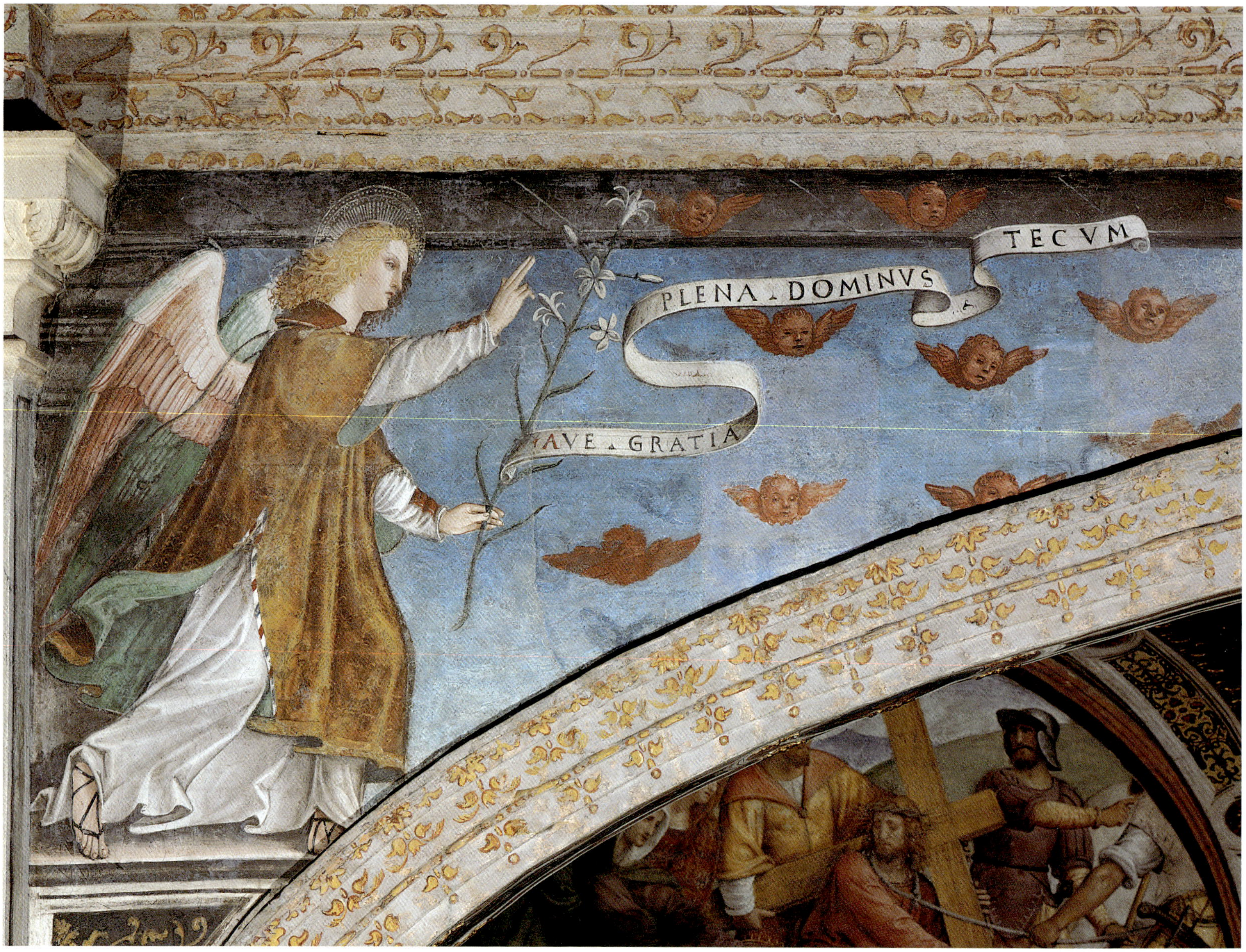

11. Lombard artist, early sixteenth century
Annunciating Angel
Spandrel of the bridge, convent hall

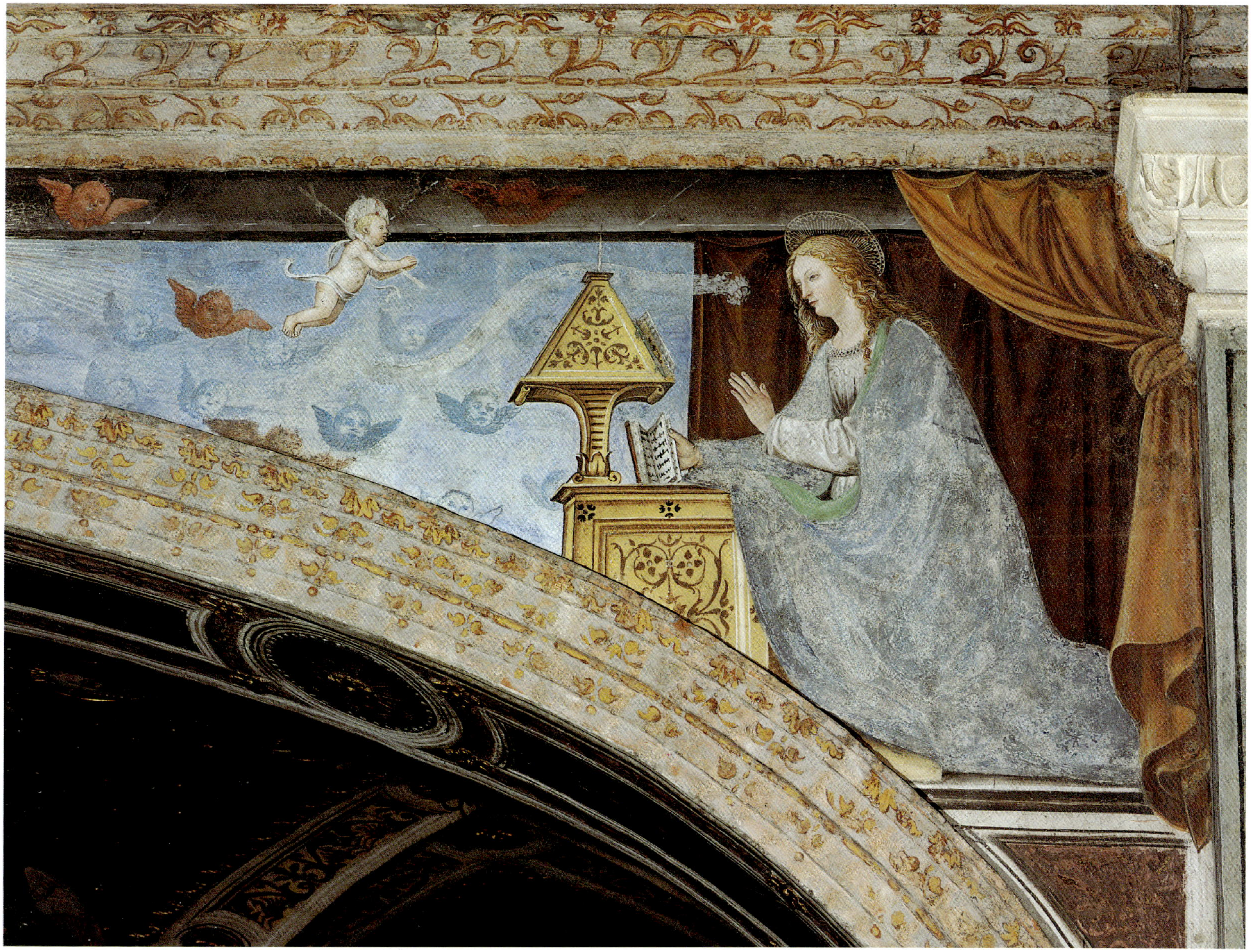

11. Lombard artist, early sixteenth century
Virgin Annunciate
Spandrel of the bridge, convent hall

Following pages
11. Lombard artist, early sixteenth century
Annunciating Angel and *Virgin Annunciate*, details

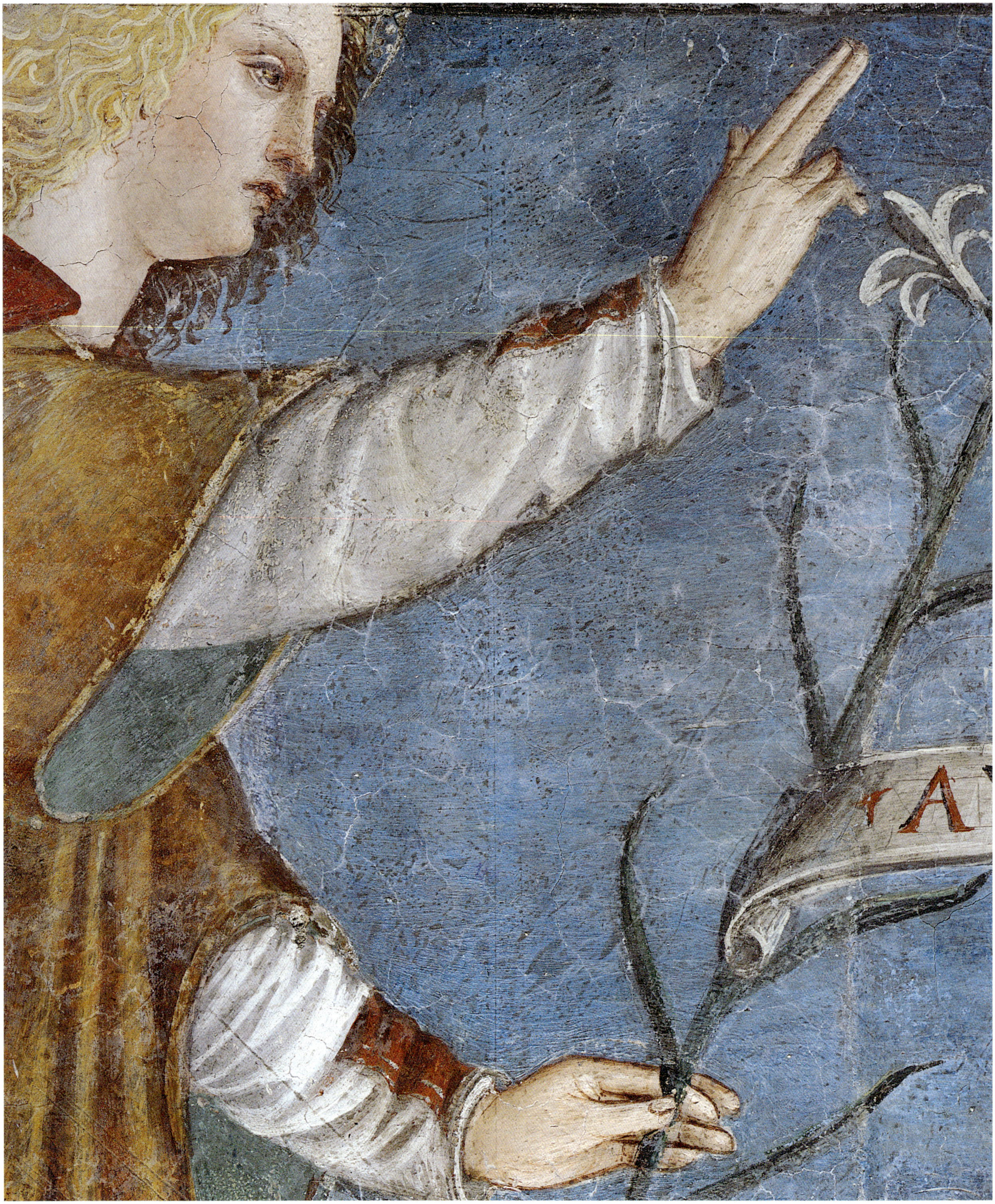
A

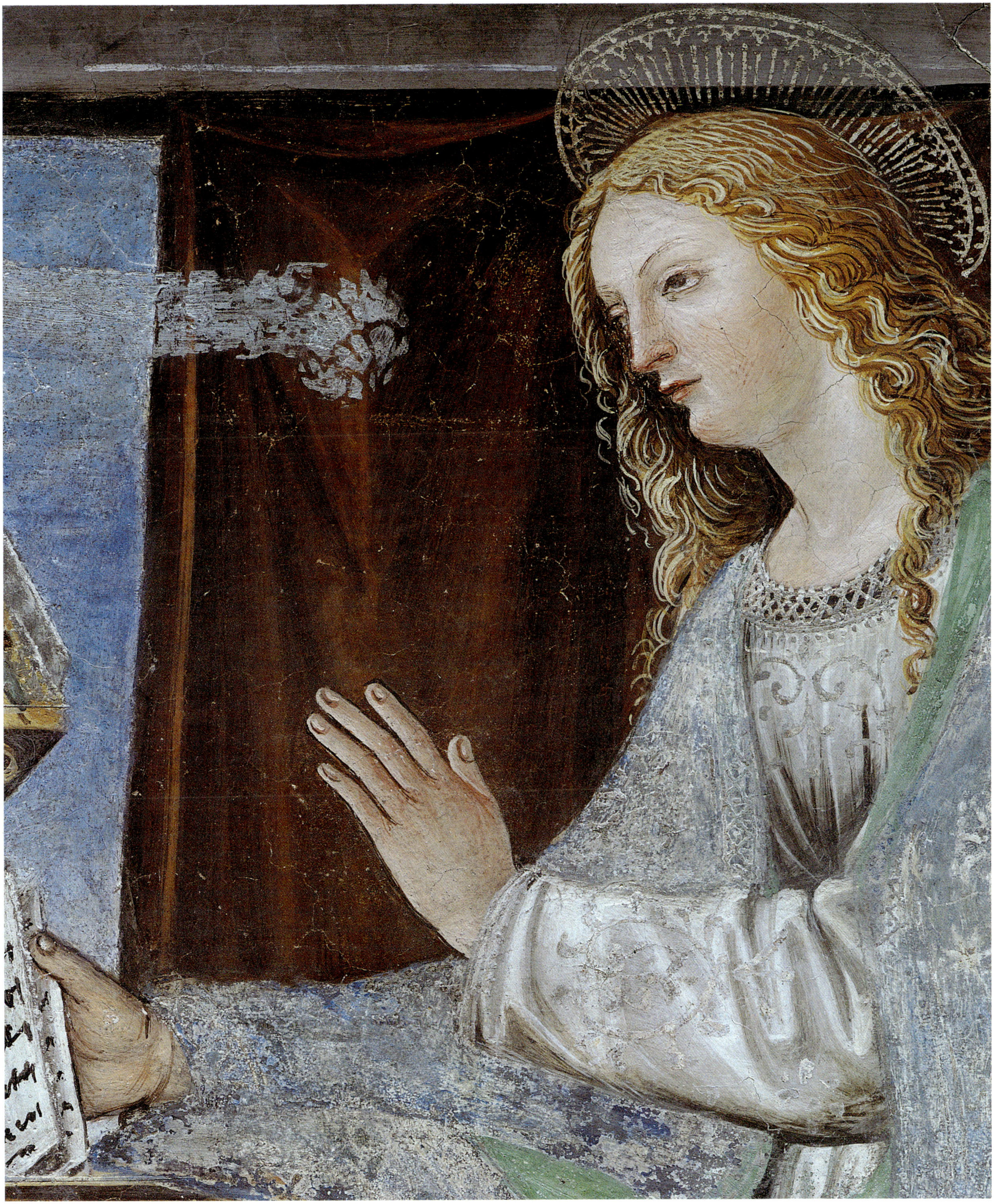

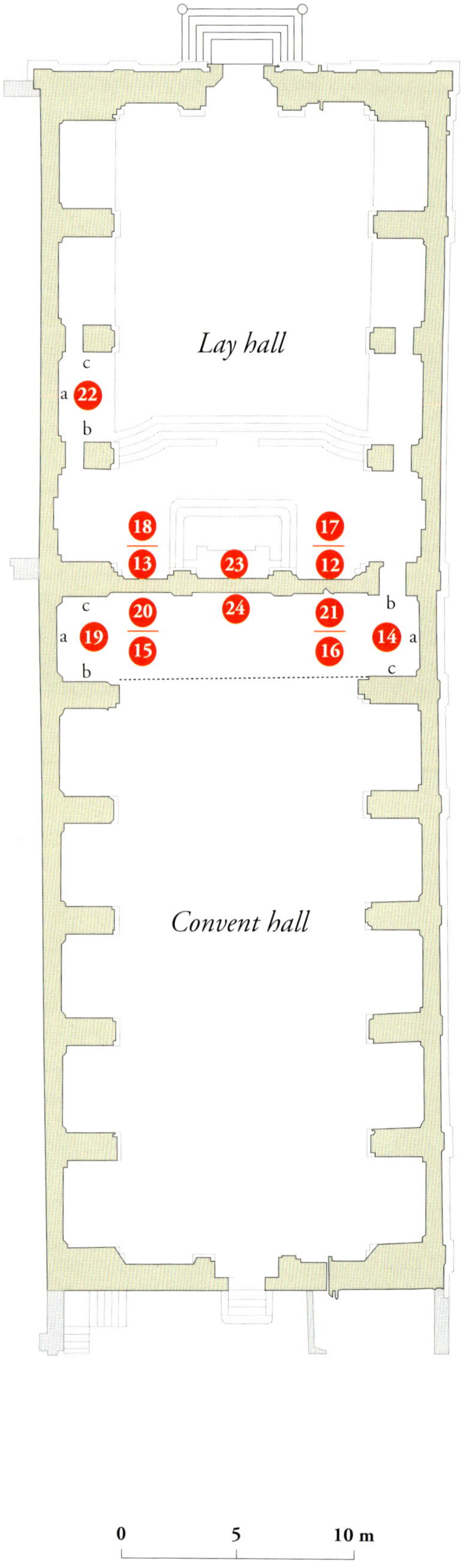

Ground plan of the church of San Maurizio al Monastero Maggiore

12. Bernardino Luini
Left side, partition wall, lay hall

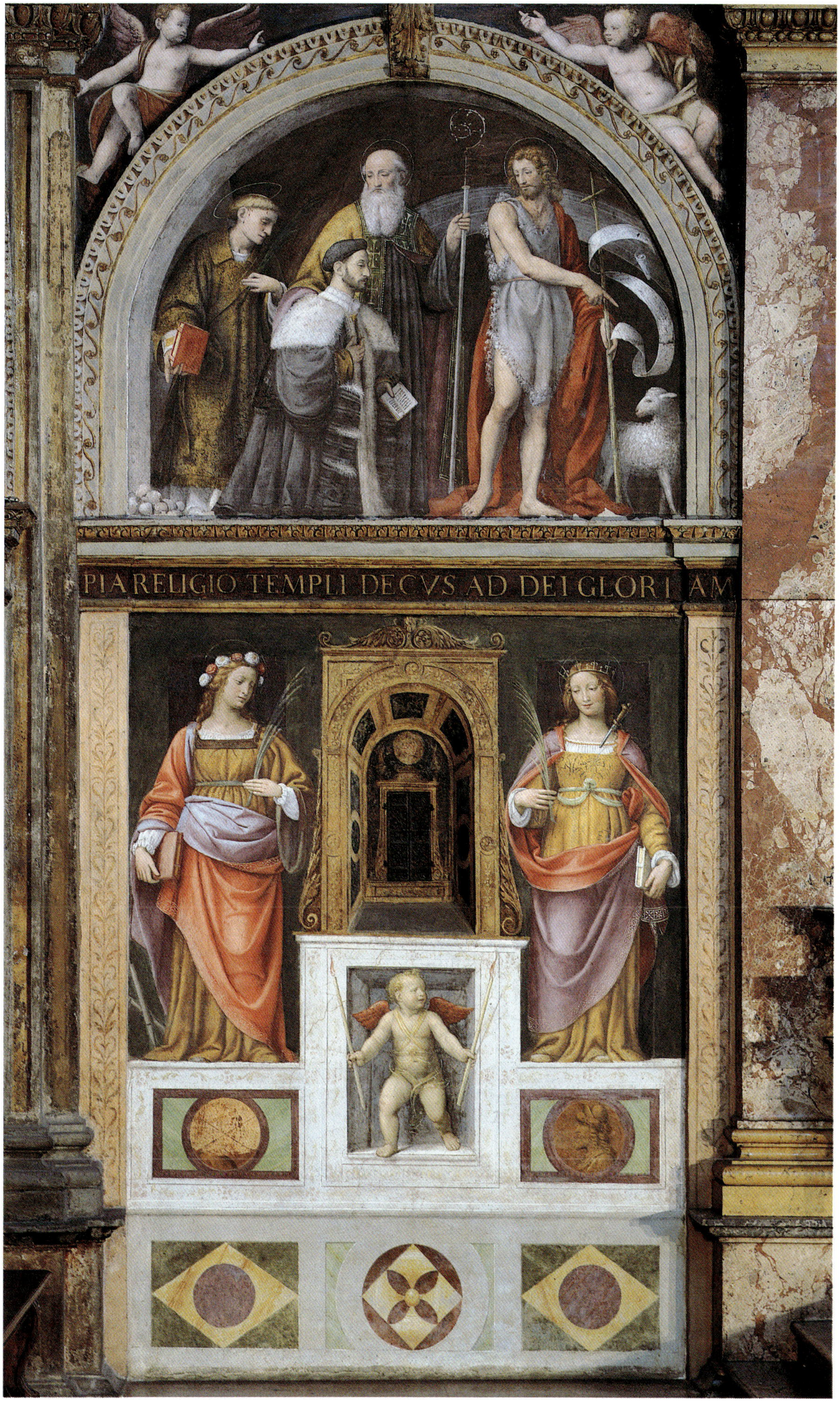

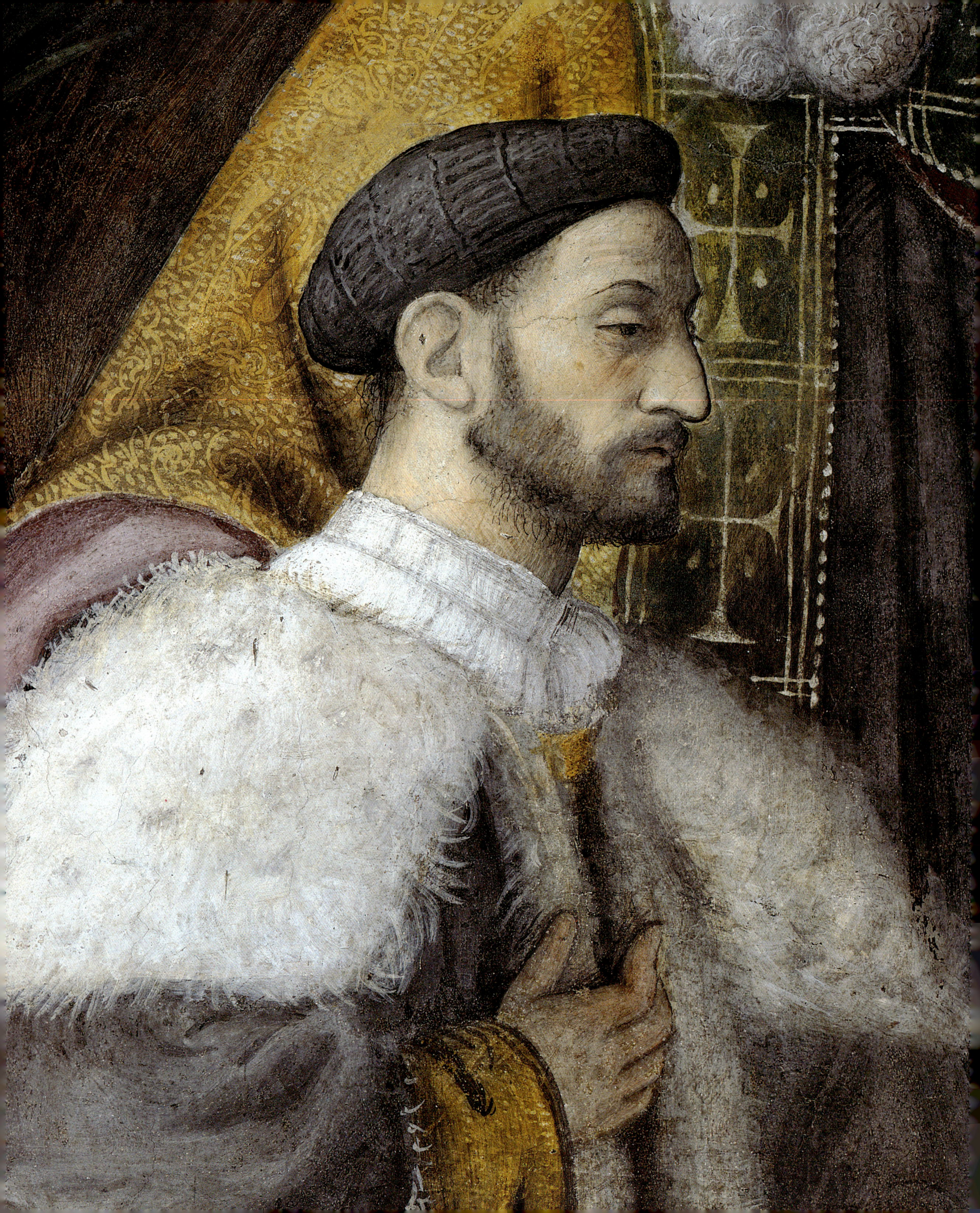

12. Bernardino Luini
Alessandro Bentivoglio among St Stephen, St Benedict and St John the Baptist, details

Following pages

12. Bernardino Luini
Angel bearing candles, detail

12. Bernardino Luini
St Ursula, detail

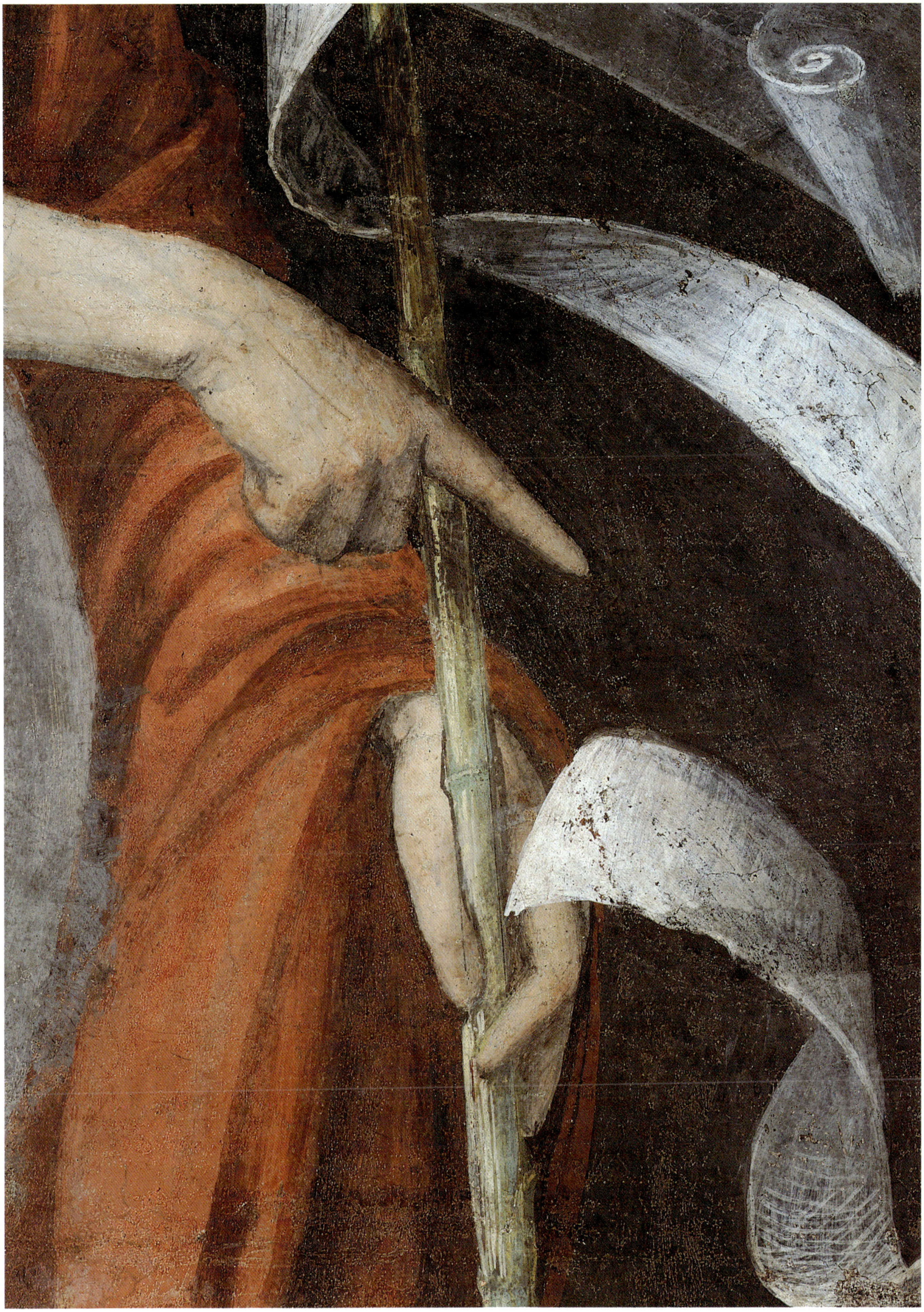

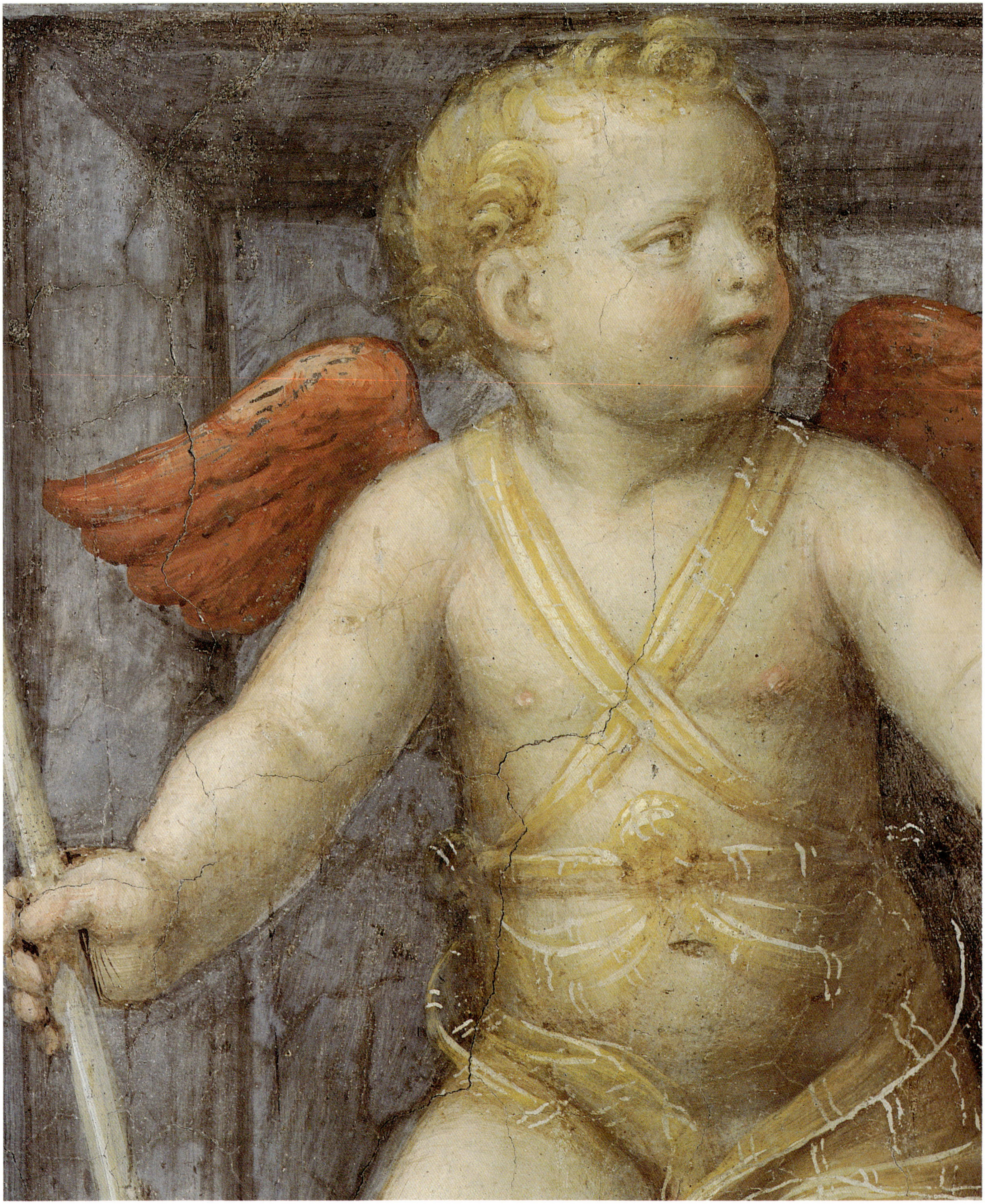

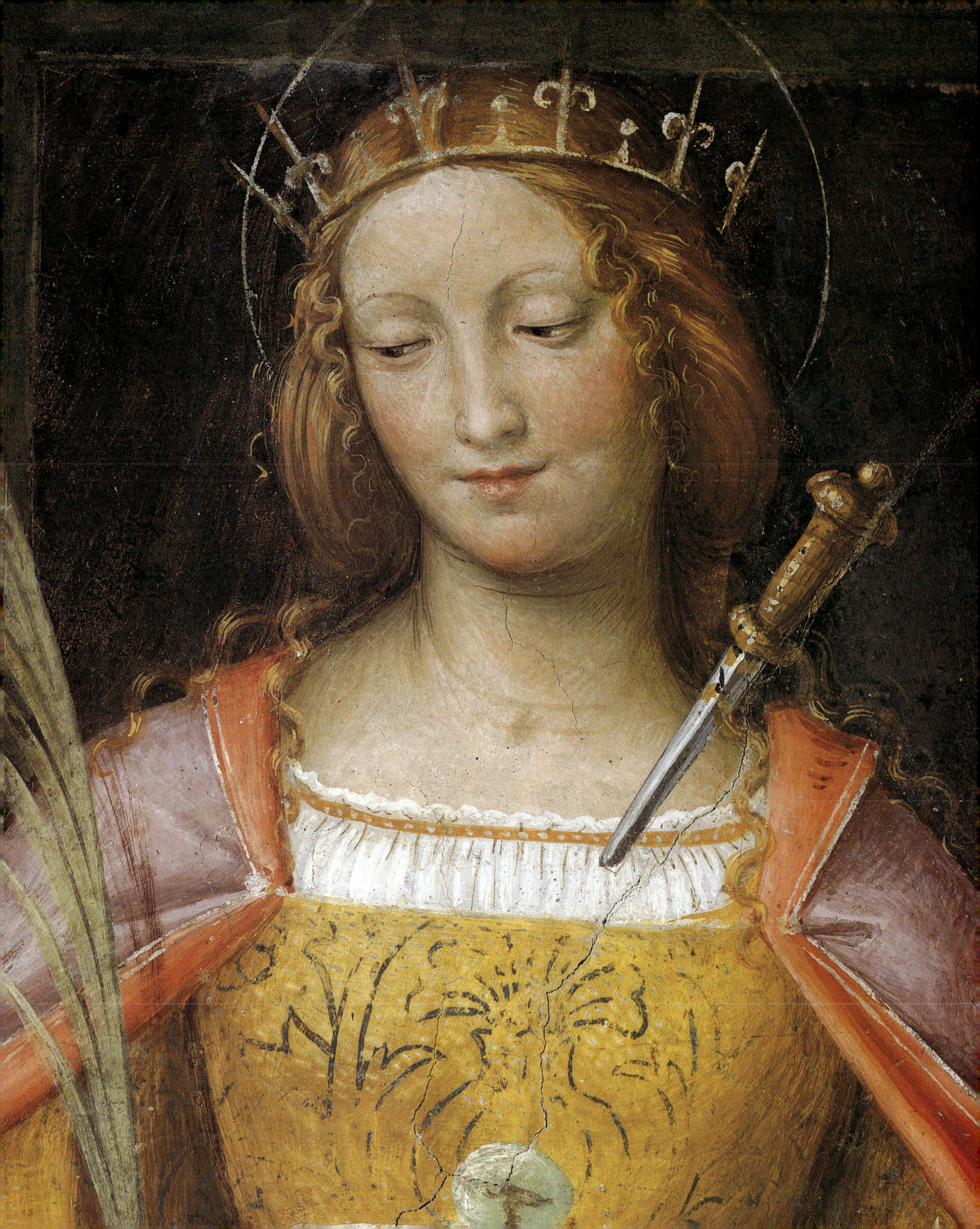

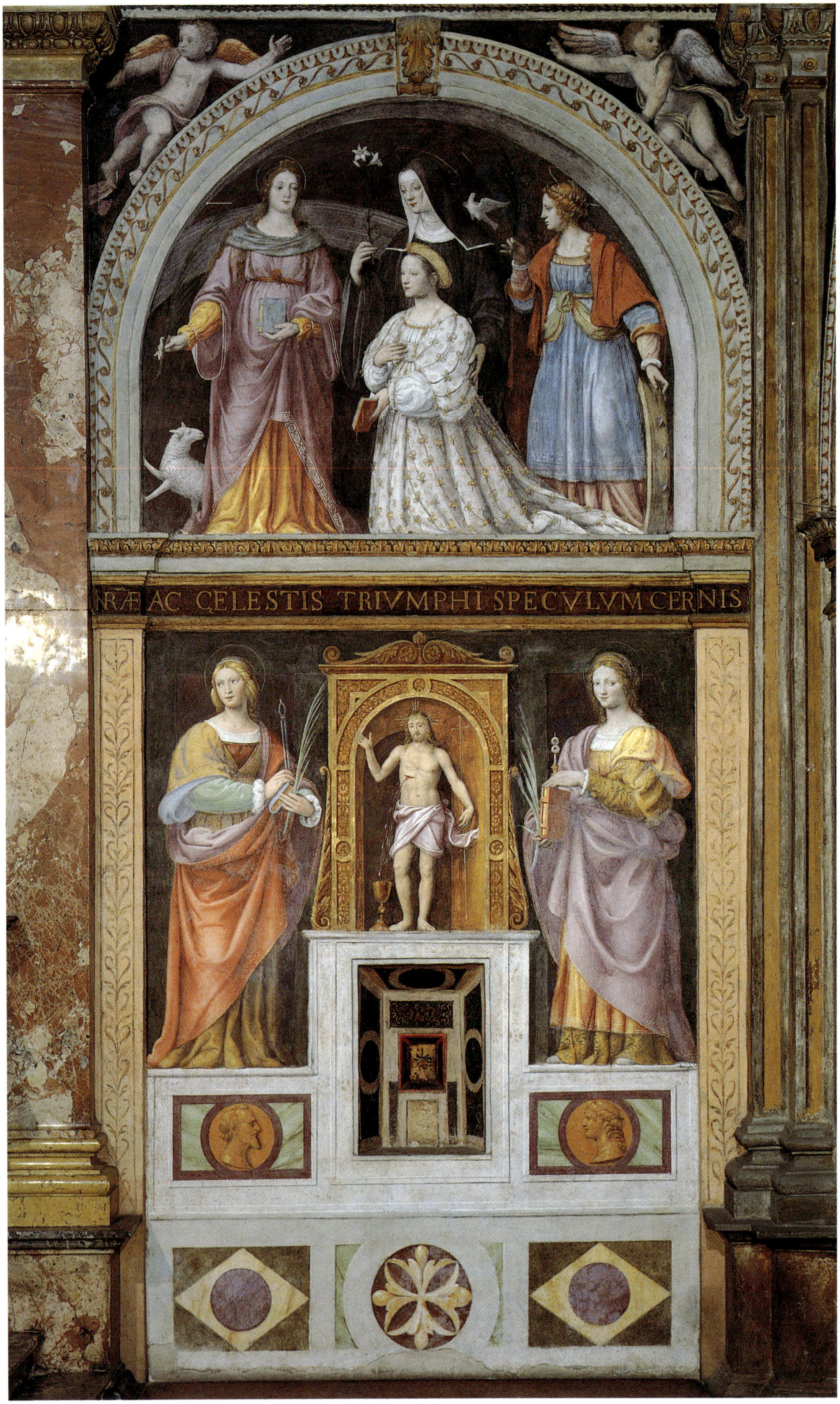

13. Bernardino Luini
Right side, partition wall, lay hall

Pages 145–147
13. Bernardino Luini
Ippolita Bentivoglio among St Agnes, St Scholastica and St Catherine, details

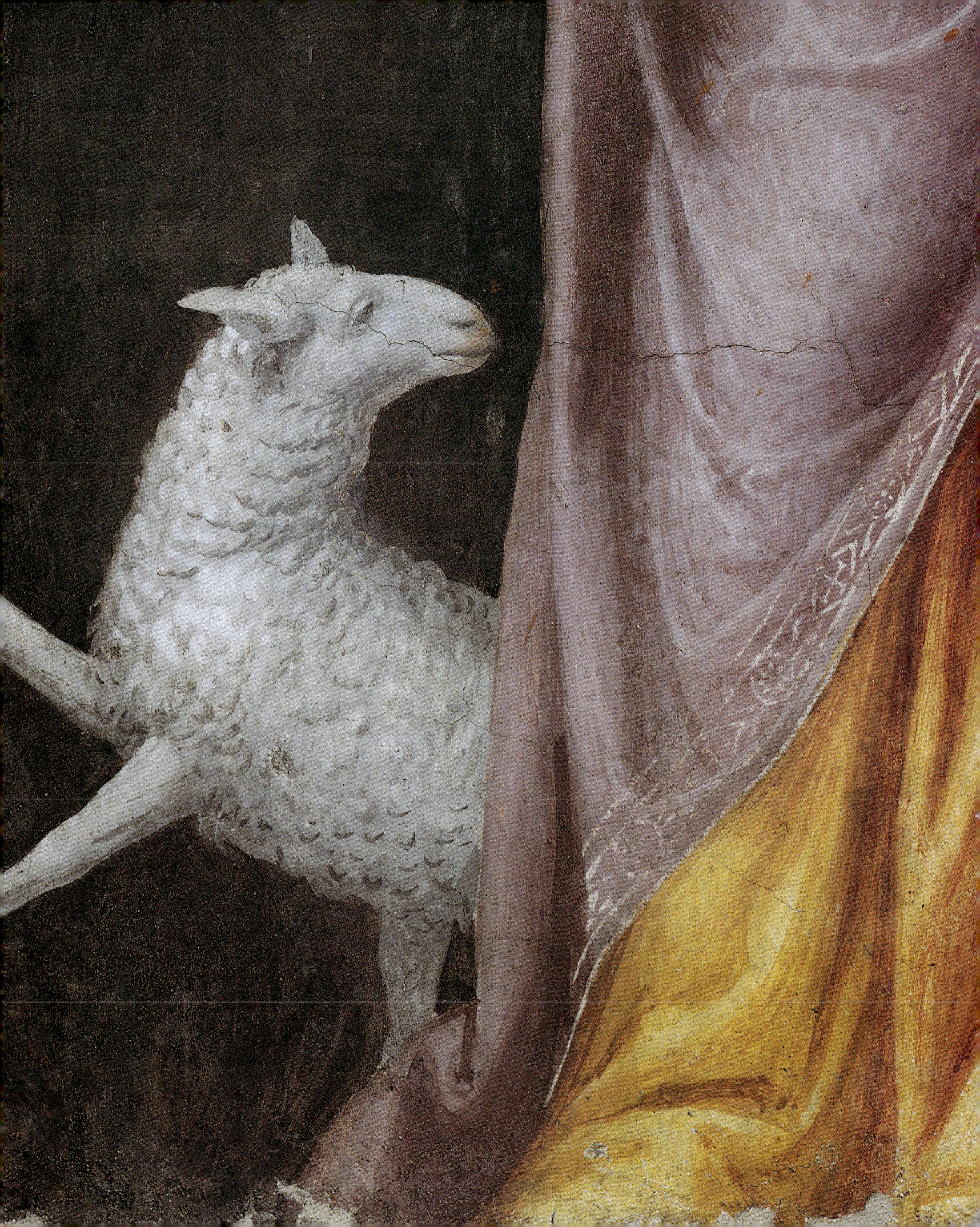

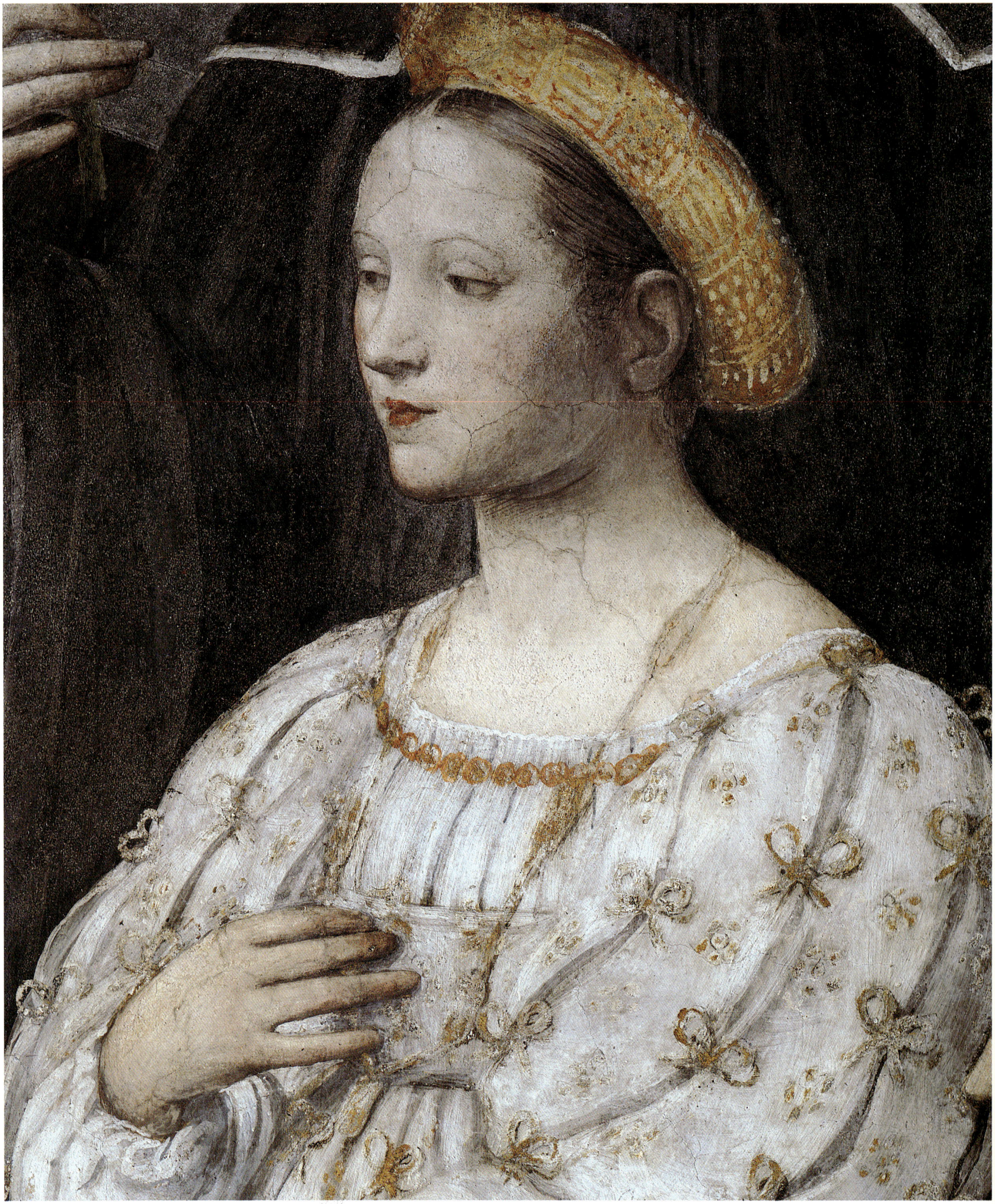

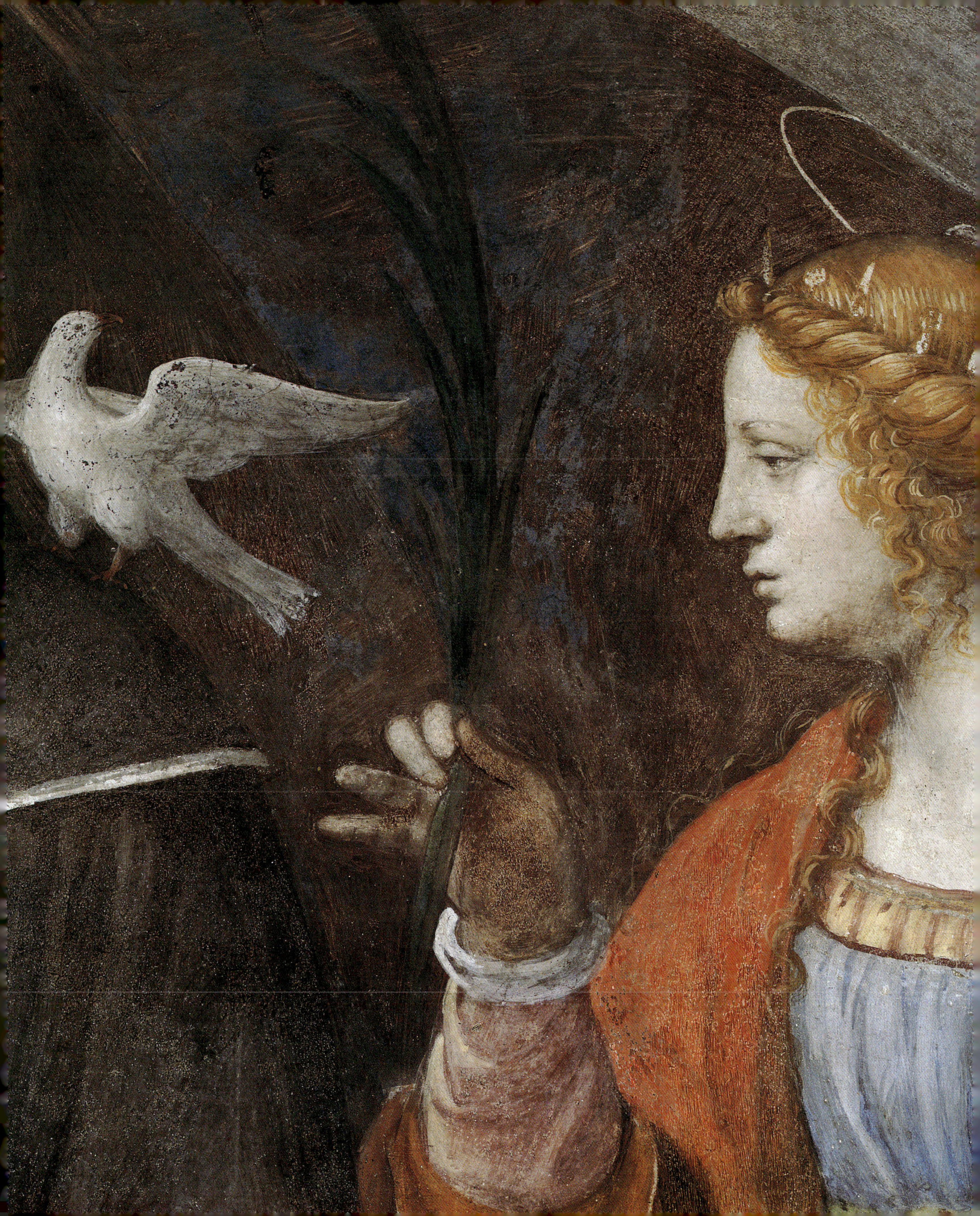

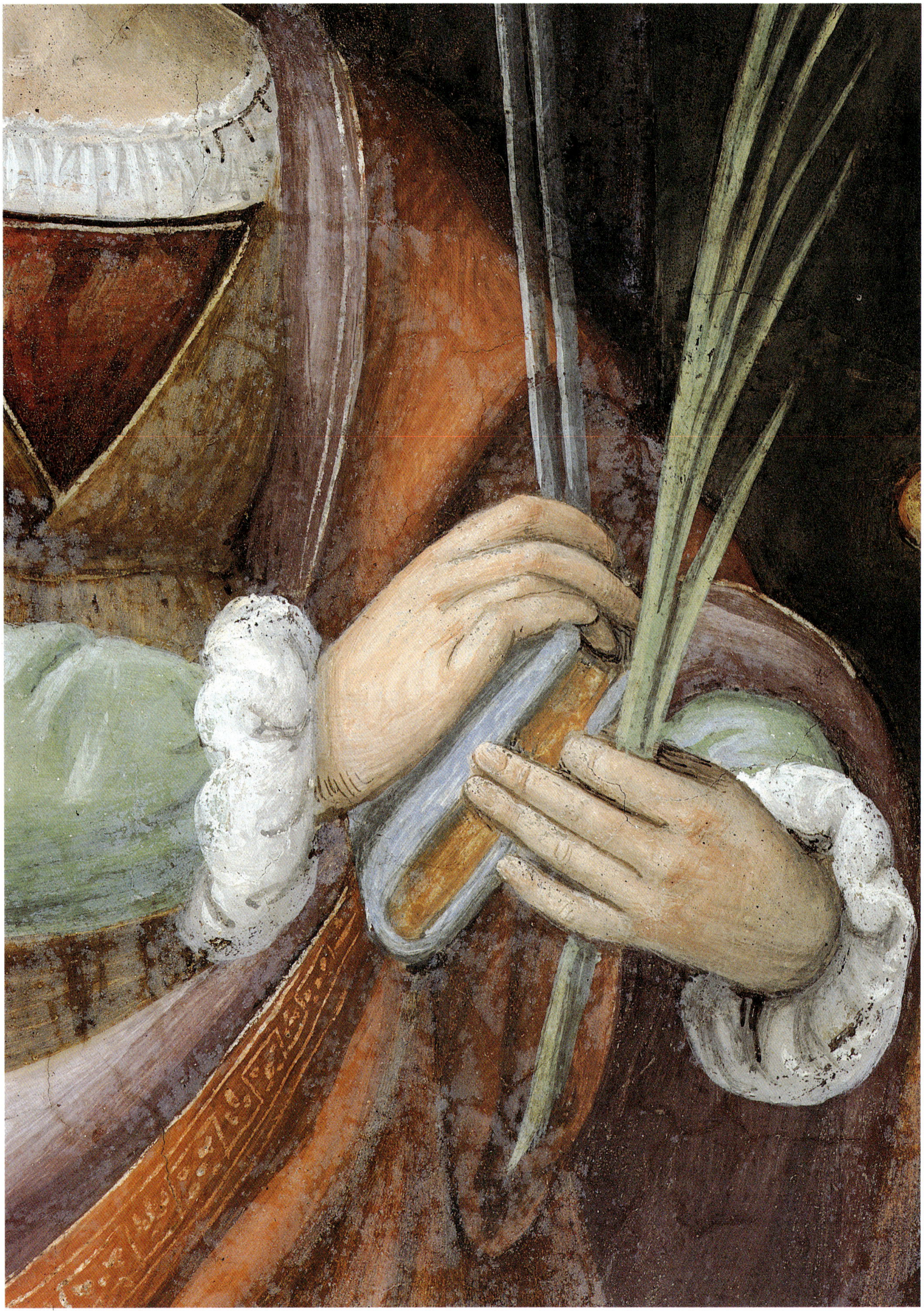

13. Bernardino Luini
St Apollonia, detail

13. Bernardino Luini
St Lucy, detail

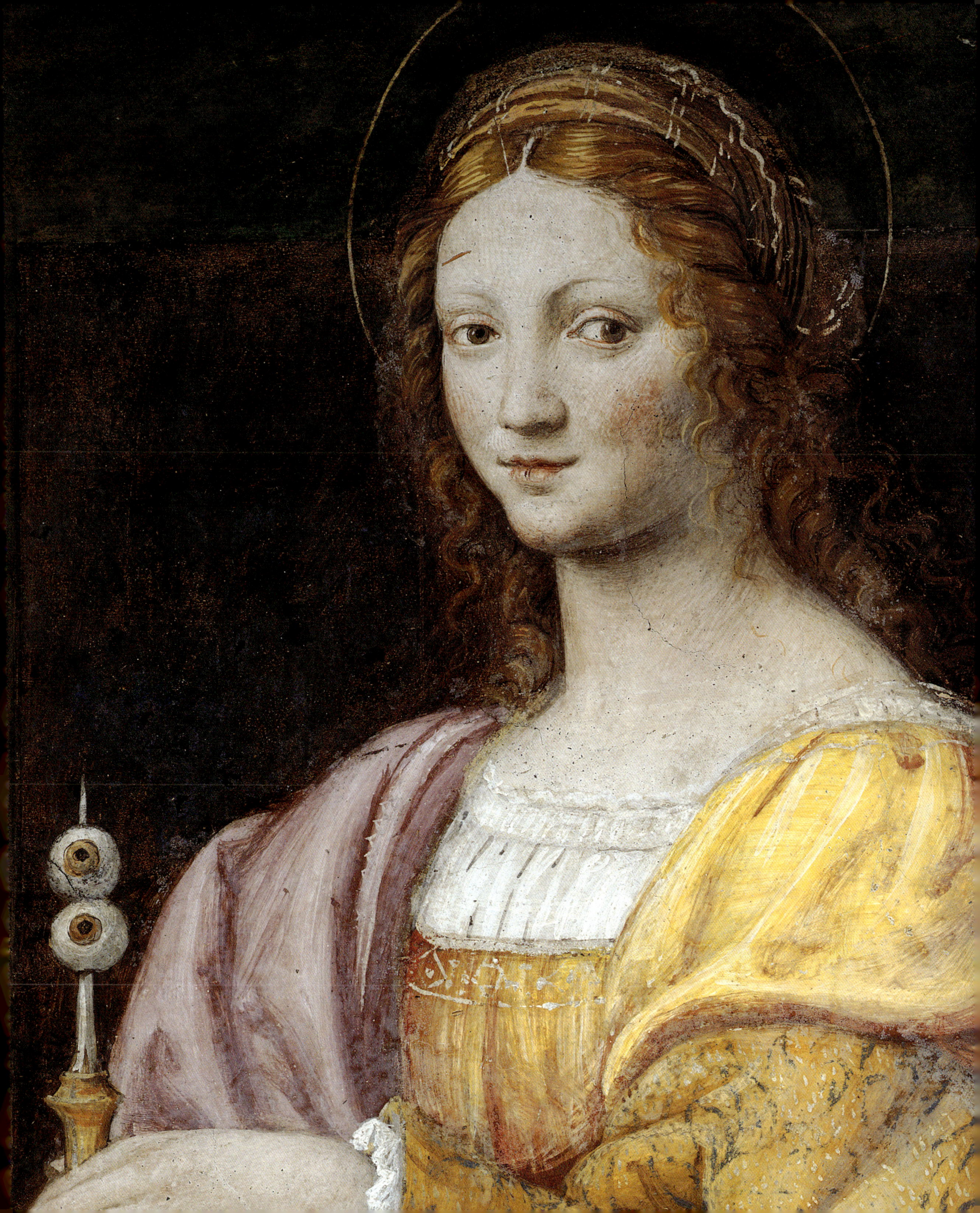

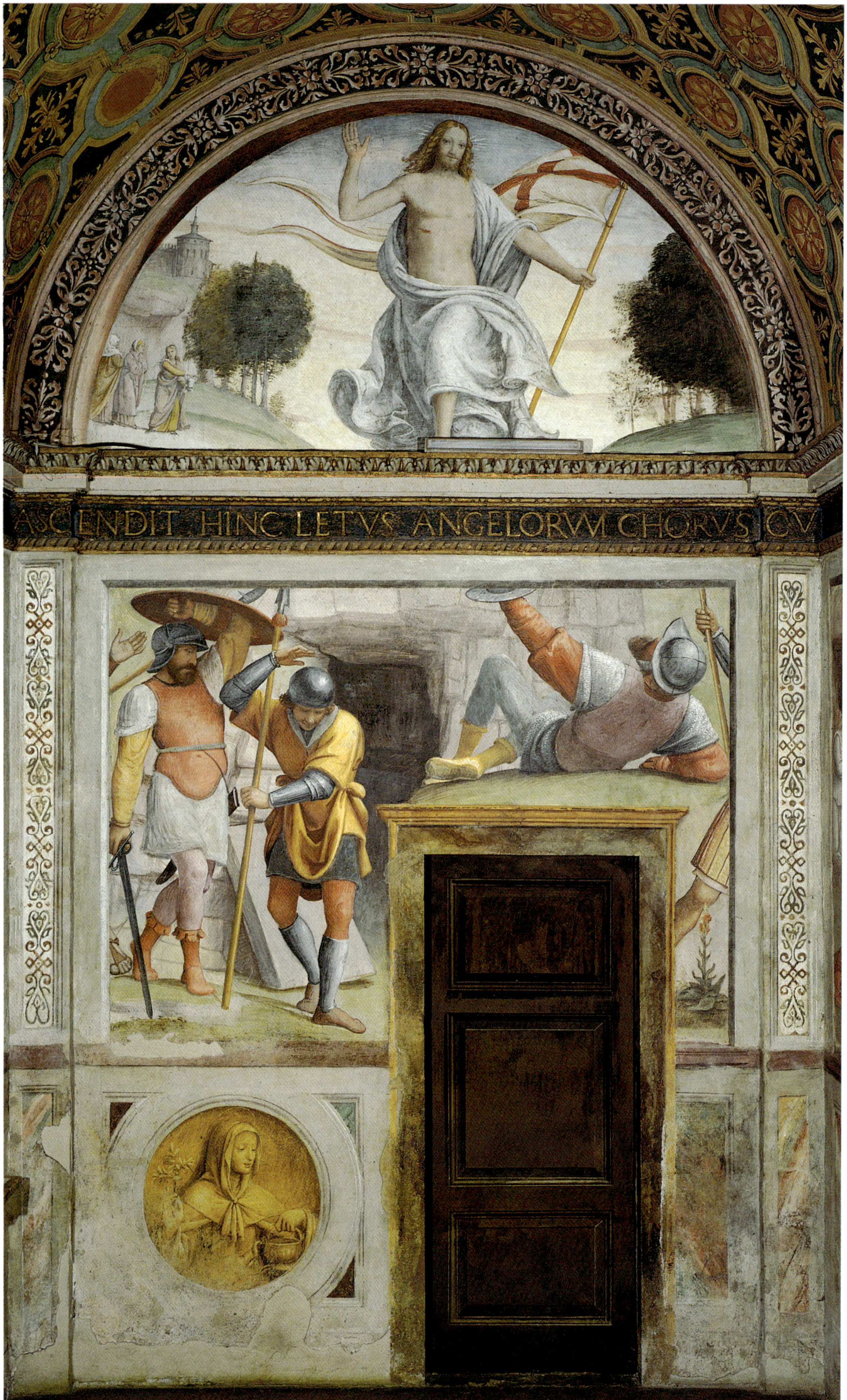

14a. Bernardino Luini
Resurrection of Christ
Convent hall

Pages 151–155
14a. Bernardino Luini
Resurrection of Christ, details

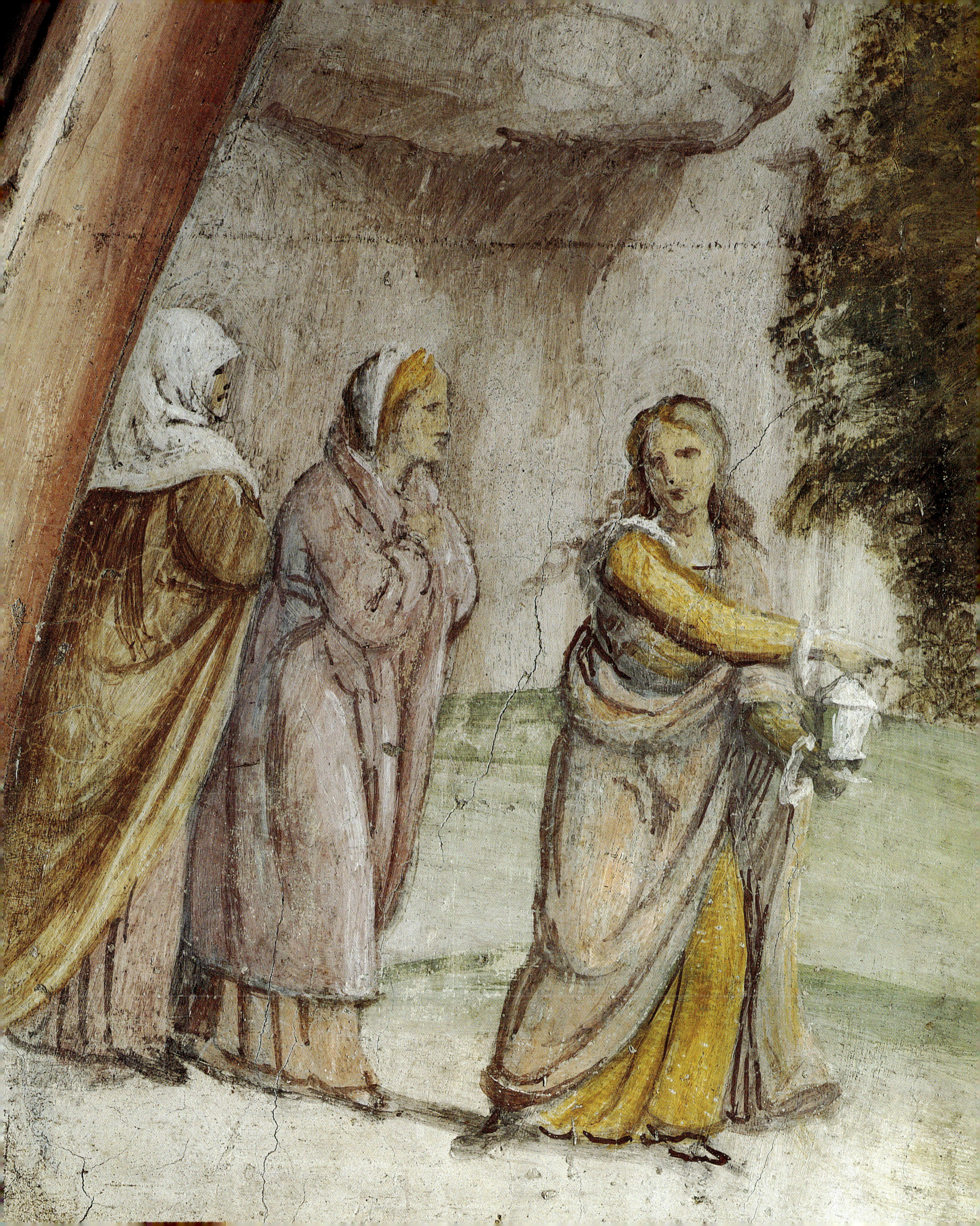

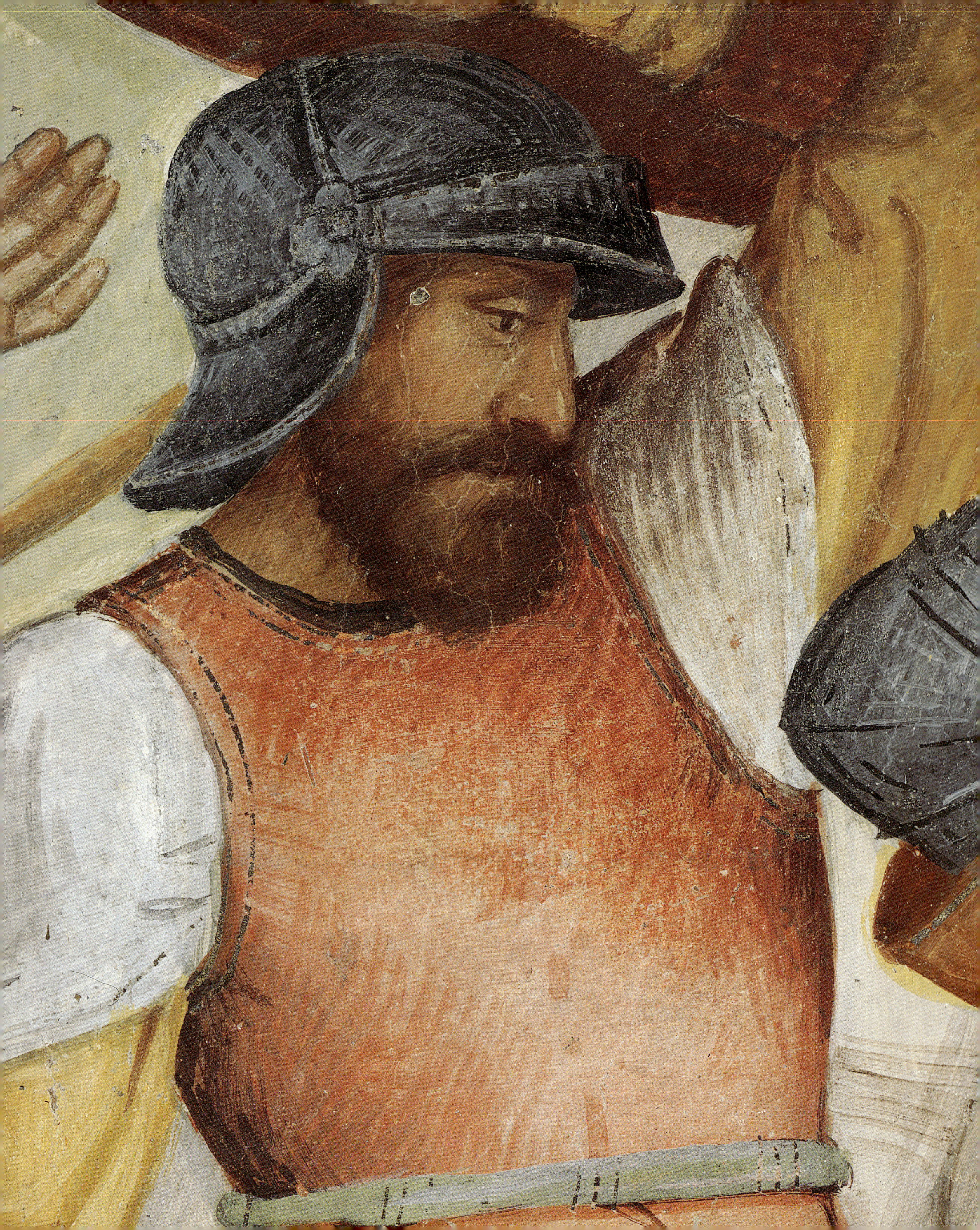

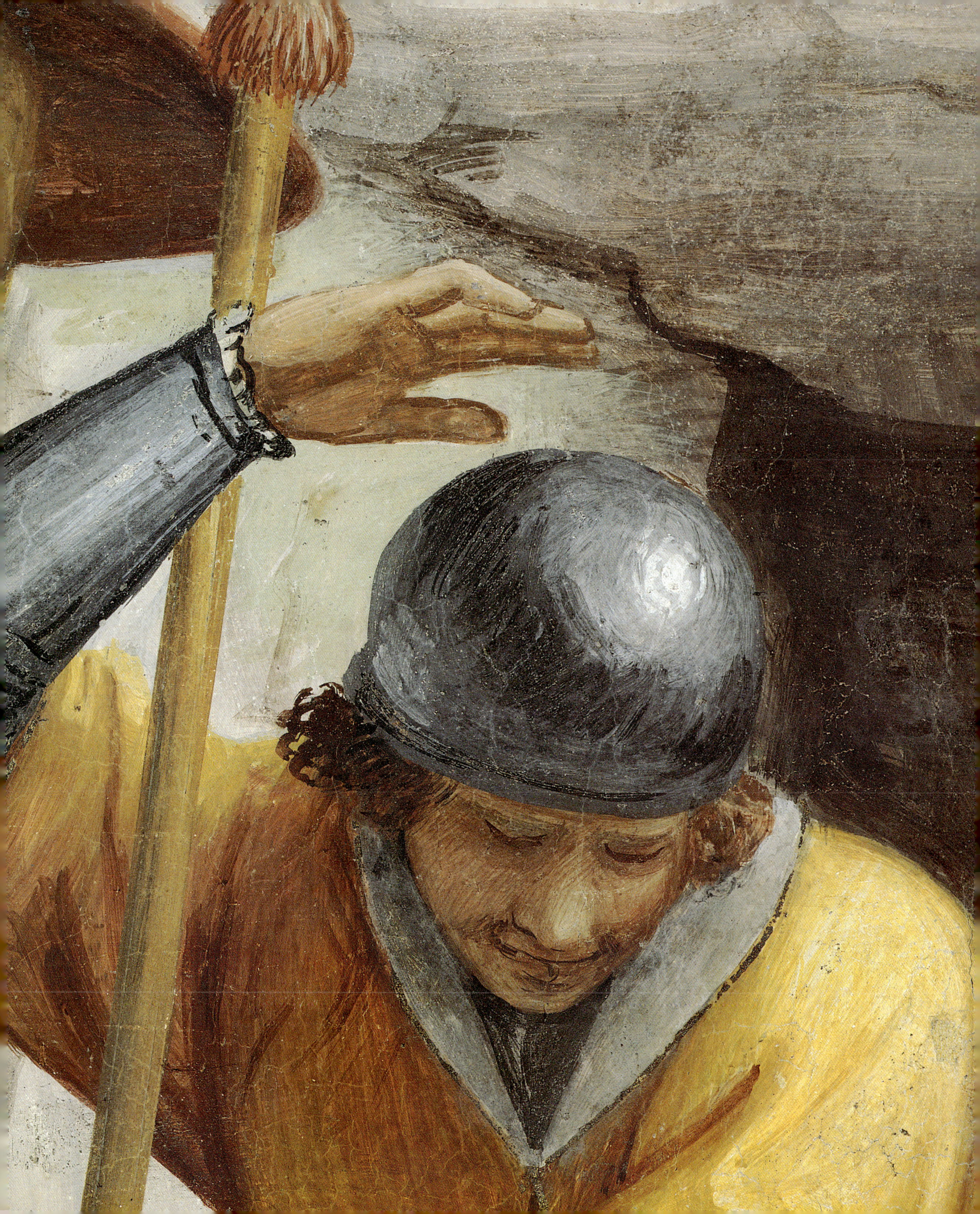

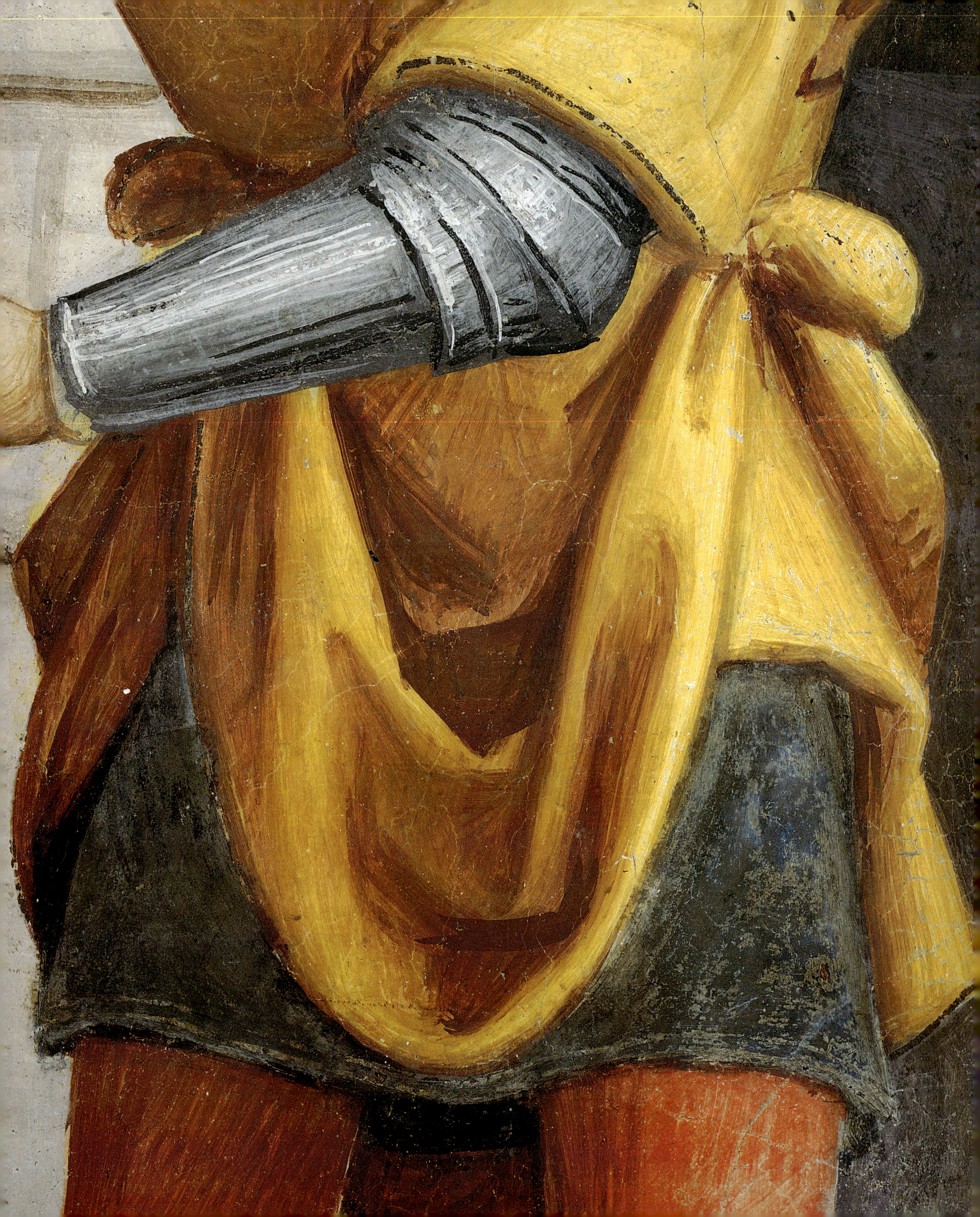

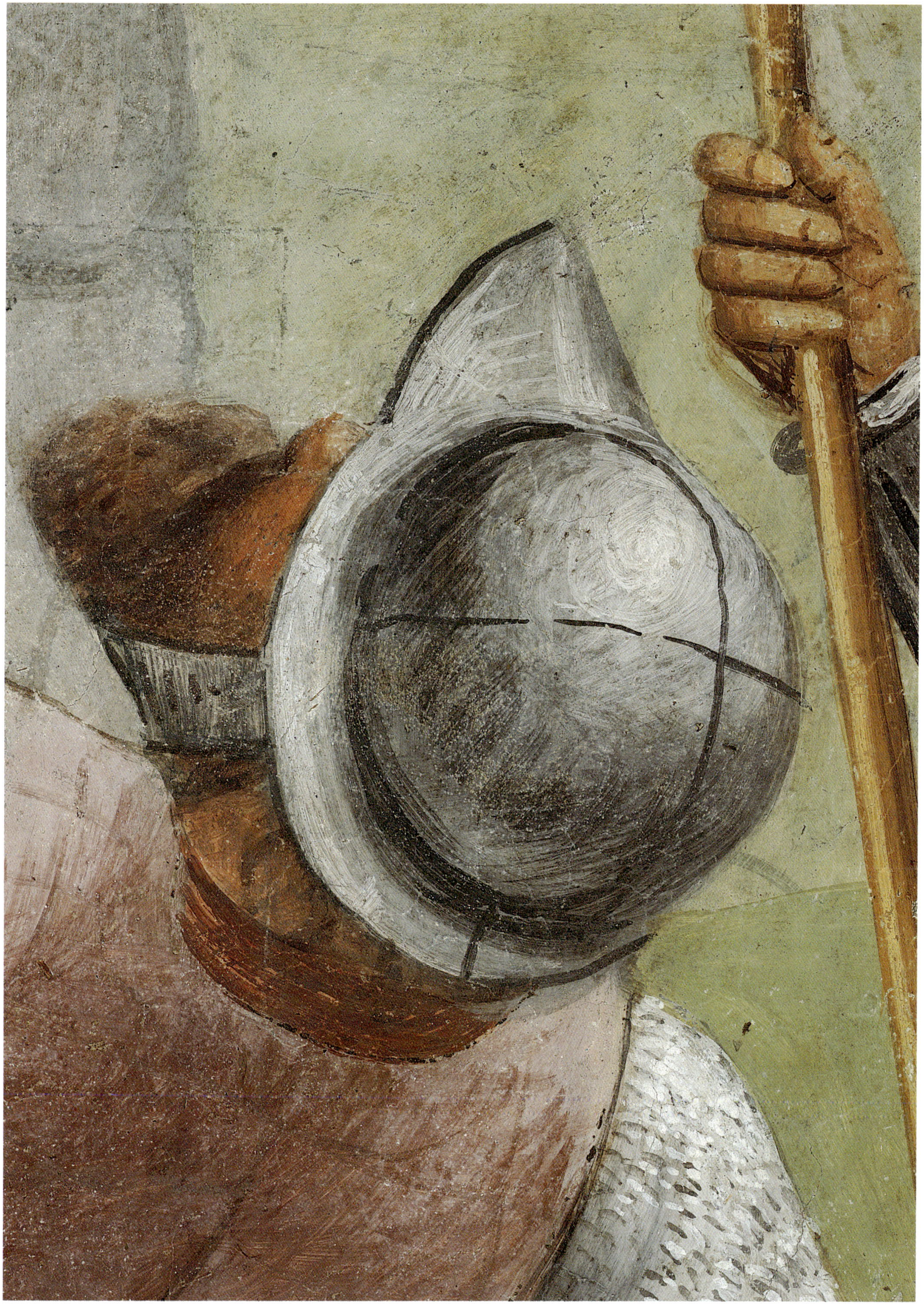

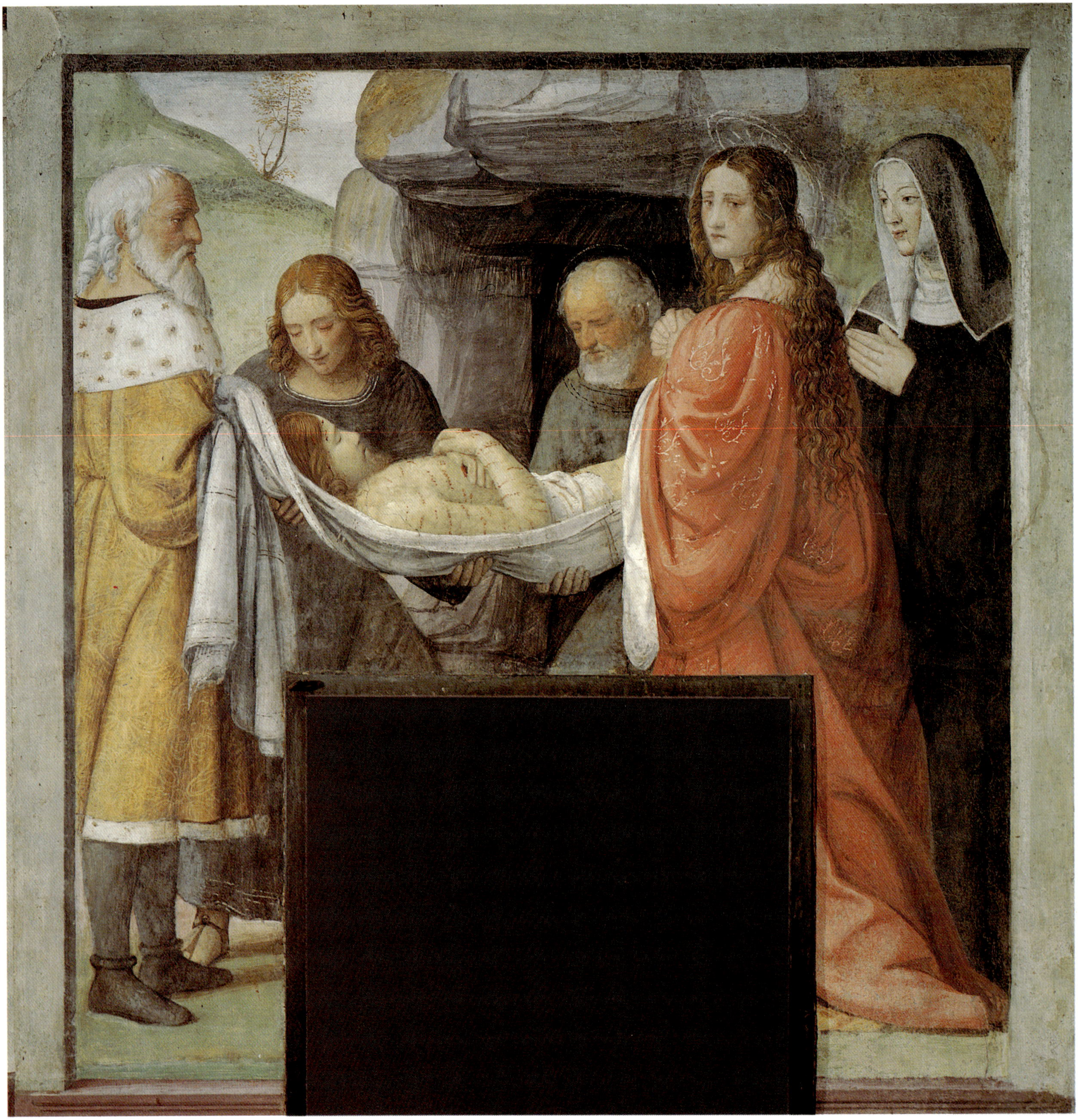

14b. Bernardino Luini
Entombment of Christ
Convent hall

Pages 157–159
14b. Bernardino Luini
Entombment of Christ, details

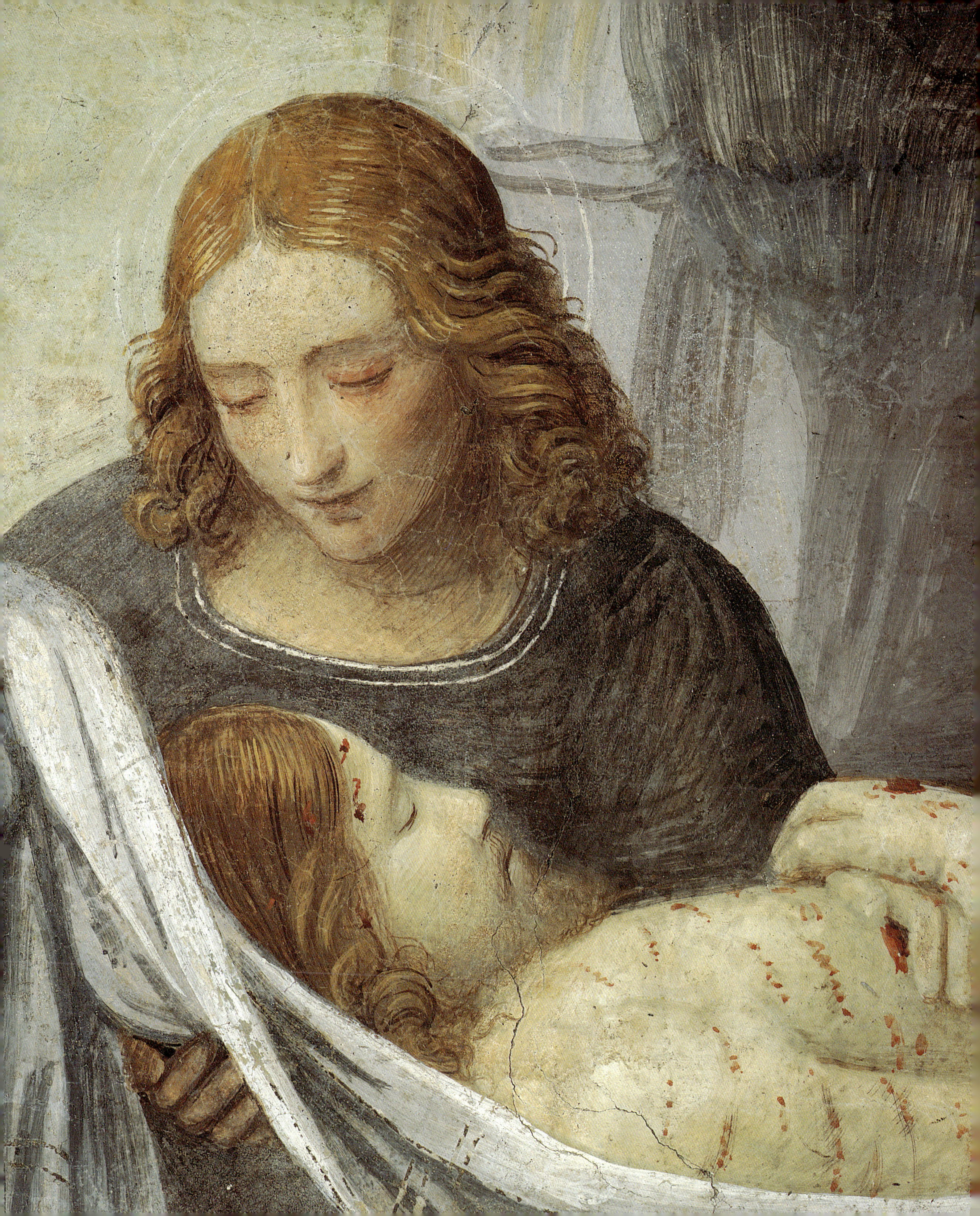

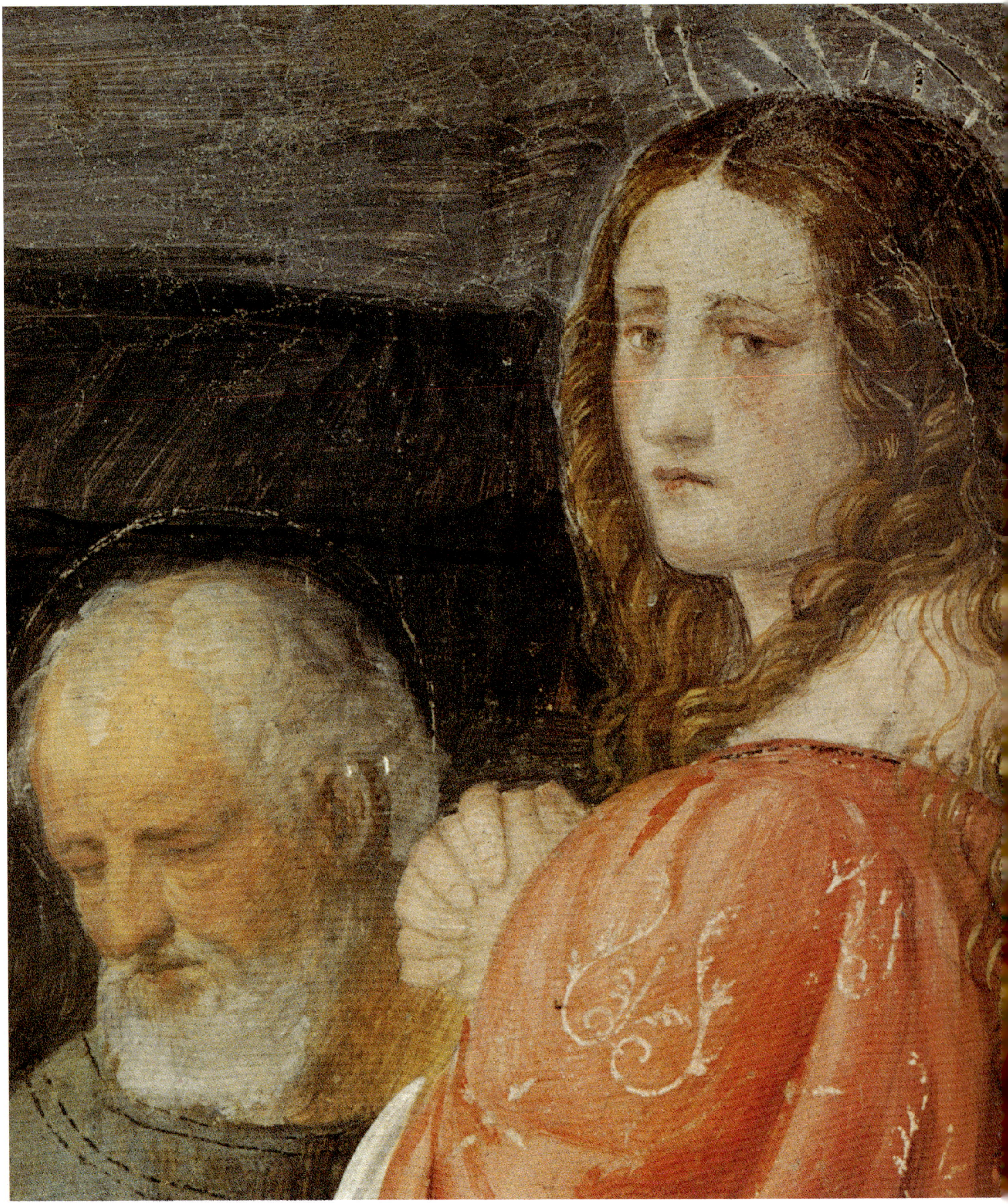

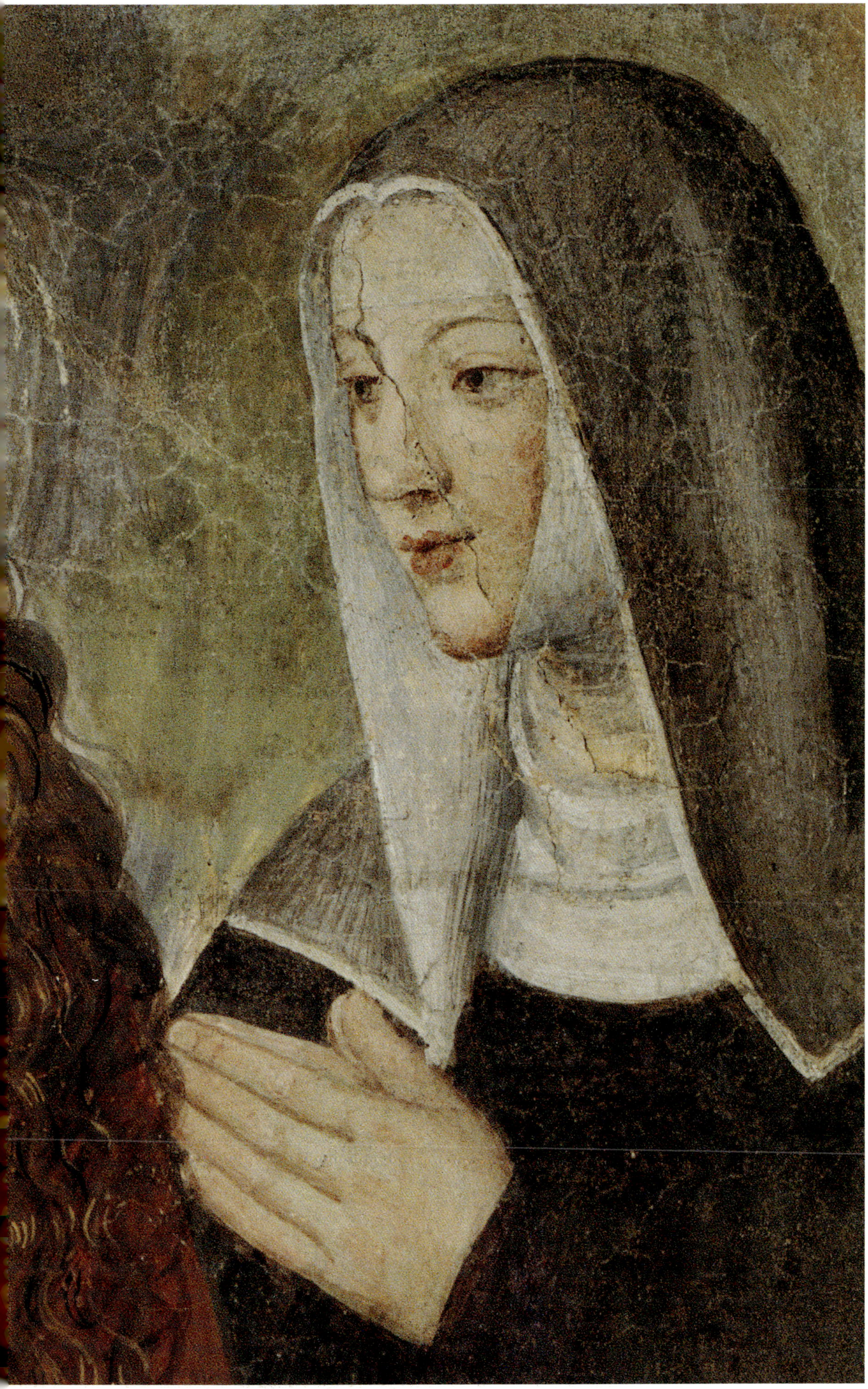

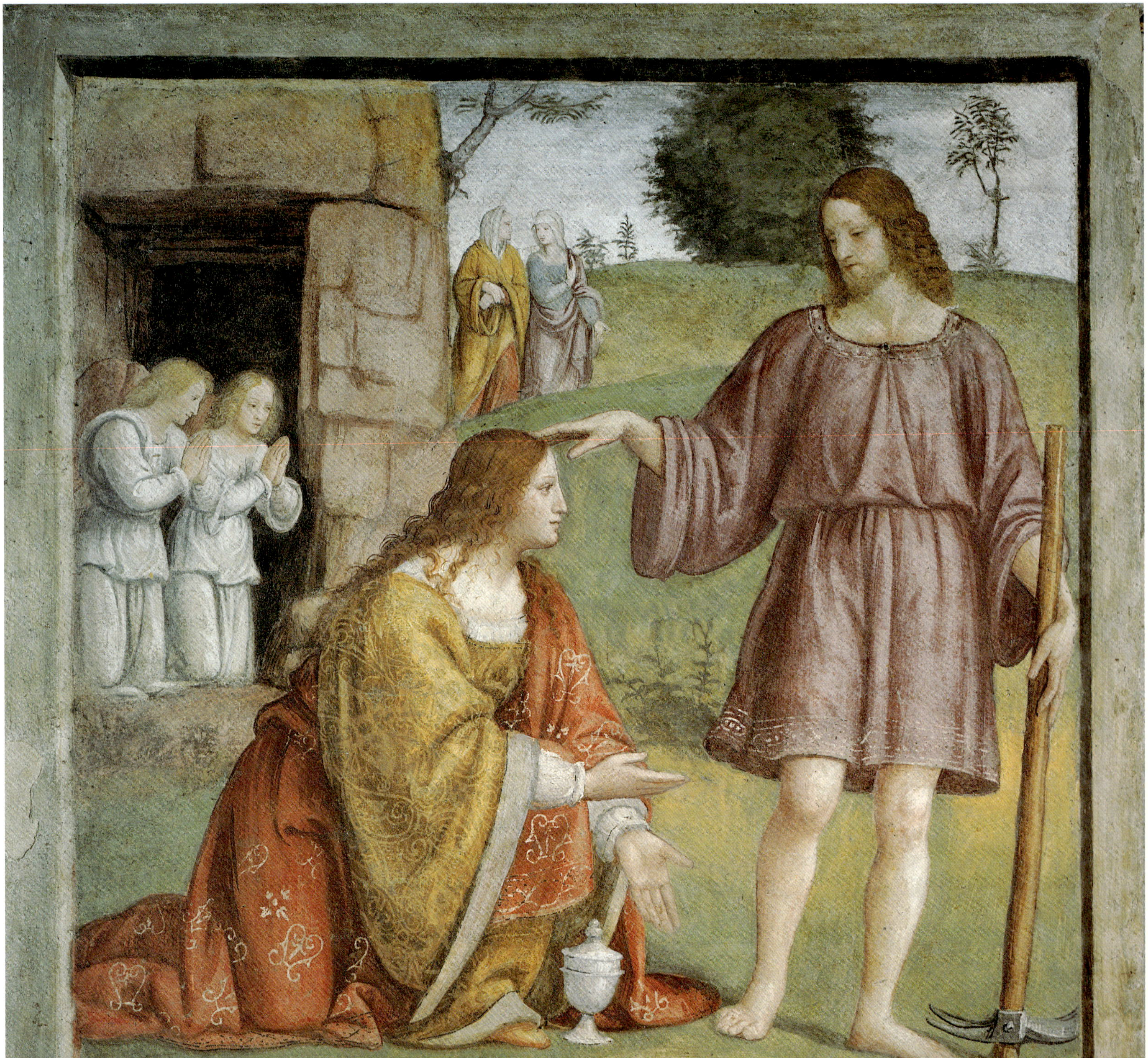

14c. Bernardino Luini
Noli me tangere
Convent hall

Pages 161–163
14c. Bernardino Luini
Noli me tangere, details

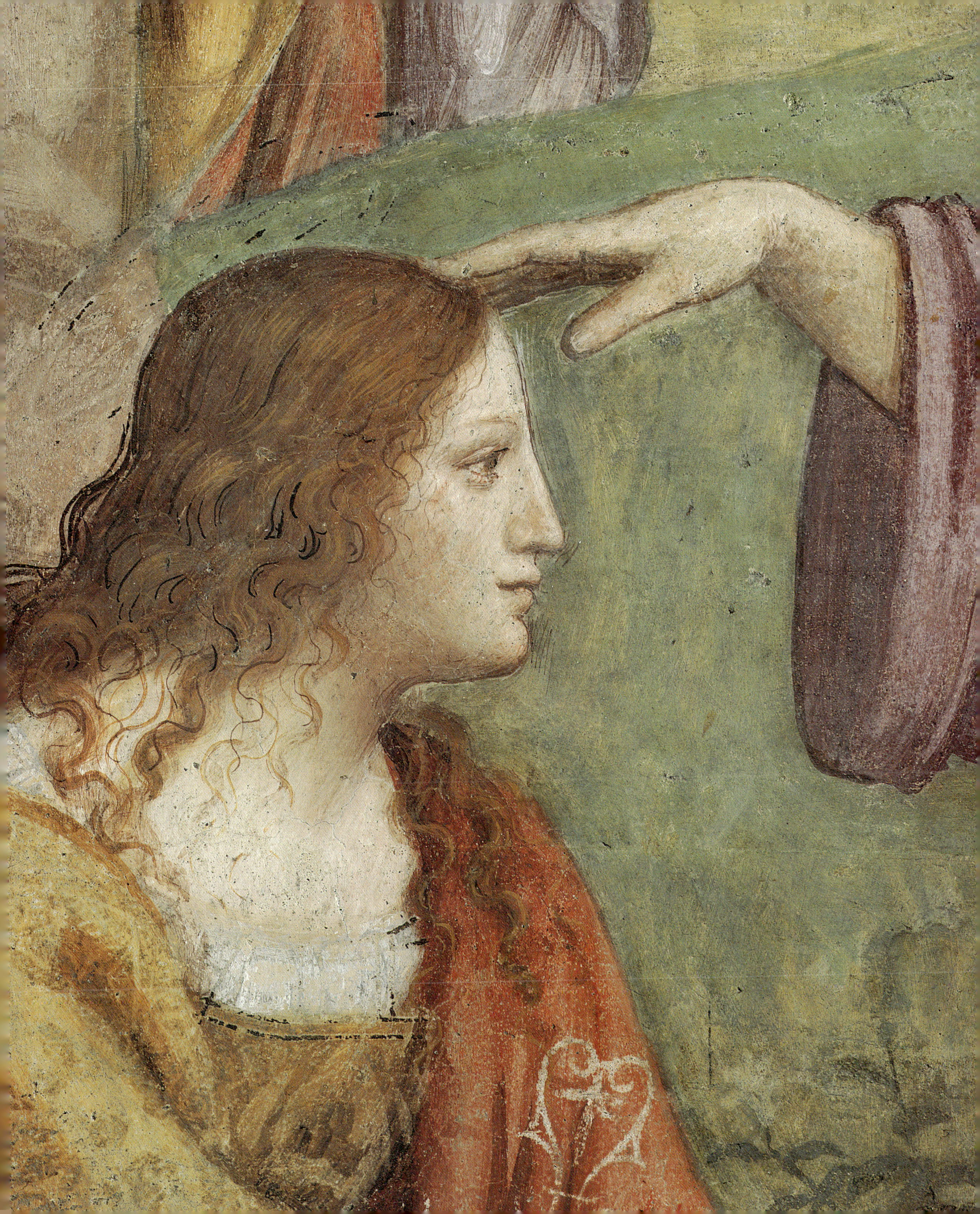

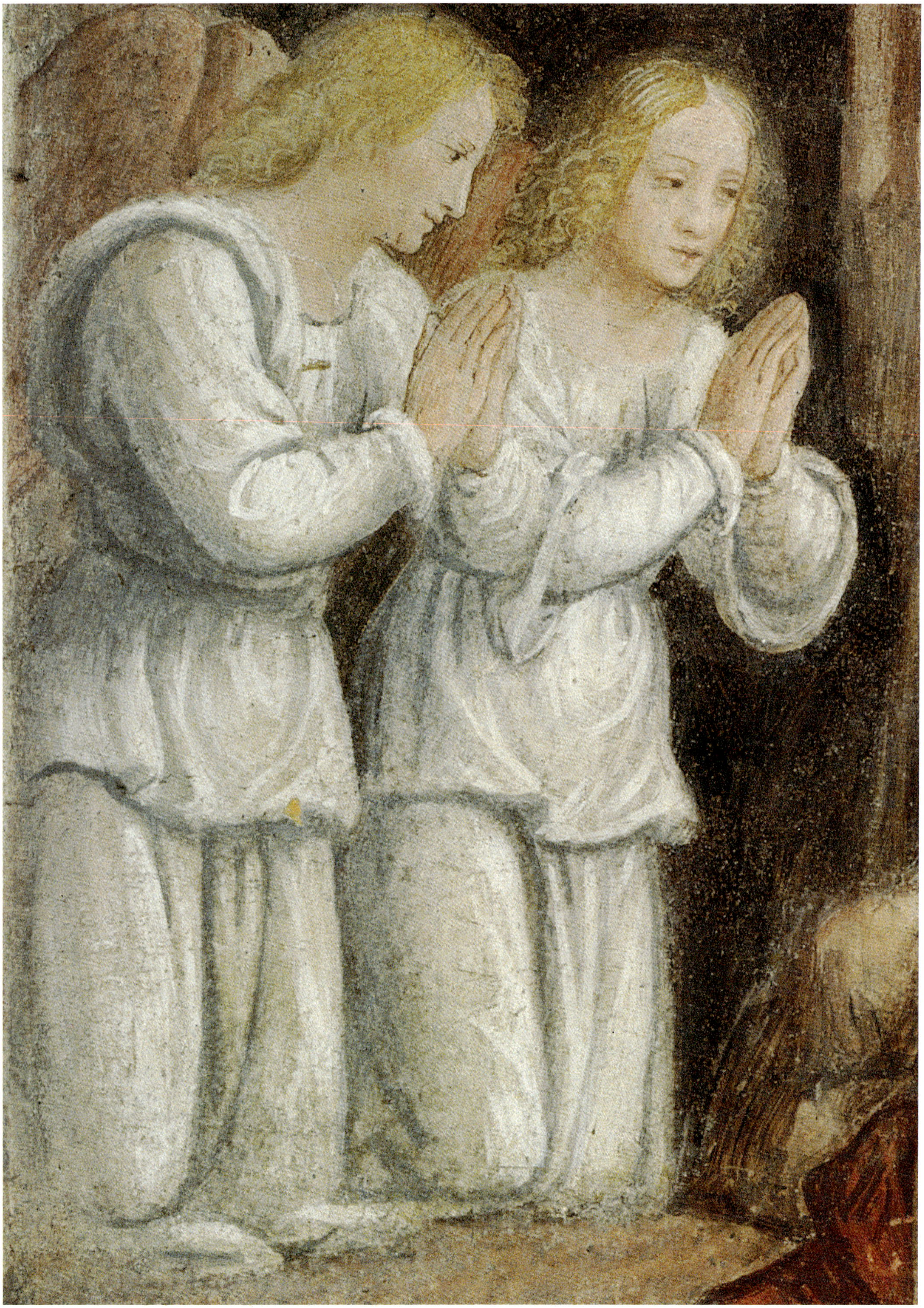

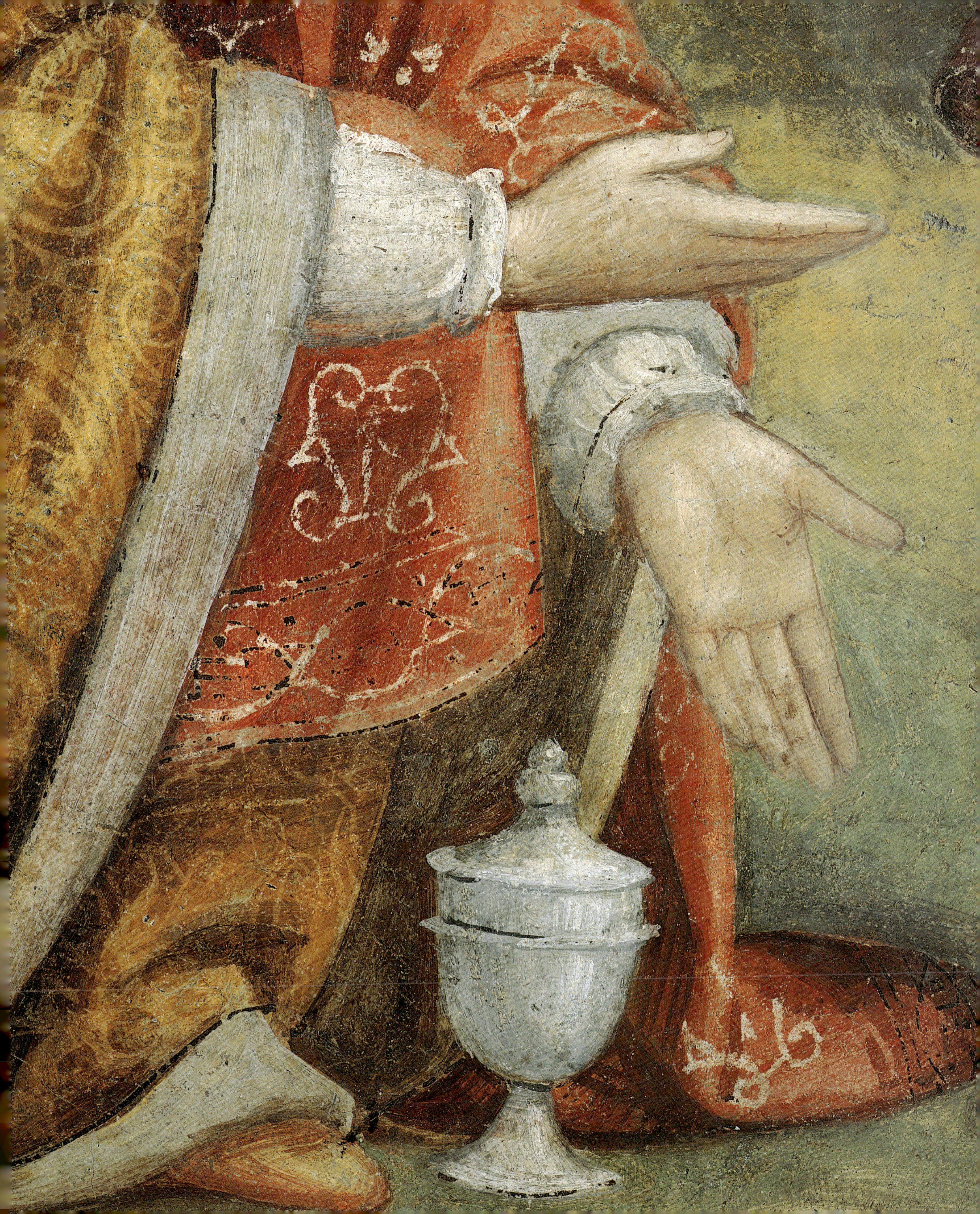

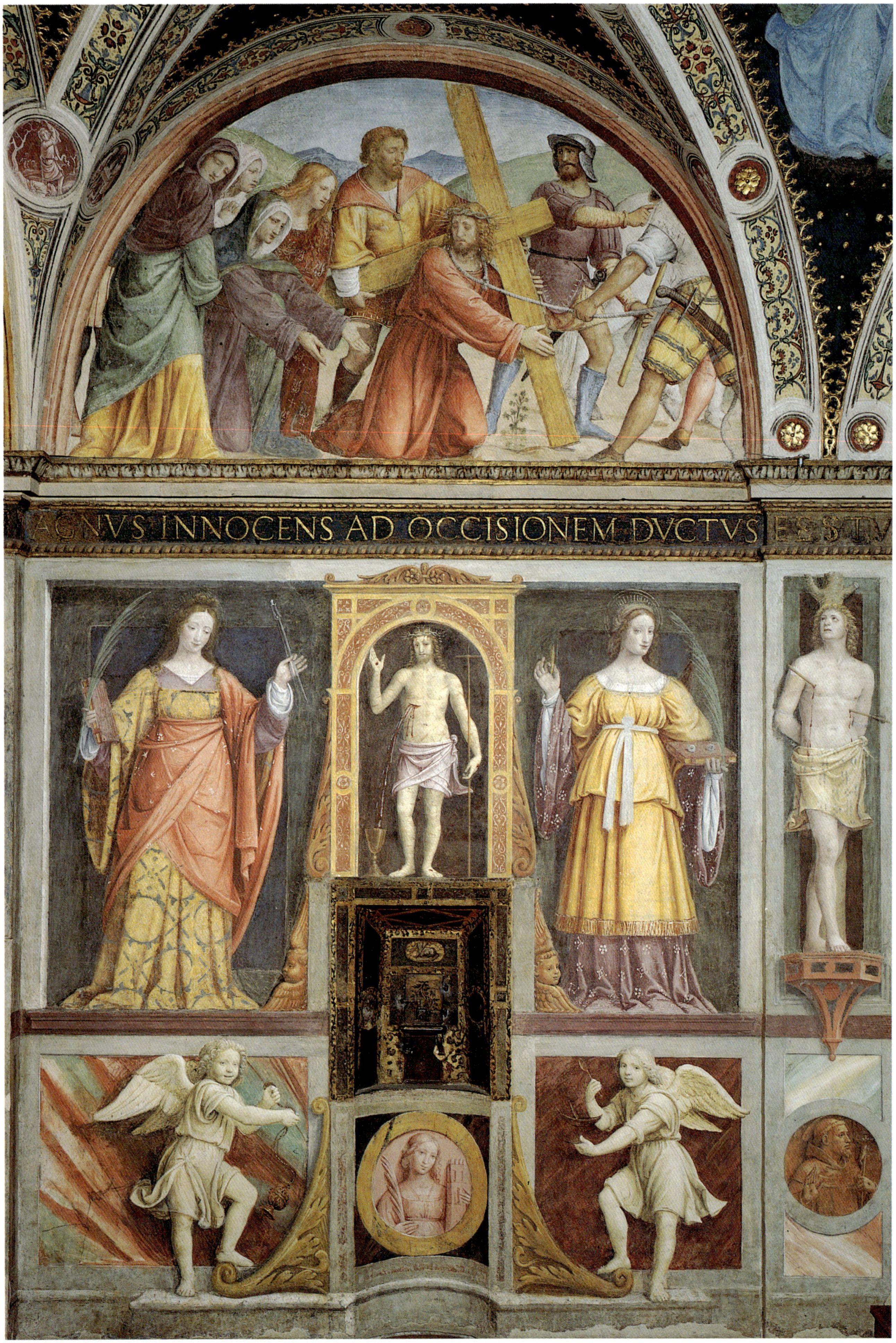

15. Bernardino Luini
Left side, partition wall,
convent hall

15. Bernardino Luini
Tondo with *St Barbara*

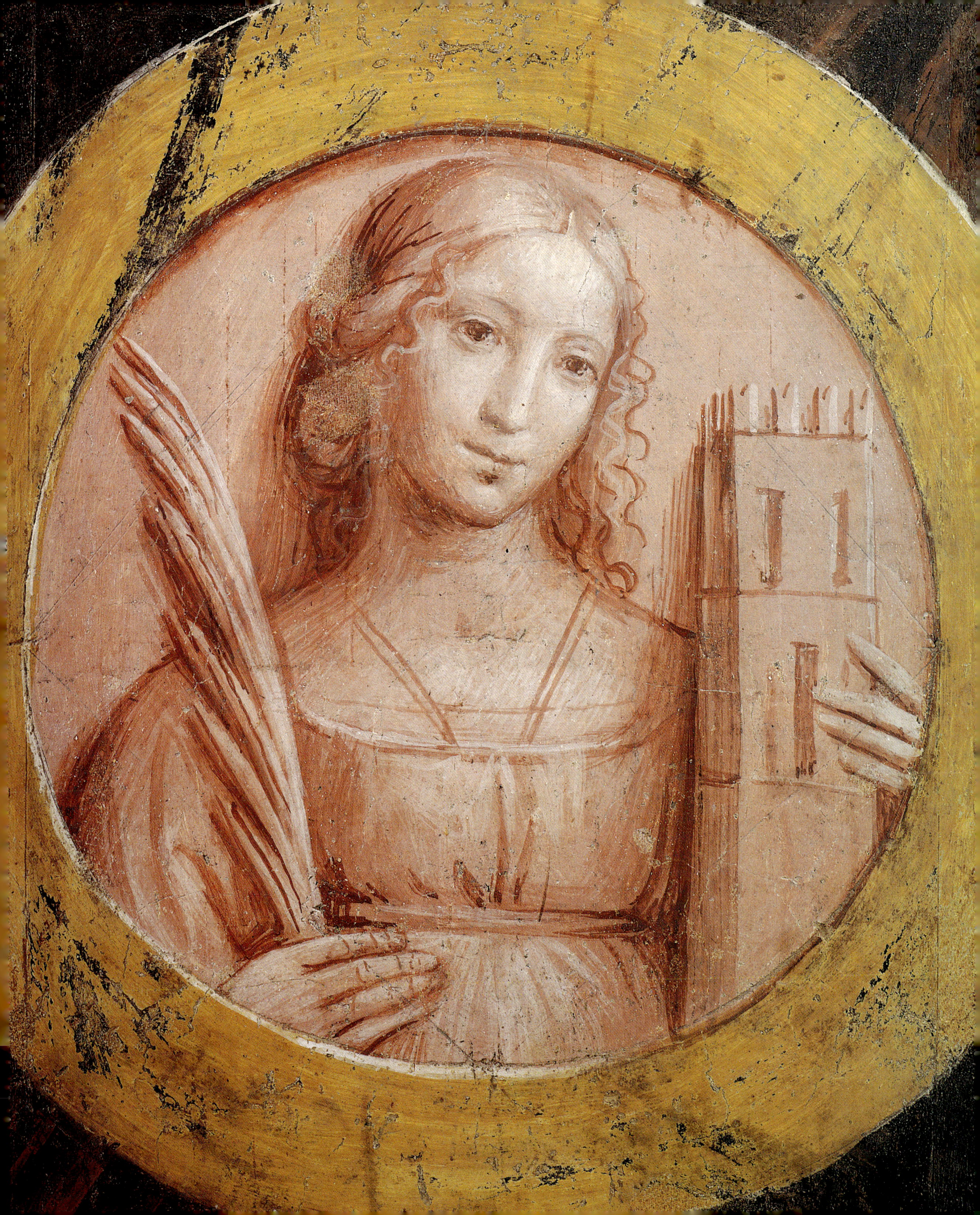

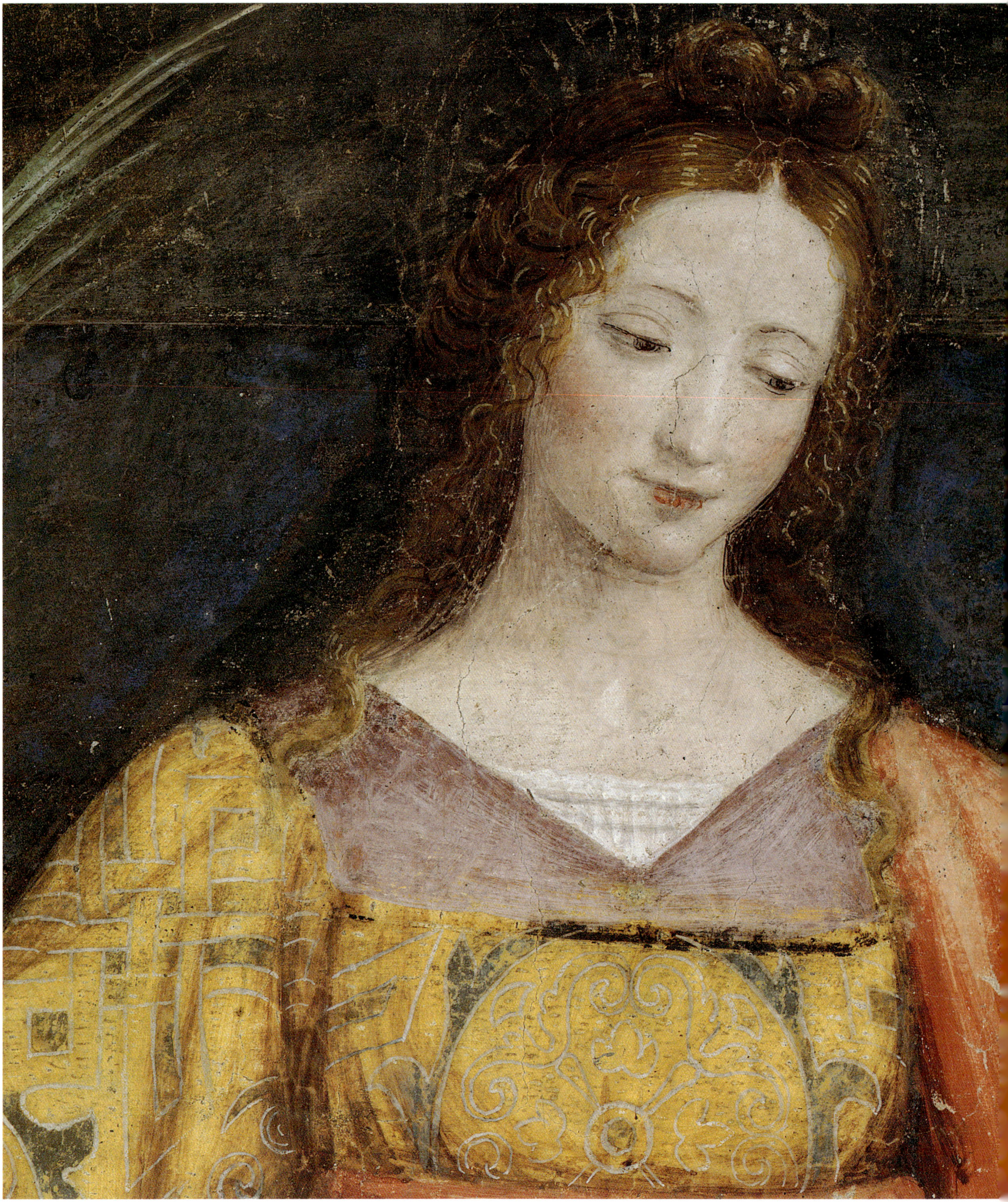

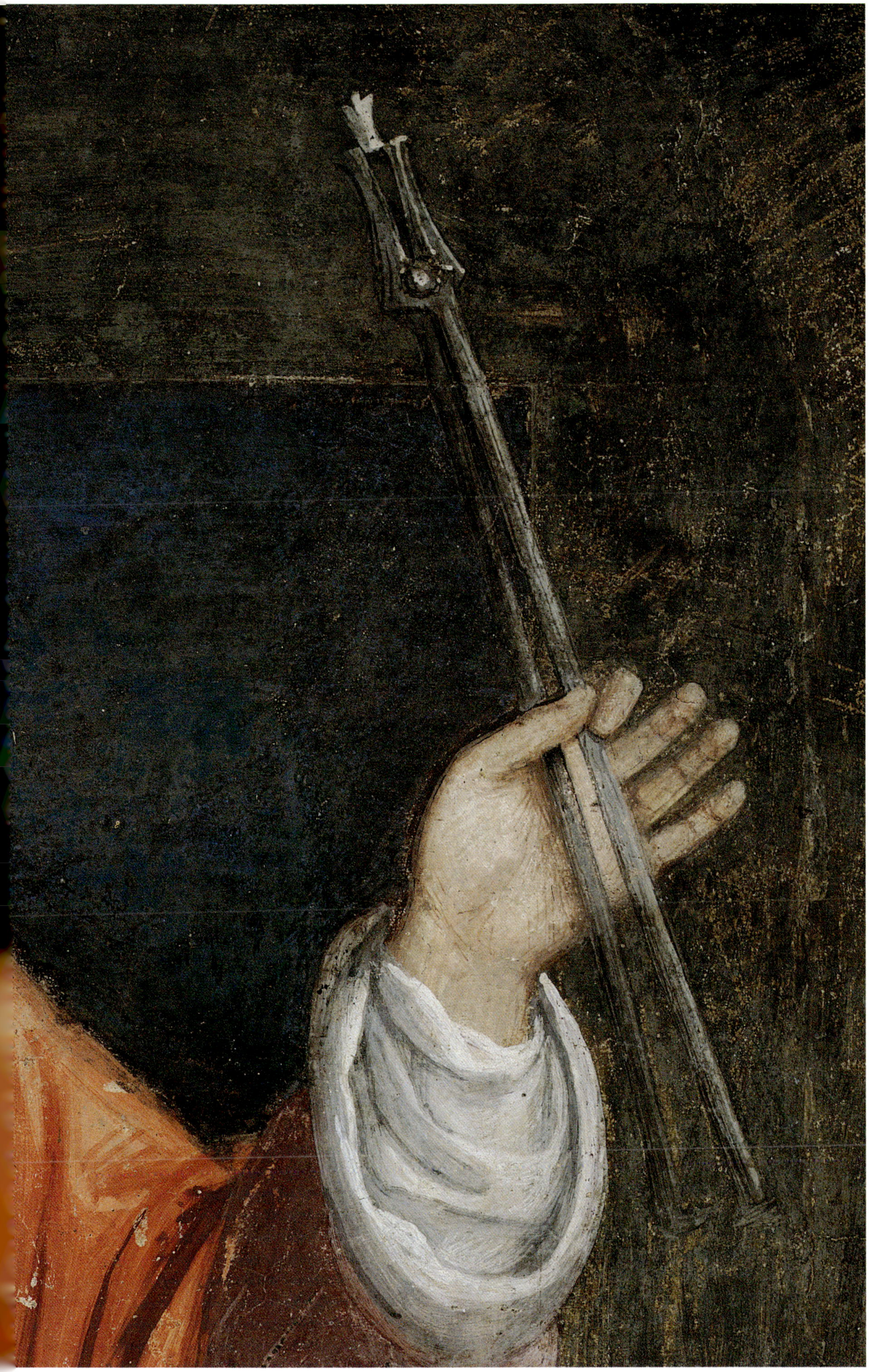

15. Bernardino Luini
St Apollonia, detail

15. Bernardino Luini
St Sebastian

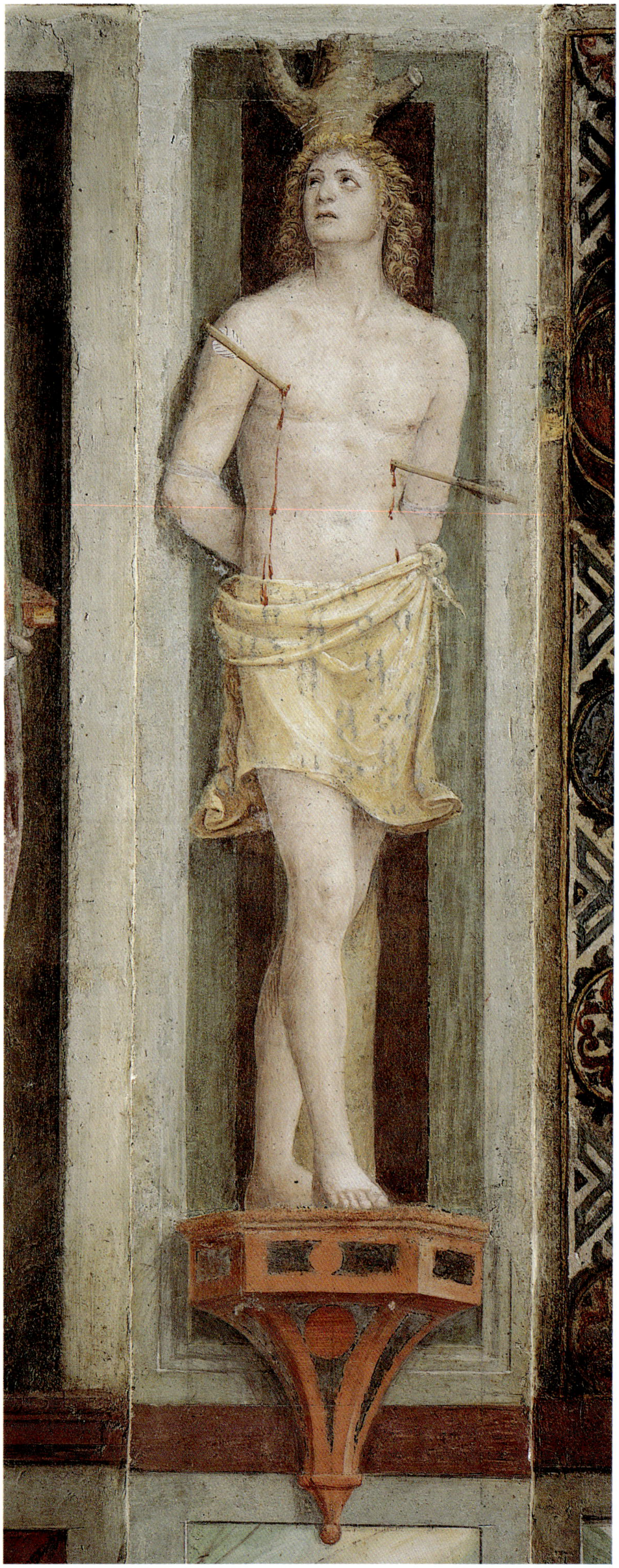

16. Bernardino Luini
Angel with incense boat, detail

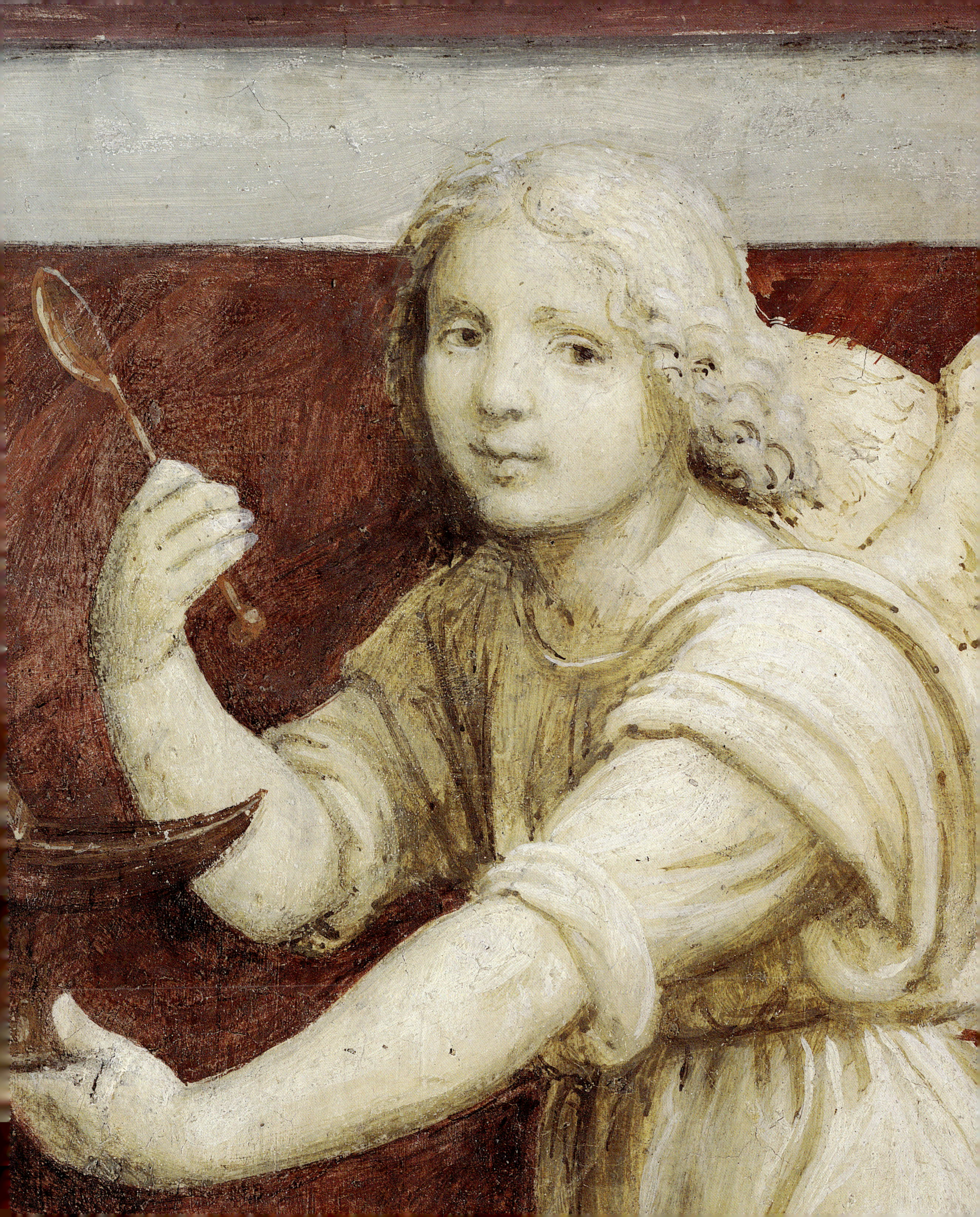

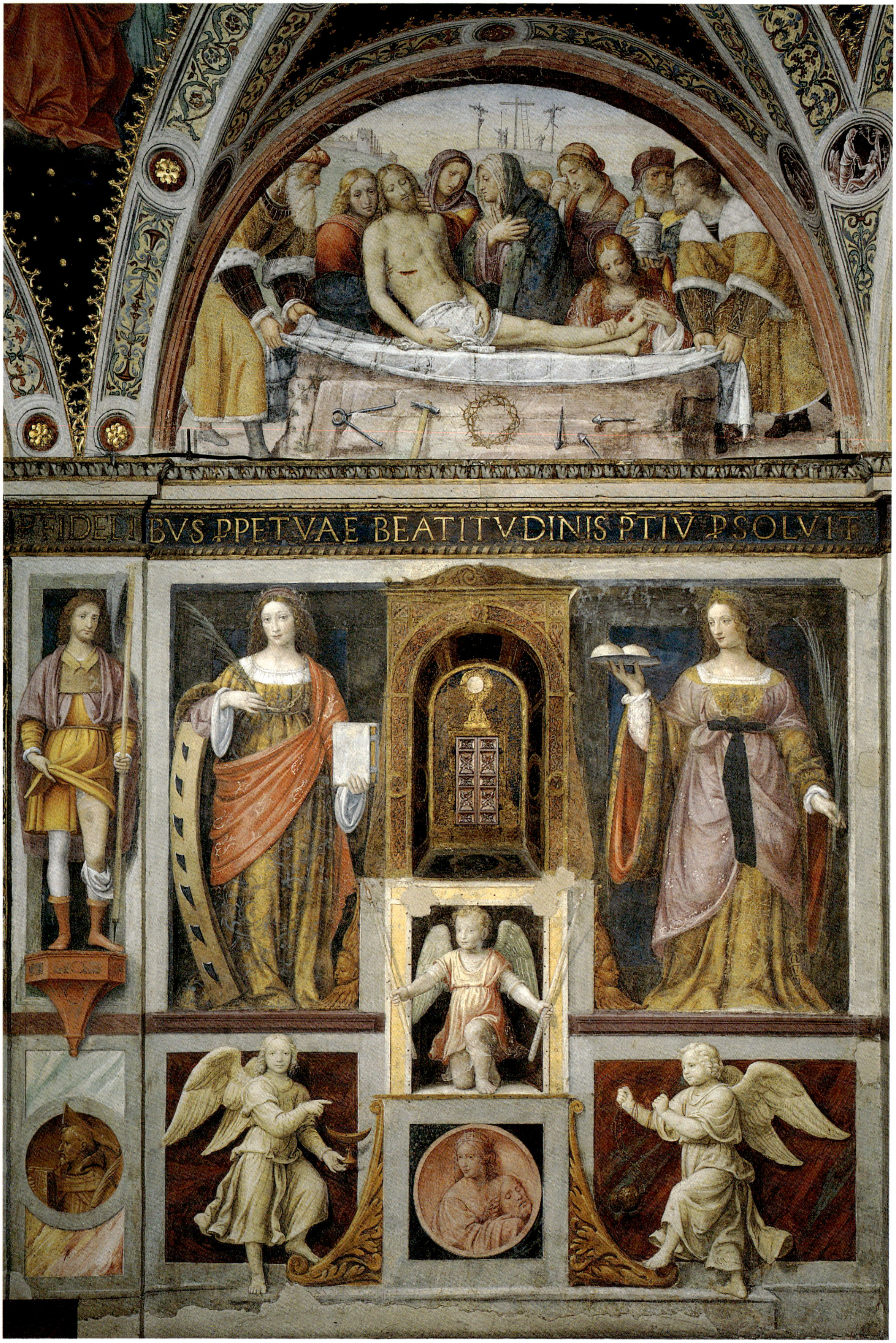

16. Bernardino Luini
Right side, partition wall, convent hall

16. Bernardino Luini
St Catherine, detail

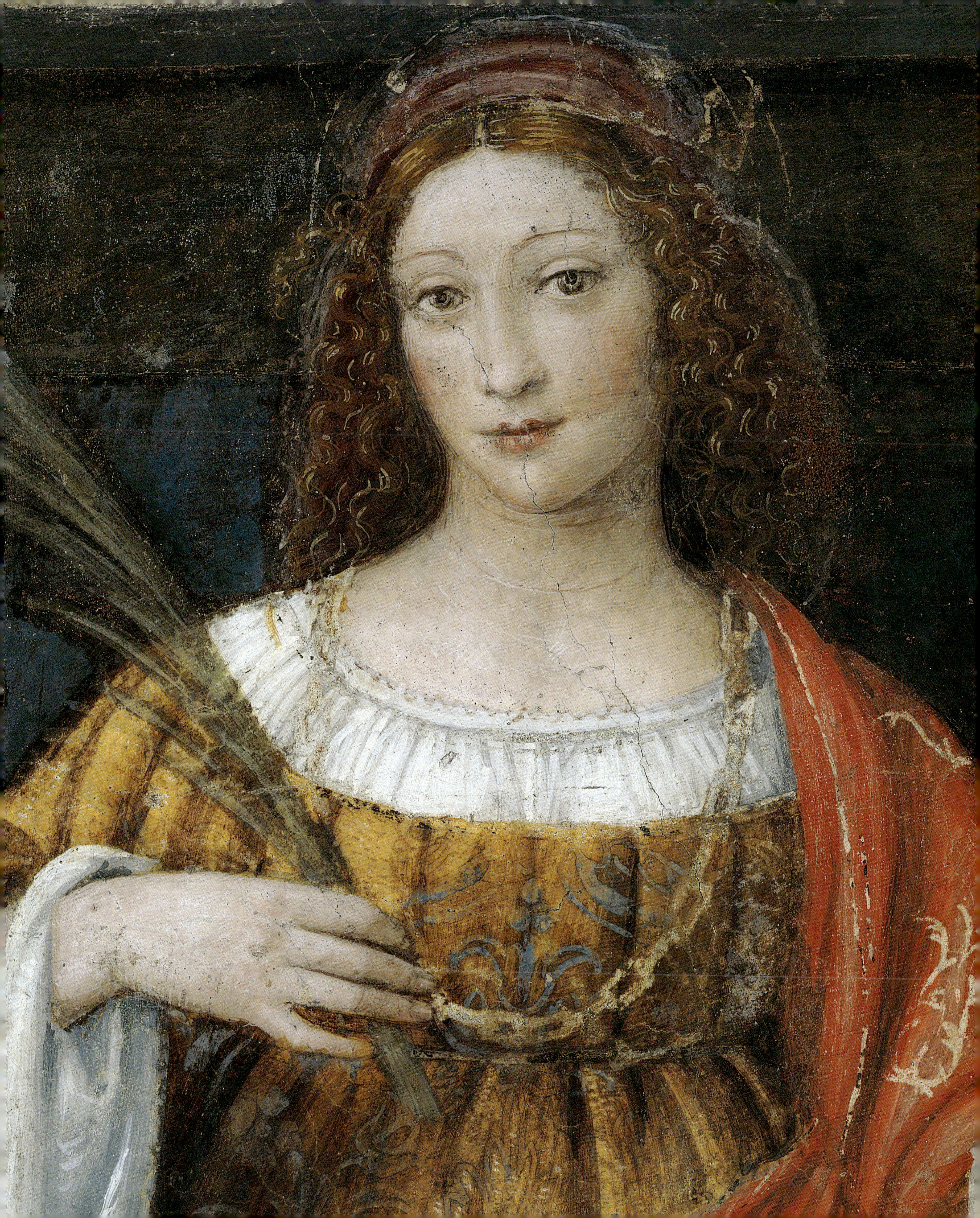

16. Bernardino Luini
St Roch

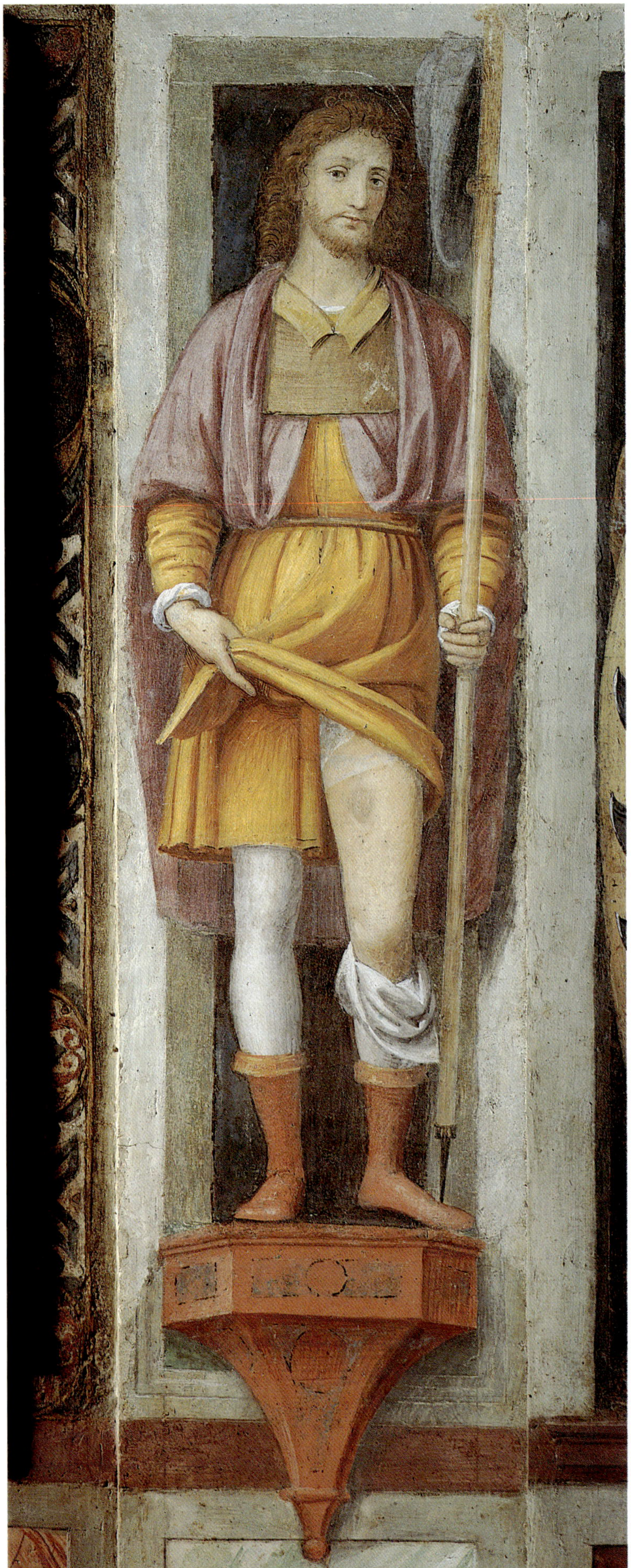

16. Bernardino Luini
Angel with incense boat, detail

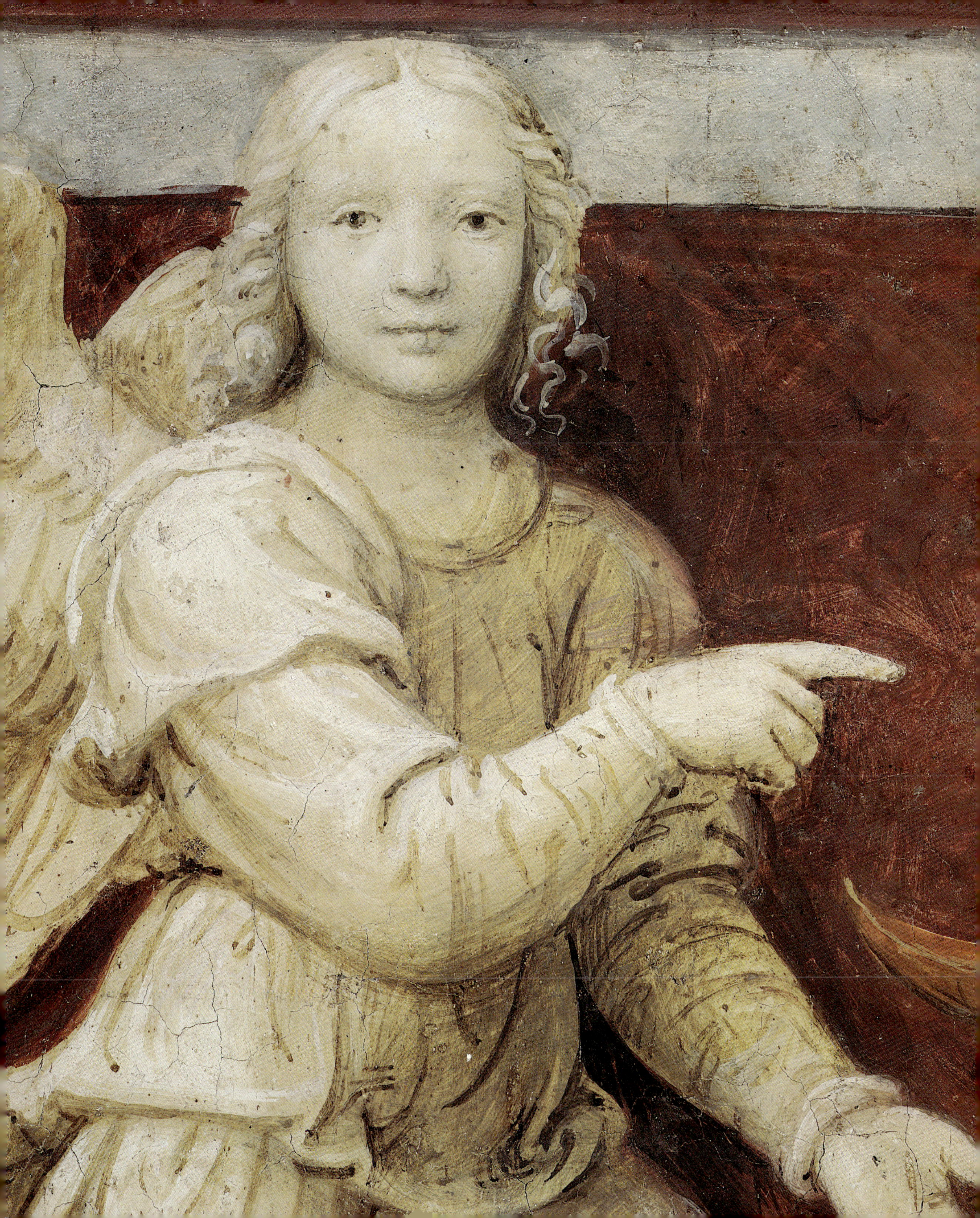

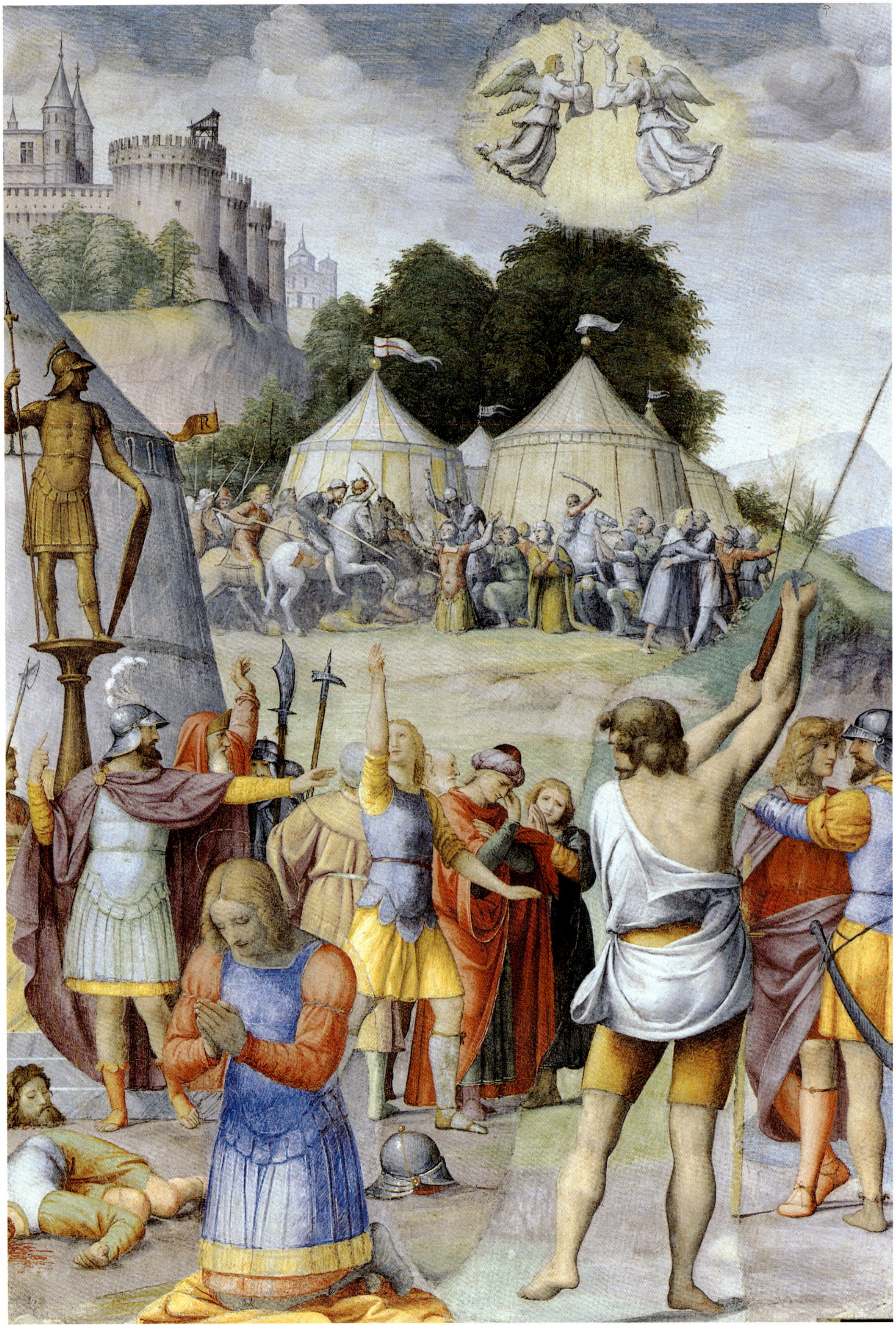

17. Bernardino Luini
Martyrdom
of St Maurice
Left side, partition
wall, lay hall

Pages 175–179
17. Bernardino Luini
Martyrdom
of St Maurice,
details

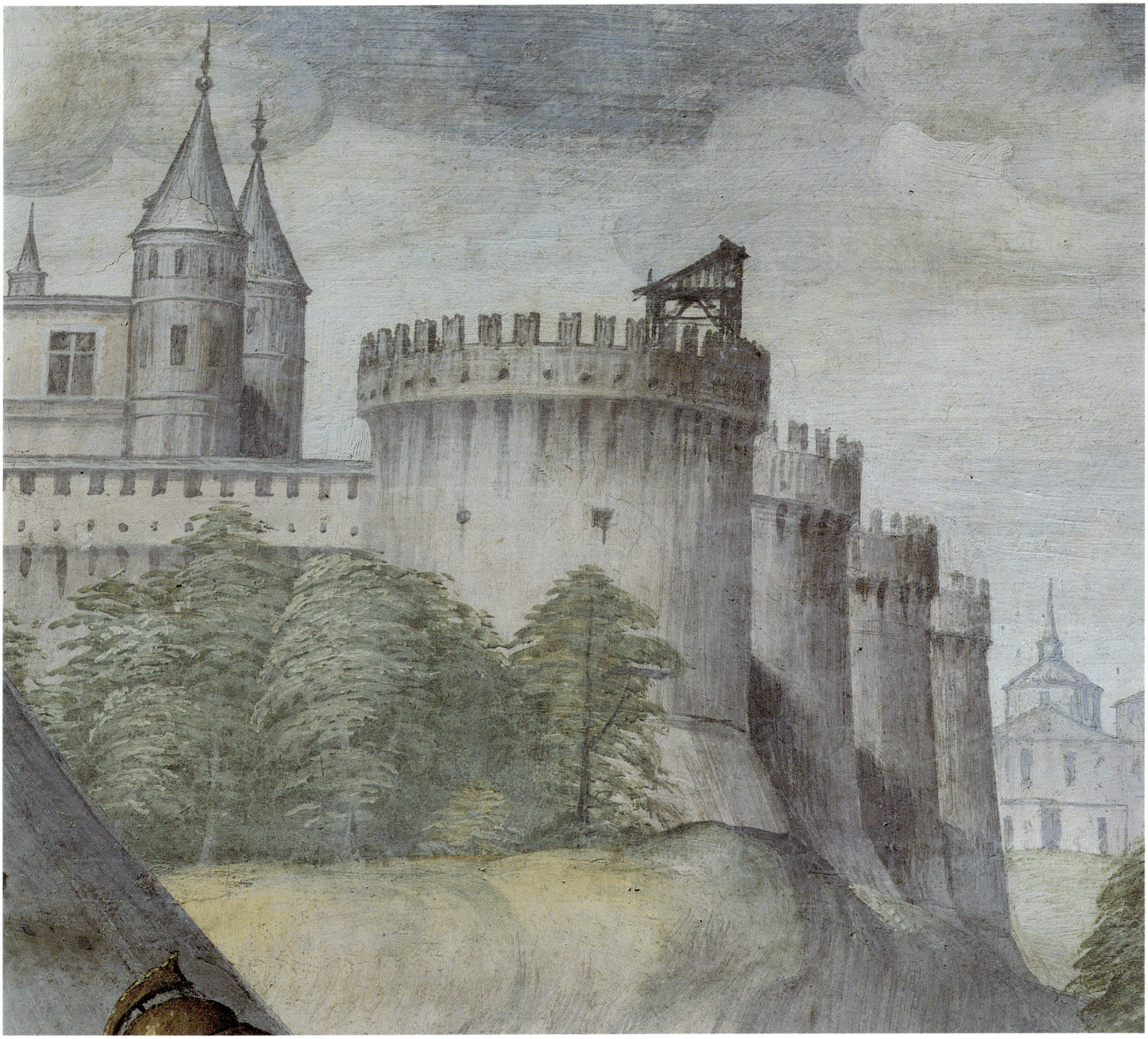

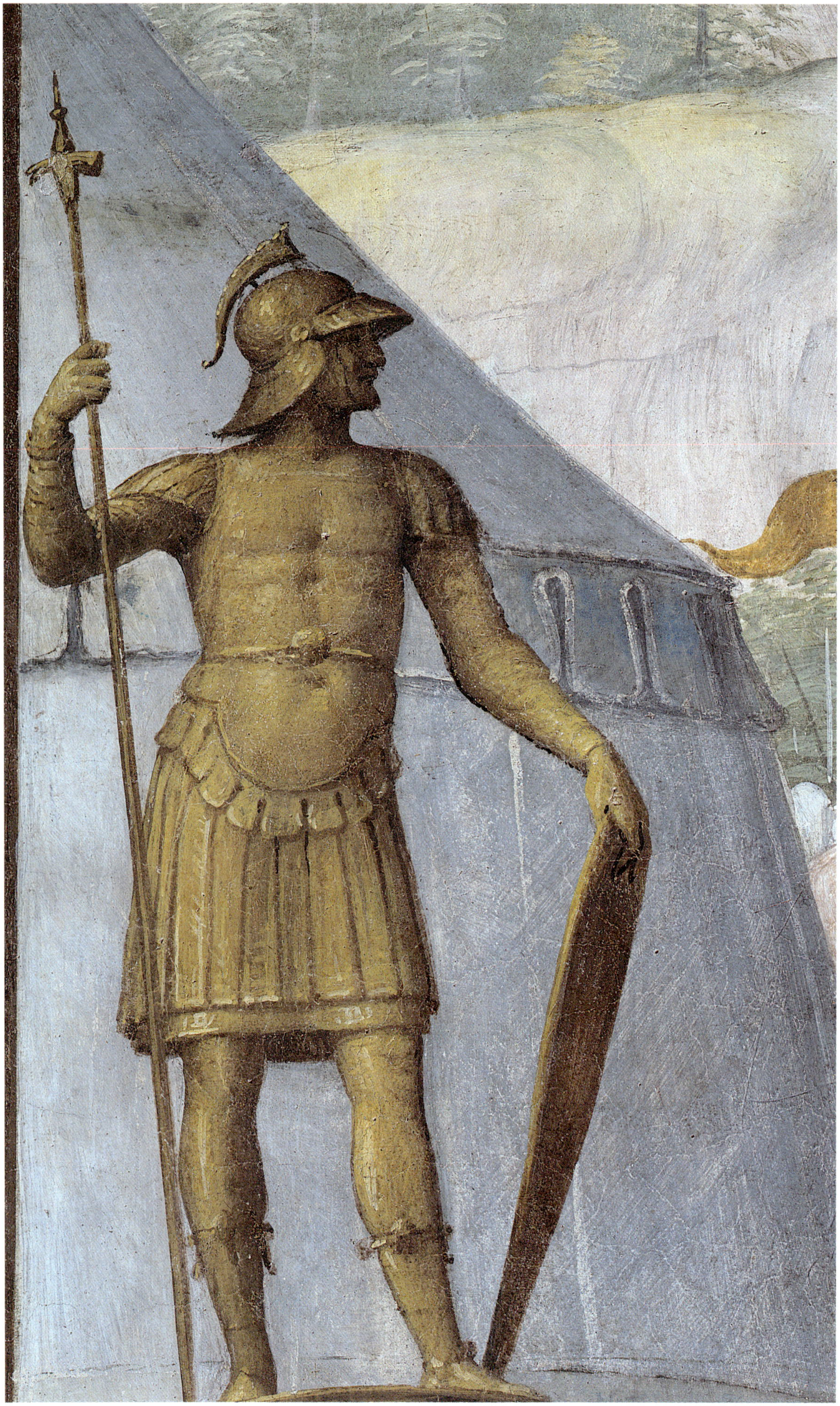

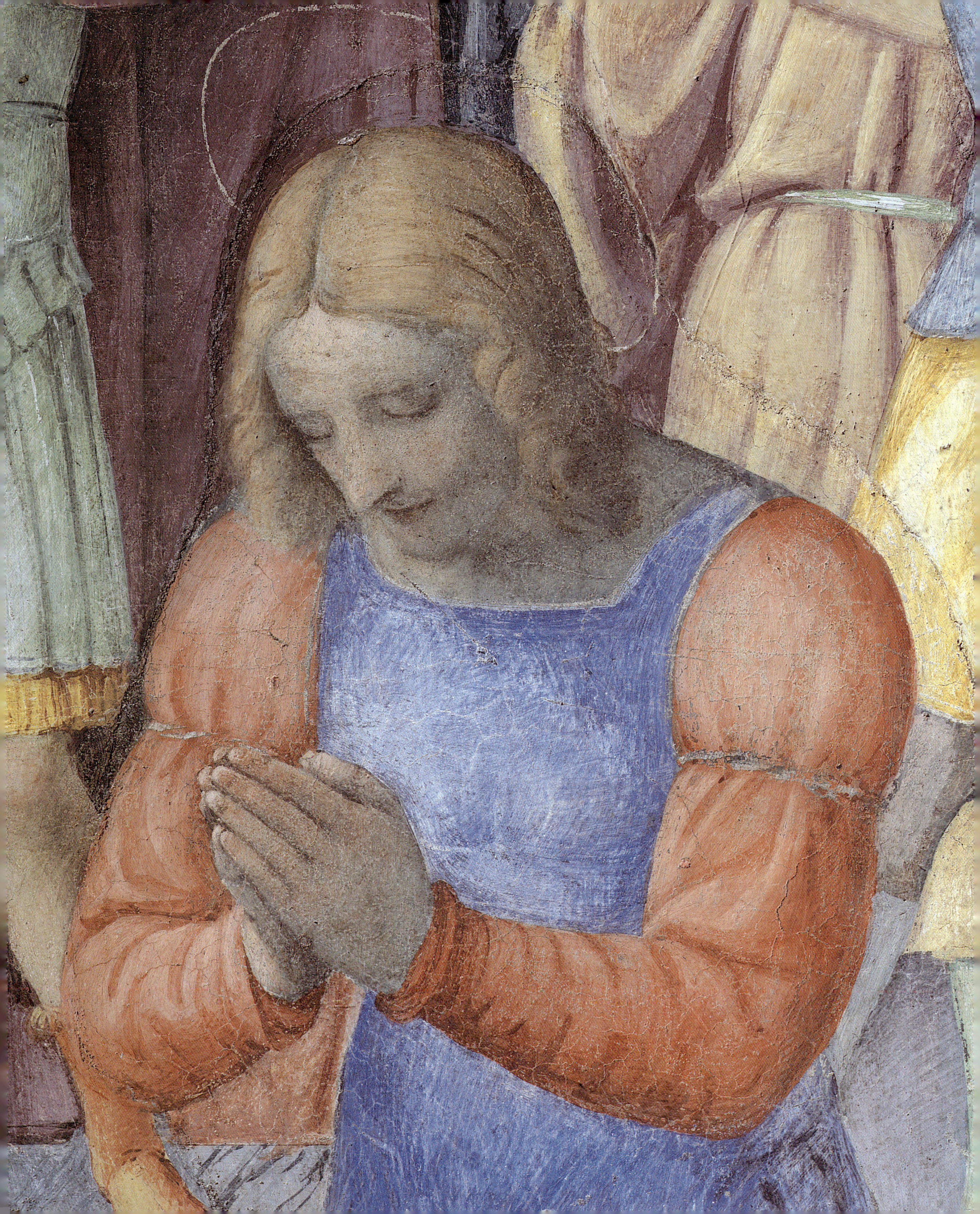

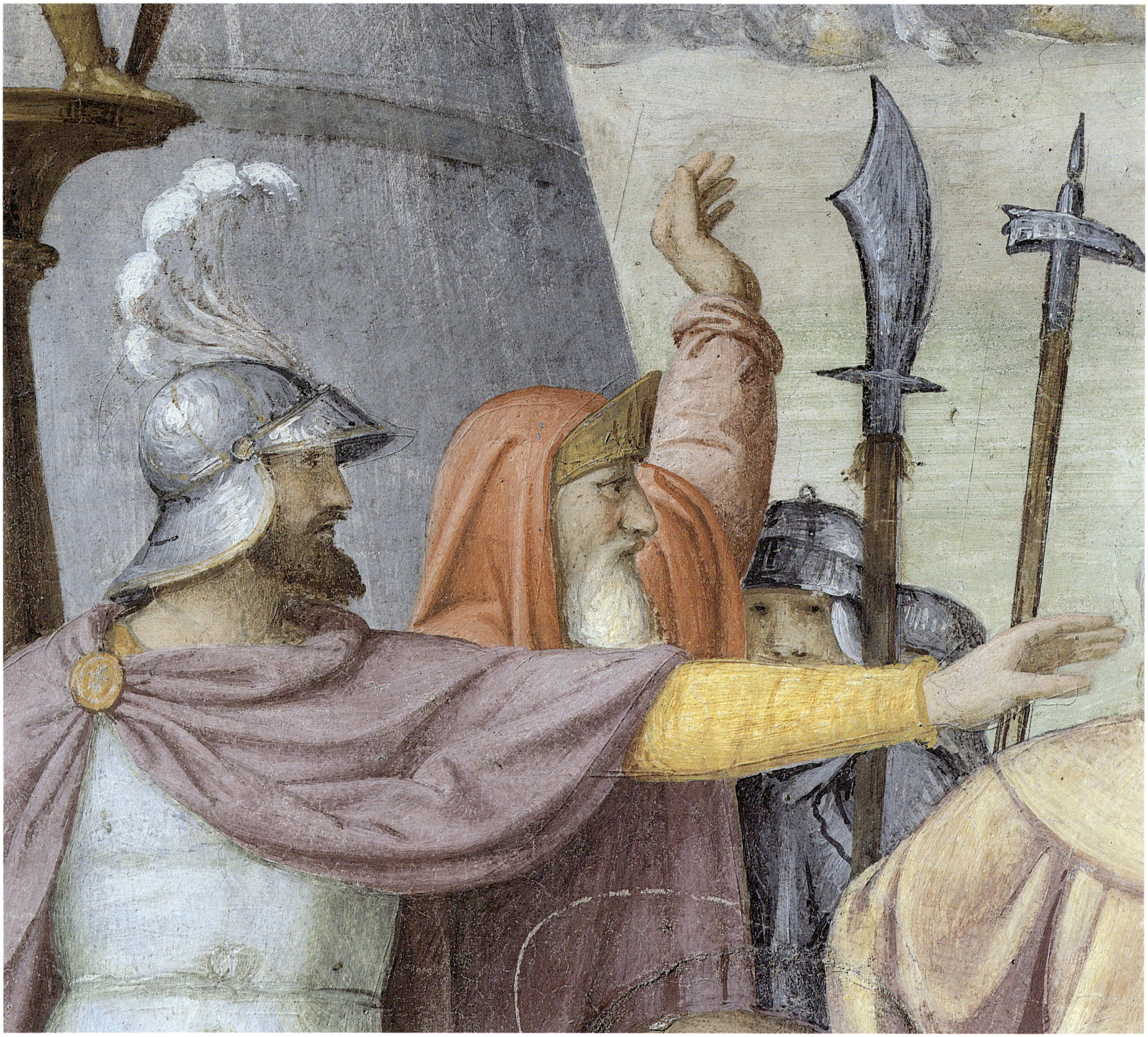

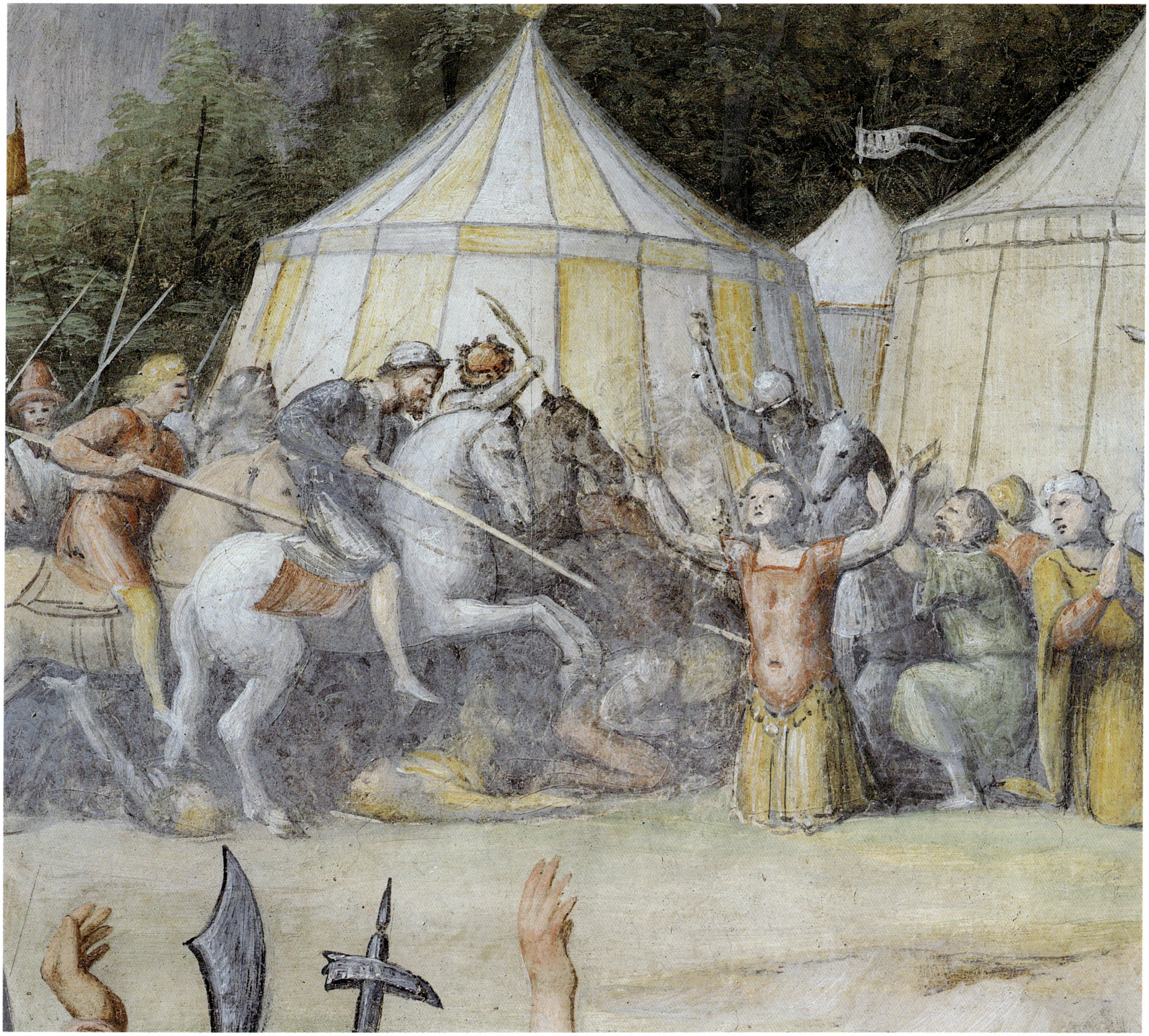

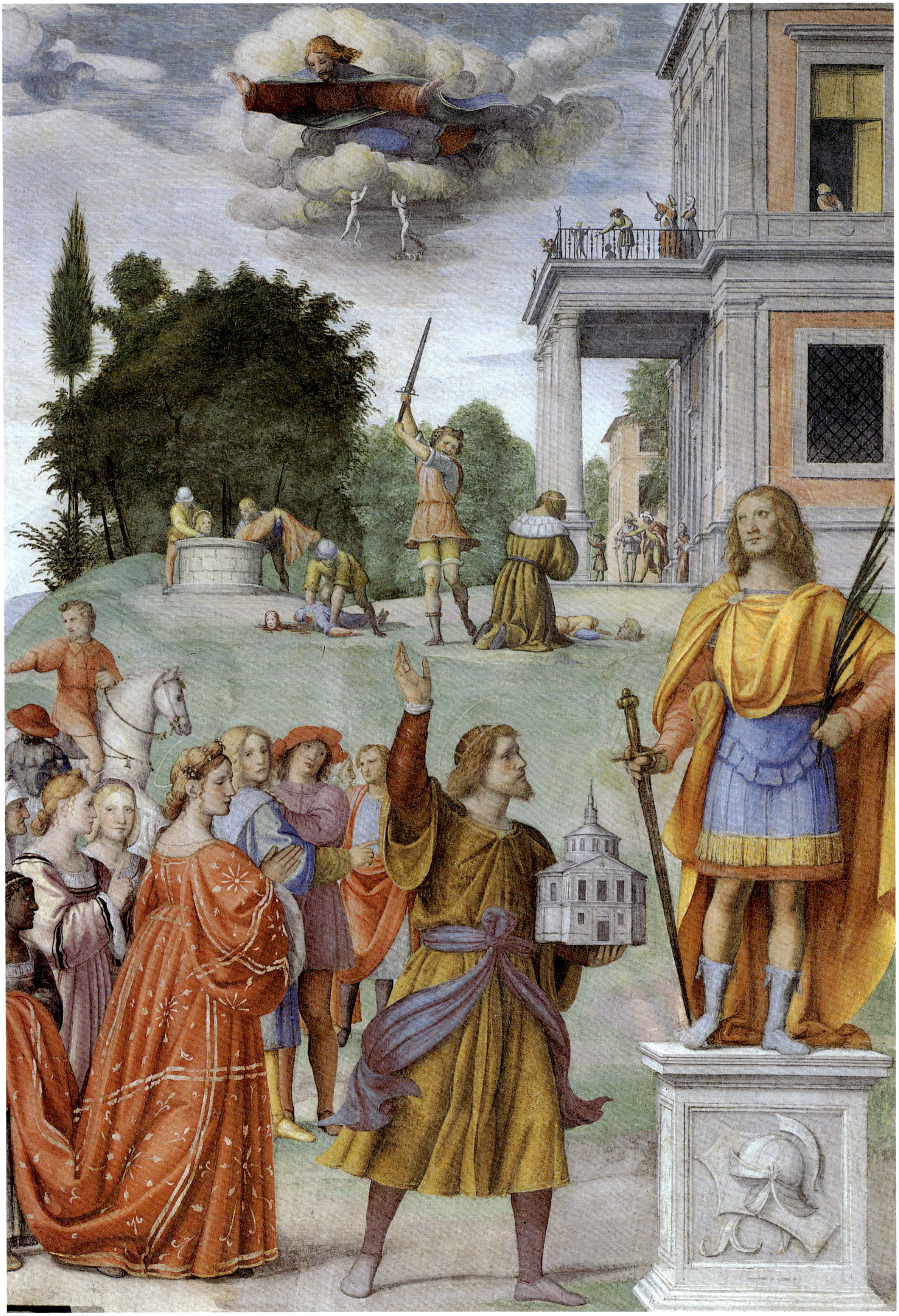

18. Bernardino Luini
St Sigismund Offering the Model of the Church of Agaunum to St Maurice
Right side, partition wall, lay hall

Pages 181–186
18. Bernardino Luini
St Sigismund Offering the Model of the Church of Agaunum to St Maurice, details

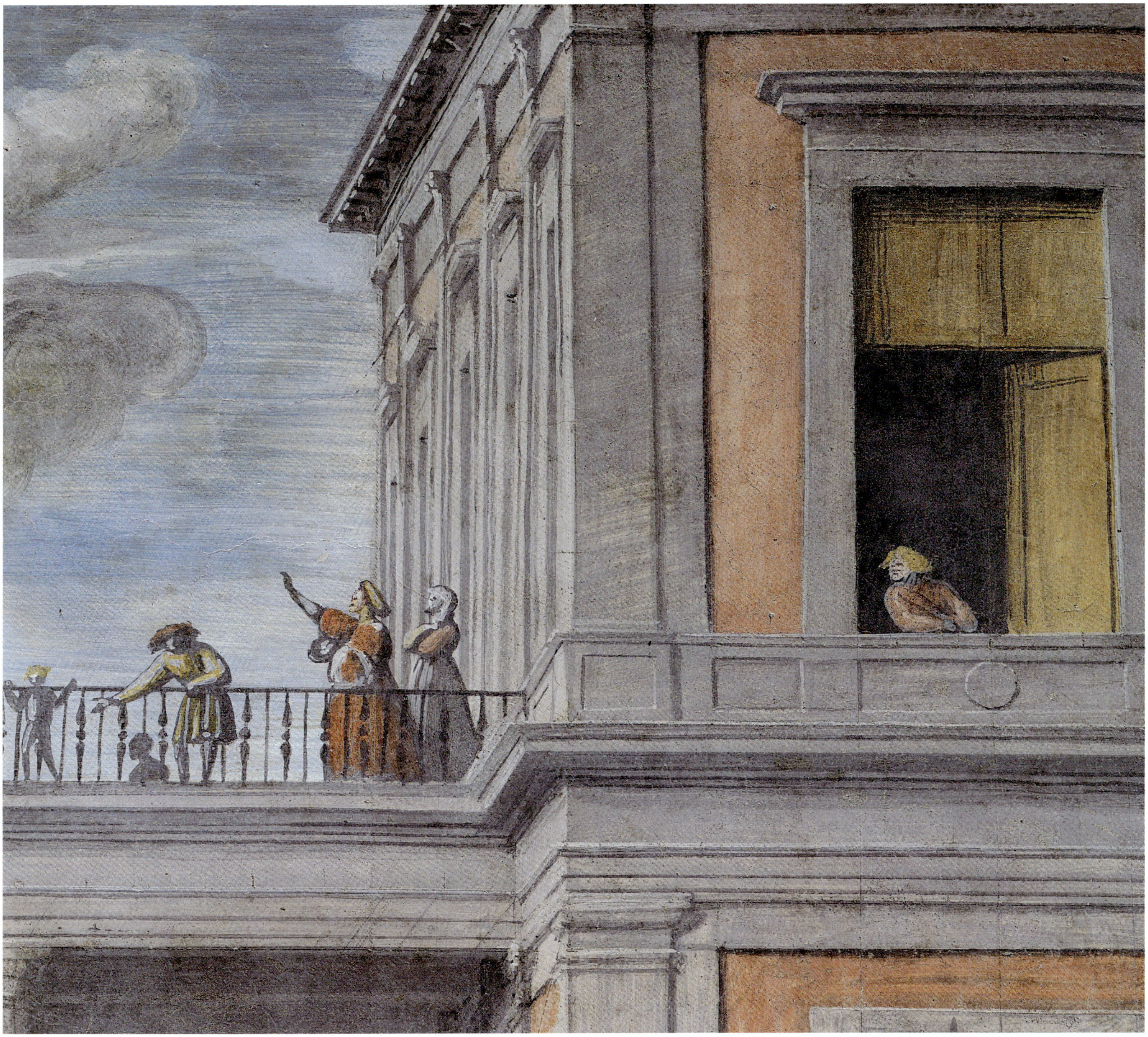

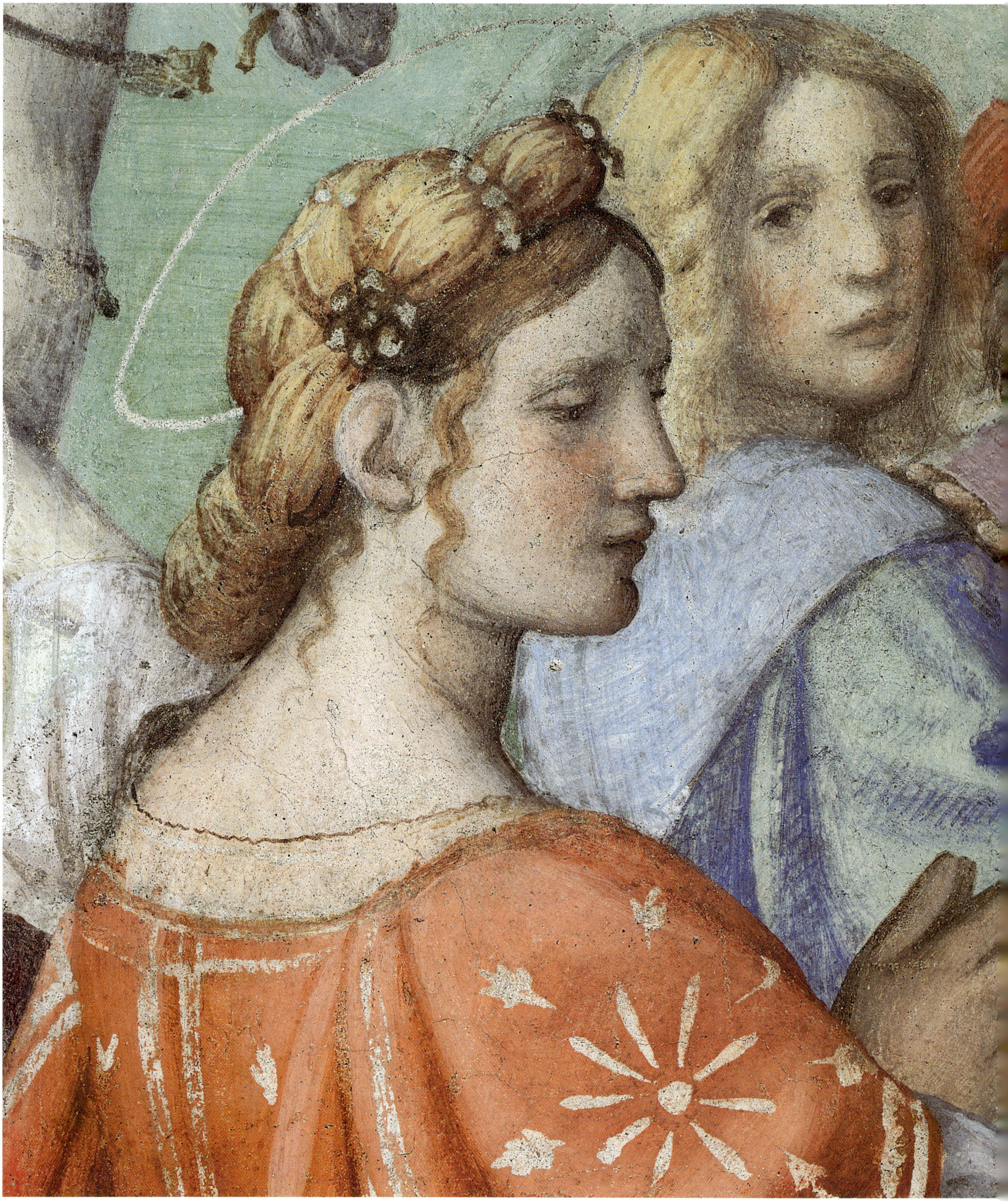

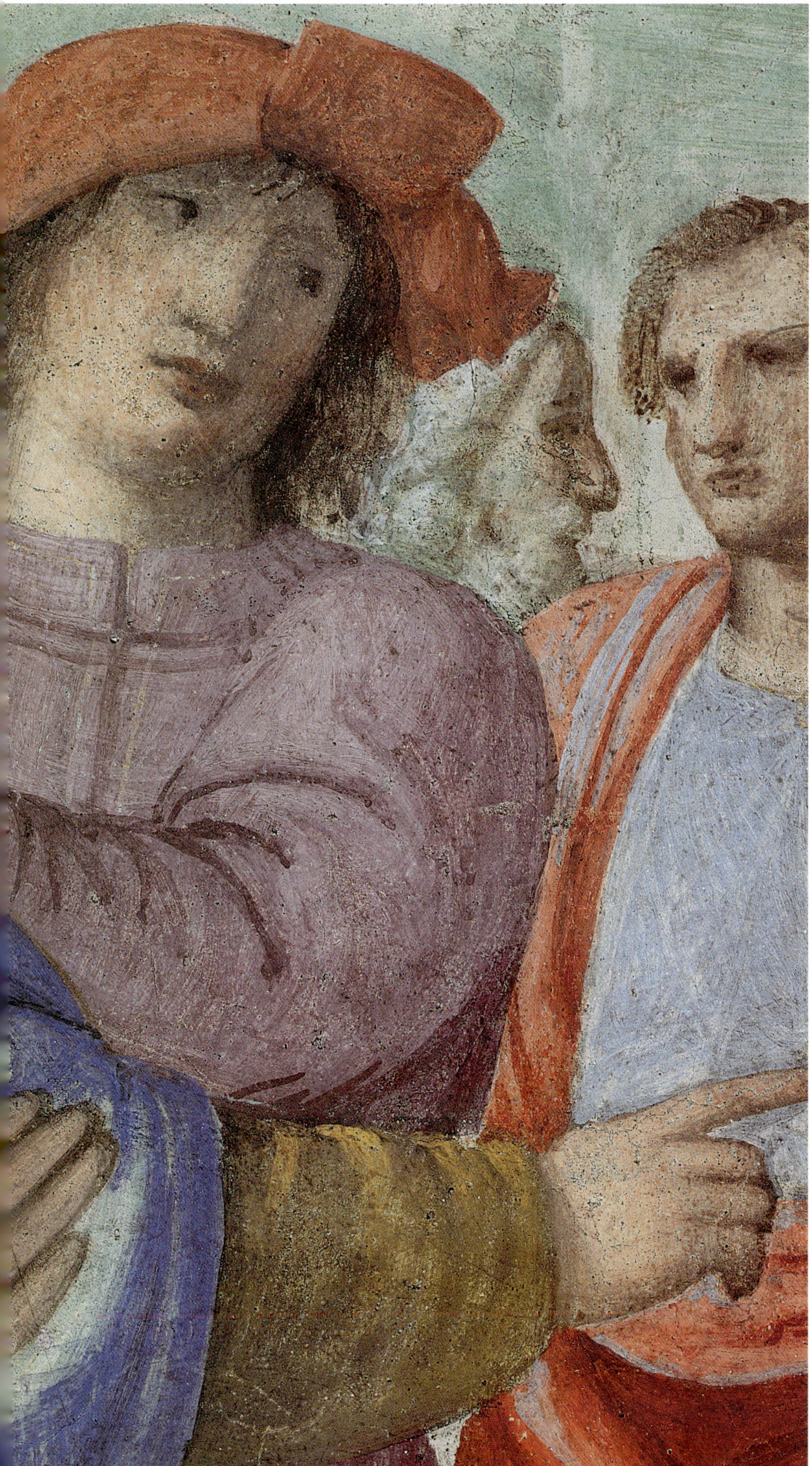

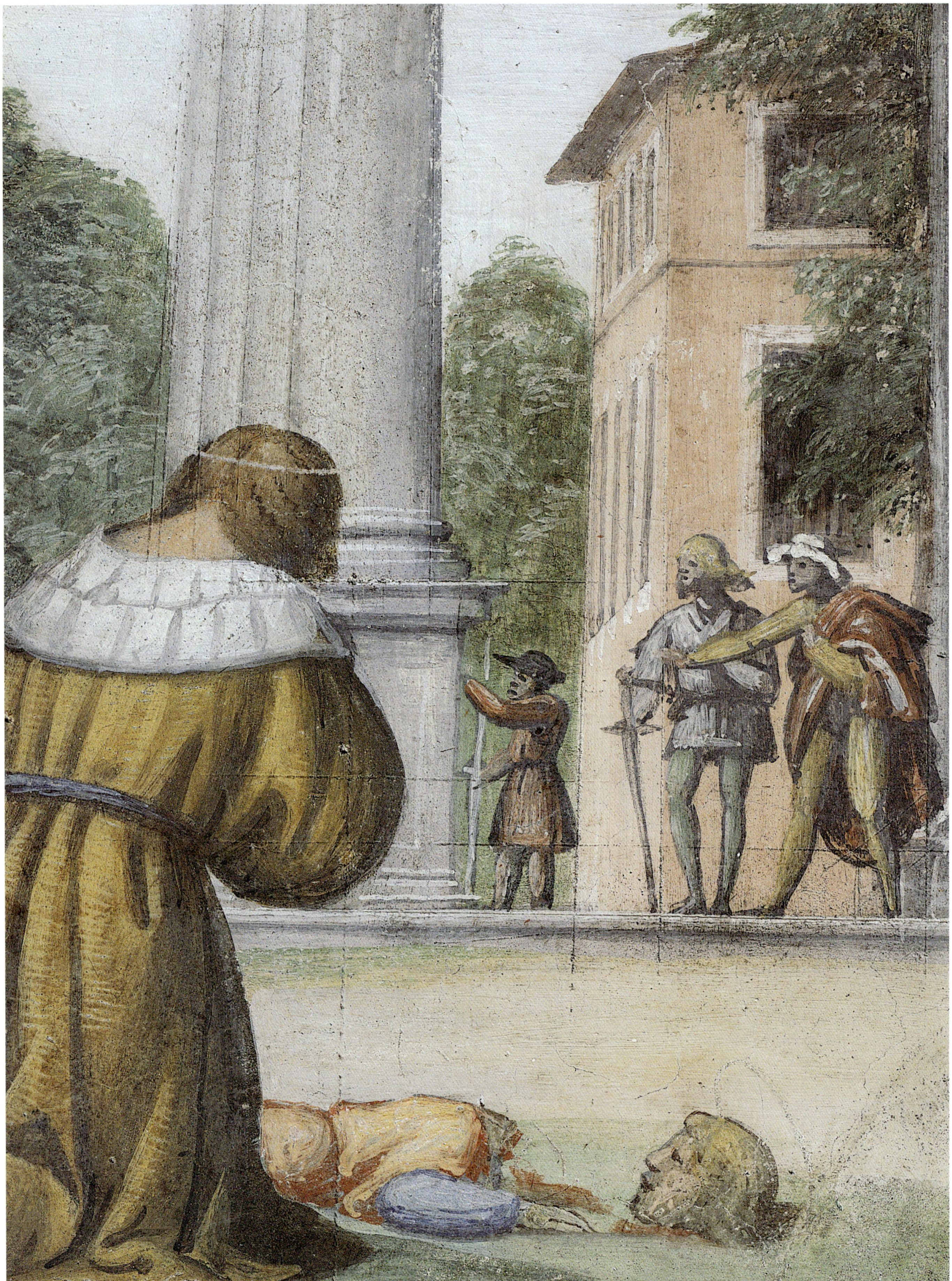

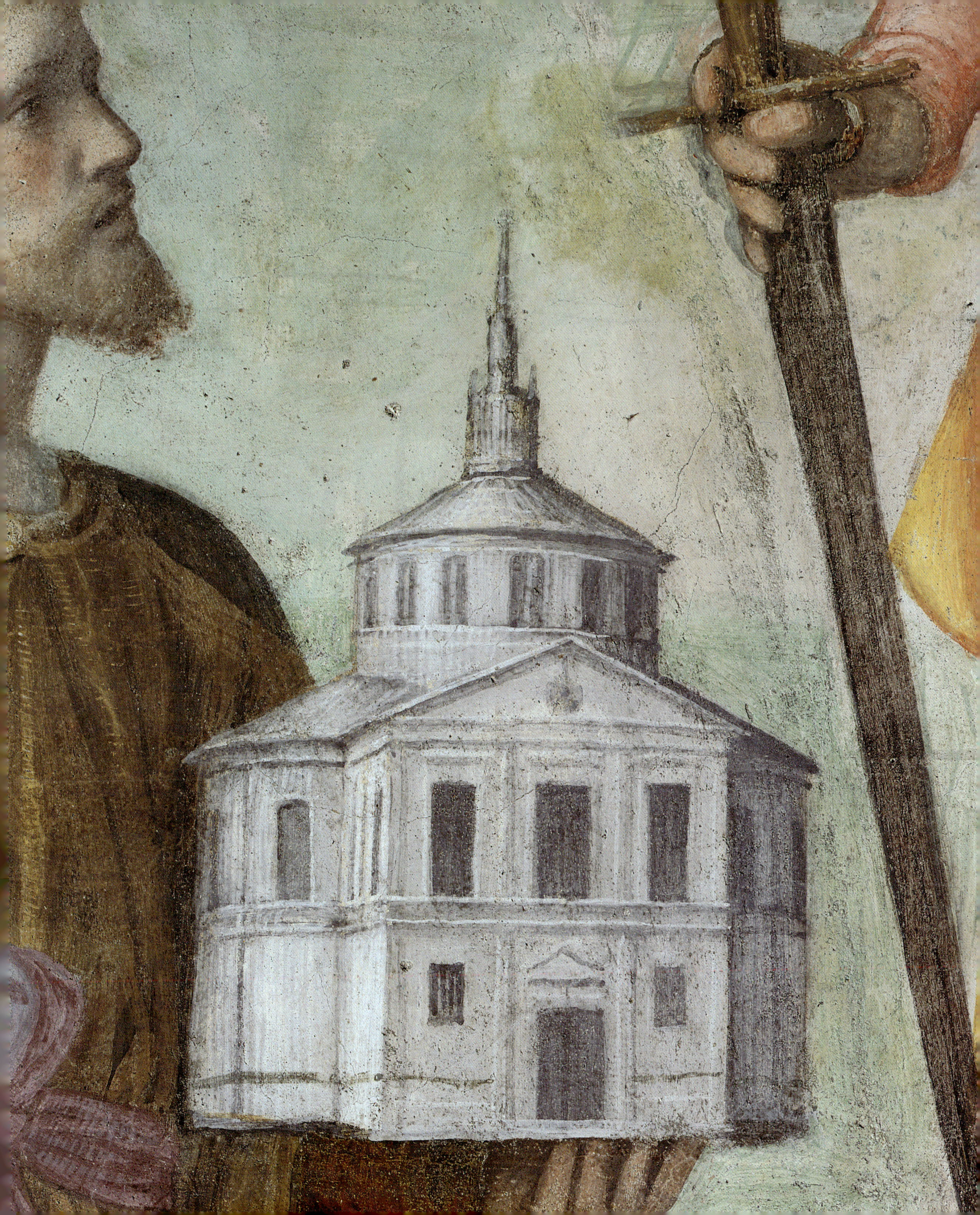

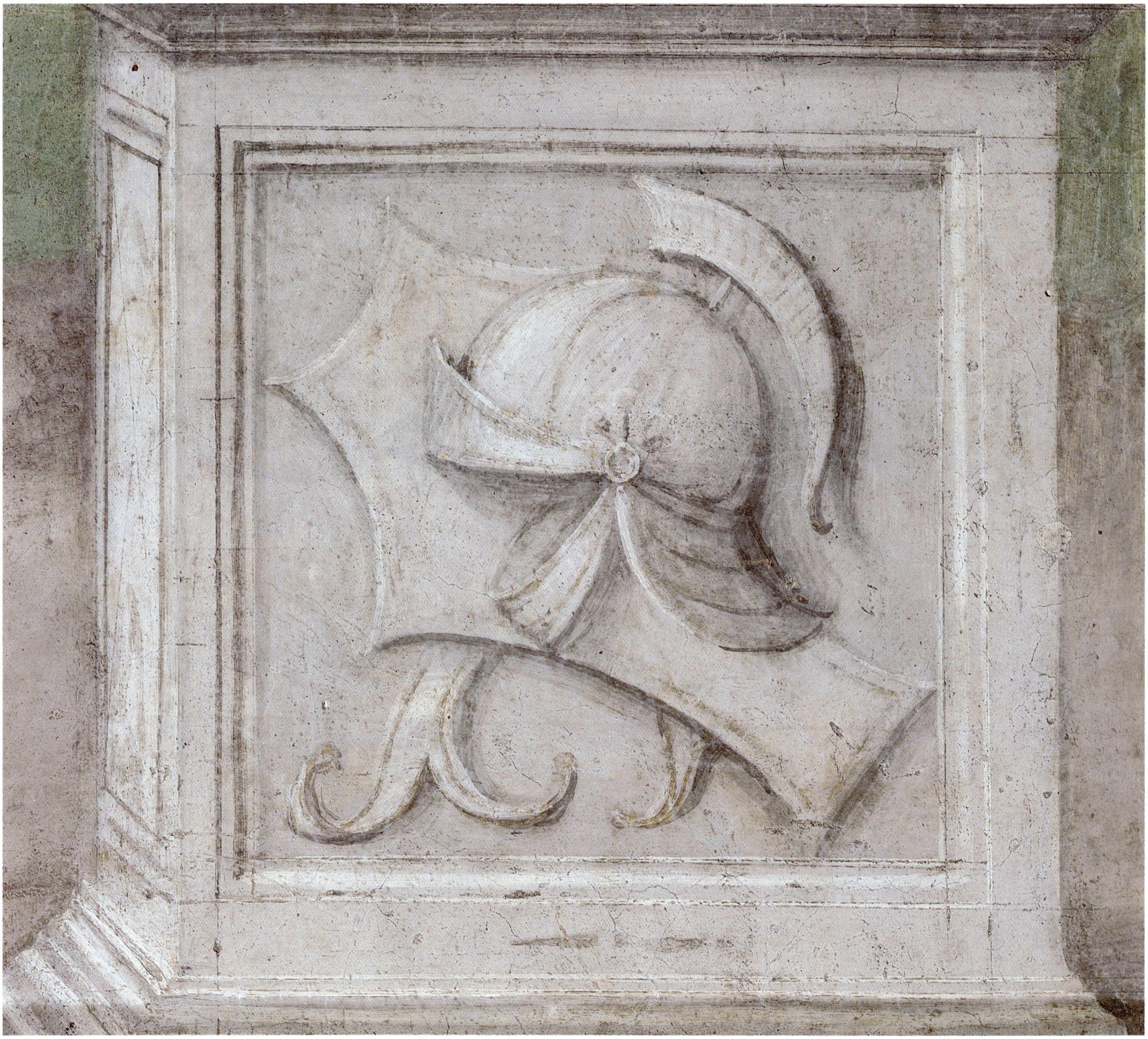

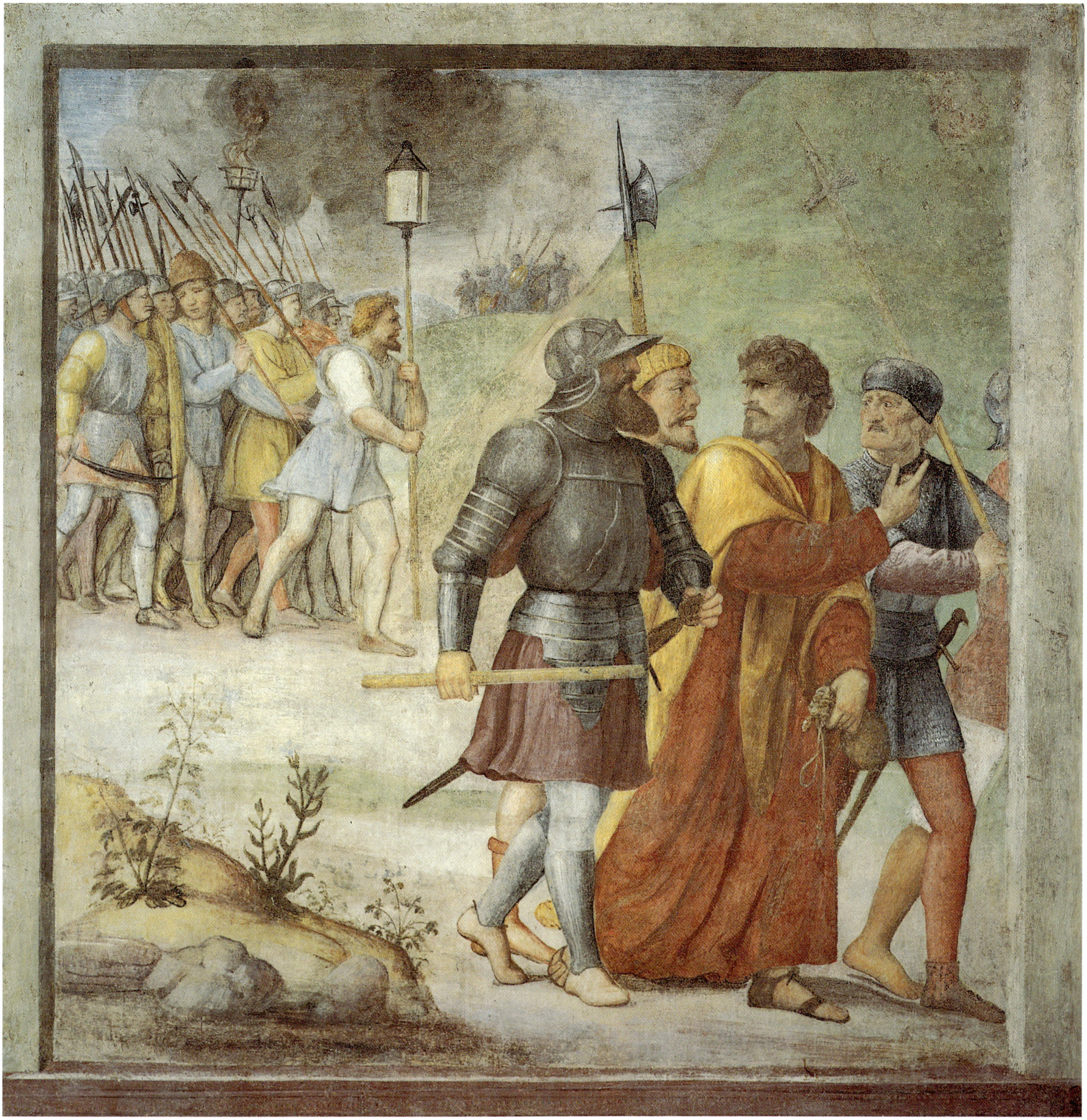

19b. Bernardino Luini
Betrayal of Christ
Convent hall

Following pages
19b. Bernardino Luini
Betrayal of Christ, detail

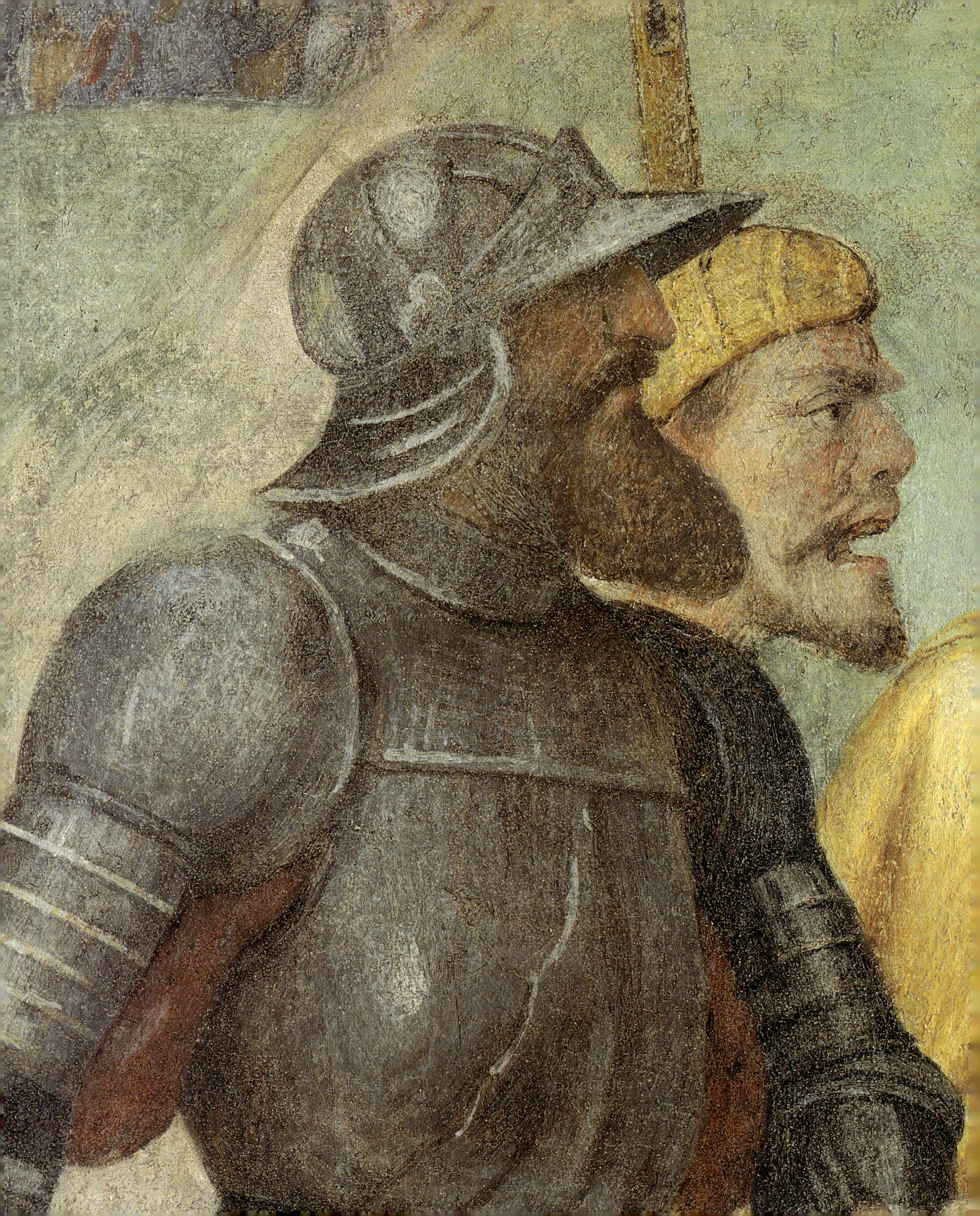

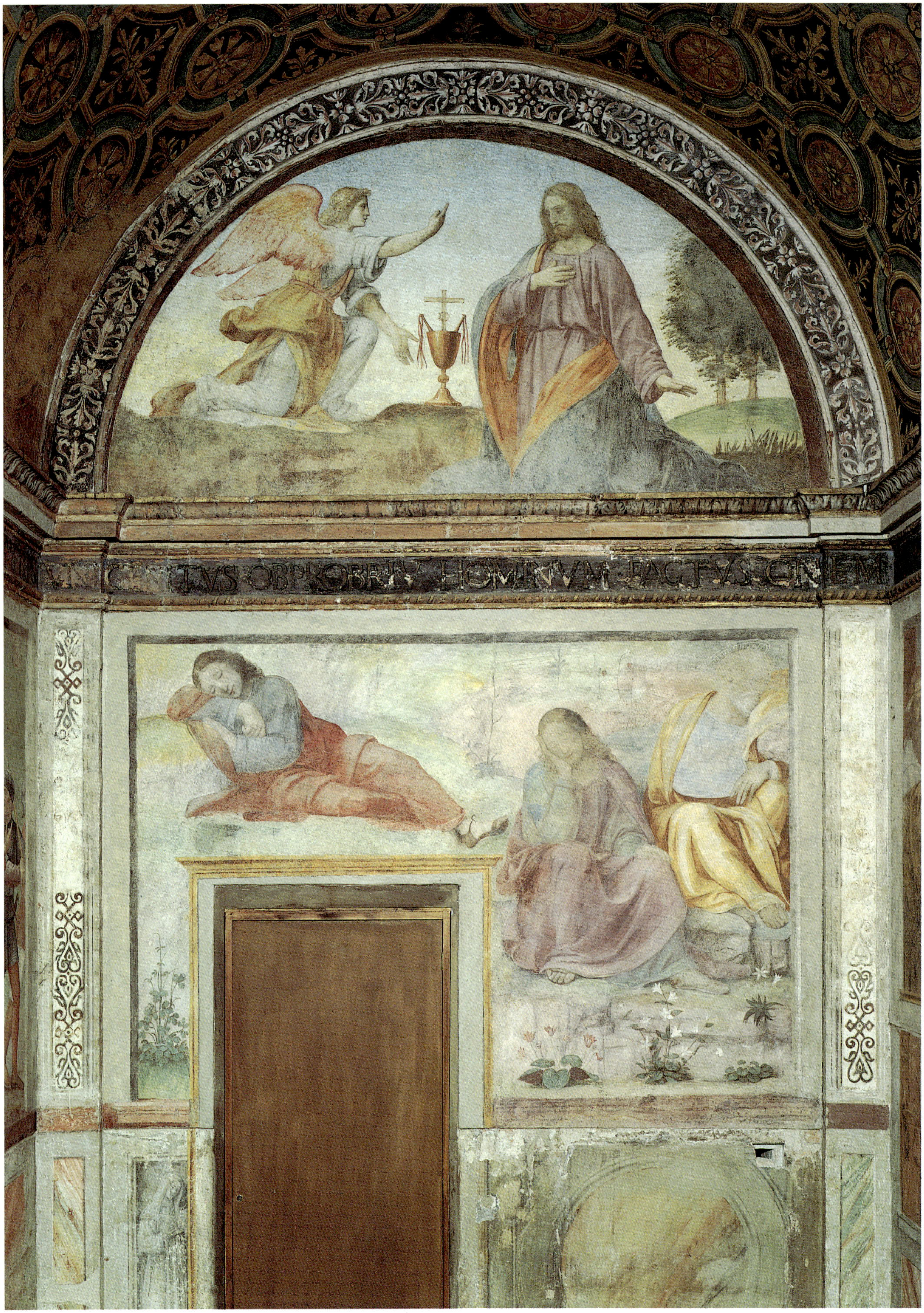

19a. Bernardino
Luini
Agony in the Garden
Convent hall

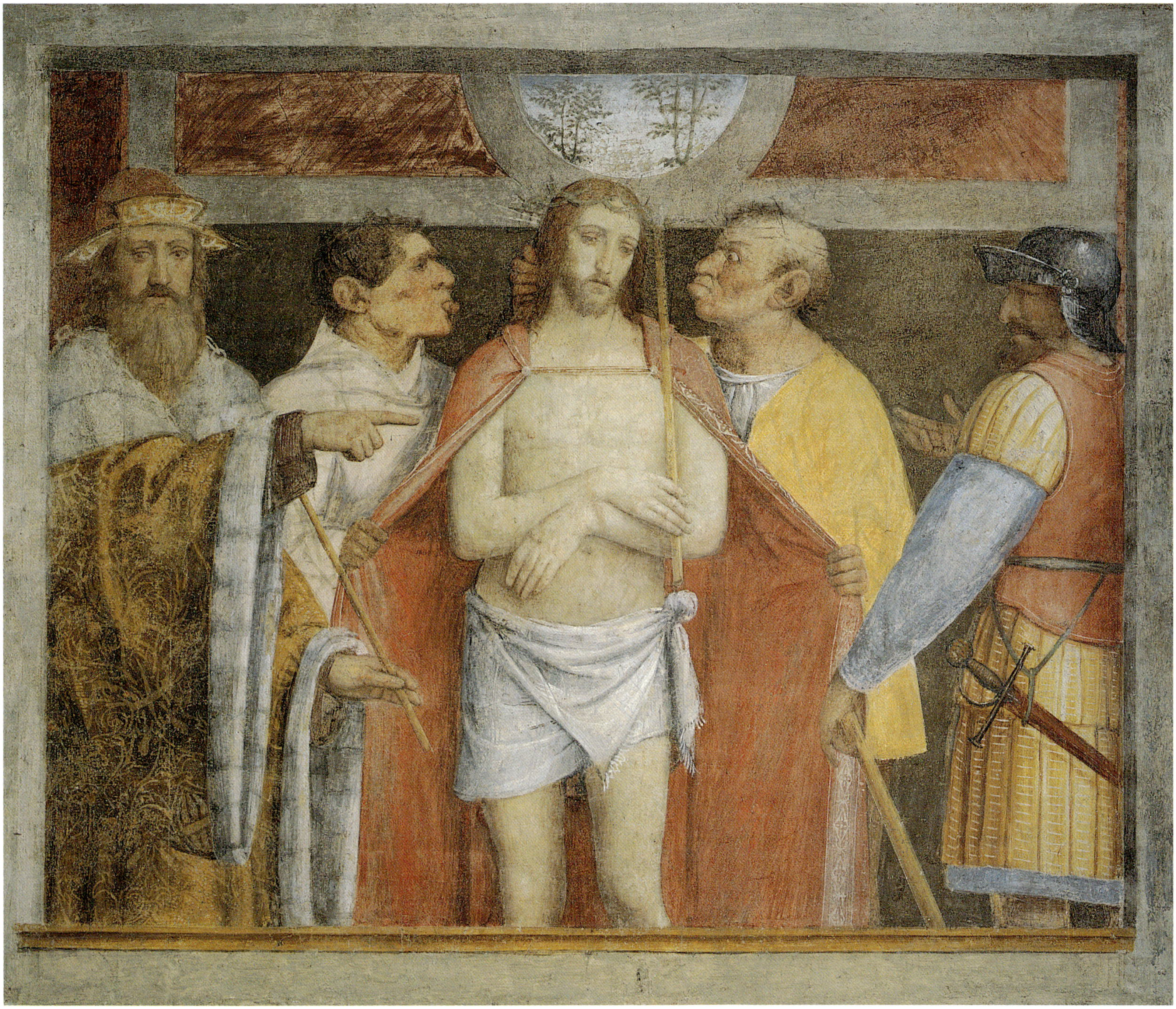

19c. Bernardino Luini
Christ Mocked
Convent hall

Following pages
19c. Bernardino Luini
Christ Mocked, detail

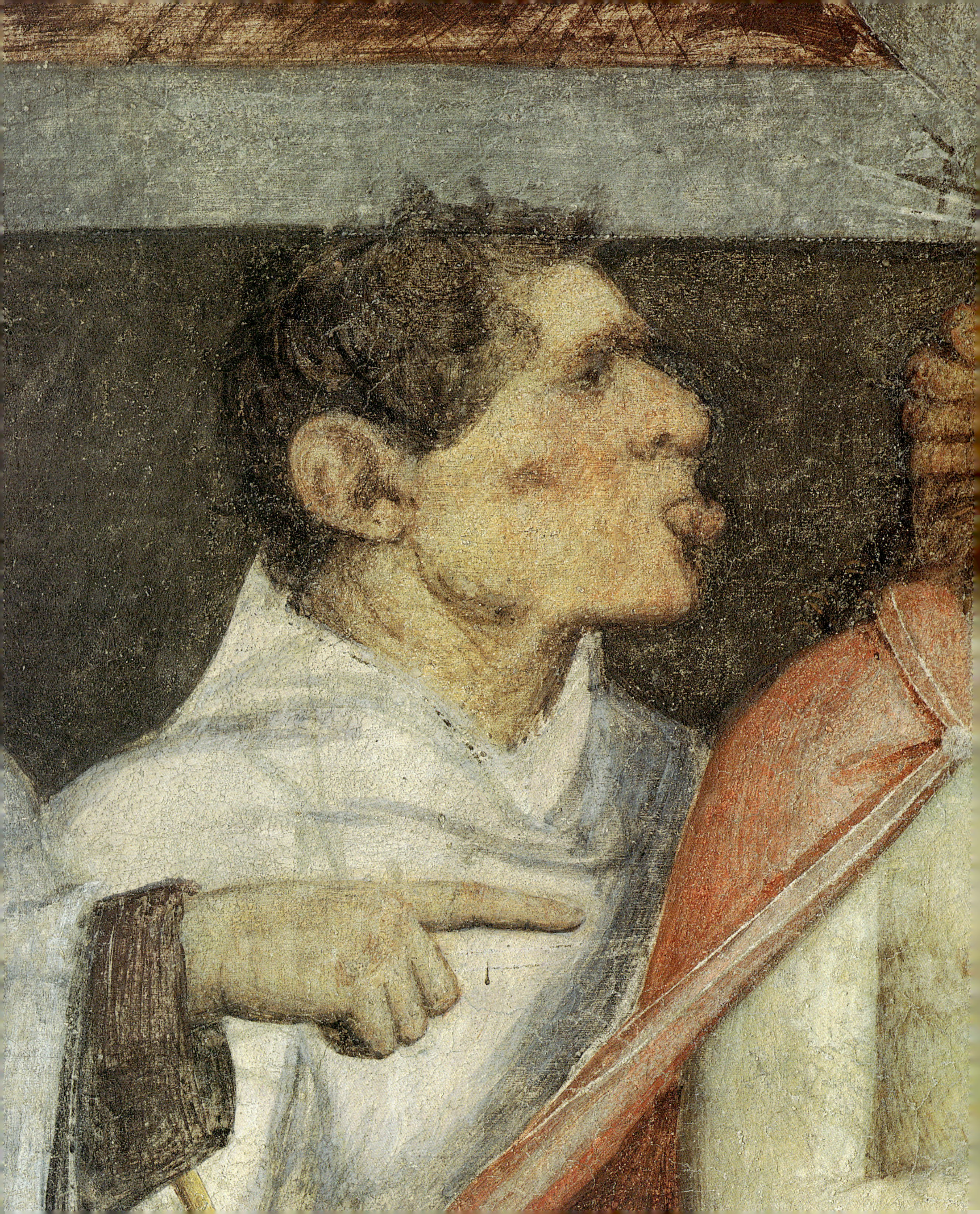

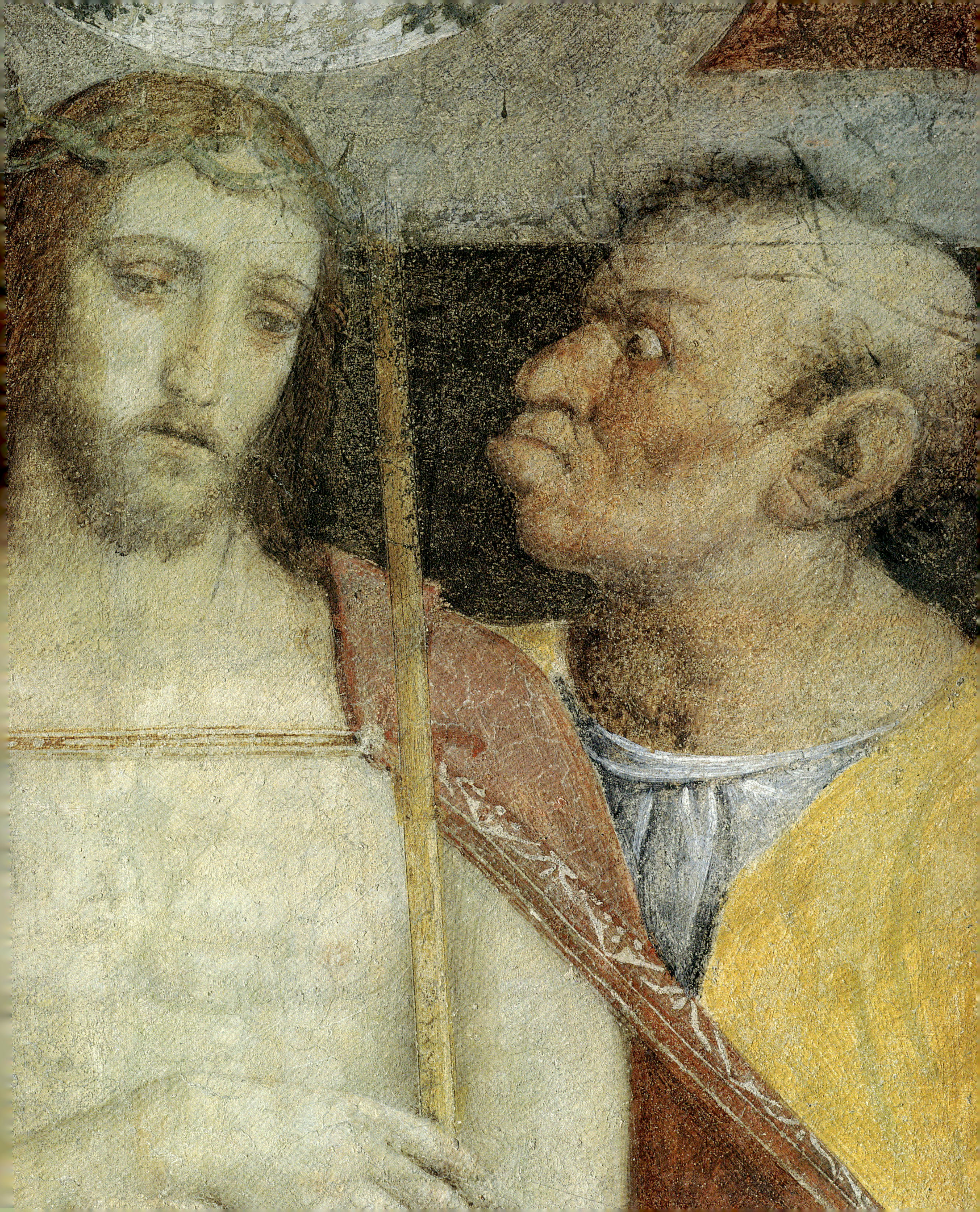

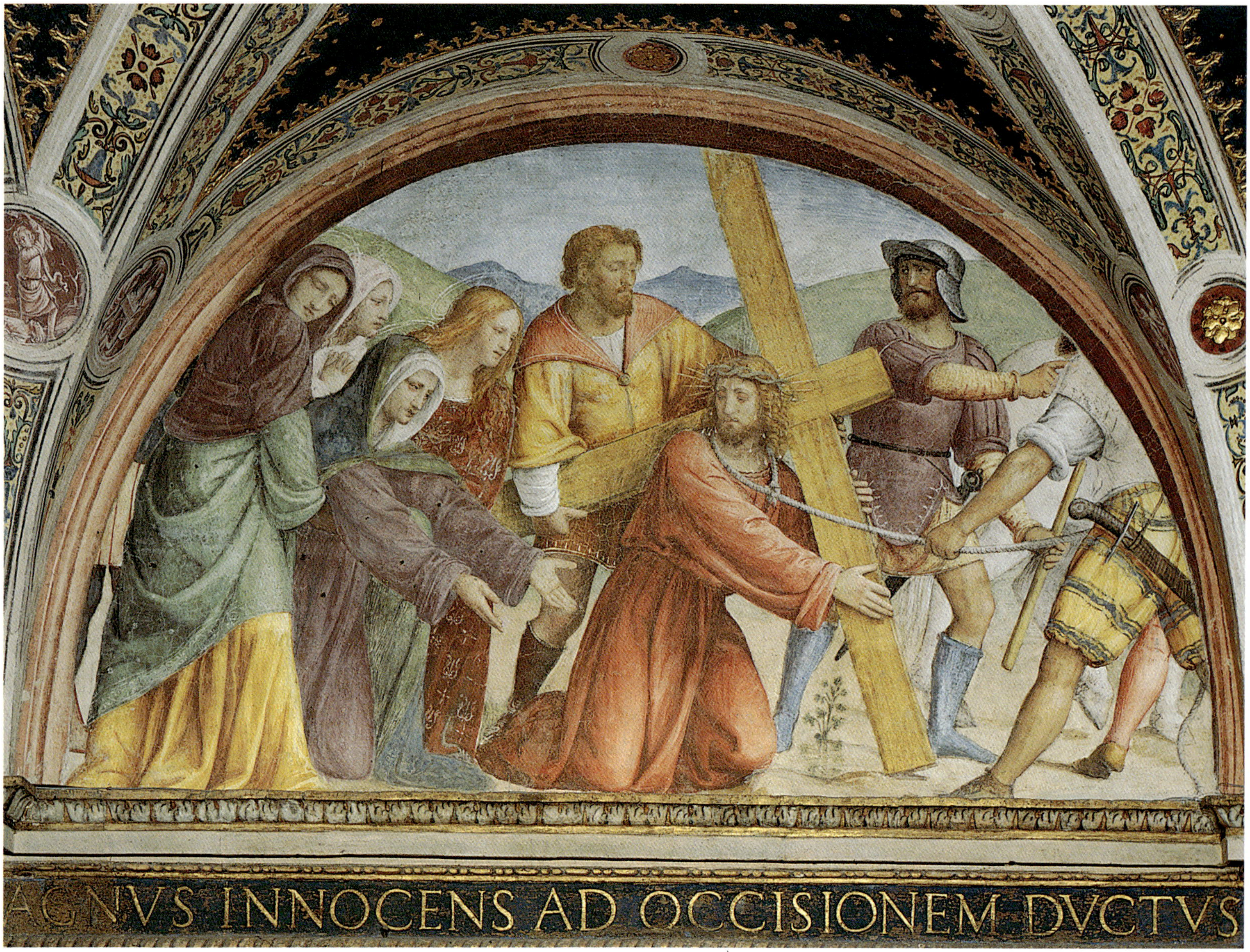

20. Bernardino Luini
Way to Calvary, with detail
Left side, partition wall,
convent hall

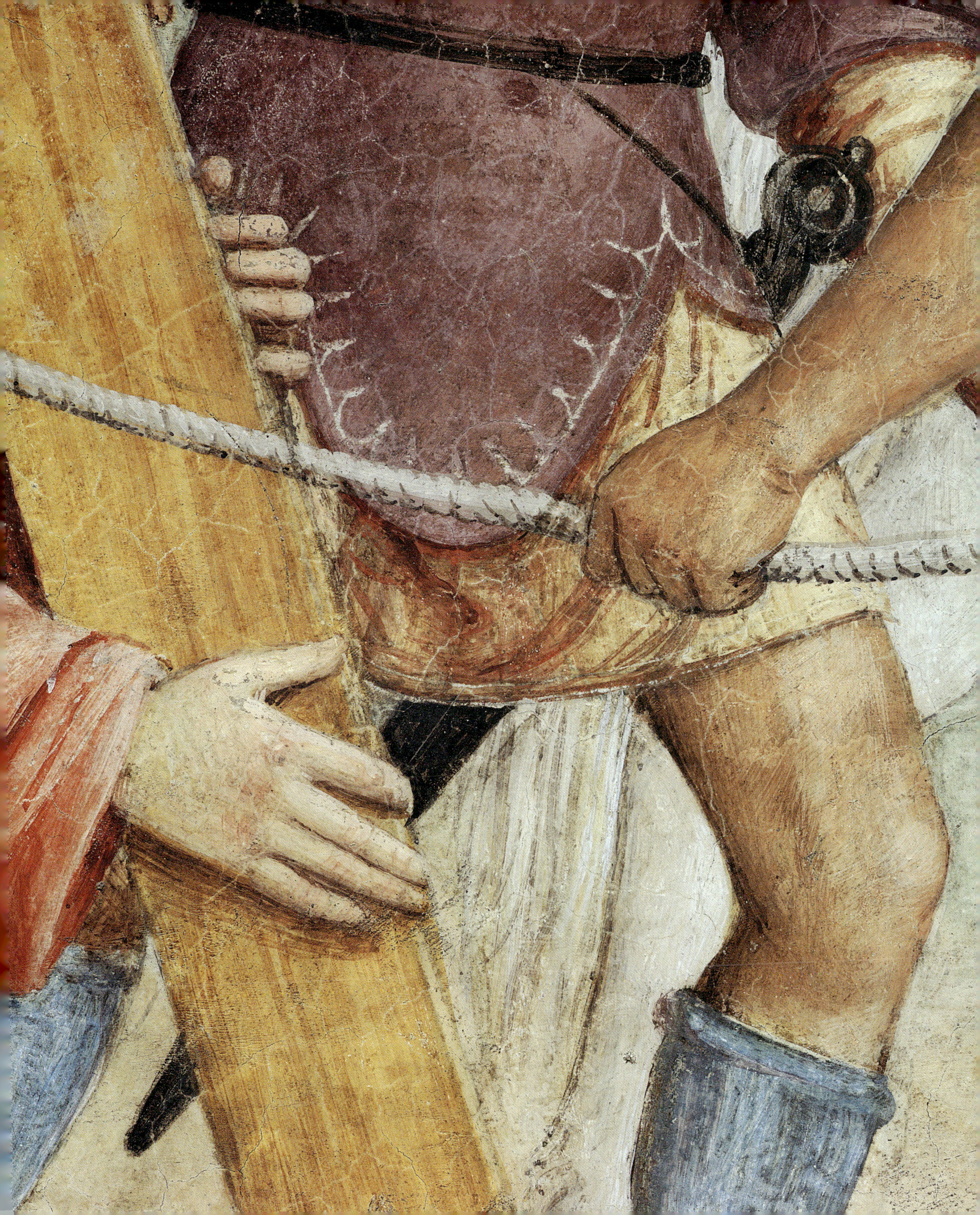

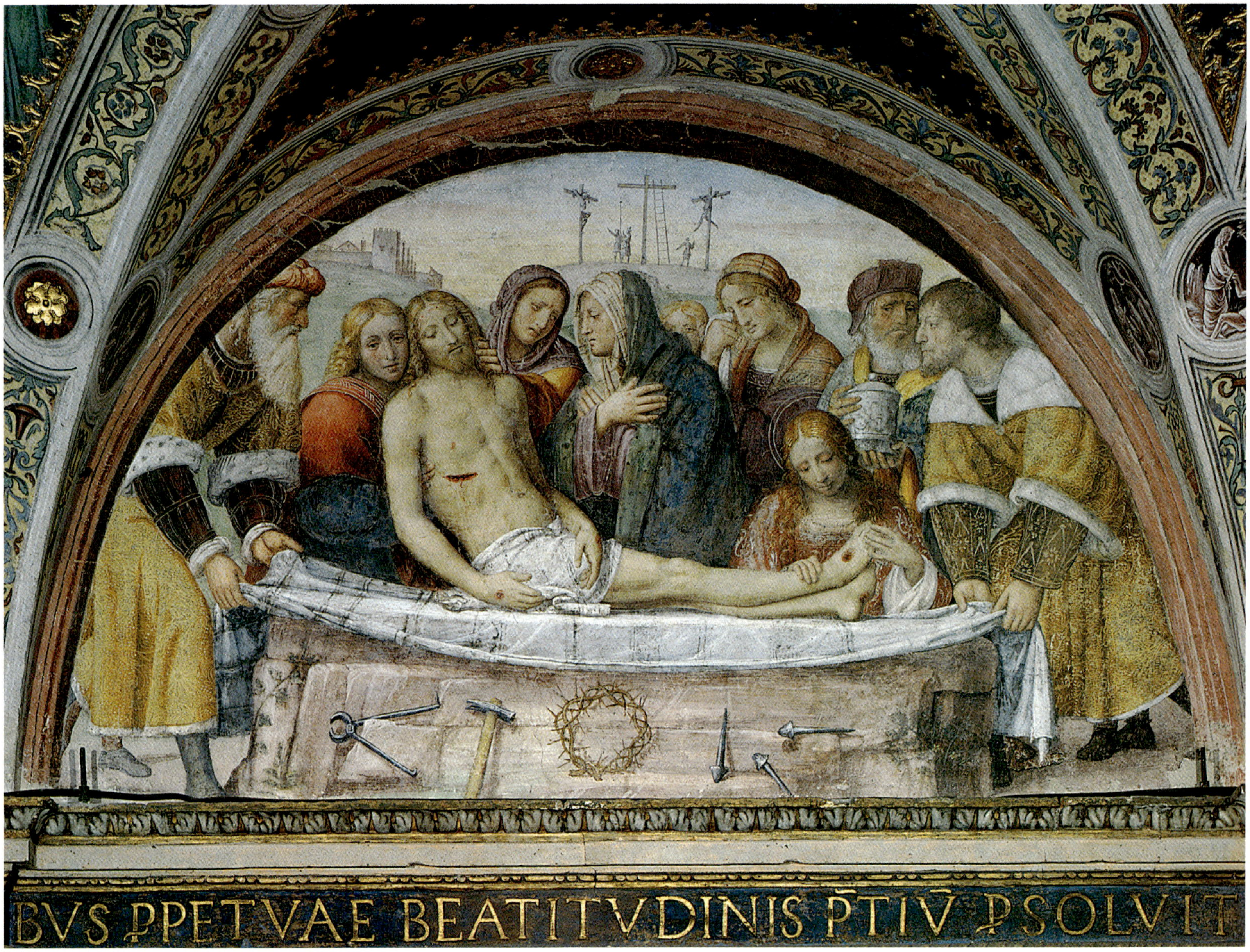

21. Bernardino Luini
Deposition of Christ, with detail
Right side, partition wall,
convent hall

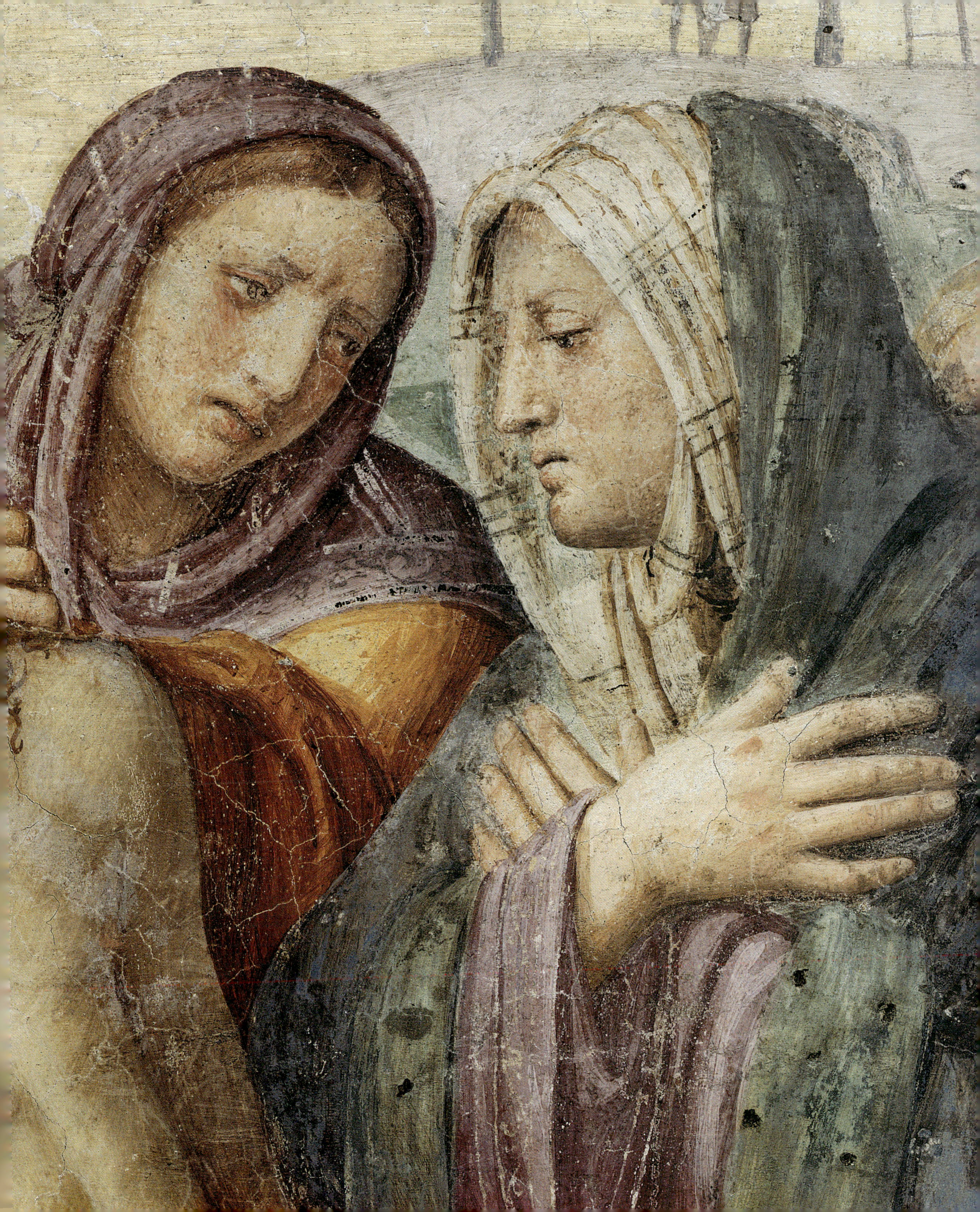

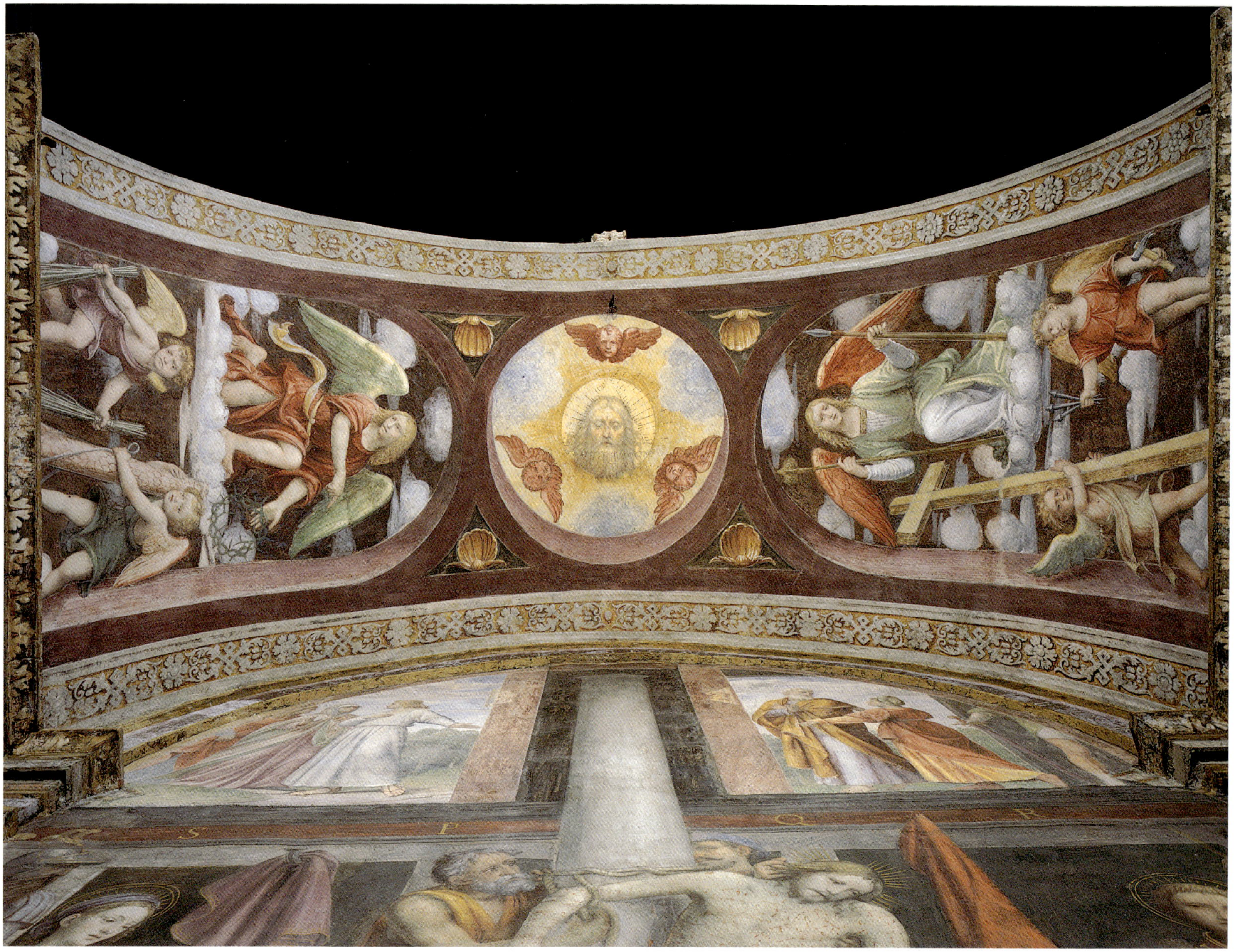

22. Bernardino Luini
Intrados, Cappella Besozzi
(or di Santa Caterina), lay hall

22a. Bernardino Luini
Christ at the Column
Central wall, Cappella Besozzi
(or di Santa Caterina), lay hall

Following pages
22a. Bernardino Luini
Christ at the Column, detail

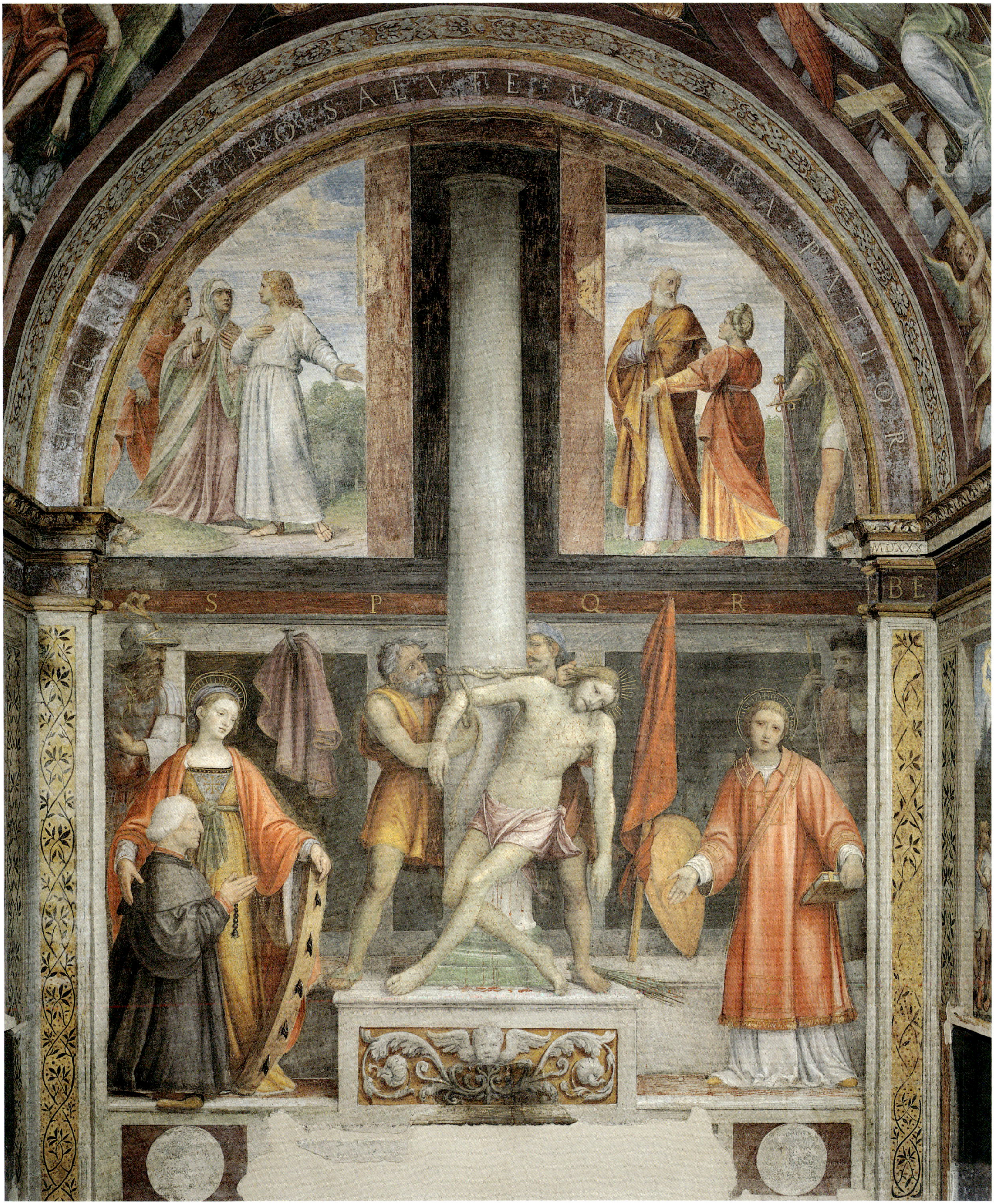
QVI PRO SALVTE VESTRA PATIOR
S P Q R
MDXXX
BE

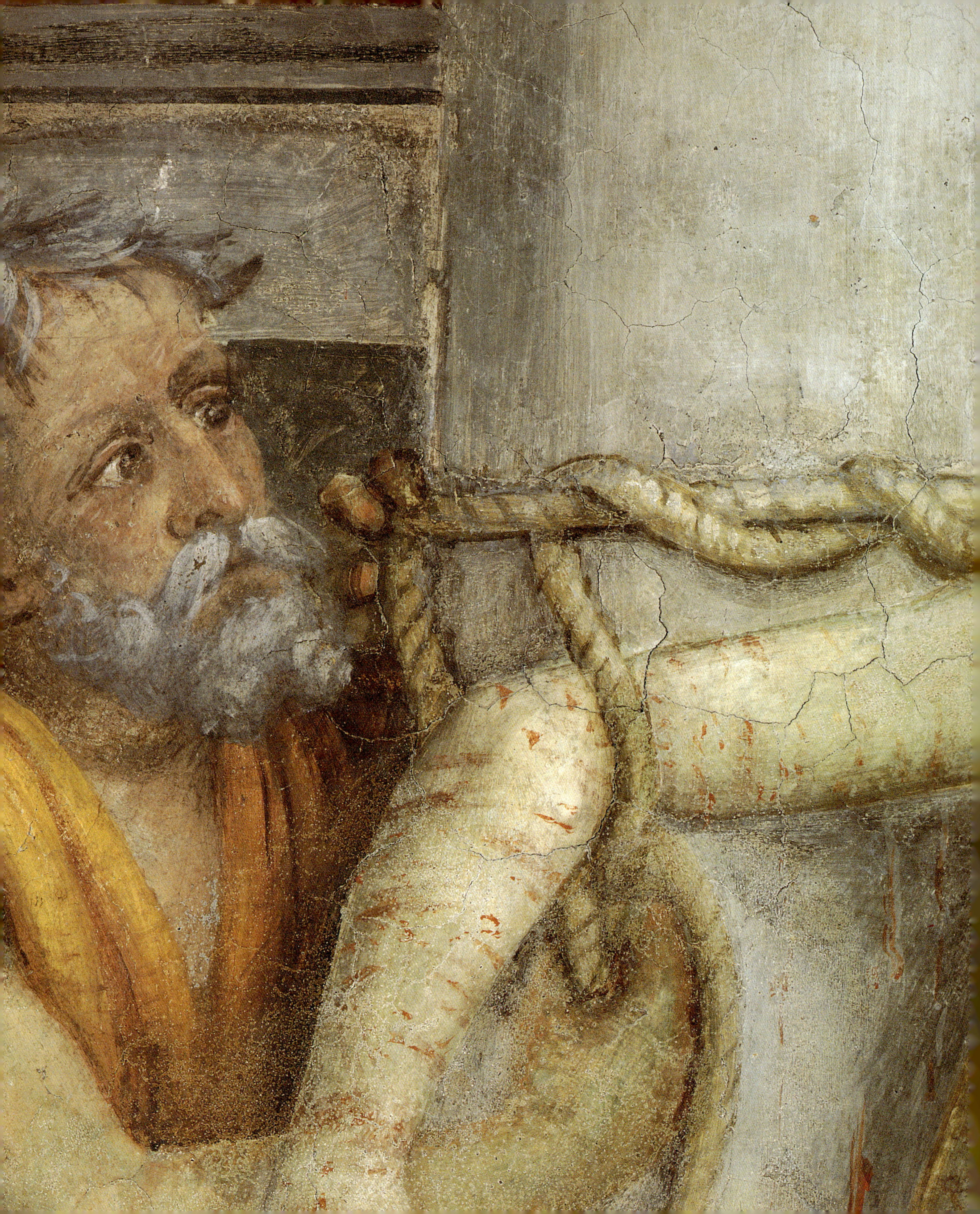

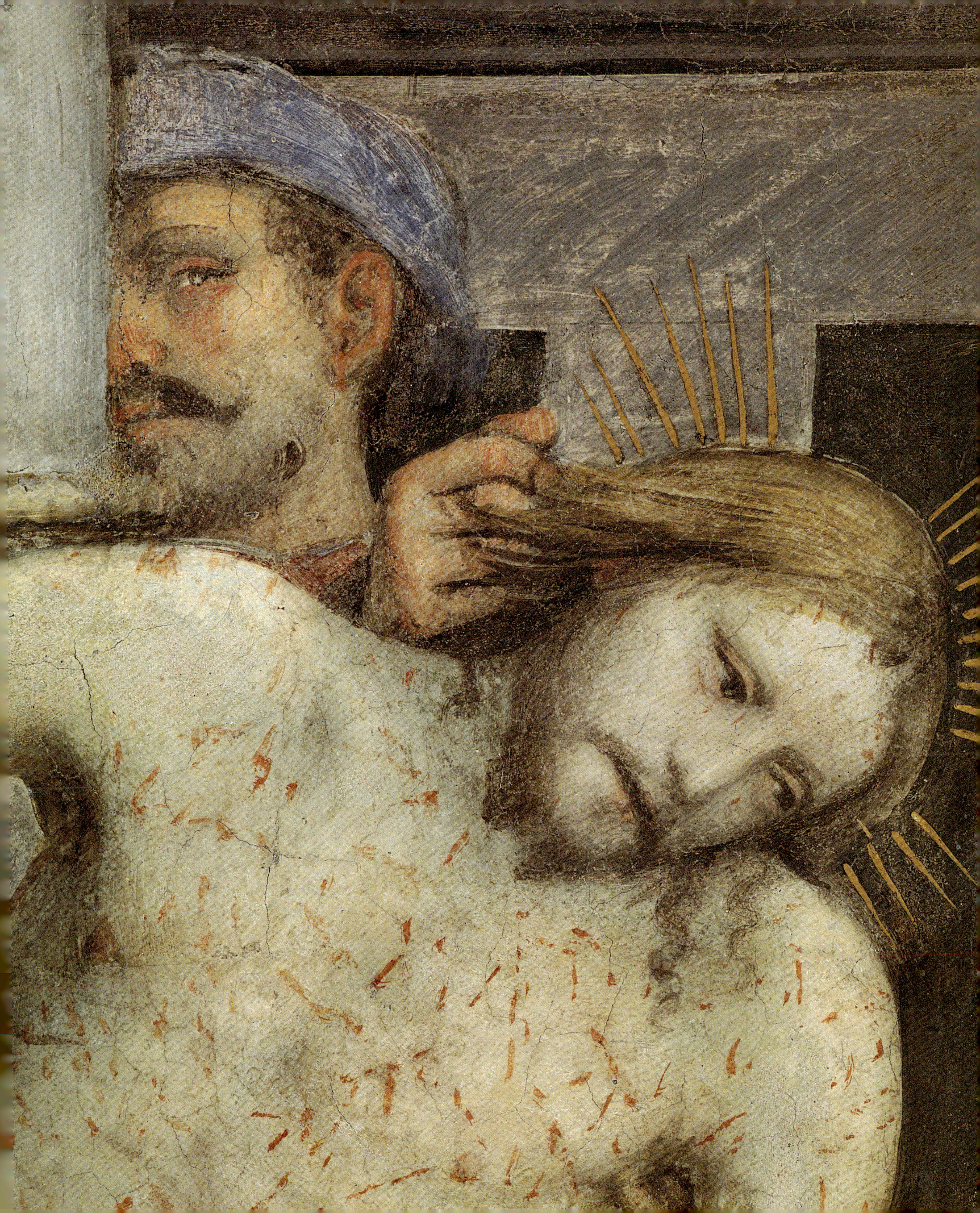

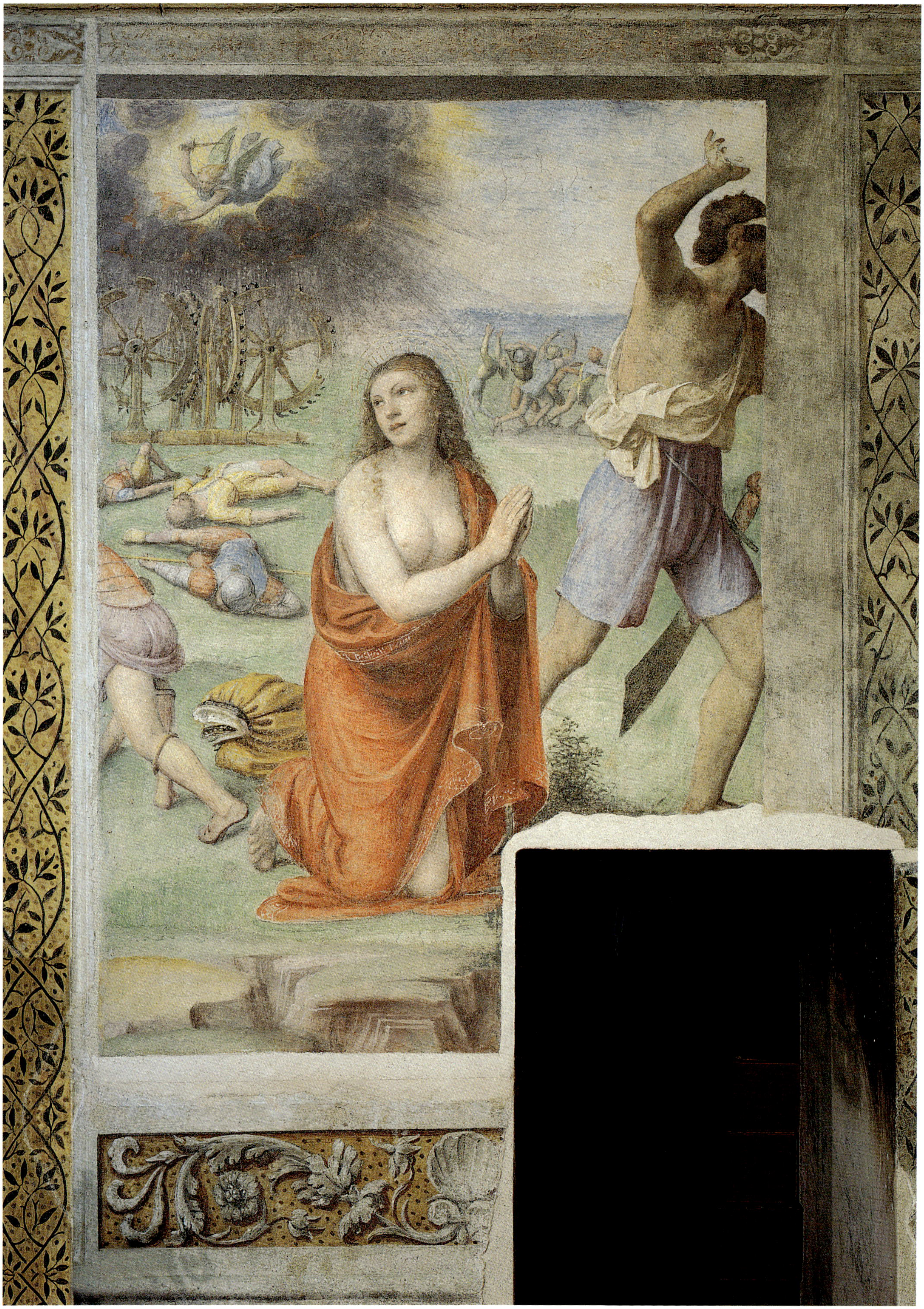

22b. Bernardino Luini
Martyrdom of St Catherine
Left wall, Cappella Besozzi (or di Santa Caterina), lay hall

Pages 203–204
22b. Bernardino Luini
Martyrdom of St Catherine, details

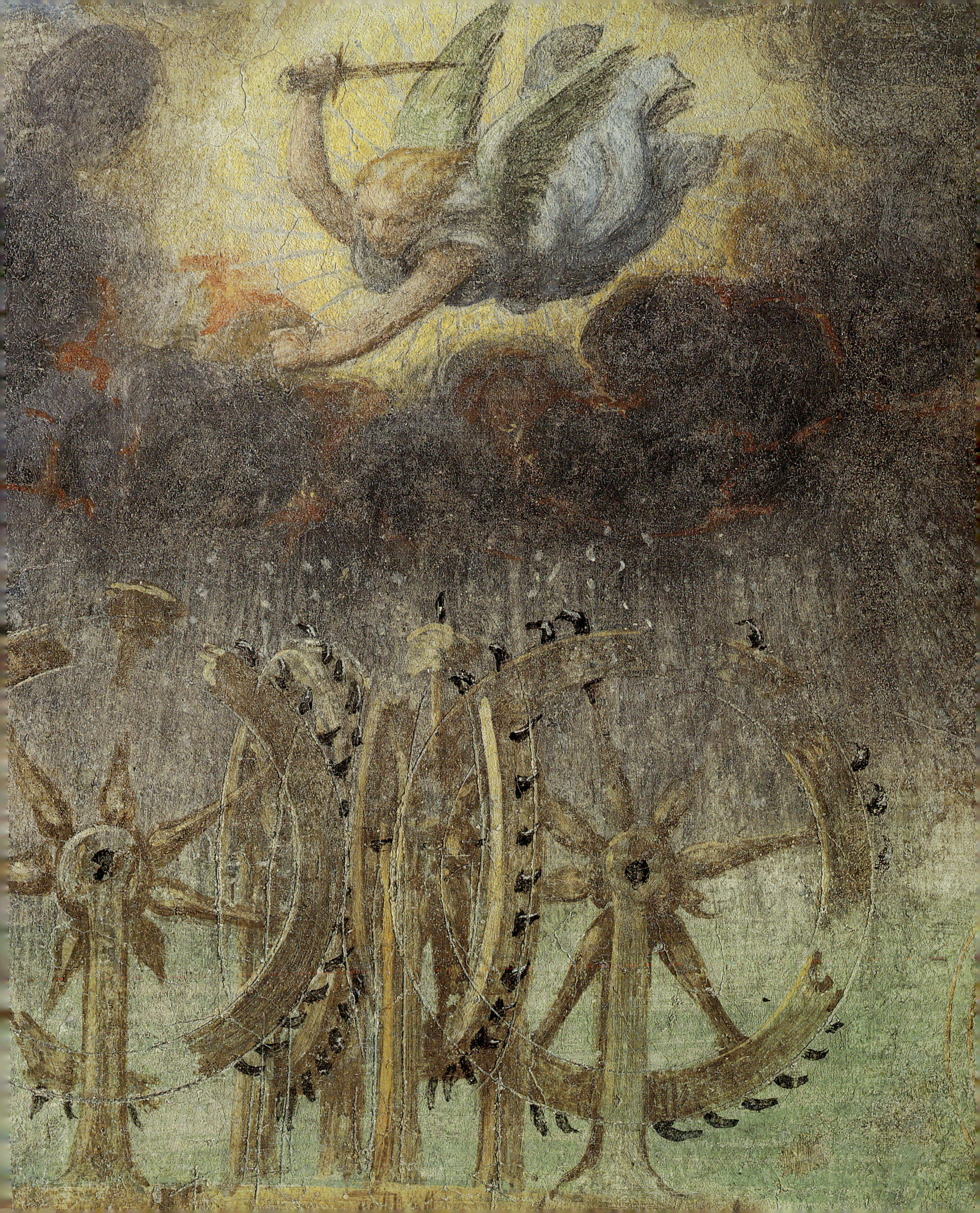

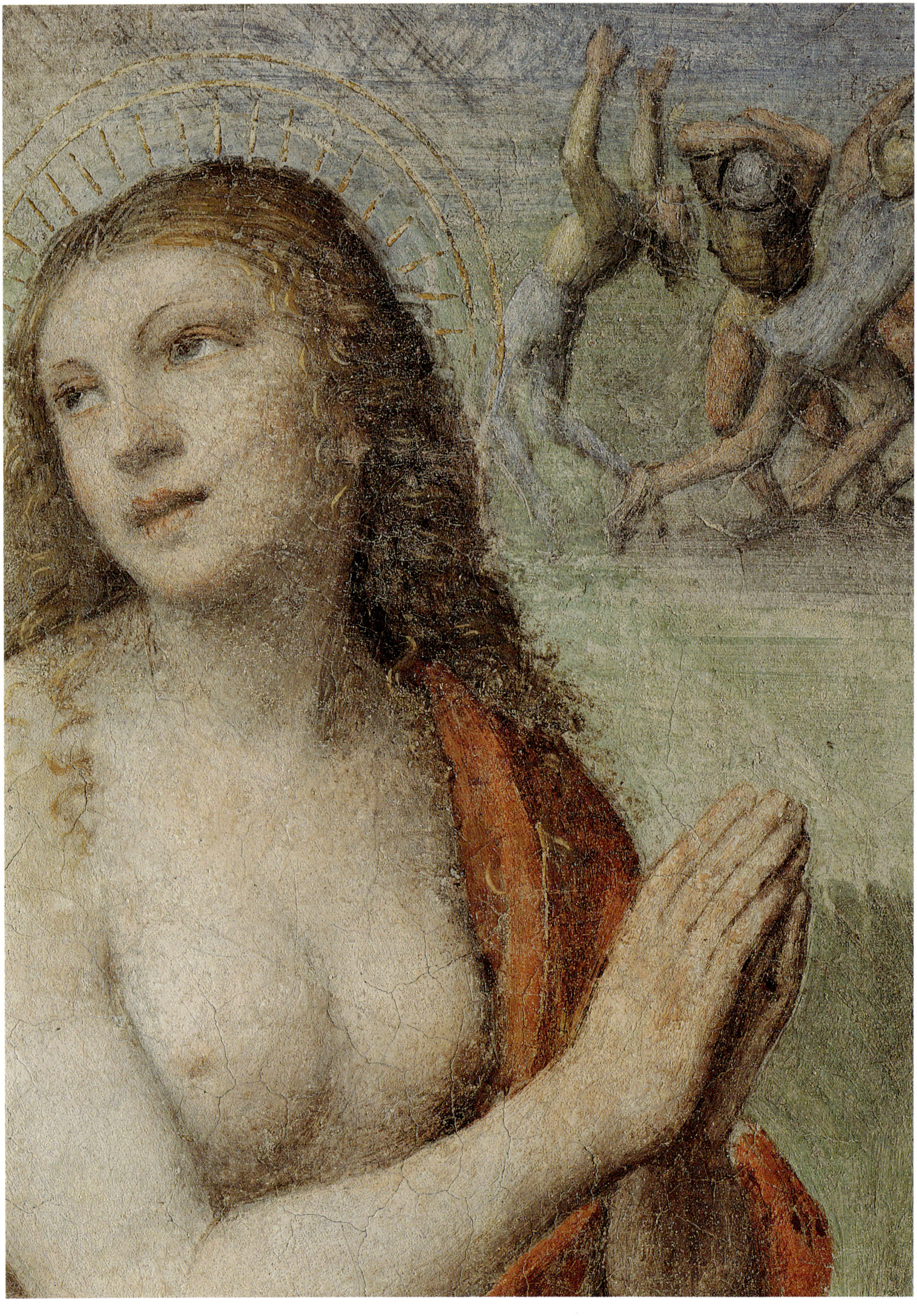

22c. Bernardino Luini
Beheading of St Catherine
Right wall, Cappella Besozzi (or di Santa Caterina), lay hall

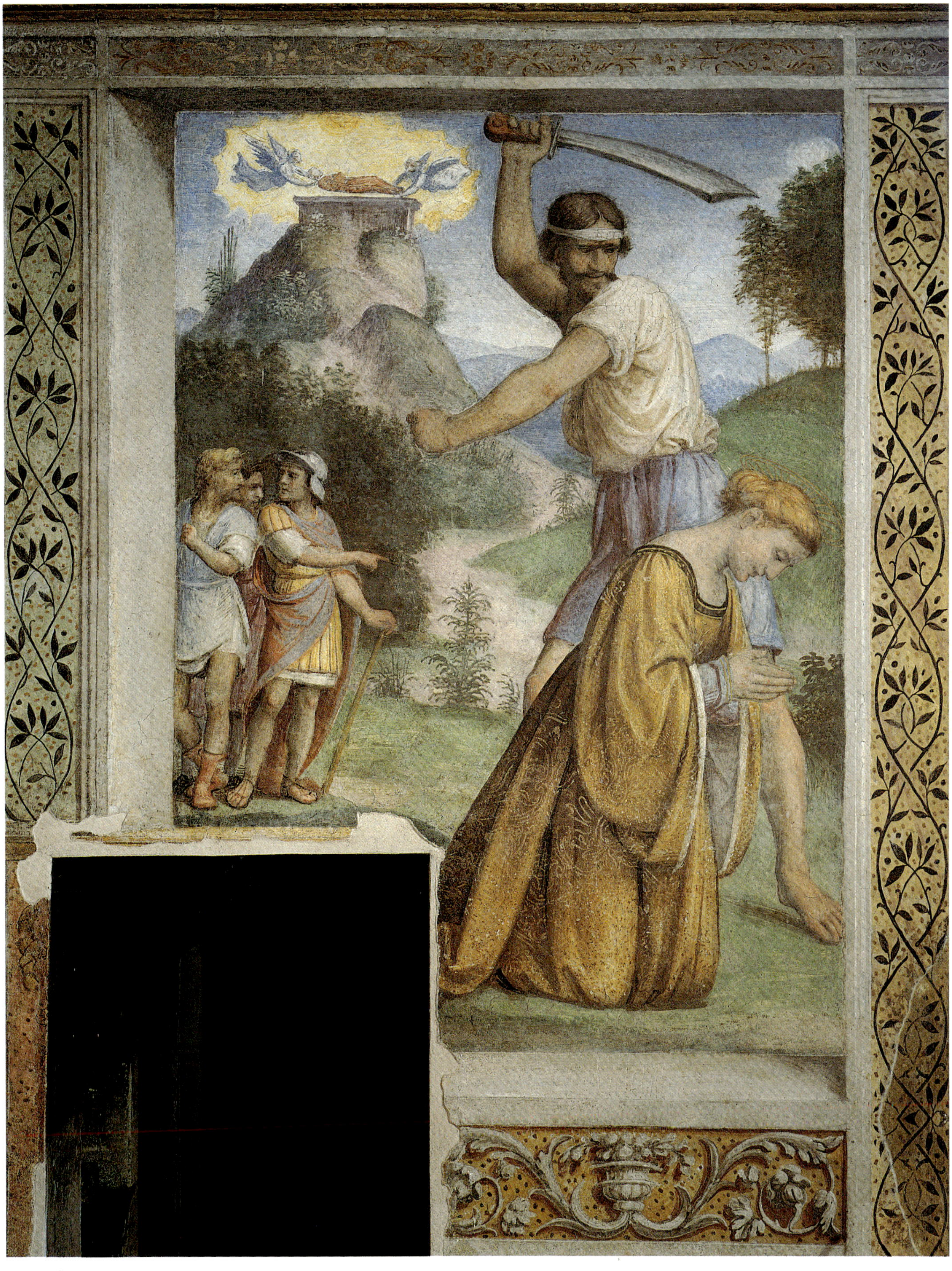

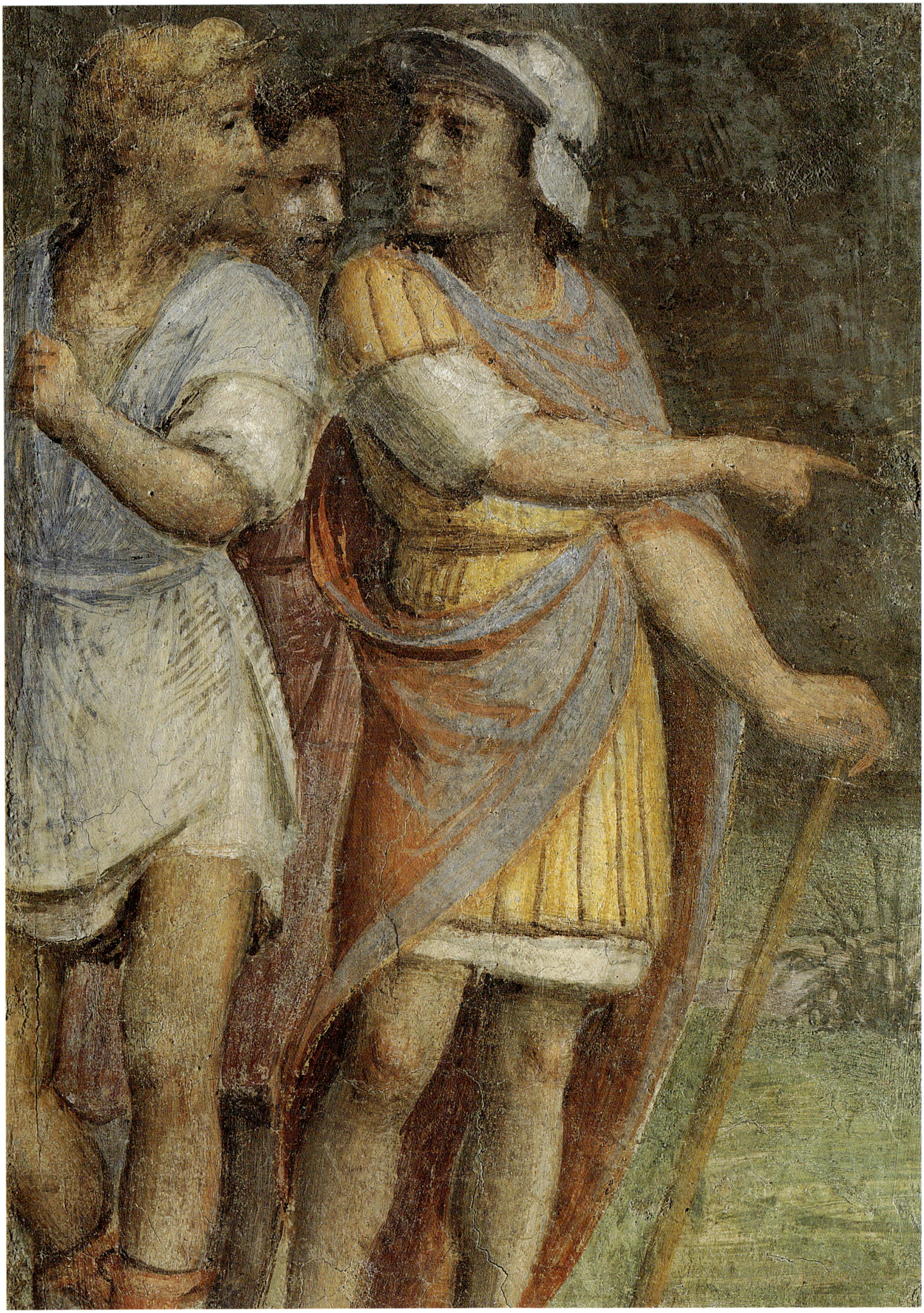

22c. Bernardino Luini, *Beheading of St Catherine*, details

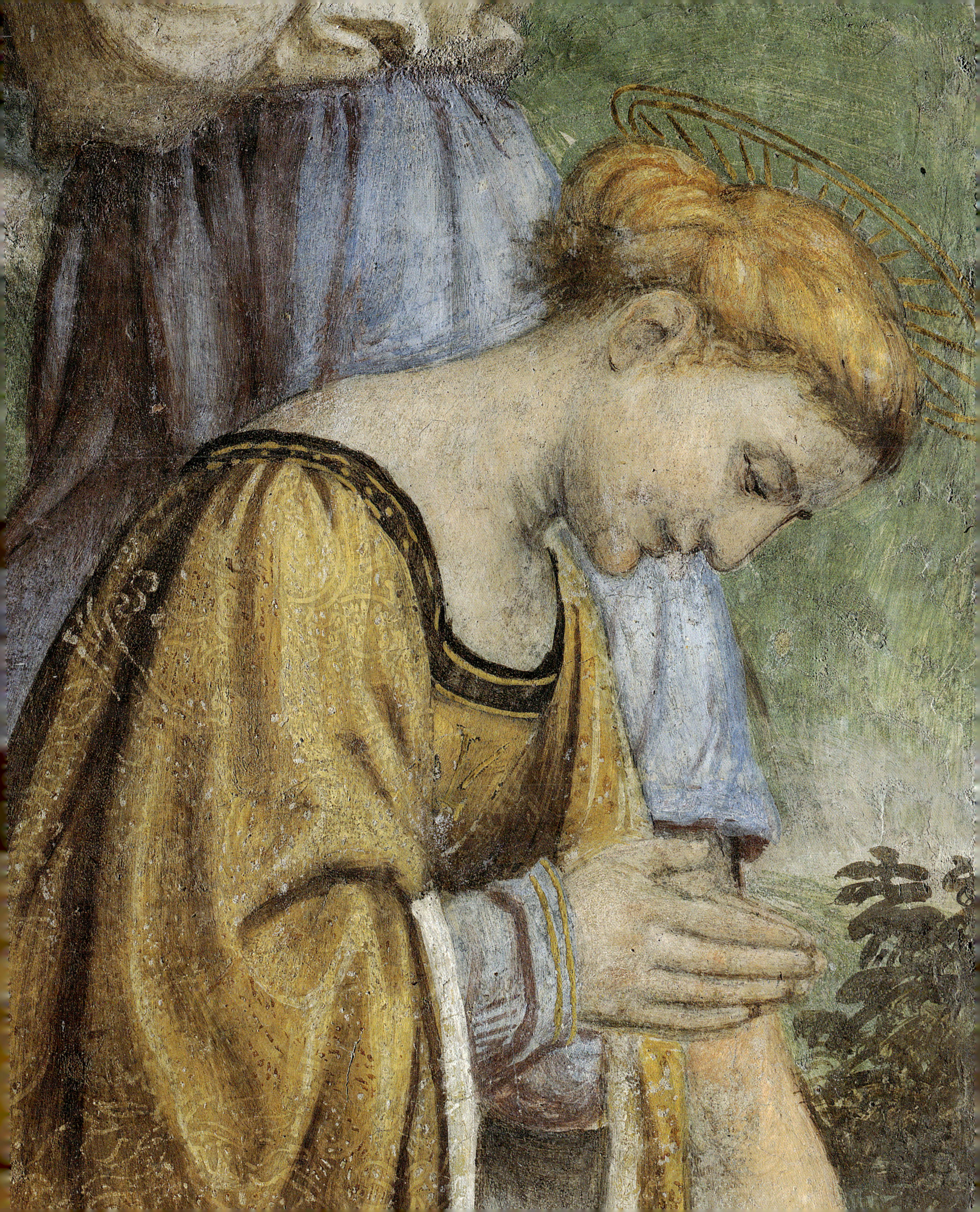

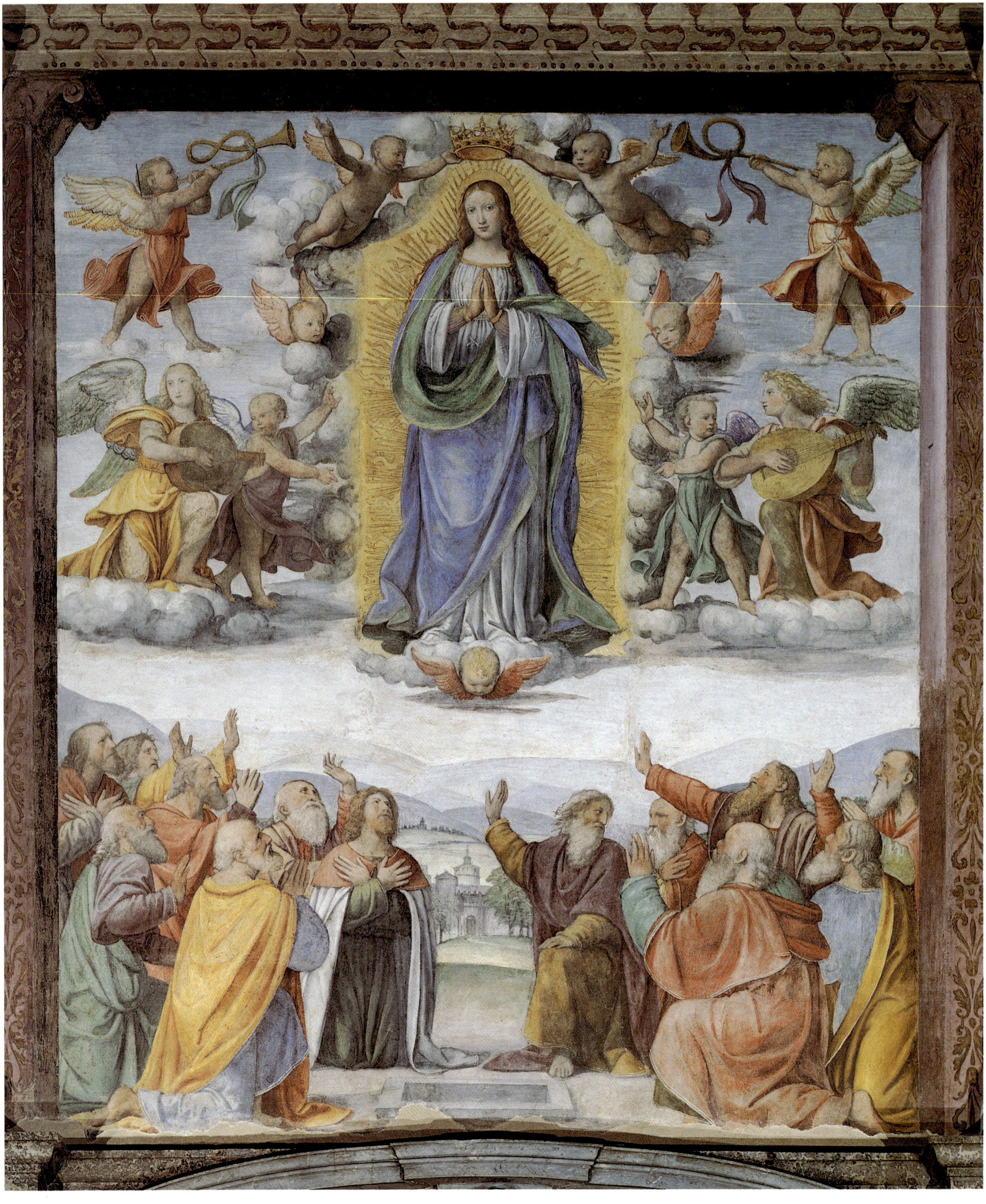

23. Bernardino Ferrari (attr.) *Assumption*, with detail Partition wall, lay hall

Pages 210–212
23. Bernardino Ferrari (attr.) *Assumption*, details

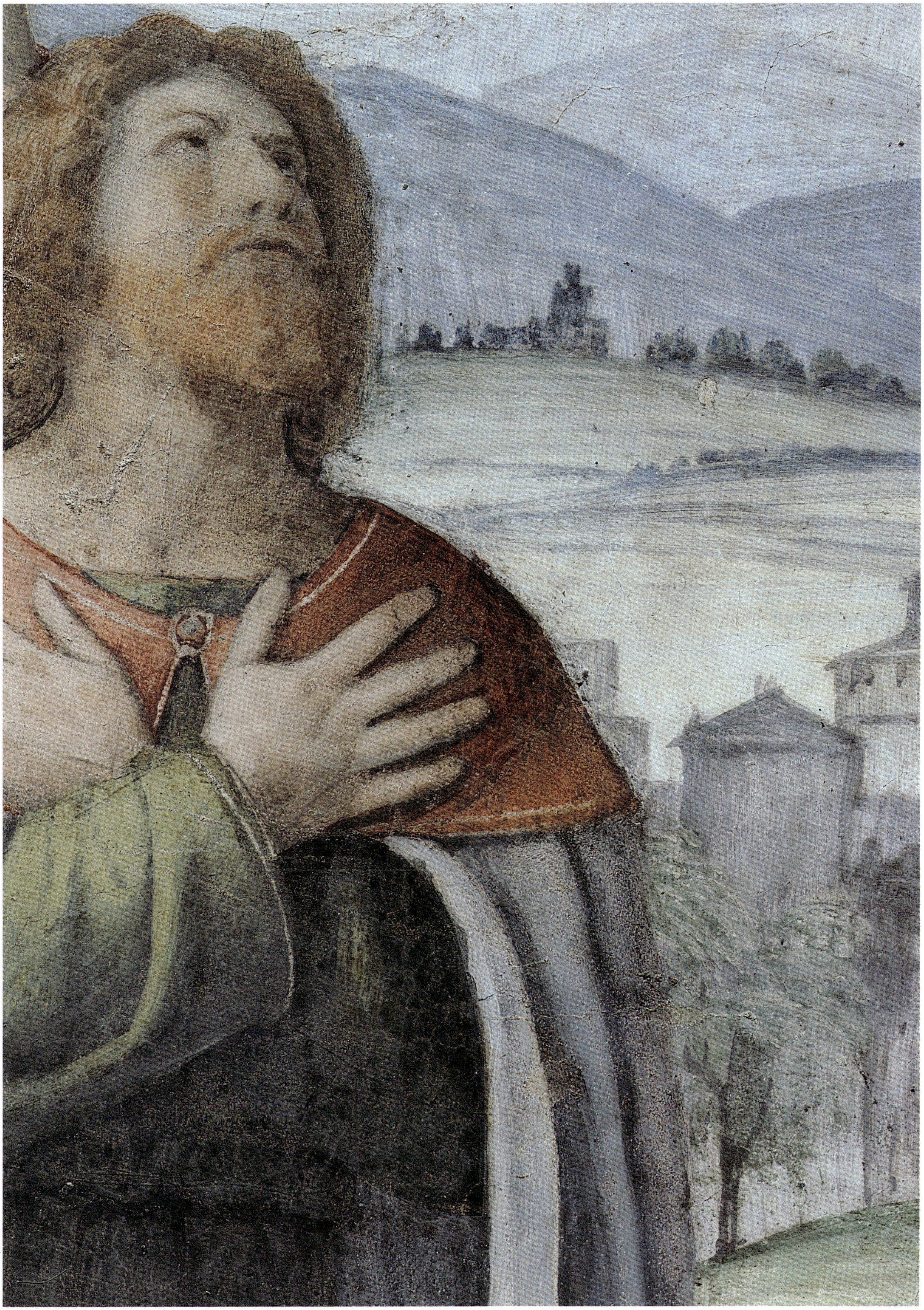

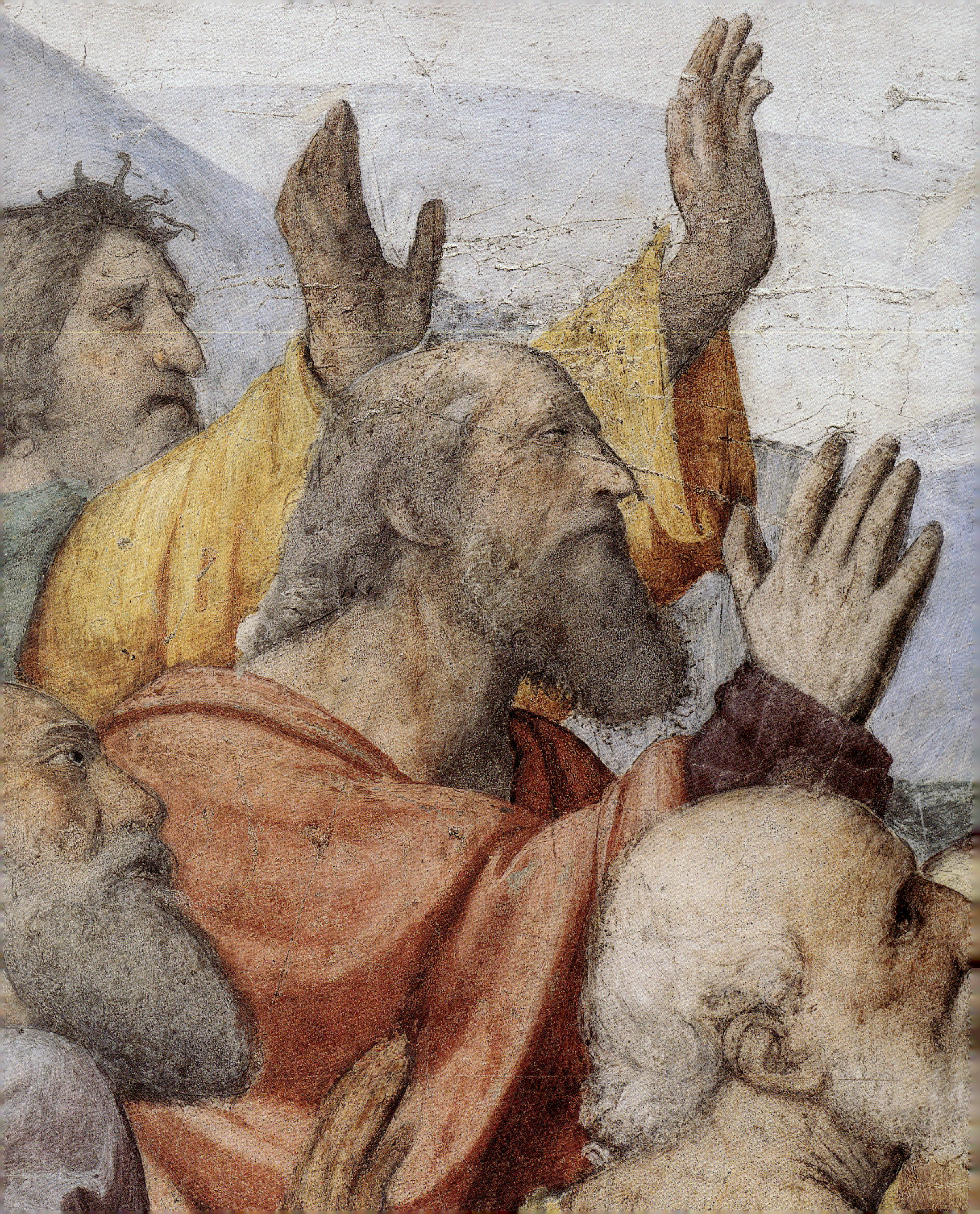

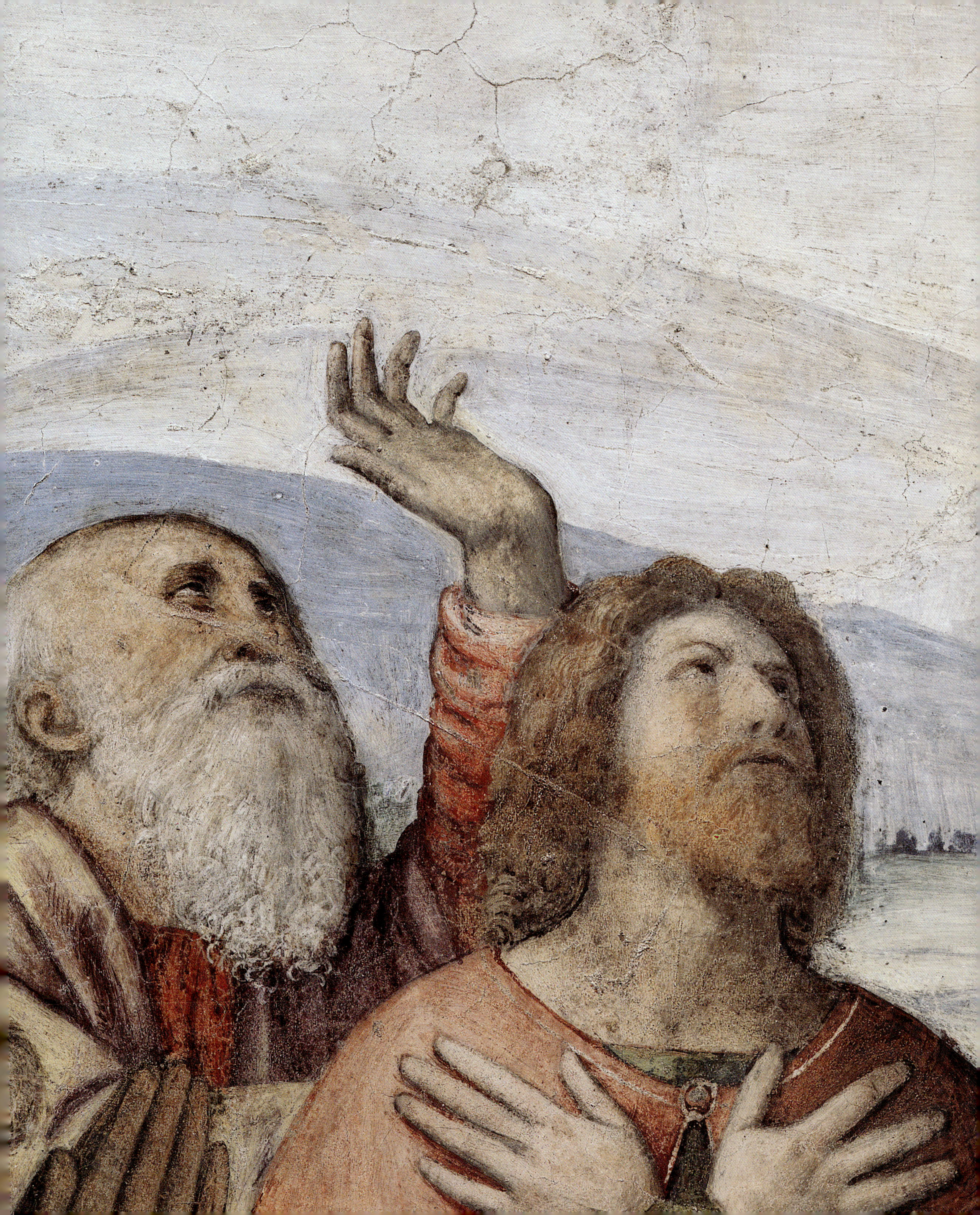

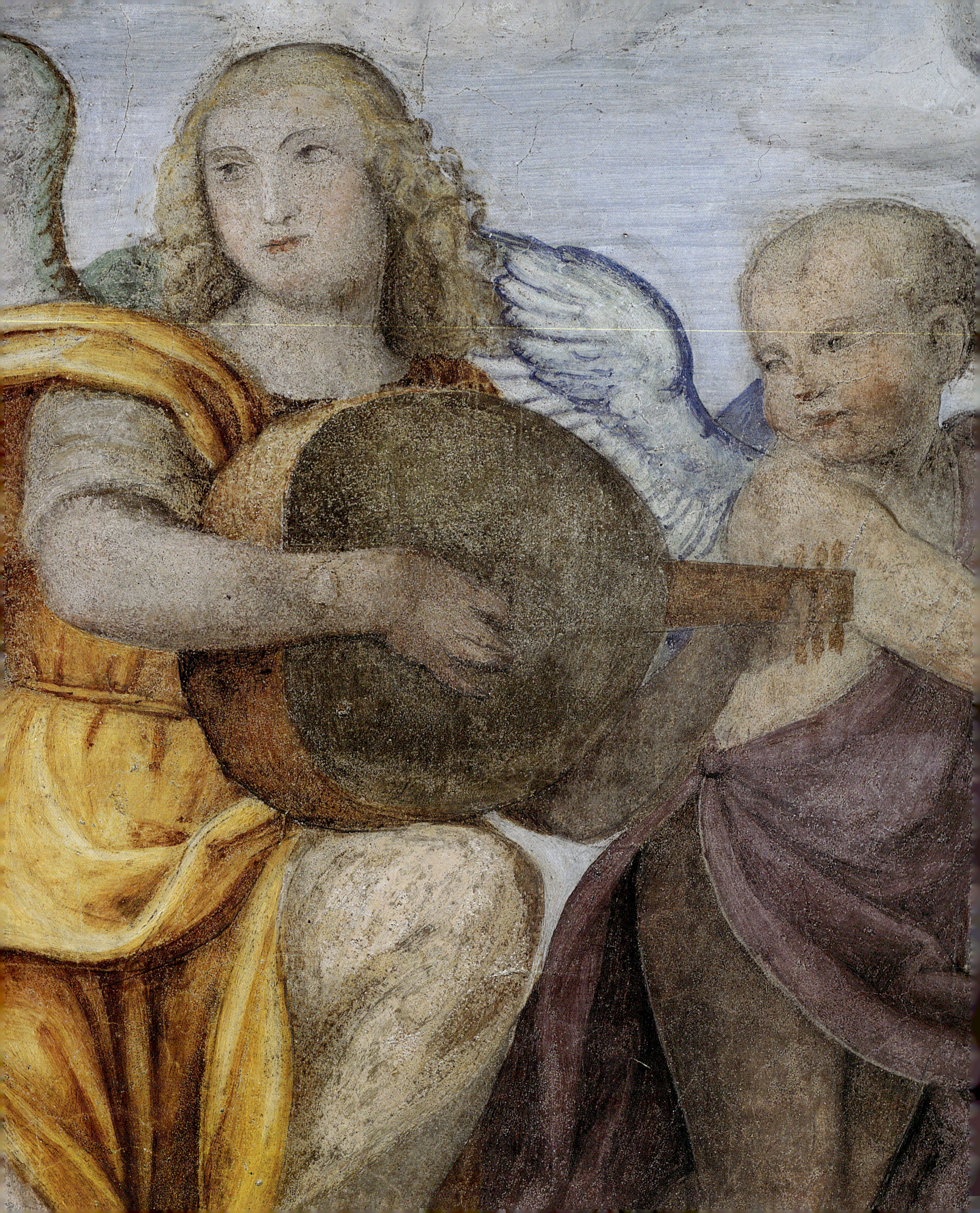

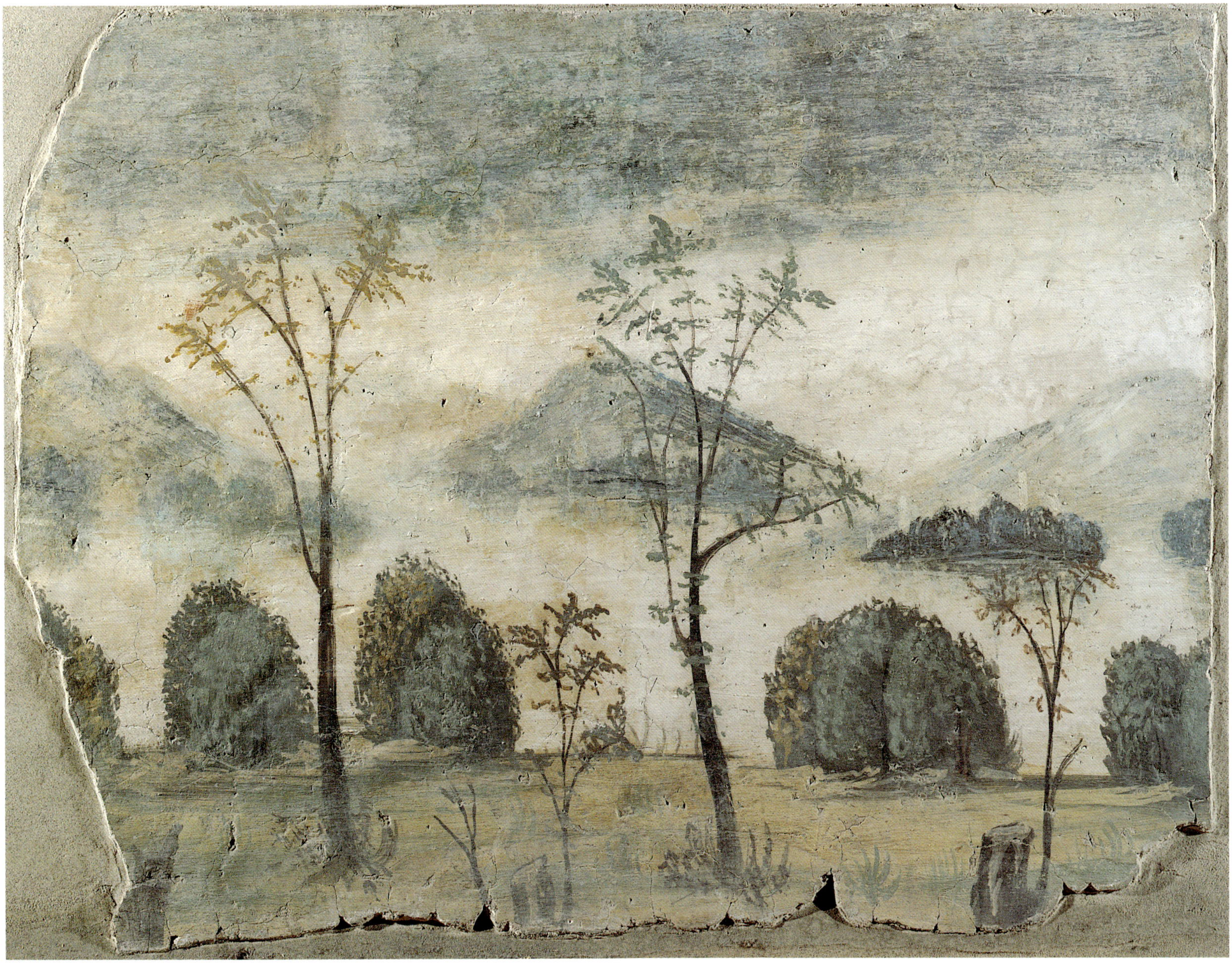

24. Follower of Bernardino Luini
Landscape
Partition wall, convent hall

The Resumption of Decoration in the Mid-Sixteenth Century by the Piazza Family and Bernardino's Sons

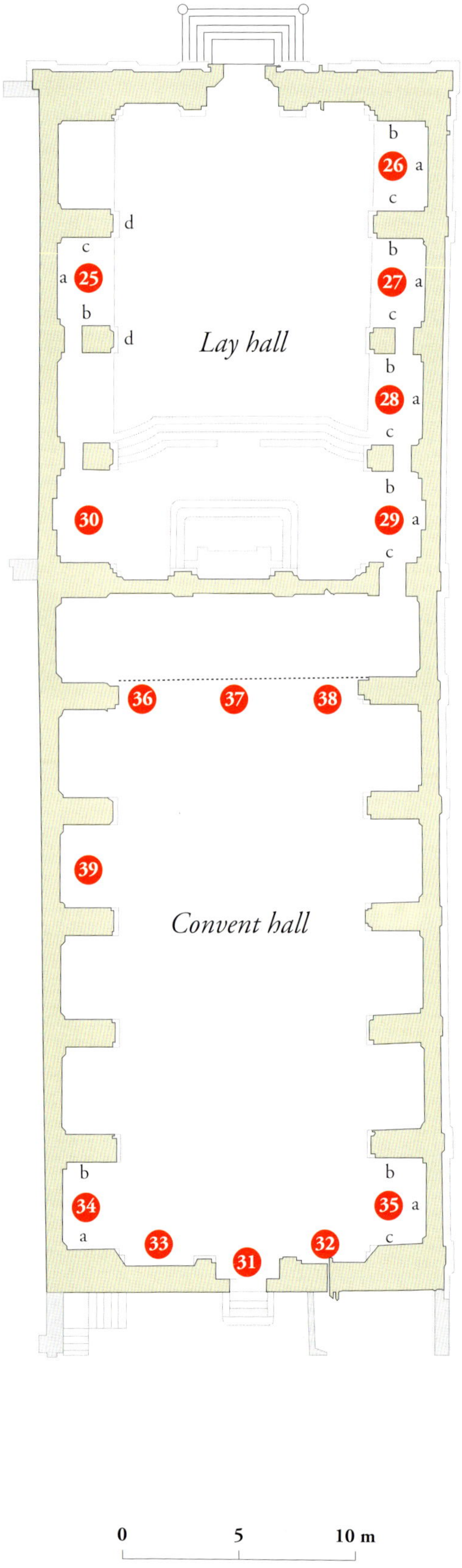

Ground plan of the church of San Maurizio al Monastero Maggiore

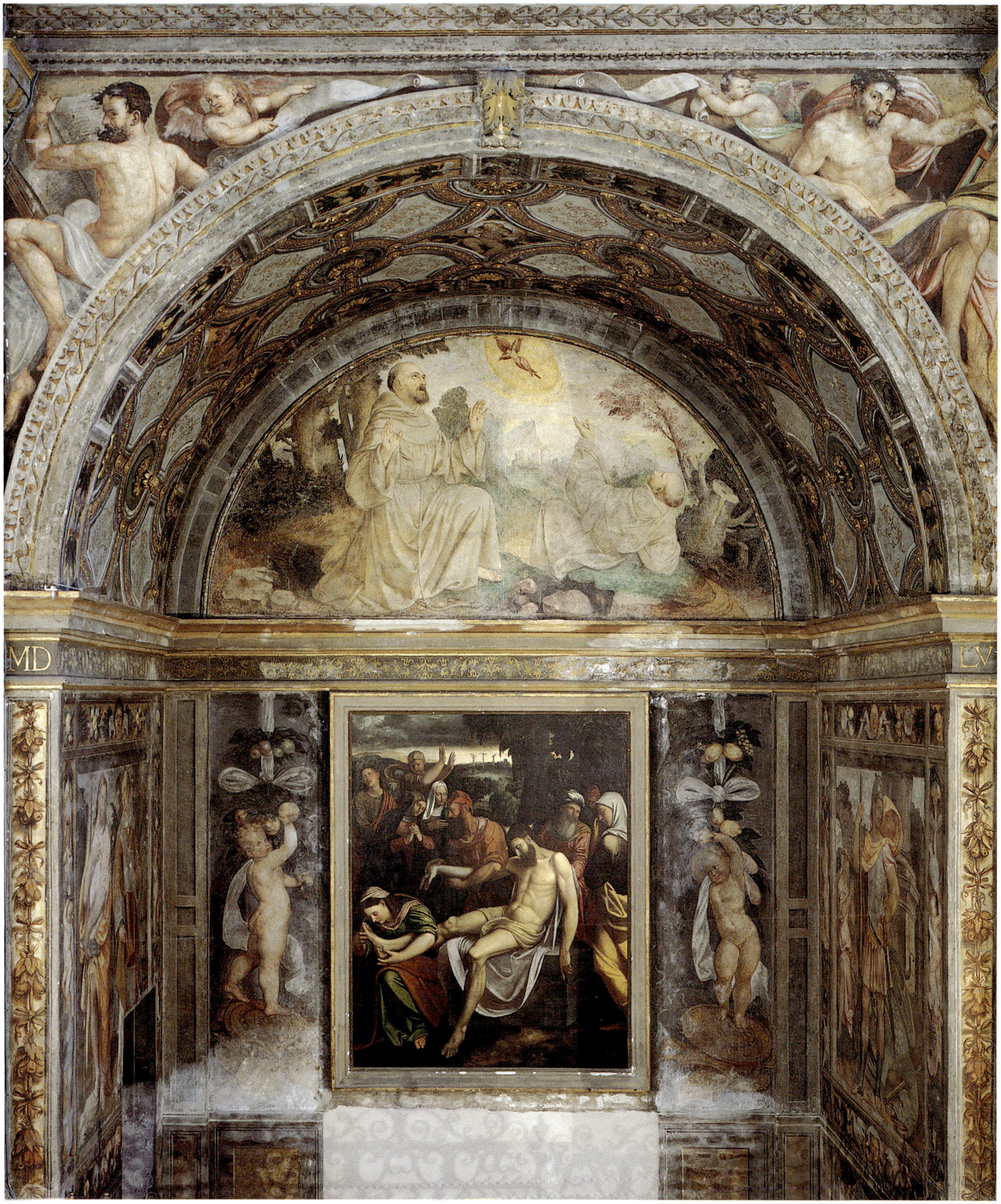

25a. Callisto and Fulvio Piazza
Central wall, Cappella Simonetta
(or della Deposizione), lay hall

Following pages
Callisto and Fulvio Piazza
25b. *St John (or James) and St Lawrence*
25c. *St George and the Dragon*
Respectively left and right walls,
Cappella Simonetta
(or della Deposizione), lay hall

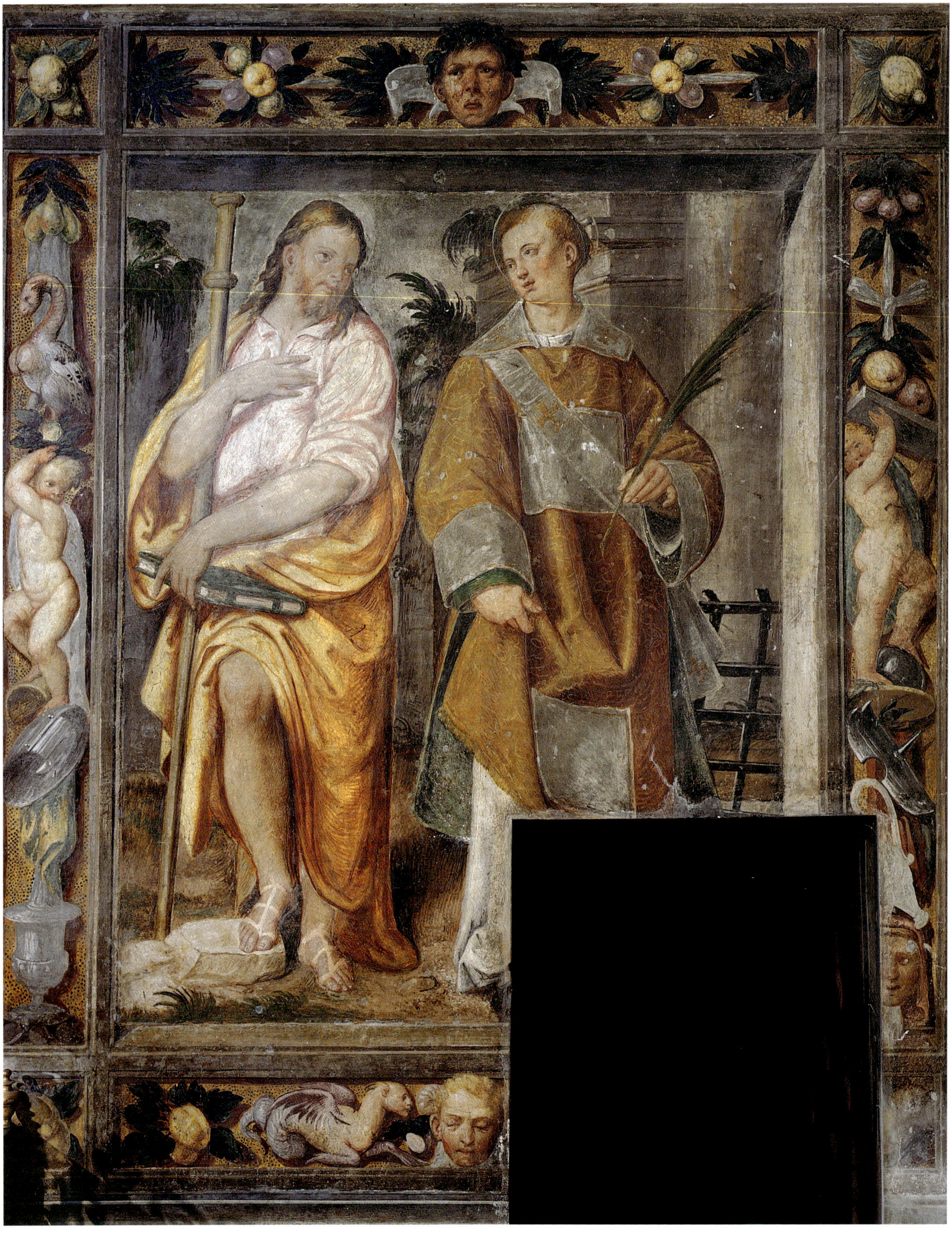

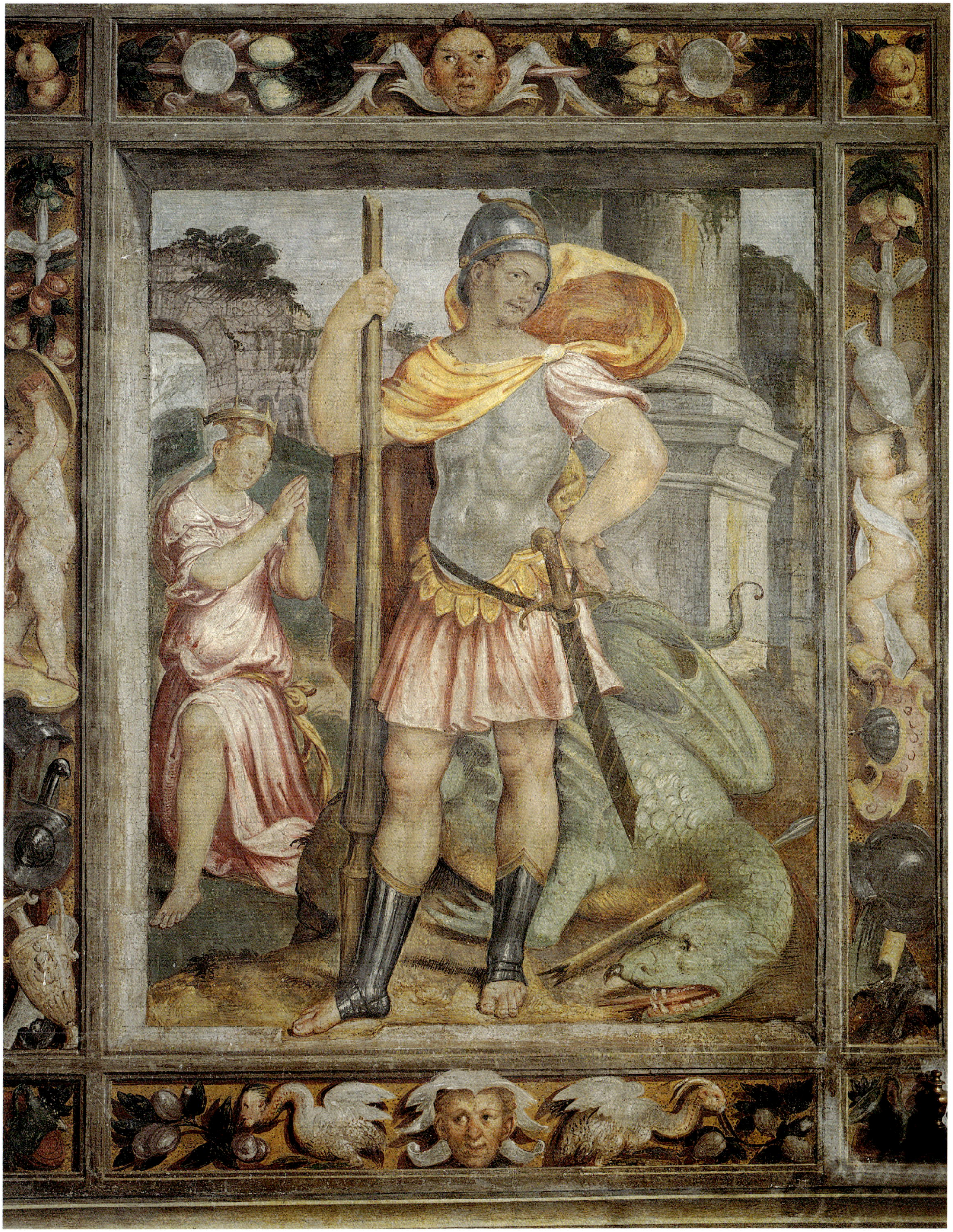

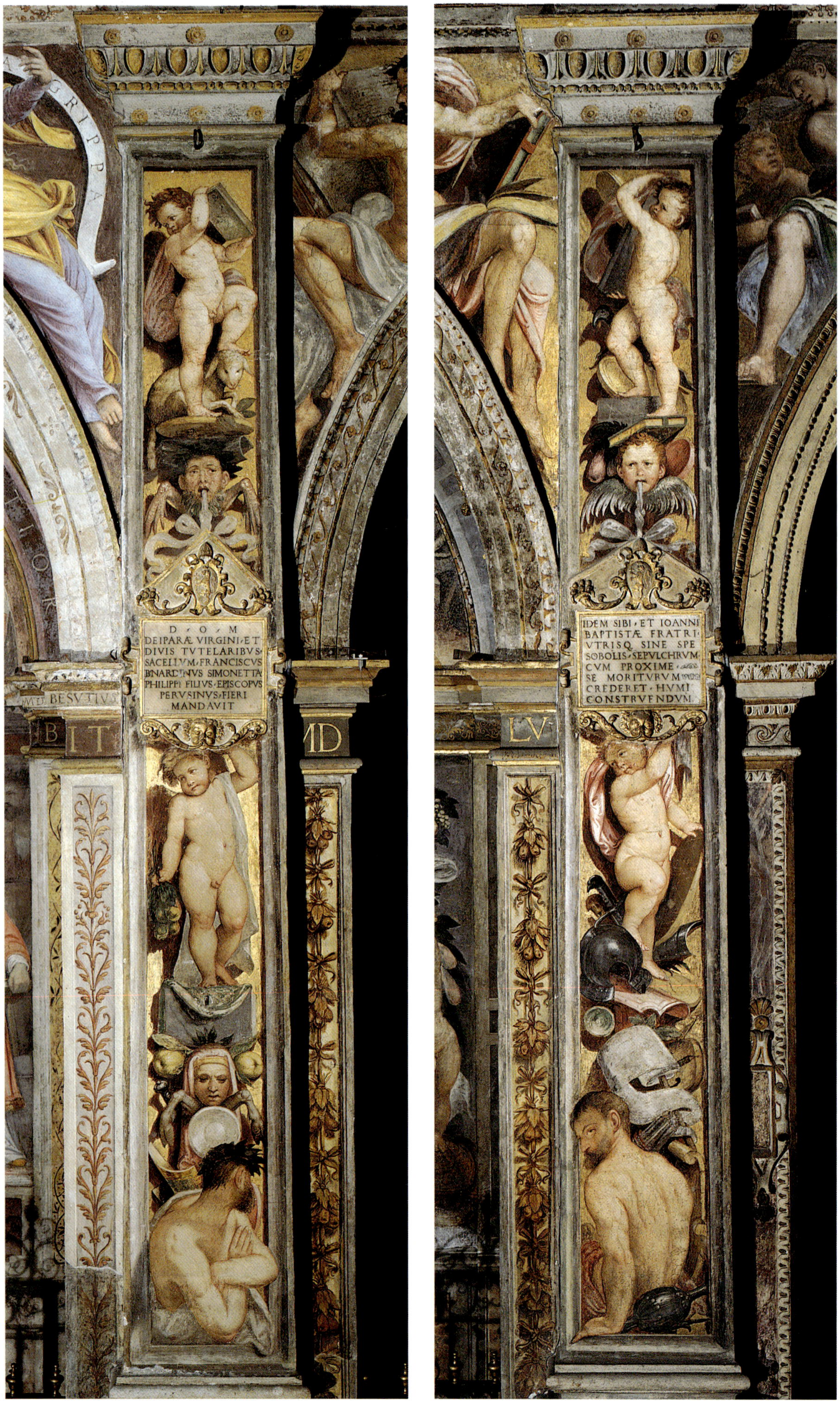

25d. Callisto and Fulvio Piazza
Pilaster strips
Cappella Simonetta
(or della Deposizione), lay hall

Following pages
25d. Details of the pilaster strips

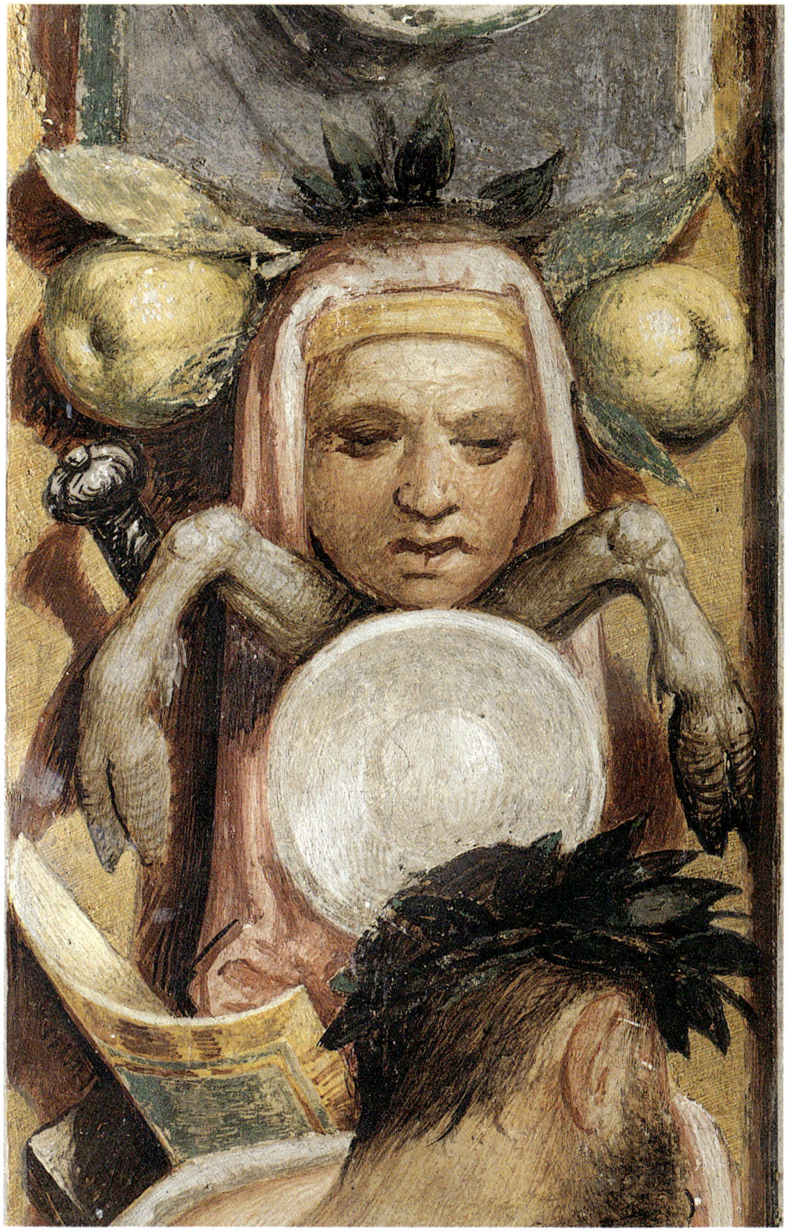

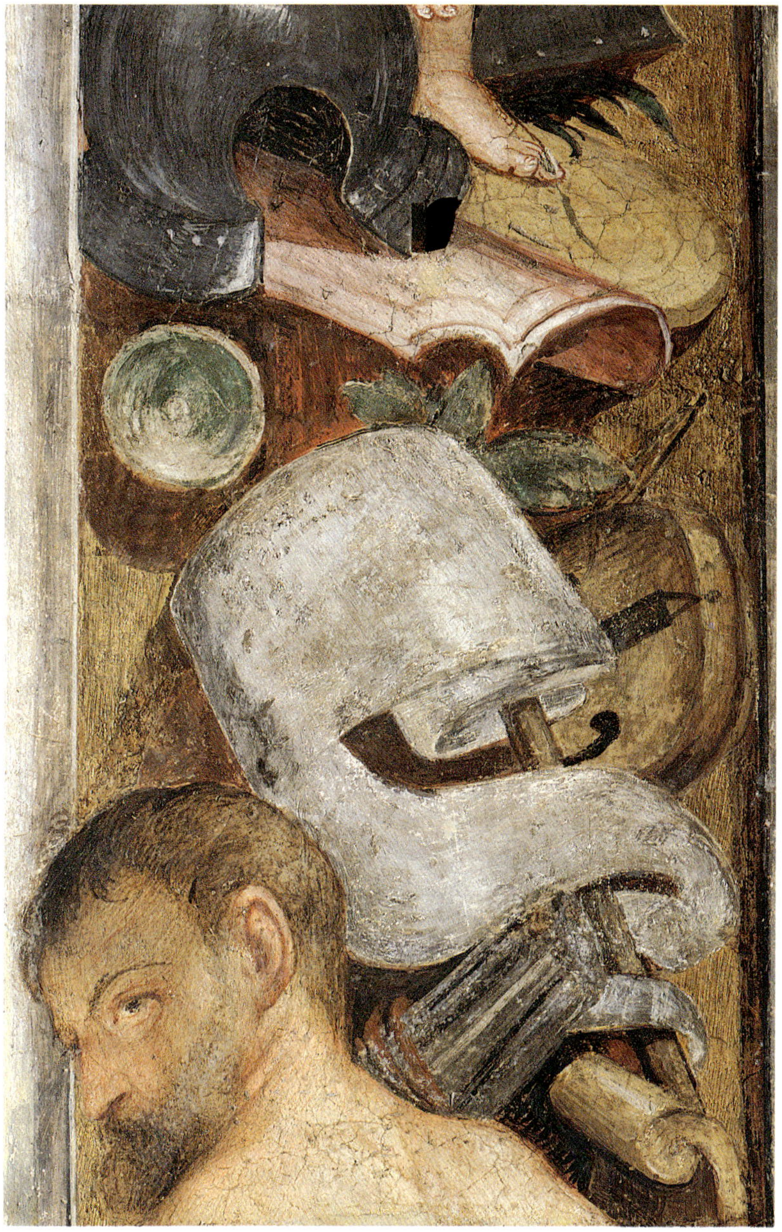

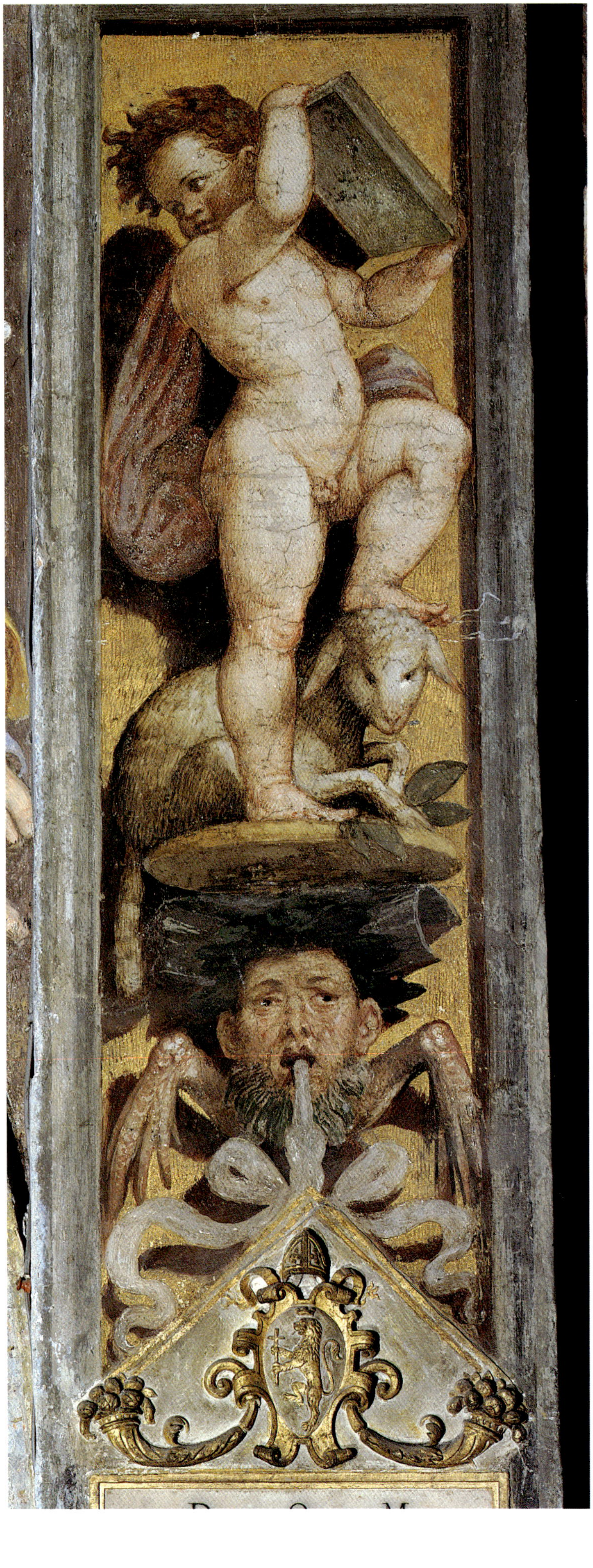

26a. Giovan Pietro and Aurelio Luini *Resurrection of Christ* Central wall, Cappella Bergamini (or della Resurrezione), lay hall

Following pages
26a. Giovan Pietro and Aurelio Luini *Resurrection of Christ*, details

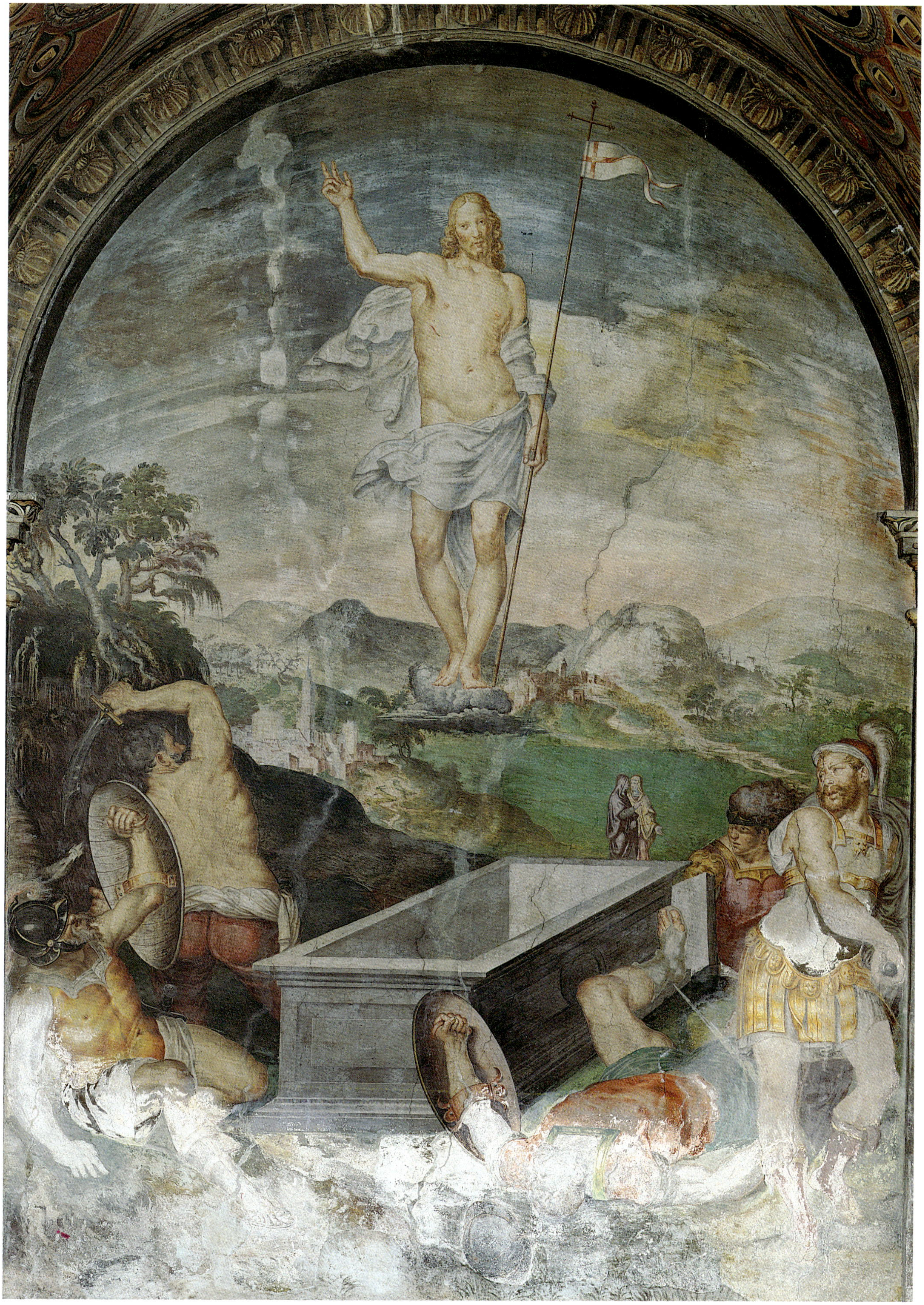

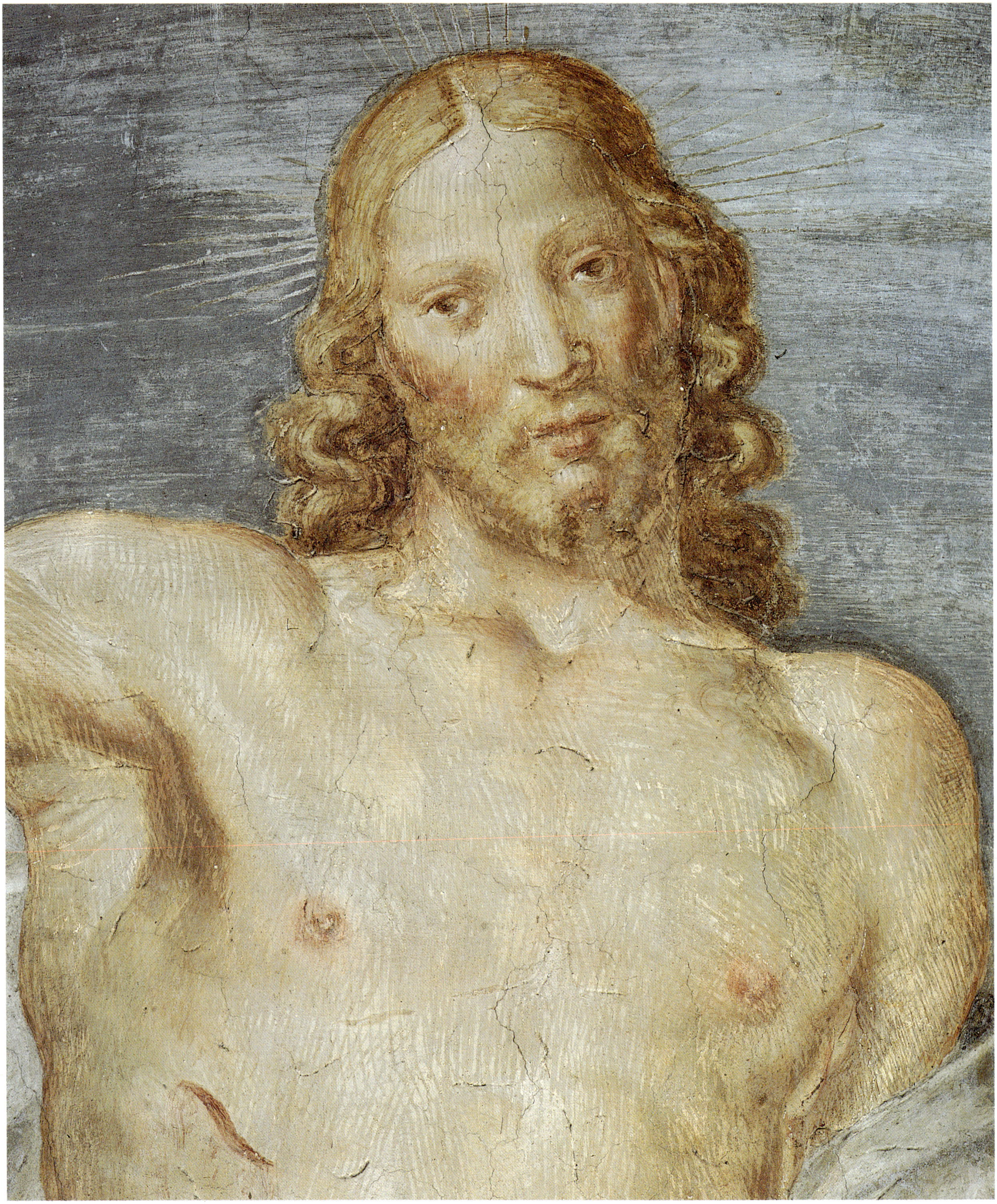

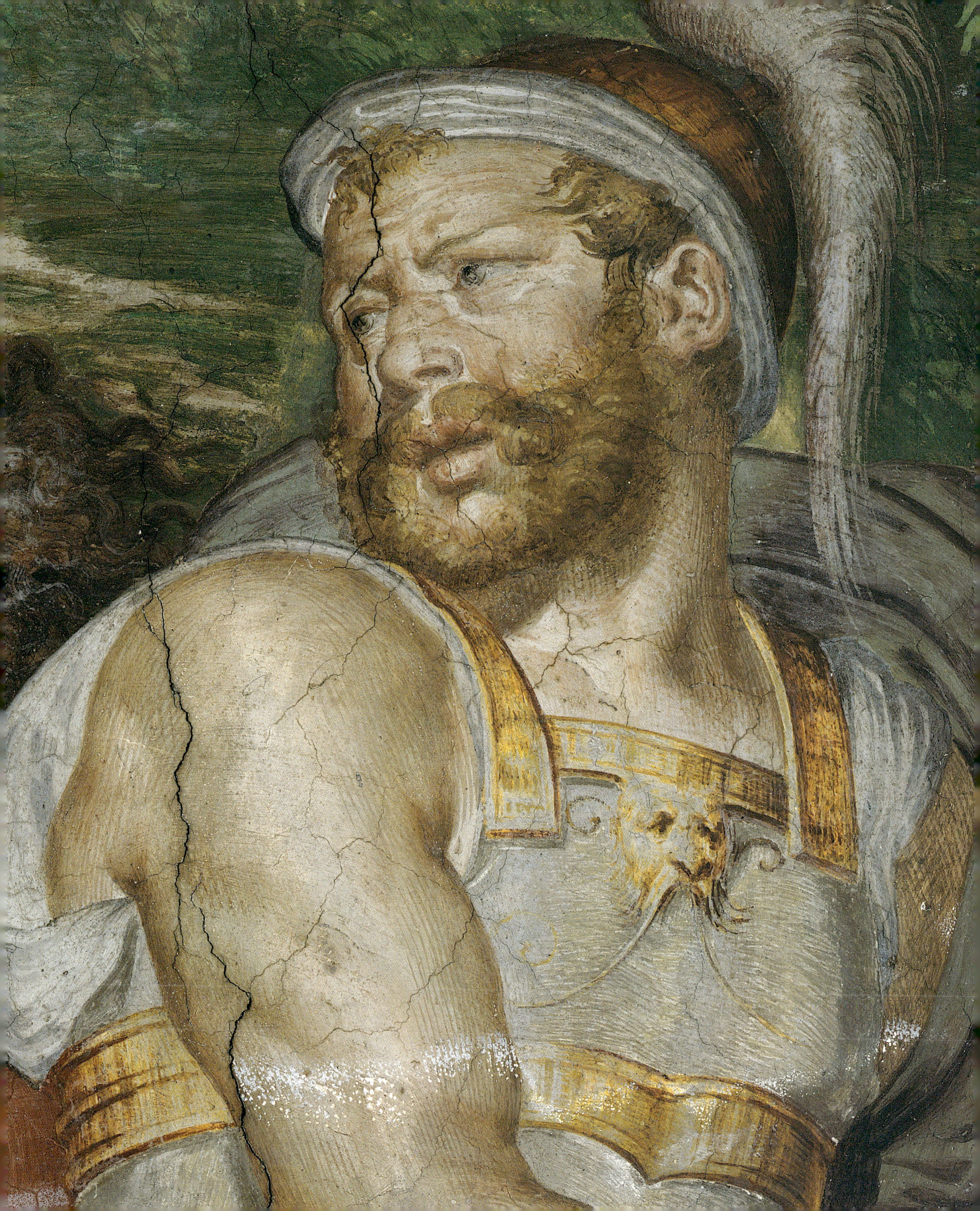

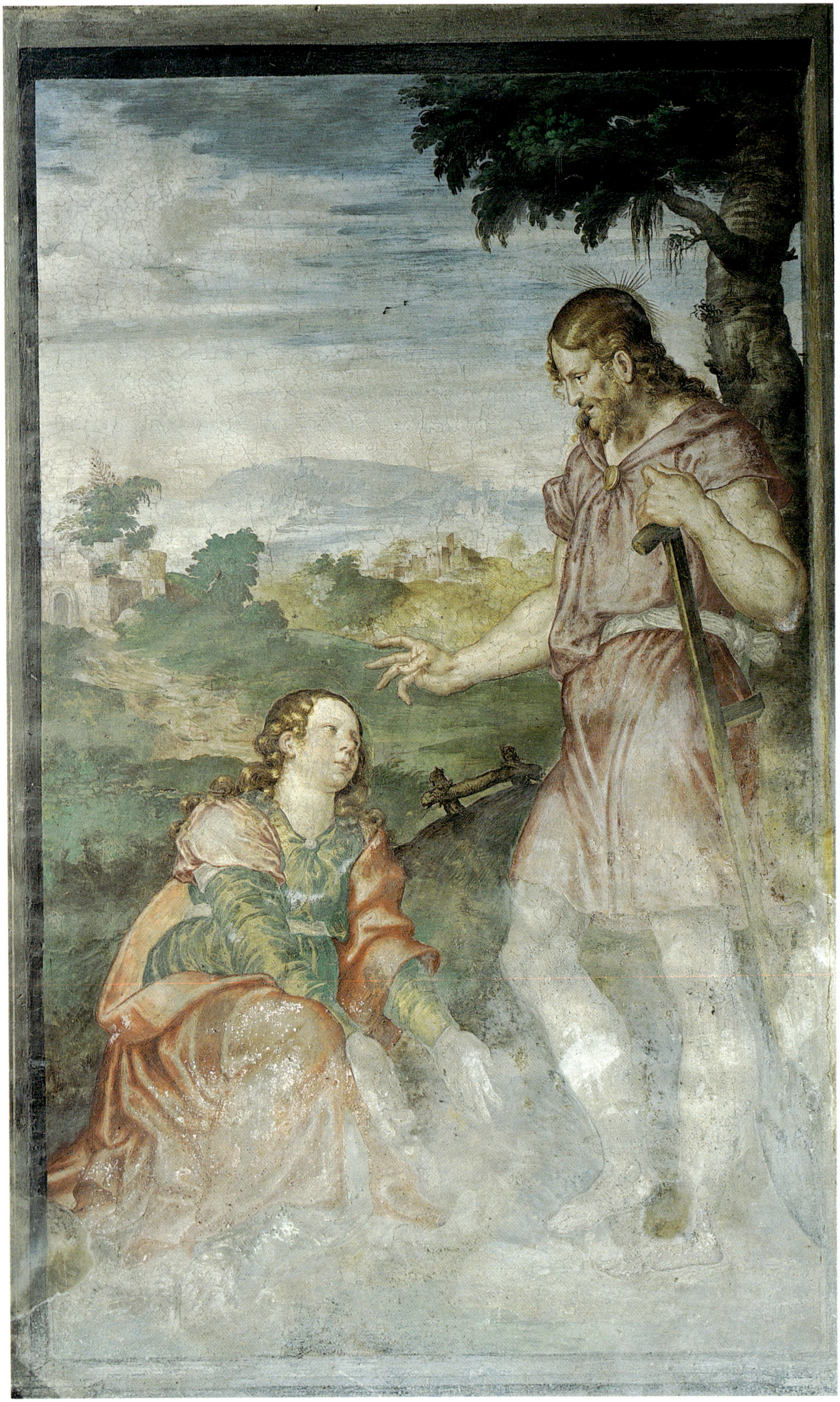

26b. Giovan Pietro and Aurelio Luini
Noli me tangere
Left wall, Cappella Bergamini
(or della Resurrezione), lay hall

Following pages
26b. Giovan Pietro and Aurelio Luini
Noli me tangere, details

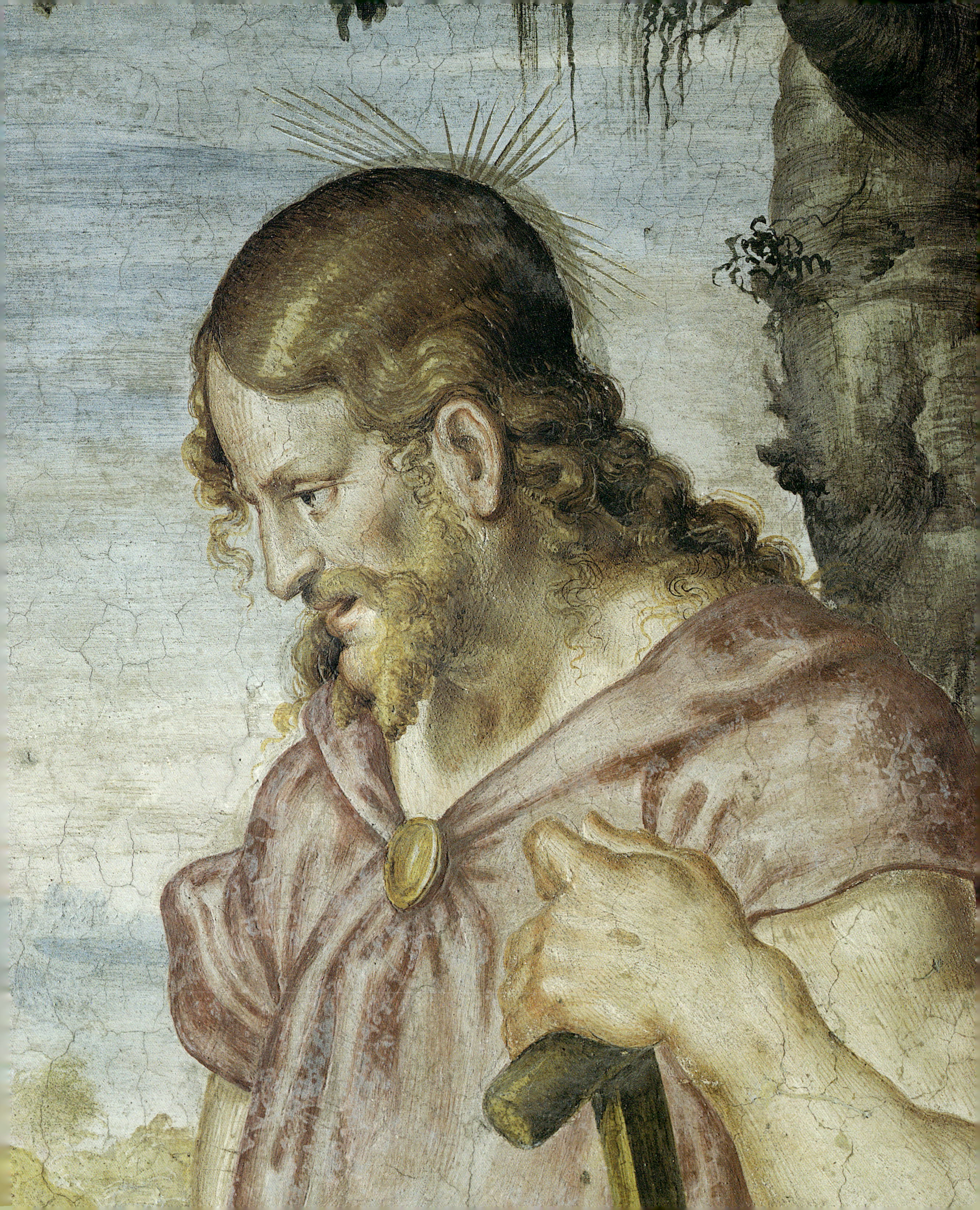

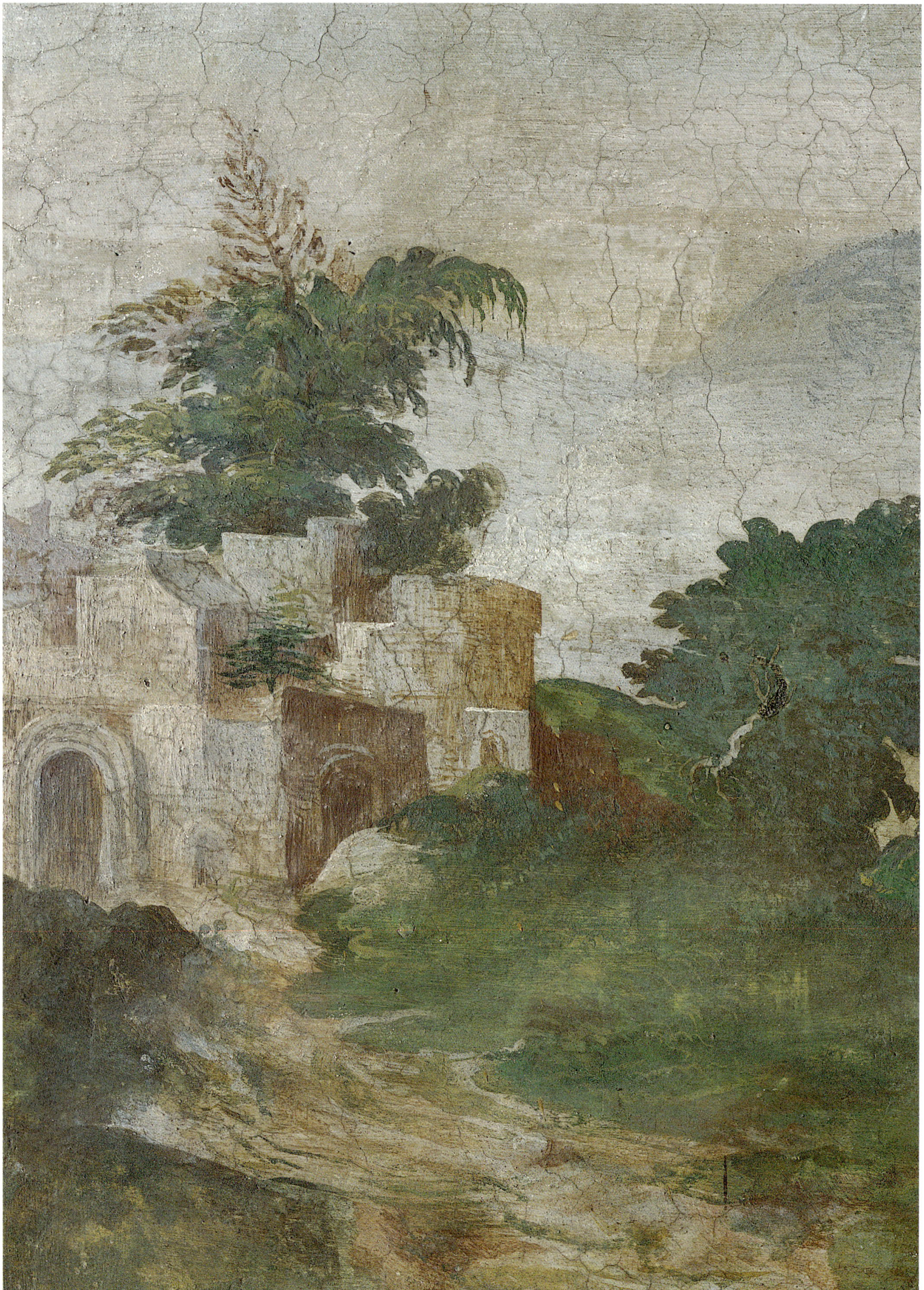

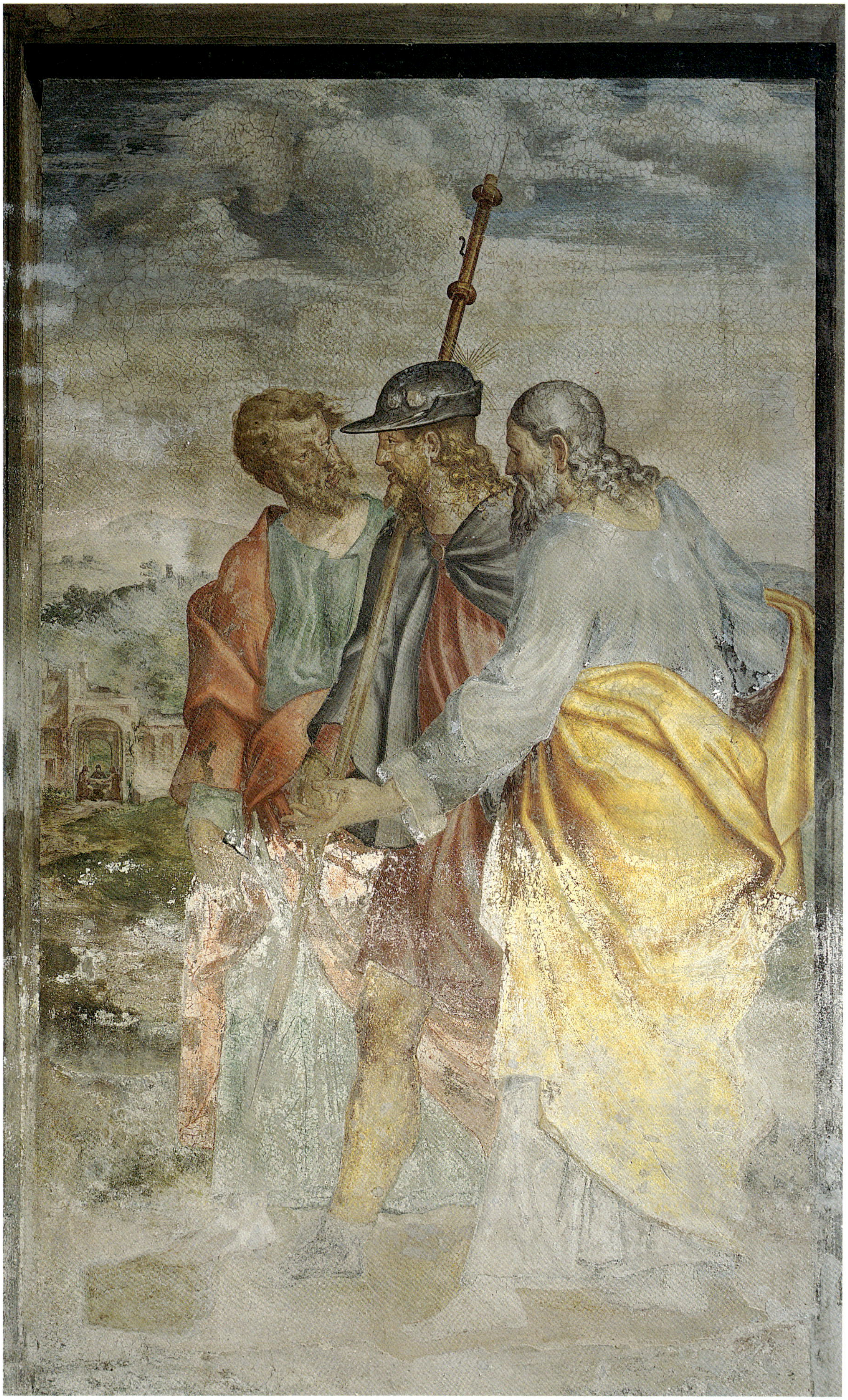

26c. Giovan Pietro and Aurelio Luini
Journey to Emmaus
Right wall, Cappella Bergamini
(or della Resurrezione), lay hall

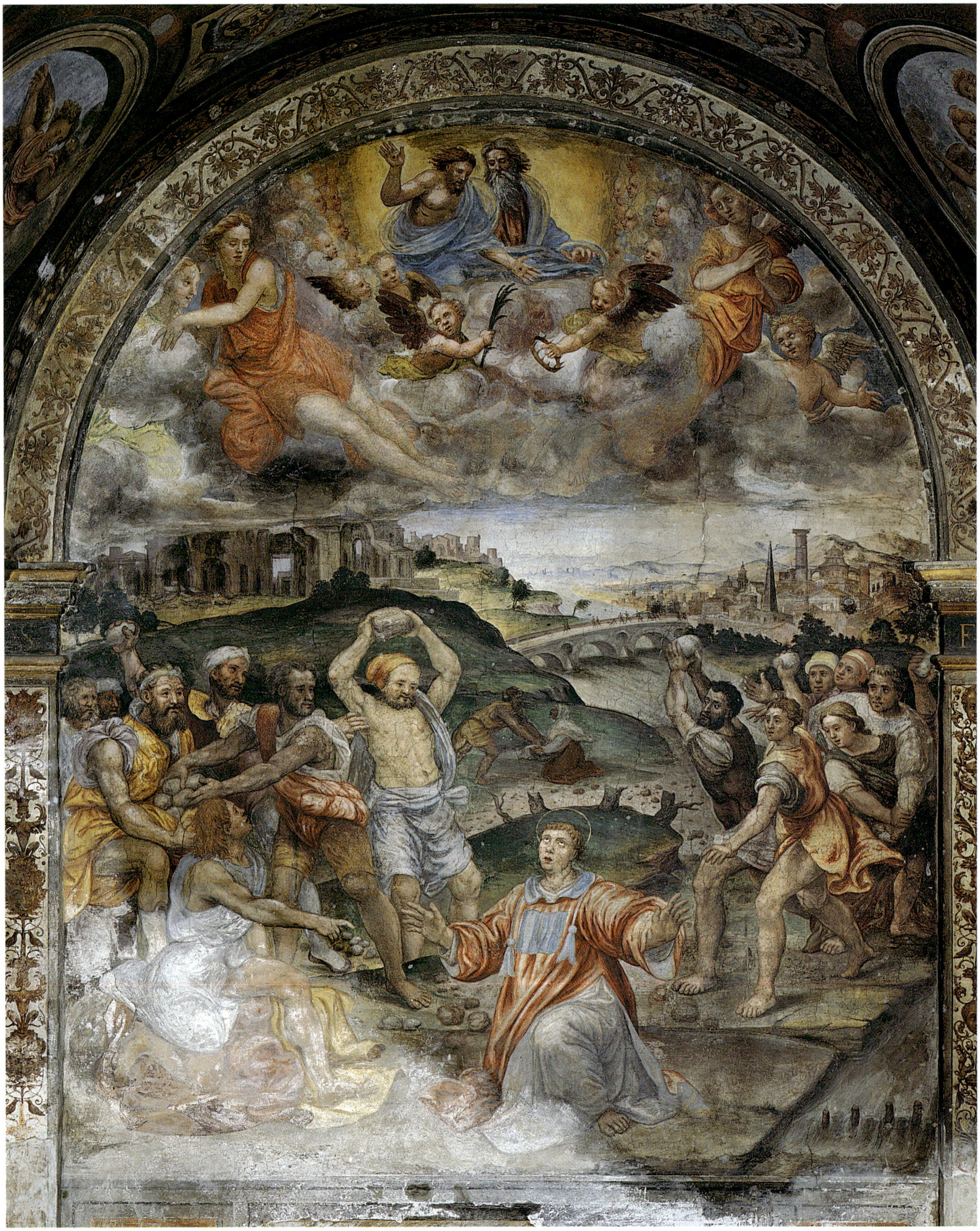

27a. Evangelista Luini (attr.)
Stoning of St Stephen
Central wall, Cappella Carreto
(or di Santo Stefano), lay hall

Pages 229–231
27a. Evangelista Luini (attr.)
Stoning of St Stephen,
details

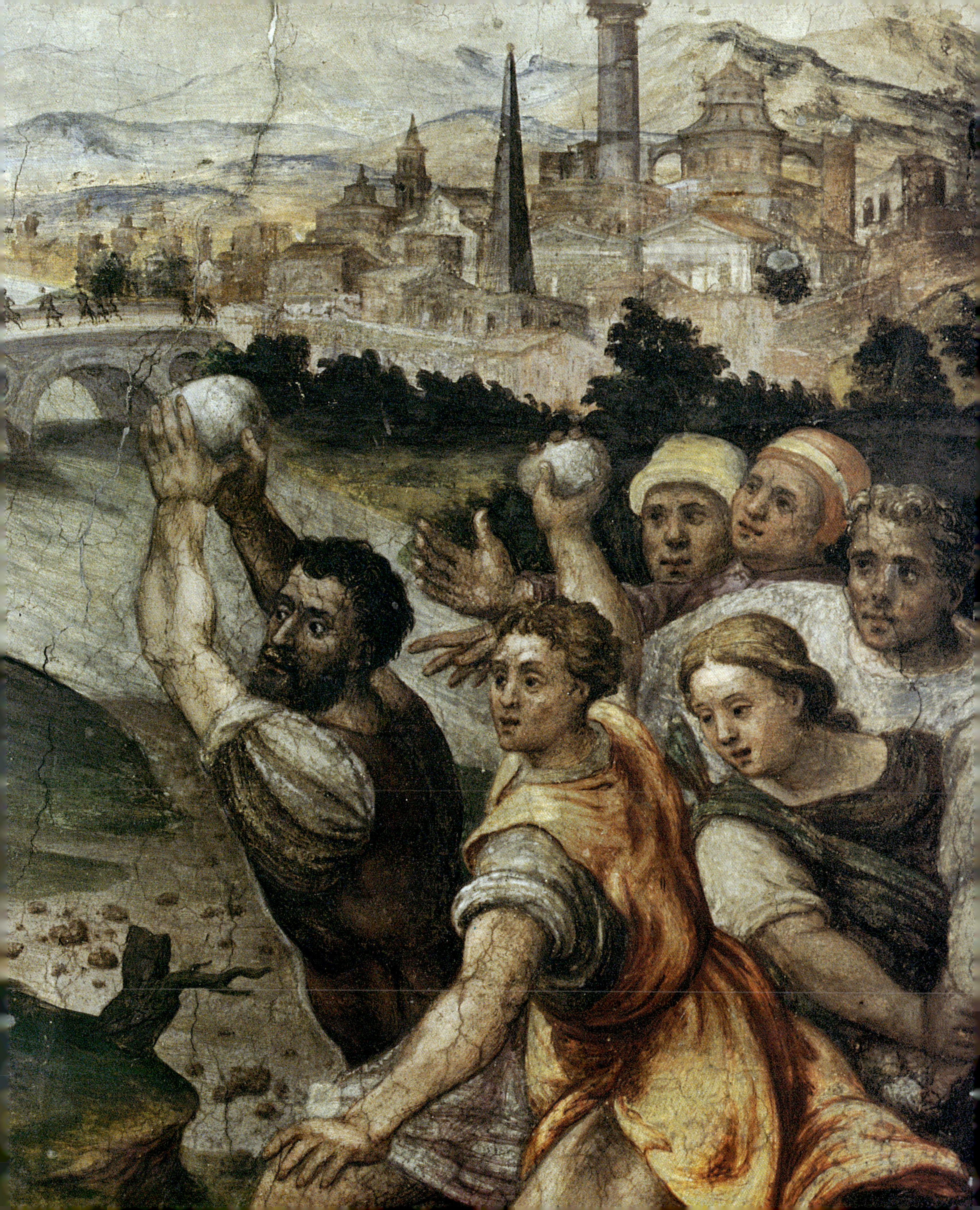

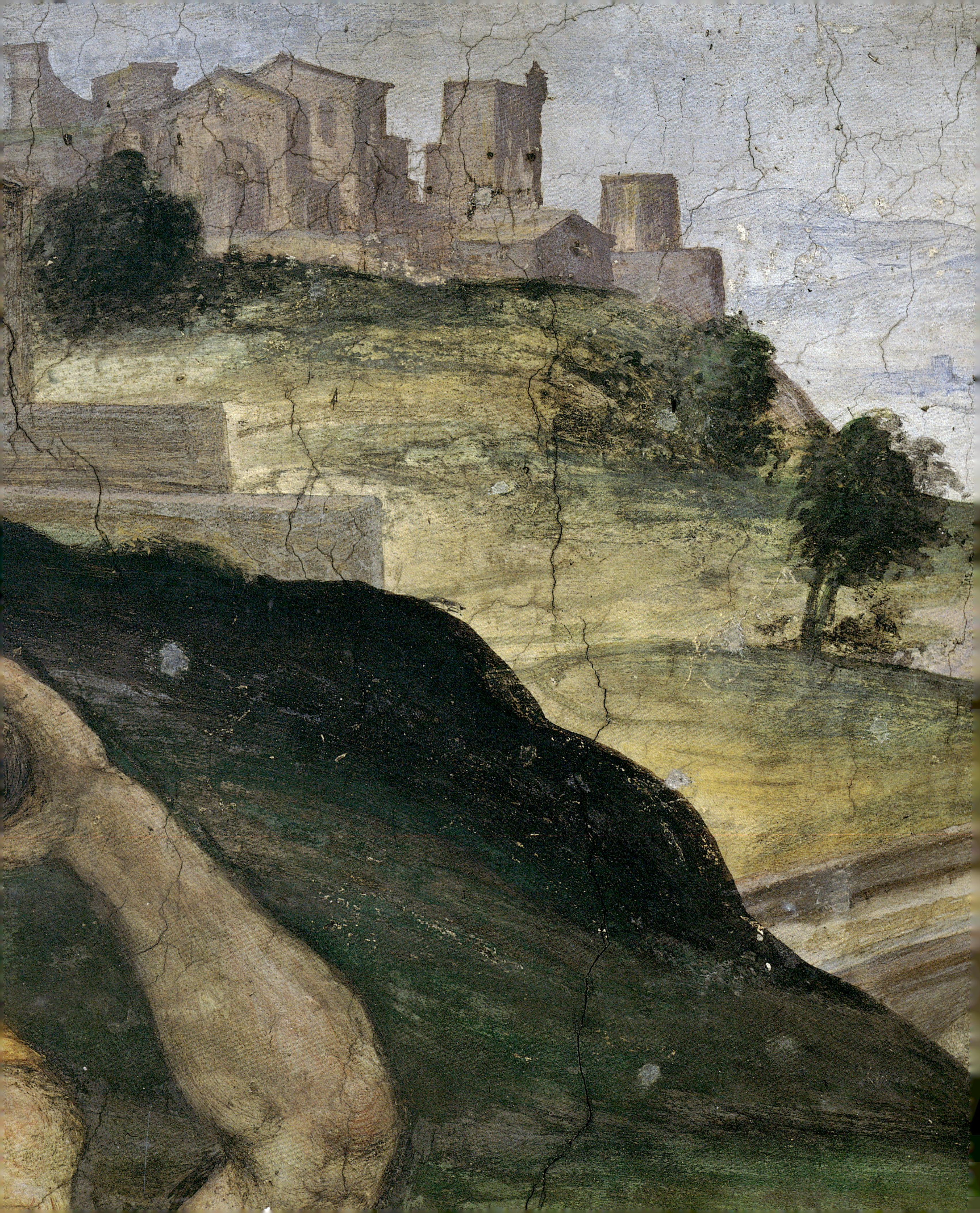

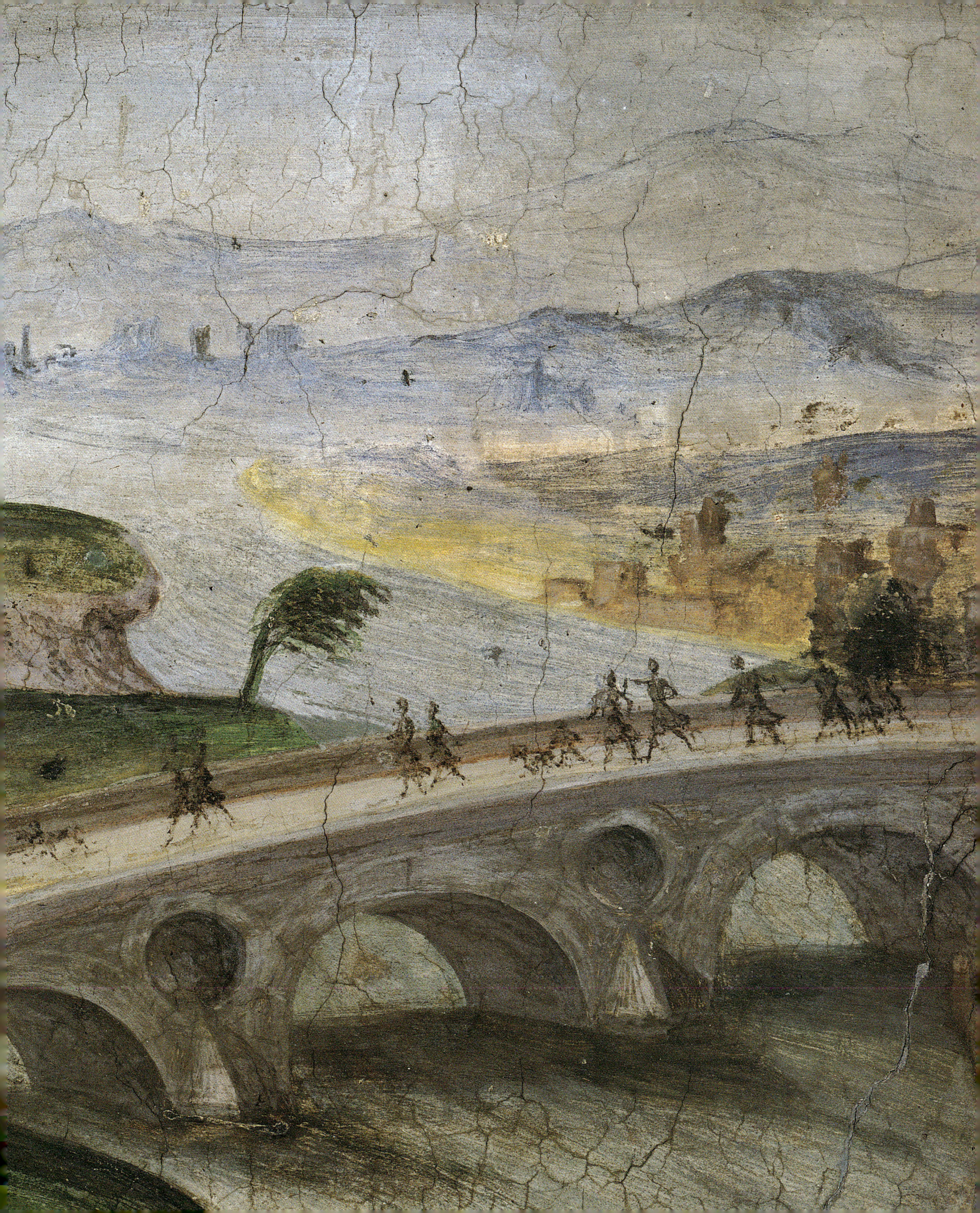

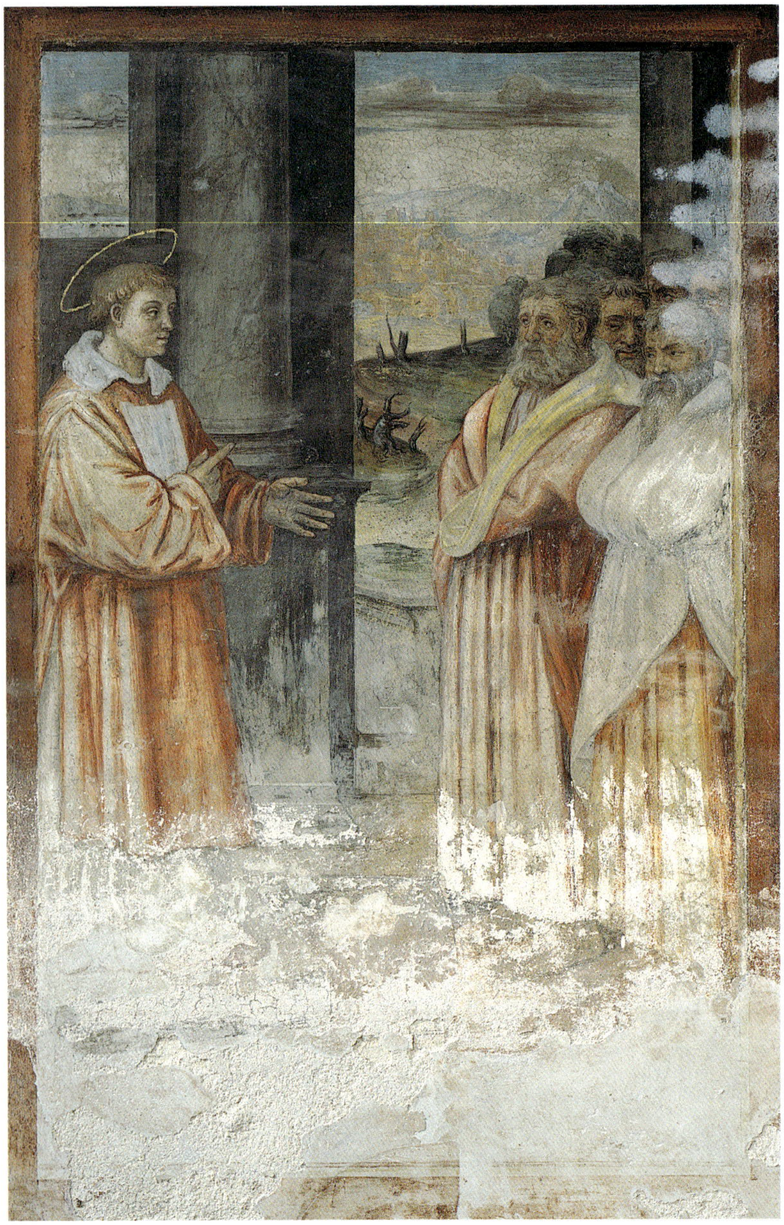

27b. Evangelista Luini (attr.)
St Stephen before the Synedrians
Left wall, Cappella Carreto
(or di Santo Stefano), lay hall

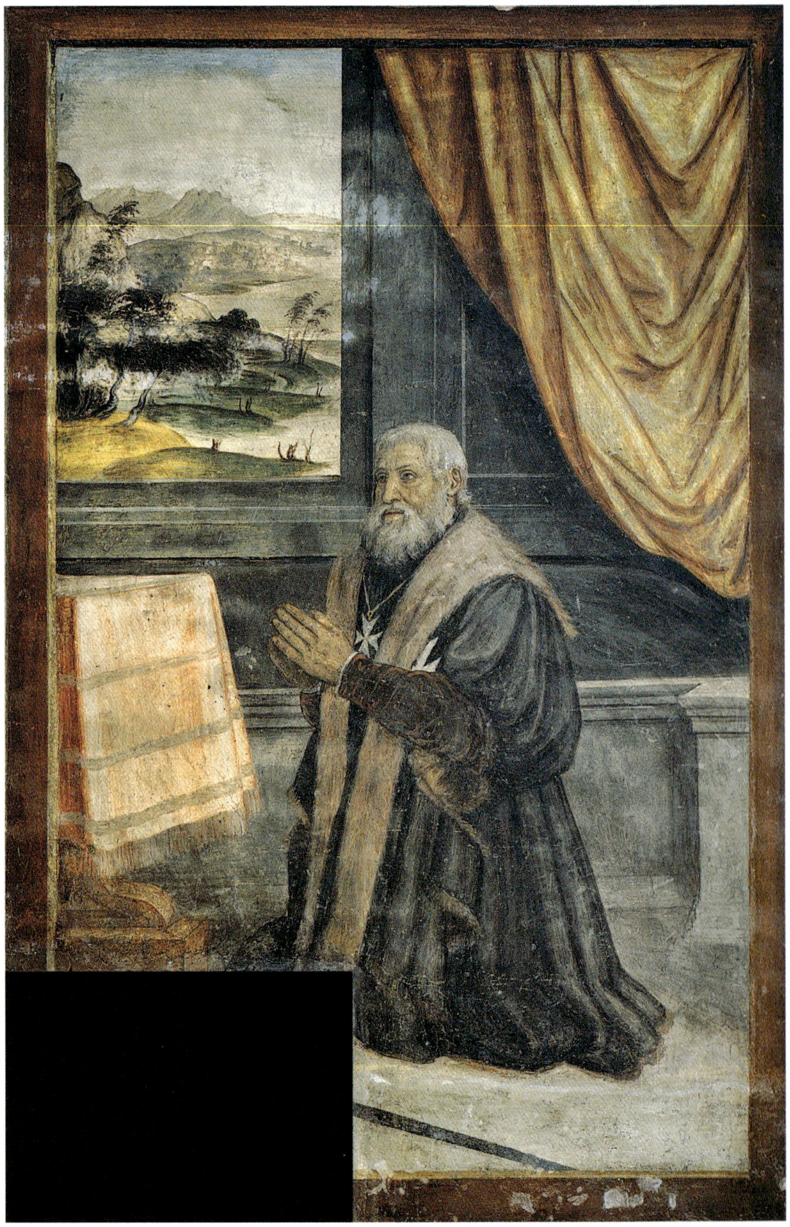

27c. Evangelista Luini (attr.)
Portrait of Francesco Carreto
Right wall, Cappella Carreto
(or di Santo Stefano), lay hall

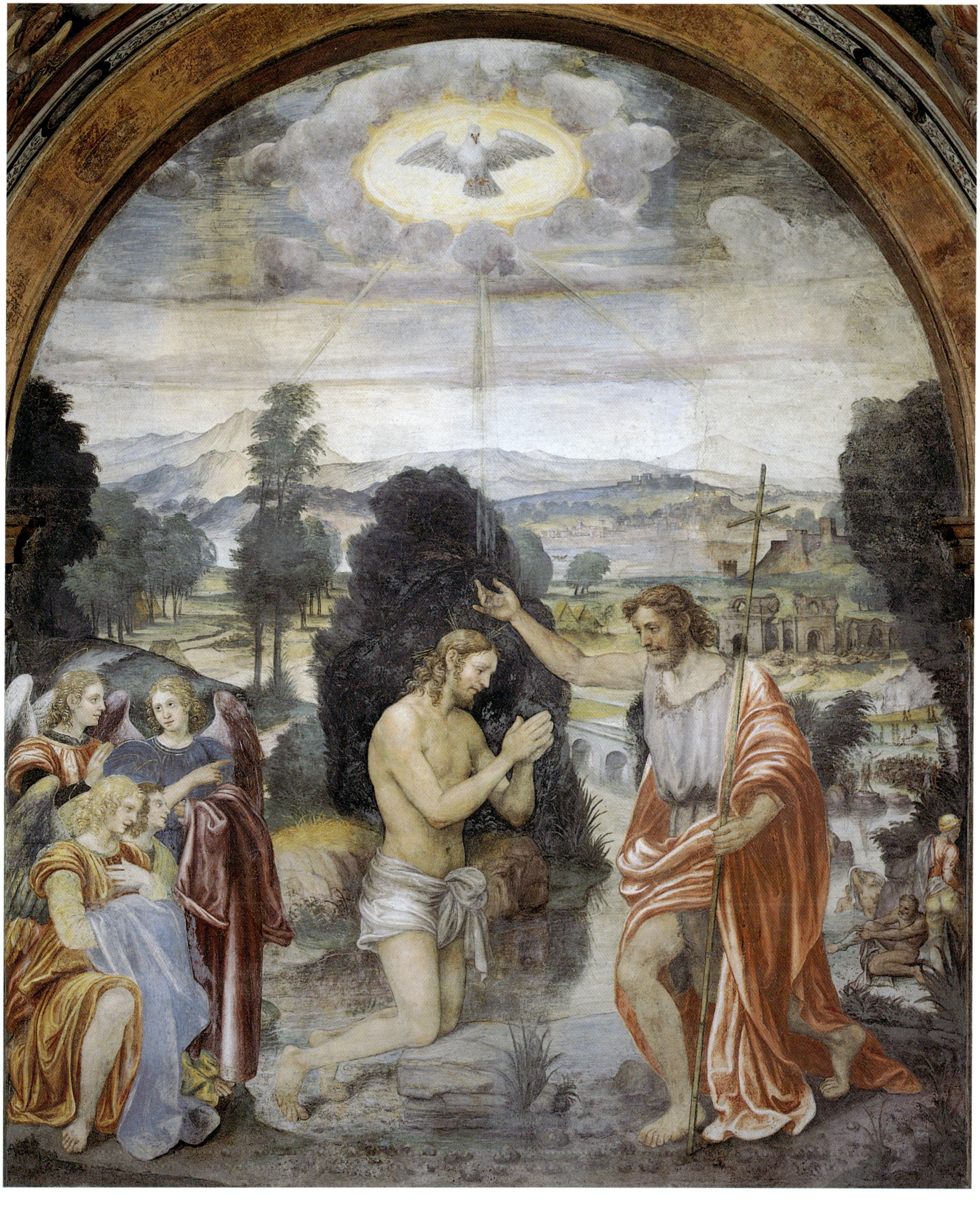

28a. Lombard artist,
mid-sixteenth century
Baptism of Christ
Central wall, Cappella Carreto
(or di San Giovanni Battista), lay hall

Pages 234–239
28a. Lombard artist,
mid-sixteenth century
Baptism of Christ,
details

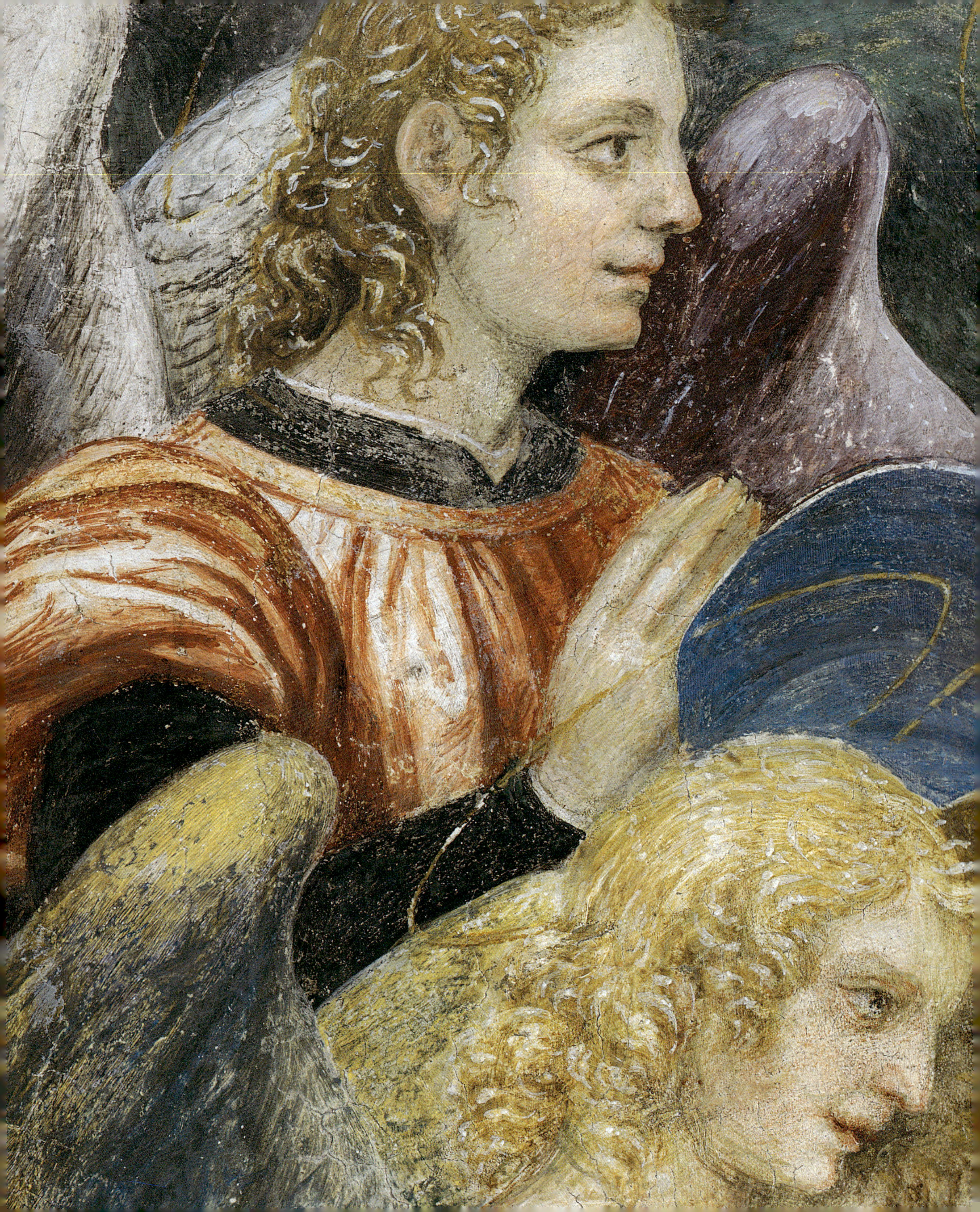

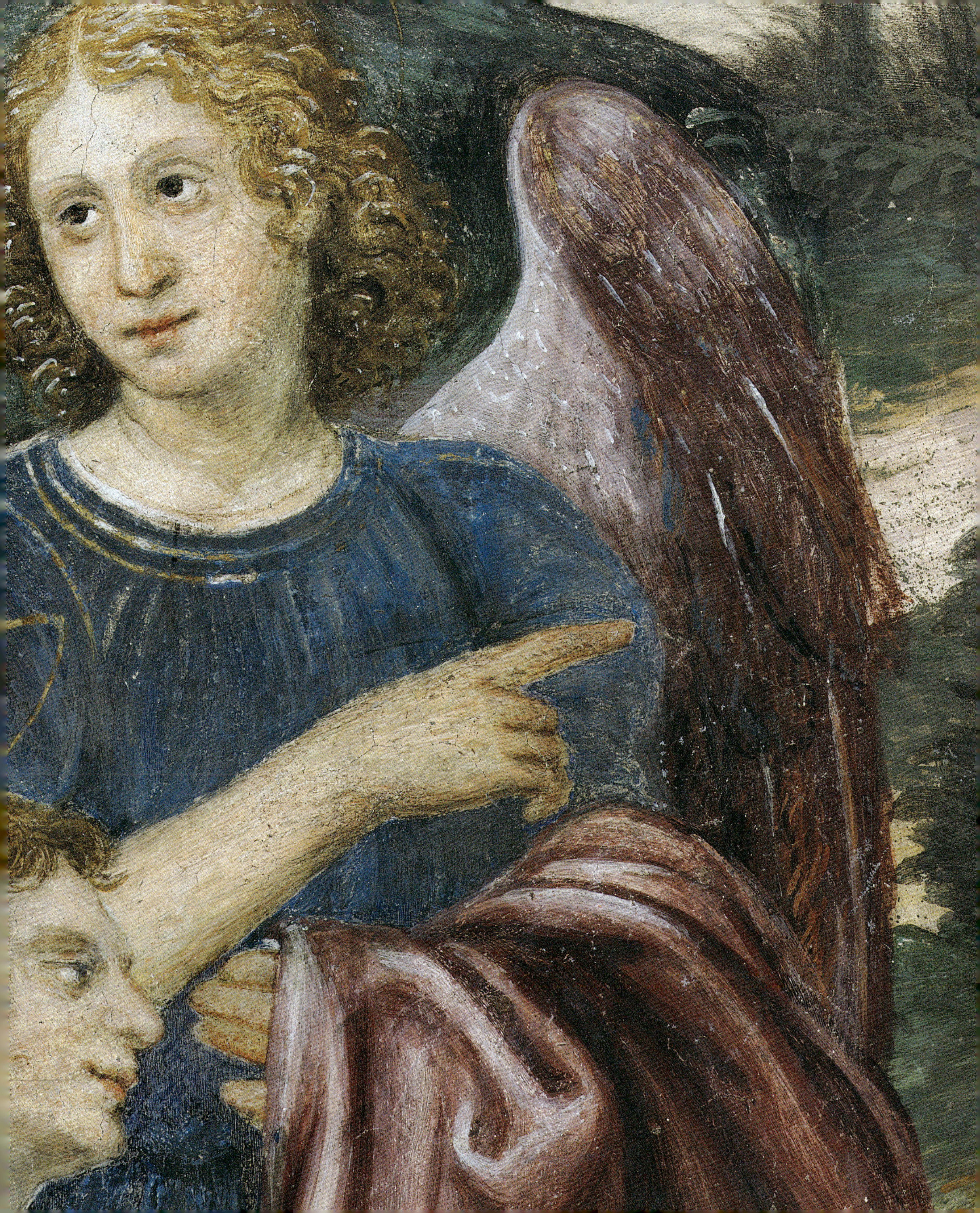

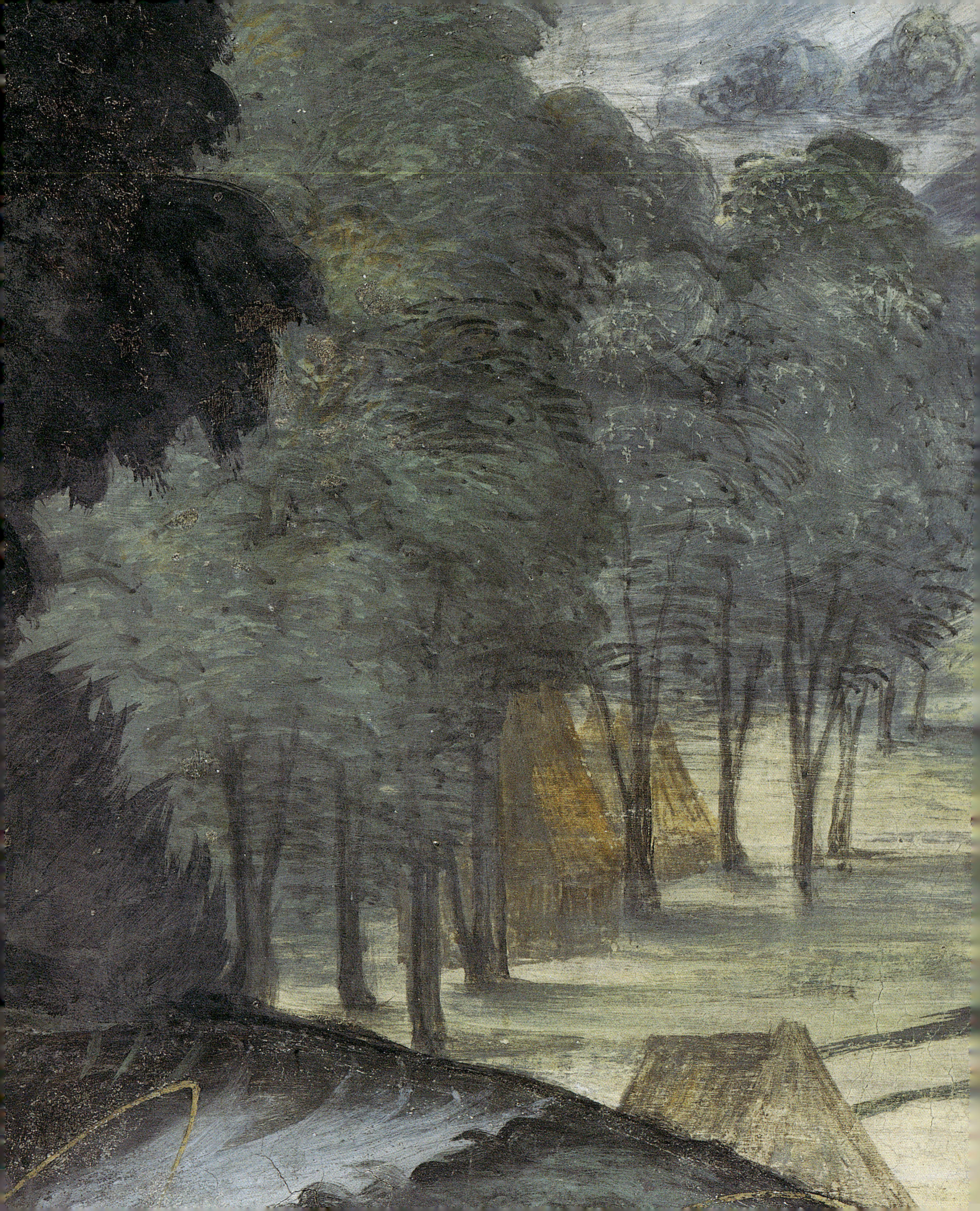

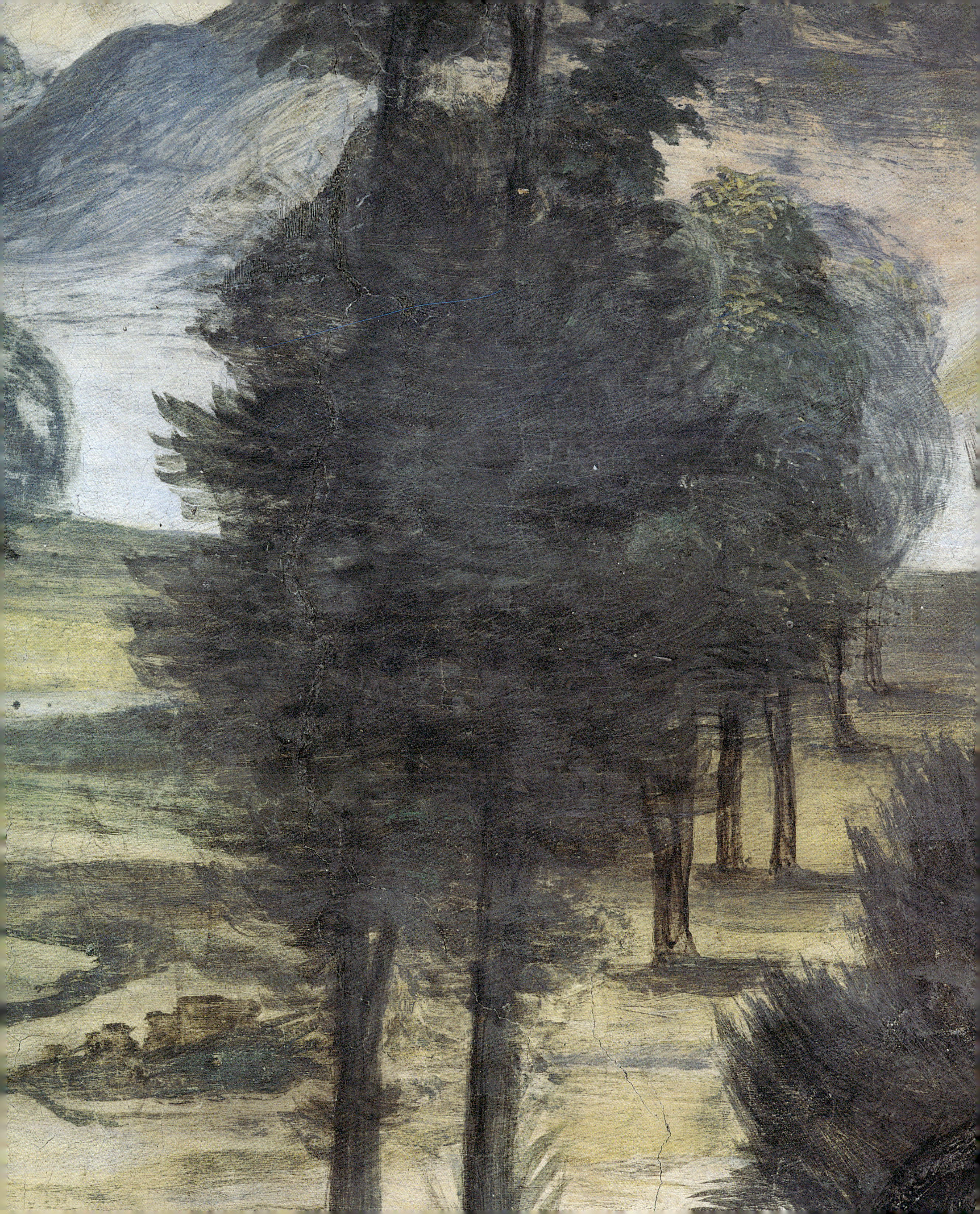

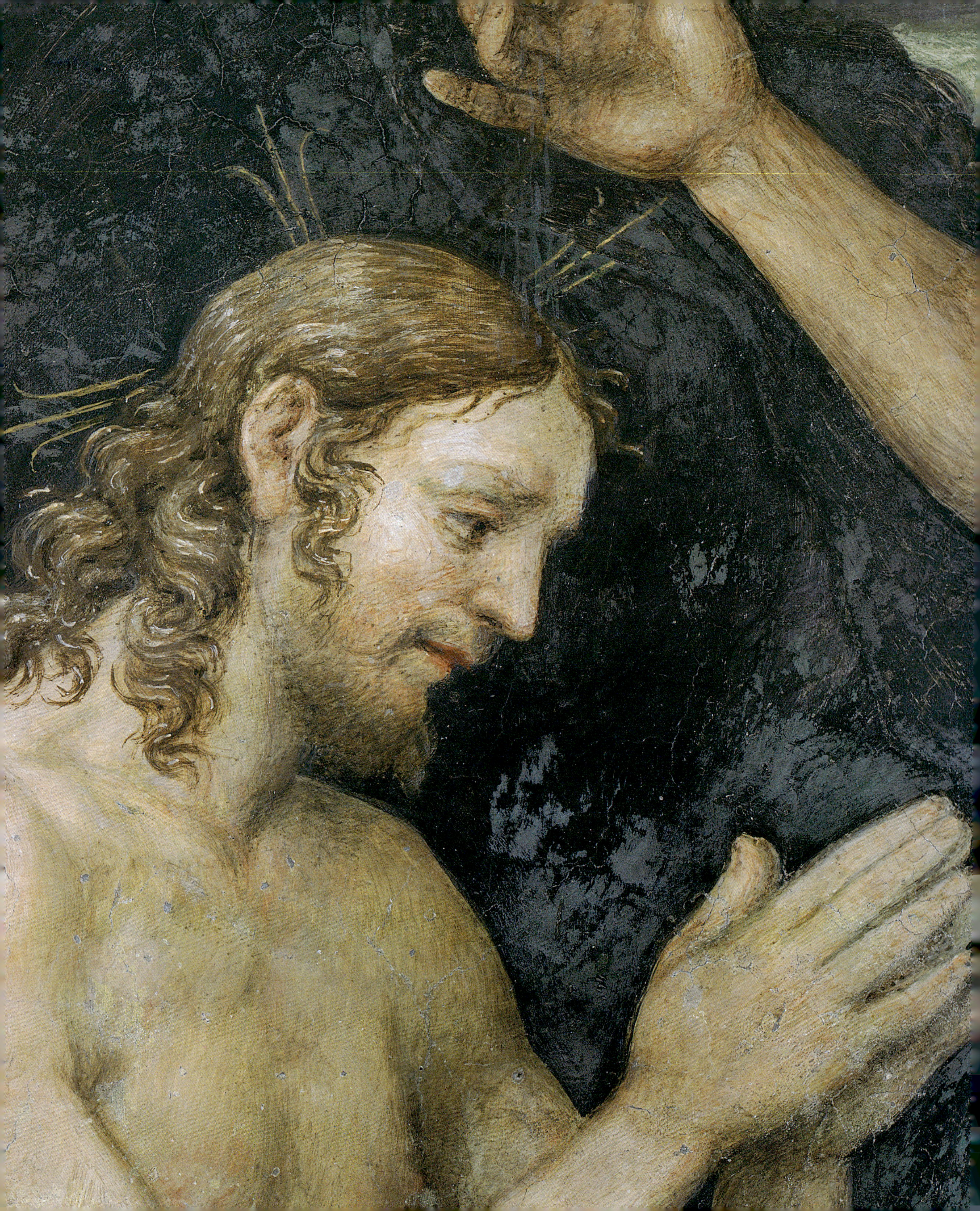

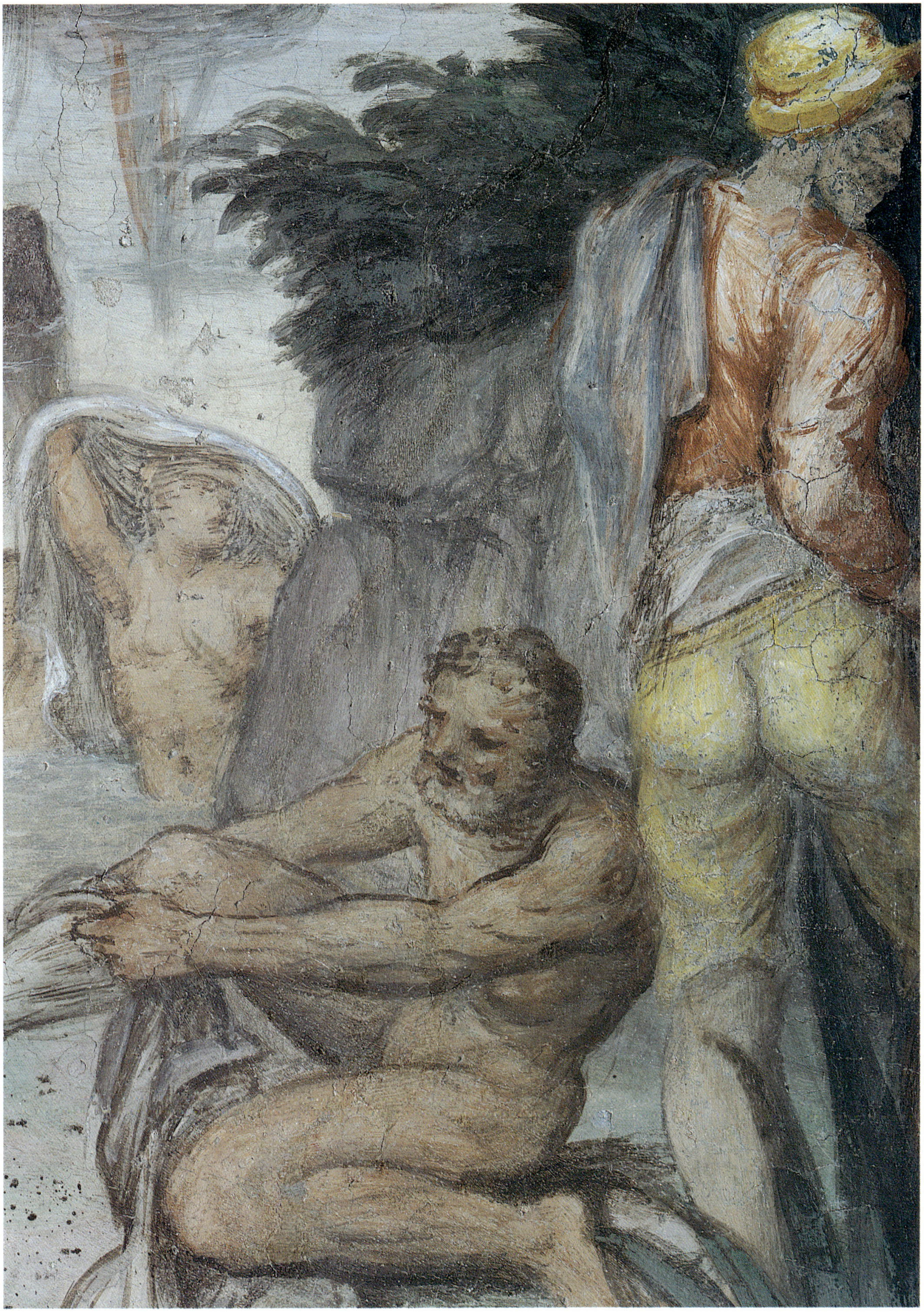

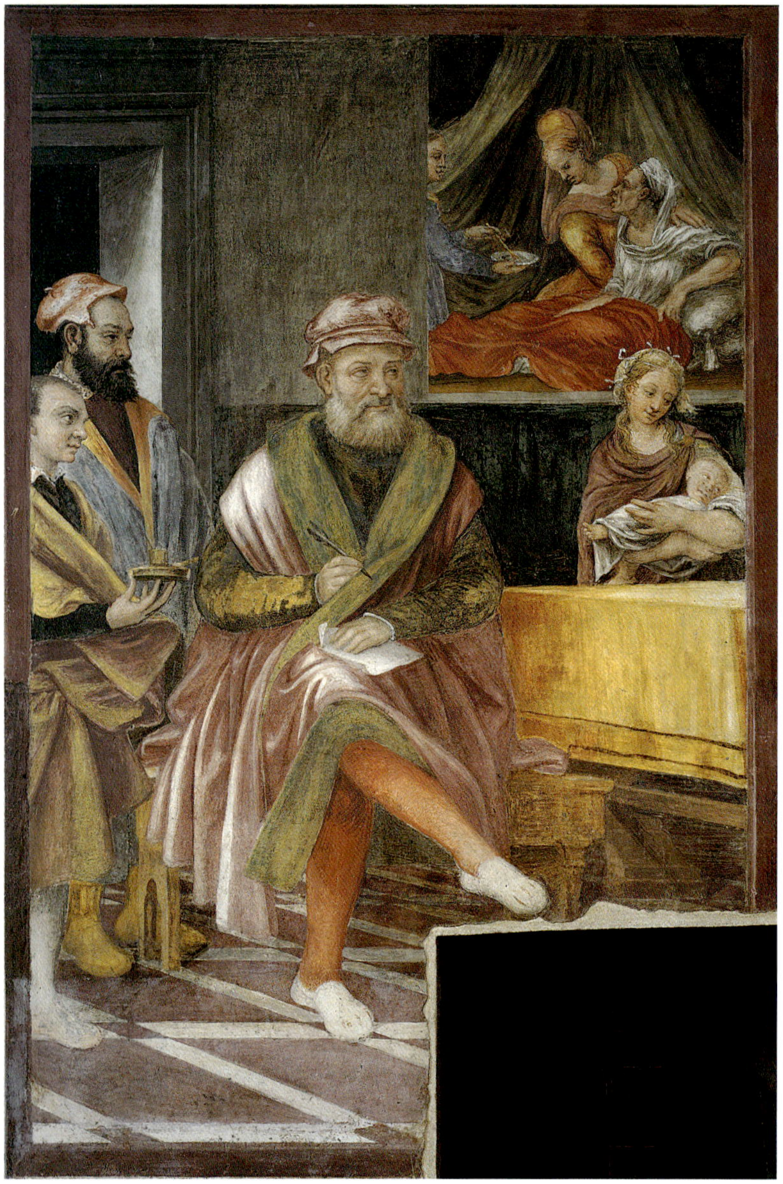

28b. Lombard artist,
mid-sixteenth century
Naming of St John
Left wall, Cappella Carreto
(or di San Giovanni Battista), lay hall

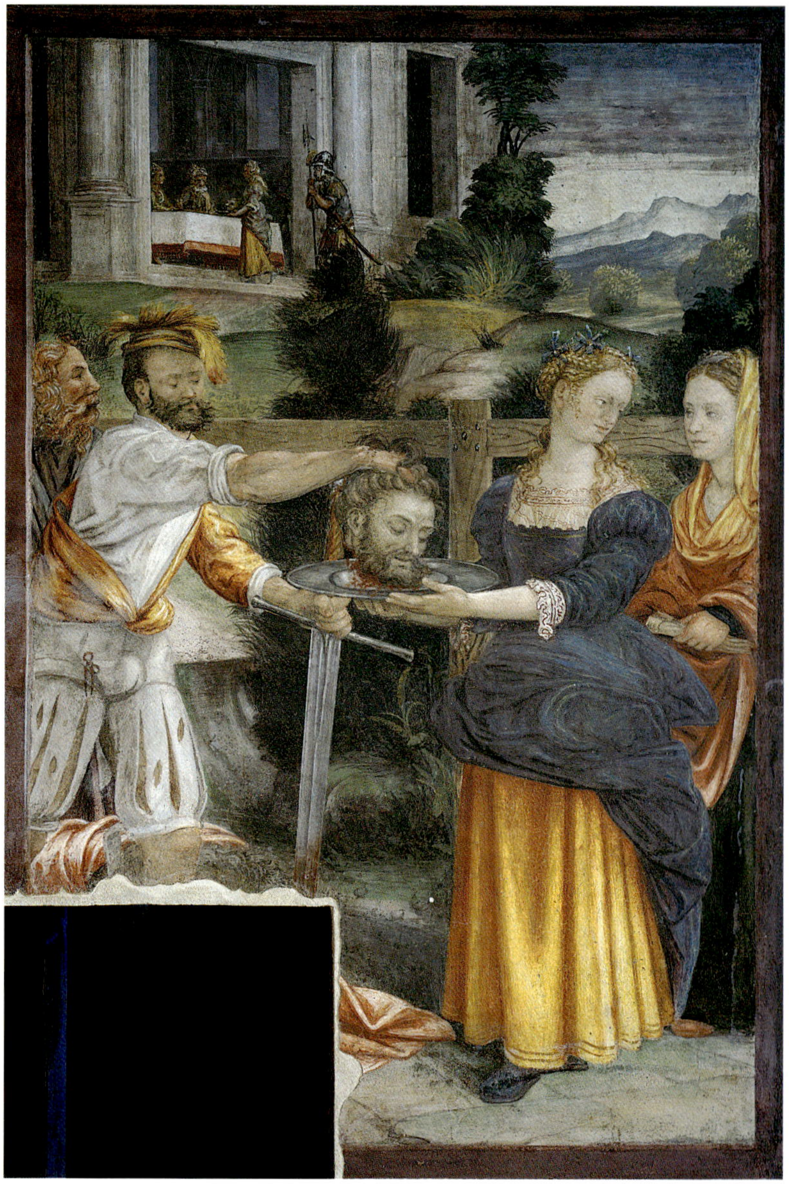

28c. Lombard artist,
mid-sixteenth century
Beheading of St John
Right wall, Cappella Carreto
(or di San Giovanni Battista), lay hall

Opposite
29a. Aurelio Luini with the assistance
of Giovan Pietro Luini
Deposition
Central wall, Cappella Bentivoglio,
lay hall

Pages 242–243
29a. Aurelio Luini with the assistance
of Giovan Pietro Luini
Deposition, details

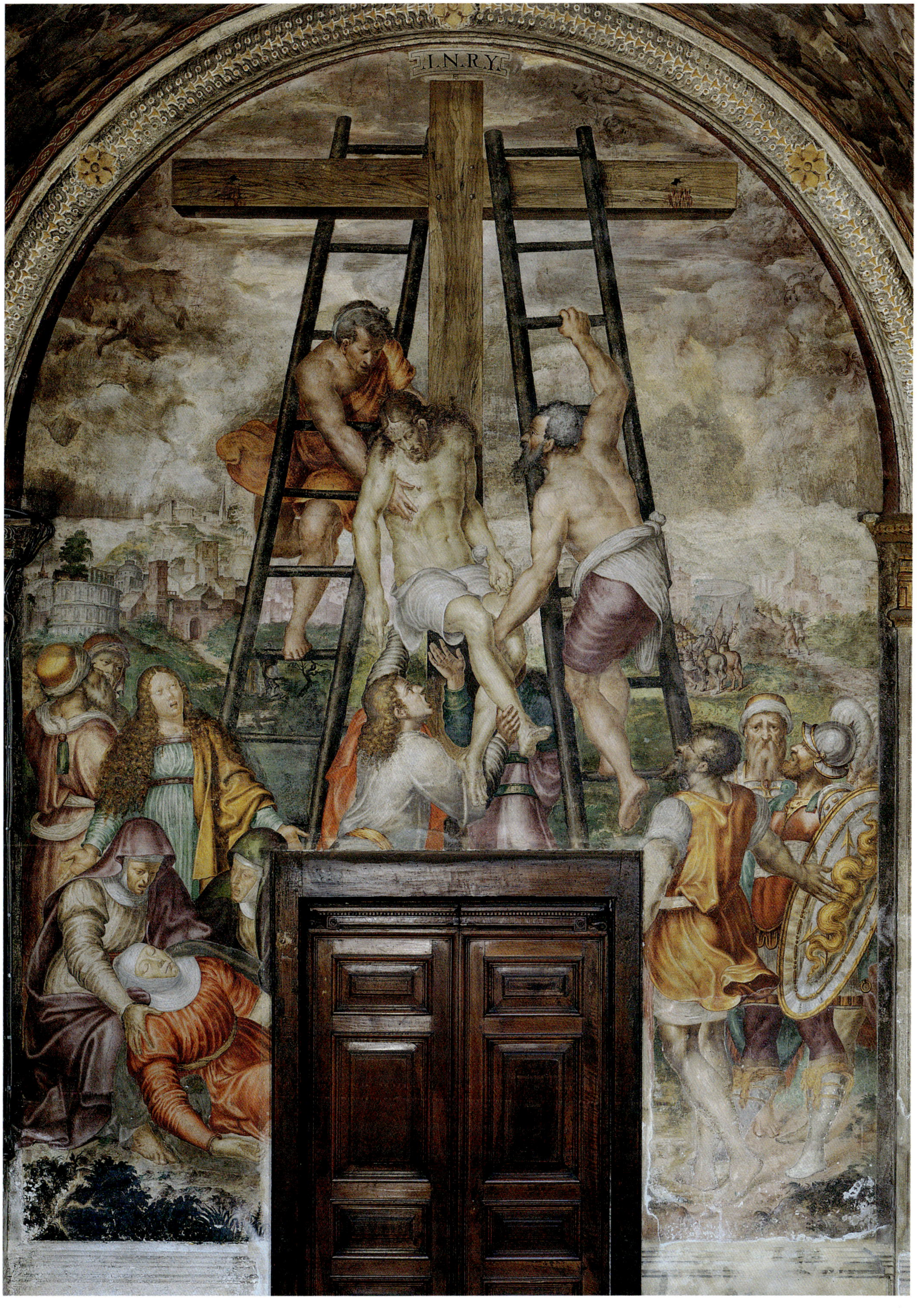
I.N.R.Y.

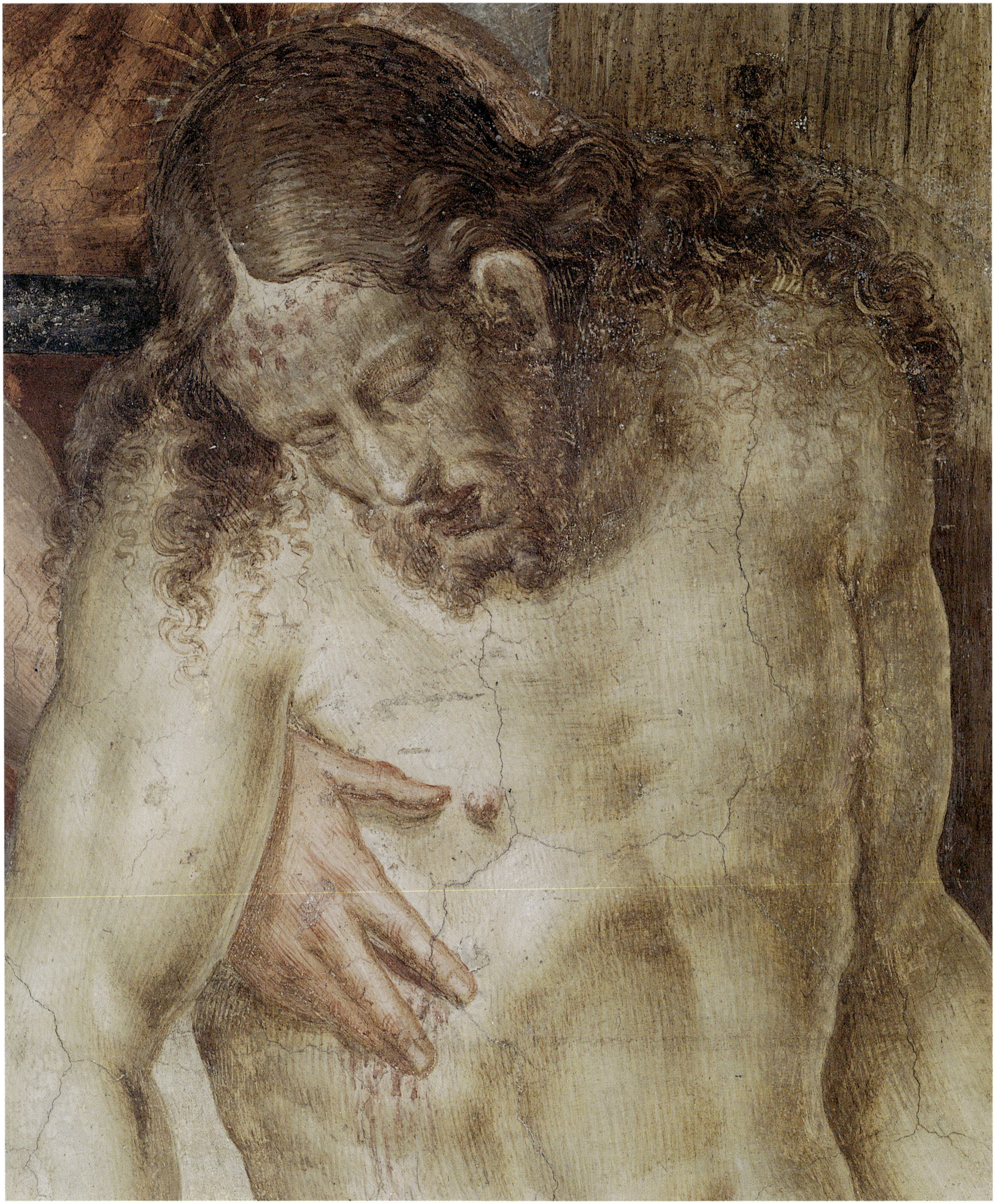

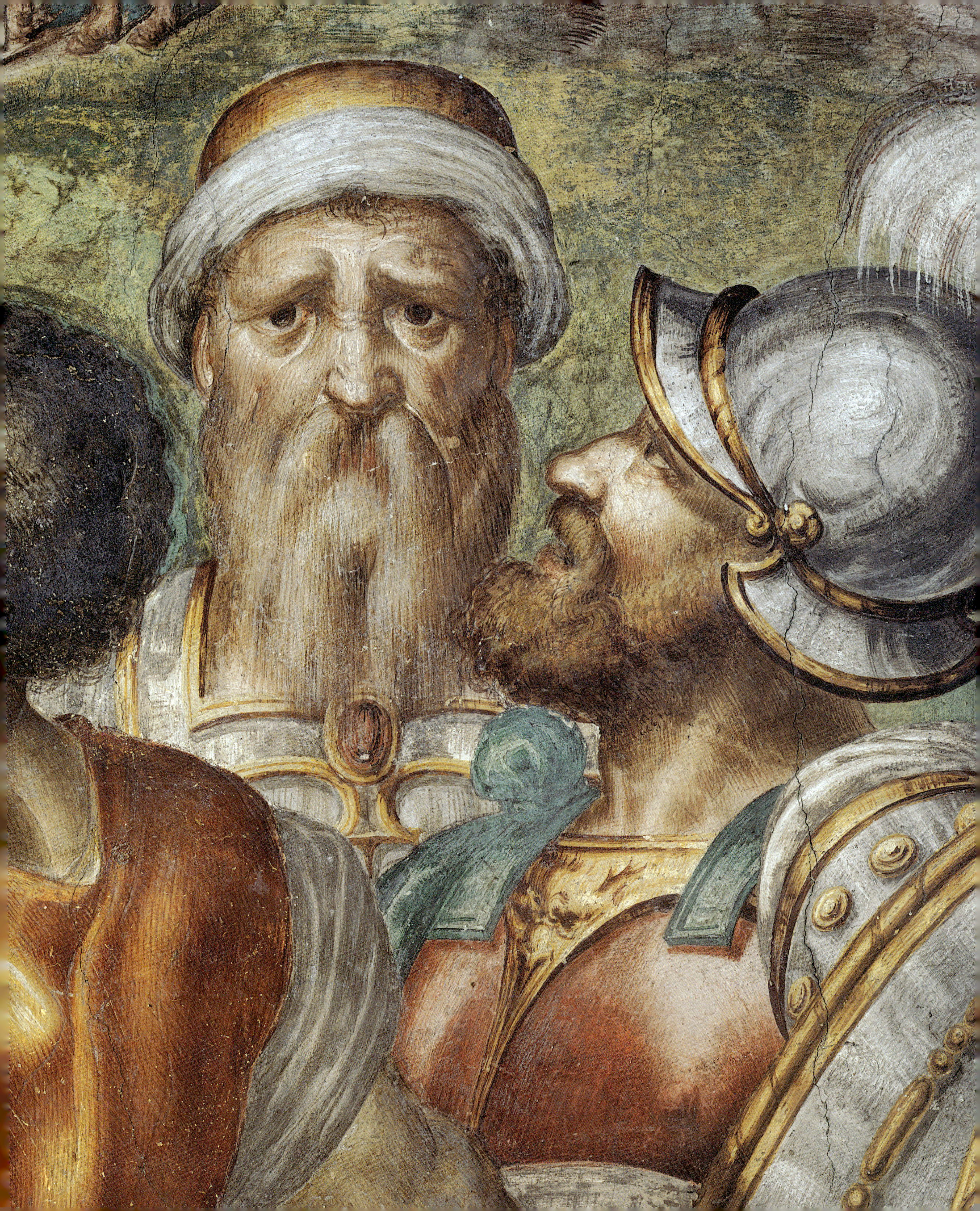

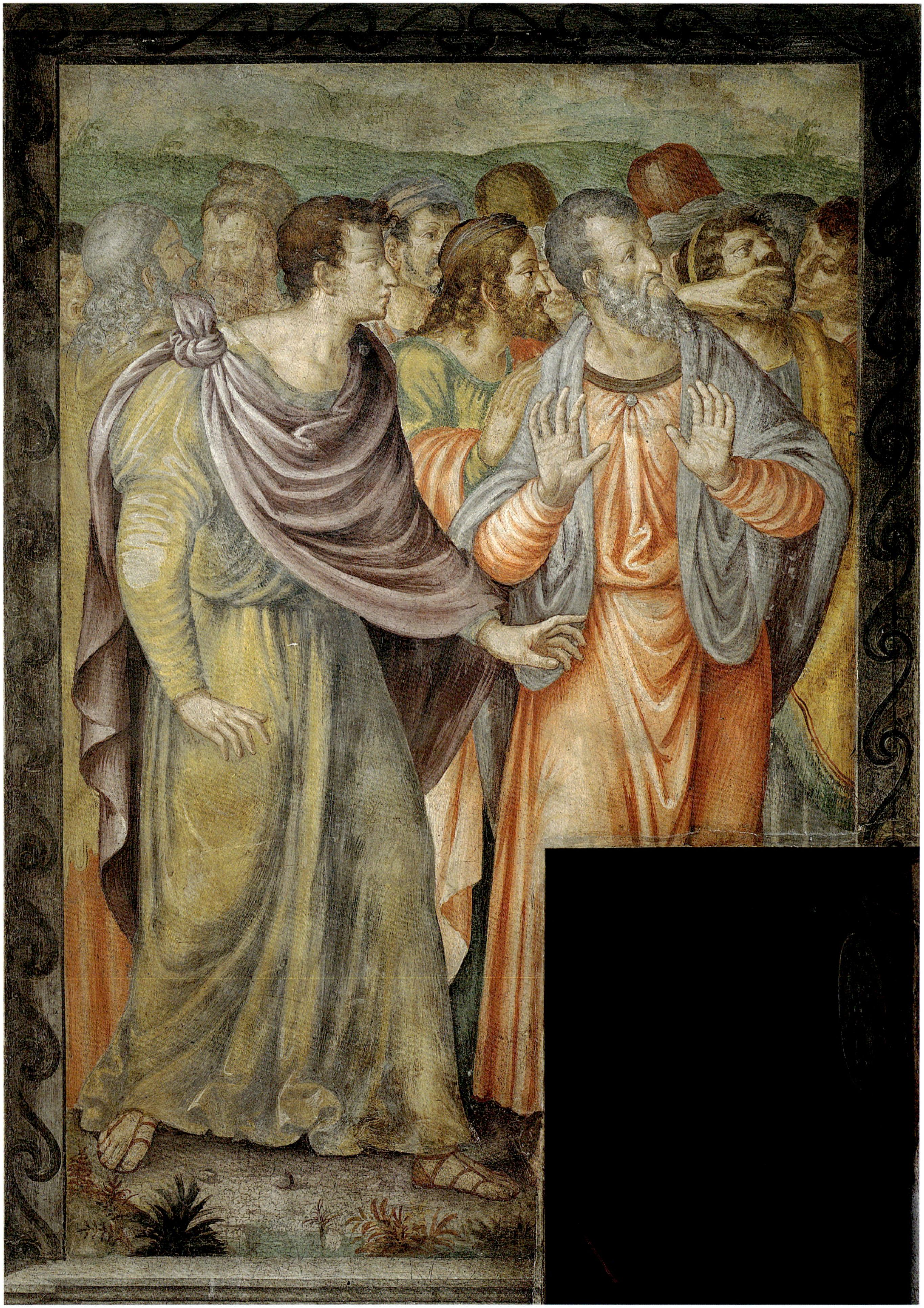

29b. Aurelio Luini
with the assistance of
Giovan Pietro Luini
Apostles
Left wall, Cappella
Bentivoglio, lay hall

29c. Aurelio Luini with the assistance of Giovan Pietro Luini *Apostles* Right wall, Cappella Bentivoglio, lay hall

Following pages
29c. Aurelio Luini with the assistance of Giovan Pietro Luini *Apostles*, detail

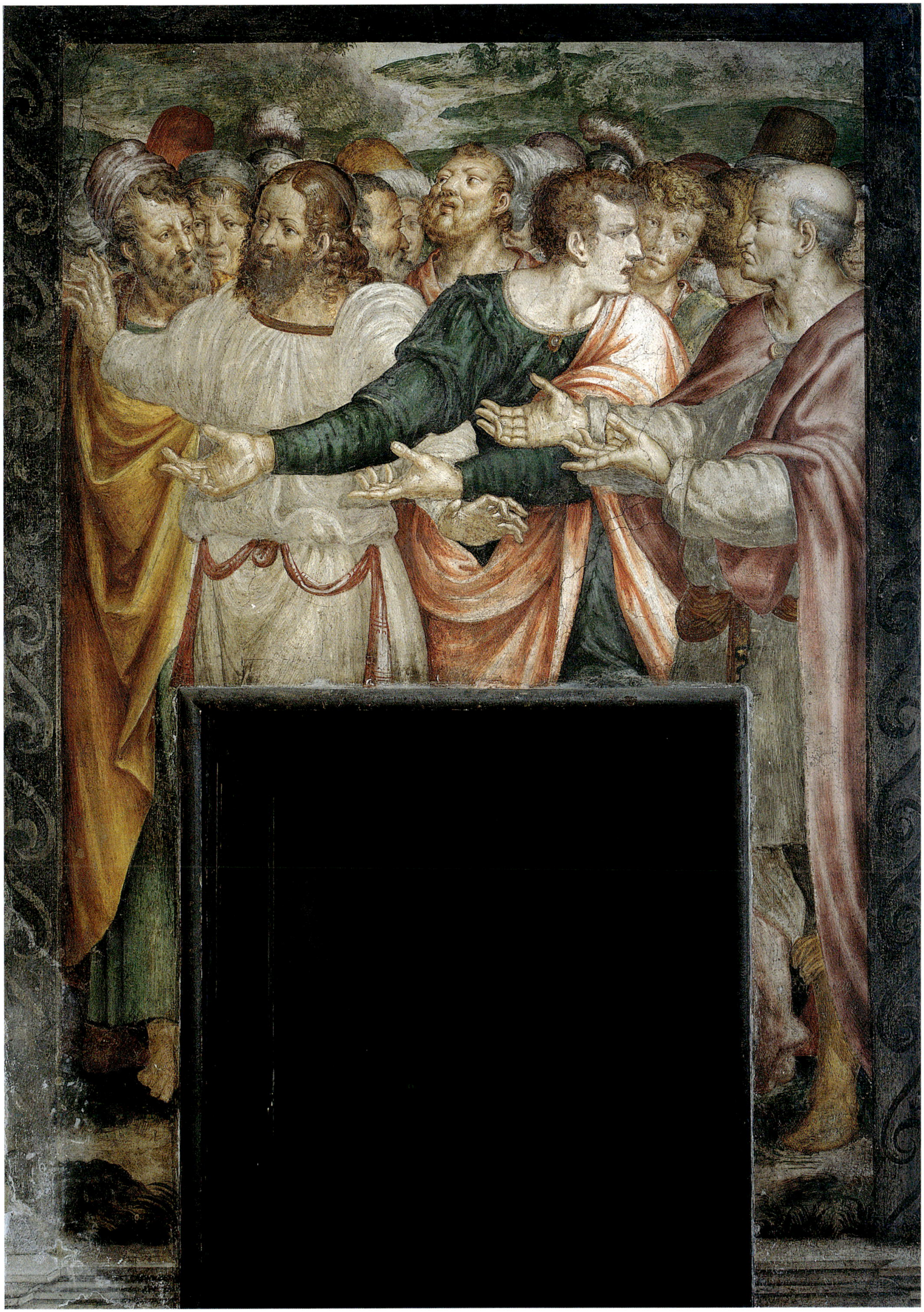

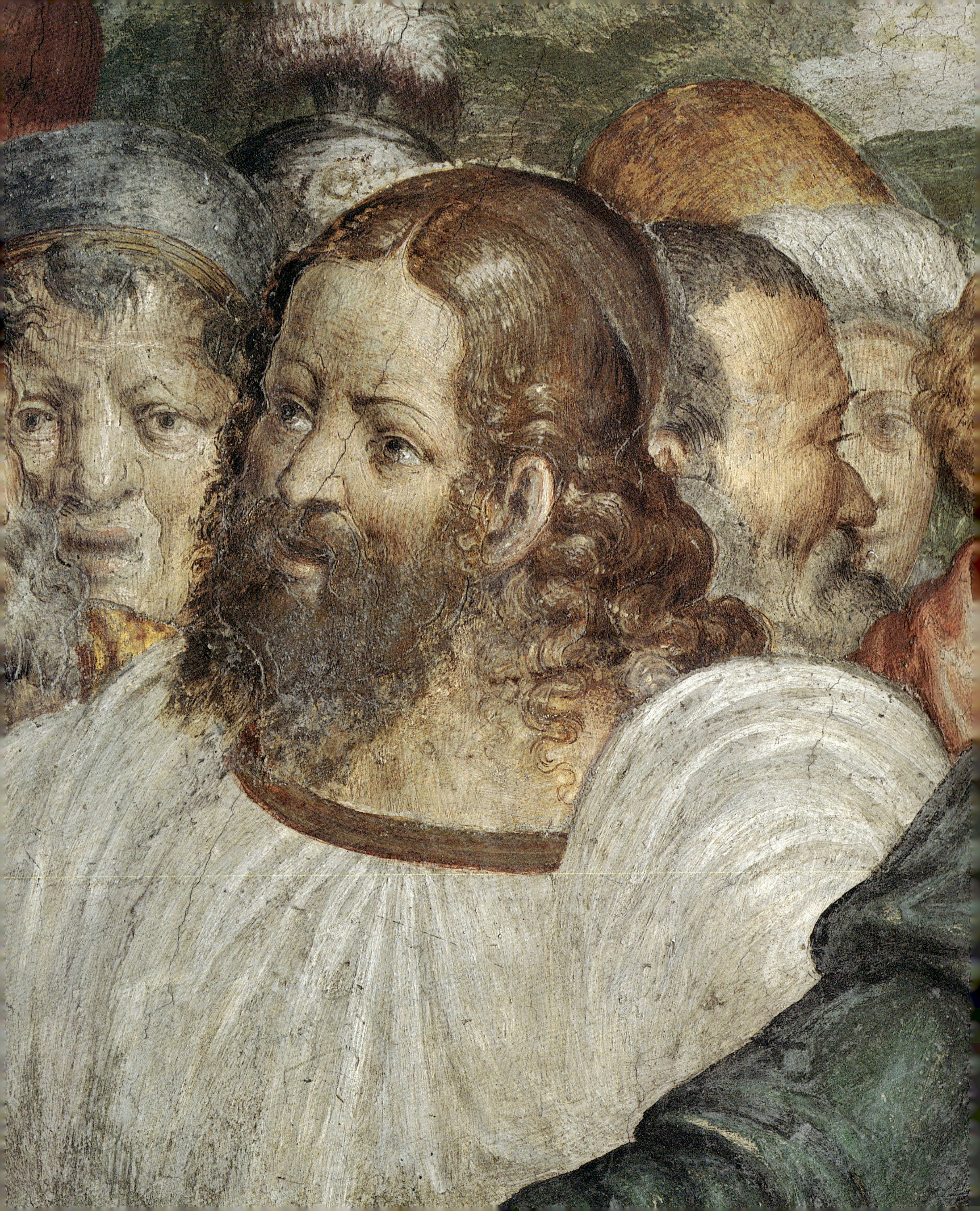

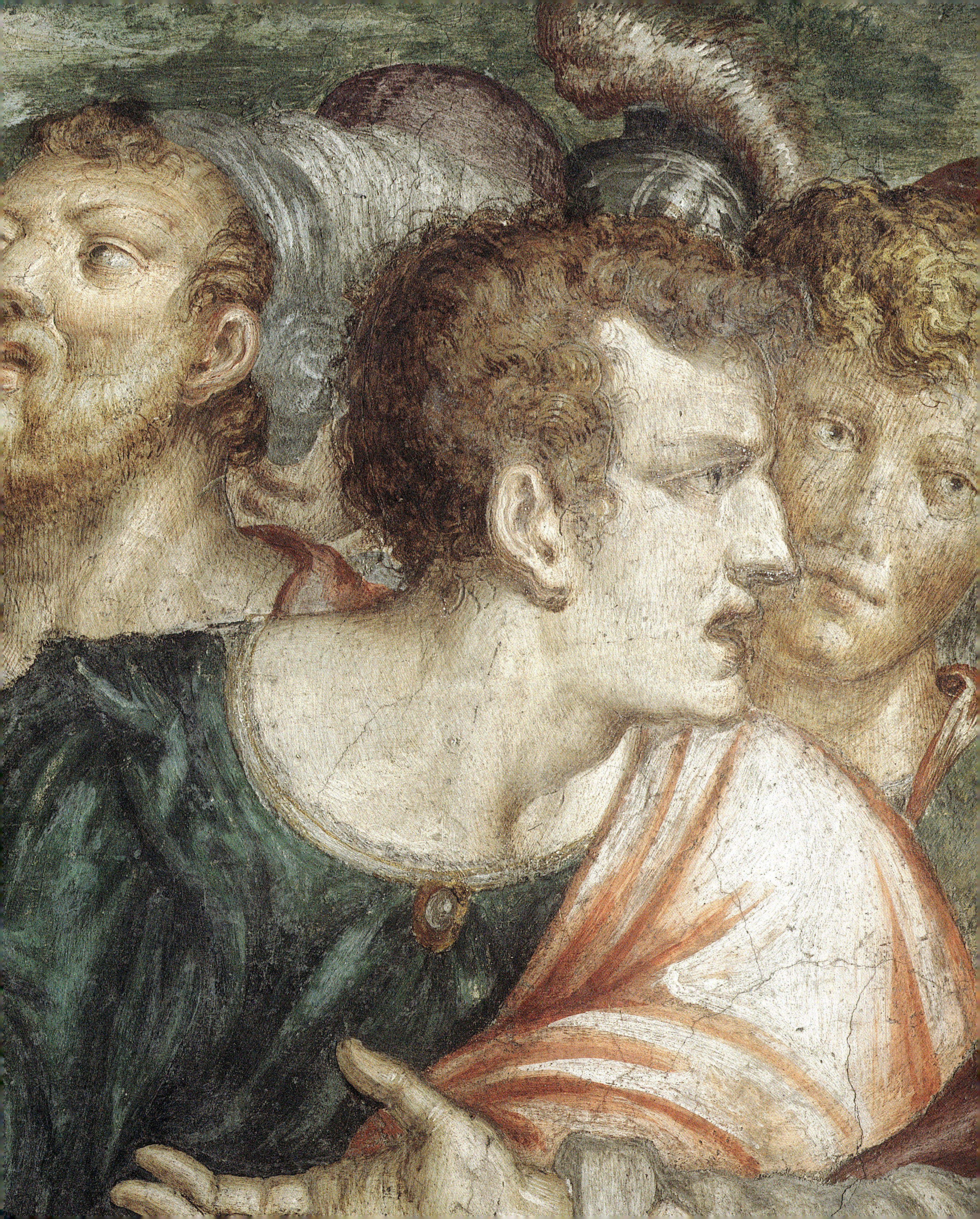

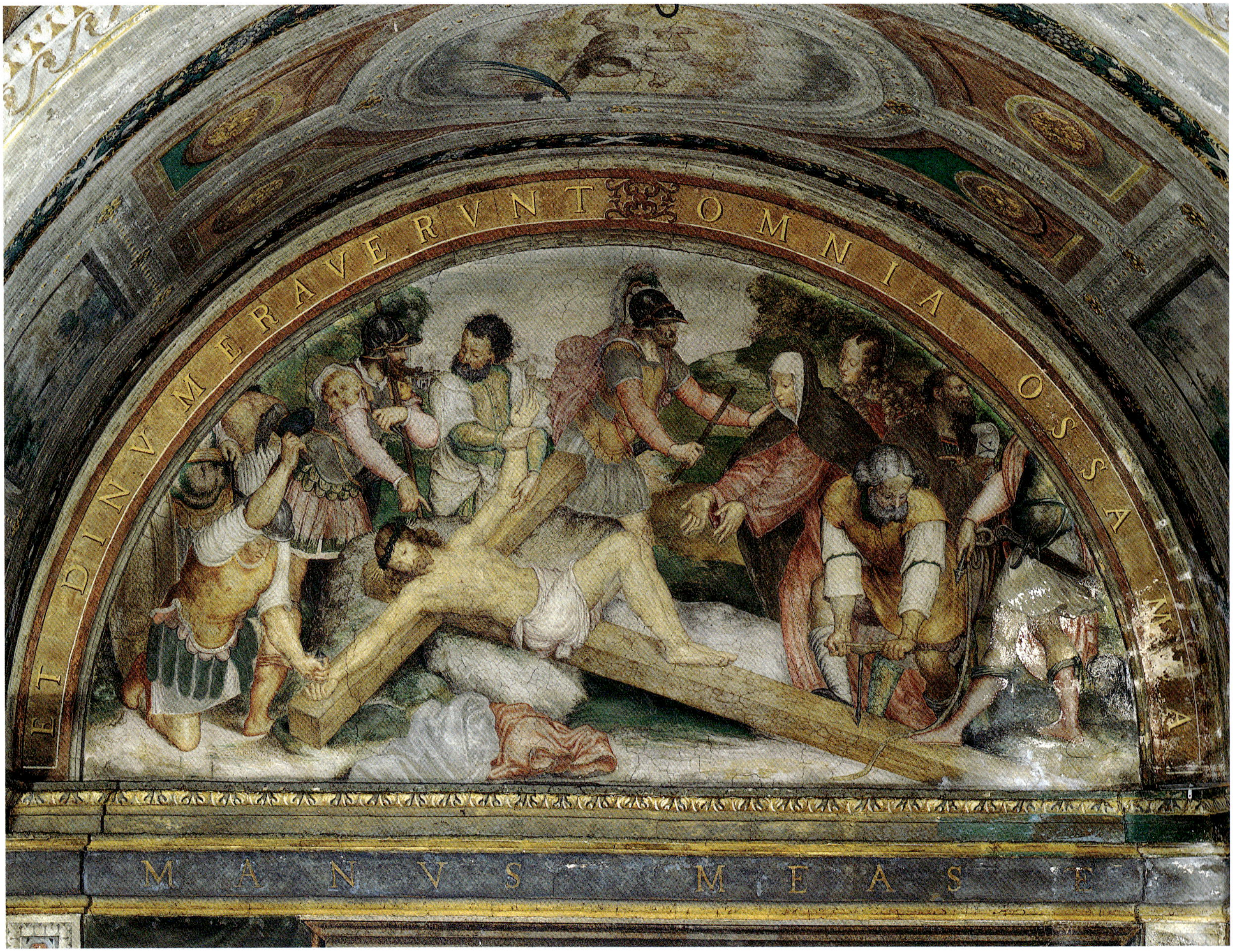

30. Aurelio Luini with the assistance
of Giovan Pietro Luini
Christ Nailed to the Cross
Central wall, Cappella Bentivoglio
(or dell'Ecce Homo), lay hall

30. Aurelio Luini
Putto drawing back a curtain, detail
Central wall, Cappella Bentivoglio
(or dell'Ecce Homo), lay hall

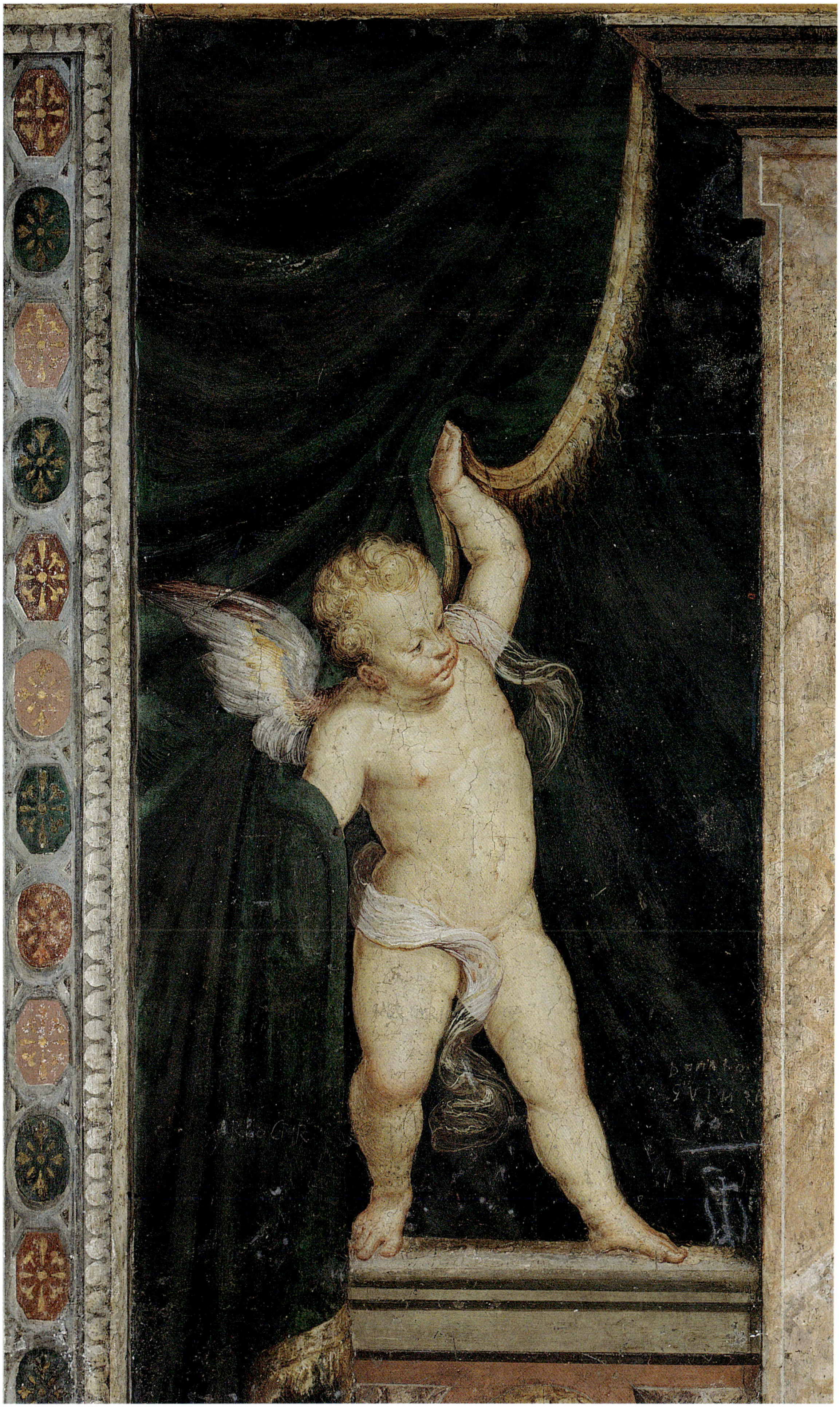

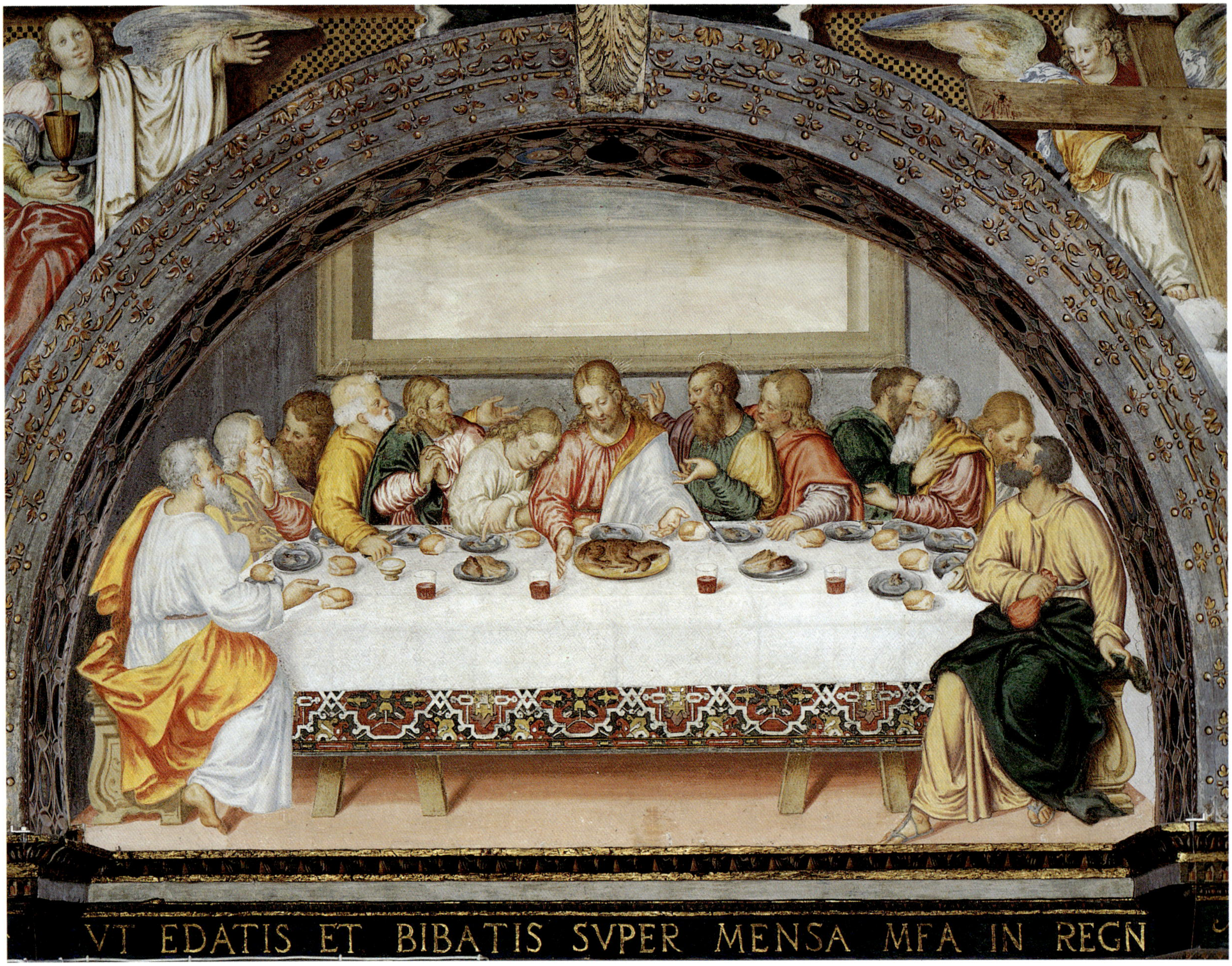

31. Giovan Pietro Luini
Last Supper
End wall, convent hall

Pages 251–254
31. Giovan Pietro Luini
Last Supper, details

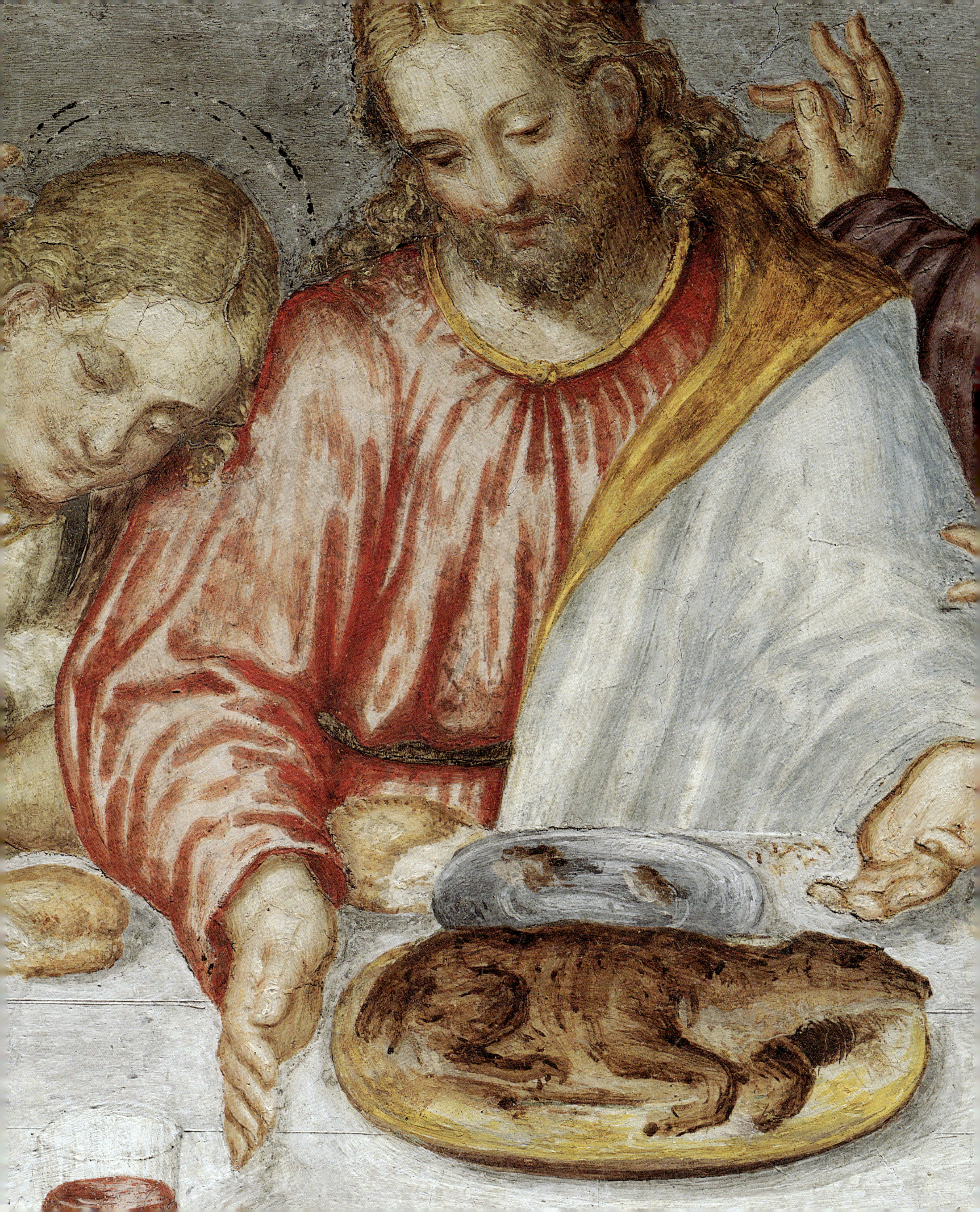

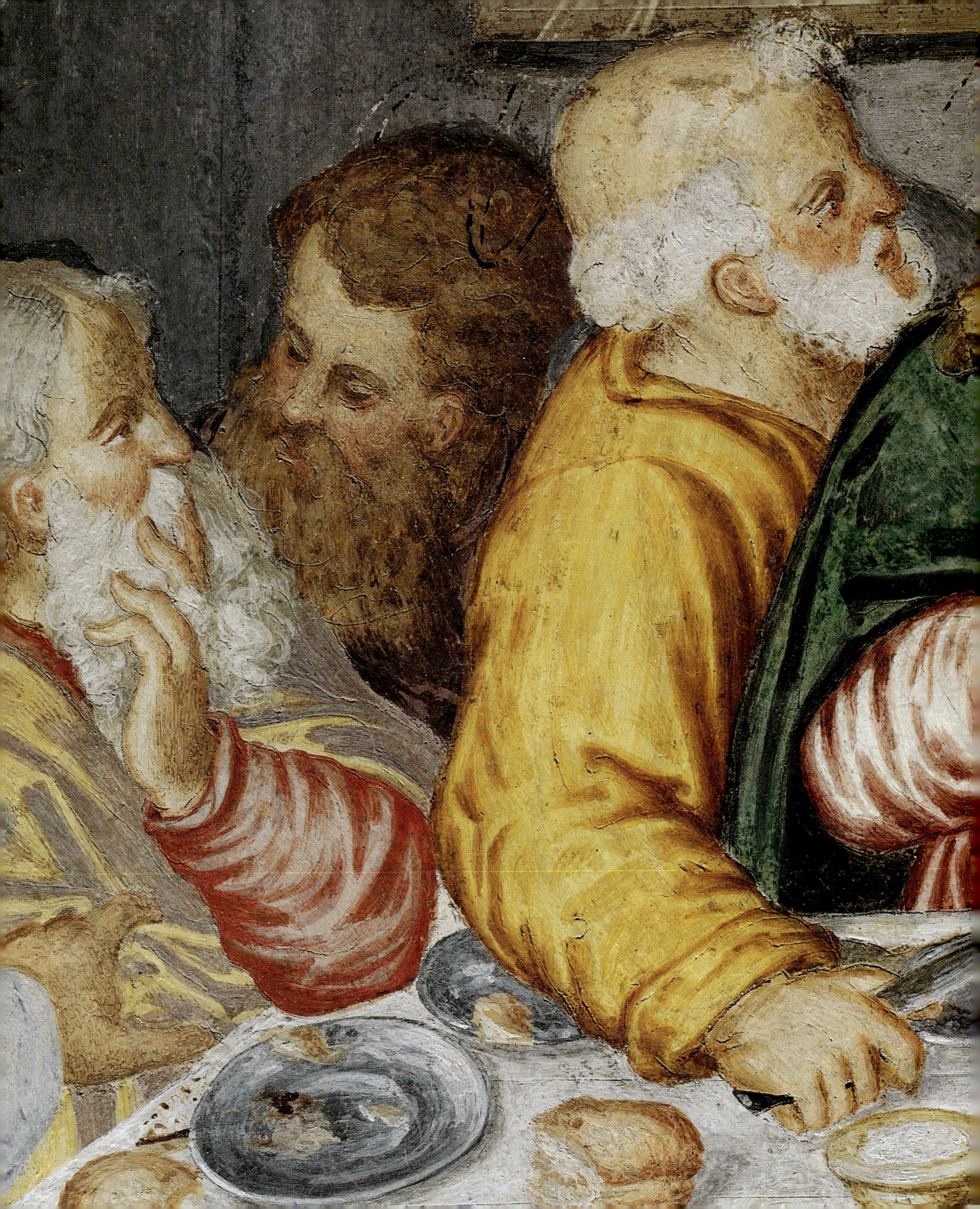

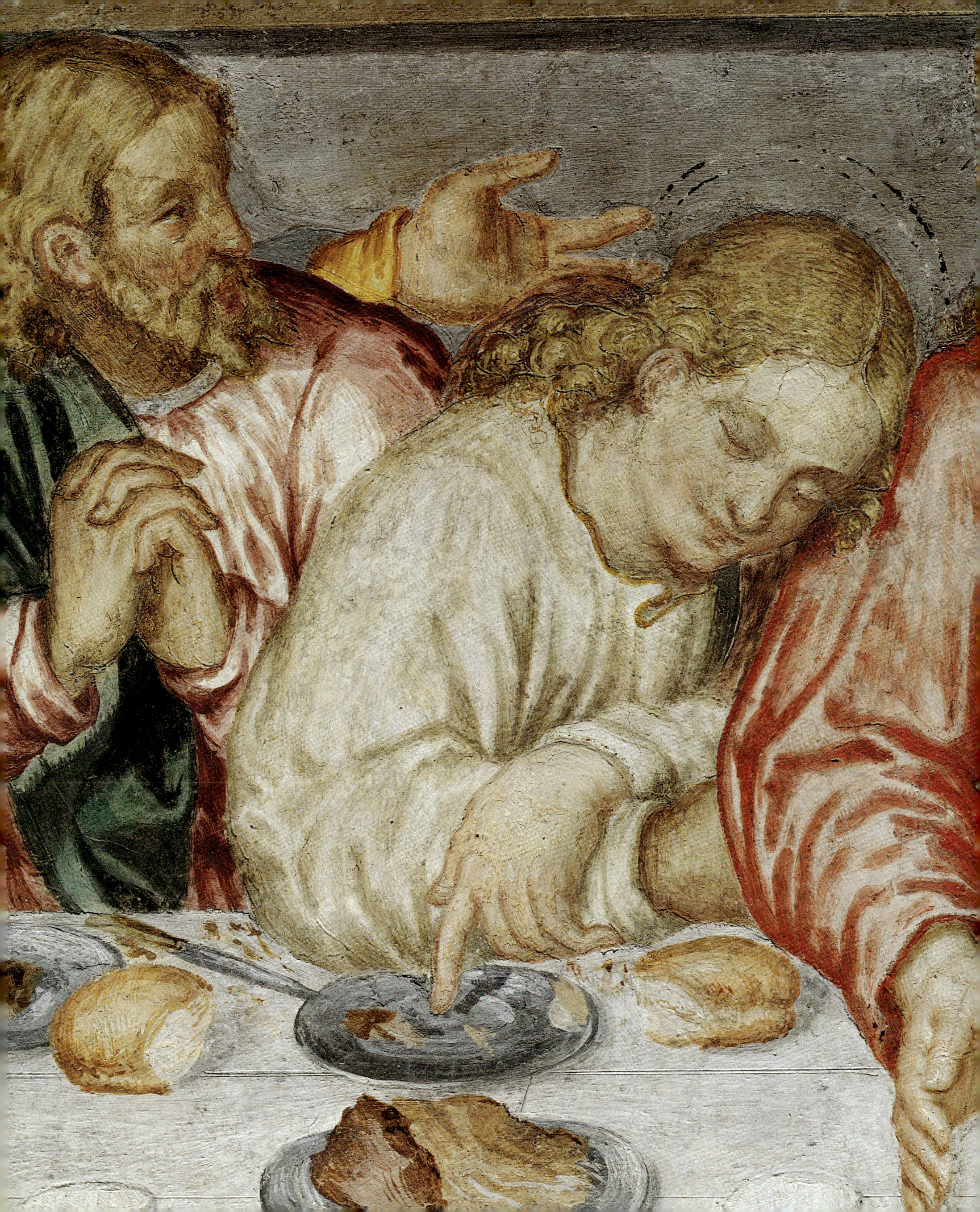

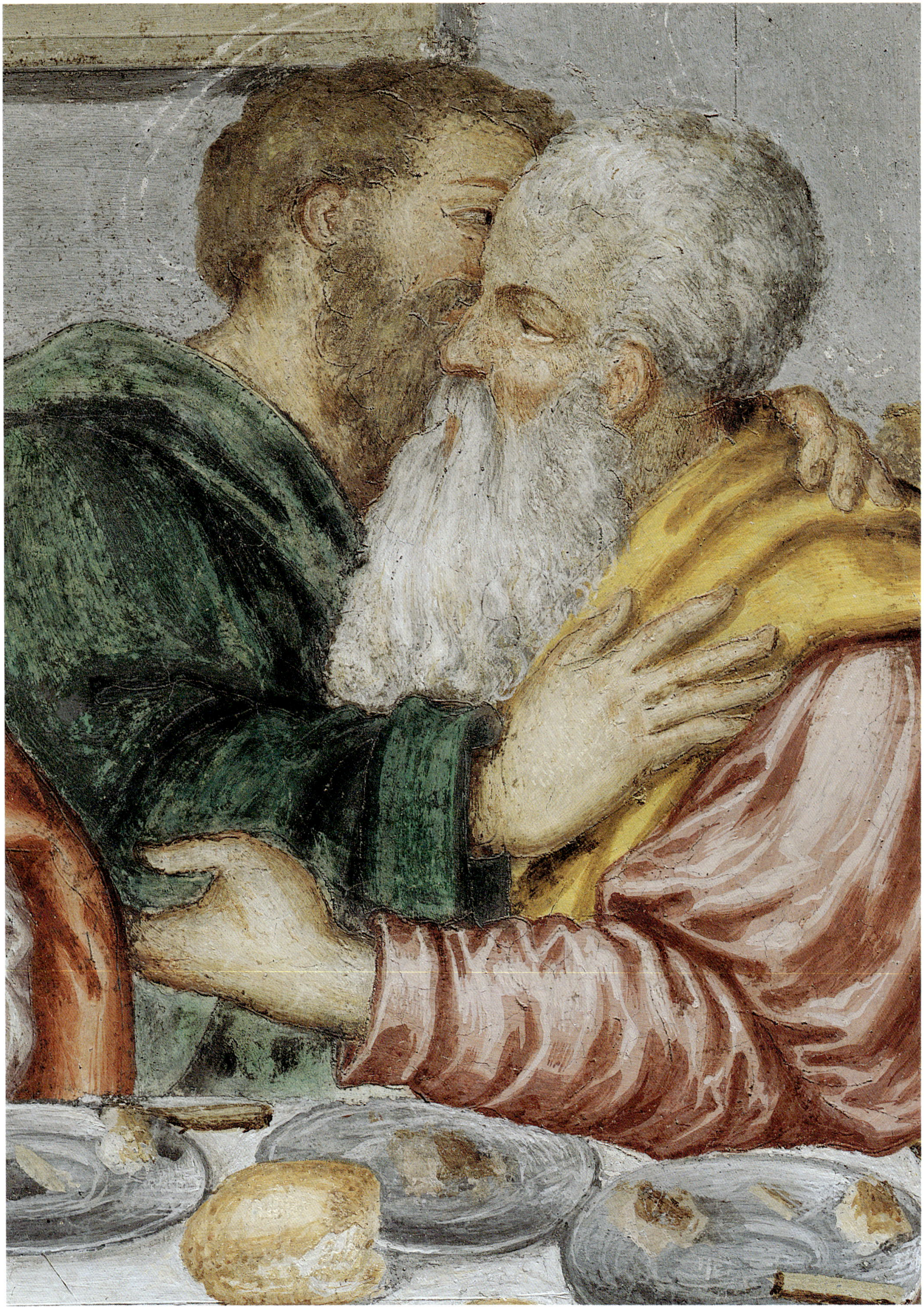

32. Giovan Pietro (and Aurelio?) Luini
Christ before Pilate
Aurelio Luini
Betrayal of Christ
Right side, end wall, convent hall

Pages 256–257
32. Giovan Pietro (and Aurelio?) Luini
Christ before Pilate, detail

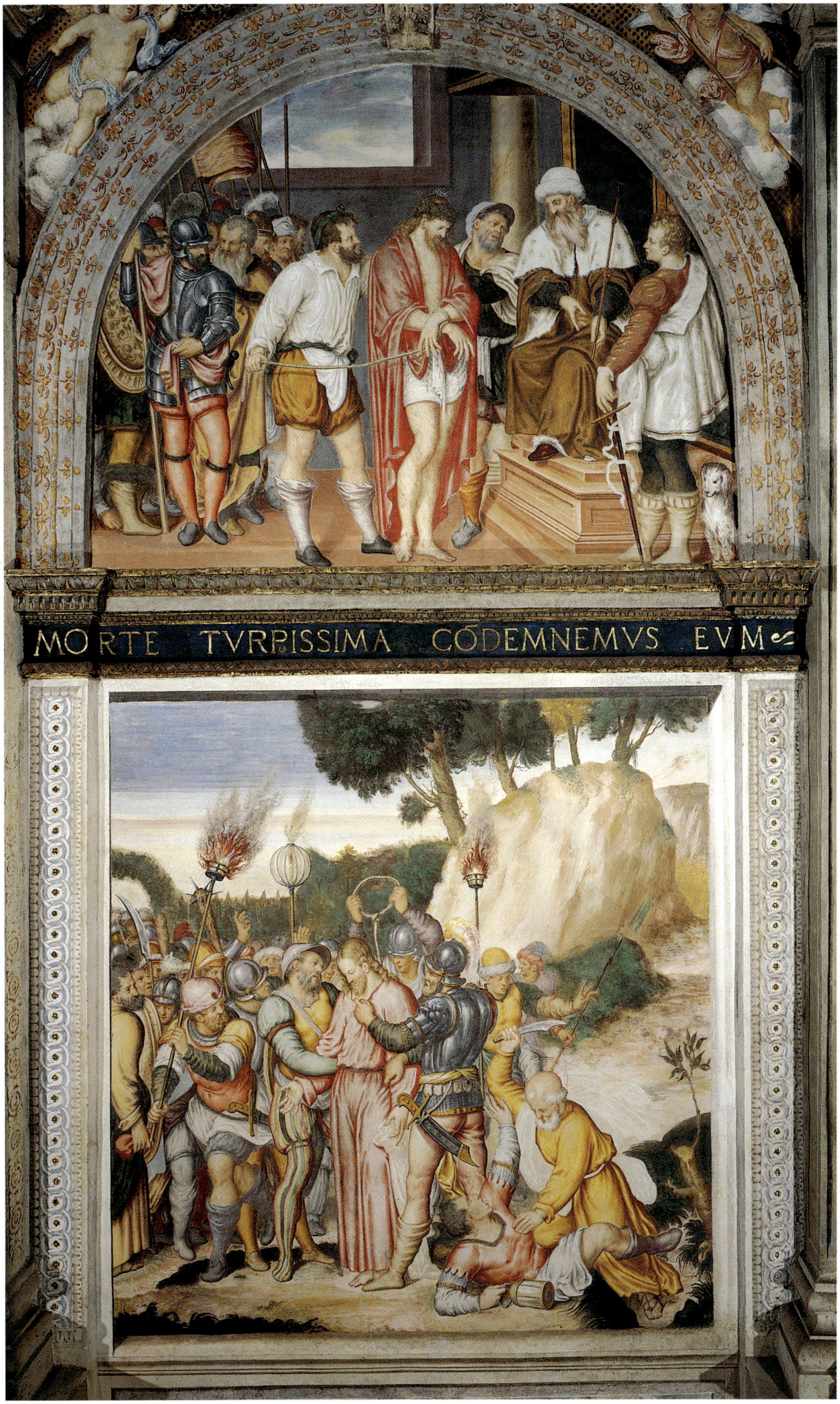

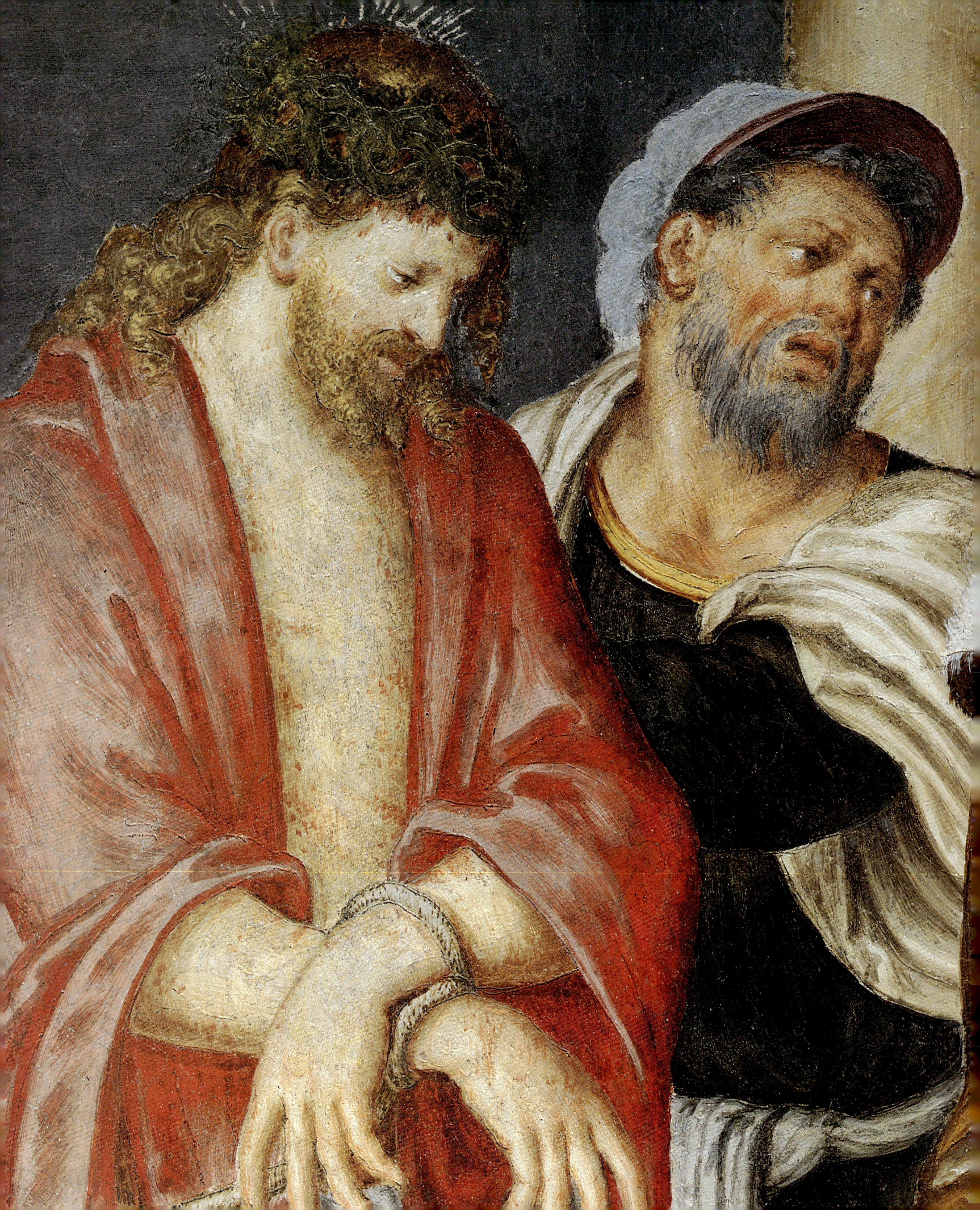

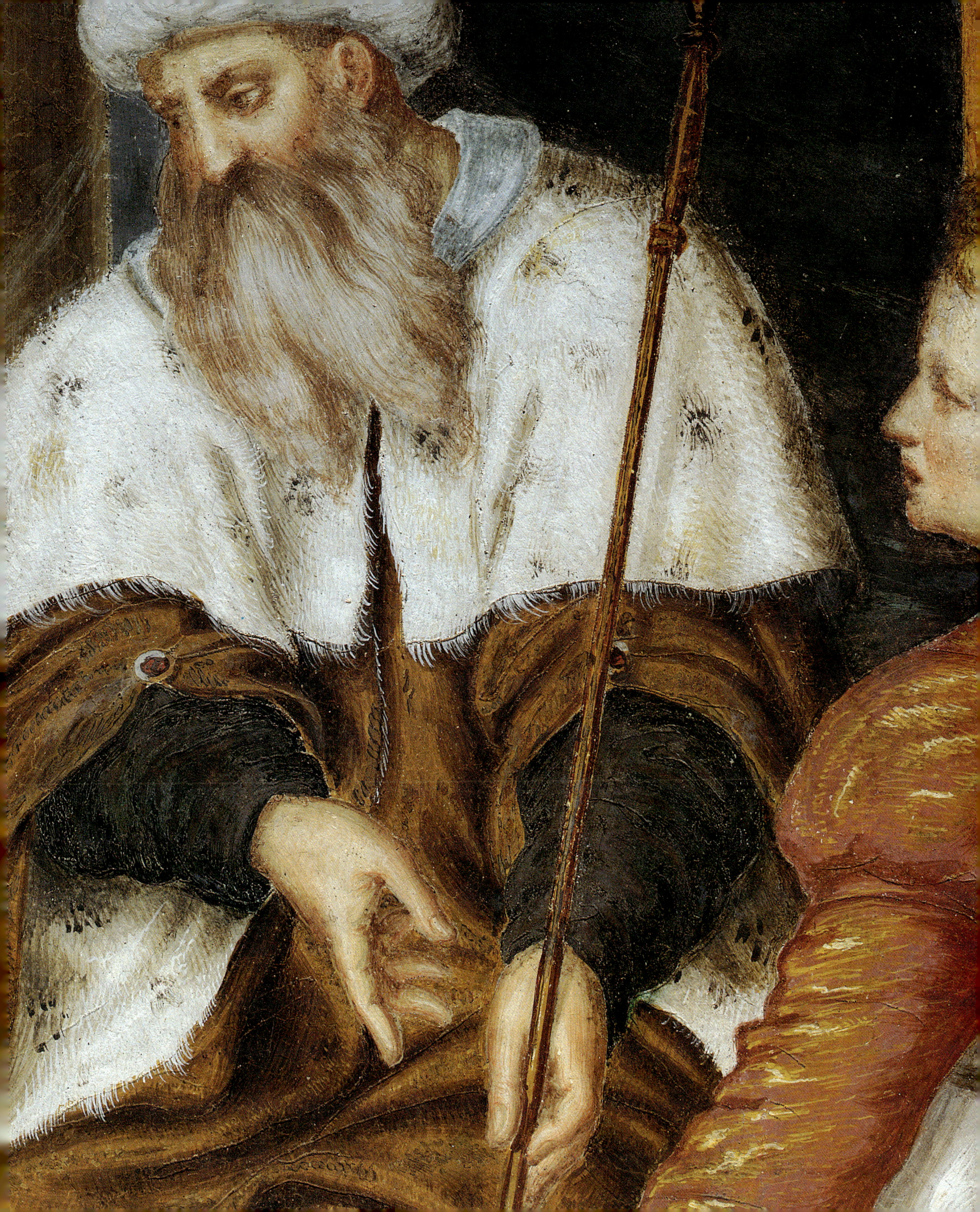

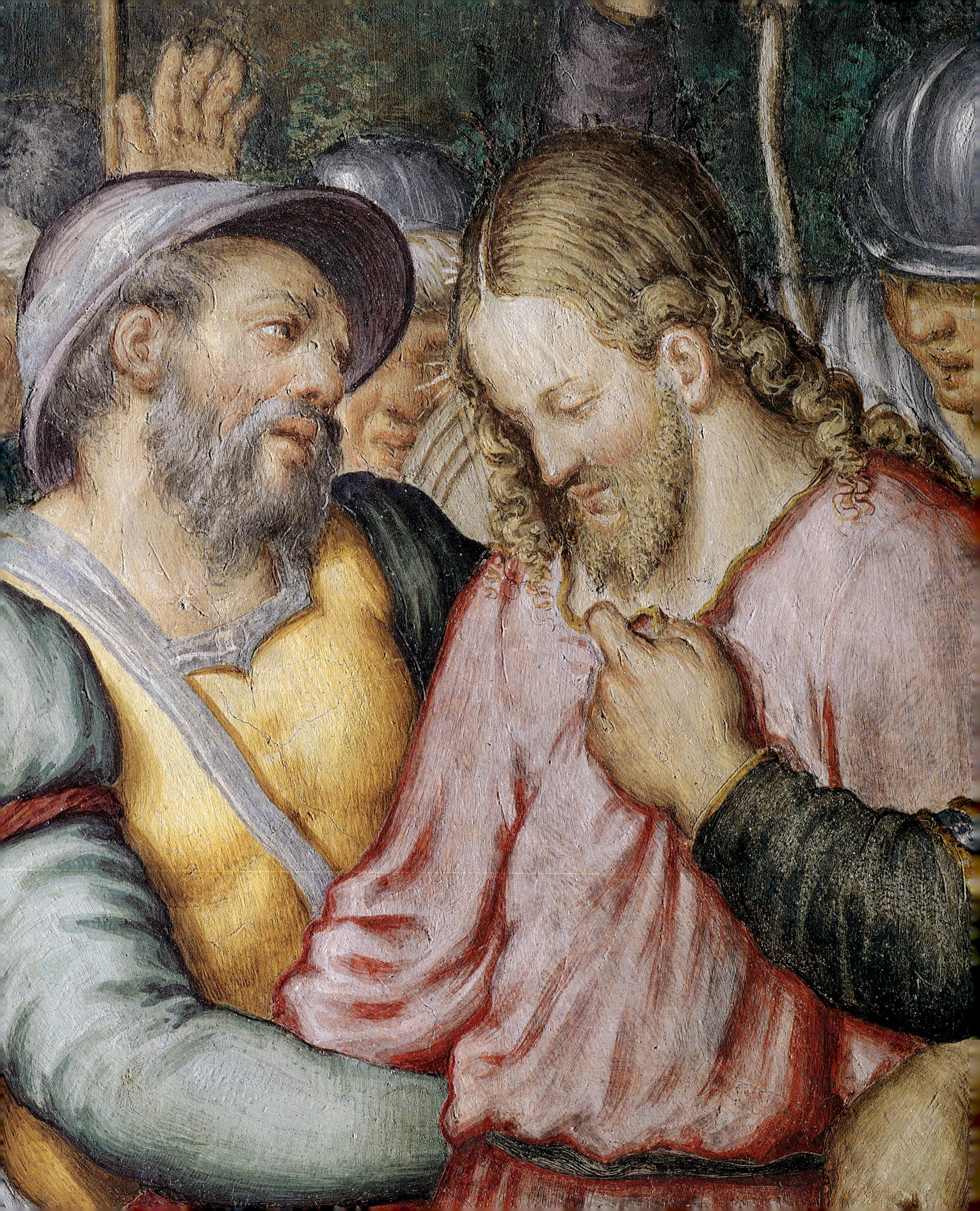

32. Aurelio Luini
Betrayal of Christ,
details

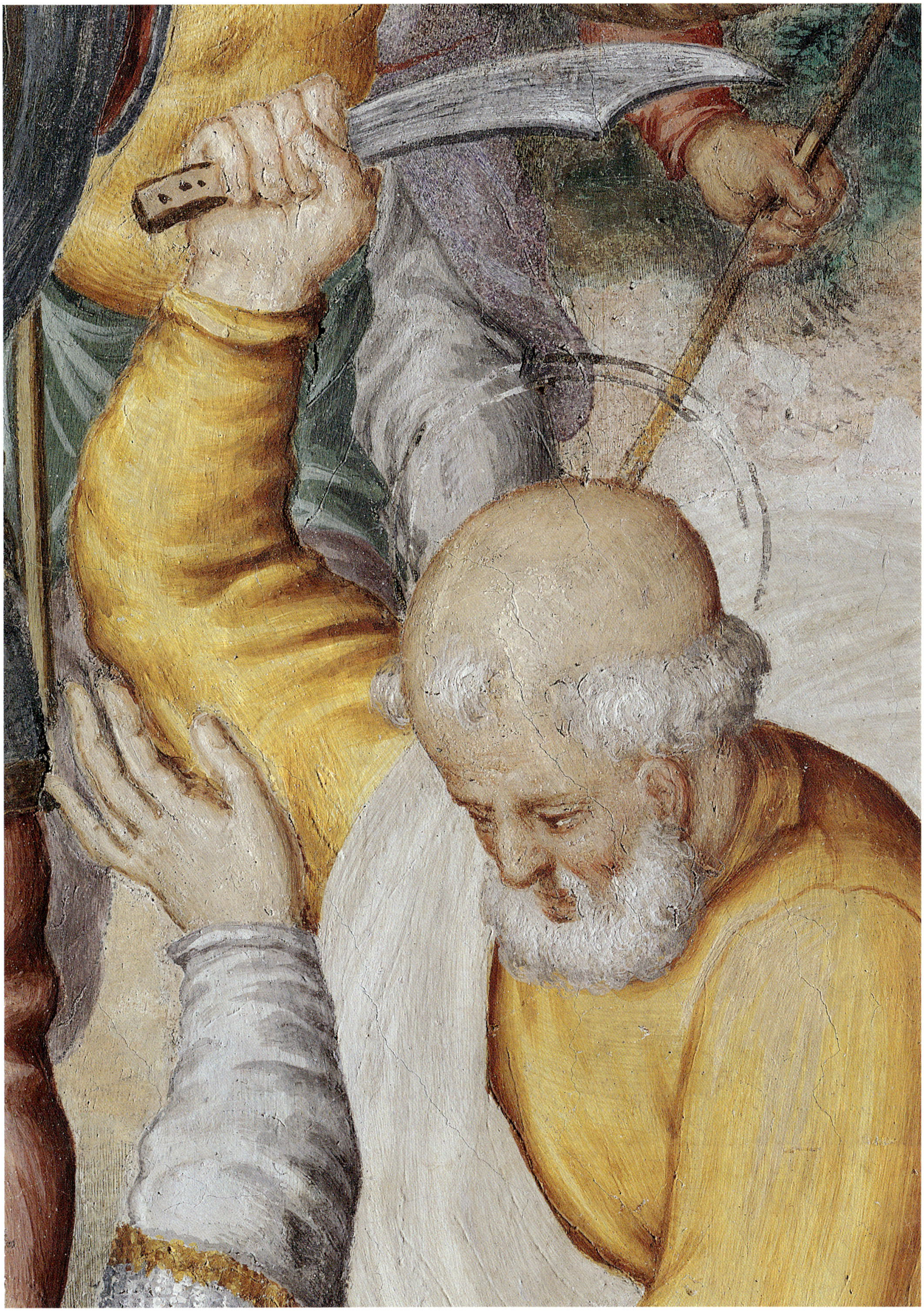

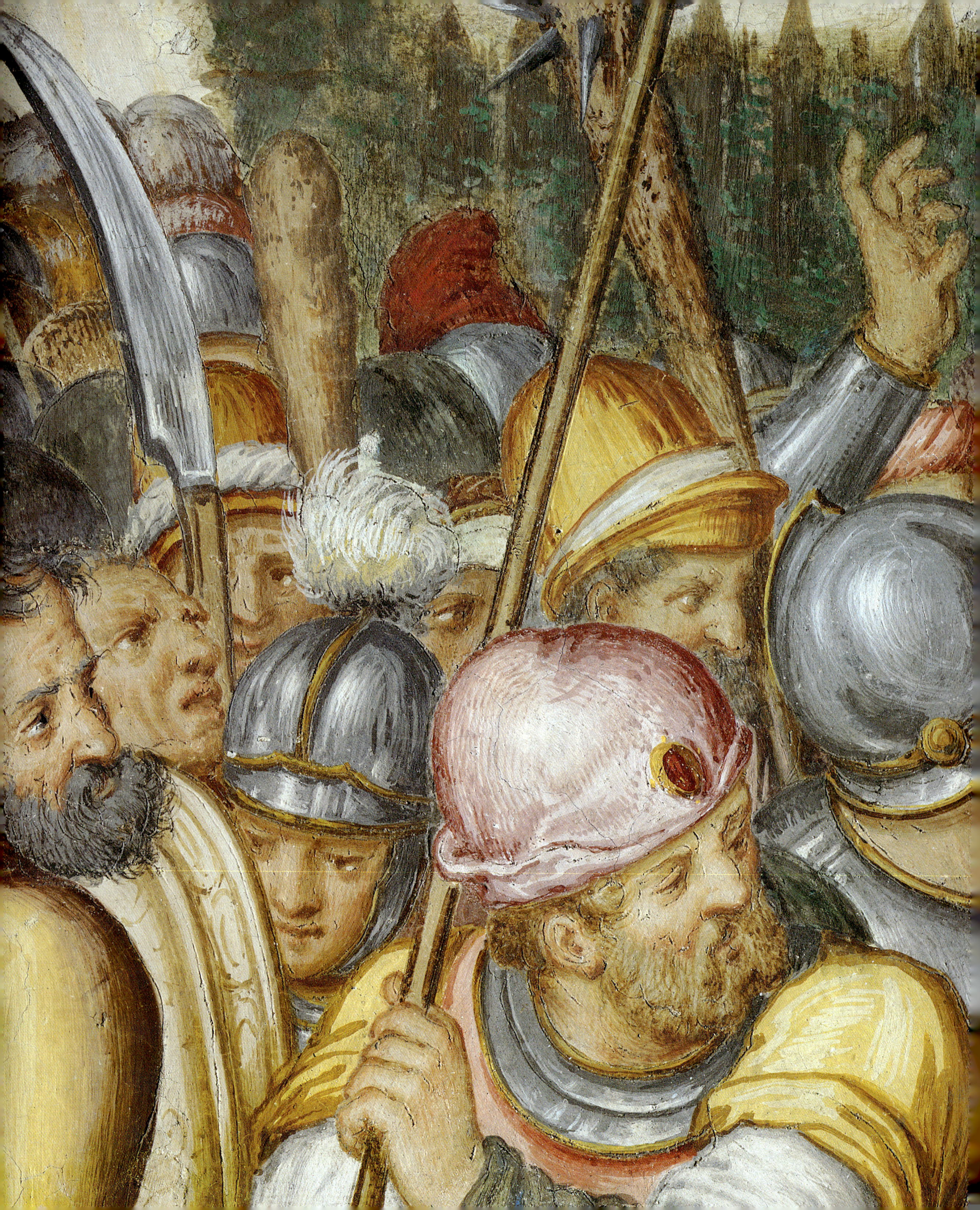

33. Aurelio Luini
Flagellation
Giovan Pietro Luini
Deposition
Left side, end wall, convent hall

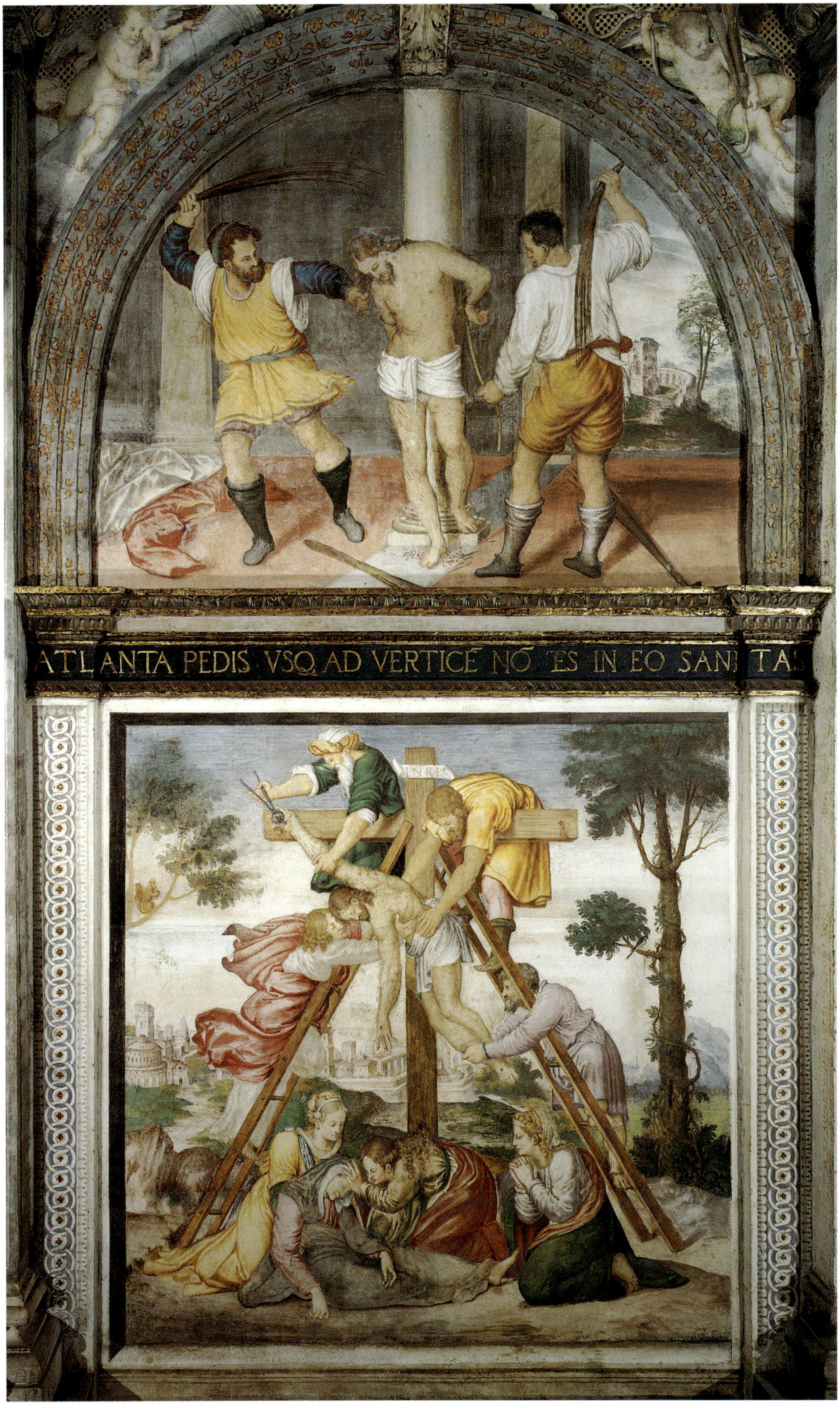

Opposite
32. Aurelio Luini
Betrayal of Christ, detail

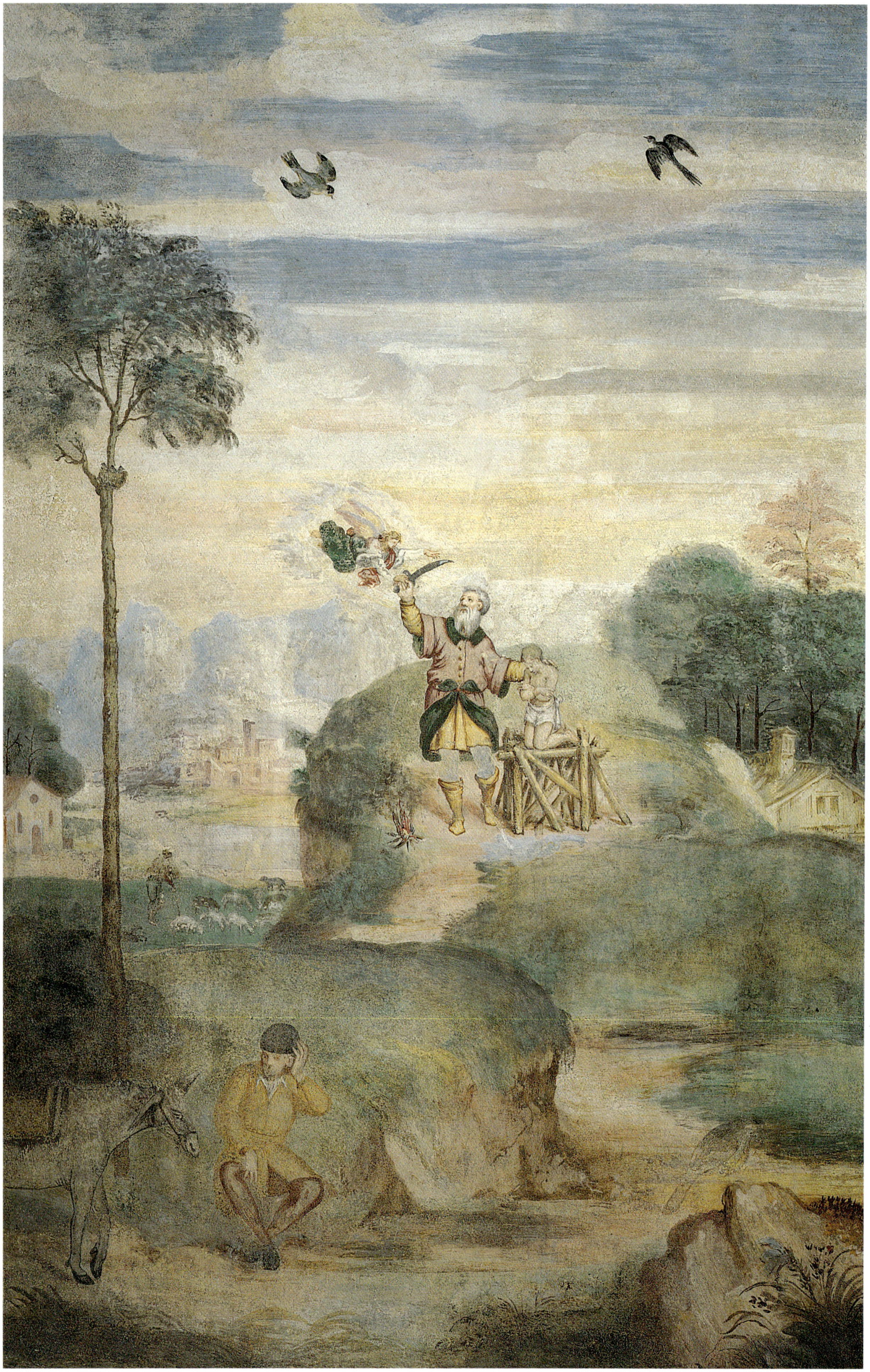

34a. Lombard artist,
end of sixteenth century
Sacrifice of Isaac
Right wall, chapel with frescoed altar,
convent hall

34b. Lombard artist,
end of sixteenth century
Fall of Man
Left wall, chapel with frescoed altar,
convent hall

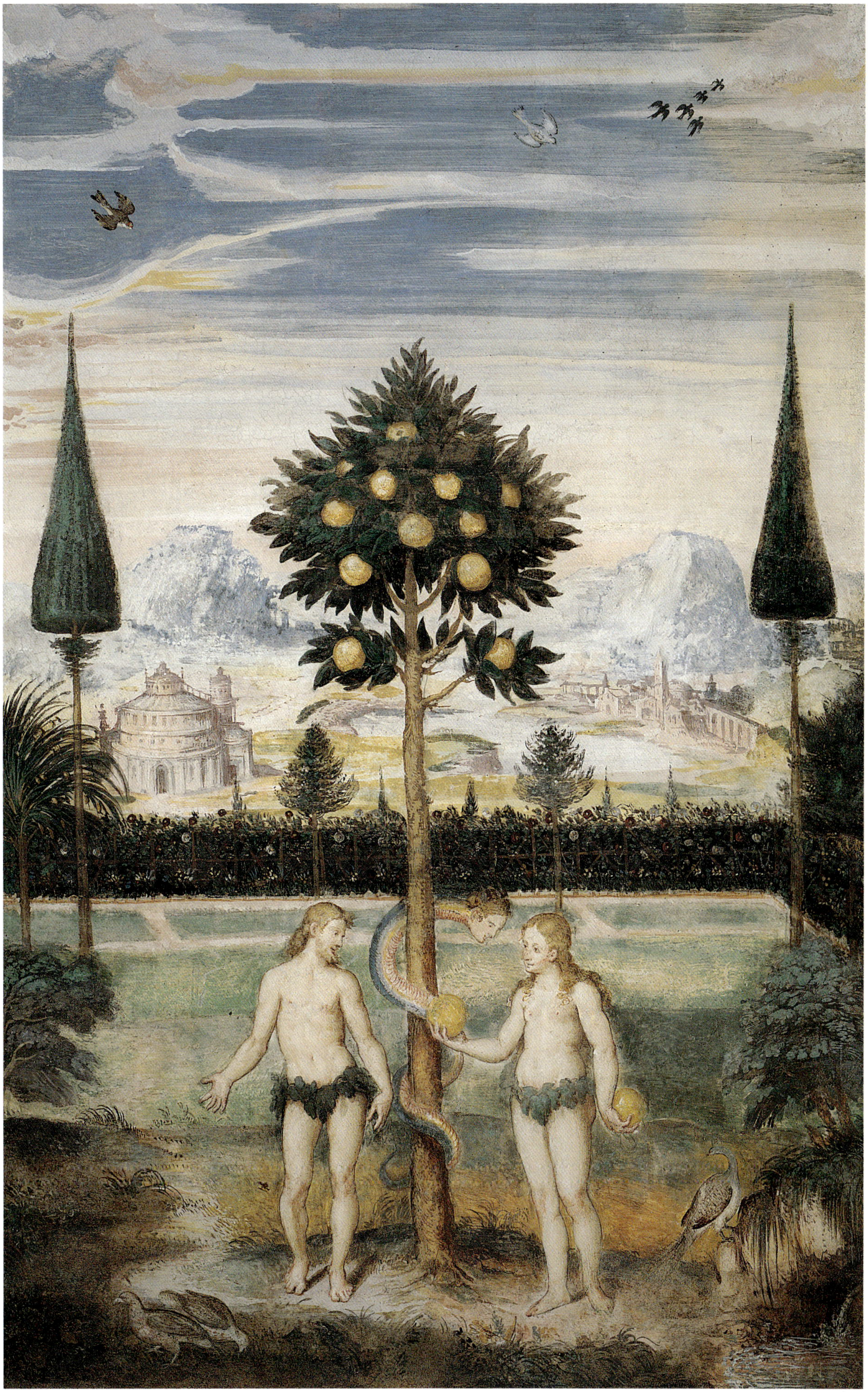

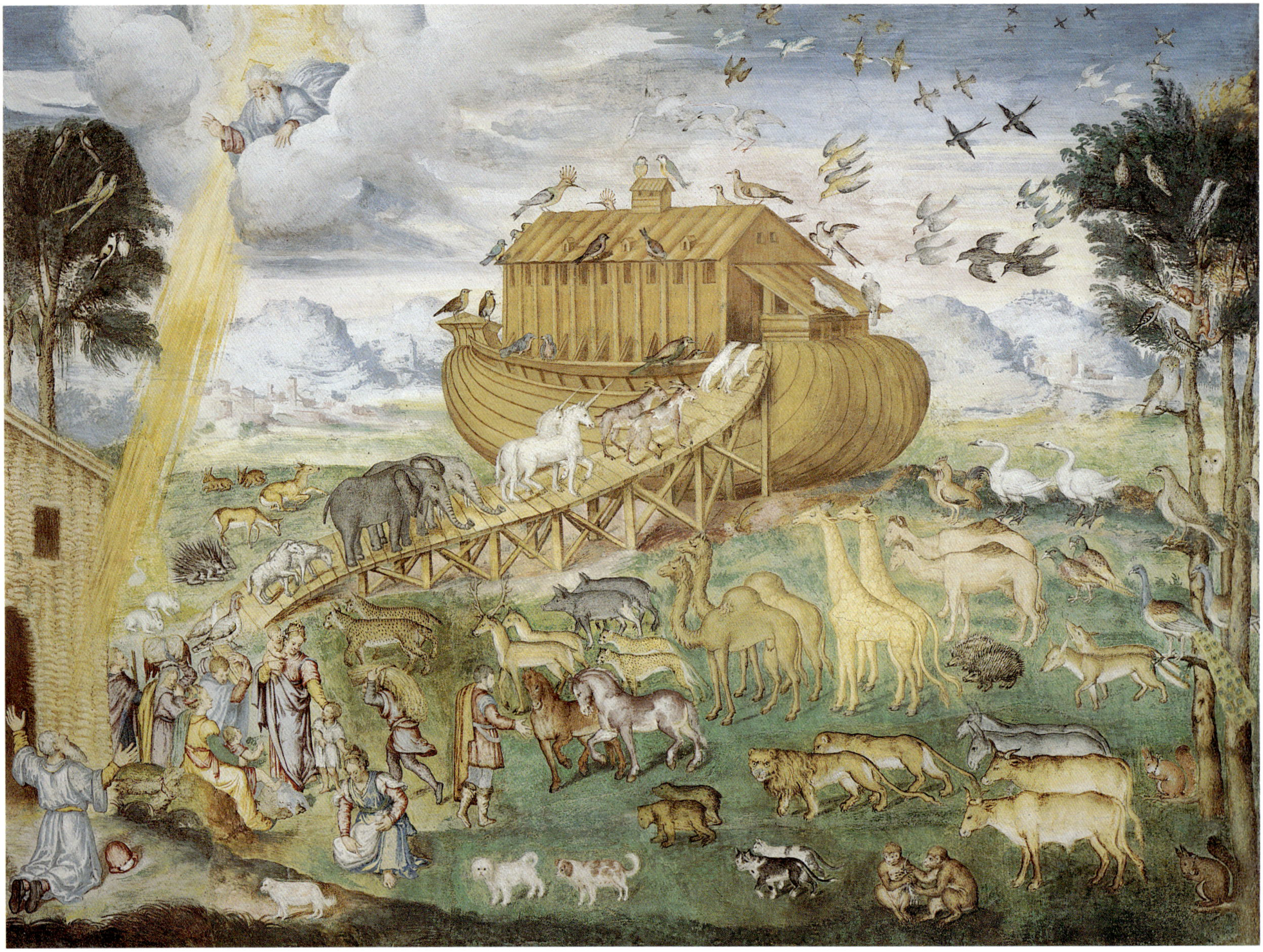

35a. Aurelio Luini
Arrival of the Animals in the Ark
Central wall, Cappella dell'Arca di Noè, convent hall

Pages 265–267
35a. Aurelio Luini
Arrival of the Animals in the Ark, details

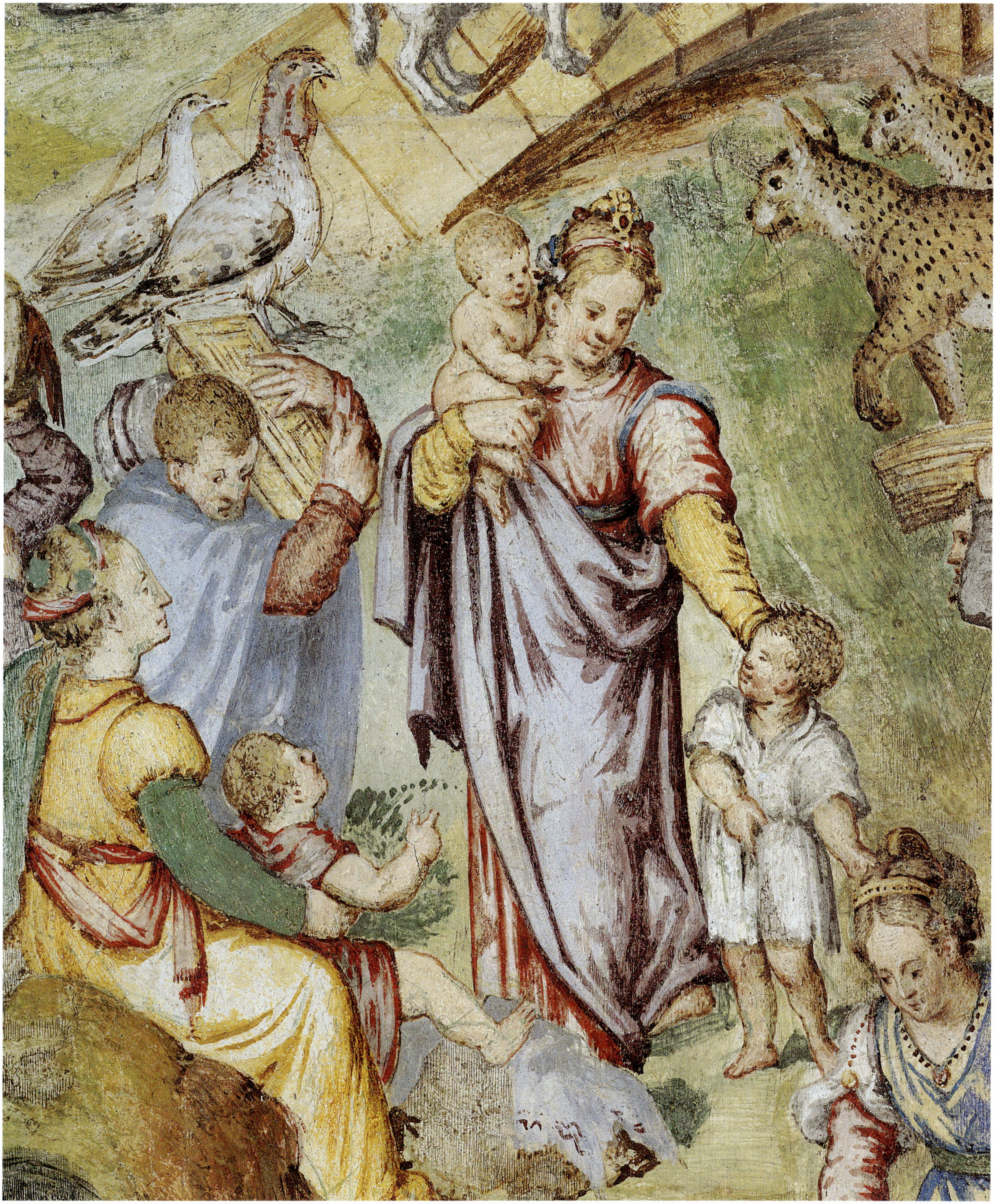

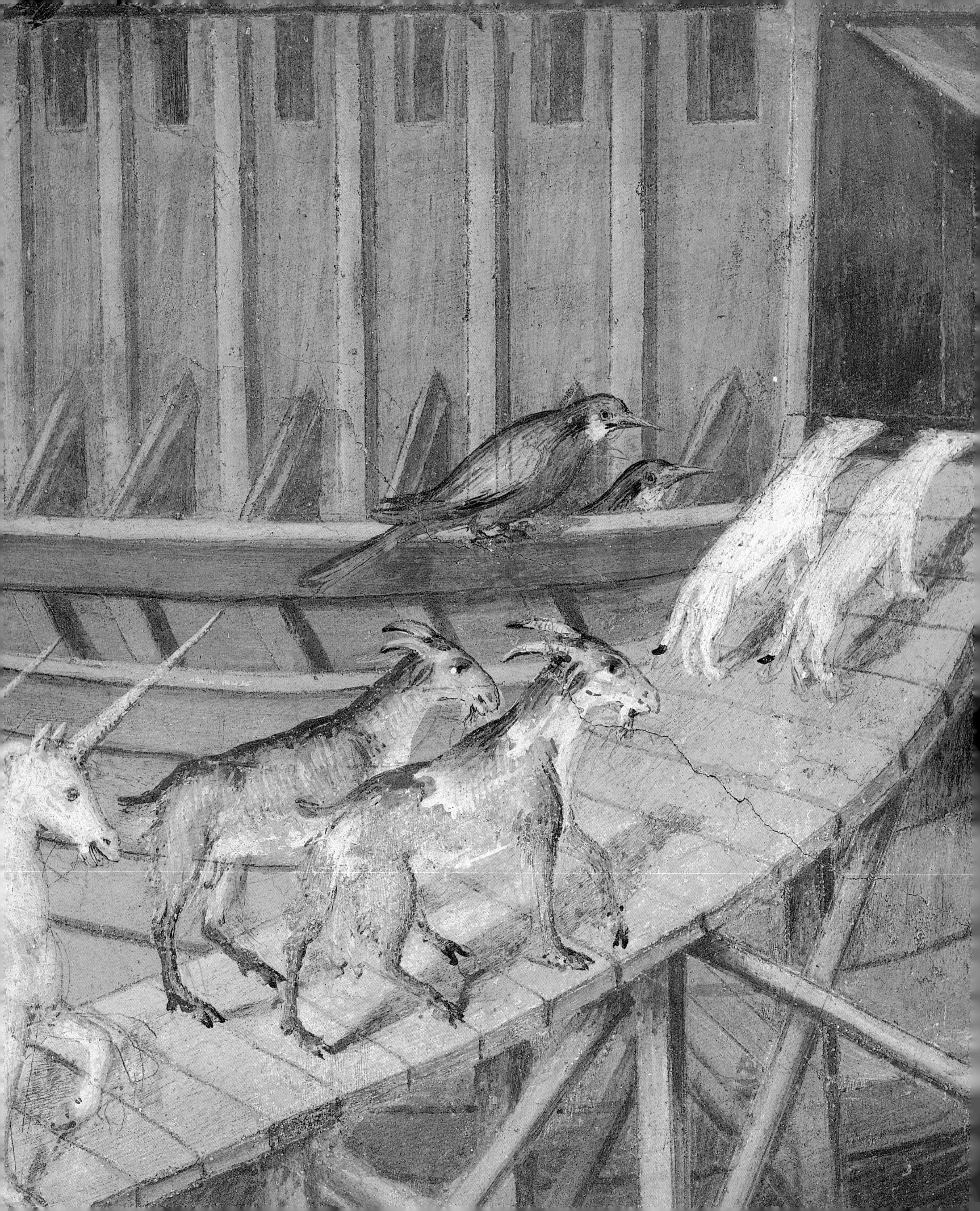

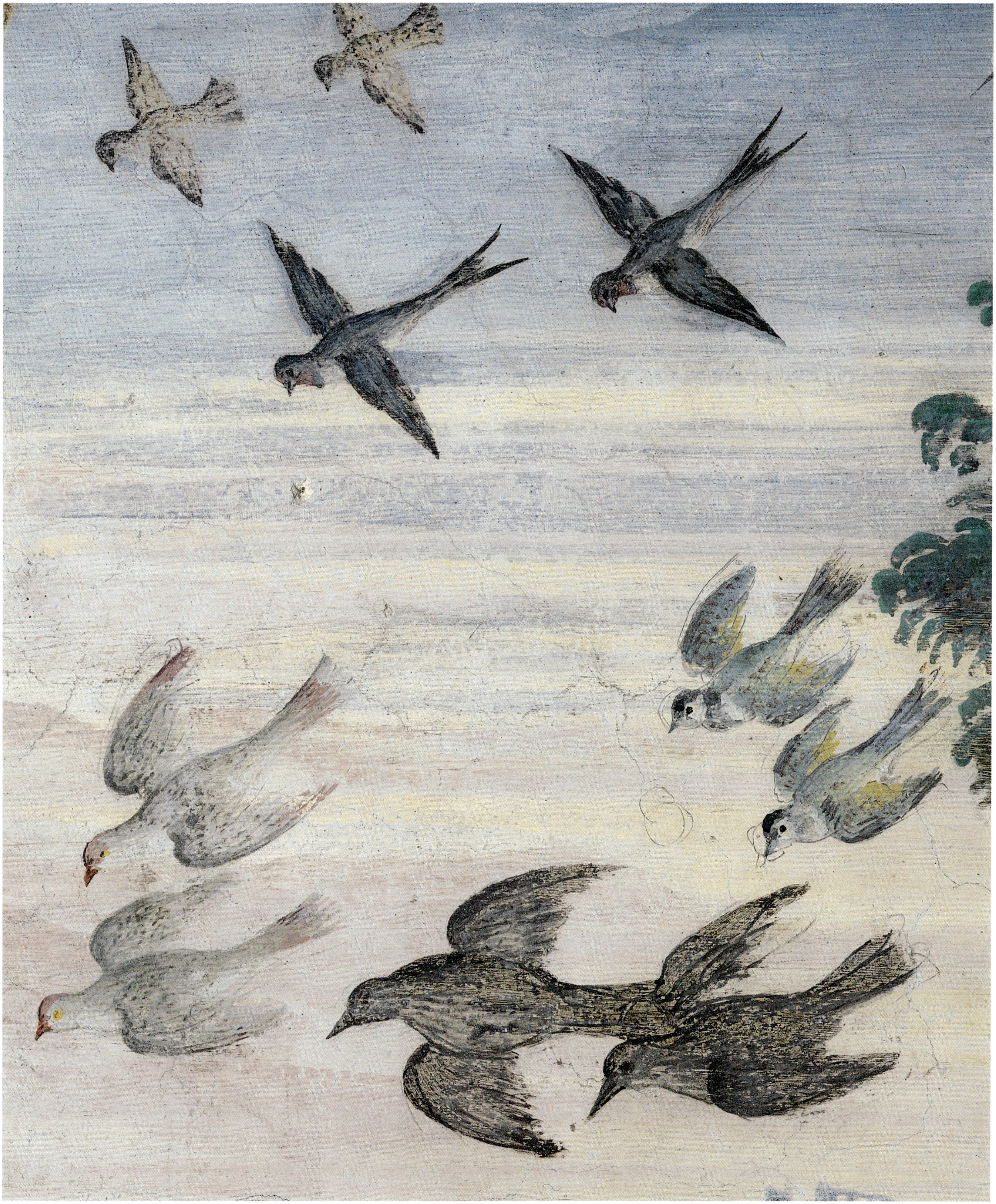

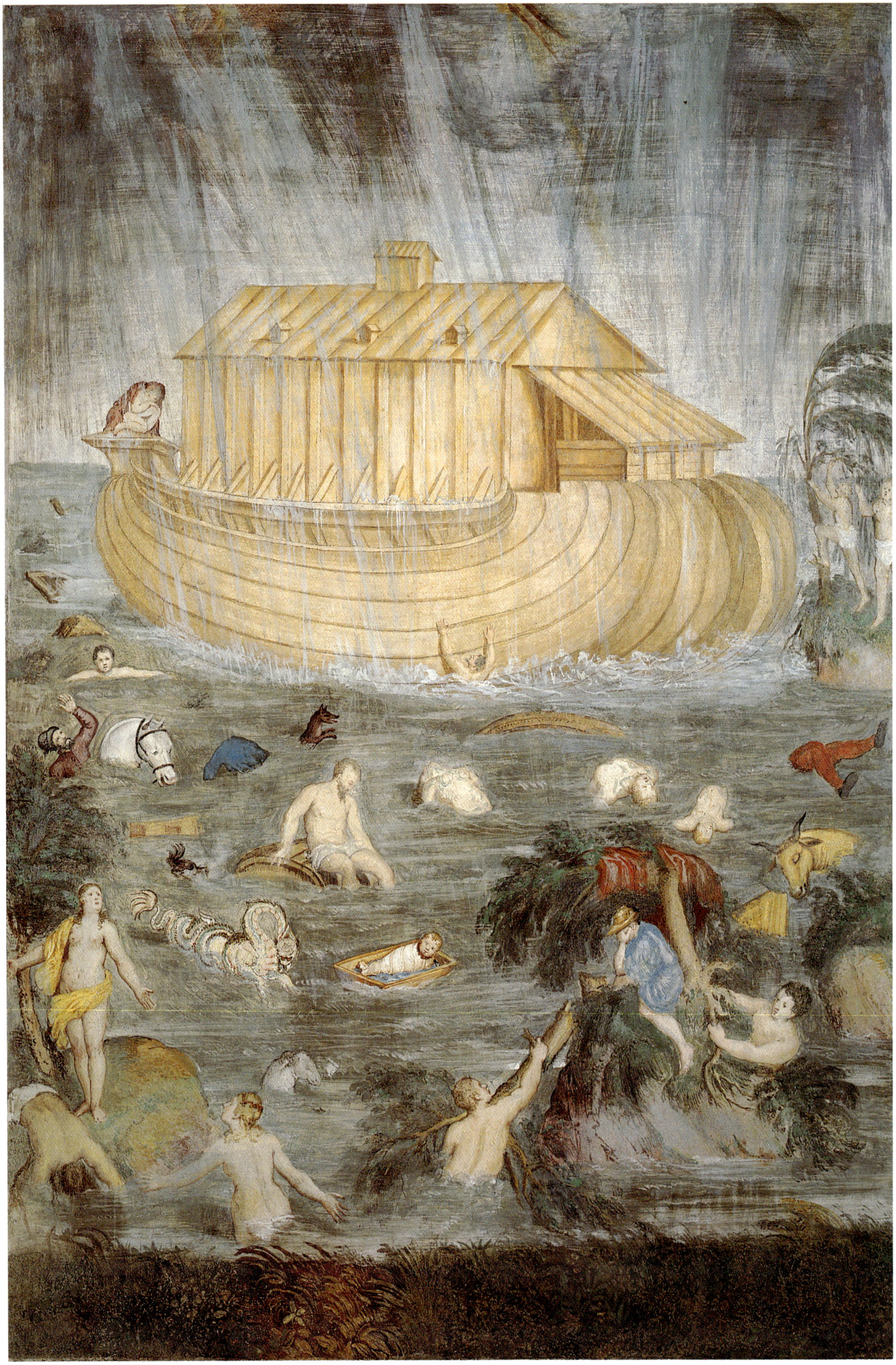

35b. Aurelio Luini
The Flood
Right wall, Cappella dell'Arca di Noè, convent hall

Following pages
35b. Aurelio Luini
The Flood, details

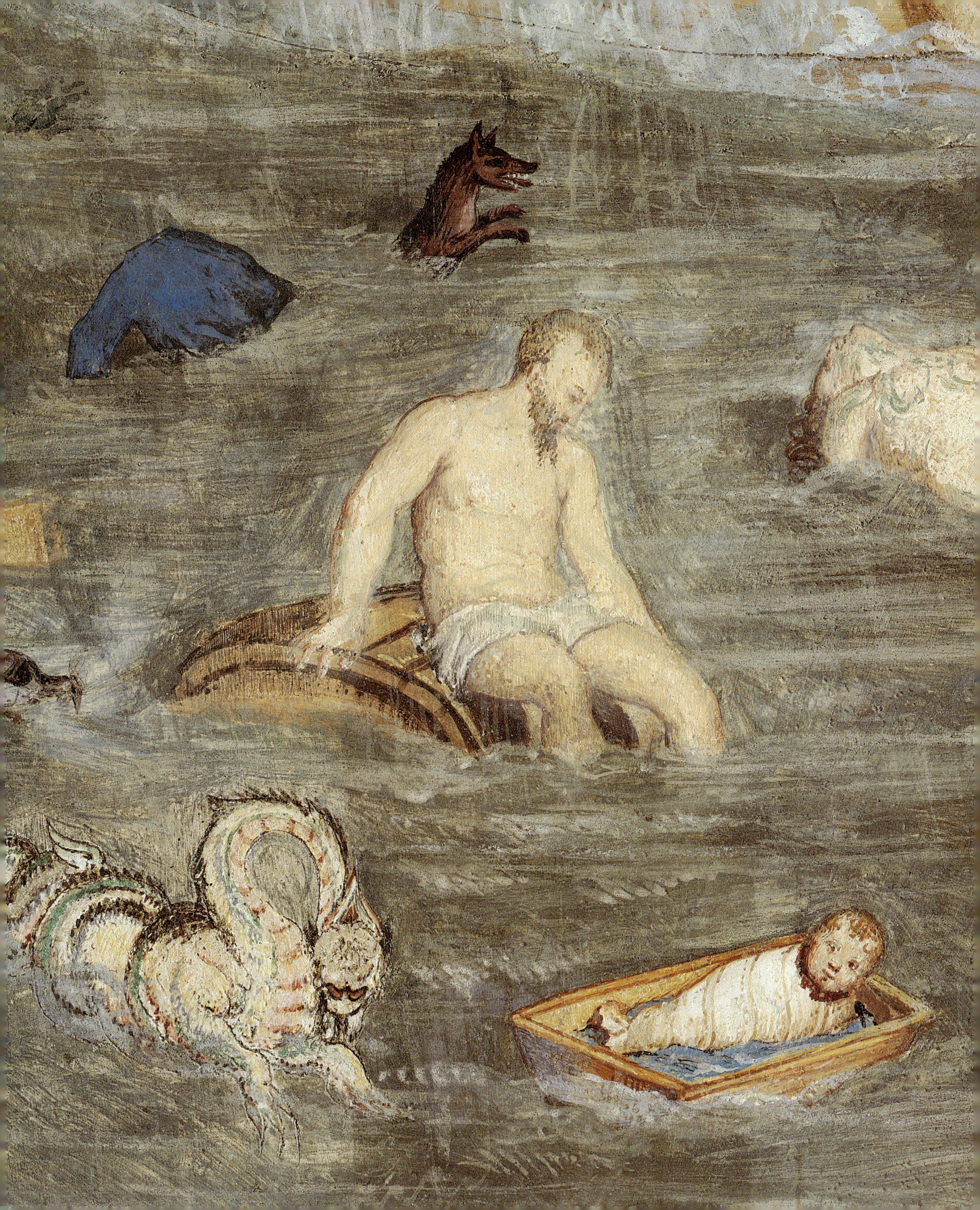

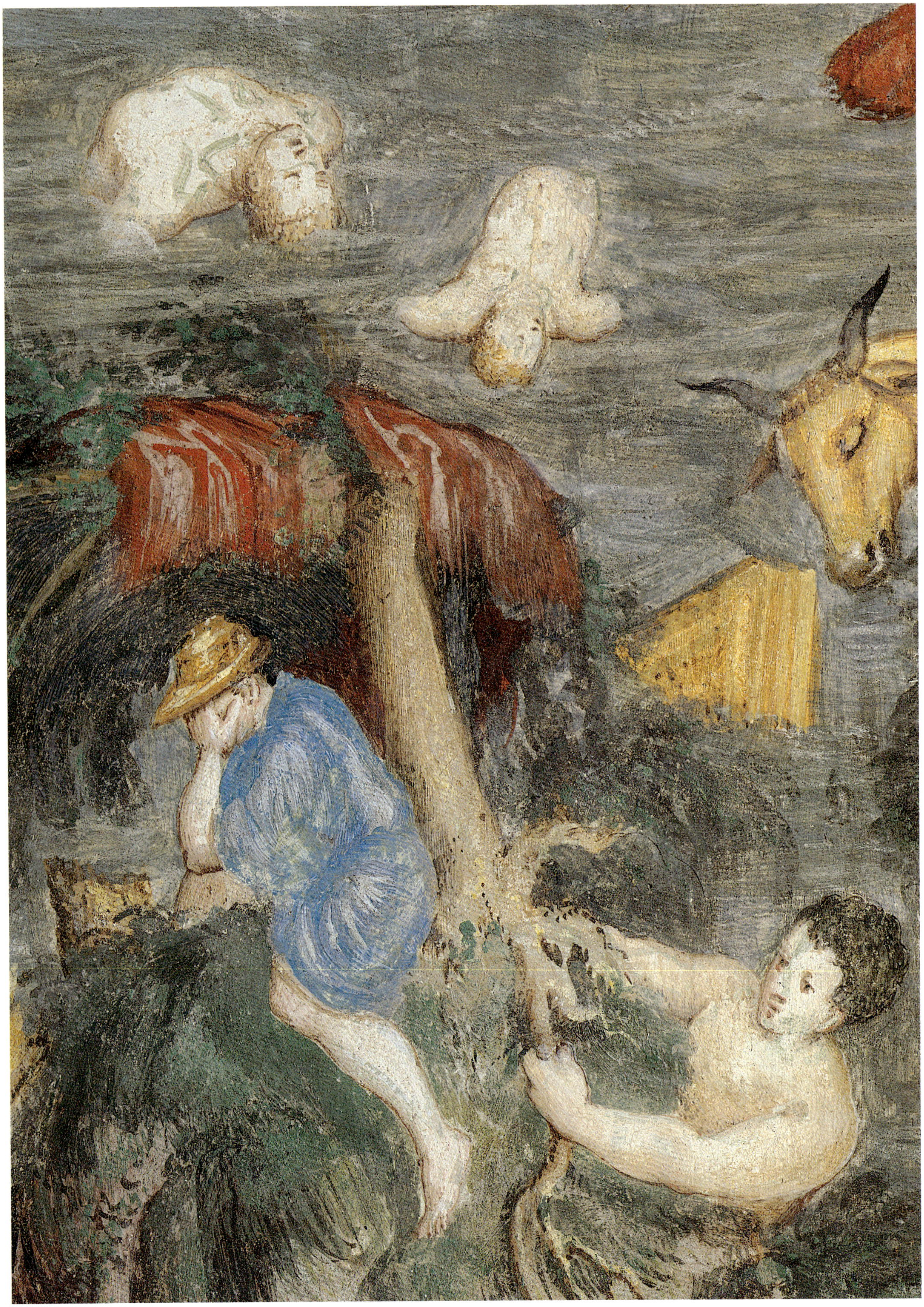

35c. Aurelio Luini
End of the Flood and the Drunkenness of Noah
Left wall, Cappella dell'Arca di Noè, convent hall

Following pages
35c. Aurelio Luini
End of the Flood and the Drunkenness of Noah, details

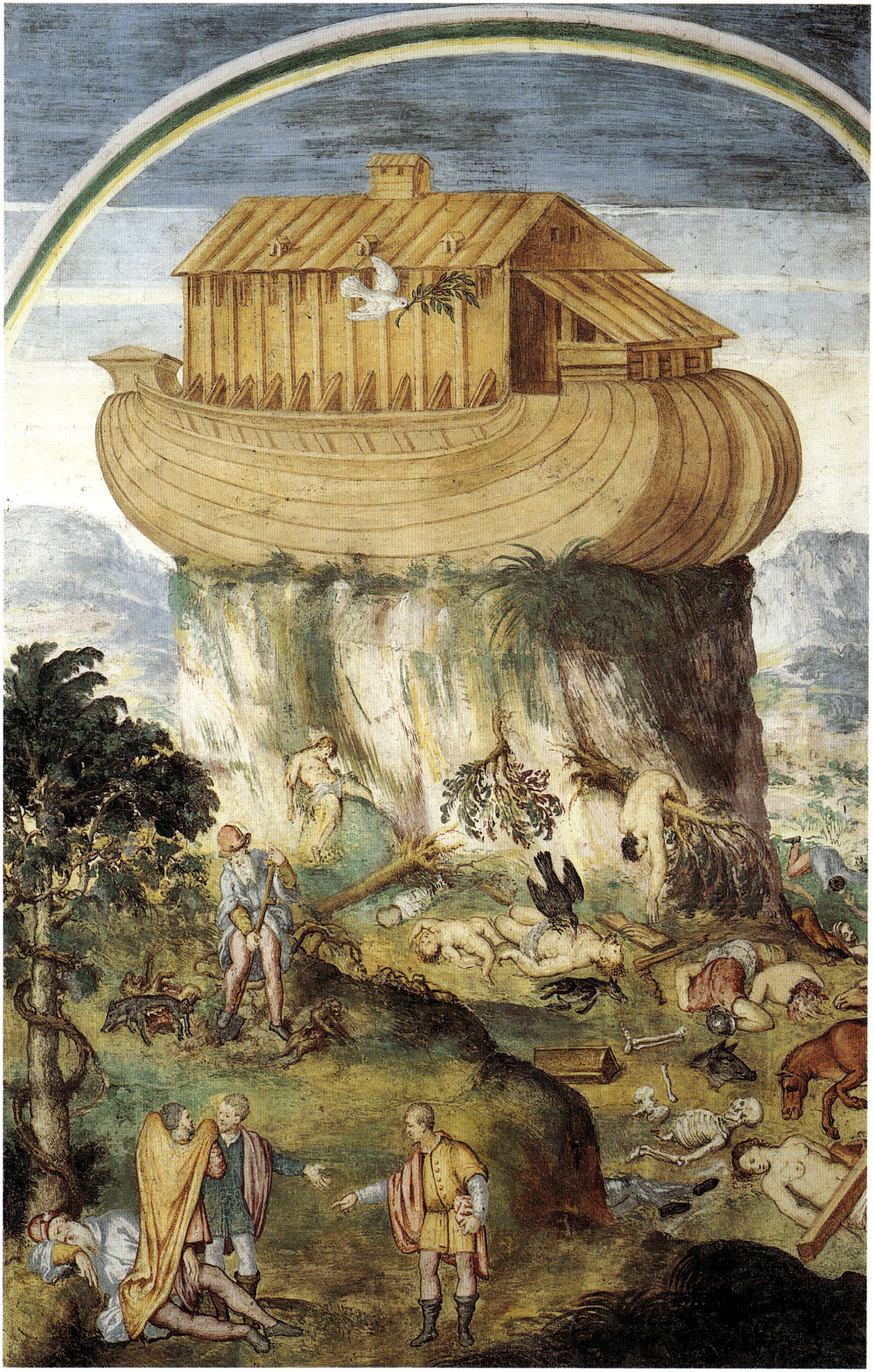

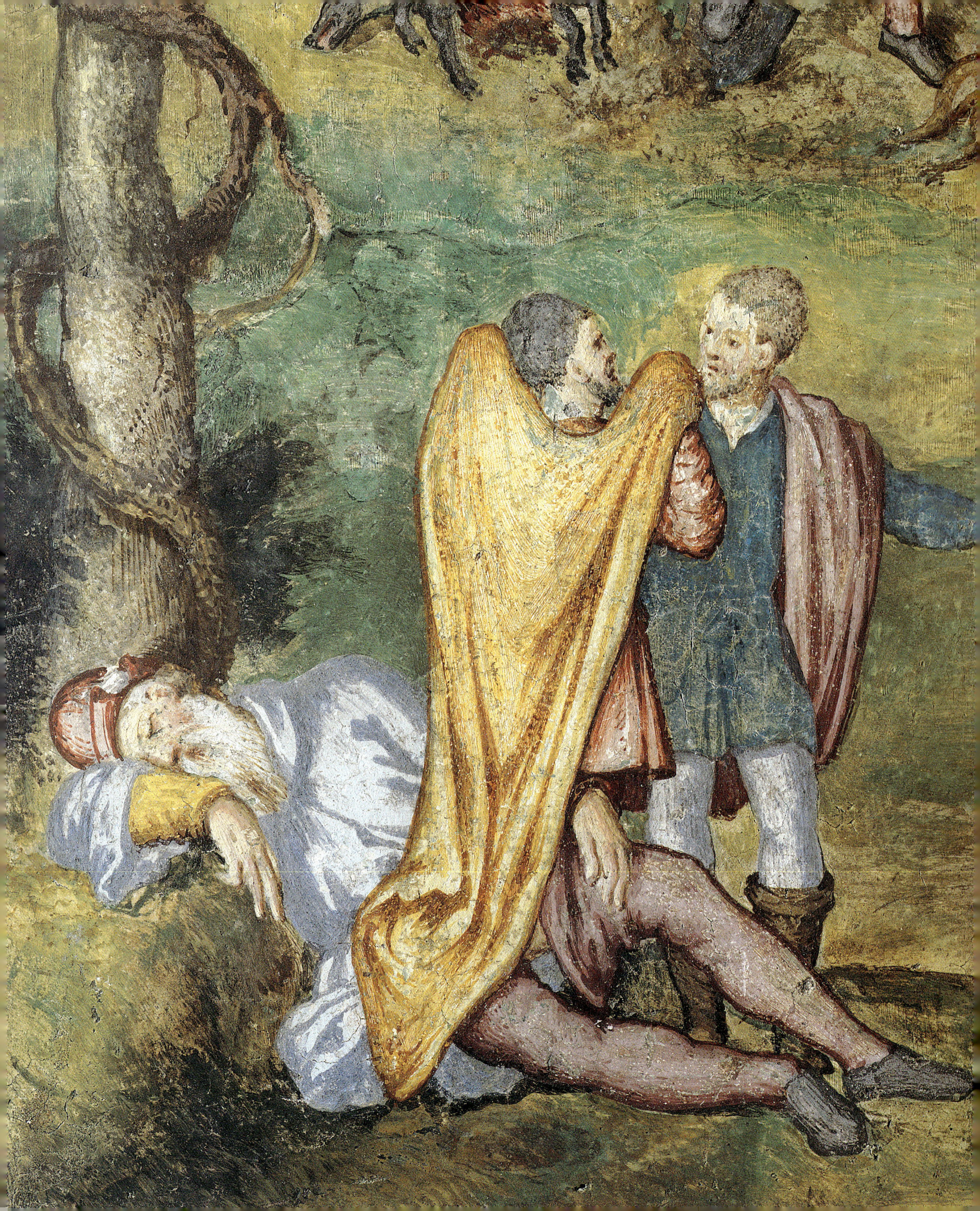

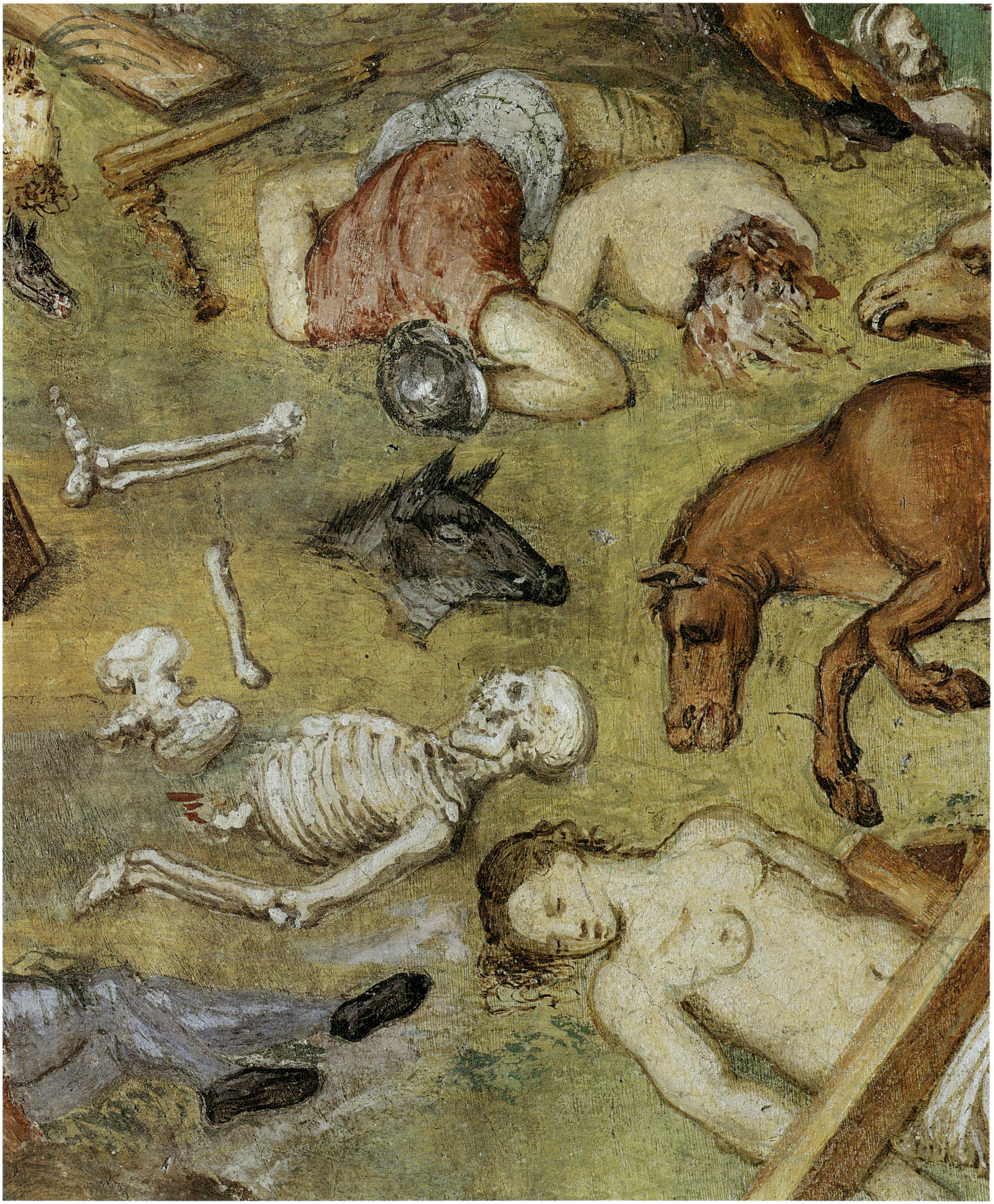

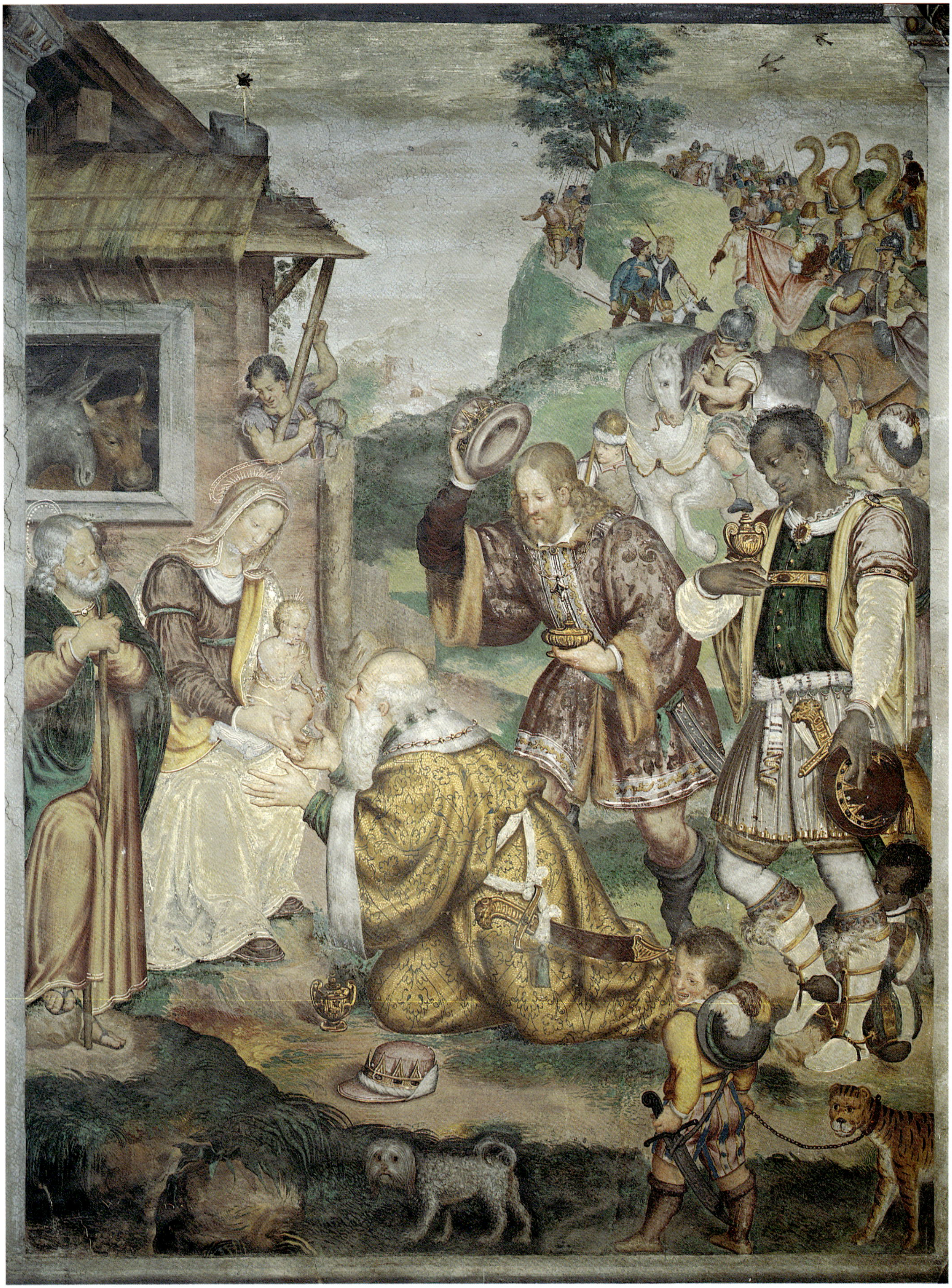

36. Aurelio and Giovan Pietro Luini
Adoration of the Magi
Partition wall, above the bridge, convent hall

Following pages
36. Aurelio and Giovan Pietro Luini
Adoration of the Magi, details

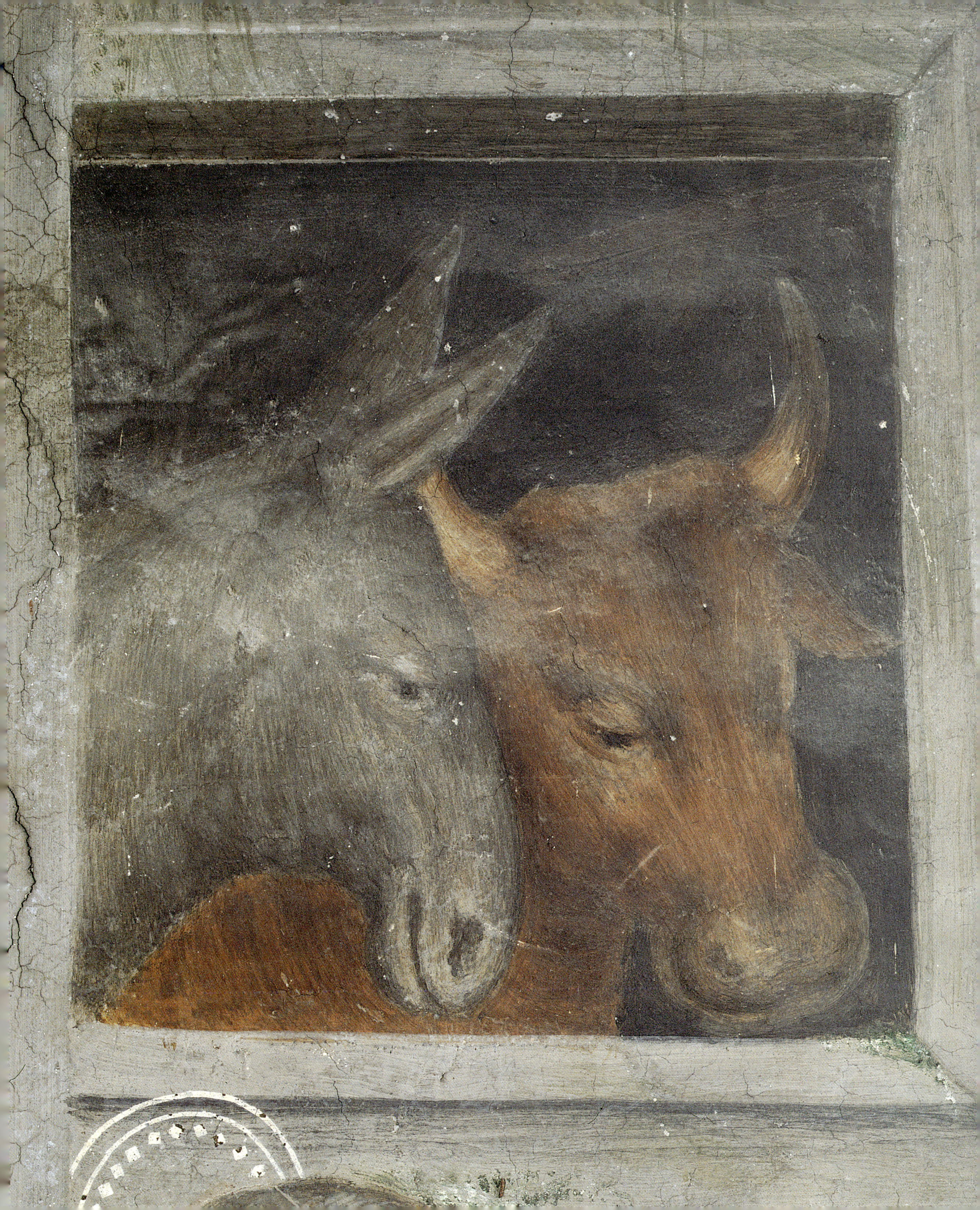

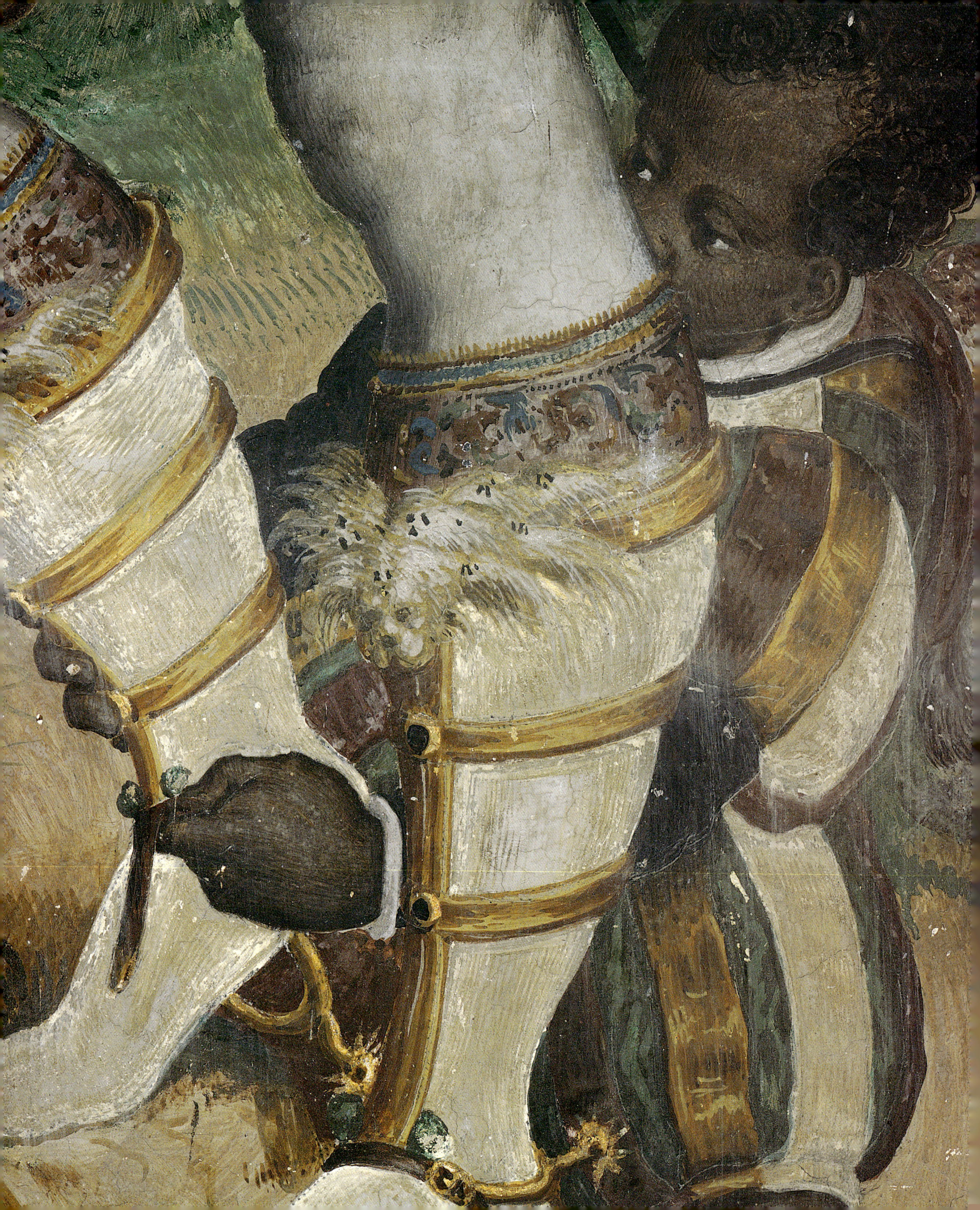

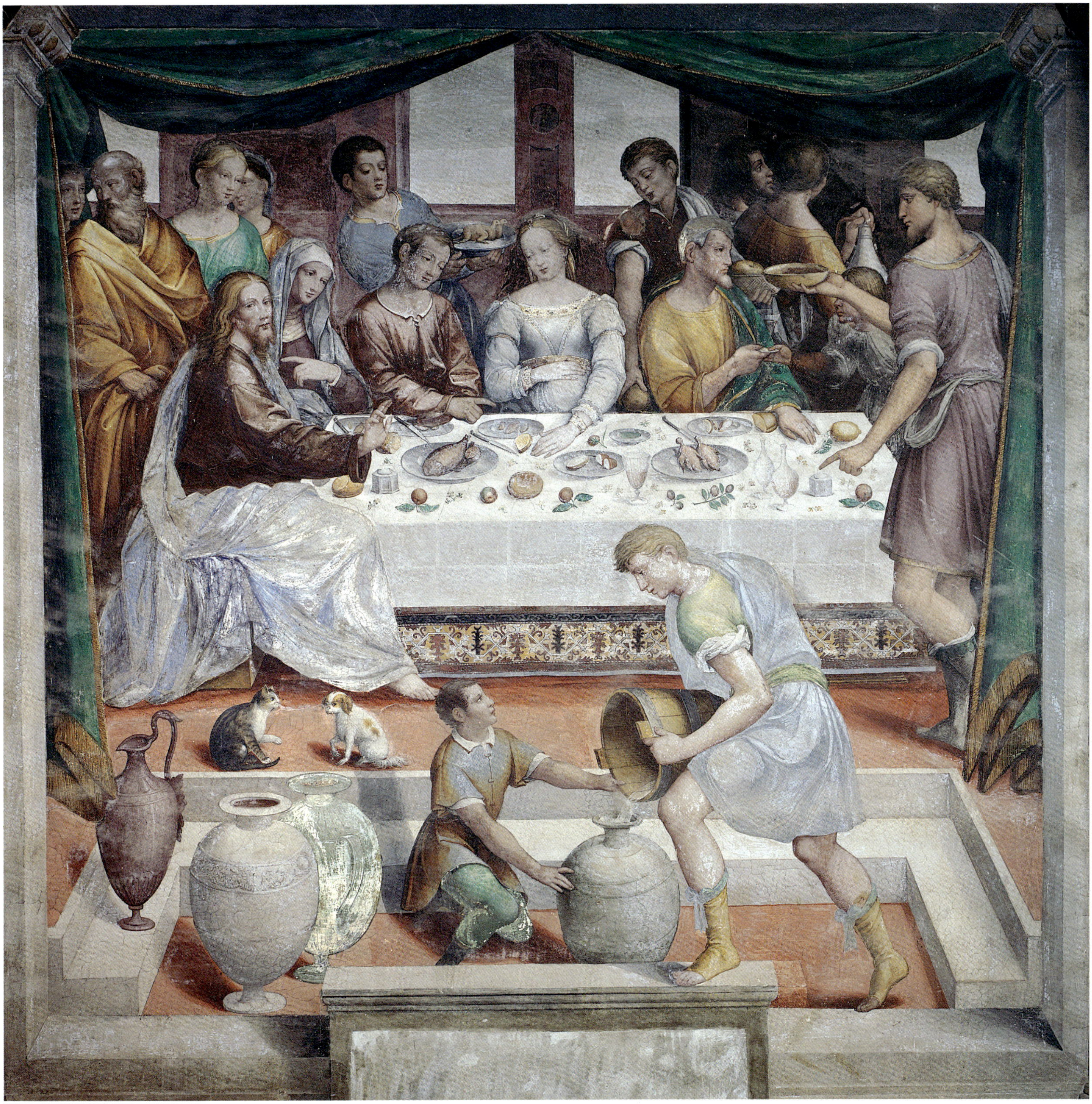

37. Fulvio Piazza
Marriage at Cana
Partition wall, above the bridge, convent hall

Pages 278–281
37. Fulvio Piazza
Marriage at Cana, details

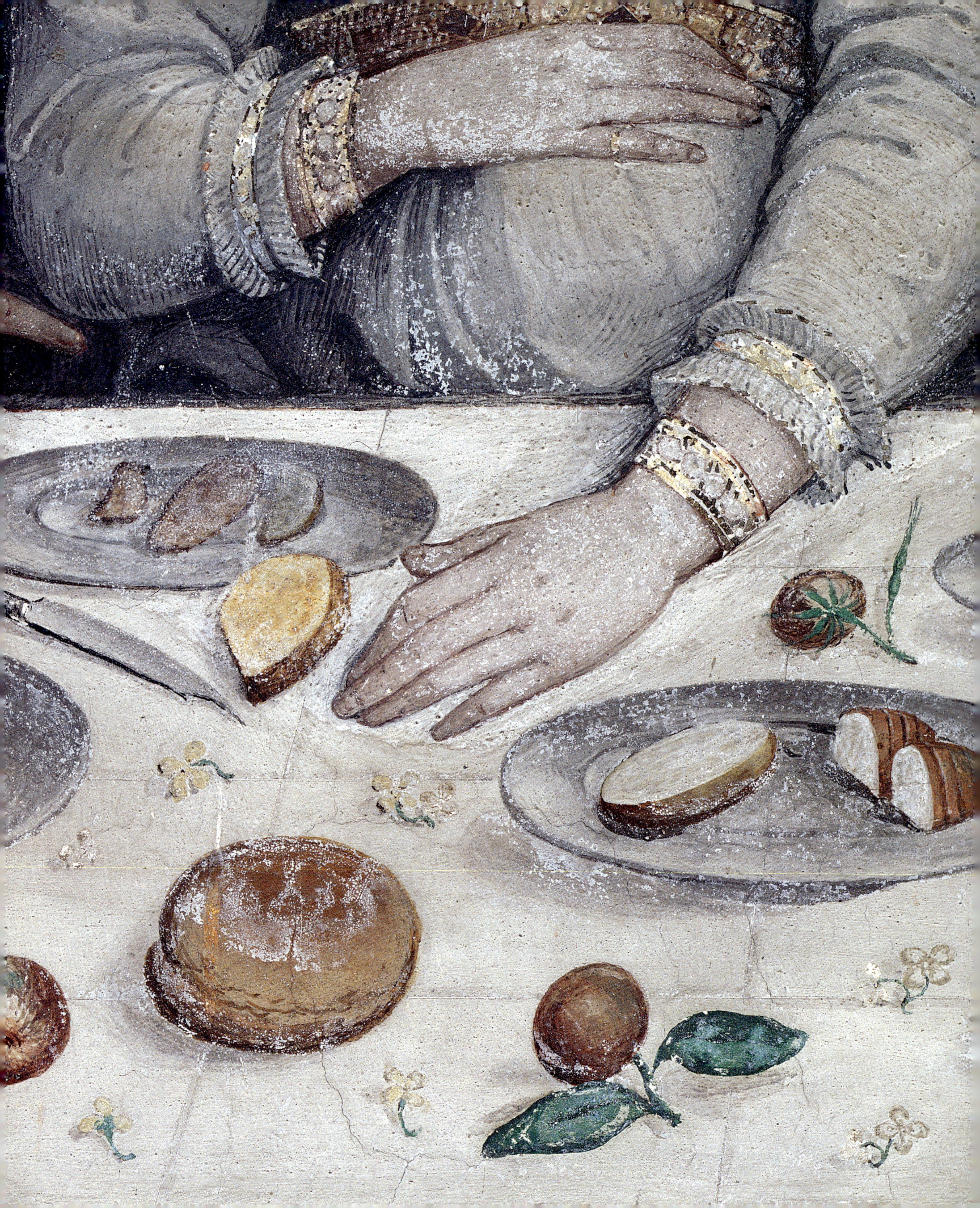

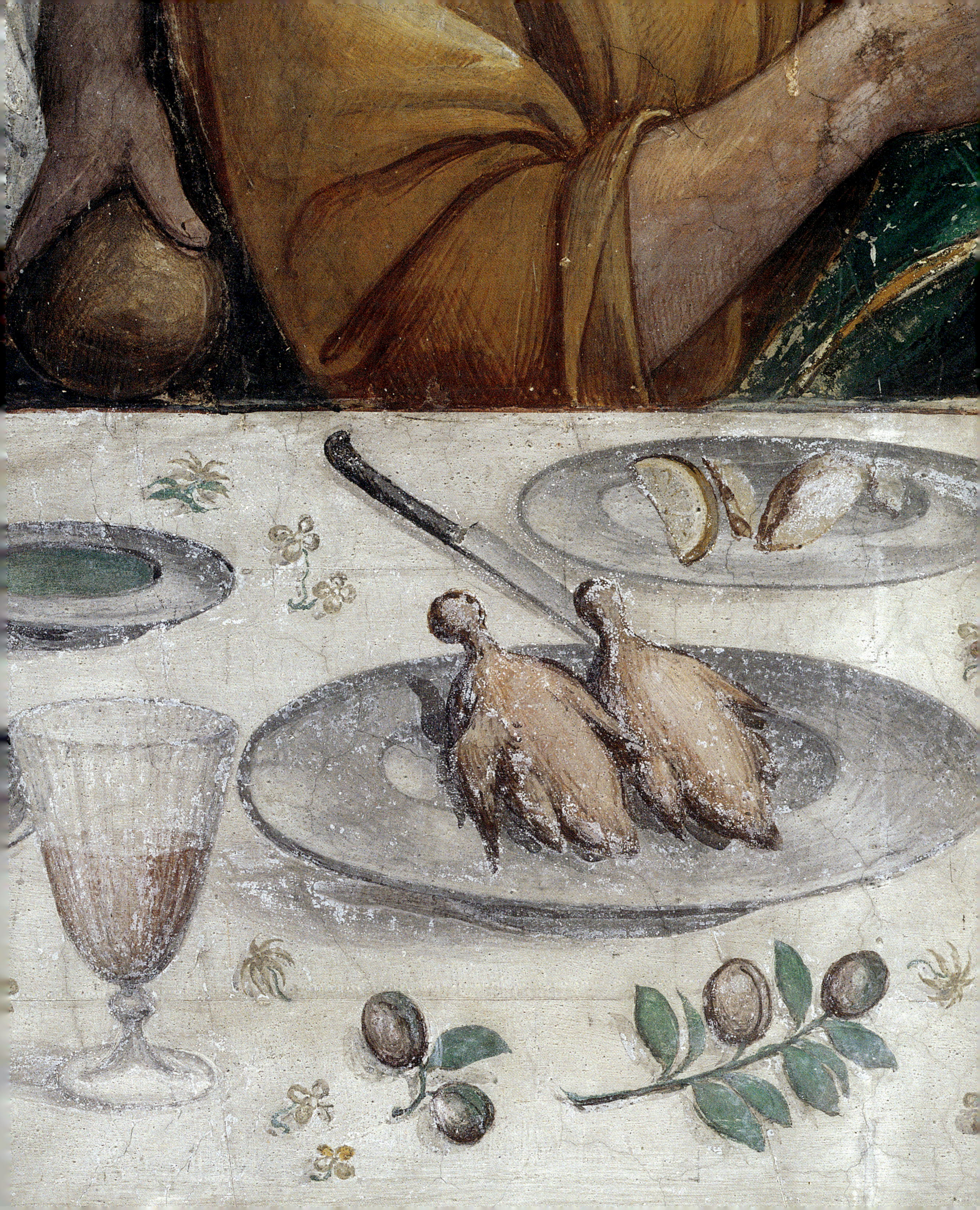

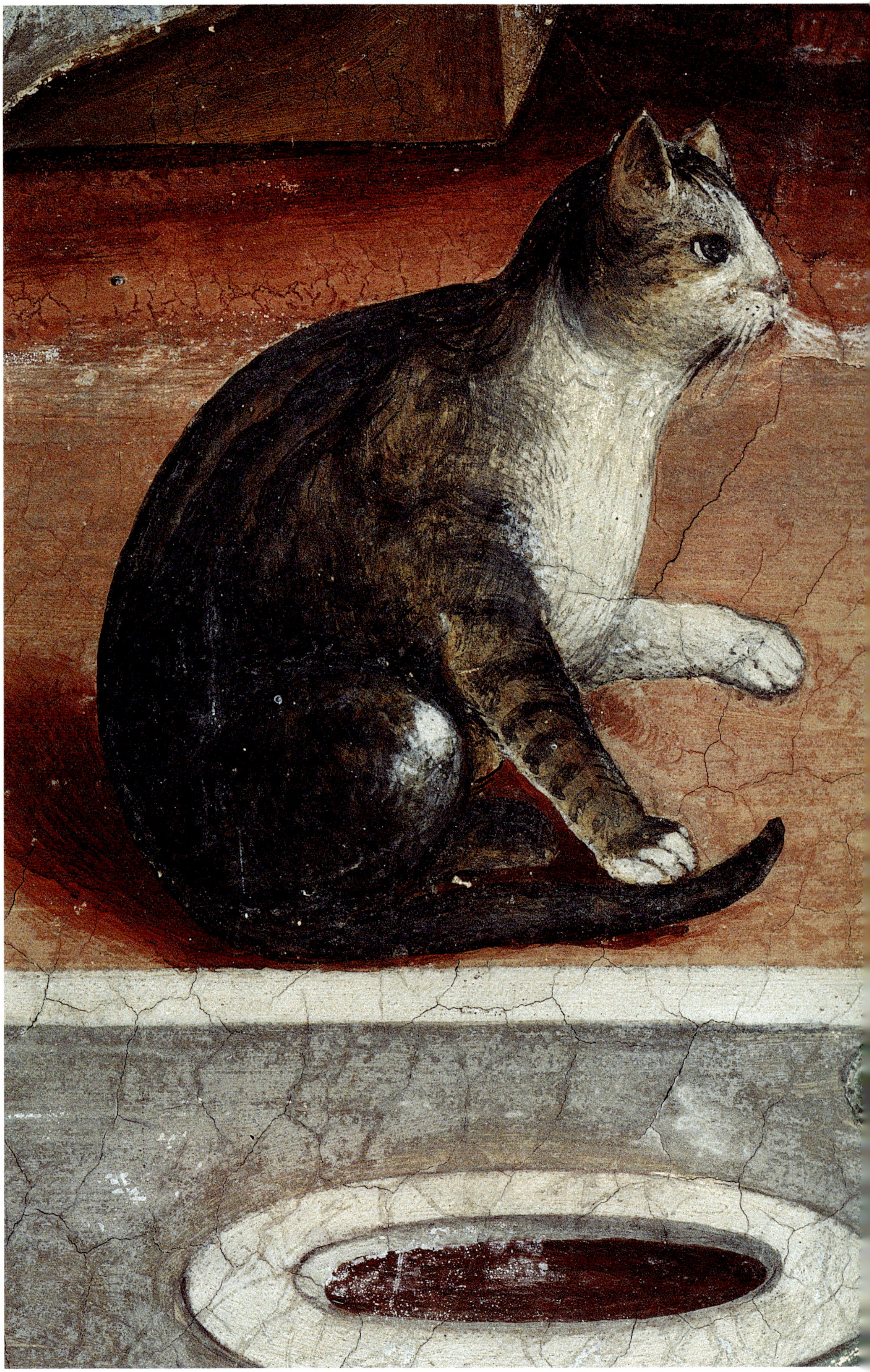

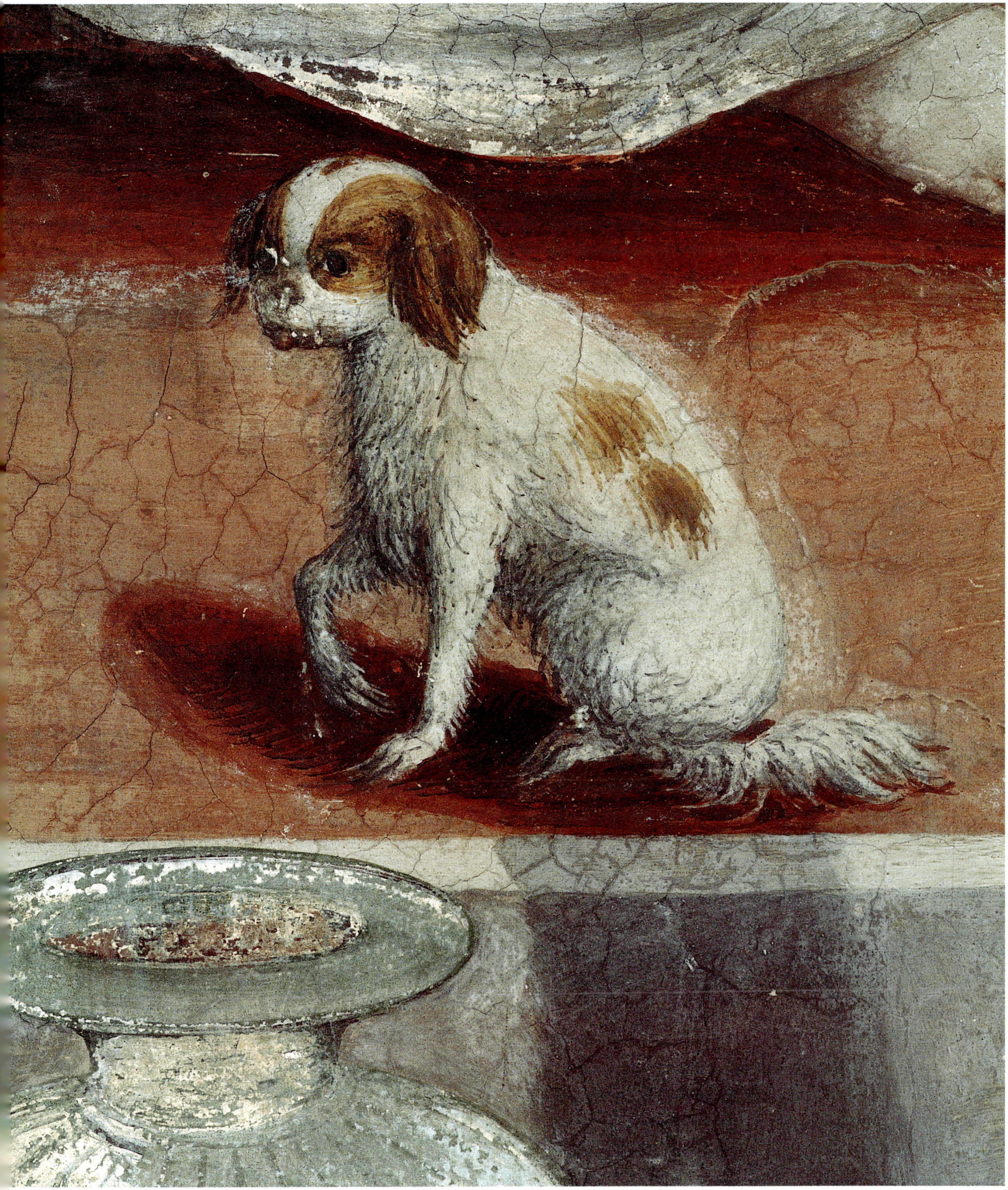

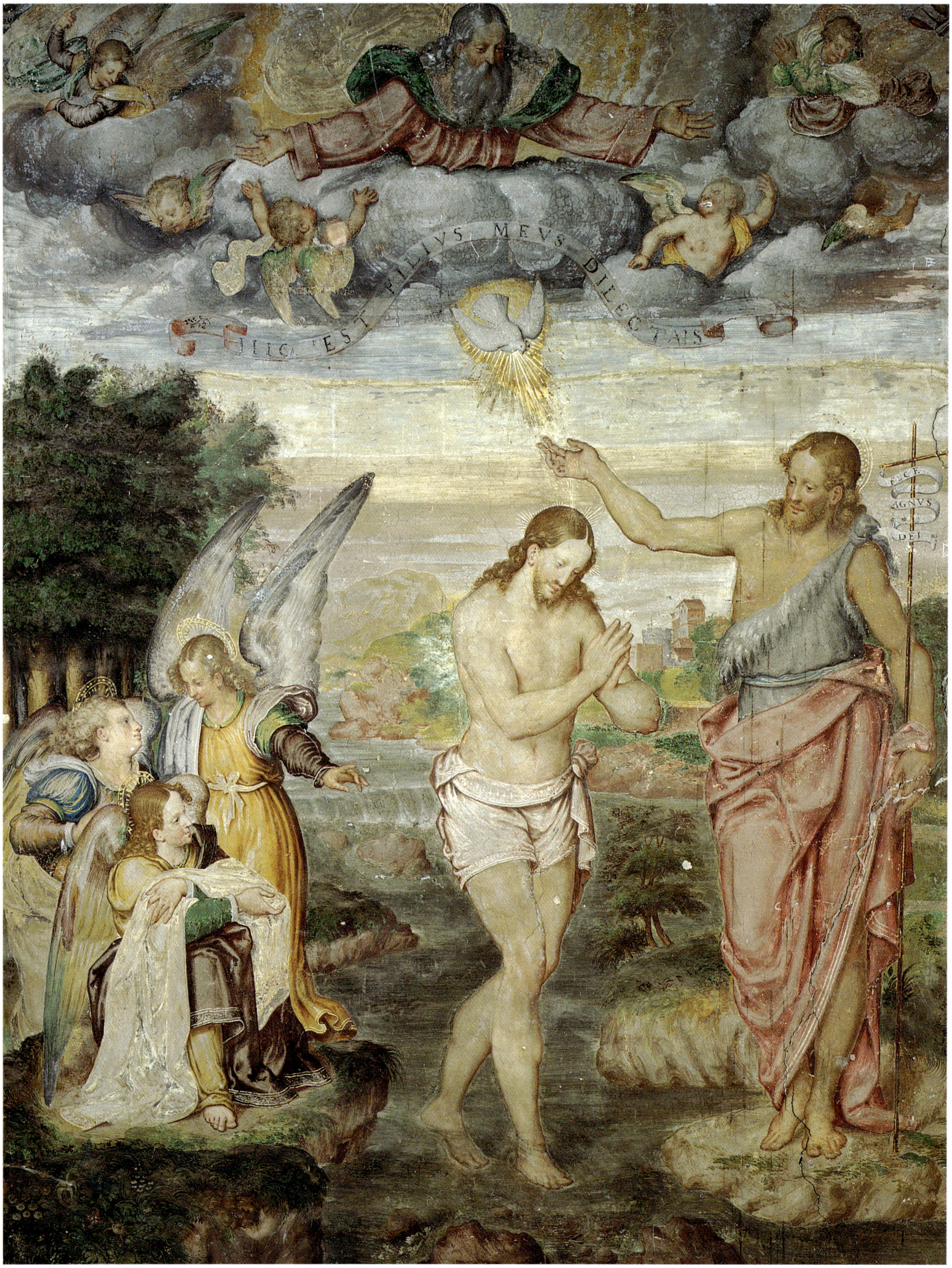

38. Aurelio and Giovan Pietro Luini
Baptism of Christ, with detail
Partition wall, above the bridge, convent hall

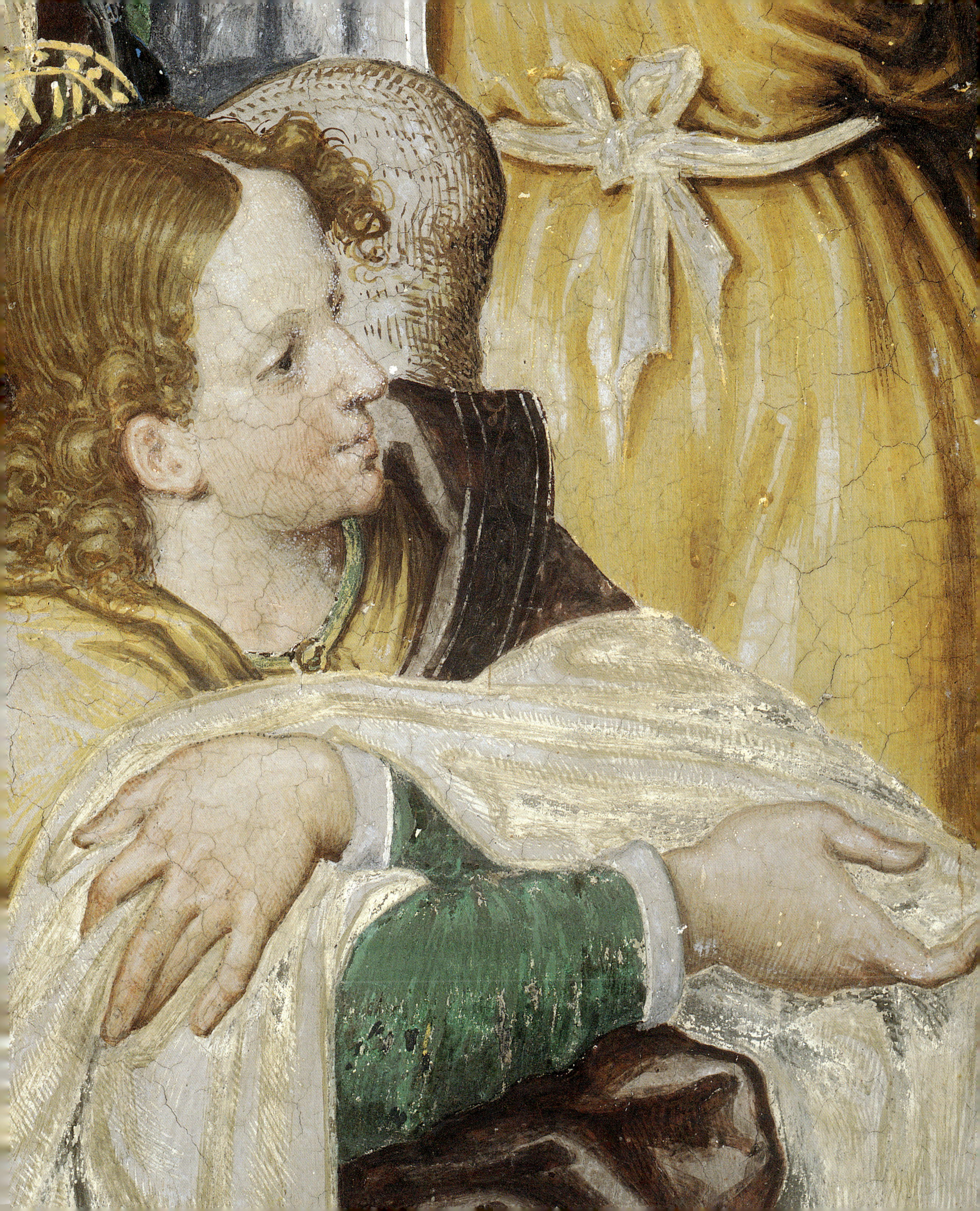

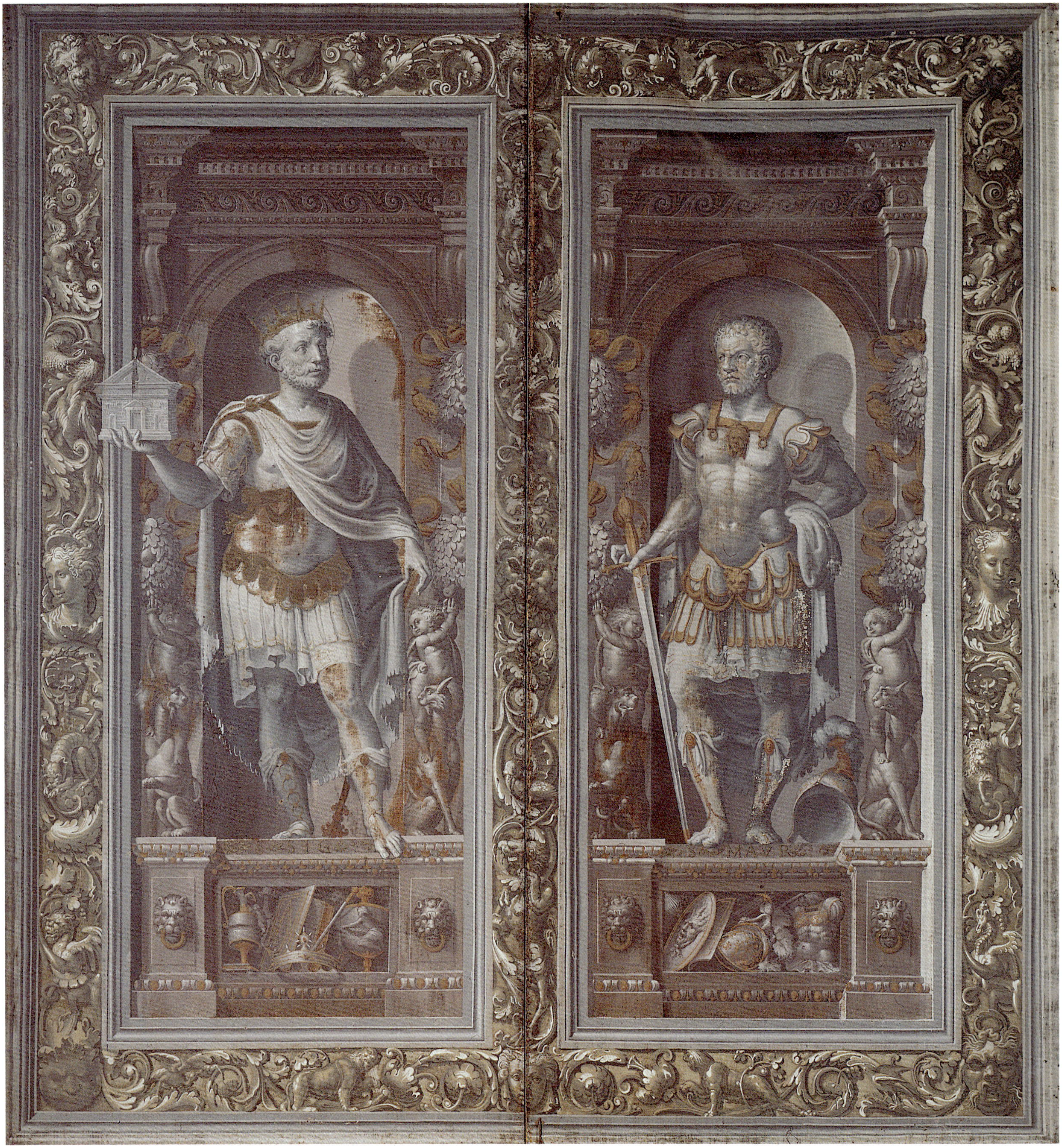

39. Francesco de' Medici
St Sigismond and St Maurice
Outside of organ shutters,
convent hall

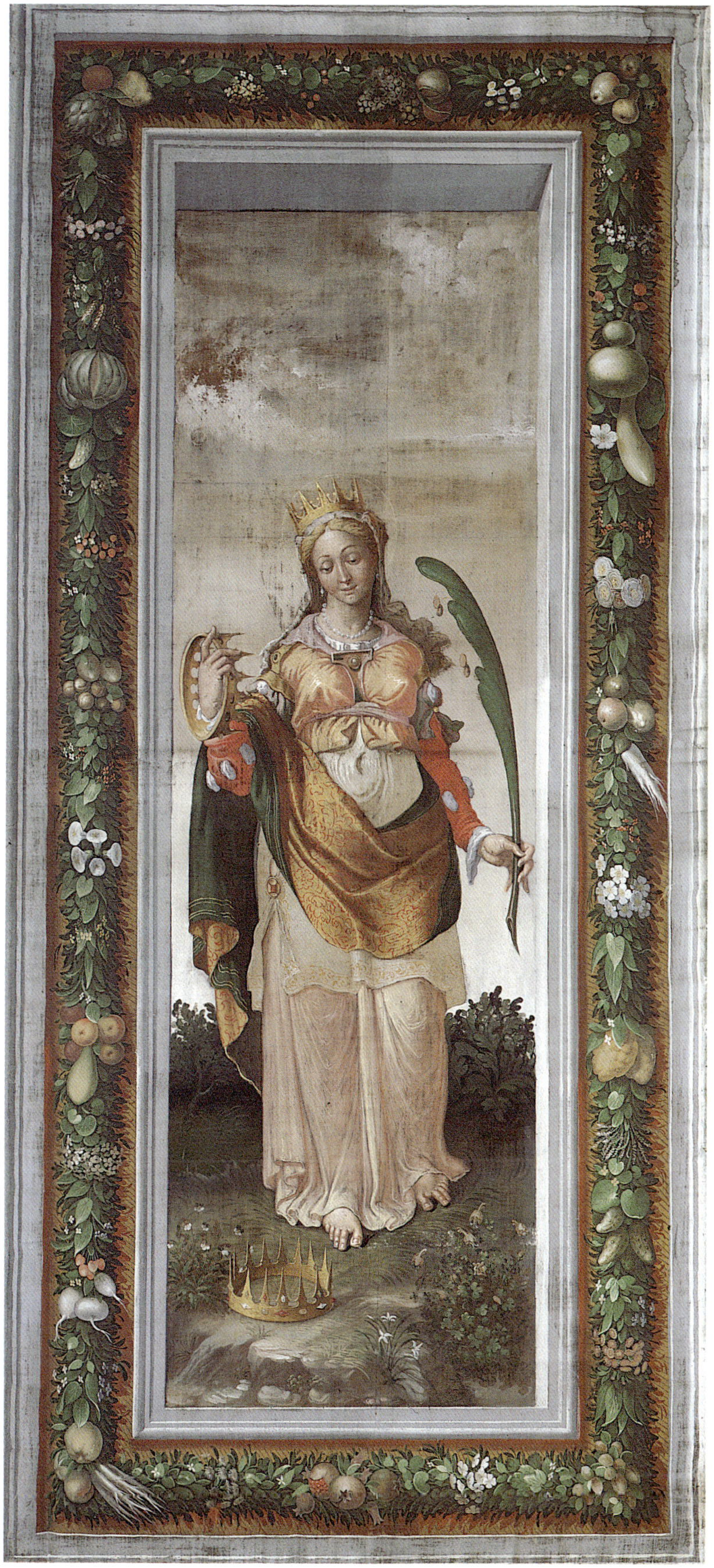

39. Francesco de' Medici
St Elizabeth of Hungary
Inside of the left organ shutter,
convent hall

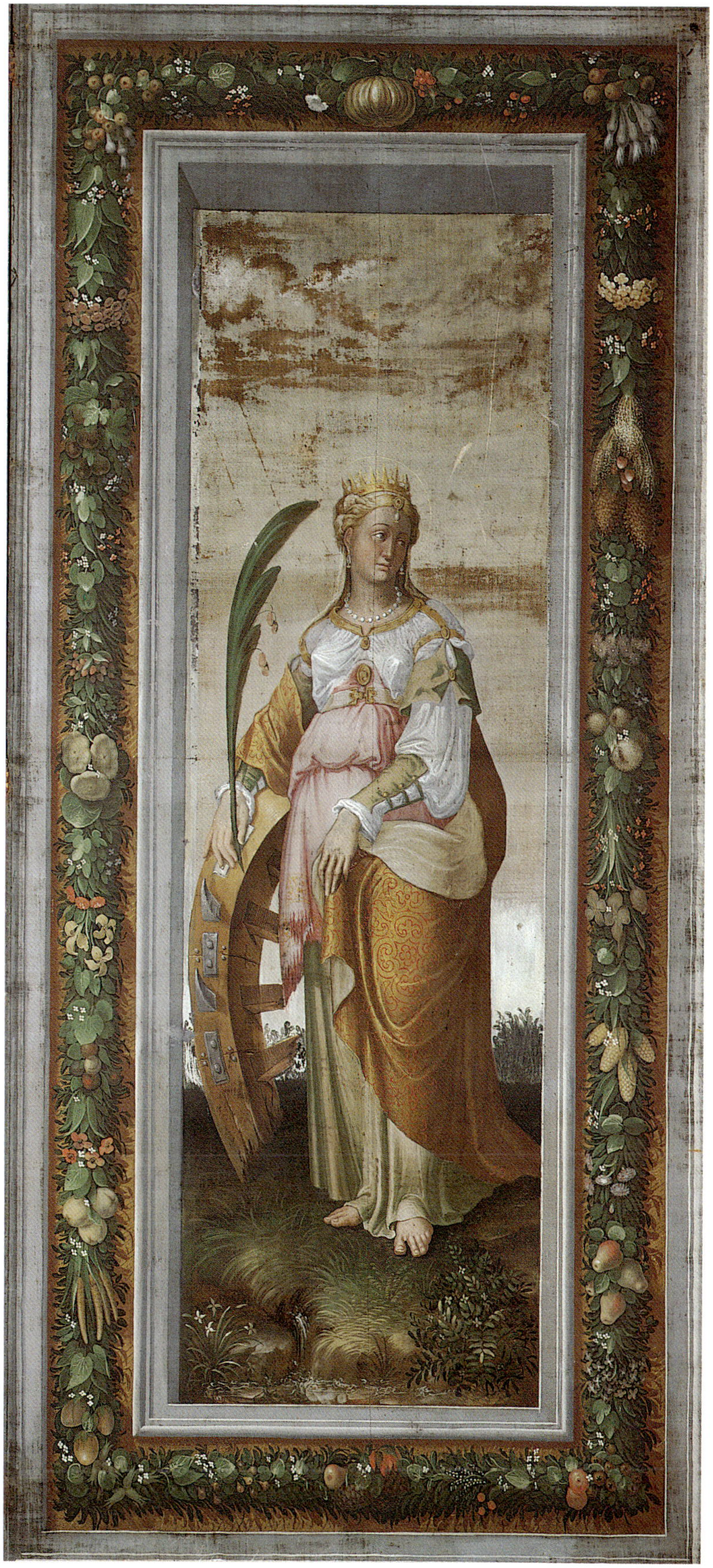

39. Francesco de' Medici
St Catherine
Inside of the right organ shutter,
convent hall

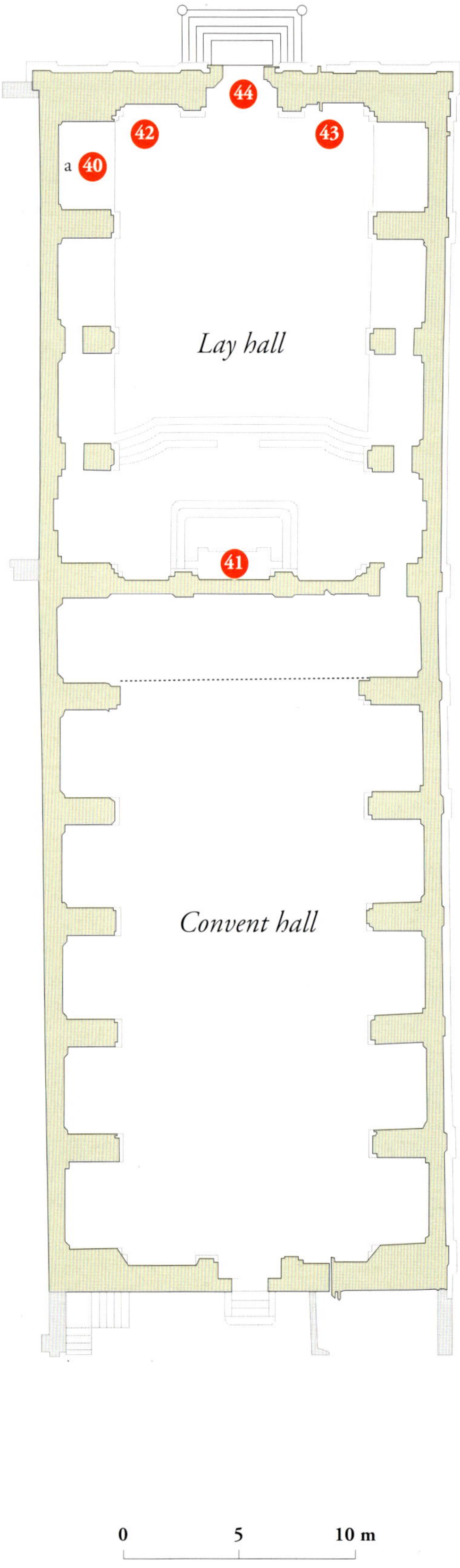

Ground plan of the church of San Maurizio al Monastero Maggiore

40. Ottavio Semino
Preaching of St Paul
Central wall, Cappella Fiorenza (or di San Paolo), lay hall

Following pages
40. Ottavio Semino
Intrados of the vault
Cappella Fiorenza (or di San Paolo), lay hall

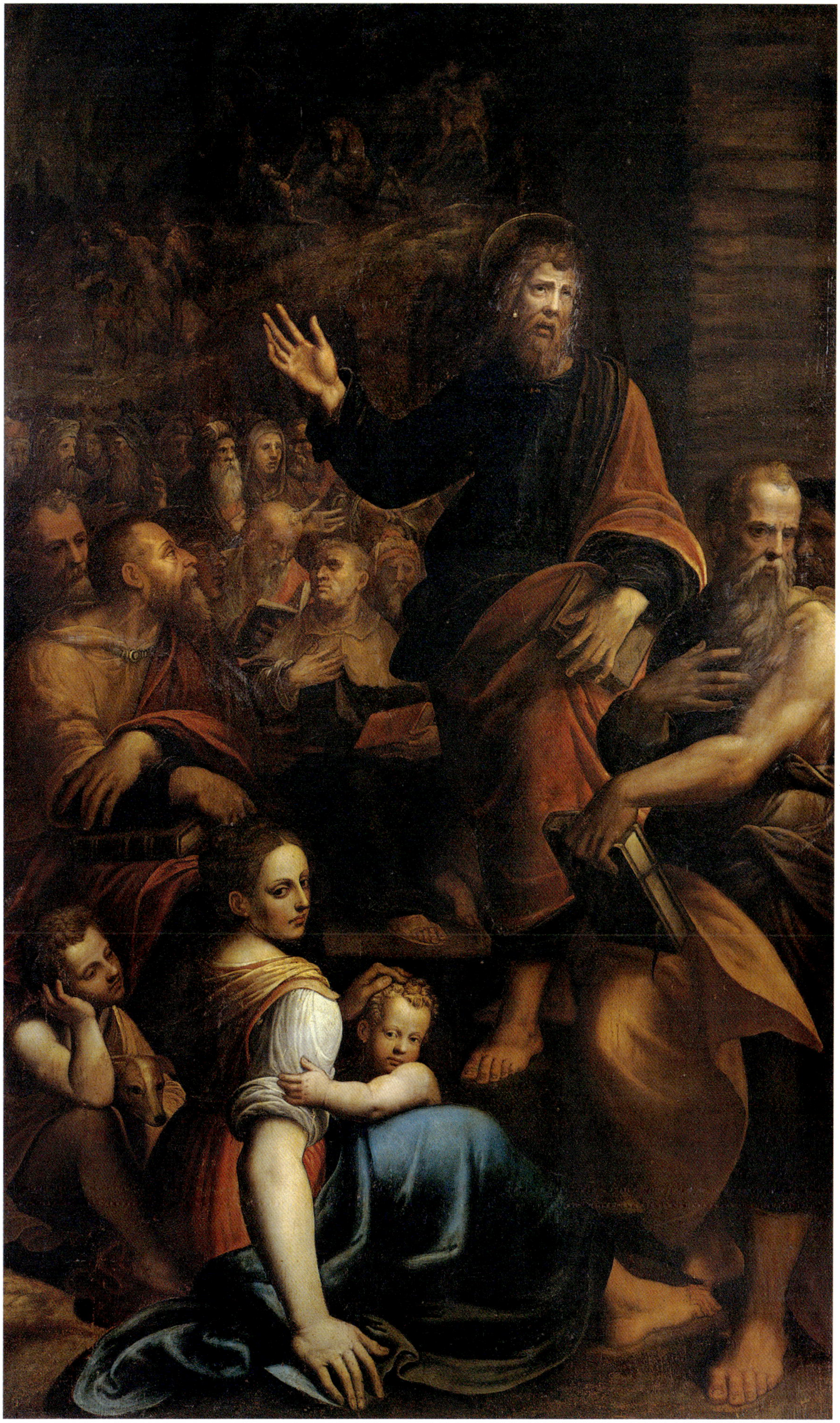

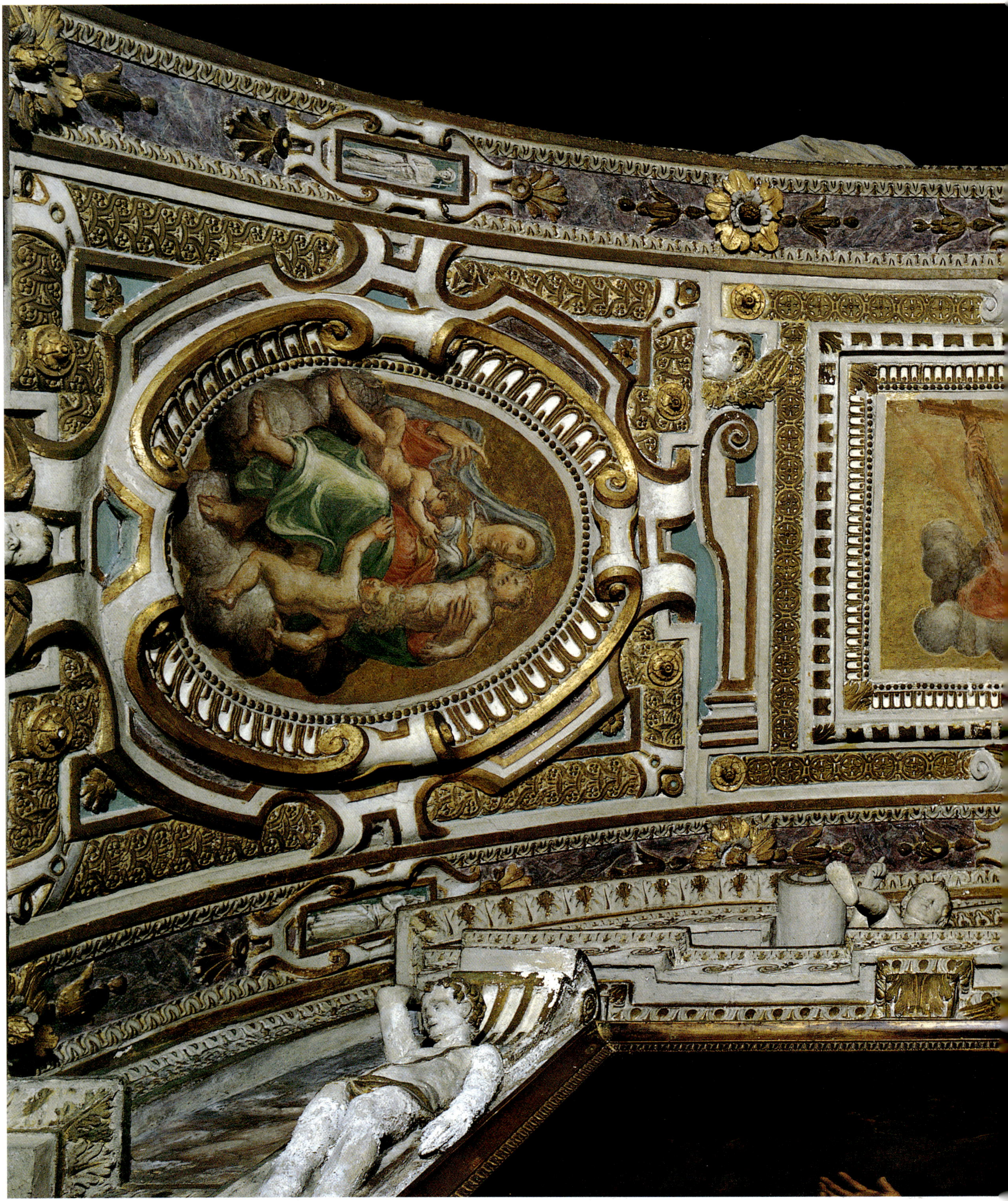

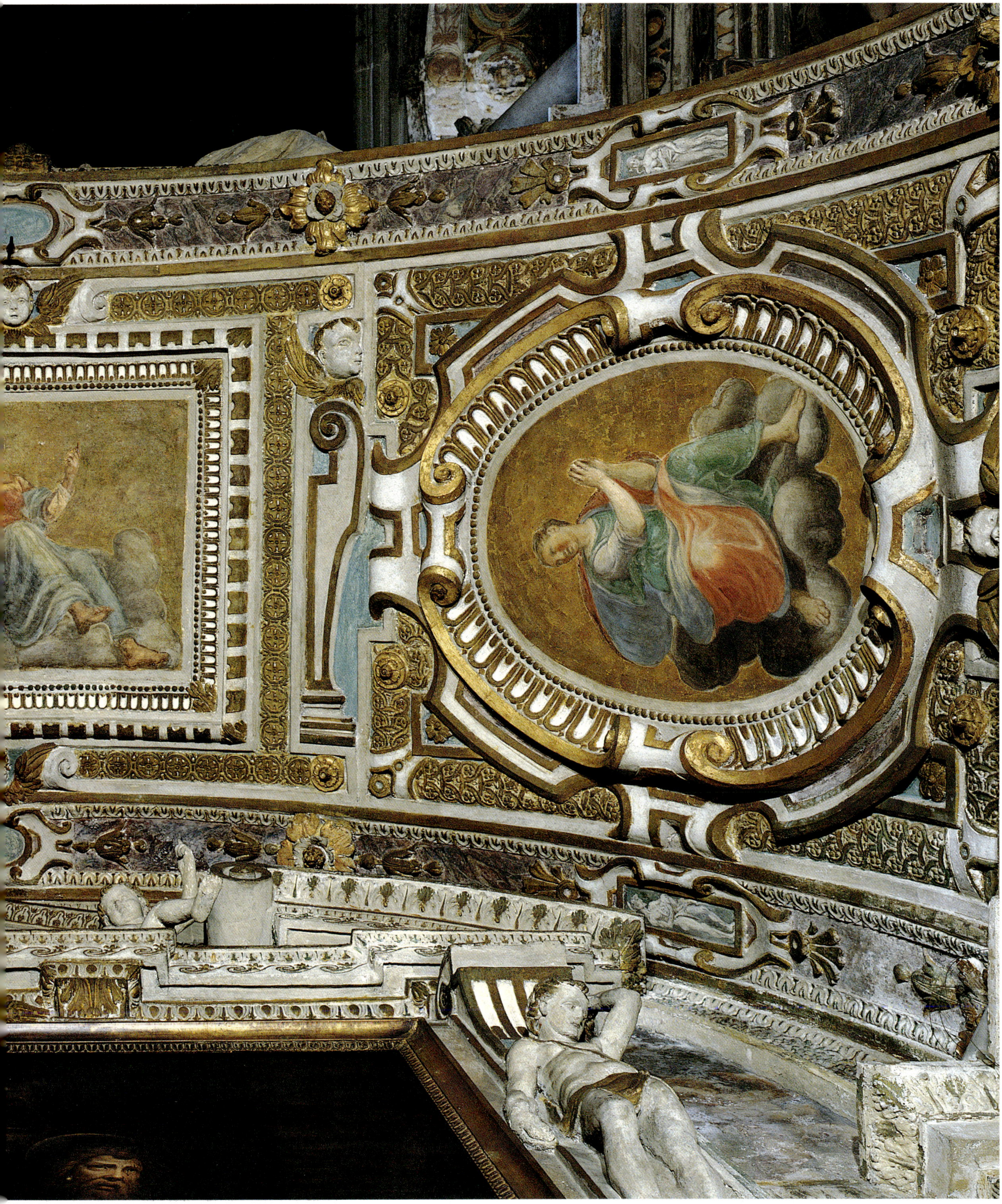

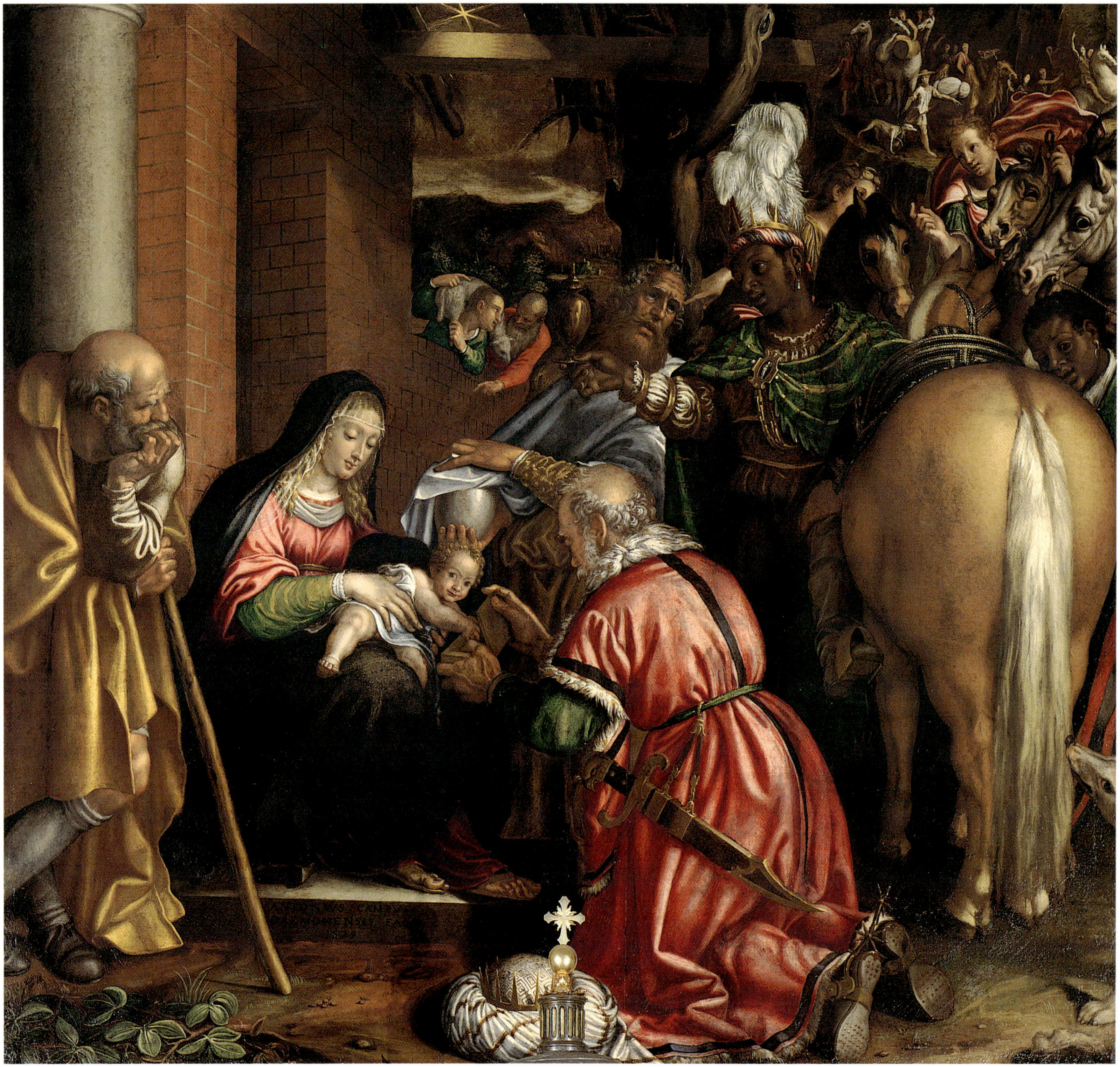

41. Antonio Campi
Adoration of the Magi
Partition wall, lay hall

Pages 291–293
41. Antonio Campi
Adoration of the Magi, details

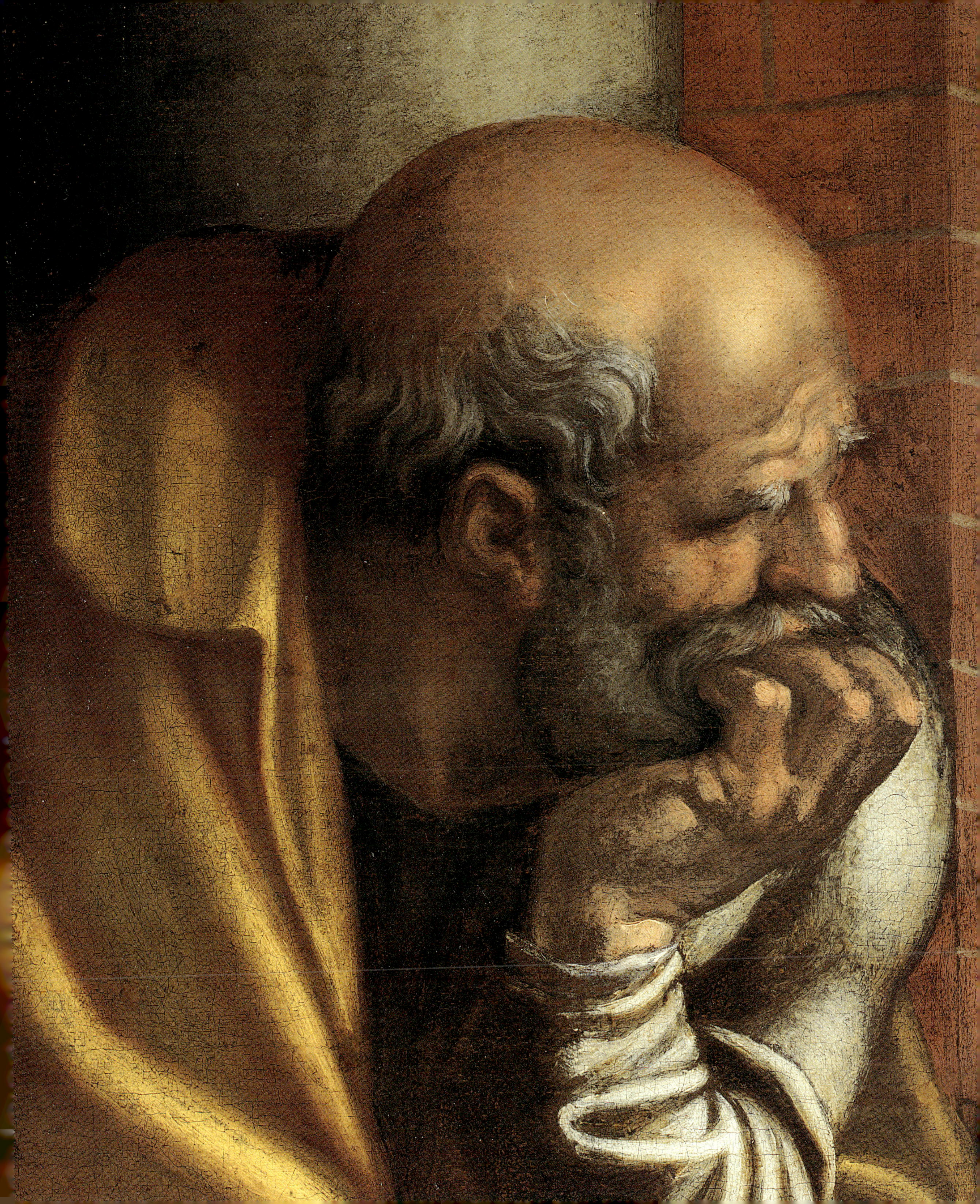

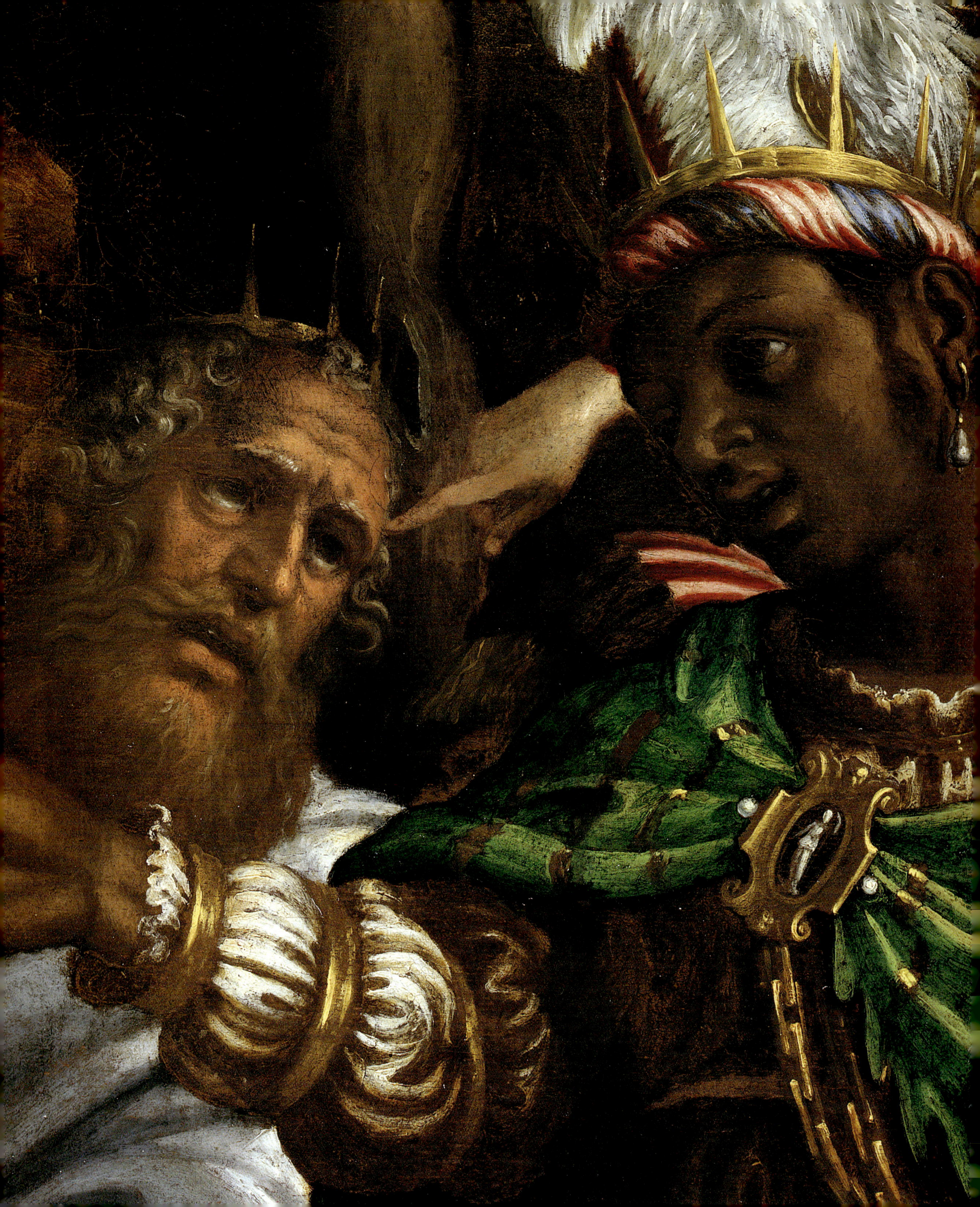

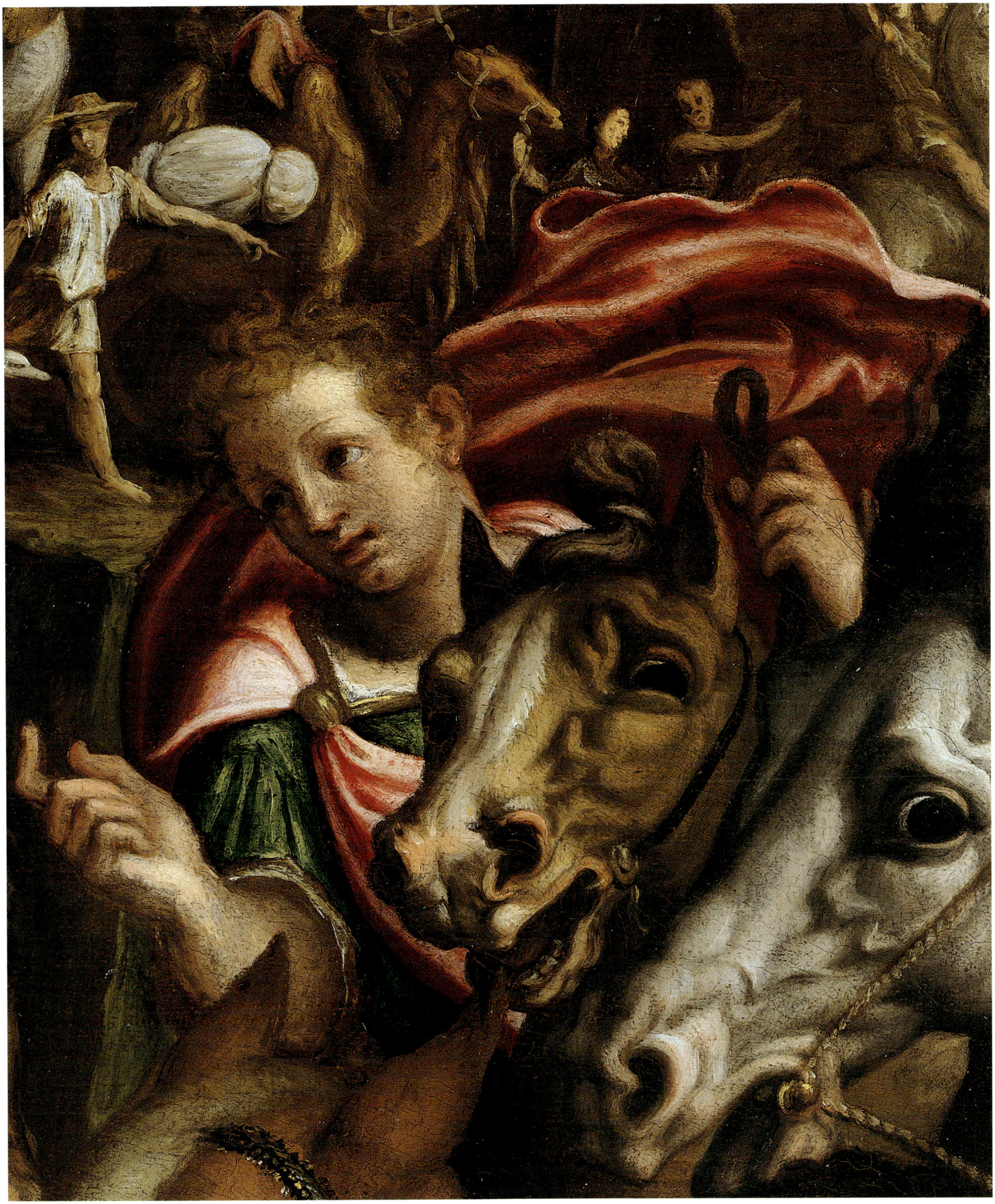

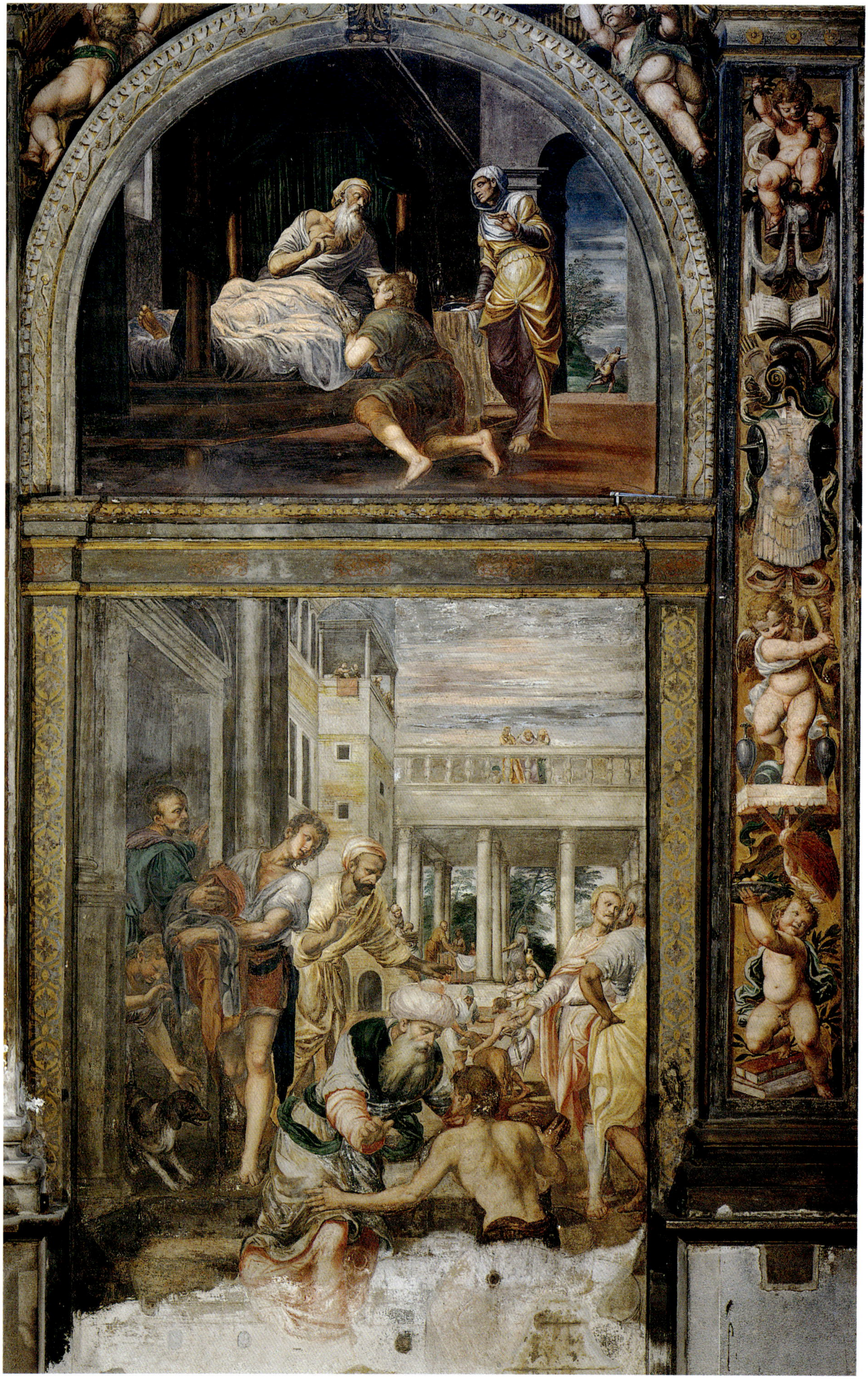

42. Simone Peterzano
Isaac Blessing Jacob
Return of the Prodigal Son
Left side, entrance wall, lay hall

42. Simone Peterzano
Isaac Blessing Jacob, detail

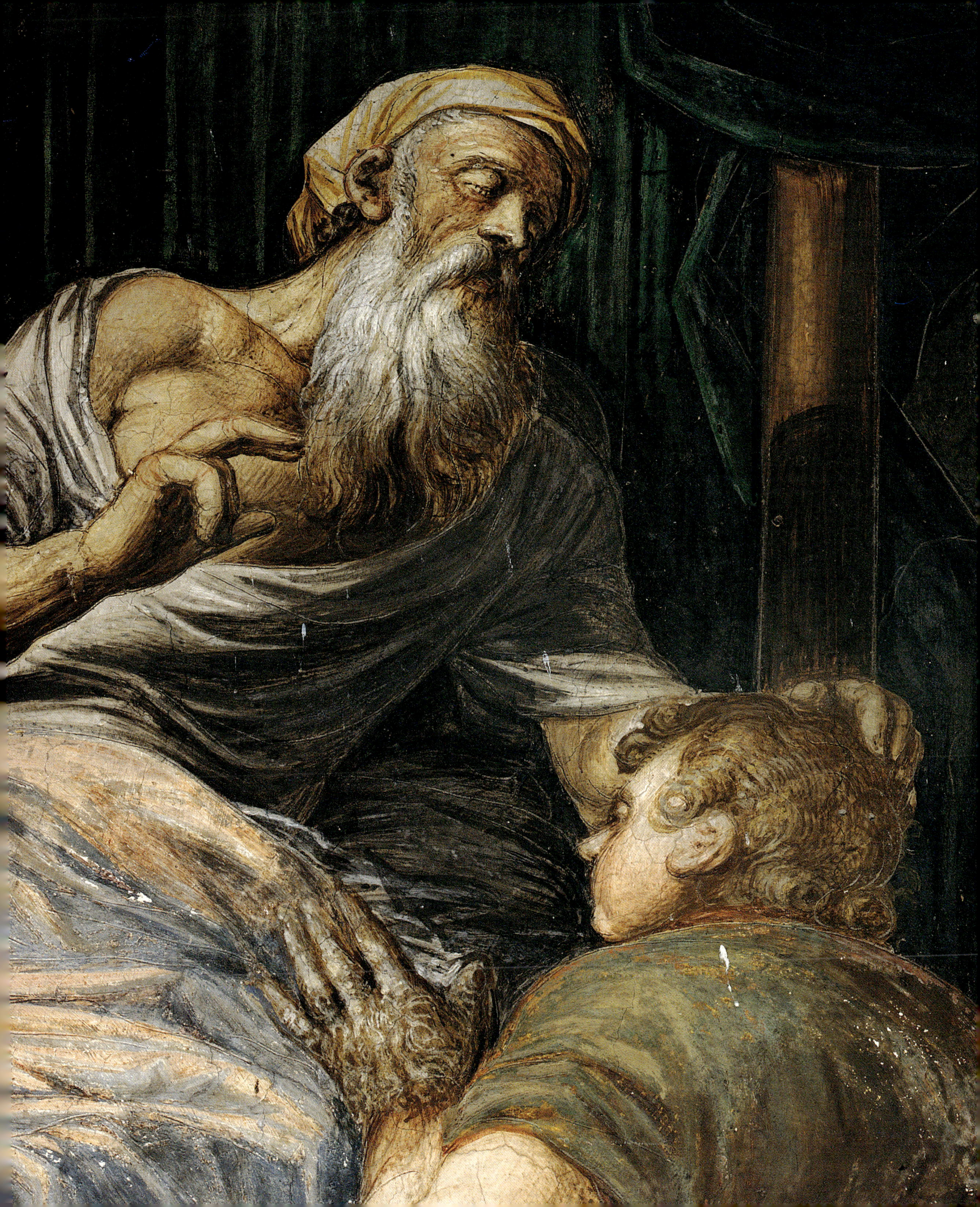

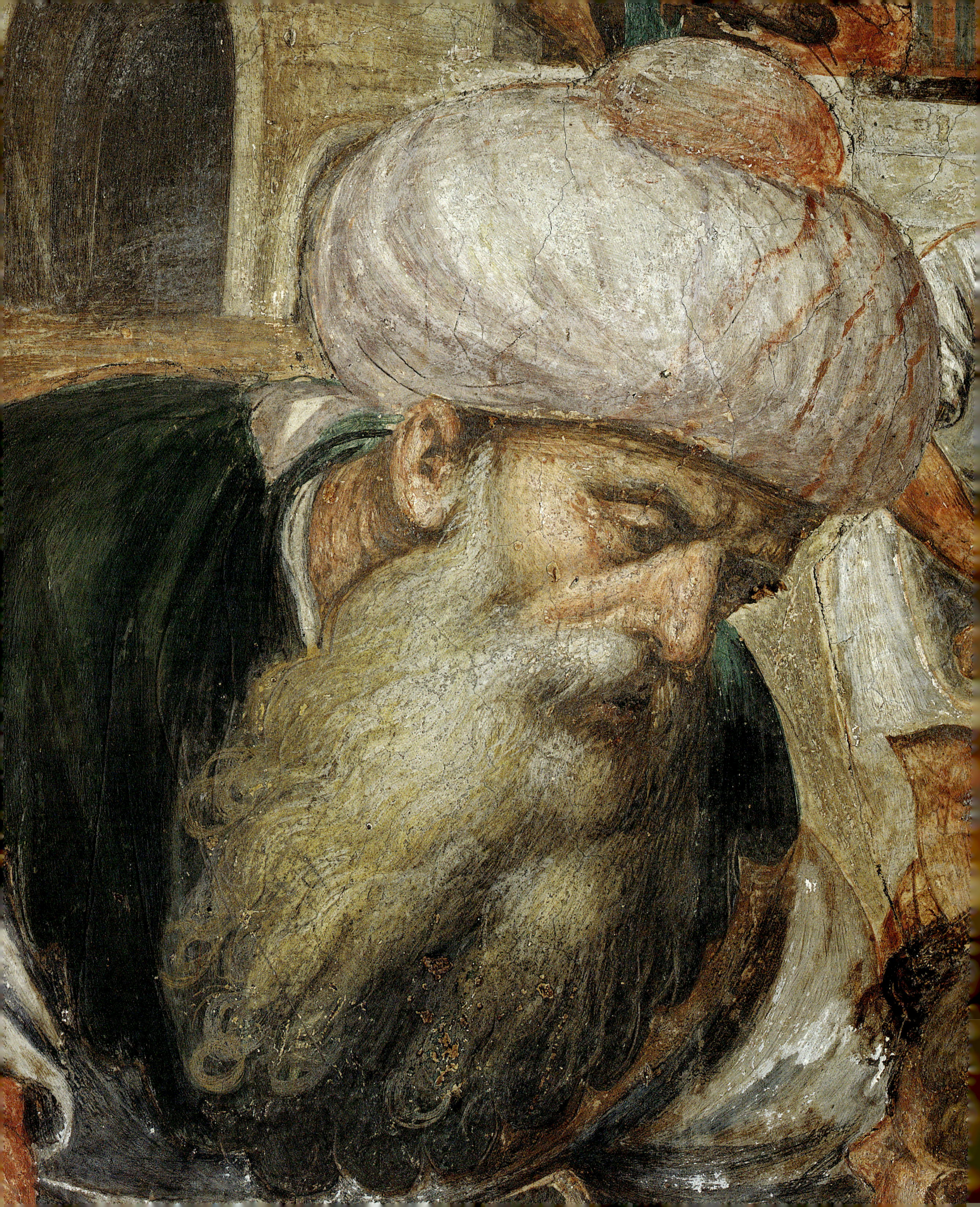

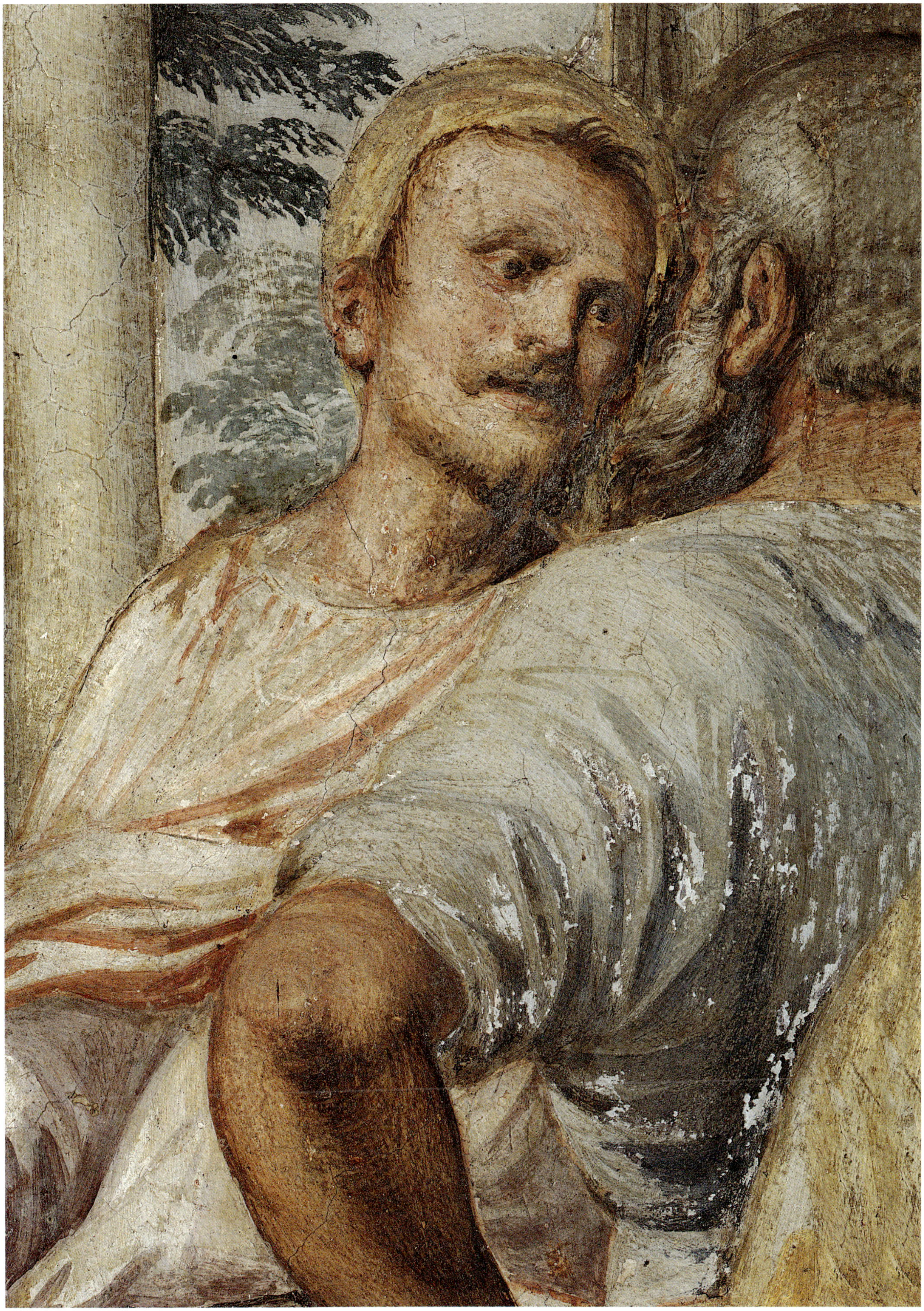

42. Simone Peterzano
Return of the Prodigal Son,
details

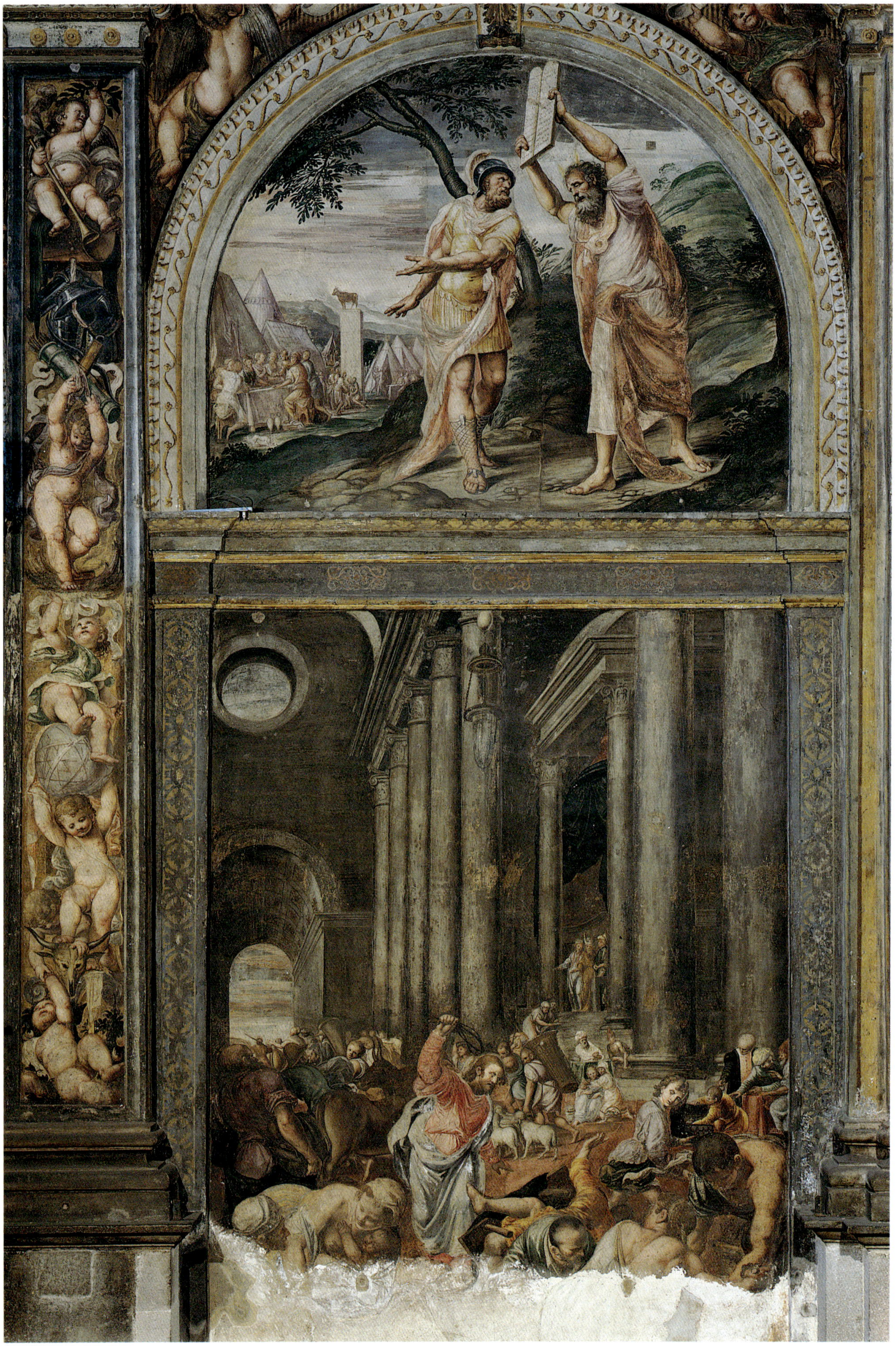

43. Simone Peterzano
Moses Breaking the Tables of the Law
Jesus Driving the Money-changers from the Temple
Right side, entrance wall, lay hall

Following pages
43. Simone Peterzano
Moses Breaking the Tables of the Law, details

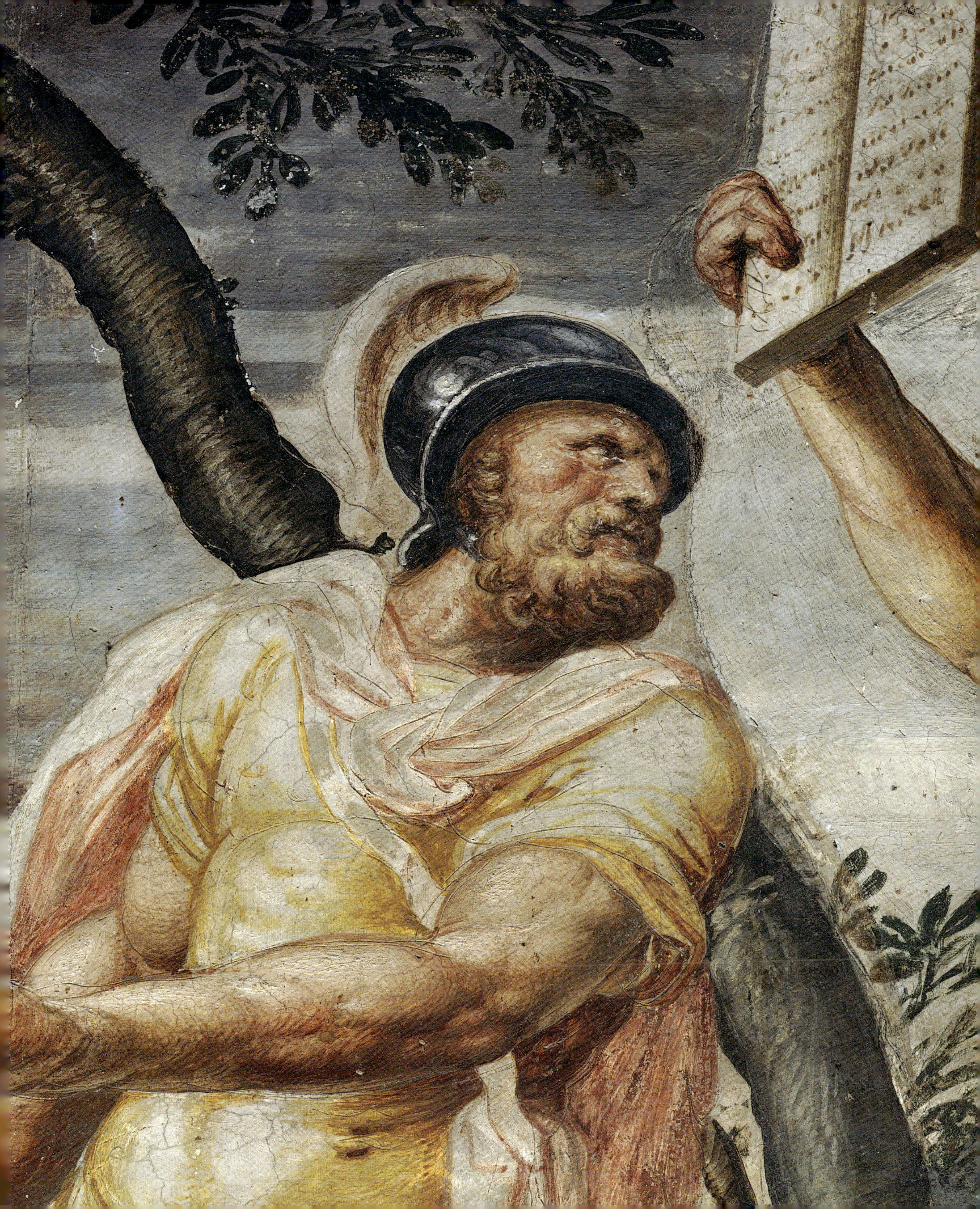

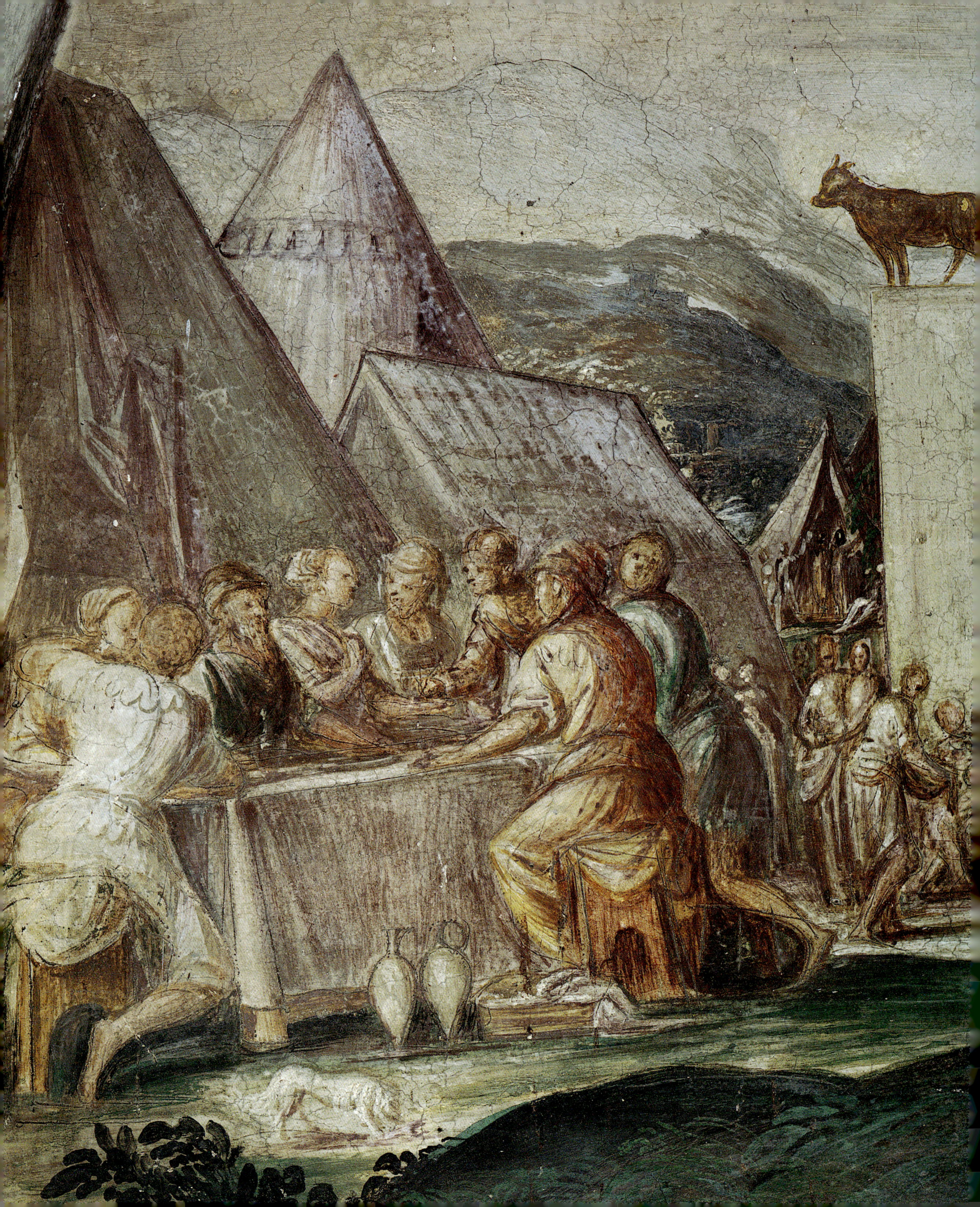

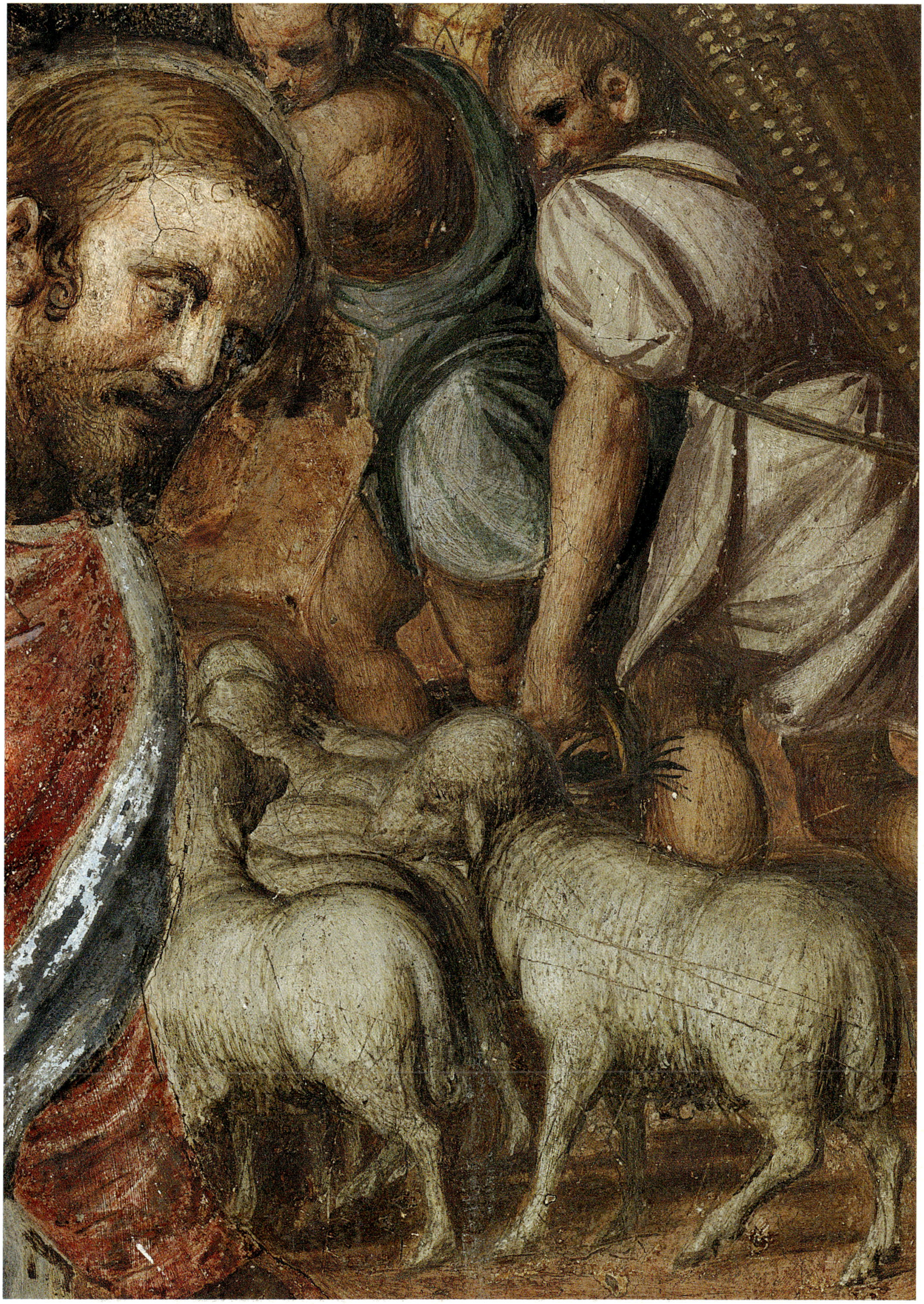

43. Simone Peterzano
Jesus Driving the Money-changers from the Temple, detail

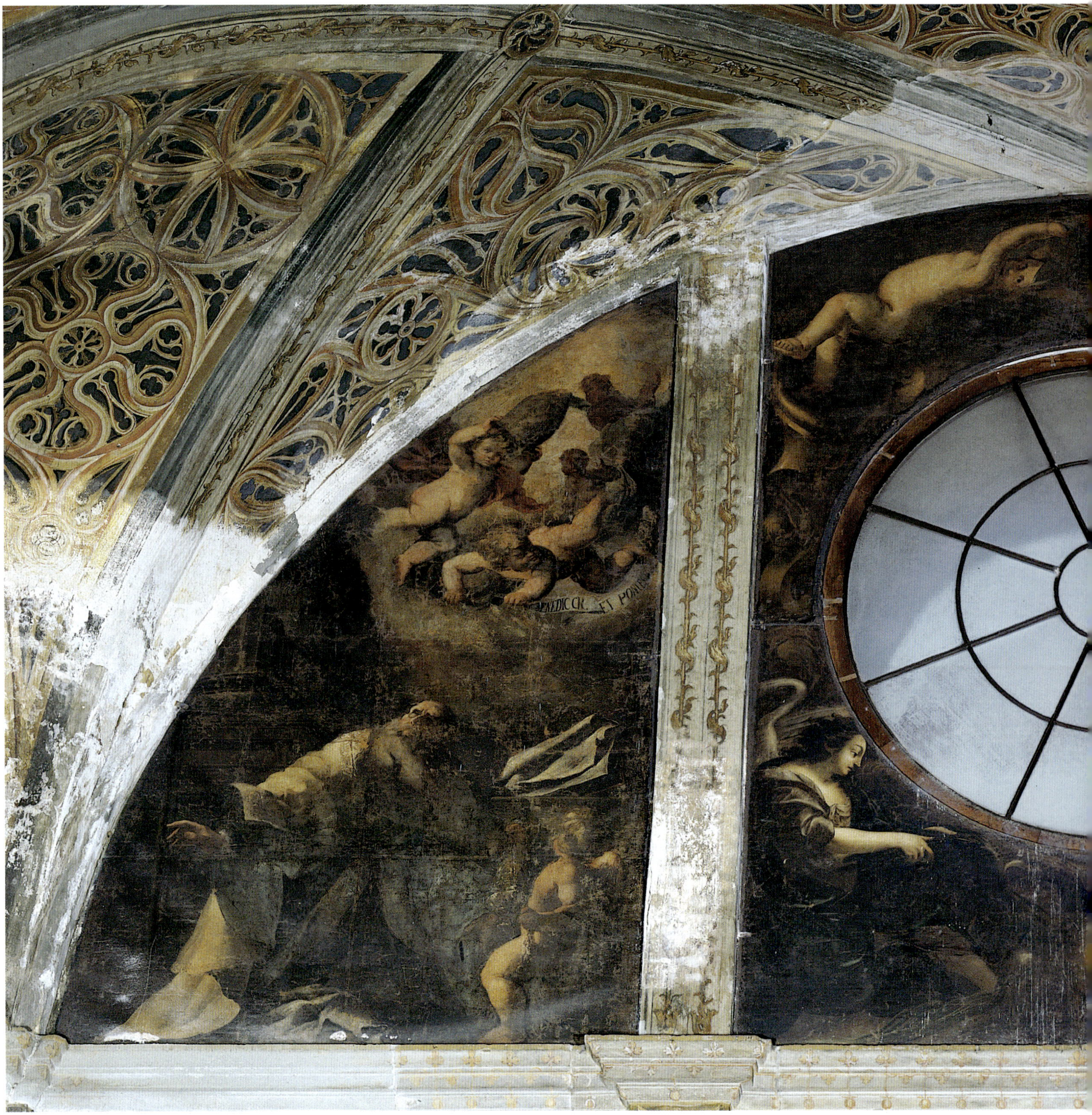

44. Lombard artist, seventeenth century
Lunette
Entrance wall, lay hall

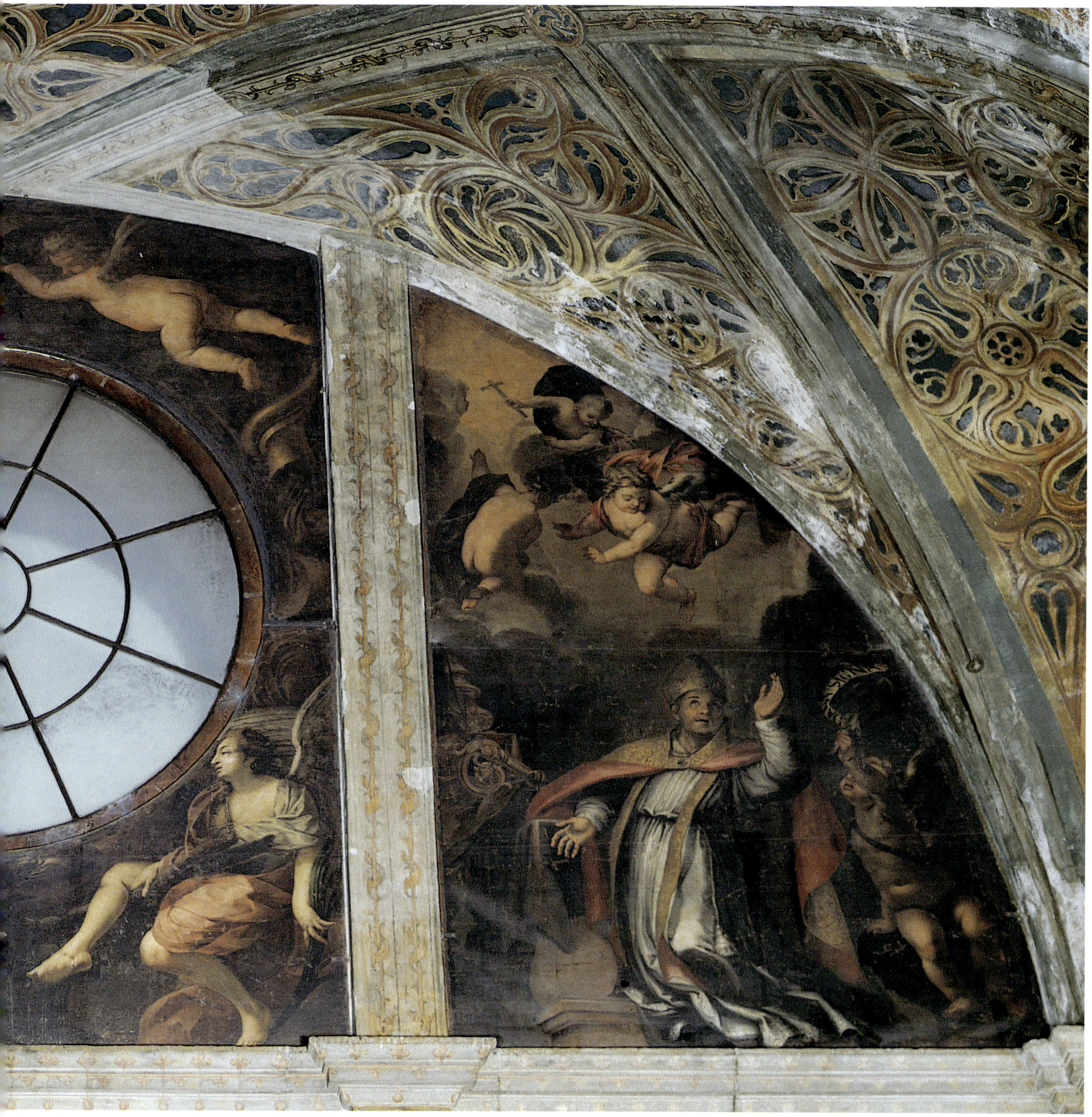

List of Documents
Related to Paintings, Decorations, and Furnishings

Abbreviations for Archives in Milan
AAB = Archivio dell'Accademia di Brera
AFD = Archivio della Fabbrica del Duomo
ASBBAA = Archivio della Soprintendenza ai Beni Architettonici e Ambientali
ASBBAASS = Archivio della Soprintendenza ai Beni Artistici e Storici
ASC = Archivio Storico Civico
ASD = Archivio Storico Diocesano
ASM = Archivio di Stato di Milano
ASMP = Archivio Parrocchiale di Santa Maria alla Porta

1487
The monastery is granted indulgence for the feast days of St Maurice, St Benedict, and St Sigismund.
ASM, *Religione p.a.* 2147: *Compre, spese...*
Sannazzaro 1989 (b), p. 64 n. 39.

1488
The monastery is granted indulgence by Cardinal Sforza Visconti for Assumption Day promulgated by Pope Innocent VIII.
ASM, *Religione p.a.* 2147: *Compre, spese...*
Sannazzaro 1989 (b), p. 64 n. 39.

1503, 20 May
Purchase of a land parcel for church construction ("pro fabricatione fiendae ecclesiae"); the list of signatories includes one "magister Antonius de Bodiis de Lonatis filius quondam domini Ambrosii porte verceline parochie sancte marie ad portam mediolani", cited among the "reverendum sacrae theologiae professorem dominum fratrem Johannem Pagnanun (ordinis: esp.) predicatorum in monasterio domine sancte marie de gratiis ibidem tantum pro tribunali sedes".
ASM, *Notarile* 4586.
Sannazzaro 1988, p. 127.

1507, 12 August
The deputies of Milan Cathedral Works opt to comply with the Monastero Maggiore's nuns' request for marble, provided Amadeo can spare it from the cathedral site that year.
"Insuper lecta supplicationem dominarum abb[atiss]e et monialium monasterii maioris Mediolani in filza diversorum posita requirente petia sedecim marmoris fini pro ornatu faciate ecclesie earum monasterii, accipientes per eas ad pradarias ab Alvisio Nostrano earum expensis, ordinatum fuit marmorem requisitum eisdem concedi debere et dari in fabrica casu quo magister Johannes Antonius Homodeus architectus fabrice [of the cathedral] iudicaverit talem marmorem non indigere in fabrica pro anno presenti, aliter non detur."
AFD, *Ordinazioni capitolari* 5, f. 131r.
Schofield Shell Sironi 1989, p. 404 (n. 1062).

1521, 6 May
The will of Ippolita Sforza Bentivoglio: "Item relinquo ven. dom. Alexandre Sfortie de Bentivolis filie me professe in monast. Majori Mediolani, et seu per eam dicto monas.rio et monialibus ejus ius et facultatem exigendi... libras millecentum et septuaginta trium sold. sex et den. octo imper., quod fit et prestatur seu fiebat et prestabatur per d. Antonium de la Somala super bonis de quibuss".
ASM, *San Maurizio - benedettine*, 461.
Rossi 1914, p. 34.

1524, 18 May
Will of Francesco Besozzi: "donationem facio, pro dote capellae Beatae Catherinae construendae in Ecclesia monalium... et sub altare ejus capellae volo fiat locus sepulchri... in quo volo reponi cadaver meum... sub tutella B. Catharinae et ut ibi remaneant ossa mea usque in diem resurrectionis electorum".
ASM, *San Maurizio* 465.
Also ASM, *Religione p.a.* 2147: *Compre, spese...*
Rossi 1914, pp. 56–57.

1545, 11 March
Cristoforo Lombardo is contracted to make the metal grille for the dividing wall window: "Cum sit que venerabiles domine abbatissa et moniales Monasteri Maioris Mediolani fieri facere telim ferrata una ante altare maius sue ecclesie ed transversa dicti ecclesie et tantum quantum durat latitudo ipsius... ordinem dandum per magistrum Cristophorum Lombardum ingenierum mediolano".
ASM, *Notarile* (Galdo da Lodi), 10021 (also 29 November 1545).
Sannazzaro 1989 (b), p. 60 n. 10.

1554, 4 September
Contract for the organ in the nuns' hall; the monastery chapter that convened at the time consisted of 93 nuns, who, "ad ferratam forestarie dicti Monasteri, ubi solent pro similibus negociis congregari... et sono campane premisso ut moris est... [the abbess Gerolama Brivio]..., domina Maura Taverna... Laura da Fiorenza... domina Francisca Violante Bentivoglio" requested "[Giacomo Antegnati] filius quondam Bartholomei porte ticinensis parochie sancti Alexandri in Zebedia" to forthwith construct "organum unum illius altitudinis et latitudinis cuius est organum ecclesie Sancti Simpliciani Mediolani, et cum illis registris et capitulis et aliis cum quibus factum est organum ecclesie maioris civitatis Viglevani", on the lines of the one in the presbytery of the ducal chapel in Sant'Ambrogio, ensuring that he "facere et construere huic ad festum Nativitatis Domini nostri Yhesu Christi anni 1555 proximi futuri", charging the organ casing to the nuns, for the sum of 200 *scudi.*
ASM, *Religione p.a.* 2147 (notary Giuseppe de Talia..., Gerolamo Mantegazza); *Notarile* (Galdo da Lodi), 10026.
Malaguzzi Valeri 1908, pp. 332–333.

1555, 6 May
The abbess Gerolama Brivio's agreement with the brothers Giovan Pietro and Aurelio Luini runs thus: "Achordo fato chon la areverenda madre badessa... per dipingere la chapela de la felice memoria de la

s.ra chontessa Bergamina nela sua gesa di fora: qual chapela li va fato dal architravo in gio come di fora li va 2 Sibile e soto la volta li va una cholo(m)ba chon li soi aragi dor claresto fato chon foiami doro parimenti, e lo architravo de la volta fato chon uno pocho dor, e il chornisono de lemposta de la volta chon or, e la facia sopra alater li va uno Christo che aresusita e tri ladroni al sepulchro, e da una banda li va quando la Madalena trova el nostro Signor vestito da ortolano, e da laltra parte el nostro Signor vestito da pelegrino chon doi apostoli quando andò in Emaus, e le pilastrate ornate de foiami e festoni o altre chose che stiano bene: e il marchato de questa opera è ... [60 gold *scudi*] ... a noi tuti doi frateli de Lovino", all written out by Giovan Pietro Luini and endorsed by Aurelio Luini, who signs in an elegant hand.
ASM, *Religione p.a.* 2147; anche *ibid.*, *Compre, spese...* ("Legato fatto per la Contessa Bergamina").
Rossi 1914, p. 77.

1556
"Spexa per dipinger la Cassa al organo al Mon.rio Mazor di M.lo fata per m.ro Francesco Medici di Seregno depinctor."
ASM, *Religione p.a.* 2147, 1556.
Malaguzzi Valeri 1908, p. 333.
"Spexa per dipingere la Cassa del organo del Monasterio Mazore de Milano facta per maestro Francesco de Medici de Seregno depinctore."
ASM, *Conventi* 439.
Rossi 1914, pp. VI–VII.

1569, 23 February
Pastoral visit of St Charles Borromeo. Specifications included: "Che nel luoco intitolato i SS.ti Martiri Nabore et Felice, non si facerà più la spetiaria, ma si facci altrove, et si lasci il luoco vuoto per oratorio di devotione, nel qual però non s'habbia da celebrar più messa, come si soleva... D. Bianca Lucia... si dia la disciplina... in Chiesa doppo i stadii del Choro, et in quel tanto l'altre monache in Chiesa dichino il Miserere".
Biblioteca Ambrosiana, D 348 Inf.
Beretta 1916, pp. 132–141.

1571, 24 July
Agreement between "s.ra Giulia Fiorenza" and "m.ro Ottavio de Ferrari detto Semino... p[arish] S. Babila" for works in the chapel dedicated to St Paul, comprising an upper frieze with cherubs "conformi a l'altro ivi vicino, et in Campo d'oro... nelli tribonatti sopra detta volta... tre Figure, cioè Fede Speranza et Charità", two Sibyls "nelli triangoli" and the altarpiece "nella angona di stucho... con le historie di S.to Paolo, cioè nel modo che li sarà dato per il s.r Franc[es]co Vesconte", with scenes either side from the life of St Paul, "se in detti lavori di stucho l'intrerà qualche camei, detto m.s Ottavio sia tenuto a farle con figure..., nelli passamenti... religati con dentro historiete in coloro di bronci", all to be completed by November, "di colori fini et laudati da persone di Giuditio et esperte in simili cose", for 40 *scudi* "su verifiche di Gio. Francesco Visconte", while the respective masonry was to be done through the month of September. Handwritten by Gio. Francesco Zurla (?), who signs on behalf of Semino, who is illiterate.
ASM, *Notarile* (Galdo da Lodi) 10029 (also 4 December 1573: convening that Paolo Camillo Landriani, son of Gerolamo, attend the workshop of Ottavio Semini "ianuansis", son of Antonio).
Sannazzaro 1989 (b), p. 60 n. 12.

1572
"Scritto di confesso fatto da Gioseffo Viagro Orefice di Milano per trenta scudi di oro in oro [sic], ricevuti dalla M.R.M.re D. Bianca Gironima Brivia con obligo di fabricare certi Candeglieri di Argento nella forma prescritta per l'altare grande della Chiesa del Monastero Maggiore come da esso."
ASM, *Religione p.a.* 2147: *Compre, spese...*
Sannazzaro 1989 (b), p. 62 n. 26.

1572, 29 August
Contract with Giovanni Battista da Vailate for the tombstone in honour of Alessandro Bentivoglio: "Jo. Batta de Vailà confesso di ricevere dalla M. Ba. Mon.ro dona Bianca Ger.a di Brivio abb.... scudi cinque d.o in oro..." for the "Monumento ch'io so a lavorare per detta...", to be placed "nella sua chiesa... prima che la preda di mezzo sarà lavorata con l'arma dei Bentivoglio di rilievo, con dui Angioli et altri ornamenti di basso rilievo et friso atorno di Cavo instucato... sopra la qual farò anch.a il suo epitafio... prometto darla finita per tutto il mese di ottobre", for the sum of 21 gold *scudi*.
ASM, *Religione p.a.* 2147.
Forcella 1890, p. 458.

1572, 10 November
Payment to Peterzano for the entrance wall frescoes: "Nob. D. Simon da Petrezano [sic] fg. Nob. Dom. Fran.ci civis venetus... de presenti moras trahens in pr. O. p. S. Stephanini ad Noxigia M.li contentus fuit... recepisse a nob. Jo. Ptero Castilliones... sindico et proc.... abb. St. monial. Mon.rii Maior M.lo... scuta viginta auri... et hoc pro soluz.e illorum scutorum triginta auri promissorum per ipsum nob. D. Jo. Petrum ipsi Simoni supra mercede picturam faciendam per dictum Simonem in ecclesia dicti Mon.ri de qua per istrum. rogatum... sub die octavo instantis mensis novembris...".
ASM, *Notarile* 10029 (Galdo da Lodi).
Sannazzaro 1989 (b), p. 61 n. 19.

1573, 11 March
Payment for work in the Cappella Fiorenza by Semino (whose workshop was later frequented by Duchino: 4 December 1573).
ASM, *Notarile* 10029 (Galdo da Lodi).
Sannazzaro 1989 (b), p. 60 nn. 12–13.

1573, 15 May
Payment to Peterzano for fresco work under way on the entrance wall: "Jo Simone di Petrazano [sic] del q.Fran.o p.o. parochie S. Stephanini di Milano, confesso avere recevuto da Bianca Ger.a di Brivio... venti d.o in oro d'Ittalia [sic], et sono in pagamento... che è convenuto della pittura che esso Simon fa nella Chiesa di esso Mon.ro conforme a una convenzione sopra ciò fatta... Io Simone confesso quanto è di sopra, et per fede ò sotoscrito di mano propria".
ASM, *Notarile* 14080 (Castiglioni Gio. Pietro).
Sannazzaro 1989 (b), p. 61.

1573, 12 June
Written acknowledgment by Giovan Antonio Ferrari and Giuseppe Prevosti of having received funds for work on the Cappella Fiorenza: "Giov. Ant. Ferrari e Josepo di Prevosti che confessano aver ricevuto... petre di castione a bon conto del l'opere... nella cappella della sig. Fiorenza... opera di stucco alla cappella della Fiorenza per opera di Giov. Antonio Ferrari... a bon conto della istugadura che siamo tenuti a far della gesa del Monastero Magior de M. nella cappella della s. Fiorenza".
ASM, *Religione p.a.* 2147.
Sannazzaro 1989 (b), p. 60 n. 12.

1573, 22 August
Balance of payment to Peterzano for the entrance wall frescoes: "Io Simone de Petrazani del q. Franc.o p.o. parochie S. Stefanino in Nosiggia de M.lo confesso avere recevuto da la molto R.da M.D. Ger.a de Brivio abb.a del Mon.ro Maggior de M.lo scudi trenta in oro d'Ittalia, et sono per saldo de la mercede della pittura fatta alla fazzada de la chiesa di esso Mon.ro, convenute in scudi 80 d'oro come per instrumento di convenzione... rogato per... Galdo da Lodi notaio di Milano a mesi passati, e per fede io sottoscritto di manu propria. Io Simone Peterzano ho sopra schrito et afermo et confesso quanto è disopra di manu propria".
ASM, *Notarile* 14080 (Castiglioni Gio. Pietro).
Sannazzaro 1989 (b), p. 61.

1574, 22 March
Balance of payment to Giovan Antonio Ferrari and Giuseppe Prevosti for work in the Cappella Fiorenza.
ASM, *Religione p.a.* 2147.
Sannazzaro 1989 (b), p. 60 n. 12.

1574, 6 August
Contract for Pietro Francesco da Como "aurifero", son of late Antonio, parish of Santa Tecla, for the execution in six months of a statue representing St Sigismund, in fine silver, one *braccio* tall, in accordance with the drawing executed by Francesco Pirovano, with a gilded brass base, gold crown, gold-tipped sceptre (in hand), gilded vestment hems; the crown, with its gemstones, was provided by the contracting nun, Paola Francesca di Appiano, "sacrestana".
ASM, *Notarile* 10030 (Galdo da Lodi).
Sannazzaro 1989 (b), p. 62 nn. 24–25.

1577, 5 July
Commission for candleholders, described in detail, from Giovanni and Francesco Bartolomeo, brothers of Toledo, goldsmiths, with variations on the previous drawings.
ASM, *Notarile* 14080 (Castiglioni Gio. Pietro).
Sannazzaro 1989 (b), p. 62 n. 26.

1578, 1 February
Payment from the abbess Laura Fiorenza for the high altar and the reduction of the dividing wall window.
ASM, *Religione p.a.* 2147.
Sannazzaro 1992, p. 108 n. 35.

1578, 17 February
"Lo meser Paolo e meser Claudio picca prede confessiamo ricevuta lire trentacinque e soldi 8, quali ebbe[ro] nel mese di decembre, et questo per compito pagamento delle prede intagliate per la ferriata del altare."
ASM, *Religione p.a.* 2147.
Rossi 1914, p. 47.

1578, 25 June
Obligation to Antonio Campi "di far di sua mano una anchona per l'altare grande del[l]a giesia... fatto sopra la tella a olio, la pictura di qual sarà il misterio della adoratione dilli tri maggi et sue circumstantie", to be delivered within a year. Acknowledgment of Antonio Campi of having received from the abbess Laura Fiorenza the sum of 50 gold *scudi* as an advance on the sum of 125, "et deta Anchona mi obligo darla dipinta di qua a uno an(n)o, comenciando il giorno di sopra".
ASM, *Religione p.a.* 2147.
Rossi 1914, p. 50.

1578, 25 August
"Ricevute dalla Badessa D. Laura Fiorenza £ 860 soldi 5 per scalini di pietra fato dal mae[stro] Paulo dei Zimini, scalini posti al altar grande dela chiesa di fora."
ASM, *Religione p.a.* 2147.
Rossi 1914, p. 47.

1578, 4 October
Acknoweldgment from Gio. Batta Suardo for payments made by the abbess for the "tabernacolo fatto per la sua giesa di legnamo et per ciò scutti 30".
ASM, *Religione p.a.* 2147.
Rossi 1914, p. 50.

1590, 2 July
Measurements and estimates by the engineer Gio. Batta Strazza [Stratta] on works realized by Cesare Pobia for the construction of the cloister refectory, including "Per la capa del camino del refetorio nuovo... con ornamento... con scartozono di cotto che religano ad efeto di ponerli tre santi... con sue piramide... Per li ornamenti fatti sopra le finestre".
ASM, *Religione p.a.* 2147 (also 2 September 1590).
Sannazzaro 1992, pp. 160–161, nn. 24–27.

1682, 16 April
Federico Perego acknowledges receiving "dall'Ill.ma e Rev.ma Mad. Anna Lucretia Arese... priora... £ 10.355 per saldo della Ancona d'argento... et oro delle dorature delle lettere et ornamenti intorno alle figure... con anco pietre per esse figure et legni dietro la cimasa... Io Federico Perego Arg(entie)ro".
ASM, *Religione p.a.* 2147.
Rossi 1914, pp. 51–52.

1683, 21 December
Giacomo Muttone acknowledges receiving 6,000 Lire "per l'ornamento in pietra fatto alla porta".
ASM, *Religione p.a.* 2147.

1705, 26–27–29 October, 6–26 November, 4 December 1706, 12–25 January
"Decreti ordinati da Noi Giuseppe del titolo di Santa Prisca della Santa Chiesa Romana Prete Cardinal Archinto Arcivescovo di Milano nella nostra personal Visita della Chiesa e Monastero delle Monache di San Maurizio detto Maggiore in P. V. di questa Città, fatta li 26–27–29 ottobre; 6–26 novembre; 4 dicembre 1705; 12 e 25 gennaio 1706." Including, "Ordiniamo a d.a R. Madre Abbadessa di far abbassare in termini di tré mesi l'organo con la sua cantoria, quali tempo fa si fecero alzare troppo vicino alla superficie del muro, che divide la Chiesa interiore dall'esteriore: e ciò, quanto bisogni, per togliere ogni veduta in d.a Chiesa esteriore; sotto pena di sospensione dall'uffizio; e di privazione di voce attiva e passiva contro le altre Monache, a' quali possa ciò spettare, overo che si opponessero... Facciansi quanto prima visitare da perito Architetto i muri della Cappella della resurrezione per potere opportunam[ent]e provvedere a qualunque pericolo di rovina. E non si manchi di far aggiustare le crepature, che vedonsi, ov'è dipinto quel Mistero... Alla fenestrella del Comunicatorio si metta di fuori frà due mesi un'Antina decente di legno, con serratura e chiave, da conservarsi dalla R. Madre Abbadessa: e ciò sotto pena a Noi arbitraria".
ASD, sez. XII, *Ordini religiosi e congregazioni* 101.
Sannazzaro 1992, p. 57 n. 65.

1790, 6 February
First drawing of the ancona: "Resta fissato il dis[s]egno più alto con la testa di Angelo sotto al timpano... Giuseppe Maria Buzzi ac[c]etto".
ASM, *Religione p.a.* 2147.
Rossi 1914, p. 52.

1791, 13 December
Domenico Aspari, teacher of drawing at the Brera Academy, brings to the attention of the official sector representative certain "opere d'arte in Milano, dipinte a fresco sul muro, quali vanno di giorno in giorno decadendo e di cui sarebbe pregio dell'opera di potere conservare la memoria", including, "molte pitture di Bernardino Luini nel Monastero Maggiore di Milano".
ASM, *Autografi* 92, 12.
Ferri Piccaluga 1990, p. 219.

1792, 29–31 May
Drawings for the high altar: elevation with notations of materials, signed by "Giuseppe Antonio Pissina ing.re e Architetto" (29 May); and plan, signed by Pissina, Giuseppe Maria Buzzi, and Antonio Giudice (31 May).
ASM, *Religione p.a.* 2147.
Rossi 1914, p. 52.

1794, 26 September
The nuns aknowledge having "fatto nell'or decorso anno di nuovo construere a Marmi lustri l'Altare Maggiore, non che pulire le Pitture nel corpo della loro Chiesa Esteriore e nel corrente anno fatto pure porre li gradini di marmo alli sei Altari laterali", asking for the bishop's pe rmission to go and inspect the work done.
ASD, sez. XII, *Ordini religiosi e congregazioni* 101.
Sannazzaro 1992, p. 118 n. 43.

1794, 28 September
Bishop Filippo Visconti authorizes the nuns to proceed "per una volta solamente" to the "Chiesa esteriore dello stesso Monastero... affine di osservarvi il bell'Altare Maggiore di novo construtto, e gli altri altari minori, e Pitture: colle condizioni però, e non altrimenti, che siano cioè in tal tempo ben chiuse le Porte si della Chiesa, che del Cortile che dalla Strada immediatamente mette al Monastero, né vi si trovi alcuna Persona Secolare che siavi il Nostro Cancelliere, e per le Monache, e il Confessore Ordinario del suddetto Monastero, amendue da Noi delegati, e che finalmente prima dell'Ave Maria della sera sieno entro la propria Clausura" ("Sortirono all'ore due e mezza del dopo pranzo nel dì 29 settembre 1794, e rientraro prima dell'Ave Maria").
ASD, sez. XII, *Ordini religiosi e congregazioni* 101.
Sannazzaro 1992, p. 118 n. 43.

1798, 22 November
"Descriptio bonorum" of the monastery, including two "Quadri letterari".
ASC, *Località milanesi* 230.
Sannazzaro 1989 (b), p. 61 n. 15.

1798, 24 November
The central authorities of Olona accept the nuns' request to continue living at the Monastero Maggiore: "il locale di cui si tratta essend'esso di pianta così irregolare, e di costruzione così infelice da doversi ritenere il meno adattato agli usi pubblici... si verrebbe ad allontanare il pericolo di danno all'annessa chiesa, che per le pregiatissime pitture, di cui è fornita, dei Luini, e Vinci, merita d'esser conservata".
ASM, *Culto p.a.* 1926.

1802, 8 December
Andrea Appiani, official of the Heritage Commission mentions "due quadri grandi di tela... molto logori", to be transported to the Brera Academy.
ASM, *Studi p.m.* 350; *Autografi* 103 (December 1802).

undated (1812?)
"Nota degli oggetti che esistevano nel coro".
ASM, *Culto p.m.* 1587; ASMP, 44/I.
Rossi 1914, p. 86.

1836, 15 March
Inventory of assets belonging to the church sacristy.
ASMP, 44/I.

undated (1844)
Request for permission to move the *Virgin* statue by Gaetano Monti da Ravanna from the chapel dedicated to St Stephen, where it had stood for some time in the chapel opposite in place of a "un quadro per cui non si ha una particolare venerazione", with a design for a gilded wooden tabernacle.

ASC, *Ornato Fabbriche* I, 18 (also 13 August 1844); ASMP 44/1 (Rossi 1914, p. 72).
Sannazzaro 1989 (b), p. 63 n. 33.

1856, 15 February
Job report by Felice Valenzani, who claims to have also repaired the *Adoration of the Shepherds*, remarking that "i fondi oscuri ed altri rapezzi sono stati eseguiti verso il 1824 dal pittore (Alessandro) Sanquirico".
AAB, *Carpi* A I /11.

1856, 3 March
For the Cappella Besozzi (previously assigned to the gilder and varnisher Felice Valenzani, who had damaged the work) the board of the Brera Academy appointed Knoller, who finished the job on 3 October.
AAB, *Carpi* A I/11 (also 18 December 1857); ASMP, 44/I (Rossi 1914, pp. 57, 62).

1859, 24 March
The board of the Brera Academy assessed Knoller's quote of 2 October 1856 for restoration work, voicing their objection to his fees and to the extent of work he proposed to undertake; in the *Flagellation* chapel, "si dovrebbe principalmente mirare allo spoglio della parte decorativa ed ornamentale dalla schifose e vandaliche ridipinture onde fu bruttata alcuni anni or sono, riservandosi di restituirla poscia artisticamente al carattere ed all'apparenza originale".
AAB, *Carpi* A I/11.

1859, 30 September
The Fabbriceria (Works Department) submitted to central administration the estimate from Giuseppe Knoller (2 October 1856), stating that the "Lesene della tribuna poste superiormente alla porta maggiore, nulla si rinvenne" were to be scraped clean and then repainted "come si crede all'epoca del scenografo Sanquirico... prosegue questo fregio al lato destro entrando con ornati ridipinti in giallo, che si direbbero moderni essendo ritoccati, ma che dietro esperimento si riconobbero di epoca antica benché non del tempo che si sarebbe creduto... Cappella della Flagellazione, la quale si è già riordinata... segue l'ultima con piccola porta d'ingresso al cortile. E queste pitture, ritenute dell'autore Ottavio Semini, altro non hanno bisogno che di qualche parziale pulimento... Quanto l'architrave come la cornice al di sotto della tribuna sono pure di fresco ridipinti".
AAB, *Carpi* A I /11.

1861, 24 August
Meeting at San Maurizio of the steering committee for the fresco restoration project.
ASMP, 44/II, 71.

1867, 23 September (24 September)
The Brera Academy advises that at 5 p.m. on 27 September an academic committee will visit the church to inspect the paintings in the chapel affected by proposed works on Via Luini.
ASMP, 44/III, 123-42; also ASCM, *Piano regolatore* (Master Plan) 1481, 27 September 1867 (Pertot 1995, p. 126).

1869, 14 January
The Fabbriceria asks the city council for funds for repairs to the down-pipes on the east flank of the church, where leaking has damaged the Luini frescoes.
ASMP, 44/II, 85-32 (also ASM, *Prefettura* 665, undated: Pertot 1995, p. 126).

1872, 10 June
Offer of purchase for four tapestries from the church.
ASMP, *Fabbriceria, Arredi sacri* 59 (also 3 June 1872, and, though undated, June–July 1872).

1872, 26 June
The painter Francesco Piana requests 1,000 Lire for "pittura a fresco" effected along the right flank of the church.
ASMP, 44/II (also 18 January 1873).

1872, 19 August
The engineer Gino Magretti, summoned by the Fabbriceria regarding the opportunity of selling tapestries for the sum of 600 Lire, expresses his disapproval.
ASMP, *Fabbriceria, Arredi sacri* 59.
Sannazzaro 2000, p. 151 n. 70.

1873, 25 January
Expenses account (185.70 Lire) for restoration works effected in the church (1872) by "Ditta Bossi, doratore e verniciatore".
ASMP, 44/II.

1886
Report on consolidation work on the building's fabric, including repairs to decorations damaged by raw plaster.
ASMP, *Chiesa di San Maurizio*.

1888
The tapestries are cited in the general inventory drawn up in the provincial fine arts department registry.
ASMP, *Restauri alle chiese*.

1892, 6 July
Gaetano Moretti remarks on the results of work carried out under Del Colla on two of the second-order archways along the church's flank, where certain "a fresco" paintwork was effected using methods that went contrary to the "regola basilare al patrimonio di ogni buon professionista".
ASMP, *Chiesa di San Maurizio*.

1895, 22 July
Authorization from the Education Department for the sale of four tapestries to Scavini from Intra (11,600 Lire).
ASMP, *Chiesa di San Maurizio*; ASMP, *Restauri alle chiese* (1896, 27 March: auth. Ministry for the Arts).
Rossi 1914, pp. 8–11.

1895, 30 July
Note on the criteria applied at the time for the inventory of the church's assets.
ASMP, *Fabbriceria* 63, *Inventari*.
Sannazzaro 2000, p. 151 n. 67.

1895–1897
"Chiesa S. Maria alla Porta, e sussidiarie di S. Maria al Castello e di S. Maurizio. Inventario cominciato nel 1895 e completato nel 1897".
ASMP, *Fabbriceria, Registri vari* 17/6 bis.

1896, 19 September
Regional office for heritage conservation informs the Education Department of its intention to carry out various operations on the church, including the restoration of the façade, with the replacement of falling cornice ledges, the substitution of the down-pipes, and the cleaning of the frescoes.
ASMP, *Chiesa di San Maurizio*.

1897, 22 June
Estimate tendered by Giuseppe Stefanoni and sons ("trasponitori di pitture e riparatori d'opere d'arte - Bergamo") for the cleaning of all the frescoes except those in the vault, for 2 Lire per sq.m (attached also quote from F. Nicora for the sum of 1,000 Lire).
ASMP, *Restauri alle chiese*.

1897, 3 November
"Quadri esistenti nella Chiesa di San Maurizio al Monastero Maggiore."
ASMP, *Fabbriceria* 63, *Inventari*.
Sannazzaro 2000, pp. 151–152, n. 68.

1897, November
"Nota degli oggetti da stimarsi dal falegname [...] San Maurizio Monastero Maggiore."
Estimate for metal fixtures.
ASMP, *Fabbriceria* 63, *Inventari*.

1897, December
"Nota degli oggetti rimasti da stimare per completare l'Inventario della Chiesa di San Maurizio al Monastero Maggiore."
ASMP, *Fabbriceria* 63, *Inventari*.

1897, 31 December
"Riassunto dell'Inventario degli Oggetti di Culto, Arredi Sacri e Mobilio della Chiesa di Santa Maria alla Porta, di Santa Maria al Castello, di San Maurizio al Monastero Maggiore."
ASMP, *Fabbriceria* 63, *Inventari*.

1899, 2 May
Detailed report on works on the church carried out by the regional office, including operations on the frescoes.
ASM, *Prefettura* 6396.
Pertot 1995, p. 133.

1900
Replacement of manuals and keys on the Antegnati organ.
ASMP, *Restauri alle chiese*.

1910, 23 December
Constitution of a special committee for collecting funds for the restoration of the frescoes, comprised in works financed by a bequest (50,000 Lire).
ASMP, *Chiesa di San Maurizio* (also ASBBAA, *Archivio vecchio* 7: Pertot 1995, p. 133).

1911, 9 April
Committee report on restoration work.
ASMP, *Chiesa di San Maurizio*; also ASBBAASS, *San Maurizio e Monastero Maggiore*, 1911, 24 June.

1911, 8 September
Luca Beltrami informs the Heritage

Commission of his withdrawal from the restoration committee, while assuring the continuance of his financial assistance and devolving a quota of the returns on his book on Luini.
ASMP, *Chiesa di San Maurizio*.

1912, 16 September
Start of work supervised by Brusconi (Heritage Commission) and Vandoni, including the restoration of the frescoes (test areas were followed by dusting and cleaning).
ASMP, *Chiesa di San Maurizio*.
Rossi 1914, p. 121.

1915-1916
Brusconi observes that below the large canvases (recently restored) there appear scant patches of painting around the large rose window, and the upper part of a saint, life-size, painted and repainted several times over ("scarse tracce di decorazione del contorno del gran rosone, e la parte superiore di un santo, grande del vero, fatta e rifatta parecchie volte").
ASBBAA, *Archivio vecchio, San Maurizio al Monastero Maggiore*.
Sannazzaro 1989 (b), p. 61 n. 20.

1916, 22 July
The Heritage Commission communicates the conclusion of the test patches of cleaning on Luini's frescoes under the arched platform on the nuns' side, where further studies were then made by Beltrami and Cavenaghi (28 May 1917), and by Ambrogio Annoni (22 July 1917).
ASMP, *Chiesa di San Maurizio*.

1917, 5 February
Consequent to surveys made on-site at the church (2 February), Ambrogio Annoni observes that in the intrados of the arched platform in the nuns' hall the minute decorative work in gold paste, such as the rays, halos, and trilobed arches, are almost completely deteriorated or depleted, leaving a white patch where the material has become detached. He recommends intervention though maintaining the dulled tone of the gilding, given that the cleaning operation being effected on the frescoes (saints) is fairly advanced. As regards repairs to the walling left exposed, he considers it too early to intervene, and not associable with operations curently under way.
ASBBAA, *Archivio vecchio, San Maurizio al Monastero Maggiore*.
Sannazzaro 2000, p. 151 n. 66.

1917, 2 April
Assent of the Heritage Commission for the sale of the church's baldacchino: the proceeds will go towards the restoration work.
ASBBAASS, *San Maurizio e Monastero Maggiore*.

1917, 22 May
Start of restoration work in the nuns' hall, in the fifth chapel right of the entrance.
ASMP, *Chiesa di San Maurizio*.

1964
Series of frescoes transferred to canvas (lunette of *St Francis*; Cappella Besozzi: *St Catherine and the Miracle of the Wheel* and upper lunette; Cappella Bentivoglio: *Christ Mocked*; nuns' hall, pair of saints flanking the first-order roundels along the right wall, and the nun-saint with dove and book in the loggia).
ASBBAASS, *San Maurizio e Monastero Maggiore*.

Bibliography
Related to Paintings, Decorations and Furnishings

1554
Bandello M., *La contessa di Cellant e il marchese Ermes Visconti. Novella storica del sec. XVI, pubblicata per cura di Massimo Fabi* (1554), Milan 1858.
1568
Vasari G., *Vite de' più eccellenti architetti, scultori e pittori*, Florence 1568, Florence 1906 (1973) ed., VI, p. 520 n. 2.
1587
Lomazzo G.P., *Rime divise in sette libri [...] con la vita dell'autore descritta da lui stesso in rime sciolte*, Milan, p. 536.
1592
Lomazzo G.P., *Idea del tempio della pittura*, Milan, pp. 8–9.
1671
Santagostino A., *L'immortalità e la gloria del pennello*, Milan 1671, p. 91; Milan 1981 ed., p. 48.
1674
Torre C., *Il Ritratto di Milano*, Milan 1674, 1714 ed., pp. 211–212.
1704–05
Biffi G., *Pitture, scolture et ordini d'architettura narrati co' suoi autori da inserirsi a' suoi luoghi nell'opera di Milano ricercata nel suo sito*, MS 1704–05, Florence 1990 ed., p. 95.
1738
Latuada S., *Descrizione di Milano*, Milan, IV, n. 170, pp. 17, 31, 410–425.
1747
Santagostino G. and A., *Catalogo delle pitture più insigni che stanno esposte al pubblico della città di Milano*, Milan, 2nd ed., pp. 81–82.
1776
Bartoli F., *Notizie delle sculture, pitture e architetture che ornano le principali città d'Italia*, I, Venice, p. 204.
1787
Bianconi C., *Nuova guida di Milano*, Milan 1787, p. 271; 1795 ed., p. 313.
1792–96
Lanzi L., *Storia pittorica d'Italia*, Milan 1792–96, 1833 ed., V.
1796
Bianconi C., *Nuova guida di Milano*, Milan, p. 312.
1802
Cenni intorno alla chiesa del Monastero Maggiore di Milano dedicata ai Santi Maurizio e Sigismondo ora sussidiaria a Santa Maria alla Porta, Milan; 2nd ed. Milan 1862.
Quadro storico di Milano antica e moderna, Milan, p. 225.
1811
Fumagalli I., *Scuola di Leonardo da Vinci in Lombardia o sia Raccolta di varie opere eseguite dagli allievi e imitatori di quel gran maestro disegnate, incise e descritte da Ignazio Fumagalli*, Milan.
1818
Bossi L., *Guida di Milano*, I, Milan, pp. 155–157.
1827
Caselli G., *Nuovo ritratto di Milano in riguardo alle belle arti*, Milan, pp. 160–161.
1831
Pirovano F., *Nuova guida di Milano*, Milan, pp. 153–157.
1833
Lanzi L., *Storia pittorica d'Italia*, V, Milan.
1869–70
Lafenestre G., "Bernardino Luini", in *Gazette des Beaux-Arts*, II, 1869, pp. 441–451; I, 1870, pp. 47–57.
1871
Crowe J.A. and Cavalcaselle G.B., *A History of Painting in North Italy*, I, London, p. 436 n. 3.
1872
Mongeri G., *L'arte in Milano*, Milan, pp. 236–248.
1875
Romussi C., *Milano nei suoi monumenti*, Milan 1875, 1912 ed., I, p. 89 ff.
1877
Milano Diamante, ed. I. Cantù and F. Venosta, Milan, p. 241.
1878
Paoli, "Über Luini's Fresken in S. Maurizio zu Mailand", in *Zeitschrift für bildenden Kunst*, II, p. 41 ff.
1880
"Atti della Commissione conservatrice dei monumenti e oggetti d'arte della provincia di Milano", in *Archivio Storico Lombardo*, VII, pp. 10, 51, 53, 70, 73, 116.
1881
Borghi, "Palazzi e monumenti", in *Milano nel 1881*, Milan.
Parravicini T.V., *Guida artistica di Milano, dintorni e laghi*, Milan ("Ricordo dell'esposizione internazionale"), p. 111.
1890
Forcella V., *Iscrizioni nelle chiese e negli altri edifici di Milano dal sec. XVIII ai giorni nostri*, III, Milan, pp. 449–460.
1891
Rotta P., *Passeggiate storiche, ossia le chiese di Milano*, Milan, pp. 135–137.
1893
"Prima relazione annuale dell'Ufficio Regionale", in *Archivio Storico Lombardo*, XX, s. II.
1894
Chiesi G., *Milano*, Turin (*La Patria. Geografia dell'Italia*, ed. G. Strafforello), pp. 101–102.
"Seconda relazione annuale dell'Ufficio Regionale", in *Archivio Storico Lombardo*, II, s. III.
Rod E., "Il Monastero Maggiore in Milano", in *Perseveranza*, 2 December (also *Journal des débats*, 22 November).
1896
Moretti G., "Quarta relazione annuale dell'Ufficio Regionale", in *Archivio Storico Lombardo*, XXIII, 12.
1897
Morelli G., *Della pittura italiana*, Milan, p. 159.
Meyer G., *Oberitalienische für Renaissance*, I, Berlin 1897, 1900 ed., II, p. 120.
1898
Moretti G., "Quinta relazione annuale dell'Ufficio Regionale", in *Archivio Storico Lombardo*, XXV, 17.
1899
Beltrami L., "Arte antica. La chiesa di San Maurizio in Milano e le pitture di Bernardino Luini", in *Emporium*, 49, pp. 51–62.
Moretti G., "Sesta e settima relazione annuale dell'Ufficio Regionale", in *Archivio Storico Lombardo*, XXVI, pp. 20–24.
Williamson G.C., *Bernardino Luini*, London, p. 129.
1900
Gauthiez P., "Nouvelles recherches sur Bernardino Luini", in *Gazette des Beaux-Arts*, 1, p. 32 ff.
1901
Beltrami L., "The Chapel of S. Catherine in the Church of S. Maurizio, Milan", in *Italian Wall Decorations of the 15th and 16th Century. A Hand-*

book to the Models Illustrating Interiors of Italian Buildings in the Victoria and Albert Museum, London, pp. 33–44.
1905
Gauthiez P., *Bernardino Luini*, Paris, p. 70 ff.
1906
Malaguzzi Valeri F., *Milano*, II, Bergamo, pp. 79–81.
1907
Berenson B., *Italian Pictures of the Renaissance. Central Italian and North Italian Schools*, London 1907, London 1968 ed., pp. 232–233, pl. 1493.
1908
Malaguzzi Valeri F., "Contributi alla storia di San Maurizio", in *Archivio Storico Lombardo*, XXXV, s. IX, pp. 325–339.
Moretti G. and Nebbia U., *La conservazione dei monumenti in Lombardia: relazione Ufficio Regionale*, Milan, pp. 84–85.
1911
Beltrami L., *Bernardino Luini*, Milan, pp. 346–350, 496–507.
Nebbia U., "Note intorno alla chiesa di San Maurizio al Monastero Maggiore", in *Rassegna d'Arte*, XI, pp. 9–12.
1912
Romussi C., *Milano nei suoi monumenti*, Milan, p. 89.
Toesca P., *La pittura e la miniatura nella Lombardia. Dai più antichi monumenti alla metà del Quattrocento*, Milan 1912, Torino 1966 ed., p. 78.
1913
Giulini A., "Su la sepoltura di A. Bentivoglio", in *Archivio Storico Lombardo*, XX, s. IV, pp. 255–256.
1914
Rossi I., *La chiesa di San Maurizio in Milano. Il Monastero Maggiore e le sue due torri*, Milan.
1915
Malaguzzi Valeri F., *La corte di Ludovico il Moro*, II, Milan, pp. 263–269.
1916
Beretta R., "Il Monastero Maggiore di Milano e la riforma operatavi da san Carlo Borromeo il 23 febbraio 1568", in *Rivista storica benedettina*, XI, pp. 127–142.
1922
Romussi C., *Milano nei suoi monumenti*, Milan, p. 89 ff.
1924
Venturi A., *Storia dell'arte italiana*, VI-II, Milan, part II, pp. 669–671, 803.
1926
Pica A., "Il Monastero Maggiore", in *Per l'Arte Sacra*, III, pp. 29–45.
1927–28
Pevsner N., "Eine Revision der Caravaggio-daten", in *Zeitschrift für bildenden Kunst*, p. 390 ff.
1928
Pevsner N., *Barockmalerei in den Romanischen Ländern*, I, Potsdam.
1929
Longhi R., "Quesiti caravaggeschi", in *Pinacotheca*, pp. 258–320.
Suida W., *Leonardo und sein Kreis*, Munich.
1930
Ponzoni C., *Le chiese di Milano*, Milan, pp. 207–215.
1933
Ansaldi G., "Il primo tempo nell'arte di Bernardino Luini", in *Nuova Antologia*, 1473, pp. 439–451.
1934
Bartoli F., "Dove probabilmente nacque un capolavoro di Bernardino Luini", in *Arte cristiana*, XXII, pp. 130–134.
Venturi A., *Storia dell'arte italiana*, IX, Milan, part VII, pp. 381–391, 483–489, 490, 501–513.
1940
Baroni C., "Aggiunte al Peterzano", in *L'Arte*, pp. 114–133.
1942
Tea E., *Architettura e decorazione nelle chiese di Milano*, Milan, pp. 23–24.
Venturi A., *Leonardo e la sua scuola*, Novara, pp. XXIX–XXX, 86–87.
1945
Sioli Legnani E. and Mezzanotte P., *Il Borgo Nuovo*, Milan ("Contrade milanesi", 1), p. 63.
1948
Mezzanotte P. and Bascapé G.C., *Milano nell'arte e nella storia*, Milan 1948, pp. 619–628, 1968 ed., pp. 316–321.
c. 1950
Baroni C., *La pittura lombarda durante la crisi manieristica*, Milan.
1953
Ottino Della Chiesa A., *Bernardino Luini*, Florence, n.p., pls. 80–82, 108–111.
Suida W., *Bramante pittore e Bramantino*, Milan, pp. 143, 223.
1954
Calvesi M., "Simone Peterzano maestro del Caravaggio", in *Bollettino d'arte*, XXXIX, pp. 122, 125, 128, 130–131.
1956
Ottino Della Chiesa A., *Bernardino Luini*, Novara.
Wittgens F., "La pittura lombarda nella seconda metà del Quattrocento", in *Storia di Milano*, VII, Milan, p. 749 ff.
1957
Arslan E., "L'architettura milanese nel primo Cinquecento", in *Storia di Milano*, VIII, Milan, p. 533.
Dell'Acqua G.A., "La pittura a Milano dalla metà del XVI secolo al 1630", in *Storia di Milano*, X, Milan, pp. 671, 678, 682–683, 692, 719.
Levi Pisetzky R., "L'apogeo dell'eleganza milanese durante il Ducato", in *Storia di Milano*, VIII, Milan, pp. 750–751.
Mazzini F., "La pittura del primo Cinquecento", in *Storia di Milano*, VI-II, Milan, p. 565 ff.
1958
Spina Barelli E., "Il Lomazzo o il ruolo delle personalità psicologiche nell'estetica dell'ultimo manierismo lombardo", in *Arte lombarda*, III, pp. 119–124.
1959
Ronchi M., "Gli affreschi di Bernardino Luini nella chiesa dei Santi Maurizio e Sigismondo", in *Città di Milano*, 6, June, pp. 376–377.
1962
Bertini A., "La giovinezza di Bernardino Luini", in *La Critica d'Arte*, IX, 53–54, pp. 20–61.
Ottino Della Chiesa A. and Reina P., *San Maurizio al Monastero Maggiore*, Milan.
1963
Bossaglia R., "San Maurizio al Monastero Maggiore", in *Arte lombarda*, VII, 1, pp. 165–166.
Gamulin G., "Qualche aggiunta alla pittura lombarda", in *Arte lombarda*, VIII, 2, p. 262.
Matalon S., *Gli affreschi lombardi del Trecento*, Milan, p. 459.
1965
Ady C., *I Bentivoglio*, Milan.
Ferrari M.L., "Calisto de la Piaza", in *Paragone*, 185, pp. 17–40, new ed. in Idem, *Studi di storia dell'arte*, Florence 1979, p. 148.
1966
Gatti Perer M.L., "Esempi di pittura rinascimentale in Valle Intelvi: il ciclo di affreschi nell'abside della chiesa dei Santi Nazaro e Celso a Scaria", in *Arte lombarda*, XI, 2, pp. 107, 111–112.
1967
Ferrari M.L., "Zenale, Cesariano e Luini: un arco di classicismo lombardo", in *Paragone*, 211, pp. 26–28, nos. 16–22.
Gatti Perer M.L., "Milano – San Maurizio al Monastero Maggiore", in *Studi e ricerche nel territorio della provincia di Milano: 50 monumenti restaurati*, Milan, pp. 151–154, 242.
1968
Reina P., *San Maurizio al Monastero Maggiore in Milano, sec. XVI*, Milan.
Tea E., *Quattrocento e Cinquecento*, Turin, pp. 757, 763, 766, 782.
1969
De Angelis D'Ossat G., "Origine e fortuna dei battisteri ambrosiani", in *Arte lombarda*, XIV, 1, p. 19.
1971
Bossaglia R., "L'arte dal manierismo al primo Cinquecento", in *Storia di Monza e della Brianza*, V, Milan, pp. 14, 16.
Mazzini F., "L'impiego di supporti di polivinile per il ricollocamento di affreschi strappati", in *ICOMOS. Il monumento per l'uomo*, proceedings of the 2nd Congresso internazionale di restauro, Bologna, pp. 343–347.
Mazzini F., "Ragguagli dell'impiego ed esperimento di nuovi materiali, apparecchi e nuove tecniche per la conservazione dei dipinti", in *Restauri in Piemonte 1968–1971*, exhibition catalogue, Turin, p. 8.
Sciolla G.C., "L'arte dei Piazza", in Novasconi A., *I Piazza*, Lodi, p. 28 n. 46.
1972
Barigozzi Brini A., *Milano. Cicli di affreschi*, Milan, n.p.
Gatti S., *Milano Cinquecento*, Milan, n.p.
1974
Asselberghs J.P., *Les tapisseries flamandes aux Etats-Unis d'Amérique*, Brussels, p. 43.
Ferrari M.L., *San Sigismondo di Cremona*, Milan, p. 146 n. 112.
Fiorio M.T., "Note su alcuni disegni inediti di Simone Peterzano", in *Arte lombarda*, 40, p. 91.
1975
Binaghi M.T., "L'immagine sacra in Luini e il circolo di Santa Marta", in *Sacro e profano nella pittura di Bernardino Luini*, exhibition catalogue, Milan, pp. 82–85.
Dell'Acqua G.A., "Introduzione al Luini", in *Sacro e profano nella pittura di Bernardino Luini*, exhibition catalogue, Milan, pp. 25–26.
1977
Bora G., "La cultura figurativa a Milano (1535–1565)", in *Omaggio a Tiziano*, exhibition catalogue, Milan, pp. 50, 54.
1979
Binaghi Olivari M.T., "I francesi a Milano (1499–1525): arti figurative e moda", in *Annali dell'Istituto storico italo-germanico di Trento*, pp. 49–76.
Bora G., "Un ciclo di affreschi, due artisti e una bottega a Santa Maria di Campagna a Pallanza", in *Arte lombarda*, 52, p. 92 n. 16.
1980
Falchetti A. and Matalon S., *Itinerari per Milano*, Milan, pp. 133–138.
Gatti Perer M.L., *Umanesimo a Mi-*

lano. L'Osservanza agostiniana all'Incoronata, Milan, p. 6.
Occhipinti E., "San Maurizio al Monastero Maggiore di Milano", in *Monasteri benedettini in Lombardia*, Milan, pp. 68–79.
1981
Sannazzaro G.B., *San Maurizio al Monastero Maggiore*, Milan.
Sironi V., "Pittura, musica e poesia in San Maurizio al Monastero Maggiore", in *La Martinella*, XXXV, pp. 183–187.
1982
Carlevaro G., "Materiale per lo studio di Bernardo Zenale", in *Arte lombarda*, 63, pp. 105–106.
Fiorio M.T., *Leonardeschi in Lombardia*, Milan, pp. 74–75, 78, 93–94.
1983
Bora G., "La decorazione pittorica: sino al Settecento", in *Santa Maria delle Grazie*, Milan, p. 168.
Leonardo e il leonardismo a Napoli e a Roma, exhibition catalogue, Florence, p. 153.
Tagliabue M., "San Maurizio o Monastero Maggiore", in *Monasteri e conventi in Lombardia*, exhibition catalogue, Milan, pp. 16–17.
1984
Bologna G., *La Trivulziana per san Carlo Borromeo*, Milan, IV, p. 16, V, pp. 14, 27.
1985
Bandera S., "San Maurizio al Mona stero Maggiore", in *Le chiese di Milano*, ed. M.T. Fiorio, Milan, pp. 85–94.
Bora G., in *I Campi e la cultura cremonese del Cinquecento*, exhibition catalogue, Milan, pp. 181–184, 300.
1986
Bisogni F., "Gli affreschi della 'torre di Ansperto' a Milano", in *Arte cristiana*, 712, pp. 3–14.
De Marchi P.M., "Nota preliminare sul Monastero Maggiore e l'inserimento delle strutture romane preesistenti negli edifici conventuali", in *Scritti in ricordo di Graziella Massari Gaballo e di Umberto Tocchetti Pollini*, Milan, pp. 351–358.
Denker Nesselrath C., "I chiostri di Sant'Ambrogio. Il dettaglio degli ordini", in *Bramante a Milano*, conference proceedings (Milan 1985), in *Arte lombarda*, pp. 54–56.
Gallone Galassi A. and Bandera S., "Conservation Treatment and Scientific Study of the Frescoes by 'Anonimo Lombardo' and Bernardino Luini in the Church of S. Maurizio al Monastero Maggiore (Milan)", in *Case Studies in the Conservation of Stone and Wall Paintings*, conference proceedings, London.
Milano ritrovata. L'asse di via Torino, exhibition catalogue, Milan, pp. 277, 494–495.
Pescarmona D., in *Disegni lombardi del Cinque e Seicento della Pinacoteca di Brera e dell'arcivescovado di Milano*, exhibition catalogue, Florence, p. 55.
Werdehausen A.E., "Bramante e il convento di Sant'Ambrogio", in *Bramante a Milano*, conference proceedings (Milan 1985), in *Arte lombarda*, pp. 35, 42.
1987
Patetta L., *L'architettura del Quattrocento a Milano*, Milan, pp. 62–66.
Sannazzaro G.B. and Sironi G., "Antonio da Lonate", in *Dizionario della Chiesa ambrosiana*, I, Milan, pp. 179–180.
1988
Forti Grazzini N., *Arazzi a Milano*, Milan, p. 91 n. 6.
Forti Grazzini N., "Gli arazzi", in *Monza. Il duomo e i suoi tesori*, Milan, pp. 114–137.
Pinacoteca di Brera. Scuole lombarda e piemontese 1300–1535, Milan, pp. 204, 209, 210, 213, 217, 319, 322, 323, 324.
Rossi M. and Rovetta A., *Pittura in Alto Lario tra Quattro e Cinquecento*, Milan, pp. 26–31.
Sannazzaro G.B., "Elementi bramanteschi nella chiesa di San Maurizio al Monastero Maggiore", in *Bramante a Milano*, conference proceedings (Milan 1985), in *Arte lombarda*, 86/87, pp. 127–131.
1989
Autelli F., *Pitture murali a Brera*, Milan, p. 129.
Bologna G., *Tutte le dame del re*, Milan, p. 62.
Bora G., "I Piazza e la fortuna della 'maniera'", in *I Piazza da Lodi. Una tradizione di pittori nel Cinquecento*, exhibition catalogue, Milan, pp. 254–255.
Marani P.C., in *Ambrogio Bergognone*, exhibition catalogue, Florence, pp. 92–101.
Marubbi M., "L'officina dei Piazza tra comprimari e presenze esterne", in *I Piazza da Lodi. Una tradizione di pittori nel Cinquecento*, exhibition catalogue, Milan, pp. 325 326.
Miller R.S., "Gli affreschi cinquecenteschi: Giuseppe Arcimboldo, Giuseppe Meda e Giovanni Battista della Rovere detto il Fiamminghino", in *Monza. Il duomo nella storia e nell'arte*, Milan, p. 228 n. 6.
Rossi M., "Il monastero di Sant'Ambrogio, i cistercensi e Callisto Piazza", in *I Piazza da Lodi. Una tradizione di pittori nel Cinquecento*, exhibition catalogue, Milan, p. 299.
Sannazzaro G.B., *Comment*, in *Florence and Milan. Comparisons and Relations*, conference proceedings (Florence 1982–84), II, Florence , p. 307 (a).
Sannazzaro G.B., "Nuovi documenti per San Maurizio al Monastero Maggiore", in *Civiltà ambrosiana*, VI, 1, pp. 59–64 (b).
Schofield R.V., Shell J. and Sironi G., *Giovanni Antonio Amadeo*, Como, pp. 58, 404.
Viotto Pedroli P., "Reminiscenze düreriane nella chiesa claustrale di San Maurizio al Monastero Maggiore", in *Arte cristiana*, 77, 731, pp. 99–103.
1990
Ferri Piccaluga G., "Eugenio di Beauharnais, conoscitore e collezionista di dipinti leonardeschi", in *I leonardeschi a Milano. Fortuna e collezionismo*, exhibition catalogue, Milan, p. 219.
Milano. Guida di architettura, Turin, p. 94.
1991
Sannazzaro G.B., "San Maurizio al Monastero Maggiore: architettura e pittura", in *Ca' de Sass*, 114, June, pp. 34–44.
1991–92
Sannazzaro G.B., "Per l'antico rosone del duomo di Monza: un possibile raffronto con affreschi milanesi del primo Cinquecento", in *Studi Monzesi*, 7, pp. 19–21.
1992
Bora G., "Tradizione luinesca da San Vittore a Meda a San Maurizio al Monastero Maggiore", in *Raccolta Vinciana*, 24, pp. 155–179.
Sannazzaro G.B., *San Maurizio al Monastero Maggiore*, 2nd ed., Milan.
1993
Sannazzaro G.B., "L'Amadeo e Santa Maria alla Fontana", in *Giovanni Antonio Amadeo. Scultura e architettura del suo tempo*, conference proceedings, Milan, pp. 305, 308, 323.
1994
Goffi L., in *Pinacoteca di Brera. Dipinti dell'Ottocento e del Novecento. Collezioni dell'Accademia e della Pinacoteca*, II, Milan, p. 310.
Savaré G., "La Commissione milanese (1877–1890)", in *Del restauro in Lombardia. Procedure, istituzioni, archivi. 1861–1892*, ed. G.P. Treccani, Milan, pp. 235–266.
1995
Bandera S., "Il recupero della cappella del Diluvio", in *Diocesi di Milano*, XXXVI, 6, November–December, pp. 60–65.
Coppa S., "Pittura e decorazione in stucco dal Cinquecento al Settecento", in *Luogo di meraviglie. Il santuario della Beata Vergine in Vimercate*, Milan, p. 224.
1996
Palmieri G., *Storia e storie del Monastero Maggiore di San Maurizio in Milano*, Milan.
1997
Cabella E., *Le attività della Fondazione Ercole Varzi di Milano 1958–1996*, Milan, pp. 65–66.
Museo d'Arte Antica del Castello Sforzesco – Pinacoteca, ed. M.T. Fiorio, I, Milan.
Sannazzaro G.B., "Per la chiesa di San Maurizio al Monastero Maggiore di Milano", in *Raccolta Vinciana*, XXVII, pp. 573–576.
Valagussa G., "Dagli inizi della pittura al Duecento", in *Pittura a Milano dall'alto Medioevo al Tardo Gotico*, Milan, p. 42.
Winkelmes M.A., "Benedectine Nuns in Milan: Claustration and Innovation at S. Maurizio", in *Picturing Women in Renaissance and Baroque Italy*, Cambridge, pp. 93–94, 102–109.
1998
Bandera S., "I cicli pittorici", in *San Maurizio al Monastero Maggiore in Milano. Guida storico-artistica*, Milan, pp. 42–83.
Bora G., "Bernardino Luini", in *I leonardeschi. L'eredità di Leonardo in Lombardia*, Milan, pp. 346–350, 353, 365–367.
Bora G., "Fra tradizione, maniera e classicismo riformato (1535–1595)", in *Pittura a Milano. Rinascimento e manierismo*, Milan, pp. 57, 60–62, and entries pp. 265, 275–276.
Frangi F., "Una traccia per la storia della pittura a Milano dal 1499 al 1535", in *Pittura a Milano. Rinascimento e manierismo*, Milan, pp. 35–36, and entry p. 242.
Manzin M., "L'organo", in *San Maurizio al Monastero Maggiore in Milano. Guida storico-artistica*, Milan, pp. 84–87.
2000
Sannazzaro G.B., "Per la decorazione pittorica nella chiesa di San Maurizio al Monastero Maggiore di Milano: suggerimenti di studio", in *Arte lombarda nel secondo millennio. Saggi in onore di Gian Alberto Dell'Acqua*, Milan, pp. 138–148.
Ghielmi L., "L'attività degli Antegnati nel Milanese", in *Gli Antegnati. Stato attuale degli studi e prospettive di ricerca*, conference proceedings (Brescia 1990), in print.

Index

Numbers in italics refer to pages on which illustrations appear